EUROPEAN ECONOMIC HISTORY

Books by Shepard B. Clough

Making Fascists (with Herbert W. Schneider)
History of the Flemish Movement in Belgium
France, 1789–1939: A Study in National Economics
An Economic History of Europe (with Charles W. Cole)
A Century of American Life Insurance
The Rise and Fall of Civilization
L'Histoire Economique des Etats-Unis
The American Way: The Economic Basis of our Civilization (revised by Theodore F. Marburg)
European Economic History: The Economic Development of Western Civilization
Basic Values of Western Civilization
The Economic History of Modern Italy
The European Past (with Peter Gay and Charles K. Warner, and John M. Cammett)
European Economic History: Documents and Readings (with Carol Gayle Moodie)
A History of Modern Italy in Readings and Documents (with Salvatore Saladina)
European Economic History in the Twentieth Century in Documents (with Thomas and Carol Moodie)
A History of the Western World (with others)
Storia dell'economia Italiana dal 1861 ad oggi (with Luigi De Rosa)

by Richard T. Rapp

Industry and Economic Decline in Seventeenth-Century Venice (forthcoming)

EUROPEAN ECONOMIC HISTORY

The Economic Development
of Western Civilization

Third Edition

Shepard B. Clough

Professor Emeritus
Columbia University

Richard T. Rapp

Assistant Professor
State University of New York at Stony Brook

McGraw-Hill Book Company
New York St. Louis San Francisco Auckland Düsseldorf
Johannesburg Kuala Lumpur London Mexico Montreal New Delhi Panama
Paris São Paulo Singapore Sydney Tokyo Toronto

To our students

European Economic History:
The Economic Development of Western Civilization

1234567890 KPKP 798765

This book was set in Palatino by Compucomp Corporation.
The editors were Robert P. Rainier and Barry Benjamin;
the designer was Anne Canevari Green;
the production supervisor was Judi Frey.
Kingsport Press, Inc., was printer and binder.

Library of Congress Cataloging in Publication Data

Clough, Shepard Bancroft, date
  European economic history.

  First published in 1959 under title: The economic development of Western civilization.
  Bibliography: p.
  1. Economic history.   I. Rapp, Richard T., joint author.   II.   Title.
HC21.C64 1975   330.9'182'1   74-16043
ISBN 0-07-011393-9

Contents

Part V *Crises in the economy of Western culture—1914 to 1974*

List of maps and charts

List of illustrations

List of tables

Preface to the third edition

The widespread success which this book has enjoyed, both in the United States and abroad, has encouraged the publishers and the authors to offer this new edition to the scholarly public.

Economic history is a field of study that is very much in motion, and the principle that has guided our revision has been to introduce into the text the newest findings of scholarship and the latest directions in historical research. For example, three areas of heated professional discussion are the relationship between population trends to economic change, the study of popular standards of living, and the analysis of the effects of long-term economic fluctuations on material well-being. We have developed these themes and others like them in the text with the hope that new findings will now reach a wider audience.

Occasionally (very often, in fact), historical debates go unresolved for a time. In order to reflect best the state of the art in economic history, when we have encountered problems that are still under active discussion, our strategy has been to present the facts and the range of possible interpretations, leaving the verdict to the reader. Many history textbooks seem to present facts about the past as if the final word about them had been spoken, whereas scholars know very well that the fertility of history is maintained by a constant turning and overturning of the soil, so to speak. We have worked to make this new edition of a well-established book mirror the vigor and dynamism of modern scholarship in economic history.

Shepard B. Clough
Richard T. Rapp

Preface to the second edition

It will hardly come as an astounding revelation to my readers that I, as a professional historian, hold man's greatest heritage to be knowledge of the past, nor will they be greatly surprised to learn that I believe all current human behavior to be conditioned by "man's experience through time." It is, indeed, my firm conviction that "the wisdom of the ages" is man's choicest possession.

If I am correct in my estimate of the place of history in life, then it follows that historians have a weighty responsibility to discharge for their fellow men. It is their task to select, record, and interpret from myriads of experiences those which are the most useful in helping men to decide what kind of a world they want and in guiding mankind in its eternal quest for that world. Of necessity this assignment requires the study both of detailed events and of exceedingly broad movements.

In the present work, I have labored long and conscientiously to understand and to present a *part* of human experience which will have meaning in the human struggle for the attainment of higher levels of civilization. In other words, it has been my intention to show the relationship of economic activity to the human drama as it has unfolded through time. In addition, I have tried to meet one of the major criticisms of economic historians, so cogently pointed out by one of my masters, the late Wesley C. Mitchell, that we have been guilty of amassing data without plan or reason and that we have made little effort to establish what the necessary relationships among those data are.[1] Specifically, I have endeavored to organize economic data around the central theme of economic growth and to relate that theme to human strivings for civilization. I have done this for that part of the world known as Western Culture, especially for Europe.

Inasmuch as the preface of a scholarly book is the one place where the author may speak familiarly with his readers, it is not improper that I should confess to them my trepidation regarding the product of my efforts which they hold in their hands. I fear that critics may complain that I have undertaken too huge a task, that specialists may contend that I have not given enough space to some hobby of theirs, and that reviewers may argue that I should have written another kind of book from the one in these covers. These are the usual foibles of men who are dedicated to the proposition that knowledge to be "sound" must be stereotyped; they have to be borne with patience and fortitude by the would-be innovator. At all events, I am of the opinion that both scholar and student should resist allowing education to become so strait-jacketed by tradition that it loses all relevance to the world about us.

I should also confide to my readers that I, like all conscientious scholars, have a fear regarding the possible appearance of errors in my work and that, like most of my kind, I have taken extreme precautions to avoid them. Not only have I spent some seven years in writing this book and over a quarter of a century in the study of economic history, but I have imposed on my friends and colleagues to help protect me from slips. Fortunately I had the expert criticism of Professor Thomas C. Cochran of the entire manuscript and that of Professor A. P. Usher of a large part of the European sections. Furthermore, Elias Bickerman read those parts having to do with Ancient history, John H. Mundy, those dealing with the Middle Ages, and Garrett Mattingly, those covering the first three centuries of Modern Times. To all of these experts I am grateful, and I hereby exonerate them from all blame for those frailties of expression or of interpretation which they did not catch or which I was obstinate enough to retain in spite of their warnings.

The enthusiastic and worldwide reception which the first edition of this work received has warranted a new edition. The text has been brought up to date, and thus deals with the economic *miracles* in several countries since World War II—miracles which provide yet again new reflections upon the process of growth. Moreover, an attempt has been made to provide more economic analysis—more cause-and-effect relationships—of economic issues in the last hundred years. The general nature of the work has, however, been maintained; that is, the central purpose has been to provide a general synthesis of economic growth in Western culture by dealing with

---

[1] Wesley C. Mitchell, "The Role of Money in Economic History," *The Tasks of Economic History*, a supplement to *The Journal of Economic History*, December 1944, pp. 61–67.

all pertinent factors, be they political, social, or intellectual, as well as economic. It is my belief that only by such a broad view of human behavior can the social scientist provide the guidance which society needs. The results may seem extremely complex to those who want easy answers, but complexity of reality seems something with which we mortals must learn to live.

Shepard B. Clough

Economic growth

1

To the reader

The subject and purpose of this book

At the outset of any scientific research it is essential both for clarity of thought and for effective analysis that the investigators state as precisely and as cogently as possible what subject is under inquiry and why the study is being made. For fuller comprehension, the reader should have this information from the beginning. Therefore, let us explain our purpose and state as explicitly as we can what phase of man's experience we have sought to elucidate in this book.

The subject of our study is the historical development of the economy of Western culture. The reasons for engaging in this pursuit are numerous but easily summarized. As we study history to achieve an understanding of the roots of our civilization, we study the various branches of history to comprehend better the separate elements of civilization past and present. The separation of branches is an intellectual convention—economic life is not disconnected from culture or politics in history or in life. Our branch of study, economic history, offers insight into the origins of modern economic *institutions* and into the process of natural selection by which institutions change or die. Further, the study of economic history deals with the causes and effects of *productivity changes* that alter human welfare for better or worse. Finally, economic history relates changes in institutions and productivity to *cultural changes*. Trade, for example, broadens the boundaries of a culture; economic well-being makes possible leisure in which to enjoy esthetic creations. Topical specialization is all very well as an expedient for intensive study, but only in history recognized as the totality of human activity is it possible to arrive at a synthesis of economic, social, political, intellectual, psychological, and geographic aspects of life in the dimension of time. We study the culture of the West because we are the heirs of that culture and because the Western economic tradition has become the most widely diffused system of production and distribution in modern times, but again it should be noted that this specialization is an expedient which must not be interpreted as a minimization of the importance of non-Western economic traditions.

To speak of "the West" as a unit has its dangers. Complete homogeneity, of course, does not exist in Western culture. Subcultures are distinguished by differences in language, literature, traditions, and political boundaries. Real as such differentiating factors as national states have been and are, Western society, including the Western economy, shows great unity. Subdividing material by national histories seems more artificial than using more functional (if more abstract) categorization. Generally speaking, behavioral variations are greater between socioeconomic groups than they are between national subcultures. Thus city merchants from France, Germany, England, and the United States have more in common with each other than, let us say, a merchant in France and a French manual laborer. This text bears that consideration very much in mind, and while separate national histories are not ignored, we have chosen to emphasize the general patterns of change in the Western economy.

Concerning economics, economic history, and economic growth

Before proceeding with our historical study of the economic development of Western culture, let us stop briefly to become oriented in some of the fundamental concepts of economics, economic history, and economic growth. These concepts will provide an organizing structure for the material to be found in subsequent chapters.

Economics is a study of goods and services which have exchange value. It deals essentially with the following questions:

1 What goods and services are produced, in what quantities, in what places, with what regularity, and why?

2 By the use of what natural and human resources, with what productive arts, and by means of what savings are these goods and services produced?

3 By what economic organizations—families, guilds, companies, partnerships, or corporations—are they produced?

4 For whose eventual use are these goods and services produced?

If these are the central issues of economics, it follows perforce that they are the major subjects of economic history. Yet between the two disciplines there is a difference of emphasis. Economics is concerned primarily with the "here and now," and only secondarily with the past. It is, therefore, interested in analyses which will throw light upon current problems and will assist in policy formation. By contrast, economic history is concerned with the problem of becoming—with development—and hence places more emphasis upon processes, long-term trends, and factors of change. Of all the subjects to which it has devoted its talents and on which it has thrown most light that of economic growth stands out as predominant.[1]

By economic growth is meant essentially an increase in goods and services available for human use. One may speak of the economic growth of a political or territorial unit, like the economic growth of France or of Vermont, or of any other segment of mankind, like the economic growth of Western culture. The implications of economic growth vary, however, within the chosen division of mankind, as the supply of goods and services increases not only in absolute, aggregate terms but also in proportion to the population. Therefore, economic growth usually signifies, and this will be our usage, not only an increase in the total supply of goods and services within a selected unit of mankind but, more significantly, an increase in goods and services per capita of the population.[2]

In recent times, goods and services produced have come to be expressed in terms of national income or of net national product. These measures are national because nation-states are the chief gatherers of the necessary statistical data. These data include wages and other compensation of employees; net income of unincorporated businesses; net interest received from private bonds, mortgages, and other loans; net rents of persons, including self-occupied homes; and net corporate earnings.[3] Unfortunately, reliable national income statistics do not exist for many years in the past, nor do many states have adequate statistical information from which to derive them.[4] Yet national income figures may be employed for making estimates that are accurate enough to show trends and to make international comparisons.[5]

For times preceding those covered by national income figures, that is,

---

[1] By antithesis, the study of economic growth includes economic decline.

[2] Some students prefer to employ the formula of goods and services per occupied person. The issue involved here is that theoretically, at least, a growing economy could have a great many unemployed young persons or a declining economy could have a great proportion of unemployed old persons with the result that goods and services per capita of the total population might not reflect accurately the productive potential of the economy. Thus the supply of goods and services per capita of the employed emphasizes the more strictly economic side of society and minimizes the demographic and social side.

[3] For a fuller statement, see Simon Kuznets, *National Income and Its Composition: 1919–1938*, vols. 1 and 2 (New York: National Bureau of Economic Research, 1941); and U.S. Department of Commerce, *Survey of Current Business*, Supplement, July 1947.

[4] The margin of error for a country like France has been said to be as much as 20 percent.

[5] See Simon Kuznets, *National Income—A Summary of Findings* (New York: National Bureau of Economic Research, 1946), part 2: Colin Clark, *The Conditions of Economic Progress*, 3d ed. (New York: St. Martin's, 1957); and *National and Per Capita Incomes: Seventy Countries* (New York: United Nations, Department of Public Information, 1949).

for those prior to anywhere from 1870 to 1918, there are statistics regarding national outputs of certain products like iron, steel, and coal; freight carried on public carriers; bills discounted by national banks; and the volume of foreign trade. For earlier periods, it is possible to arrive at some idea of expansion from port transactions, the development of individual businesses, the number of inventions made, the introduction of new techniques, and the rise in real wages as derived from price-wage statistical time series. For still more remote times, general impressions may be had from a variety of written and archaeological records. For example, some notion of economic growth may be derived from very long-range increases of population, for more people could not be housed, fed, and clothed if there were not an increase in production. Some idea of development may also be gained from the growth of cities, on the theory that urban centers grow in size in direct proportion to the increase in production. And a notion of economic progress may be obtained from improvements in the standard of living of the people as reflected in better clothes, better food or food supply, better houses, and the production of great buildings and works of art.

The task of explaining economic growth, or what the economist would call the analysis of growth, is exceedingly difficult, for different factors and forces, and different combinations of them, have in different times and places and under varying circumstances affected growth. Here, as in so many other cases, no monocausal explanation of what is complex can possibly be adequate. The task of the economic historian is then to explain economic growth in terms of many factors (multiple variables)—to explain what they were, their quantities, and the timing of their coming together. From his findings a theory of growth may be constructed, but perforce this theory will not be a simplistic one.

The economic historian may organize his historical analysis around the basic questions of economics—why goods and services are produced, with what natural and human resources, with what productive arts, and with the use of what savings. Obviously the *desire* for more production of goods and services on the part of a population is essential to the finding of ways and means to effect growth. Clearly better techniques of production mean greater output per unit of human input. Patently the easy acquisition of materials for processing facilitates the productive process. And logically society must have some reserve on which to live while it experiments with new ways of doing things. The historian has some guiding principles with which to launch his investigation—some hypotheses—even though he does not have an ironbound theory.

Why goods and services are produced depends up to a point upon physiological requirements, that is, upon the desire either to maintain one's own life and health or that of persons for whom one accepts some responsibility, like children, parents, or friends. To meet these basic requirements it is necessary in most climates and conditions to store goods against future emergencies like nongrowing seasons of the year, droughts, or destructive plagues; hence in most societies, even primitive ones, surpluses are produced although they may not be used in such a fashion as to produce still more goods. Beyond the satisfying of bodily needs, people may produce goods to meet some culturally inspired desire, such as tools, an amulet, an opera house, a steel factory, or a four-car garage. Here the range is obviously very great and depends not only upon the ideologies which a culture has built up but upon the productive potential of the society. In any case there is much evidence to indicate that only those cultures which do not have the means of increasing their material well-being minimize the desirability of wealth and establish as determinant ideologies religion, physical asceticism, and indolence.

If the acquisition of material things constitutes an important goal in a culture, the attainment of the goal will depend upon a great range of other factors. Among these the availability of natural resources per capita of the population plays a very significant role. Land, plant life, and animal life have been throughout history the most extensively and universally used resources. In fact, economic growth in the known past was first marked in those places where land was extremely fertile, as in the Nile, Tigris and Euphrates, and Indus River valleys. Subsequently development was great in areas which could draw upon the resources of other areas by trade, as in the case of Greece. Still later man began to dip into what has been called "nature's capital"—to exploit, often ruthlessly, inorganic substances stored up in the earth's crust over aeons of time. In all cases, however, the actual exploitation of nature has depended very largely upon techniques. Coal, iron, uranium, and even wheat were not natural resources in an economic sense until man wanted them and had enough knowledge of the productive arts to obtain and use them. Only when desire for goods is accompanied by ability to get them do the bounties of the earth take on great significance for economic growth.

Of crucial importance, also, has been the directing of human resources to the production of goods and services. The larger the proportion of a population which devotes its energies to the productive process and the harder it works, the larger the quantity of goods and services which it can expect to turn out. Furthermore, the greater the proportion of natural resources to the population, the greater will be the chances of producing surpluses which can be invested for the production of still more goods. Populations in the past have outstripped a society's productive potential, and they may well do so again in spite of modern man's seemingly inexhaustible ingenuity in finding ways to turn into useful goods what only yesterday was worthless rubble. Yet population growth and economic growth cannot go on indefinitely until people are packed on the earth's crust like living sardines in a box.

A knowledge of the productive arts is an essential factor in economic growth, for they determine very largely the amount of human input that has to go into a unit of output. So important are techniques, indeed, that the theory has been advanced that they lead in effecting all economic and social change and that all other aspects of life have to adjust themselves to such alterations in the ways of performing tasks.[6] Although this theory overstates its case, it points to a crucial force in economic growth, to the entire question of "leads" and "lags" in change, and to the process of adjustment.

New techniques may originate within a society (indigenous or autonomous origin) or may be obtained from others (adaptive origin). In the former case, they usually come about as the result of some socially felt need, the gradual accretion of a great nunber of related details, and the putting together of these details in such a manner that a new process comes into being. In the latter case, they may be borrowed voluntarily or may be imposed by a more advanced culture upon a more backward one. The process of diffusion usually takes place first in those under-developed areas which are culturally close to an advanced one and where an exchange of goods and ideas is already taking place. Subsequently it involves more background districts as the developed areas seek more raw materials and foodstuffs. What techniques and institutions are diffused is determined by what is demanded by the two parties and by the adaptability of what is transposed to the recipient's existing productive processes and knowledge. Simple things facilitating the production of basic goods and services, like transportation, usually precede the complex and the luxurious, and those requiring little capital ordinarily go ahead of those demanding a great amount.

This brings us to the role of savings in economic growth. Inasmuch as greater production is obtained chiefly from better methods and better equipment, expansion requires excesses out of current production for developing those methods or for providing that equipment. Thus instead of devoting all its energy to producing goods for immediate consumption, a society that would grow economically must devote some of its energy to making capital or producers' goods. Such savings may be voluntary, or they may be forced.[7] But whatever their nature, savings are facilitated if

---

[6] See William F. Ogburn, *Social Change* (New York: Viking, 1952).

[7] Savings are said to be forced when they are not effected willingly. Thus they are forced when money is inflated, for someone, in our society the state, has spent its funds to obtain goods and services beyond the ability to pay for them in the usual medium of exchange. Similarly, savings are forced when an entrepreneur borrows money to build a factory and is subsequently unable to pay off his loan. His creditors have involuntarily come into the possession of capital goods.

the economy has a recognized, nonperishable measure of value for exchange, like gold, for accumulating savings, has institutions for safeguarding these stores, and has mechanisms for combining the savings of many persons, for creating credit, and for making investments.

The organization of business enterprise next becomes an important element in the analysis. Here much depends upon a division of labor, that is, upon the extent to which producers specialize in those things which they can turn out with less human input by doing only part of a job than they could if each did the entire task himself, as, for example, in the manufacture of automobiles. A division of labor necessitates the development of commerce, and those societies today which have the largest incomes per capita have a relatively larger proportion of their labor force in commerce and transport than do backward areas.

Finally, there are three other crucial factors in economic growth. The first of these is entrepreneurial leadership. Whether or not leadership is talented will depend upon the methods of recruitment (by merit, family ties, or force), upon training, and upon motivation. The second is that purchasing power should be divided equally enough that there will be an effective demand for goods on the part of the masses, for a sustained demand will encourage entrepreneurs to risk their capital and their resources in the production of more goods. Thirdly, the functioning of any economy will depend upon general conditions conducive to orderly operations. Thus, periods of peace, social harmony, and political stability permit a greater devotion of energies to the economic process than do periods of strife.

Scholars have devoted much time and energy in trying to ascertain which one of these factors has been determinant in setting off a chain reaction of economic growth. Some have argued that if a given percentage of national income (say 10 percent) is devoted to investment in plant and equipment, economic growth will ensue, and it will be sustained because investing this much of national income will become an established pattern of socioeconomic behavior. Others have contended, however, that economic change comes about very gradually and that sudden breakthroughs can be understood only by knowing the long-term development during which all the pieces needed came into being.[8] Some have held that economic growth has come first in particular sectors of the economy, for example in the textile industries, in foreign trade, or in transportation, and then has spread to other sectors. Others have maintained that economic

---

[8] Much of this controversy is surveyed in W. W. Rostow, (Ed.), *The Economics of Take-Off into Sustained Growth* (New York: St. Martin's, 1964). See also Simon Kuznets, *Six Lectures of Economic Growth* (New York: Free Press, 1959).

growth has tended to be more even and that the spread of growth features from one sector to another has been very rapid.[9]

Both economic analysis and historical evidence indicate that all the factors of production which have already been mentioned must be present if economic growth is to take place. Furthermore, it seems clear that these factors have developed over a very long period of time. If, as some archaeologists believe, man appeared on the earth some million years ago, then it took him some 990,000 years to discover how to smelt ore—to utilize what is today a very common natural resource. It took him some 6,000 years to get from the metal scythe to the reaper. And it took him 2,300 years to get from the first coins in which the metallic content was guaranteed by states to banknotes issued by central banks. Small accretions have been added to what existed until a new synthesis was possible—a synthesis that made an important breakthrough in man's ways of doing things.

Also it seems apparent that economic progress in the sense of more goods and services per capita has come in relatively sudden bursts, as in the age of copper from 5000 to 3000 B.C., in the period of the supremacy of Greece in the first millennium B.C., in the Industrial Revolution in the hundred years after 1750, and in the period since World War II. In each of these experiences changes have come in clusters. Yet the lead was usually taken in one sector of the economy, while "lags" were to be observed in others. In the course of time, changes in one sector usually led to changes in others, so that over time an equalizing process took place, although it might not be complete.

Thus, the economic historian does find recurring regularities in his study of economic growth, but he is reluctant to use them for establishing a hard-and-fast theory. He realizes that every historical event is in some respect different from every other, for the individuals involved are different, or they come to the new event with knowledge acquired from the last one, or they have had different kinds of breakfasts that day, or the food settled differently in their stomachs. He knows that he is dealing with analogies from human experience, and he has learned from elementary logic that analogies are for purposes of illustration and not for purposes of proof. Consequently he is wary of believing that any pattern of behavior which he discovers will be continued with mechanical regularity and unfailing certainty in the future. The mere fact that man behaved in one way under given circumstances may mean that when similar conditions arise he will use his experience to avoid what he did not like in what he did before. That man may profit from his experiences in attaining more fully

[9] One of the chief exponents of uneven growth has been Albert O. Hirschman. *The Strategy of Economic Development* (New Haven, Conn.: Yale, 1958). An exponent of even growth was Ragnar Nurske, *Problems of Capital Formation in Underdeveloped Countries* (Oxford: Blackwell, 1953).

the kind of a world he wants justifies on pragmatic grounds the study of the past.

In the history of economic growth, the historian finds that noneconomic factors have a great impact upon economic phenomena and that he must encompass them in his view. He discovers that change affecting the economy may originate in any part of society—in a change in the size of a population in a given geographical region, in a religious revival, in a new philosophy of production which may deride hard work, or in a drought which reduces the food supply or the purchasing power of farmers. In order to get the *total* picture of economic growth—to achieve the great synthesis of human behavior over time which is his highest and ultimate goal—he must have a wide knowledge of all aspects of history and an open mind to all possible forces at play in a given situation.

One of the most useful guiding concepts in his quest for knowledge about change comes from sociology. It is that changes in society will depend in large part upon how rigid the structure of that society is. If a people has fixed ways of doing things, has absolute taboos against adopting what is new, and has leaders who can maintain their positions only if nothing changes, changes conducive to economic growth will be much less readily introduced than among a people that looks upon the latest and newest as best, has advertisers who drum this notion eternally into their heads, and has leaders who stand to gain from the introduction of the new. Actually, the analyst is concerned with trying to ascertain what extends the range of opportunities for alternative decisions regarding the use of human and natural resources, and he finds that societal rigidities are some of the most stubborn barriers to change. Indeed, the range of opportunities for alternative decisions may be the key to understanding economic growth.

Having considered the fundamental elements of economic growth, we come to the question, for whose eventual use are goods and services produced? Here a distinction must be made at once between capital or producers' goods—things which are capable of being used to produce more goods—and consumers' goods—things which individuals use up at a rapid rate in the process of living.[10] Also one must distinguish between goods which are designed to destroy what man has made, as in the case of war matériel, and those which are intended to add to the accumulation of the ages.

In a rapidly expanding economy, a larger part of national income goes into producers' goods than in a stable or declining economy, as has already been suggested. What happens is that people forego the joys of present

---

[10] The difference between the two is not always sharp. There is a twilight zone between the two types, illustrated by the "jeep," which may be used for pleasure and for plowing.

consumption for future gain. In a growing economy they are willing to do this, because with expansion their standard of living rises, and being satisfied with some improvement, they do not demand for immediate use all that is economically possible. In a sense they get their cake and eat it too. Also, it is essential, as we have previously seen, that economic benefits do not go only to a very small group in society, be it a religious organization, members of a political hierarchy, or a social class, for the basic economic wants of a few are soon met, and when they are, expenditures tend to be for luxuries rather than capital goods. A wide distribution of purchasing power has the effect of sustaining demand and of encouraging expansion.

The way the ownership of goods is held also has a bearing upon economic growth. Here the goal is to get enough concentration to obtain maximum efficiency of operation, but not so much that a group will have enough power to extort unreasonable sacrifices from others. Apparently some form of competition is desirable to prevent any one group from attaining a position that it can abuse. Finally, too great a concentration of ownership of goods may prevent the creation of incentives to work effectively, whether these incentives are wages, the attainment of status in society, or the sheer personal joy of creating something.

Desirable as economic growth may be, it cannot be expected to continue indefinitely, to infinity. It creates certain counterforces which tend to curb it. In the past the most important of these retardative factors have been:

1   The growth of large populations beyond the technological capacity of the economy to support them
2   The exhaustion of natural resources
3   The rigidification of institutions, inhibiting technical change and curtailing the ability of the economy to respond to exogenous forces

In no case in history has there been a straight-line progression of economic expansion. Having a simplistic idea of progress which fails to recognize backward steps in productivity and human welfare would be a great hindrance to properly understanding Western economic history.

In the following pages we shall endeavor to find the beginnings of those ideologies, institutions, and techniques which first gave Western culture its economic characteristics, a search which will lead us to scrutinize our heritage from the ancient past. Then for the time span since the twelfth century we shall endeavor to keep before our readers the relationship between material well-being and levels of civilization.

The Ancient and
Medieval worlds

Economic achievements in the Ancient world

Inheritance versus invention and discovery

So impressed are modern men in Western culture with their own achievements that they seldom recognize the importance of their cultural heritage. They stand entranced by such notable accomplishments in their own time as the development of airplanes which exceed the speed of sound, the splitting of the atom, and the extension of life expectancy at birth by some 20 percent in one generation. Even in their moments of contemplation, their minds are actively at work in the search for ever more grandiose ways to extend control over their social and physical environment. In some instances Western man has become so impressed with his own achievements that he has displayed symptoms of a paranoid condition of superiority—a condition perhaps best relieved by shock therapy.

For the mental health of the Western world a consideration of the tremendous accomplishments of the past is definitely indicated as a specific. A realization that many early achievements, given the existing level of knowledge, were as great as anything seen in our time might give modern man a becoming degree of modesty, if not what we in Western culture consider to be socially desirable humility. In any case, Western man would do well to realize that knowledge both of the physical world and of society has been an accumulative process of which he is the chief beneficiary, and that all of his wonderful achievements would not be possible if it were not for this rich legacy. It is probably not too much to say that no important technique for producing goods, either agricultural or industrial, that no solution of mathematical or engineering problems, and that no important information regarding our earth has ever been permanently lost. Western man has, indeed, been able to build upon a very rich inheritance from the past.

Furthermore, Western man would also do well to consider the experience of man through time—to learn how progress has been made in the period of some 5,000 years for which we have written and relatively abundant archaeological records. If experience is indeed the best teacher, it can well be that modern man may learn to build even better than his forebears and to avoid some of the pitfalls which have brought other cultures to their economic doom.

The beginnings of man's long climb upward

At the beginning of man's long climb up the scale of civilization, by some estimates a million years ago, Homo sapiens was very close to the animal both in his knowledge of the world about him and in his way of life. In fact, if one assumes, in conformity with current evolutionary theory, that man is descended from some of the higher forms of animal life, the gap between man and animals must at one time have been very small. And if one has had any experience in trying to tame or train even the most advanced animals, one can imagine how uncivilized early man really was.

Although anthropologists, who specialize in the study of primitive man and his cultures, have relatively little evidence on the subject, they believe that remains which have been unearthed and the behavior of the most primitive people now extant indicate that the first men on earth had practically no tools, could not control fire well enough to have it always available, followed animal traits in their relations with their fellowmen, and were primarily food gatherers rather than food producers. They picked berries, harvested nuts, and foraged for tubers, the eggs of birds and reptiles, and the seeds of plants, which came to be called grains. They did some hunting, clothed themselves, if at all, in skins, and sought shelter in caves, thickets, or trees. They had little surplus to allow for pursuits other than the satisfying of bodily needs. Indeed, it is probable that, much like hibernating animals, they had to rely on their own fat rather than on stores of food to get them through the unproductive seasons of the year.

Obviously primitive man's greatest problem was to secure freedom from want, that is, so to extend his control over his physical environment that he could diminish the threat of imminent starvation. This meant, first, better tools and weapons and, secondly, growing foodstuffs rather than merely gathering them. Both of these things were crucial to economic advance, but to materials used in tools and weapons have gone the honor of furnishing names for the early ages of history. Thus we have the Paleolithic Age, in which tools and weapons were made of crude, chipped stone; the Neolithic Age, when polished stone was used; the Age of Copper, when copper tools and weapons prevailed; and so on through the Age of Bronze and the Age of Iron.

The dates for these various ages cannot be fixed with finality for all the world, for there seem to have been parallel developments in many places and different people advanced at different rates. Indeed, throughout the world today it is possible to find man at nearly every level of civilization. In the district which stretches from the eastern Mediterranean to the Persian Gulf, whence most of the heritage of Western European culture came, the Paleolithic Age extended from the early days of man's appearance on earth down to about 10,000 years ago; the Neolithic, from 8000 B.C. to the fifth millennium B.C.; the Age of Copper, from the fifth through the fourth millenniums B.C.; the Age of Bronze, from the end of the fourth millennium to the end of the second; and the Iron Age lasted through the first millenium B.C.

That the Paleolithic Age was the longest of these periods indicates how difficult it was for man to effect basic changes in his way of life—how difficult it was for man to take some of what seem to us very elementary steps forward. In fact, it is striking to the historian how rarely in the past just the right human talents, social drives, proper materials, and other factors came together with such a timing and in such proportions as to break through "resistance points" of advance. It is amazing to us how long it took man to find his way by the stars, to conquer oceans, to develop numerical notations, to grow annual crops, or to get energy from wind, waterfalls, or steam.

However difficult Paleolithic man found his problems, archaeological evidence shows that slowly but surely he solved some of them. He began to control fire and developed ways of producing it at will. His first crude weapons and tools, which were chipped from some hard stone, like flint, were gradually improved in quantity and workmanship, and they came to be differentiated for different tasks. In the course of time man added bones and ivory to the materials which he used for tools and weapons, and he stored food in horns and skins. Still later he devised hooks and lines for catching fish, domesticated the dog so that he would have some help in the chase, employed rotary motion for drilling, utilized the principle of the lever and fulcrum for moving heavy objects, and invented the bow and arrow, the first composite mechanism of which we know. It is probable, too, that Paleolithic man had some means of transporting himself on water, whether it was on a crude raft, a log canoe, or a kayak. He did not have yet, however, the principle of the wheel, and when he moved by land, as he frequently did in search of food because of droughts or "overpopulation," he carried his few belongings on his back, dragged them on poles, or pulled them on sledges.

Apparently primitive man, especially in those climates and areas where nature was not so bountiful as to provide steady sustenance and moderate temperatures, established a very definite ideology about economics—he had a most intense desire to avoid want. In the religions of people who live under conditions of uncertain food supply, there are almost always found prayers, spells, rites, and incantations to the totem beseeching assistance in the hunt or aid to the supplicant in his efforts to overcome some economic trouble.

The universality of such practices, the doctrine that "gods help those who help themselves," and the very logic of a precarious food supply suggest that Paleolithic man was not averse to altering his ways, if change would make him more certain of the morrow. Finally, conditions became propitious for reform. Sometime between 10000 and 8000 B.C., as the northern ice sheets of the last glacial period were receding, the steppes and tundras of Europe were transformed into temperate forests and the prairies south of the Mediterranean and of Hither Asia were converted into deserts with oases and fertile river basins. As a result food gathering and hunting in these southern areas was poor, and the men who went to them had to find a new solution to their problem of food supply. This they did by domesticating grains and by taming animals, in short by raising their own food and thereby for the first time creating settled agriculture. Here was one of the major technological revolutions of all time.

Man (or woman, more often than not) devoted more time and labor than ever before to raising food. The rewards of these changes were longer life, increased population, and the release of some (very few) members of society for specialized pursuits. Civilization, by the standards of Western culture, begins with this greatest of technical changes.

With the beginning of settled agriculture man entered the Neolithic or New Stone Age. Tools were now improved by polishing, were given finer edges, and were further differentiated. The hoe and the sickle appeared, for they were needed in the cultivation and harvesting of grains. The earthen pot was shaped by hand for storing grain; other pots were developed because grains, unlike meat, could not be cooked over an open fire on a spit but had to be contained in some sort of vessel. Fermentation was discovered (and probably encouraged). Clothes came to be made out of animal and vegetable fibers, because hides were too warm in summer and not in large supply; the use of fibers led to the invention of the spinning stick and the loom (Figures 1 and 2). Bodily decoration gave evidence of a greater concern for aesthetics.

Undoubtedly the most important of the cultivated grains were related to our wheat and barley and were selected from the seeds which food gatherers had been gleaning from mountains and marshes. In certain places Neolithic man had rice, millet, Indian corn, yams, manioc, and squash. Besides the dog, he numbered goats, sheep, cattle, and pigs among his animals.

Figure 1
Primitive spinning. One of the earliest
techniques that required a composite
mechanism had to do with the making of
cloth. On this Athenian vase of the sixth
century B.C., the process of turning wool into
loose bands is shown by the major figure on
the right. The central figure is spinning. The
left hand holds the distaff with the loose
wool while the right hand twirls and drops a
heavy weight to which the thread is attached
and so twists and draws out the fiber. The
author has seen this same method employed
in recent years in modern Delphi. On the left
of the vase two women are folding and
packaging finished material. *(From the collection of
the Metropolitan Museum of Art, New York. Fletcher
Fund, 1931. Reproduced with permission.)*

Figure 2
Primitive weaving. On the same vase that was
represented in the preceding figure, a
primitive loom is portrayed. The threads of
the warp run vertically rather than
horizontally as on more highly developed
looms, as shown in the figure on page 296. The
operator on the right is passing a spindle with
the wool thread between the threads of the
warp.

Important as was the agricultural revolution of the Neolithic Age, it could not produce much of a surplus or effect much of a division of labor. Foodstuffs were too perishable to be stored for long. Tools were too elementary to provide much of a division of labor, since individuals could for the most part shape what they themselves needed. Transportation was too inadequate to make distant trade feasible, and man had not yet learned to make use of either animal or mechanical energy.

The technological revolution of the Age of Copper

Important as was the advent of settled agriculture in the march forward to higher levels of civilization, men of the Age of Copper between 5000 and 3000 B.C. witnessed still further changes which were to revolutionize the economic existence of humankind. The most important of these innovations were:

1   The development of a technology of smelting and of working copper and later tin and lead
2   The growth of trade and the perfecting of instruments of exchange
3   The effecting of a greater division of labor than had ever been realized before
4   The founding of more and larger settlements

These innovations were introduced primarily in that great heartland of civilization from which Western culture was to inherit so much—the area bounded by the Sahara and the Atlantic on the west, by the Himalayas on the east, by the Caucasus and Hindu Kush Mountains on the north, and by the heat of the torrid zone on the south (Map 1).

That this area should have pushed through the points of resistance to economic progress, while so many other areas failed to do so, is one of the great facts of history. Among the reasons for the advance were the following: This region had unproductive seasons so that surpluses had to be provided for a portion of every year. It possessed extremely fertile land in oases and in great river valleys. It was protected against invaders by mountains and deserts. It had rivers for transporting goods over long distances, and access to seas navigable for relatively crude boats. Moreover, the necessity of controlling the waters of rivers for agricultural use may well have required a social organization that would make people obey rules for the general good of all. Periodic floods and long voyages meant that people had to acquire knowledge of the seasons and of the heavens so that they would plant at the right time and so that they could safely traverse trackless deserts, high mountain passes, and wastes of seas.

Conducive as such general conditions were to the changes which took place, it must be remembered that the geographic and climatic characteristics of the area had existed for a long time before any alterations in the economy were effected and that other more immediate and specific innovations must of necessity loom large in any explanation of what took place. Of these innovations the development of copper metallurgy was exceptionally significant. It set off a chain of technological changes in the fifteen hundred years before 3000 B.C. which may be considered to have had more far-reaching consequences than any subsequently arrived at up to the seventeenth century A.D.

Probably the first copper was found in its relatively pure state as a glistening metal in rocks or in the residue of some exceptionally hot fire which had been built on copper ore. But whatever the occasion for man's discovery of it, we know that Chalcolithic man, that is, man of the Age of Copper, was by about 4000 B.C. smelting it with charcoal in furnaces, heating it in crucibles, and pouring it into molds. He thus had a metal for tools and weapons which was far superior to stone, for it was lighter and less fragile, took a sharper edge, and could be more easily shaped to produce a greater variety of products. Of special importance was the fact that people were acquiring knowledge about the skills in metallurgy which were applicable with minor variations to a great number of metals. Thus they were laying an essential foundation for the use of materials which

Map 1
Cradles of civilization, 3000 B.C.-1000 B.C.

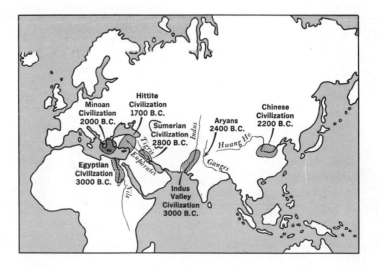

were more efficient and more durable than anything known hitherto, and tapping large sources of supplies—those which had been stored up over aeons of time in the earth's crust. Without these advances neither the high machine speeds of today nor the large amount of energy from inorganic sources, which we now take for granted, would be possible.

In addition to metallurgy, however, the Age of Copper witnessed the development of other techniques of the greatest moment. Pottery, which had previously been shaped by hand and fired for greater durability, began to be made on the potter's wheel and to be baked in special kilns.[1] The wheel, which is essential for the transmission of mechanical power and for the reduction of friction in land transportation, began to be used on the cart.[2] Furthermore, bricks fired in kilns date from 2500 B.C. in India. Wooden plows appeared in Egypt and in Mesopotamia about 3000 B.C.; oxen began to be used as draft animals, which meant that manure could be husbanded for specific use.[3] Carrying by water became more efficient because of the use of the sail (circa 3000 B.C.), which was one of the first instances of the employment of inorganic power for economic purposes, the construction of larger boats, and improvements in methods of steering[4] (Figure 3).

The combined effect of these innovations was greatly to increase economic activity. Smelting and working copper, turning pottery on the wheel, making kiln-fired brick, and constructing plows and wheels required skilled craftsmen who became specialists in their trades and who exchanged their products for agricultural goods. Better tools and agricultural techniques meant an increase in the output of foodstuffs per worker on the land, and hence the accumulation of surpluses which could be used in securing such amenities as earthen jars or copper sickles through channels of trade. And new techniques of transportation at one and the same time made possible and reflected an extension of commerce.

Thus, a division of labor, which is the *sine qua non* of high per-capita output, was taking place. Surpluses of different areas were being exchanged so that economies which were deficient in certain products had their outputs complemented by goods coming from afar.[5] And commerce

---

[1] This invention seems to have appeared first in Hither Asia before 3000 B.C., to have reached Egypt by 2700 B.C., and the Indus River valley by about 2500 B.C.

[2] Wheeled vehicles appeared in Sumer about 3500 B.C., in the Mesopotamian Valley generally by 3000 B.C., in India before 2,500 B.C., in Egypt by 1600 B.C., and in China and Sweden by 1000 B.C. Incidentally, the Mayan, Incan, and Aztec cultures never made economic use of the wheel, although it appeared in toys.

[3] Camels, asses, and horses were used primarily as pack and riding animals.

[4] At this time the oar or oars used for steering were fixed on one or both sides of the stern of the ship. The hinged rudder, installed directly astern, was to come much later.

[5] For example, the copper used in Egypt came mostly from the Sinai Peninsula; that employed in Mesopotamia came at first from Oman on the Persian Gulf. Furthermore, Mesopotamia obtained lead and silver from the Taurus Mountains of Asia Minor. Finally, finished goods seem to have been traded in this period between such centers as Sumer on the Lower Tigris and Euphrates Rivers and Egypt.

was leading to diffusion of knowledge which of itself tended to extend the vision and the imagination to new horizons. Withal, the range of opportunities for alternative decisions regarding the employment of human energies and other resources in economic activity was greatly extended.

Change in the Age of Bronze

Change in the Age of Bronze, unlike that in the Age of Copper, cannot be traced directly to a metallurgical innovation despite the fact that the new period was named after such an advance. To be sure, bronze, a mixture of copper and tin, provided a harder and more durable metal for tools and

Figure 3
Model of Egyptian yacht. This model of an Egyptian vessel from Thebes of circa 2000 B.C. illustrates many of the problems that were involved in early water carrying. The ship was so designed that it had a small hold. It was so constructed that it could be rocked to get it off sand bars and to facilitate getting it on and off landings. The paddlers constituted a good deal of the "payload." The steering apparatus is not a hinged rudder but consists of a steering oar lashed to a post astern. *(from collection of the Metropolitan Museum of Art, New York. Museum Excavations, 1919–1920; Rogers Fund supplemented by contribution of Edward S. Harkness. Reproduced with permission.)*

weapons, but it was not so much better than copper that it could do more than accelerate developments already initiated. The economic revolution of the Bronze Age was effected primarily by the invention of money (Figure 4), which, I am prepared to argue, was one of the most important inventions of all time in that it greatly facilitated the exchange of goods, and thus a division of labor, by the development of systems of writing and of numerical notation which made possible the recording and the transmission of data and ideas, and by the rise of cities and the great river-valley empires which established rules of conduct or laws for more orderly relations among people. Let us look at each of these developments in turn.

Economists usually define money as a medium of exchange, a measure of value, and a store of wealth. With the growth of trade it was essential to have some such instrument, for when one produces for unknown buyers, one cannot be certain that the purchasers will have goods to exchange which are really wanted in the market. Money is acceptable, however, in any market, because it is exchangeable for anything that is for sale. This is particularly true if money has the confidence of all, and early money had this confidence, for it consisted of pieces of metals, like gold, silver, and copper, which in themselves were in universal demand. Moreover, money permitted the amassing of wealth and the borrowing from many sources for the financing of large-scale enterprises, like distant trading expeditions, the construction of large buildings, and the execution of drainage and irrigation works.[6]

[6] Incidentally, the metallic content of money was not guaranteed by states until about 700 B.C.

Figure 4
Roman coin. This illustration is a denarius of T. Carisius of 48 B.C. The profile of Juno Moneta, patroness of mints, is clearly delineated. Profiles were used because they could be well rendered. Note the hammer and tongs on the reverse side of the coin. This particular piece has been mutilated by clipping the edges. Yet it was imperfectly struck in the first place. The denarius is the ancestor of the penny, the symbol for which was d. *(From the Moneys of the World Collection of the Chase Manhattan Bank of New York. Used with permission.)*

With the increasing use of money, banking came into being and with it the practice of charging interest. The former innovation meant that there were businessmen who specialized in the safekeeping of funds, in the accumulation of money from diverse savers, and in the lending of sums to those who would engage in business enterprise. Interest taking meant the creation of an incentive to hold savings in money, and this practice made mobile wealth available for those who would pay to use others' savings in the hope of making a profit. Here were added features of the monetary system which were almost as important to economic growth as money itself.

We specify one point in time as the age of the creation of money, but certainly mediums of exchange and measures and stores of value did exist beforehand. The *systematization* of these functions into a handy and efficient mechanism is the innovation. It suggests that the Bronze Age market for the interchange of goods and services was so developed in complexity and geographic extent as to require a monetary system to reduce the risks and costs of making transactions.

The second group of advances of the Age of Bronze, as has already been noted, was the development of writing, the establishment of numerical notations, and methods of obtaining knowledge, all of which seem, from the archaeological information that we have, to have stemmed from economic activity. The earliest forms of writing and of numbers were developed in the keeping of records of business transactions. Temple priests, for example, became engaged in such numerous and complicated operations that they could not possibly retain the details in their heads and made such long-term contracts that, the span of life being what it was, others than themselves had to know about the commitments made.[7] Also, in business agreements quantities had perforce to be employed; this gave rise to the use of agreed-upon weights and measures.

Then in the acquiring of knowledge, people of the Bronze Age effected a particularly significant revolution. Science, the search for general laws which consistently explain the relation between cause and effect, began to develop. With it mankind laid the very foundation for mastery over its physical and social environment.

Evidence of the advances made can be illustrated from arithmetic, where the multiplication table was developed, and from geometry, where proofs were sought to explain why given conditions always gave the same answers. From such beginnings it eventually became possible to construct

---

[7] The earliest forms of writing were pictograms. Then came in turn hieroglyphs, which are conventional signs for things; ideograms, which are symbols for ideas; phonograms, which gave sound values to ideas and things; and finally, in the nineteenth century B.C., the alphabet.

large buildings with accuracy. The Great Pyramid of Cheops (2420–2270 B.C.), for instance, contains 2,300 blocks of stone, some of which weigh 350 tons, has a base of 777¾ feet on each side, and has less than an inch of error in either length or level. Also, celestial observation led to a development of astronomy, which permitted the accurate measuring of time, the seasons, and points of the compass. Accordingly sundials for regularizing human activity were invented and a calendar of 365 days was created.

All these revolutionary innovations of the Bronze Age made possible a greater division of labor, a greater output of goods and services per operative, the concentration of economic surpluses in different localities, and finally the establishment of cities. The first urban centers of which we have knowledge came into being somewhat prior to 2500 B.C. in the three great river valleys of the Nile, the Tigris and Euphrates, and the Indus, and a little later along the Yellow River in China. The largest may have had populations of some 20,000, which is small by modern standards, but which was enormous compared with the size of argicultural villages of earlier times.

The same economic growth which made cities possible also led to the formation of great empire civilizations, such as those of Sumer, Babylonia, Assyria, Egypt, Mycenae, Phoenicia, and Crete. Social and economic relations in them came to be regulated by rules of conduct, known as laws, such as the Code of Hammurabi in Babylonia sometime around 1750 B.C., and by the creation of political powers which could make subjects adhere to their edicts. Most of these civilizations made important strides forward in architecture, that of Egypt especially expressing great refinement with its courts, its colonnades, and its pleasing proportions. Sculpture became more naturalistic, especially in Mycenae; paintings in tombs displayed a search for perspective and the use of bright if monotonous colors. Music became more refined with the use of the heptatonic (seven-note) scale and the construction of better instruments, such as the flute, the harp, and the lyre.

In spite of the progress realized in the Ages of Copper and of Bronze, all the leading economies showed signs of decay by the end of the second millennium B.C. Inasmuch as the tools and weapons made of the new metals were expensive, many persons did not possess them; those who did had a great advantage in production and thereby were able to effect a considerable concentration of wealth and power. Eventually a very wealthy class of kings, lords, or priests developed, with a very poor class of slaves, serfs, tenants, or freemen. The demands of the former upon the latter were very great and these demands came to be sanctioned by custom and laws and enforced by mercenaries.

Because of the distinction in classes, the rich became separated from actual production and took very little interest in it. They bent no energy to the solution of technical problems, for they knew very little about them and cared less, nor did they plow back part of their surplus into capital goods, for they had no real reason to do so. They were largely content with spending such surplus as they had upon luxuries, such as tombs and temples, personal adornment, and pleasures of the flesh. In the very process of becoming civilized, they turned so much of their energies away from economic activity that they contributed to economic decay.

The poor, on the other hand, did next to nothing to increase production by developing new techniques or by improving their organization of work, because they had no leisure in which to experiment on new methods, no resources for such experiments, and no incentive to turn out more goods. They knew all too well that whatever increase they might produce would be taken away from them in one way or another.

Consequently, during the Bronze Age itself little progress was realized in the techniques of production, save for the development of clear glass in Egypt and for improvements in the ship. What economic progress there was came chiefly by the diffusion of techniques within and among the main centers of civilization, by the concentration of wealth in larger enterprises, by trade, and by the establishment of peace among warring lords.

Then, to make matters worse, other peoples borrowed the production and war techniques of the leading economies. This fact led to the growth of economic rivals, to contests of strength among the great, and to intermittent raids on the centers of wealth by peoples on the frontiers. Indeed, the destruction of war and the political and social disorders which accompanied it were primary causes of decline. In fact, the Age of Bronze was to end with a series of wars and of mass migrations of warring peoples—the "Peoples of the Sea"—who came from the Balkans and the Black Sea regions into more civilized societies. Hence the Iron Age was inaugurated by economic decline and by a cultural dark age.

The Age of Iron and the supremacy of Greece

With the coming of the Age of Iron at about the beginning of the first millennium B.C., the center of economic life was to shift from the early river-valley cultures to Greece—the first great civilization upon the European continent. This event was of great import for Western culture, for it was from Greece that the West was to receive many of its richest legacies.

Undoubtedly the greatest technological event of the Bronze Age was the discovery of iron; in a very real sense, this one achievement compensated largely, in the broad perspective of the past, for the two millenniums of relative technical stagnation. The earliest use of iron is still shrouded in mystery, but there is evidence that a tribe in the Armenian mountains was employing iron even before 2000 B.C. At all events iron tools and weapons began to be widely used in Palestine, Syria, and Greece by 1100 B.C. and thence spread to other lands.

The development of iron metallurgy and the use of iron products constituted in itself an economic revolution (Figure 5). Unlike copper and tin, iron ore is quite abundant in nature and widely distributed; thus iron tools and weapons were relatively cheap in terms of human input and came within the reach of nearly everyone. At last even rather poor people could avail themselves of equipment that was in most respects as good as that of the well-to-do. Iron was in Ancient Times, as it is today, a plebeian metal, and it had a democratizing effect, at least from an economic point of view. It also made possible an attack upon the forests of Europe and the opening up of that continent to settled agriculture.

A long list of old tools, including shovels, spades, forks, mattocks, axes, and scythes, were now made of iron, and new tools made their appearance,

Figure 5
Primitive forge. The black-figure painting shown on this Attic vase of the sixth century B.C. pictures the kind of forge which was used in the metallurgical industry of Ancient Greece. Similar forges were found in many other cultures. The metal was worked into a "bloom," that is, a molten mass in the fire at the base of the forge. The upright furnace provided a draft for the charcoal fire. The fuel was put in from above. Note the tongs and hammers above the workers. *(British Museum, London, Greek Vase, 507 B.C. Adapted from photograph. Courtesy of the Trustees.)*

such as pickaxes for road work and sheep shears for cutting the wool which had previously been plucked from the poor animals. In general, therefore, agricultural workers were able to increase their production, particularly in those areas like European Greece where an exaggerated concentration of wealth had not taken place and where socioeconomic rigidities had not become established. As farmers built up bartering or purchasing power, they were able to demand more industrial goods from specialized crafts-men—from ironworkers, potters, weavers, and carpenters.

The demand for craft goods had, in turn, an impact upon industrial techniques. By 500 B.C. carpenters had such new tools as the iron saw and, by 50 B.C., augers and planes. In addition, existing tools previously made of copper or of bronze, like chisels, drills, hammers, and adzes, were now made of iron. Smiths, who in the working of iron had to spend long hours hammering iron into desired shapes (Figure 6), because it could not be heated sufficiently hot by ancient methods to make it liquid enough to be

Figure 6
Primitive metalworking. After metal had been "smelted," it had to be hammered to drive out impurities. This hammering was a tedious task and was not made lighter until the invention of a water-driven trip hammer. Note the products of the smith: a saw, knives, hammers, weapons, and a pitcher. *(From T. Schreiber, Atlas of Classical Antiquities, Ed. by W. C. F. Anderson, London: Macmillan, 1895, pl. 69, fig. 6. Reproduced by permission.)*

cast in molds, soon invented hinged tongs better to hold their blooms while they worked them and developed a great variety of specialized hammers. Shortly after 200 B.C. they built special anvils for making nails and blocks for drawing wire. Masons, too, had better tools; most importantly, they developed the pulley (eighth century B.C.), which allowed the construction of cranes and blocks and tackles. Thus building was made more efficient, and it became possible to bore tunnels and to construct aqueducts.

Furthermore, iron made possible improvements in various types of machines that did not stand up well when made of wood or the more fragile copper. Among these mechanisms was the water-raising wheel for irrigation and drainage; this consisted of a wheel fitted with pots or with chains holding pots that, as it turned, dipped water at the bottom of its arc and dumped it at the top. Because of its great resistance to friction, iron made new machines possible. Indeed, one of the most notable mechanical devices of the Iron Age was the rotary quern for grinding grain into flour. It consisted of two circular stones, the upper one of which turned on an iron pivot protruding from the center of the lower, which crushed the grain between them. By the fifth century B.C. this mechanism was being turned by animals hitched to a lever attached to the upper stone, which was the first use of animal power save for draft purposes (Figure 7). Once the principle of using non-human energy in industry became established, it was possible to conceive of employing inorganic sources of energy for power. It is not strange, indeed, that the water wheel, developed sometime

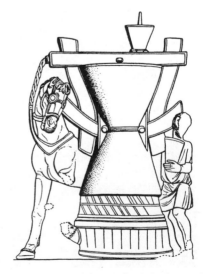

Figure 7
The quern driven by horse. The quern in this drawing is exceptionally large. The upper stone is being rotated by a horse which has been hitched to a wooden frame attached to the stone. Grain was placed in the upper part of the top stone, which thus served as a hopper, and was ground as it worked its way down between the stones. The flour would fall into a trough at the base of the quern and be collected by the workman. This picture is from a Roman sarcophagus of the second century A.D. *(From A. G. Drachmann, Archaeol.-Kunsthistoriske Meddelelser, vol. 1, p. 143, fig. 9, 1932–1935, Copenhagen, Det Kongelige Danske Videnskabernes Selskab. Reproduced by permission.)*

after 100 B.C., was first applied to the grinding of grain and continued to be used almost exclusively for this purpose well into the Middle Ages.

Lastly, in the Iron Age, more attention was given by the educated in society to economic matters, and one begins to get written descriptions of various kinds of mechanical devices. Archimedes (287–212 B.C.), one of the greatest mathematicians of all time, described the theory of the lever and thereby laid the foundation for theoretical mechanics, albeit building on his work was slight until the end of the Middle Ages. He also wrote about the screw pump, which he may have invented, and he developed many military devices, especially the launching of stones by the elastic power of twisted ropes. Hero of Alexandria (circa 50 B.C.) described a number of gadgets, many of which were mere toys, such as pumps, the syringe, a fire engine, devices for adjusting the wick on a lamp, a windmill arranged to drive a bellows of an organ, and a contraption moved by the expansive power of steam. The Roman Vitruvius in about 1 A.D. wrote a famous book on architecture and mechanics, nearly all of which had been borrowed from the Greeks, which discloses that Rome had knowledge of all the principles thus far mentioned, as well as a solution to the problem of the transmission of power by gears. Then, in the allied field of mathematics, Euclid published his *Elements* of geometry in about 300 B.C., Apollonius of Perga (247–205 B.C.) prepared his geometry of cones, and Hipparchus (160–125 B.C.) invented plane and spherical trigonometry.

The developments mentioned here meant not only that people in the Iron Age experienced economic growth through their ability to increase individual production, but also that there was an ever greater division of labor than there had been in the Age of Copper. Indeed, the demand for iron tools and weapons was so great and the techniques of ironmongering so specialized that ironworkers, among others, could concentrate upon the production of goods for unknown buyers. Finally, there was an enlargement of productive enterprises, for we find establishments employing twenty or even a hundred workers, and a thousand were at work in the Laureion silver mines of Athens.

As has already been stated, the area which profited most fully in an economic sense from the new methods of production was mainland Greece, in spite of the fact that the area is about the size of the State of New York and that only 20 percent of its surface can be cultivated. Greece produced specialized agricultural products, like olive oil and wine, which could be grown on its hilly land, and sold them in foreign markets, which were easily reached by sea. Subsequently it also turned out specialized industrial goods, such as iron tools and weapons, pots, and works of art, for which there was a foreign demand. By exporting such goods, Greece was able to pay for the foodstuffs and raw materials which it lacked. In this exchange it benefited, for then, as is generally the case, industrial products required the expenditure per unit of value of less human energy than did raw materials and foodstuffs. Moreover, the home market, at least in Athens, tended to grow because of a fair degree of economic equality and the absence for a long time of the subordination of labor by force to a slave status and hence to something approaching a subsistence level (Map 2).

Undoubtedly the wealth built up by great cities like Athens and Corinth provided much of the surplus which allowed human energies to be devoted to the arts, to philosophical speculation, and to technological improvements. Both in material and intellectual achievement and in their socioeconomic organization, the Greeks met in high degree the various conditions prescribed by Western culture's concept of civilization.

Why the Greeks did so well, or how any society achieves a high level of civilization, is one of the great problems of history. In this regard it is not without significance that the height of Greek civilization came at the conclusion of or shortly after the period of greatest economic growth, that is, between 600 and 400 B.C. Furthermore, the Greeks built upon the excellent art forms of Mycenae, developed rules of justice, had a social system that allowed men of talent to assume positions of leadership, and for a long time avoided stultifying rigidities.

Unfortunately this happy state of affairs was not to endure indefinitely, for Greece, like other societies which have attained a position of economic and cultural primacy, generated destructive forces within itself. Its superior agricultural and industrial techniques were diffused to other lands in the process of trade and colonization, particularly to the eastern Aegean and Mediterranean Seas, to Sicily, to Magna Graecia in southern Italy, and

Map 2
Ancient Greece and its trading areas

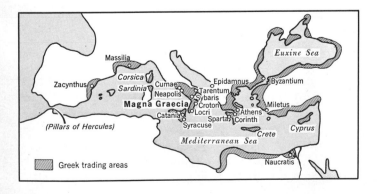

to the Black Sea area. Eventually these regions produced both for themselves and for Greek markets abroad the very goods that had previously been furnished by Greece itself. This development meant a decline in production in Greece, difficulties in getting sufficient food supplies from foreign lands, unemployment, a fall in real wages, and the development of rigidities, of which slavery was an outstanding example. A slave labor force meant that the internal market for goods declined, and there was less incentive than there had been earlier to adopt laborsaving devices or to apply animal or inorganic power to machines.

Moreover, Greece was badgered by political problems that ate away its strength. For one thing, Greece never achieved real political integration, but remained divided into city-states, which reduced the size of its domestic market, mitigated against an extension of the division of labor, and led to rivalries which resulted in intermittent wars. Finally, Greece was invaded by people on her northern frontiers and by Persians, and the ensuing wars were extremely devastating. Even though Alexander the Great was able to conquer most of the known world between 334 and 324 B.C., his efforts did little to revive a society that was on the way down.

The rise and fall of the Hellenistic East and of Rome

By the last half of the fourth century B C , economic primacy and the center of civilization were moving away from Greece proper to Hellenized cities of the eastern Aegean and eastern Mediterranean Seas. Here Greek treatises on husbandry were widely read and Greek practices imitated; here, too, olive oil, one of Greece's main export products, was produced in such quantities that it captured Greek markets. Moreover, cities in Asia Minor and on the Black Sea became important sources of iron tools and weapons. Cotton cloth, first known to the Greeks in the fourth century, was made in Egypt and Phoenicia. Parchments and papyrus sheets on which to write were made, respectively, by Pergamum and Egypt. The curing of fish, long practiced by the Greeks, was adopted by others, and luxuries, which had previously been supplied by Greece, began to come primarily from the Hellenistic East. Trade also flourished in economically developing regions, as is evidenced by the use of larger ships, some of which reached 5,000 tons burden, by the construction of lighthouses, like the famous one at Alexandria, and by the greatly increased use of money in exchange.

Undoubtedly Greece profited briefly in the third century B.C. from this general economic activity, but the revival was not enough to allow her to regain her former position. Throughout the Hellenistic period, from 338 to 30 B.C., the highest levels of economic prosperity and of civilization were attained in such places as Ephesus, Pergamum, Rhodes, Antioch, and especially Alexandria. Nearly all those who described new techniques at the end of the Iron Age, to whom reference has already been made, were from non-Greek cities—Archimedes was from Syracuse, Hero, from Alexandria, and Vitruvius, from Rome. Much of the sculpture of antiquity which has come down to us was from the Hellenistic East, such works as the "Dying Gaul" from Pergamum, "Laocoön" and the "Victory of Samothrace" from Rhodes, and the "Venus de Milo" from the Alexandrian school. Alexandria, with its library of some 500,000 rolls, its medical school, and its observatory, was the honored successor of Athens as the intellectual center of the world. It was thence that much of the knowledge of antiquity, even that of Greece, was transmitted to the West.

By the second century B.C., the Hellenistic East, in its turn, began to show signs of economic stagnation; in the first century B.C., it was manifestly on the decline. Here the age-old concept that the monarch owned the land and could collect dues from whoever worked it had the same effect as earlier—the exploitation of workers of the soil to a point where they had little incentive to increase production. Moreover, kings and their favorites got control of the more important industrial and commercial establishments and in their management of them made profits which were used for the owners' pleasure and culture rather than for the extension of economic activity through investment. Social disorders were numerous, and wars between parts of Alexander's former empire were frequent. Gradually, Rome entered the scene, sometimes upon the invitation of a wealthy group which wanted help, and once there used its position of power to its own economic benefit. Indeed, the chief aspect of the political history of the last part of the pre-Christian era was the absorption of the Hellenistic East by the Roman Empire.

Rome profited, as had the Hellenistic cities, from the various agricultural, industrial, and commercial techniques which it acquired from Greece or inherited from an earlier civilization of north-central Italy—the Etruscan culture. Thus, in the formative period of Roman history, from about the beginning of the first millennium B.C. to 270 B.C., an economic surplus was developed from greater agricultural output, from the manufacture of such goods as pottery at Arretium, the modern Arezzo, of spears, javelins, swords, picks, scythes, and chisels at Puteoli, the modern Pozzuoli, of the ubiquitous pots and pans at Capua, and from trade and the division of labor. Rome itself produced practically no new productive techniques, but it did organize well. It built numerous roads and ports which facilitated commerce, and it constructed great aqueducts for irrigating the land. In this period, too, the lower classes were given full citizenship, could participate in the most important political decisions, and could aspire to the highest offices of the state. Many of them owned their own land or small shops and hence had an incentive to increase output.

In the next period of Roman history, from 270 B.C. to 14 A.D., Rome
extended its sway over Carthage, Macedonia, Syria, Greece, Egypt, all of
Italy, southern Gaul, and some of Spain. This great empire the Romans
administered politically to their economic advantage. Not only did the
conquered lands have to pay tribute to Rome in one way or another, but
they took Rome's specialized products in return for foodstuffs and raw
materials—grain from Sicily, North Africa, and Egypt, copper, silver, lead,
tin, wool, and hides from Gaul and Spain, salt fish from the Black Sea, and
wool and dyestuffs from Asia Minor (Map 3). Roman cities grew in size
because of this activity; the population of Rome has been estimated at
from 650,000 to 1,200,000 in the Augustan Age that stretched from 31 B.C.
to 14 A.D. Urbanization gave a fillip to economic development, for persons
living in great agglomerations had to have services performed by others,
as in the case of providing food and water, which led to a greater division
of labor and trade. Also their demands were more diversified than those
of country folk. With the formation of cities, moreover, Romans devoted

Map 3
Rome and its empire at the end of the reign of Augustus

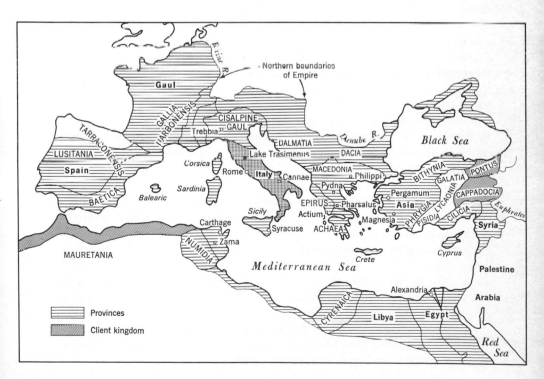

more of their attention to the arts, particularly architecture, sculpture, and letters. In fact, the height of Roman civilization was probably reached at the end of the Augustan Age and in the first century A.D., at the time of or just after the economic activity of Rome had reached its peak. In this respect the experience of Greece was repeated.

Once again, as in the case of previous economies, Rome developed forces that led to its undoing. Land became concentrated in great estates, the *latifundia*, whose owners lived in luxury in cities and whose workers got so little for their labor that they had no incentive to increase output. Techniques were exported and used to produce in conquered lands what had been obtained from Roman cities—a development that was particularly marked in Gaul. Imitation Arretine pottery from Gaul drove the home product from the marketplace. The lamps and glasswares and metal crafts of the Italian peninsula were buried under a flood of imports originating in sites as remote as Britain and Africa—strong testimony to the declining productivity of domestic Roman industry.

Social tensions increased in urban agglomerations as employment declined, and even the policy of providing "bread and circuses" to keep the people quiet proved to be only a temporary expedient. Parts of the empire found their production impaired by overcropping, as in North Africa, and could not make necessary deliveries of grain; other areas revolted and refused to continue the payment of tribute. Wealthy Romans invested less capital in producers' goods, but spent their surplus on luxury products for themselves. Many large landowners tried to make their estates self-sufficient and thereby they injured trade and the division of labor. Finally, the incursions of new migrant populations, both peacefully and, at times, violently, caused the withering of Roman central administration. The event of the year 476, the pensioning off of the last Roman Emperor of the West, was a transition of patent insignificance; few residents of the Western Empire had reason to care at all about it, for their daily lives were entirely unaffected.

Explaining the decline and fall of Rome has been a historical preoccupation for centuries. Christianity, depopulation, moral decay, racial mixture, overextension of empire, slavery, bureaucracy, soil exhaustion, military mismanagement, and class struggle are only *some* of the causes that have been proposed in our own century. Only one thing is certain: No single cause will ever be so convincingly advanced as to make consideration of alternative explanations obsolete. Without saying therefore that Rome's fall was of exclusively economic origins, we may still contribute a catalog of economic failings and misfortunes that befell the late Empire.

Agriculture, the foundation of national income, declined. Italian lands since the time of the Republic had been put to inefficient and harmful use as the peninsula came to rely on foreign grain supplies. Absentee landlords of oversized latifundia cared only for maximizing revenues in the short run so that money could be spent in Rome. The agricultural labor force was tied to the land, but this did not prevent a continual abandonment of acreage as soil productivity failed.

Taxation to support governmental excesses and to pay for the protection of overextended frontiers was oppressive. The urban middle class (the *curiales*) was yoked to the task of tax collection. Some chose slavery rather than submit to a life of trying to drain blood from stones.

Economic mobility was outlawed. Professions became hereditary by law, and investors were likewise forbidden to transfer capital from one business to another. The efficient allocation of factors of production terminated and industry ossified.

Inflation and currency debasement became endemic. At the beginning of the fourth century A.D., Diocletian, the last effective ruler of the Empire, attempted reforms which seem familiar to modern observers. Uniform gold and silver coins from the imperial mint replaced the welter of provincial issues. To check a runaway inflation, an edict of wage and price controls was issued, setting a maximum price for every good and service and a maximum for all wages, fees, and stipends. These measures provided temporary solutions, it is true, but at the same time the Emperor's new tax programs, based on units of income-producing real estate (*jugum*) and on labor and livestock (*caput*), provided the basis for even more effective fiscal oppression.

All these factors contributed to the economic decline of Rome. Falling productivity, population, and standards of living were the consequences. Certainly this combination was as lethal to the continuance of Roman hegemony as "barbarians" at the gates.

In antiquity a pattern of economic growth and of economic decline was established, which was repeated several times. The Ancient world's experience contained many lessons of importance, but none was more significant than how to maintain economic development over long time spans. How the successors of the ancients tried to solve this problem will be the theme of the remaining chapters of this work.

The agrarian economy
of the Middle Ages

The Middle Ages: the formative period of Western culture

The term "Middle Ages" was coined in the Renaissance when Western
Europeans were rediscovering the glories of Greece and of Rome. Their
choice of an appellation for the years that stretched from the fall of Rome
to the close of the fifteenth century had something derogatory about it.
The coiners of the term were of the opinion that they were emerging from
a millennium in which civilization had been at a low ebb, that they were
leaving behind them a dark age, and that they were experiencing a great
cultural revival. Subsequently in the Enlightenment of the eighteenth century their characterization of the Middle Ages received further confirmation, for writers like Voltaire condemned what they believed to be the
dominant aspect of the Middle Ages—the superstition and irrationality of
its religion and the poor taste of its people for things aesthetic. Even the
great architecture of the Middle Ages was dubbed Gothic, as though it
were the creation of the Goths and hence barbarian and decadent.

The expression Middle Ages was, however, a gross misnomer for the
thousand years after Rome was invaded by the peoples on its frontiers. It
was not a time of waiting for a new and glorious future but rather the long
formative period of Western culture, comparable in many respects to the
formative periods of the civilizations of both Greece and Rome. It was the
childhood and perhaps even the period of puberty of the West. It was the
time when some of the basic ideologies of Western European culture were
being established, when attitudes regarding economics, society, politics,
and philosophy were being formed, and when many of the institutions of
Modern Times had their beginnings. The Middle Ages comprised, therefore, a period not to be scorned, but a period to be studied if one is to
understand much that is fundamental to the Western world.

The Renaissance writers who coined the expression "the Middle Ages" and their successors who confirmed and added to their concept did a further disservice to a comprehension of the era by lumping all the thousand years together and by applying their characterizations with little discrimination among times and places. In fact, most modern European languages even today use the singular Middle Age instead of the plural Middle Ages, thus implying that this was a static period with little social change. Indeed, in many histories of the Medieval world generalizations regarding life, work, and thought are presented as though they were equally valid for all of Western Europe during an entire millennium.

The Middle Ages did not, however, constitute a single unit. There were several acts to the drama, several scenes to each act, and several "off-stage" performances accompanying the main show. For at least the economic history of the Middle Ages, it is possible to discern four major periods: the first, from the fifth to the eleventh centuries, when a manorial economy was being established and when extensive trade over large areas was slight; the second, from the twelfth century through the thirteenth, when there was a revival of trade, an expansion of industry, a renaissance in arts and letters, and the beginning of a breakdown of manorialism; the third, in the fourteenth and early fifteenth centuries, when wars and the Black Death ravaged particularly France and England and when there were signs of economic stagnation; and the fourth, the latter part of the fifteenth century, when there occurred a Renaissance—particularly in Italy and the Low Countries—and also a new activity in commerce and in Portuguese and Spanish explorations and discoveries overseas. Even this periodization is, however, based upon the most typical aspects of what was taking place and does not mean that the same changes were taking place everywhere, for they were not.

Clearly one must beware of those hoary generalizations which are applied to all the Middle Ages and to all Western Europe. For the Medieval period we can subscribe to Voltaire's aphorism that "all generalizations are false, even this one." Fortunately the aphorism has an escape clause, of which we shall take advantage.

The economy of the Middle Ages is usually characterized as having been essentially agrarian—an agrarianism based upon the relatively self-sufficient manor and employing crude agricultural techniques. To an extent all this was true, but one should not lose sight of the fact that all economies, except very local ones, prior to the nineteenth century were predominantly agricultural, that the self-sufficient agricultural estate had appeared in the late Roman period, and that remnants of the manorial system were to remain far into Modern Times. Moreover, within the Middle Ages there were many changes in manorial life. Many varieties of agricultural enterprise existed. Improvements were made in agricultural techniques; and after the twelfth century there was a trend toward farming for a profit—toward capitalistic agriculture. Undoubtedly the changes which took place resulted in output per agricultural worker that was in general higher than it had been in the Ancient period. If there were a dark age for agriculture in the West, it was most marked at the time of the Germanic invasions when settled agriculture was disrupted.

Frequently the Middle Ages are characterized as having had little trading over a large area. To some extent this generalization is also correct, especially in the eighth and ninth centuries when the manor was largely self-sufficient, when political conditions made travel uncertain, and when Western Europe's commercial activity on the Mediterranean was severely reduced. Yet even in these centuries there were cities, like Venice, that lived almost exclusively from trade. The Scandinavians carried on trade through Russia with the Byzantine Empire. And certain products necessary to life, like salt, were distributed throughout the West. Later on, in the twelfth and thirteenth centuries, trade actually staged a great revival, and though it fell off in the fourteenth century, it was on the way to recovery in the fifteenth century.

In a similar fashion, medieval industry is frequently represented as having been organized into guilds, whose members charged a fair price for their goods, and as having been conducted on most primitive lines. To be sure there were guilds, but they varied so greatly in time and place that it is difficult to generalize about them except to say that they endeavored to regulate the production of goods and to monopolize the local market. Moreover, from the thirteenth century onward, particularly in large towns and in expanding branches of industry, there was a tendency for guilds to evolve in such a fashion that master craftsmen's shops produced for more than the local market and employed for wages workers who had little chance of becoming guildsmen. The so-called "just price" was in essence a customary market price rather than an arbitrarily low price and was aimed at those who tried to take advantage of special circumstances, like invasions, to charge unusually high prices.

Some industries were never organized along typical guild lines, and by the twelfth century, some manufacturing was conducted in fairly large units, as, for example, the silk industry at Lucca and the woolen industry in Flanders. Nor were the medieval craftsmen's techniques so very backward. They included all that the Ancient world had used and many new things besides. When one compares the summary of ancient techniques by Vitruvius with the writings of Leonardo da Vinci at the end of the Middle Ages, one finds a world of difference, particularly in the field of mechanics.

As regards the overriding ideologies of the Middle Ages, many of which loom large in Western culture, we may agree with the universally accepted view that they stemmed mostly from the accepted Christian religion and that man's main concern was to get into heaven, where he would find his true reward for having lived in conformity with Christian principles. It is true, too, that he was told that avarice was a cardinal sin, that the accumulation of wealth implied avarice, and that the Bible bluntly stated that it was more difficult for a rich man to get into heaven than it was for a camel to pass through the eye of a needle.

Yet, in spite of all this, ideologies which stemmed from the flesh rather than from religious teachings were not unknown. Wealth is, after all, a relative matter, and it was possible to rationalize the possession of it by the use to which it was put. Indeed, St. Augustine thought that wealth was excellent if employed for the common good. The Church itself sought riches and indulged in some very sharp practices, like the collection of relics in such abundance that there was enough wood of the "true cross" to build a fire, and like the sale of indulgences on such a scale that there was a "real estate boom" in Purgatory. The Franciscan order, established in the thirteenth century by the humble St. Francis, who would do no harm to man or beast, became wealthy in the generation after its founder's death. The Benedictine order preached the virtue of orderly work, and the Cistercians organized large farms which they operated in part to satisfy market demand. Lords and bishops were often given to ostentatious displays of material well-being.

From the twelfth century onward burghers managed in one way or another to find excuses for circumventing the Church's rules against taking interest and making profits. To be sure, the slogan of the medieval man was not "get rich quickly," perhaps because it was so difficult to do so, but neither was it, with few exceptions, to glorify the soul by abasing the flesh in poverty nor to renounce completely this world for the next. Here, as in so many phases of medieval life, there were contradictions between theory and practice. At least toward the end of the Middle Ages the trend toward investing surplus for individual gain, which is the basic ideology of the capitalist system, was being generally accepted. Here was an attitude that was to become dominant in Western culture.

Another cliché regarding the Middle Ages is that society was organized on a hierarchical basis in which every man was born into a given station from which it was difficult, if not impossible, to emerge. Such a generalization implies great social rigidity and the lack of opportunity for those of low birth and high talents to achieve an elevated status in society. This contention embodies some truth, especially with the firm establishment of feudalism by the ninth century and by the creation of guilds by the twelfth century, yet here again there is need for qualification. Although there was much less social mobility then than there is, for example, in present-day America, some mobility did exist. It was possible for the lowly born to achieve status within the Church or in monastic orders, for them to rise in the service of lay lords, and later, when trade became more general, for them to acquire status through wealth. In fact, it was the growing power of men of wealth—the bourgeois—that was to overthrow the basic hierarchical structure of the Middle Ages. It is difficult to say why the medieval bourgeois maintained their economic creativity so much longer than their predecessors in the Ancient world, but the range of opportunities open to them proved to be great and they managed in one way or another to play along with those in political power so that they were not squeezed to death.

It is also frequently stated that the Middle Ages were characterized by the universality of culture, the universality of the Latin language, and the lack of political centralization. There is much truth to all these allegations, for basic Christian doctrines were universal. Much of the literature, like the Arthurian cycle and the *Romance of the Rose,* available to the few who could read, was enjoyed throughout the West. Gothic architecture was the standard from the twelfth century to the Renaissance. Latin was the universal language of the Church and of scholars, and there was no general political power that embraced large parts of the West. Yet, when this has been said and emphasized, one must add the usual qualifications. Within Christian philosophy different schools of thought developed, and the very debates on religious issues led to questioning of the faith and ultimately to heresies. Even some of the propositions of St. Thomas Aquinas, today the very symbol of Catholic conservatism, were condemned after his death by the Archbishops of Paris and Canterbury; and Dante's *De Monarchia* was put on the *Index* in the sixteenth century.

Literature, too, in spite of its early universal character, began to be written in vernacular languages, and to be more characteristic of the places of its origin. Latin, particularly toward the end of the period when "humanists" tried to purify it, gave way to national tongues. Thus, in the Middle Ages two important steps were taken which were to contribute much to the rise of nationalities—the literary use of national languages and the creation of national literatures. Eventually, too, Gothic architecture gave way to a revival of Greek and Roman forms. Last but not least, as feudalism waned, one feudal lord began to extend his sway over others, so that even in the political sphere the dream of a universal empire, attempted by Charlemagne in 800 A.D. and again by the German Otto in 962 when the new Roman Empire (which was called the Holy Roman Empire in the twelfth century) was founded, was not to become a reality.

Our main concern here is not, however, with religion, with art, or with politics, but rather with economic and social history, to which we must return. What we have been attempting to do is to show that the Middle Ages were not so completely static nor from the twelfth century onward, at least, not so backward—not so dark—as has often been maintained.

Furthermore, we have aimed to indicate that traditional generalizations about the Middle Ages must be examined critically. Finally, we have suggested that many basic ideologies representing material well-being of the modern Western world had their beginnings in the Middle Ages, and that along with them there appeared in formative fashion some of our fundamental economic institutions.

The establishment of the manorial system

We begin our more detailed consideration of the economic history of the Middle Ages with an analysis of agriculture, not because in this segment of life were to be found the chief factors of economic growth, but rather because, as has already been said, agriculture was almost the sole economic activity of man in the early part of the Medieval period. Although few trustworthy statistics are available regarding the population of Medieval Europe and although we lack quantitative data regarding the distribution of the population by occupations, what evidence we have indicates that at the beginning of the fourteenth century between 80 and 90 percent of the people of France were making their living directly from the land, and probably this proportion was approximately the same in other countries. Incidentally, this occupational concentration in agriculture was not to be much reduced for the whole of Western Europe until the nineteenth century.

In the study of medieval agriculture it is almost essential to begin with the organization of the manor, for this institution gave life on the land its dominant characteristics. In brief, the manor was a large estate, where the land was owned by a lord, where the common people were attached to the land which they had a right to work, and where these serfs paid the lord for the use of land and for protection in stipulated amounts of goods and services, and later in money.

The concentration of land in large estates was nothing new. Great estates had been formed in the Italian peninsula during the period of Rome's expansion, in part as a result of land grants to important personages, including military leaders, and, in part from inheritances, purchases, marriages, and seizures of a political nature. Large estates also existed in Gaul well before the Romans came to give the "barbarians" a model to follow. Furthermore, on the great holdings both in Italy and in Gaul a portion of the land was set aside for the use of the owner, and the rest was divided into numerous plots to be worked by the rank and file of society —the *coloni*. Only a few districts, notably those that were very mountainous or those that were swampy or very heavily forested, escaped this development. And what was more, the Roman estate or Gallic *villa* pattern of agricultural life remained intact throughout the German invasions and well into the Medieval period.

As time went on, however, and as commerce diminished almost to a standstill, a change came over the large estates. Even in late Roman times, as we have seen, there had been a tendency for the estate to become self-sufficient, and this trend was accentuated particularly in the eighth and ninth centuries. As the estate produced mostly for its own needs, both its economic arrangements and social relations became more rigid.

One aspect of this growing rigidity was the institution of feudalism. In essence, feudalism was a system whereby all lay members of society had obligations to someone above until the supreme authority of the king or emperor was reached. Thus the serf owed services and goods to his lord; lesser lords, like knights, owed allegiance to some superior lord, like a count or baron; and the highest-ranking lords owed fealty to the king.

This infeudation of society resulted from a whole series of complicated factors. With little economic expansion, or commerce, or money, and with a considerable amount of disorder, the common people wanted above all else land and protection. Emperors, kings, and other politically ambitious personages, for their part, wanted power in order to be able to enforce their wills on others, to maintain order, and to live well. In order to raise armies for defense or to perform certain other public services, these political leaders invoked the time-honored dodge of claiming title to all land and of making grants to those who would perform for them certain specified services, such as furnishing soldiers in case of need. The recipients of large holdings, in turn, made smaller grants to those who would do the hard work in field and forest, but made them on condition that these grantees would perform certain services for and deliver certain goods to them. Other leaders, however, simply established local governments in response to need for order in the absence of any other strong authority. At all events, princes got the means of establishing an armed force to maintain order; the lords got a labor supply for their holdings; and the lower classes got land for their own use.

To make these arrangements as binding as possible, one had to swear not only to be loyal to one's superior, but also in essence to recognize that it was impossible to free oneself from one's obligations. All society thus became bound together by an intricate system of agreements, the sanctity of which was recognized by custom and supported by force. The lower classes were not slaves in the sense that they could be bought and sold,[1] but they were serfs who were not free to leave the land nor to break

---

[1] There were cases, however, in which serfs were sold along with the land. Some household workers were also slaves. See the study on this subject by Charles Verlinden of the University of Ghent, *L'Esclavage dans l'Europe médiévale* (Bruges: De Tempel, 1955).

their ties to their lords. On the other hand, the upper classes were not free to effect changes in the arrangements with their underlings and in addition had to assume a certain responsibility for their serfs in times of famines, plagues, and wars. Kings and emperors, although in origin heirs to Constantine and Charlemagne, were little more than lords who had established their domination over other lords and had to rest content with a rather ephemeral political existence. The political system of feudalism meant, above all else, decentralization and localization of power.

By the twelfth century this system had come into full flower. At that time many estates were 10,000 acres in size, although the very large ones of important lords, of bishoprics, or of monastic orders ran well over this figure. Inasmuch as these great estates had been built up of smaller holdings through marriages, gifts, inheritances, conquests, and mortmain, the holders of them usually owed allegiance to several superiors. It sometimes happened that these superiors were rivals, and when this was the case the raising of fighting forces through land-tenure obligations could not be relied upon to produce the desired results. Furthermore, the lands comprising the very large estates might be separated from one another by miles of intervening estates, a condition which precluded the possibility of operating the estate as a whole. The effective productive agricultural unit was the manor.

The establishment of feudalism was, in essence, the solution to a dual problem of administration and communication. Granting benefices in return for military and administrative services was a means of extending control over far-flung and sparsely populated regions in the absence of rapid transportation and communication upon which modern centralized governments rely. Great lords and their lesser vassals both benefited from the arrangement. But the manorial relationship, that between manor lord and agricultural peasant, is harder to account for in terms of costs and benefits, though not for lack of trying by economic historians. Basically, two differing viewpoints emerge.

The first view might be called the *theory of contractuality,* espoused jointly by experts in medieval law and some modern economists (strange bedfellows!). Its premise is that the relationship between lord and serf was of mutual benefit and was in the nature of a contract freely arrived at over centuries. The contract, varying in conditions from place to place, became the most powerful of medieval social bonds, the "custom of the manor." The lord's share in the arrangement was support (for himself and his military retinue) without his having to do agricultural labor. The serf's share was protection from invasion, pillage, and other violence from within and without the village. Further, as the custom of the manor prescribed the tenant's payment largely in terms of workdays, not produce or money, the contract insulated the serf from loss of land rights resulting from an inability to "come up with the rent." Both the landowner and the tenant thus shared in the risks of agricultural life. Serfs could not be evicted, and if the harvest was meager, both lord and serf suffered losses.

The second opinion concerning the manorial relationship might be called the *theory of coercion*, for it asserts that serfdom was but a variety of slavery. In this view, the key fact of the establishment of manorialism was the elimination of all labor-force mobility, thereby abolishing any labor market, however rudimentary. In the view of the economist Evsey Domar, recourse to labor coercion in agriculture results from the following preconditions:

1   "Free" land, the abundant factor of production, in the hands of a limited landowner class (the lords)
2   Scarce labor, the result of low population density
3   Political power of the landowners to work their will

Without coercion (serfdom) a market for agricultural labor to work the land would bid up the price of labor (in terms of a high wages or generous tenancy rights) and so largely eliminate landowner profits. The manorial contract thus became a mechanism of slavery by which a cheap, fixed supply of labor was guaranteed to each landlord.

Fortunately for us, the two views of the manorial relationship, while contradictory, are not mutually exclusive. No one would deny completely either the element of bondage to the soil in serfdom or the elements of mutuality built into the customs of the manor. Those who have experience with similar historical debates will know that a final and conclusive resolution in favor of one view over the other is very unlikely. The danger, in fact, is to become too convinced by any one generalization. The "typical" manor is a fiction; the variations from location to location and from time to time were so great as to preclude any single right answer.[2]

Description of the manor

Although manors differed from one another according to variations in terrain, fertility of the soil, the kind of crops grown, and manorial contract, it is possible to present a composite picture of them (Figure 8). In the center of the manor was the manorial village, dominated by a castle, manor house,

---

[2] For two important interpretations of the manorial relationship see Douglass C. North and Robert Paul Thomas, "The Rise and Fall of the Manorial System: A Theoretical Model," *Journal of Economic History*, vol. 31, Dec. 1971, and Evsey Domar, "The Causes of Slavery or Serfdom: A Hypothesis," ibid., vol. 30, March 1970.

Figure 8
Medieval village with open fields. The distinction between a town and a village was in the later Middle Ages determined by whether or not the place had a degree of political autonomy or even independence from the overlord. The distinction was not determined, as is sometimes maintained, by whether or not the place was fortified by a wall

or monastery, built for protection upon a height, or in flat country with a large moat around it. Attached to it were barns for livestock and for storing grain and hay and other buildings for housing the lord's bakery, smithy, and winery, brewery, or cider press, according to the local drink of the people.[3] Nearby the castle was the church, the size and general importance of which depended upon the wealth of the community and upon whether or not the manor belonged to a lay or religious lord.

---

[3] Fermented drinks were customary because by rule of thumb the people had learned that their water supply might not be sanitary. As a rule, wine was preferred to other drinks, but because grapes could not be grown in the colder climates, recourse was had to cider, beer, or ale.

Clustering around the manor house and church, but in a more exposed position, were the dwellings of the serfs. These were usually built of stone or of wood and mortar, had tile, wood, or thatched roofs, and had few windows, because glass was dear and parchment let in little light. They were often designed, as is frequently the case even to the present, so that livestock in stalls or pens on the ground floor would provide some warmth in winter for the living quarters upstairs, unless, indeed, animals were taken directly into the household. Attached to these houses there was usually a garden, with an outhouse located nearby.

Then somewhere within the village there was a well or a fountain where people fetched their water. The streets were sometimes paved with stone blocks, but they were more frequently simply made of packed dirt and gravel, which became quagmires in the rainy seasons and dust bowls in the dry ones. There was also the lord's gristmill, located along a stream, if there were one that could turn a water wheel, or in an advantageous place to catch the wind, if the millstones were run by a windmill. Finally, around the whole there might be a stone wall with heavy gates of wood reinforced with iron, which were closed at night to keep out marauders.

Outside the village or town was the manor's forest, pasture, meadows, and arable land. The forest belonged to the lord, but peasants had the right to get their firewood there and sometimes to cut wood for buildings. The pasture or "commons" was opened to the livestock of all, but the number of head which any one person might turn into it was limited, because a too-numerous herd in the possession of one peasant would mean that there would not be enough feed for the livestock of others. The meadows were also common to all, and there peasants might cut hay which would help get their livestock through the winter months.

The arable land was, of course, the most important part of the manor's existence, for it was the source of most of the people's food supply. Usually the arable land was divided into two or three large fields, which in turn were partitioned into small strips. Some of the strips were set aside for the exclusive use of the lord and constituted his demesne where he grew food for his household and household workers. Others were divided among those serfs who had a contractual right to land and varied in size, depending upon the fertility of the soil, from 5 to 20 acres, which was supposed to be enough to sustain a peasant family. Because typically one of the large fields was allowed to remain fallow each year, that is, was not cultivated but grazed, so that it might recover some of its fertility, the strips of both the lord and the peasants were scattered among these fields. Finally, the strips of one individual in each of the fields might be dispersed in order that each holding might be of equal fertility.

The holdings of a peasant had great stability and still give to the cultivated land in some parts of Europe a patch quilt character. This rigidity resulted from the fact that although peasant holdings could usually be inherited on the making of certain payments, they could not be sold nor could they, as a rule, be consolidated by marriage. Nor was there much incentive toward larger peasant holdings, for without markets in which to sell surplus products, except in times of famine, the chief purpose for having more land was to increase one's supply of consumers' goods. Thus what economic differences there were among peasants with land usually came about through harder work, better planning, thrift, and good luck and were manifested by better houses, better clothes, a better table, and more livestock. Investment for more than a modicum of greater production was, therefore, almost unknown among peasants and for that matter among lords.

Some serfs, as has already been suggested, were not fortunate enough to have any land other than garden plots to cultivate, and this class was filled by the younger children of peasants for whom there was no inheritance. Some of these people were cottagers or cotters and worked on the lord's land or on the land of well-to-do peasants in return for payments in kind. Others were the lord's servants, who could sometimes be sold. Some were shepherds or herdsmen; others were artisans who worked in the lord's mill, smithy, or ale- or winehouse. A select few were employed by the lord as overseers, the chief of whom was the seneschal or bailiff, whose office came to be hereditary.

The entire structure of society, based as it was on an inflexible landholding system, was a rigid one, and this rigidity was maintained both by the lack of economic opportunity and by restrictions imposed by the lord on the individual activity of peasants. Since it was, indeed, in the lord's interest to perpetuate a system that supplied him with a satisfactory existence and that maintained relatively friendly relations among his serfs, he was at no loss to find ways to control affairs to suit his ends. Thus the lord established various claims upon the peasants and their lands, and when these did not suffice he sat in court over issues at stake and rendered decisions which favored the kind of world which he wanted.

In the course of time there came into being under this system a number of "dues," some of which were very burdensome, which the peasant owed the lord for the use of land. Among the most important of these were week work, boon work, and deliveries in kind. Thus the ordinary serf might have to work for his lord from one to five days a week, three days out of six being the most common. Inasmuch, however, as the rule was that each holding should provide week work, the serf might send a grown son to fulfill his obligation, but he might have to furnish at the same time a team of oxen or a cart and thus was temporarily deprived of the use of his capital equipment. In planting and harvesting seasons, the serf was required to give additional services to his master, but this boon work was measured in tasks to be performed rather than by time. Thus the peasant might have to plow part of the demesne, or cut grain on one of the lord's strips, or thresh a given quantity of grain. Furthermore, the serf had to deliver to his lord some of the produce of his own land, maybe fish or honey, or a lamb in the spring, a pig in the late fall, a duck at Christmas, and eggs at Easter. If the manor was owned by a monastery or if the lord had many workers in his shops, deliveries in kind consisted more of basic foodstuffs.

In addition to fulfilling these regular requirements, the serf was subject to additional payments upon special occasions. When he gave a daughter in marriage, he had to make a payment in goods or money, although this exaction, known as *formariage,* was levied in France as a rule only when the daughter was wedded to a man from another estate. When the lord was in great need, as for example when he was at war, the serf had to pay a *tallage* or *taille,* an unspecified amount determined arbitrarily by the lord and hence subject to considerable abuse. The peasant was also subject to the *champart,* a part of his field crop, a survival of the Roman public tax, that theoretically went to the territorial prince but which was often simply confiscated by the serf's immediate superior. For the use of the lord's gristmill, drink-making equipment, and bakery, he had to pay fees, called banalities, which consisted of a part of whatever was being processed. Upon his death, a serf's heir or heirs had to deliver their best animal or some other object of value to the lord (*heriot*), and if a serf died without direct heirs, the lord got all his property (*mortmain*). Last but not least, the peasant had to pay a tithe to the Church, which was in theory at least a tenth of his annual produce.

The lot of the serf was thus not very brilliant and that of freemen was not much better. Even they had to provide week work, boon work, and deliveries in kind to the lord. In fact they were free only in the sense that they were not subject to servile restrictions and that they could leave the land if they wished. What made the situation of the tillers of the soil particularly burdensome, at least from our modern point of view, was the practical impossibility for them to improve their condition. They could run away and join bands of vagrants who roamed the forests, but such a life, even if one were a Robin Hood, was a precarious one and not for the masses.

One should not, however, represent the life of the serfs as utterly miserable. They did get land to work, and they got help from the lord in times of famine and other misfortunes. They also had time for play, which must have been very robust, if one may judge from the literary accounts and pictorial representations of their fun. Their greatest difficulty, especially as regards economic growth, was that they were in a box which was kept tightly shut by convention—by the various contractual and customary bonds which we have described.

Production on the manor

The political forms of manorialism in all their rigidity should not be allowed to overshadow the technological importance of manor cultivation, particularly the development of three-field agriculture that began in the eighth and ninth centuries in manorial Europe.

Two-field agriculture (or two-course rotation) means that land is alternately cultivated and left fallow on an annual basis. Fallow land is left open to grazing so that fertility might be replenished by manuring as well as by "resting" the soil from tillage. The three-field system (or three-course rotation) is a more productive method whereby a given parcel of land is left fallow only one year in three, rotated between winter crops (wheat or rye) and spring crops (oats, barley, beans, peas) during nonfallow seasons. Intensity of land use is thus increased. Likewise the amount of labor devoted to tillage (in terms of man-days per year) increases with the adoption of semiannual sowing and reaping of nonfallow fields. The transition from two-field to three-field agriculture in Northern and Central Europe happened largely in the Middle Ages. The impact was a large increase in the productivity of the land with reduction of fallow. The steady rise in the population of Europe that dates from the eleventh century is linked to the rising productivity of the soil, the effect of the new agrarian technique.

The exact nature of the link between population growth and agricultural productivity is a "chicken or egg" problem (which came first?), which recurs periodically in the history of rural life. Simple logic tells us that population increases must be supported by greater food supplies. This is particularly true when part of the growing population leaves the land for nonagrarian pursuits. Ergo, agricultural growth precedes and sustains demographic growth. But it has been argued convincingly that growth in numbers of persons causing pressure on food supplies is the main cause of technological change in agriculture. Farmers, it is reasoned, can be induced to farm more intensively and to work longer and harder—as intensive techniques invariably require—only when threatened by population pressure.[4]

---

[4] The general thesis of population pressure as the source of increased productivity on the land is the work of Ester Boserup in *The Conditions of Agricultural Growth* (Chicago: Aldine, 1965). Her argument covers the full gamut of changes in cultivation from primitive slash-and-burn agriculture through the total elimination of fallow in Modern Times. For the details of medieval cropping see B. H. Slicher van Bath, *The Agrarian History of Western Europe, A.D. 500–1850* (London: E. Arnold, 1963) part 2; and Lynn White Jr., *Medieval Technology and Social Change* (Oxford: Oxford University Press, 1962), Chap. 2.

Table 1 Estimates of Europe's population, 400 B.C.–1950 A.D. (in millions of inhabitants)

Year	Population estimate	Year	Population estimate
400 B.C.	23	1400	45
1 A.D.	37	1450	60
200	67	1500	69
700	27	1550	78
1000	42	1600	90
1050	46	1650	103
1100	48	1700	115
1150	50	1750	125
1200	61	1800	187
1250	69	1850	274
1300	73	1900	423
1350	51	1950	594

SOURCES: Merrill K. Bennett, *The World's Food* (New York: Harper & Row, 1954), p.9; B. H. Slicher van Bath, *The Agrarian History of Western Europe, A.D. 500–1850* (London: E. Arnold, 1963), p. 78; Fernand Braudel, *Civilisation Matérielle et Capitalisme* (Paris: Colin, 1967), p. 26; United Nations, *The Determinants and Consequences of Population Trends,* Population Studies No. 17 (New York: United Nations, 1953), p. 11.

Clearly the question of which came first is secondary; a spiral of increasing magnitude between both interacting factors—population and food production—is a more plausible model than a simple cause-effect relationship between one and the other. The important fact to note is that agricultural change and population growth are inextricably linked. The Middle Ages, despite the social and political rigidity of the period, emerge as a time of economic dynamism founded upon improvements in productivity on the manor.

The chief natural resources in agricultural production are fertile land, water, warmth, and sunshine; accordingly upon these ingredients depends in large part the output of the individual farm worker. Western Europe was particularly well endowed with these factors of farm production. As can be grasped from Map 4, Western Europe had large plains of fertile land, such as the Po Valley in Italy, the plain between the Pyrenees and the Massif Central, that from the Massif Central to the Vosges, Ardennes, and Jura Mountains, and the Rhône Valley in France, the flat land of the Low Countries, and the Rhine Valley, the Danube Valley, and the great rolling stretches in Germany and Austria. Here was a vast area, quite different from the limited arable land found in the mountain valleys, coastal plains, or plateaus of central Italy or of Greece or from the narrow strips of

Map 4
The topography of Europe

productive land along the Tigris and Euphrates or Nile Rivers.[5] Furthermore, the natural fertility of much of this land was enhanced by the fact
that it had not been exhaustively cultivated over centuries, but had been
fairly recently reclaimed from forests, marshes, and heaths.

Also, Western Europe was blessed, as it still is, with plenty of rainfall
and a temperate climate, and although droughts and too much rain were
not unknown, they were usually relatively local in character. Sufficient
rainfall in the growing seasons meant that seeds germinated quickly and
thus diminished the chances of erosion, that crops were lush, and that
pasture grass, except in mountain areas and in the colder regions, was
available to feed livestock out of doors for large portions of the year.[6] In
general, European climatic conditions were almost perfect for growing the
grains which constituted the staple food and for the husbandry of those
animals which were most important to human consumption—cattle,
sheep, pigs, and hens. The chief drawback was that winters were longer
in Western Europe than in the Mediterranean regions, but wood for fuel
was plentiful; grains could be stored and meat cured for the unproductive
months. After the fireplace and chimney, which reached Northern Europe
in the twelfth century, replaced the brazier, it was possible to protect
oneself from the cold indoors without being suffocated by smoke.

Differences in soil and climate within the European continent led to
differences in the adoption of three-field agriculture and of the manorial
system. The region which today comprises northern and central France, the
Low Countries, and Germany west of the Elbe River, with its rich soils and
four distinct seasons, was the heartland of the manorial system. Even in
this favorable territory the diffusion of the new agricultural method was
by no means uniform or rapid. Agriculture changed very slowly, for the
risks associated with trying out a new style of cultivation were high. An
experiment which failed could bring starvation. The political extension of
feudalism to more remote areas such as England and northern Italy brought
variants of the new agriculture in its wake, but large areas of Europe
(Iberia, southern Italy, Scandinavia, and Eastern Europe) continued to
employ farming methods which were more rudimentary but better suited
to local soils, climate, and population density than the "classic" three-field
manor.

Output does not depend only on available natural resources, as we have
previously indicated, but also upon a knowledge of the productive arts—
upon techniques and technology. In this respect the farmers of the Middle
Ages knew about all the ancient methods of cultivation and had all the

---

[5] The fertile land along the Nile south of the Delta averaged only 12 miles in width in Ancient Times.

[6] In some parts of Europe one sees, even today, few large barns for the storage of hay or for the stabling
of animals in the winter.

ancient tools. In their borrowing from their predecessors they simply adapted what had already been developed to a new environment, improving where necessary. The Middle Ages witnessed the development (between the tenth and twelfth centuries) of a harness for the horse that did not choke the animal when it pulled. It also saw improvements in the plow —the introduction of the coulter up front to cut the sod, an iron plowshare that could dig into heavy soils, a moldboard that turned over the earth instead of just scratching it, and wheels that steadied the implement, made the plowing of a straight furrow much easier, and lessened the labor of the plowman. In fact, by the thirteenth century the modern walking plow had assumed its general form, although it was not yet made of the more durable steel. Lastly, the Middle Ages made progress in threshing, which is one of the more arduous of farm tasks. Up to the eleventh century grains, beans, and peas had been separated from their stalks, shells, and hulls by beating them with straight sticks or by driving animal-drawn sledges or rollers over them. But at that time the hinged flail came into use. If handled with dexterity, this was a great labor-saving device; if used inexpertly, it might crack the operator in the back of the head.

One of the greatest technological handicaps under which medieval agriculturists labored was lack of knowledge of how to maintain the fertility of the soil. To be sure, they recognized the value of manure on the land, but there was usually a shortage of it. This lack resulted from the pasturing of animals for long parts of the year in the open, and only rarely were animals confined in limited pens so that the droppings could be concentrated. However in Mediterranean lands, where animals were, and still are, kept in stables for most of the year because of the lack of pasture in the dry summer months, farmers had supplies of manure that they put on the lands which were to be seeded. In times of high prices for grains, such as from 1150 to 1300, and in those places which were producing for market, farmers might buy "night soil" (human excrement) from the cities or hen droppings from neighbors, and they might marl their land, that is, put on it a soil rich in lime and clay.

Yields in the Medieval period were very low, although they varied greatly by year and place. The yield of wheat was not far from 4 bushels to each bushel of seed sown and that of rye was only a little more, compared with some 14 bushels today. Animals were also small: even as late as 1710, sheep sold at the Smithfield Fair in England averaged only 28 pounds and beef cattle 370 pounds; whereas at modern slaughterhouses they run 135 and 1,800 pounds, respectively. Under the common pasture system, improvements in breeds were difficult and took place mainly in areas where cattle were isolated and feed was so scarce that it had to be husbanded carefully for only the best animals, such as on the islands of Guernsey and Jersey and in the lowlands of Holstein and Friesland. Under most circumstances fodder was in short enough supply that the fall was a time for slaughtering, except those animals which were kept for breeding or for work or those, like chickens and cows, which produced all winter.

From a study of medieval agriculture, one reaches the inevitable conclusion that, from the standpoint of the individual peasant, no great improvement in the standard of living attended technical change. The land-tenure arrangement was harsh and the work load, if anything, increased. Diet was still a monotonous succession of bread, garden produce, and thirst-making salted meat and fish in small quantities. The vagaries of climate kept most of agrarian Europe under the perpetual threat of death by famine. The bounty of increased yields went to feed an ever-increasing number of mouths. Thus, paradoxically, the roots of the decline of the manorial system lay in its early successes.

Economic expansion and the decline of the manor

The chief force that upset the manorial system was the economic growth fostered by productivity increases. Above all there was population growth. Although estimates of the continent's population are unavoidably imprecise, it can be stated with confidence that the inhabitants of Europe doubled in number between the eighth and fourteenth centuries (Table 1). Where population density increased, the self-contained manor became an anachronism. Self-sufficiency became less necessary for survival as regional markets for food and other goods developed. Enforced bondage to the soil became an outmoded form of land tenure as the agricultural labor force expanded.

Related to the demographic expansion, a second important force in the decline of the manor was the revival of commerce and the growth of towns. In the eleventh century there was renewed activity in Western European trade in the Mediterranean, in the North and Baltic Seas, and along the land routes which joined the riverain countries of these two areas. With the revival of commerce on a larger scale, towns came into existence, and with the towns, there appeared industries which produced goods for unknown buyers in far-off lands. With trade of this kind, money reappeared in greater volume than formerly, and economic relations came to be expressed more and more in terms of money prices instead of in goods, services, and land.

Thirdly, the rapid decline in population in the fourteenth century, when the medieval expansion came abruptly to an end, created a temporary labor shortage that had an effect upon the manorial system, particularly in England. And finally, the increased use of money and the consolidation of political power in the hands of kings with some authority led to a shift from armies composed of knights who owed military service to their lords to armies composed of soldiers paid with moneys raised by taxation.

Most of these factors operated together to undermine feudalism and the medieval manor; thus it is quite arbitrarily that we consider first the effect of the increase in population. As might be expected in an agricultural system that had little flexibility, there was a limit to the number of stomachs which could be filled on the manors. As population grew, the excess, usually the younger sons, simply had to go elsewhere. Some of them took off on conquering expeditions, like that of the Norman adventurers in Sicily at the end of the eleventh century, or William the Conqueror's invasion of England in 1066, or Crusades to the Holy Land. Of more importance to the decline of the manorial system was the fact that others, in the twelfth and thirteenth centuries particularly, went to the towns to participate in the growth of commerce and industry and that still more moved to unsettled lands where a different form of agricultural organization was created. Both the opportunities for and better terms of employment in these new outlets for population made manorial arrangements seem particularly burdensome and in the long run proved them to be untenable.

In the next chapter we shall see in more detail what the condition of town workers was; here it is sufficient to state that these men were free and that they had a chance to improve their economic status by hard work and enterprise. For the present, we shall concentrate our attention upon the opening of new lands to cultivation. This movement becomes visible by the twelfth century, when recently founded religious orders, like the Cistercians, as well as enterprising secular lords, took advantage of the available labor supply created by the increase in population to found new farms on land that had not yet been brought into cultivation, whether by clearing forests, by draining marshes, or by seizing territories beyond the frontiers.

So anxious were protagonists of the new agricultural settlements to attract labor that they indulged in current forms of advertising, which painted a rosy picture of the conditions on their lands, and what was of still greater importance, they offered favorable terms of employment to those who would come to work for them. Thus on the new agricultural units freedom was granted to any serf who would stay on the job for a year and a day[7] and there, in fact, serfdom hardly existed. Here there was seldom any oath of fealty to the lord; there was no labor service comparable to week work and boon work; and there were no requirements like mortmain, heriot, and *formariage.* Inasmuch as the workers got by perpetual

---

[7] A lord did not usually, however, extend this rule to apply to his own serfs, for he did not want to destroy existing manorial arrangements so long as they were of some advantage to him.

and inheritable contracts the right to cultivate a stipulated amount of land or the right to given quantities of goods produced, they were required to make certain payments to the owners of the land, whether lords or religious orders. Some of these dues were held over from the earlier manorial system, like tallage, the necessity of performing military service, and banalities, but these were all less arbitrary and less burdensome than they had been formerly, and the last-named was actually rent for the use of capital equipment. The chief payment under the new arrangements was *le cens,* which was usually a fixed amount of money and was essentially what we today would call rent. Because this payment was a stipulated amount in a long-term contract, the burden of it was reduced as prices went up, which they were to do over the next centuries, for with rising prices the sums owed represented fewer goods.

As these fundamental changes in the relationship of lords to peasants were taking place—changes which were in the direction of establishing monetary relations between owners and workers—lords began to alter their attitudes toward agricultural enterprise. They were less interested than formerly in simply securing goods for their own consumption and more in getting goods for sale in the market in return for money or in receiving money payments for the use of their land. Their ends might be attained by dividing the land into strips or into unified farms and then of receiving salable products or *le cens* from the landholders, a system described by the German term *Landherrschaft.* But they also might manage the farm enterprise themselves and try thereby to produce not only enough to support their workers but also an extra amount for the market, a system known as *Gutsherrschaft.* Small, unified farms with the peasant living on the land were found, for example, on the reclaimed land of the Low Countries: whereas large estates farmed as units predominated on the conquered land east of the Elbe, a characteristic of this area which was to be maintained until after World War II.[8]

One further aspect of the inroads being made into the old manorialism was visible in the laws and customs of the new agricultural villages. In some places they received charters from their lords which were copied from those that had previously been granted to commercial towns. Hence the *hôtes,* literally the guests, who came to settle in the new agricultural villages had a status something like that of the burgesses in the commercial towns, had the right to nominate a mayor, and had some administrative autonomy. Of special importance was the fact that the harsh seneschals or bailiffs of the manorial system were no longer present, for if peasants were treated as badly as they had been, they would simply pack off and

---

[8] The lands of Cistercian monasteries were also farmed as large units on the *Gutsherrschaft* principle.

the lord would be left with no labor. The new management had to have some semblance of being reasonable in order to be successful.

The territories into which this new organization of agriculture spread were of various kinds. In France from the Loire to the Meuse were to be found the new agricultural villages of which we have been speaking, and south of the Loire, *bastides,* or estates developed by lords. In Spain, lands taken by Christians from Moslems were colonized along military lines. In Italy, where feudalism was never very firmly established, changes took place as Saracens were driven out and as the civil wars of the tenth century came to an end. In the Low Countries, lands settled in the new manner were largely those reclaimed from the sea, the so-called polders, by building levees or dikes to keep the rivers within bounds and in some places to keep out the sea. The practice of building dikes was so successful that Flemings and Netherlanders were called upon to carry their arts to the lower reaches of the Elbe, and thence to settle Mecklenburg and Brandenburg. Indeed, Flemish colonists went to Thuringia, Saxony, Lausitz, and Bohemia. By the end of the twelfth century Mecklenburg was completely settled and by the end of the thirteenth, so, too, was Brandenburg. Then the Teutonic Knights, from 1230 onward, pushed into East Prussia, Livonia, and Lithuania, establishing the system of *Gutsherrschaft,* while Bavarians and Rhinelanders spread out to Bohemia, Moravia, Silesia, the Tyrol, and even to the frontiers of Hungary.

With the extension of an agricultural system where large farms were operated by lords to produce goods for the market or where single farms were rented for money to individuals who lived on them instead of in villages, there developed some specialization in production—some division of agricultural labor. Thus from the twelfth century the Cistercian monasteries in England concentrated upon the production of wool; peasants and lords in the Bordeaux region of France specialized in wines; and lords east of the Elbe applied themselves to the growing of grain. In each of these cases, as in many others, much of the produce was sold in distant markets.

This new kind of farming was eminently successful, so long as agricultural prices were rising, compared with that of the old manorial system. There custom-bound practices provided little surplus that could be sold, and lords whose lands were thus encumbered eventually sought ways to free their estates from peasant claims. For their part, serfs were anxious to improve their lot, which seemed to them much worse than that of workers in towns or of those under the new agricultural system. Accordingly serfs were often freed for a monetary consideration. Many of their dues were commuted to money payments, and the rules of heriot, *formariage,* and mortmain were lightened. Demesne lands were sometimes sold to capitalists but more frequently were rented to free peasants for money or for a share of the crop. Crop sharing, or the *métayer* system as it came to be called in France, became particularly popular in southern France and in central Italy, where it is still practiced. When labor was in very short supply, as it was in England after the Black Death in the fourteenth century, these arrangements were particularly advantageous to the peasants, for lords had to attract peasants to their lands.

In these ways, and logically enough, actual serfdom in the feudal sense, and also manorialism, broke down most completely and most rapidly in those places where trade and industry were most highly developed. Thus in Lombardy, Tuscany, northern France, and Flanders they were definitely on the way out by the middle of the twelfth century; whereas in England they did not show signs of decay until the end of the thirteenth century, and in isolated places were not very much altered until later. Furthermore, periods of changing prices, now that agriculture was at least partially geared to a price system, meant an additional pressure for alterations in agricultural procedures. Incidentally, grain prices rose sharply in the twelfth and thirteenth centuries, fell from 1300 to 1450 as the population was decimated by famines and the Black Death (1316, 1347–1351, 1360–1370, and 1400–1401), went up again slowly from 1450 to 1550 and then more rapidly until approximately 1650, declined until about 1720, and then climbed until 1819.

Despite the decline of the early manorial system, connected as it was with feudalism, and of the growth of capitalist farming for profit through money rents or through the sale of goods in the market, various remnants of the earlier arrangements were projected into Modern Times. Lords still had nominal title to the land, except where it had been sold clear of all restrictions, and these titles gave the lords certain rights. As we have already seen, they could collect rents and some services from their peasants. They exercised justice over their people. They collected banalities, and where changes had been slight, they might have some rights of heriot, mortmain, and *formariage*. The Church still collected tithes from the peasants and the growing political states began levying taxes upon them. Peasants had little voice in public affairs and many of them were confronted with problems of trying to farm widely scattered strips with time-honored techniques. Thus with the beginning of Modern Times, there were agricultural reforms to be effected before all agriculturalists were freed of all obligations to overlords and could operate with entire liberty in a money economy. But changes there had been, and the trend was clear. Agriculture was on the way to becoming a capitalist enterprise in which profits could be made and a surplus could be invested for the making of still more profit.

4

The fall and rise
of medieval commerce

Economic decline to the eleventh century

In recent years many economic historians of the Middle Ages have been
inclined to represent commerce as the touchstone of medieval economic
activity.[1] Their fundamental contention has been that the lack of trade
from the early Middle Ages to the eleventh century accounted for economic stagnation in this period; hence the revival of commerce in the
twelfth and thirteenth centuries was largely responsible for the economic
growth which took place within this two-hundred-year span. Persuasive
as their arguments and data are, the position taken here is that numerous
factors, of which commerce was only one, interacted in such a way as to
have an accumulative effect of decline in the first half of the Middle Ages
and of revival and growth in the second half. Indeed, even the facts
presented by those who stress the overwhelming role of commerce suggest
that the simplistic explanation should be eschewed for the more complex
one, that what was important in causing a decline and then a growth was
the result of many factors working upon one another.

That there was a decline of commerce in Western Europe in the first
half-millennium of the Middle Ages is uncontestable. It is evidenced by
the falling into disrepair of Roman roads, by the decline of towns, and by
the lack of archaeological evidence in the form of goods or coins of any
wide exchange of products. This lack of trade may be regarded, however,
in part as an effect of economic decline rather than as a main cause of it.

---

[1] For example, see the work by the great Belgian medievalist Henri Pirenne, *Economic and Social History
of Medieval Europe* (New York: Harcourt, Brace, & World, 1956). For a discussion of the Pirenne thesis, see
A. F. Havighurst (Ed.), *The Pirenne Thesis: Analysis, Criticism, and Revision* (Boston: Heath, 1958).

As we have already seen, commerce within the Roman Empire had fallen off drastically before the Goth Odoacer replaced the last Roman emperor in 476 A.D., because Rome's production of exports was insufficient to offset imports, because internal disorders connected with the weakening power of the state made the transport of goods precarious, and because the tax-collecting system and public financial burdens had induced landowners to create self-sufficient estates. Furthermore, the treasure in precious metals which Romans had amassed through trade and conquests was so completely drained off, especially from the second century A.D. onward, by payments which Rome had to make for foodstuffs, that sufficient bullion to support a satisfactory coinage system did not exist. In fact, as the treasure dried up, Syrian merchants came less and less often to Rome and finally disappeared altogether from Roman markets.

To a large extent similar conditions existed in Britain, Gaul, and Spain. To these areas the loss of Rome as a market was a severe blow. Moreover, it was accompanied by a series of in-migrations, usually known as the "barbarian invasions," which were reminiscent of the migrations of the Peoples of the Sea at the beginning of the first millennium B.C. In the third century A.D., Franks crossed the Rhine barrier and pillaged as far as Spain before they came to a halt. Then the West Goths, after sacking Rome in 410, moved into Gaul and Spain. Vandals from Eastern Germany drove through the same countries to North Africa, whence they attacked Rome in 455. Huns raided Gaul and Italy in the middle of the fifth century and then vanished into Eastern Europe. East Goths migrated to Italy (489–493) and were ultimately absorbed there. Finally, Jutes, Angles, and Saxons from northeastern Germany invaded Britain. Burgundians came into southeastern Gaul, and more Franks came into Gaul in the fifth and sixth centuries. Even though these great migrations were more gradual and less violent than had once been supposed, their massive movements did upset the established system and, with it, commercial intercourse.

Moreover, no sooner had the migrations come to an end than Western Europe was threatened by a new and perhaps even more disturbing force from the outside—the Moslems. In the sixth century an Arabian camel driver, known in history as Mohammed, claimed that he was the true prophet of God and shortly acquired a band of faithful followers. His religious sect grew by leaps and bounds and in the seventh century, fired by religious zeal, embarked upon conquests to win the world to its persuasion. Within a hundred years after their prophet's death Moslems had created a vast empire which stretched from the western bounds of India through Persia and Arabia and across the north of Africa. In the seventh and eighth centuries they overran Spain and, unsuccessfully, attempted an invasion of France. They occupied the Balearic Islands, Corsica, Sardinia, Sicily, and certain ports of southern Italy. In 846 they raided Rome. In the tenth century, they had a military outpost at Garde-Freinet, a short distance inland on the French Riviera, whence they preyed on pilgrims and merchants taking the land route between France and Italy. This encirclement of Southern Europe by Moslems was made even more complete by their intermittent raids along the coast, such as their pillaging of Pisa in 935 and 1004, their destruction of Barcelona in 985, and their incursions into the Gulf of Lyons and into the Bay of Genoa.[2]

As a climax, Western European life was disrupted by invasions of marauding Hungarians in the tenth century and of pillaging Normans in both the tenth and eleventh centuries. Under these circumstances what little trade had been maintained between Gaul and the Mediterranean was still further reduced. The lack of accounts of merchants traveling these routes from the south to the north and the absence of Arabic coins found in trading centers on them offer strong evidence of what was taking place. Towns that had lived on Mediterranean commerce were no longer important, and their decline was felt far inland. Fairs were now almost entirely of a local character, only that of St. Denis on the outskirts of Paris attracting buyers and sellers from a distance. The creation of an economy based on land was hereby given a new reason for being.

The decline of commerce and the growth of the manorial system had, in turn, a decided impact upon industry. With little opportunity for selling surpluses in distant markets and with the chief demand for industrial goods being on the large estates, industry came to be almost as exclusively manorial as agriculture itself. This fact meant that Europe produced next to nothing which was in demand in the markets of the eastern Mediterranean. Thus the circle in the downward spiraling of distant commerce was complete. On the manor the people raised their own sheep for wool and raised their own flax for linen, spun these fibers into thread, wove the thread into cloth, and fulled and dyed their finished product. Nor was this work in textiles done by specialists in workshops. Rather it was carried on as a domestic enterprise by peasant women, children, and men in their spare time, especially in the winter months when work in the fields was slack. Furthermore, peasants could do most of the rough carpentry work which they needed, could process nearly all their own food, and could make their own clothes and some few of them their own shoes. Even the few things which they could not produce for themselves, largely because they lacked equipment, were for the most part furnished by the lord's mill, winery or alehouse, and smithy. In fact, about the only goods obtained

---

[2] Moslems increased their own supply of precious metals not only by raids on Christian churches but also by booty from their conquests in Syria and Persia, by pillaging the tombs of the Pharoahs in Egypt, and by trading with gold-producing areas of Africa, like the Sudan, Nubia, and Abyssinia, and with silver-producing regions, like Khurasan and Transonania in the Near East.

through commerce were salt, iron, glassware, and pottery. Yet, the relatively wide distribution of salt in the sea and in mines, the many outcroppings of iron ore, and the prevalence of clay suitable for pots resulted in many small establishments which produced for nearby markets. Hence, it is not surprising that industrial techniques changed little during the first half of the Middle Ages—that the great medieval inventions came after the eleventh century.

Nor is it strange that the concentration of economic life on the manor should have had repercussions on the use of money, credit institutions, and attitudes toward the accumulation of wealth. With the localization of economic activity on the manor, money ceased to be an important store of wealth and was used primarily as a medium of exchange for the few purchases peasants had to make. Even lords had no great accumulation of mobile wealth, and when in desperate financial need, as in times of wars and famines, had to have recourse to borrowing. Evidence of the decline in the use of money for other than small transactions is to be found in the coinage system established by Charlemagne. By the ninth century, the gold solidus of the Roman Empire had become so rare that a new money had to be brought into being. This money was based upon silver, obtained largely from older coins and from the melting down of silverware, rather than upon the dearer gold. Its basic measure was the pound (livre, libra) weighing 491 grams, which was divided into 20 shillings (sous, solidi), each of which was, in turn, divided into 12 pence (deniers, denarii). The significant thing about these measures was, however, that only pence and halfpence coins were ever issued, pounds and shillings being used only for bookkeeping purposes. This system, adopted in all the territories under Charlemagne's rule, was for the times satisfactory, since it provided the small change needed for purchases. Incidentally, these divisions of money lasted in most European countries until the French Revolutionary and Napoleonic period and until most recently (1971) in Great Britain.

In spite of Charlemagne's efforts to establish a usable money for his empire and of the continued employment of his pound, shilling, and pence system, a state of anarchy befell money after the dissolution of the Carolingian Empire and the collapse of public administration in the monarchies which were created from its remnants. Feudal princes were quick to assume the privilege of striking coins, and kings frequently bestowed the right of minting on churches. As a consequence there were soon throughout Western Europe almost as many different pennies as there were large fiefs; to make matters worse the pennies were of varying degrees of fineness and weight. In the beginning of the eleventh century, a mark, probably of Scandinavian origin and weighing only 218 grams, was introduced into the Germanies, but it did not help stabilize money, for all kinds of pennies were used to make it up.

Furthermore, those who had the right to mint were given to "crying the money down," that is, calling it in, issuing new coins of less value in their stead, and paying those who had brought in their coins penny for penny in the debased money. This was a very profitable operation and recourse was had to it with great frequency. For example, in the thirty-two-year reign of one German prince this act of prestidigitation was performed on the average of three times a year. Moreover, so much copper was ultimately mixed with silver, even less than 10 percent of silver, that coins soon turned black and were dubbed "nigri denarii." Finally, existing techniques of minting by hammering out pieces of metal and then stamping them with a die hit by a hammer were unable to achieve standard weights, sizes, and shapes. The differences in coins which resulted from the use of such methods invited both counterfeiting and such common practices as clipping edges and "sweating" silver coins, that is, shaking them in a leather bag until a certain amount of dust could be recovered. Little wonder that coins were looked upon with suspicion, were tested with the teeth for hardness before being accepted, and were sometimes weighed to check on tampering. If commerce had been thriving, such money would have been intolerable. Indeed when trade revived, monetary reform was the order of the day.

With all the rest of economic decay in the first half of the Middle Ages, there was also a decline in the use of credit and the adoption of a hostile attitude toward it. Churches and monasteries now had the chief accumulations of gold and silver, for one of the ways for the faithful to express their piety was to bestow their riches upon those institutions which held the keys to eternal salvation. Most of this wealth was in relics, ornaments, and adornments of various kinds, but it could be rendered mobile by melting it down and minting it. Recourse to such extremities was not rare, for when lords were in dire need of funds they borrowed from churches and monasteries. As can readily be imagined, they pledged repayment in the only wealth at their command—in revenues from their lands. If these revenues, or part of them, went to reduce the principal of their debt, their pledge was called a "live gage" (*vif gage*), but if they were pledged to the creditor without reducing the principal, the contract was called a "dead gage," or mortgage.

Invariably these debts were incurred to acquire consumers' goods rather than to purchase capital equipment for the purpose of producing still more goods. Inasmuch as this was the case, the religious lenders could hardly take advantage of the misery of the people to exact heavy tribute for the use of their savings. Thus it came about that the Church did not lend at interest or usury, as it was then called—a term which acquired all the discreditable overtones that it bears even to the present day. In time the Church supported its practice of not taking interest with the doctrine that money was in itself unproductive, that it was, in fact, "sterile." With such arguments it was able by the ninth century to forbid the laity to take interest and to reserve to ecclesiastical courts jurisdiction over questions involving usury. If these steps had not been taken, spendthrift lords and princes would undoubtedly have borrowed much more than they did for purposes of ostentation. Moreover, heavy consumption debts would have resulted either in such a rapid change of or concentration in ownership that society based upon land, feudal loyalty, and manorial production would have been upset. Indeed, changes in the practice of borrowing for investment, in the taking of interest, and in the Church's attitude toward it came only with economic expansion and the need of capital for the conduct of business.

From all the evidence which has thus far been presented, the economy of most of Western Europe in the first half of the Middle Ages can be characterized as having been first in a state of decline and then of stagnation—as having evolved a socioeconomic system based on land in which rigidities prevailed and the "range of opportunities for alternative decisions" was extraordinarily limited. There were, however, two parts of Europe which did not conform to the pattern thus far laid out: they were certain Italian cities of the Adriatic and in the southern part of the peninsula, on the one hand, and specific ports of the Baltic and North Seas, on the other. In them long-distance commerce was being carried on when it was almost nonexistent in the West, and accordingly in them there was not such an extensive decline in business and business institutions as there was where manorialism was triumphant.

The focus of the trade of both these areas was Byzantium or Constantinople, a fact which requires a word of explanation. As is well known, the Strait of the Bosporus had for centuries been the location of trading centers because of its situation at the juncture of transportation routes between the Black Sea, with all its great tributaries, and the Aegean and Mediterranean Seas with their vast littorals. During Roman times Byzantium rose to great importance. At the end of the third century A.D., when Diocletian divided the empire into two parts, he chose this most important center of commerce as his capital in the East. Then in the fourth century, when conditions in Italy were particularly disturbed, Constantine moved his capital from Rome to Byzantium and rechristened the city in honor of himself. Although "barbarians" subsequently made inroads into the Eastern Roman Empire,[3] they never upset the applecart as they did in the West. When they attained to the emperorship, they maintained authority, the dignity of their office, and their frontiers. Moreover, Moslem attackers

---

[3] They defeated the Emperor of the East at the Battle of Adrianople in 378.

who laid seige to Constantinople in 719 were turned back and were never able to dominate either the Aegean or the Adriatic Sea. As a matter of fact, many Italian towns—Naples, Gaëta, Amalfi, Salerno, Bari, and above all Venice—continued a rather tenuous recognition of the Emperor of the East until the eleventh century.

Throughout all this period the economy of Byzantium continued to be vigorous. In the eighth century, Constantinople had a population of a million people and was thus by far the largest city of the known world. Furnishing this great agglomeration of people with the basic necessities of life was in itself a major enterprise and required the tapping of supplies over a vast area. But what was more, many people in Constantinople possessed enough wealth to indulge in luxuries and semiluxuries, ranging all the way from elegant churches, like St. Sophia, down the scale to fine clothes and trinkets. The resulting active demand for industrial products kept the local craft shops and bazaars busy and attracted goods from far and wide. Indeed, Constantinople was a great entrepôt for such Eastern products as silks, spices, dyes, and perfumes and for such European goods as furs, amber, timber, and iron. Money was used in this trade and was free from gross tampering; credit practices, inherited from Rome, were maintained; and neither interest taking nor other forms of profit making were frowned upon.

So great was economic activity at Constantinople, so strong was its commercial magnetism, that it is not strange that Europeans were drawn into its orbit. Those most completely affected were Venetians at the head of the Adriatic Sea. Their city had been established at the time of the invasions when people of the mainland in need of protection sought refuge on the sandy lagoons off the coast. As time went on Venetians, having no other source of livelihood except fishing, turned to shipping and commerce. In both they were eminently successful.

At an early date Venetian merchants were trading with Constantinople and were finding this business particularly lucrative. There was always a good market for the silks, spices, and other luxuries which they brought back in exchange for their exports of timber and iron, both of which were in short supply in the Eastern Empire. Gradually they accumulated wealth, an important fleet, and enough power so that they became virtually autonomous in the eighth century and formed an independent republic in the ninth—a republic which lasted until 1797. When the Moslems threatened to extend their sway, it was in the interest of the Venetians to repel them, and they collaborated with Byzantium in doing so. By the beginning of the twelfth century they had rid the Adriatic of Dalmatian pirates and had control of the eastern coast of that sea. And in the eleventh century they stopped Norman expansion eastward and by so doing eliminated the competition of the rival ports of Naples, Gaëta, Salerno, and above all, Amalfi.

Meanwhile, Venetian traders became so important to the Eastern Empire that they were exempted from paying certain import duties (992), were allowed to establish numerous trading stations (*fondachi*) in many Eastern ports, and in 1082 were given the extraordinary privilege of not paying any commercial taxes—a privilege that citizens of the Empire did not enjoy. Furthermore, Venetians were not above trading with the infidel Moslems and established commercial relations with Egypt, Syria, and North Africa. In this trade they added to their standard articles of export Slavs from Dalmatia and the Black Sea, hence the word "slave." Evidence of these early trade connections with the East survives in elements of Venetian architecture and city nomenclature to the present day.[4]

Because of the commercial activity of Venice, with which most of its population was in one way or another connected, there was never any question there of establishing serfdom or of adopting a hostile attitude toward profit making. Interest was taken in one way or another; money was lent for investment rather than consumption. Fairly advanced forms of business organization were employed, like multiple partnerships and the *commenda* (collegantia), and literacy among laymen, which was then an indication of the scope of economic activity, was extensive, for otherwise it would have been impossible for merchants to keep their complicated accounts or to receive written reports from their agents.

To some extent, conditions resembling those in Venice existed in other Italian towns that traded with the East, especially Bari and for a time Amalfi. Moreover, Venetian commerce eastward was bound to have repercussions westward. At the end of the ninth century, the district around Verona and many places in the Po Valley were trading with the Queen of the Adriatic; in the tenth century, Pavia, Treviso, Vicenza, Ravenna, Ancona, and many other places had been affected. Certainly by the eleventh century, German products were coming through the Brenner Pass in the Alps and Eastern products were making their way northward in return. In Venice itself there began to be signs of manufacturing, especially luxuries like glass, playing cards, and chessmen, that had hitherto been imported for far-flung European customers. Finally, certain other cities like Pisa and Genoa began to awake to the facts of economic life and to indicate a desire to break into the Venetian commercial act. Thus, from the principal Western trading center of the first half of the Middle Ages there radiated an idea and a practice which were to lead to a revival of commerce and to economic change throughout the West.

---

[4] The great cathedral of St. Mark's was built along Byzantine architectural lines in the eleventh century. Within, a crypt is said to contain the body of Venice's patron saint. According to the traditional story, the apostle's remains were smuggled from Alexandria by two Venetian merchants in the year 829.

The main waterfront promenade of Venice is called the *Riva degli Schiavoni*, recalling the presence of Dalmatian sailors.

In addition to the economic ferment that grew from Venetian trade with the East, there was also, as has previously been stated, another area of economic activity in the first half of the Middle Ages—that in the Baltic and North Seas. Here the Northmen developed ships and the seafaring ability which carried them far and wide. Not only did they reach Iceland, the British Isles, and the French and Netherlandish coasts, but even got to America about 1000 A.D. Most of their early excursions were of a raiding character, but in the course of time these people turned from robbery to trade—in the minds of some wags an easy transition. In the tenth century Hamburg on the Elbe, Thiel on the Waal, and London were all frequented by them. In the same century they established themselves in Normandy, whence their descendants, the Normans, conquered England and Sicily in the eleventh century. As was logical, they established commercial relations between their old settlements and the new, and in time this trade attained proportions which were to have an impact upon the settled ways of economic life.

While the Northmen, or Norsemen, or Vikings, as they were also called, were thus building up an area of commerce in one direction, Swedes were active in another. From the Baltic they penetrated Russia and worked their way down the Dnieper River to the Black Sea—a route that in Ancient Times had been followed by Greek traders seeking Baltic amber. From the middle of the ninth century they established fortified trading posts, called *goroda* in Russian, along this artery of commerce, and in these places they accumulated honey, furs, and females for Moslem harems. Each year a trading fleet left Kiev in the spring for the Black Sea and thence sailed on to its final destination at Constantinople. At the same time, other traders went down the Volga to the Caspian Sea and exchanged goods with Jewish and Arab merchants from the Moslem Caliphate of Bagdad. How important trade to these two centers was is difficult to estimate, but we do know that it must have been fairly large, for from the ninth century that with Byzantium was regulated by treaties, and the Russians, as the Northern merchants were called, had a special quarter in Constantinople assigned to them. Moreover, it was through these commercial contacts with the East that Russia got its writing with Greek letters, its Byzantine style of art and architecture, and the Eastern form of Christianity.

The merchandise which came back from the two markets in the East and which consisted primarily of spices was concentrated in the Gulf of Bothnia, for here the two trade routes converged. Thence the goods were distributed throughout the Baltic, but there was a western entrepôt on the island of Gothland, where Eastern products were available to Northmen for sale in their sphere of interest. Eventually, however, the flow of Eastern goods through these places declined, for costs of transportation via the arduous Russian routes were much higher than those via Venice and, after the twelfth century, via the Strait of Gibraltar. Yet, while this trade lasted, it kept alive a desire for profits and a familiarity with business practices. It provided a basis for greater economic activity at a later date.

Revival of economic activity in the twelfth and thirteenth centuries

Although trade over long distances existed in the Adriatic and in the North and Baltic Seas during the first half of the Middle Ages, most of Western Europe's economy was moribund, based as it was on a rigid land tenure system and upon production for immediate consumption. By the end of the eleventh century, however, there were many signs of economic growth and in the twelfth and thirteenth centuries a revival took place which was to break the older rigidities and greatly extend the range of economic opportunities. Many forces, such as the growth in population, the rise of towns, greater industrial production, and more extensive trade, initiated this change. To attribute to any one of them the ultimate cause of what took place is to raise the problem of whether the hen, the egg, or the rooster came first to the poultry kingdom. The fact is that they all came together, and one would have been meaningless without the others.

We have already seen how the growth of population affected agriculture and how expanded cultivation on old manors and newly reclaimed lands supported growing numbers of people on the land and a flow of people into the towns. The expansion of agricultural enterprise created a demand for industrial goods. Settlers on new land in Europe, like all others both before and after them, were in need of capital equipment in order to make themselves self-supporting; and for a time they even had to buy consumption goods in the market. Thus there was pressure on the means of production for such producers' goods as tools, plows, builders' hardware, and textile equipment and for such consumers' products as cloth and shoes. This pressure was reflected in an increased and geographically concentrated output of these very things.

Another factor of change had its origins largely in political conditions. Moslem and Norman invasions which lasted from the eighth to the eleventh century, atrocious cavalry raids of Hungarians at the beginning of the tenth century, and struggles among rival lords led feudal princes to build great fortified castles or *burgs,* frequently on the site of some earlier town. In these fortresses there was a garrison of knights and a kind of donjon for the special security of the lord. As trade revived, itinerant merchants came to seek shelter at night and protection in time of need in these places and while there did a certain amount of business with the local people.

In the course of time, trade became so great that there was not enough room in the old feudal or monastic town for merchants, and they had to establish themselves outside the burg, that is, in the *faubourg*. The inhabitants of the *faubourg* came to be known as *poorters* (Dutch) or portmen (English), for they were living in land *ports* of trade. Eventually, however, they became so numerous that they completely surrounded the old burg and themselves built a wall around their district for protection, thus creating a new burg. Accordingly, they came to be known as burghers, burgesses, or bourgeoisie, and because they were engaged in business instead of in agriculture, these terms came to mean men of affairs.

The concentration of merchants in towns and the new requirements of agriculturalists for tools and of lords for weapons created an active demand in towns for labor. By the eleventh century there was a definite drift of surplus manorial population to these new centers of production. Such a development was particularly marked in Flanders where clothmaking moved from the countryside to the towns. Here merchants were prepared to supply wool, fuller's earth, dyer's soap, and dyes to textile workers and to take finished products for sale elsewhere. Gradually weaving passed from the part-time occupation of women to the full-time job of men. In Italy, silk, which had been introduced from the East, moved into cities, as in the case of Lucca, and fustians, mixtures of linen and wool, began to be produced in places like Milan and Florence. Even the making of finished iron and copper products became concentrated in cities in spite of the locational disadvantage of having to bring in both ore and fuel. The skilled and specialized town labor force made it worthwhile.

As these changes took place, townsfolk began to acquire a legal status which made a deep inroad into the seignorial regime. In the first place, since these people did not hold land from the lord, they were under no obligation to him on that score. Secondly, for the conduct of their affairs they needed to be able to come and go as they pleased and hence to be free of attachment to the land. And thirdly, they required a government which would be less arbitrary than that of the lords and which would provide services which would further their own interests.

Certain things townsmen demanded, and gradually they were able to get their demands recognized as valid. Although most workers came of unfree parents, once they were off the land and were getting nothing from the lord, they were freed from paying anything to him. Thus by the late eleventh century the rule became established that if a serf remained a year and a day in a town, he was free. As the Germans said, *Stadtluft macht man frei*.

Furthermore, the sheer need of regulating affairs among the merchants led, by the early eleventh century, to the creation of a *jus mercatorum*, the beginnings of a commercial law, and to the establishment of merchant courts, called piepowder in England, where traders with their feet still dusty from the road (*pieds poudreux*) could get a fair judgment of their differences. By the twelfth century, these embryonic judicial bodies were becoming regularized by the formation of local town courts of aldermen whose members were chosen from among rich merchants. Also the need for defense measures required a governmental organization to manage the construction of walls, the raising of armed forces, and the building of markets. These things all necessitated the expenditure of funds and hence the establishment of a tax system. By the eleventh century, councils of burgesses were being elected to perform the various functions of government and thus to create an organization distinct from that of the lords. Some seigneurs, particularly ecclesiastical princes, looked askance at this turn of affairs and frequently offered considerable resistance to it. Yet, most of the lay lords realized that the towns indirectly increased their well-being by permitting the collection of tolls and the manipulation of money, and many ecclesiastical princes gave way to bourgeois demands when their position was weakened by disputes between the Papacy and the Holy Roman Empire.

The town charters of the eleventh and twelfth centuries manifest in their contents the origins of "civil libertarianism," a movement always associated in Europe with the cities and with the city middle class. The charters were contracts between new towns and local lords, each of the parties optimistic of future benefit in the new arrangement. In the provisions of the charters, townsmen seem to plead: "Exempt the townspeople from the rigidities and military strifes of agrarian feudalism, leave us free to conduct our trade and manufacturing, and profit for all (including the lord) will be the result." To achieve the appropriate ambiance for profitable enterprise, the preconditions of civil liberty, social mobility, and a leveling of arbitrary privilege were deemed necessary.[5]

During the twelfth century, the laws and government of the *faubourgs* were extended to the old burgs, and thus all townspeople, except the clergy, had the same status. Accordingly a new estate or class, the third estate, came into being and took its place alongside the previously existing estates of clergy and nobility. Only later were country folk accepted as members of the third estate, but when they were taken in, they were made to accept an inferior political position.

---

[5] See, for example, the charter of the town of St. Omer (1127) translated in D. Herlihy (Ed.), *Medieval Culture and Society* (New York: Harper & Row, 1968), pp. 180–184, and the discussion of its significance in Henri Pirenne, *Medieval Cities: Their Origins and the Revival of Trade* (Princeton, N.J.: Princeton, 1970). "Civil libertarianism," as originated in medieval town charters, did not guarantee equality in either a legal or economic sense to all citizens. It meant the removal of feudal privilege and restriction such that men and their wealth might become mobile and unencumbered by traditional obligations between men such as prevailed in the countryside.

The development of long-distance commerce

Clearly the growth of towns and the breakdown of rigidities within them, the development of industry, the expansion of agriculture, and the growth of population all formed part of a pattern which was changing economic life. But certainly the revival of trade between distant parts of Europe was an important factor in, as well as a reflector of what was taking place.

In the late eleventh century, commercial expansion was apparent in many places, but it was particularly pronounced in northern Italy and in the Low Countries. Mediterranean commerce, which had been so rudely interrupted by the Moslems, except for that carried on by Venice and a few south Italian cities, began to show signs of life. Toward the end of the tenth century, Pisa and Genoa decided, first, that they ought to get into the trade which had made Venice so prosperous, and secondly, that it was their mission to wage a holy war against the Mohammedan intruders. When they began to put these thoughts into action, Dame Fortune deserted them. Nevertheless, they persisted in their efforts and finally their luck changed. In 1015, they were able to establish themselves on the island of Sardinia. In 1052, they destroyed the Moslem arsenal at Palermo in Sicily, and in 1087, they seized the Moslem city of Mahdia in North Africa. Inspired by these victories, Pisans undertook the construction of their famous cathedral; and they financed the undertaking by booty taken from Islam and from trade with conquered areas.

Their successes against the followers of Mohammed were continued by crusades to the Holy Land. In 1097, the Genoese sent a fleet to support members of the First Crusade in their siege of Antioch and for their services got the privilege of establishing the first of many *fondachi* or trading centers in the eastern Mediterranean. Subsequently, all the Crusades were waterborne, and by carrying and provisioning men fired with religious zeal, Genoese, Pisans, Venetians, and Marseillais reaped a rich harvest. Even Barcelona grew wealthy by capturing Moslems on crusades in Spain and selling them to Christian buyers (Map 5).

Some idea of the profit-making motives connected with these enterprises is well illustrated by events of the Fourth Crusade (1204). Venetian shippers were engaged to transport the would-be liberators of the Holy Land to Palestine, but the pilgrims were unable to pay the price of the carriers, so the shippers took command of the entire expedition and diverted it to Constantinople, where they had so long plied their trade. The city was seized and sacked, and both Venetians and pilgrims brought back great amounts of booty. Among the rest were the famous gilded horses which to this day stand over the entrance to St. Mark's Cathedral.

By such exploits Western Europeans got control of the Mediterranean and began rapidly to develop trade upon it. Crusaders were free and easy

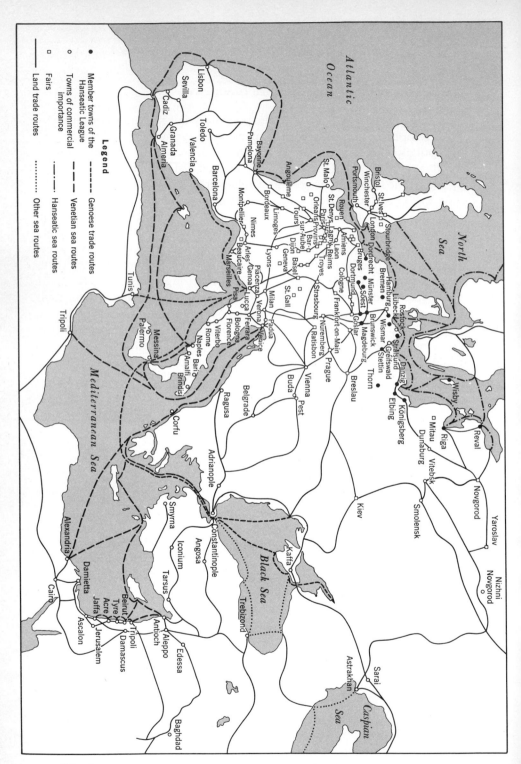

Map 5

Economic map of Europe, A.D. 1300

in dispensing trading privileges in their ephemeral states, and Europeans soon had *fondachi* throughout the eastern Mediterranean and the Aegean. The Byzantine Empire was no longer strong enough to keep them out. The Turks, who easily wrested the Holy Land from the Crusaders in the twelfth century, found it to their advantage to do business with the Christians. Besides they had no fleets with which to contest mastery of the seas until the fifteenth century. Thus, Europeans had even larger supplies of Oriental goods than ever before to distribute at home, and soon trade in these products was being carried on far inland. Ports like Marseilles, Montpellier, Narbonne, and Barcelona developed trade into their hinterlands. Pisa began to share its prosperity with Lucca, Florence, and Siena. Genoa developed its commerce with Piedmont, with Savoy via the Mont Cenis Pass, and with the Rhône Valley. And Venice strengthened its ties with Germany via the Brenner, the Septimer, and the Saint Bernard Passes, and in the thirteenth century, via the Saint Gothard by the construction of the first suspension bridge in Europe.

While these changes were taking place in the Mediterranean littorals and their hinterlands, commerce was also being built up in the North and Baltic Seas on the foundations already established by the Norsemen and Swedes. Here Flanders was the unquestioned leader and the port of Bruges on the Zwyn River became the great trading port of the region—the "Venice of the North." Through it came English wool for Flemish looms, Bourgneuf "bay salt" from the Bay of Biscay, wines from Bordeaux and La Rochelle, and fish and grain from the Baltic. Then, beginning in 1314, Venetians and Genoese sent annually organized fleets to the city via the Strait of Gibraltar. Bruges thus became the entrepôt for silks, rice, figs, dyestuffs, alum, cotton, spices, and other Mediterranean luxuries. Paradoxically enough, it was the coming of Italian ships with their deep draught which led to the development of the deeper ports of Damme and then of Sluys at the mouth of the Zwyn and it was competition from these places more than the silting up of the river that was responsible for the ultimate decline of Bruges.

In the north as in the south, the hinterland of North Sea ports was affected by the growth of trade. On the Rhine, Cologne and Mainz, in the Meuse Valley as far as Verdun, and on the Scheldt and its tributaries, Ghent, Antwerp, and even Tournai developed active trade. Then in the Baltic, commercial towns were established, largely to supply the agricultural colonists of eastern Germany with the many things which they needed and to serve as entrepôts for trade with the North Sea. Thus Lübeck was founded in 1158 on the banks of the Trave; Wisby was begun in 1160 on the island of Gothland; and Stralsund, Danzig, and Riga came into being in the early thirteenth century.

Development of transportation, fairs, and hanses

As can easily be imagined, the extension of commerce in the twelfth and thirteenth centuries was accompanied by important improvements in transportation. Nor is it surprising that the most dramatic changes occurred in seafaring, for the bulk of goods moved by water. By the twelfth century, Mediterranean seamen were using astronomical tables especially prepared for their needs. By the thirteenth century, they were employing a primitive compass, probably derived from China, had the astrolabe for finding latitude by astronomy, and were beginning to make accurate maps—the *portulani*[6] —based upon actual observations rather than upon fancy. Most significant of all, however, was the invention in the thirteenth century of the rudder to replace steering oars. This instrument, located directly astern, gave much better control of a vessel than had been possible earlier, for steering oars were difficult to manage in heavy seas. Moreover, it made possible sailing closer into the wind and construction of larger vessels. Galleys, in which oarsmen and supplies for them occupied much of the pay space, were to become obsolete for trade. The larger ships which were built could no longer be pulled up on beaches for repairs, nor could they find refuge in many of the small ports that had formerly been in use. Because they required deeper and better-protected harbors and because such places were few in number, shipping came to be more concentrated than in the past. This centralization, in turn, led to the construction of better port facilities with cranes, docks, and warehouses.

Important as such innovations in shipping were, inland transportation also improved. Between the ninth and twelfth centuries, the horse collar and iron horseshoes were developed and their use diffused, which greatly increased the effectiveness of the horse as a draft animal and made large-scale farming more feasible. Also, the lowly wheelbarrow was invented in the thirteenth century, and although it was used mostly on farms, it was employed in towns for short hauls of light loads. Old roads were rebuilt and new ones laid out, usually at the expense of merchants or of burgesses of the towns. Bridges were built at such a rate that this industry experienced a veritable boom. Canals began to be dug in Lombardy in the twelfth century, the *Naviglio Grande* which was constructed between 1197 and 1257 from Milan to the Ticino River being 31 miles in length. In the thirteenth century, the Low Countries started their network of man-made

[6] In the Early Middle Ages map making had fallen to a low level, for cartographers in the absence of knowledge gave free rein to their imaginations. They represented the earth as a flat circle with Jerusalem in the center, with the east at the top where the Garden of Eden was supposed to be. There were three almost shapeless lumps representing Africa, Europe, and Asia surrounding the Mediterranean Sea. Because a perfectly straight Nile bisected the Don River, they formed a "T". Hence the maps are referred to as "T in O" maps.

inland waterways which revolutionized their methods of transportation. Although locks were not invented until the fourteenth century, water levels were maintained by the construction of dams over which barges were drawn by means of winches.

Some effort was also made to remove man-made obstacles to trade. Territorial princes began to realize how valuable trade was to their lands and took steps to protect it. They conducted campaigns against "robber barons" (*Raubritter*) and by the thirteenth century had driven them to remote places. They even sold or otherwise abolished some of their tolls, although enough were left to constitute an obnoxious abuse down to the nineteenth century. The right of wreckage, whereby a lord could claim anything that the sea cast up upon his shores and which encouraged putting lights in the wrong places to cause disasters, was abolished or regulated by agreements. And arrangements were made to guarantee foreign merchants freedom from arrest for the debts of their fellow countrymen.

To facilitate merchandising, lords encouraged the establishment of great fairs within their territories. These institutions should be distinguished from the local, weekly, retail markets which frequently went under the name of fairs, for the great fairs were meeting places of merchants coming from distant parts with wares which they sold at wholesale to buyers from both far and near. The great fairs began to appear in the eleventh century and prospered until the end of the thirteenth—in the period when distant trade was of a peripatetic nature. In fact, they declined when merchants began to establish fixed places of business in centers like Bruges, and they never developed in cities like Venice where merchandising had always been sedentary.

The most important of the great wholesale fairs came into being along the land routes traveled by merchants coming from the two main economic centers of Europe: the Low Countries and Northern Italy. They reached their fullest flowering where the two currents of trade met, that is, in Champagne in northern France.

An individual fair was established by act of the territorial prince in whose lands it was situated, and this act of creation usually granted to merchants highly cherished privileges. For example, those who went to the fair traveled under a "safe conduct" of the prince, were exempted from reprisals for crimes committed or debts contracted outside the fair, and were not subject to escheat, that is, to the lord's right to claim their property in the case of their death. Moreover, lawsuits or acts of execution against merchants were suspended during the "peace of the Fair" and above all the canonical prohibition of usury was temporarily set aside.

A fair was held as a rule only once, or at most twice a year, but various towns in Champagne managed to organize a series of these trading sessions

which covered nearly the entire year. Because of concentration of wholesale trading marts it was practical for merchants coming from different
parts of Europe to have permanent residences in several of the fair towns.
At the fair of Troyes, for example, the Germans had their own "house,"
and traders from Montpellier, Barcelona, Valencia, Rouen, Auvergne, Burgundy, and Geneva had their own stalls or inns. At Provins there were
special lodgings for Lombard, English, and German merchants, and the
same was the case at the fairs of Bar-sur-Aube and Lagny. In the wake of
merchants, students and travelers went to France and became well versed
in French culture. This fact accounts in large part for the spread of French
Gothic and French literature throughout Europe in the twelfth and thirteenth centuries.

As trade over large areas became important, merchants began to form
associations for security and for advancing their mutual interests. By the
eleventh century these bodies, known variously as merchant guilds,
hanses, *charités,* or *compagnies,* were in evidence throughout Europe. Their
main goal was to become powerful enough that they could establish
monopolies and get special privileges in the towns where they operated.
In addition, they created rigorous rules of conduct for their members and
made entry into their closed circle much sought after and difficult of
attainment. When members of a merchant guild embarked upon a trip,
they formed small armed caravans for protection under the command of
a "captain." Sometimes they bought and transported merchandise in common and divided the profits according to each man's investment.

In the course of time, these hanses or guilds began to specialize in certain
kinds of activity in given regions—the Paris Hanse of Water Merchants,
for example, limiting its operations to transportation on the Seine between
Paris and Rouen, and the London Hanse of Flanders, to trade in cloth and
wool between Flemish towns and London. Also wholesale merchandising
became more sedentary, because the need of convoying land shipments
decreased, wealthy merchants wanted to avoid weary travel, and other
ways were worked out for selling and buying. Merchants began to operate
through agents, partners, or factors in far-off places, like Bruges, Lübeck,
Venice, or London. They also began to have enough confidence in one
another that it was possible to do business on the basis of samples, which
was the foundation for those bourses or produce exchanges which were to
be so important in Modern Times. Finally, by the end of the thirteenth
century, a considerable division of labor had developed among merchants,
some specializing in just one product, like wool or woolen cloth, and
almost all making a sharp distinction between trade and transportation.

With these new developments, the concept of trading associations was
never lost sight of, even though merchant guilds as such became less
important in town life as rich merchants got political power into their own

hands. Association was still the rule in maritime trade and here merchants frequently banded together to form "companies of merchant adventurers" for exploiting certain markets. In these companies, merchants shared the expenses of shipping and warehousing but traded for their individual profit in goods which they themselves owned. Association also took the form of leagues, or hanses, of towns for furthering their common interests.

The most important of these leagues of towns was the Hanseatic League. It began when Lübeck, seeking protection for its merchants in the half-conquered territories in which they operated, made a treaty of friendship and free trade with Hamburg (1230). Subsequently nearly all the shipping towns in the North and Baltic Seas from Cologne northward became joined in the pact and thus constituted a potent force. At its height the Hanseatic League had one of the largest *kontors* or trading centers at Bruges, was established in the Steelyard at London where it enjoyed special privileges, reached out to Novgorod in Russia, and traded deep into continental Germany via the Rhine, Weser, Elbe, and Oder Rivers. It was the agency that took Prussian wheat, Russian furs, and Baltic timber, tar, and salted herring to the West and that brought back woolens, hardware, salt, and Oriental luxuries to its customers.

Although cities of the Hanseatic League enjoyed a prosperity unequaled by any other part of Germany, trade along the Rhine and in the southern part of the country was by no means insignificant. Here association was largely among individual merchants rather than among towns, and they managed to set up trading posts in the great commercial centers, like the *Fondaco dei Tedeschi* at Venice. Only in the Late Middle Ages, however, did south Germany reach its medieval economic heights, for only then did the salt works at Salzkammergut and Luneburg come into large production, and only then, too, did the mines of Bohemia and of the Tyrol become important.

The area of greatest commercial revival in the twelfth and thirteenth centuries was along an axis that ran from Italy to the Baltic. Here goods of various kinds and of widely distant origins moved in some quantity. Here trade organizations were the most advanced. Here the manorial system broke down most completely. And here, as we shall see in the next two chapters, the most important developments took place in industry, in the use of money, and in business organization.

5

The revival of industry and business institutions

Industrial growth in the twelfth and thirteenth centuries

Hardly less impressive than the commercial revival which we have been discussing was the revival in the twelfth and thirteenth centuries of industrial production. In fact, these two segments of Europe's economy went forward *pari passu,* and it is scarcely conceivable that this should not have been the case. Because of the heavy costs of transportation, much of the trade by land was in goods of high value per weight that could not be produced locally, like fine woolen textiles, silks, metal wares, glass, clocks, and spices; except for spices, they were products to which considerable value had been added by "manufacturing." Even trade by sea was in goods that had undergone or were destined to undergo some processing, as in the case of salt, wool and woolens, and even grain, timber, wine, and dried or salted fish.

Secondly, the growth of population and especially the increase in the size of towns, attributable in part to the concentration of industry in them, created a new demand for industrial goods. Although data regarding population are scarce before the fourteenth century, what evidence we have has permitted estimates that suggest Europe's population went from 27 million in 700 A.D. to 73 million in 1300 and then fell back because of malnutrition and the Black Death to 51 million in 1350 and 45 million in 1400. From this point it rose to 103 million in 1650, to 125 million in 1750, and to 187 million in 1800.[1]

The most urbanized part of Europe was certainly the Italian peninsula.

---

[1] See Table 1.

Venice, Milan, Naples, and Florence each had between 50,000 and 100,000 inhabitants in the fourteenth century, and all of these centers had populations of over 100,000 in the fifteenth century except the last, which had between 50,000 and 60,000 as did also Rome, Genoa, Palermo, and Bologna. In 1328 Paris is thought to have had between 70,000 and 90,000 persons, although estimates of its size run as high as 200,000. London in 1377 had between 35,000 and 45,000; Brussels had 25,000 in 1374; Bruges had between 35,000 and 50,000 in the fourteenth century and Ghent somewhat more in the middle of the century. The population of Antwerp rose from 5,000 in 1374 to 20,000 in 1440, and to 50,000 in 1500.[2] In 1450 Nuremberg had about 20,000; Cologne, some 40,000; Louvain, 25,000; and Strasbourg, 26,000. The mere building of dwellings to accommodate these people, the clothing and the feeding of them, and the equipping of their places of work required for the times a tremendous industrial effort.

Thirdly, foreign wars, such as the expeditions into eastern Germany, the struggles with the Moslems for control of the Mediterranean and of Spain, and the Crusades, created a new and concentrated demand for military equipment. The agricultural expansion at home and the agricultural colonization beyond the frontiers of Western Europe necessitated the production of all kinds of farm equipment. Finally, increased transportation and the general needs of commerce required a greater output of harnesses, horseshoes, carts, wagons, and ships.

With this greater industrial production, it is not surprising that there was a concentration of production in certain parts of Europe and that there was some division of labor. It was not mere coincidence that the greatest industrial growth in the second half of the Middle Ages was located in the major areas of trade and of town development—in northern Italy, in Flanders, and in northern France. Nor is it to be wondered at that most of the advance in industrial techniques was realized in these same places, and from the twelfth century onward, and that the acquisition of new methods of production in these main centers proved to be a powerful factor in perpetuating their industrial preeminence.

In the course of economic history those industries which have pioneered in progress from primitive to more advanced techniques have been, at least until recently, connected with the production of food, clothing, and weapons, in part, because of the universality of demand for these things and, in part, because of a general familiarity with the fundamental processes upon which new techniques have been based.[3] This was certainly true in

---

[2] Roger Mols, *Démographie historique des villes d'Europe du XIVe au XVIIIe siècle* (Gembloux: J. Duculot, 1954–1956), vol. 2, pp. 505 ff.

[3] A qualification is introduced to this generalization because in our times very advanced economies have imposed other industries on backward areas in their search for such raw materials as petroleum.

the Middle Ages. In the production of food we have already referred to the development of the plow for use on the heavy soils of Europe, to the invention of the collar which made the horse a useful draft animal, to the use of iron shoes for both horses and cattle, and to the change in the crop rotation system (technology means more than mechanical devices!). To this list should now be added water and windmills for grinding grain. Although the water wheel was not new, its use was greatly extended from the tenth century onward, while the European windmill, perhaps adapted from Oriental predecessors, appeared in the twelfth century. At least by the end of the Medieval period, wherever grain was ground in large quantities, as near the towns of the Low Countries, northern France, Italy, and England, gristmills were always in evidence. By 1086, so it is said, England had over five thousand mills, most of which were water-driven. If each mill did the work of a hundred men per day, as has been estimated was the case, then there was available on the average the work equivalent of one man to every four or five members of the population. For the first time on any appreciable scale the industrial capacity of man was being increased by the inorganic forces of nature. This was a fact of the greatest moment, because it was this kind of power which was to contribute in such large measure to the enormous economic growth of Western culture after 1800.

In the textile industry progress was also marked in the second half of the Middle Ages, particularly in Flanders and northern Italy. Here there was early specialization, a great development of trade, and the invention of new techniques. In Flanders, there had been an important production of woolens from early in the Medieval period, and Charlemagne had made gifts of them to foreign potentates whom he was trying to impress. In the tenth century Norsemen traded in them, and in the eleventh and twelfth centuries itinerant merchants used them as one of their staples of trade, notably at the fairs of Champagne, for "no other woolens equaled them in texture, finish, or color." In the thirteenth century Hanse towns bought Flemish stuffs for sale throughout the Baltic and even to Russia. Italian merchants purchased them for their Eastern trade, and the two famous woolen guilds at Florence, the Arte di Calimala and the Arte della Lana, bought them for final finishing and dyeing.

Gradually Flemish production of woolen textiles reached a point where locally grown wool was insufficient to meet the demand of spinners, and English wool began to be imported in large quantities. By the twelfth century Flanders was already heavily specialized in textiles, and the industry was becoming firmly established in the neighboring districts of northern France—in towns like Amiens, Beauvais, Châlons-sur-Marne, and Provins.

At the other end of the axis of long-distance trade, in northern Italy, the development of woolen textiles was comparable to that of Flanders.

Here Florence was the outstanding center, although Milan, Padua, and Verona were also important. Like Flanders, the City of Flowers early became famous for its stuffs, having good customers among Churchmen and lay nobles and among Pisan merchants who sold to the East. In the course of time the members of its woolen guilds acquired capital, and they seem to have reinvested much of their earnings in their businesses. So successful were they that at the beginning of the fourteenth century Florence was annually producing 80,000 pieces of cloth which were worth about a million gold florins and was giving employment to some 30,000 of its 100,000 people.[4] Indeed, from the trade in woolens came much of the wealth that permitted the formation of the great Florentine banks and that made possible the great artistic achievements of the Renaissance.

In addition to woolen textiles, the second half of the Middle Ages witnessed the rise of the silk industry and in a lesser degree that of cotton. Silk had been known in China as early as the third millennium B.C., but only reached Constantinople, probably through the efforts of Christian missionaries, in the sixth century and Greece in the seventh century. Subsequently the techniques of silk manufacturing, like many other Eastern processes, were brought by merchants from Northern Italy to their cities of origin, for they wanted to profit in producing as well as in merchandising articles for which there was a great demand.

Efforts to introduce the silk industry into Italy met almost at once with considerable success. By the second half of the ninth century, silk was being mixed with wool at Lucca, and shortly silks were being produced in half a dozen places. In 1272 the process of reeling the fine silk thread from cocoons was mechanized at Bologna, and this invention gave the West a great advantage over the East. Cities began to foster the industry by granting it subsidies and attempted to force landowners to plant mulberry trees. Lucca was particularly successful in its efforts, but so, too, were many other cities, particularly Venice. In the early fifteenth century, it was claimed that the Queen of the Adriatic had 25,000 workers engaged in the trade.[5]

The cotton textile industry was, like silk, introduced into the West from the East. It was brought to Spain by Arab Moslems, and the Spaniards learned the techniques of production from their conquerors. Barcelona became the first center for cotton cloth, but by the fourteenth century the

---

[4] Although contemporary documents credit the Florentine wool industry with the support of one-third of the city's population, the estimate includes a medieval perception of what economists today call "linkages." Probably less than 1 in 10 of Florentine workers was *directly* engaged in wool manufacture. But it was recognized then as now that the industry supported smiths, carpenters, boatmen, wagoneers, bankers, brokers, and many other suppliers of goods and services.

[5] The same considerations apply as in footnote 4, above. The actual number of workers directly engaged in silk manufacture in Venice was on the order of between 2,000 and 5,000.

industry had reached Milan and Venice and subsequently made its way northward. If raw cotton had been more plentiful or more easily grown in Europe, this textile would have had a brilliant success, for it had the great advantage over wool of not being itchy in the heat of summer. As it was, the cotton industry only came into its own when cotton could be produced cheaply on the virgin soils in the New World.

As textile industries expanded and production became concentrated in cities, technological improvements were realized that accounted for still further growth. The most important of these advances was in spinning. Up to the thirteenth century such short fibers as wool, cotton, and flax were made into thread by hand-feeding them onto a twirling stick, spindle, or falling weight that twisted them to the desired fineness. These threads were then run onto bobbins by use of a quilling wheel. This instrument consisted of a large wheel, rotated by giving the spokes a push with the fingers, which was connected by a belt to a small wheel to which was affixed the bobbin that turned very rapidly. By 1298 the quilling wheel had undergone slight alterations which permitted spinning and winding to be combined on one machine and into one operation. In other words, the spinning wheel had come into being. In the fourteenth century the rotary crank was applied to the large wheel and was turned by a pedal worked by the spinner. Here was an invention of the first magnitude, for the task of spinning was reduced almost by one-half. Finally, in the sixteenth century, if not before, a "flyer" or fork was placed over the spindle in order to wind the thread evenly on the bobbin. This machine was so successful that it remained virtually unaltered until the eighteenth century.

In other phases of textile production, improvements were also made, although none was quite so dramatic as in spinning. Weaving was advanced by the construction of better shuttles, heddles, and reeds, and the draw loom was introduced from the East which permitted the making of patterns, like damasks. In the fulling of cloth, that is, the beating of it in water to shrink it in order to increase its density and durability, technological progress was marked. Fulling had been done by beating the cloth with sticks and was a most arduous and wet task. In the twelfth century it began to be done by machines which worked on the trip-hammer principle. Great wooden plungers were rigged up so that they would be lifted by a peg in a shaft turned by a water wheel, and let fall when the peg reached the top of its arc. Furthermore, new dyes were brought into use, some of them coming from finds in the glass industry, and Florentines pioneered in making dyes fast, particularly by the use of alum.

In the last half of the Middle Ages there was also expansion in the production of tools and weapons. The greater use of machines, like water wheels, created a demand for rapidly moving parts made of metal; the expansion of agriculture meant a greater need for metal tools and builder's hardware; and wars against the Moslems, the Crusades, conquests in Eastern Europe, and internecine troubles of various kinds resulted in an increased market for instruments of destruction and of defense. Then with the introduction of gunpowder from China, where, incidentally, it had been used mainly for fireworks, there was a demand for a new arsenal of weapons.

Although there was less concentration in the metallurgical industry than there was in textiles because of the location of production near the many outcroppings of ore, increased production was marked in the foothills of the Alps in northern Italy, in the Walloon part of the Low Countries, and at Hildesheim and Nuremberg in Germany. It was in these places, too, that the most important technological changes in the metal trades occurred. In them was developed in the late twelfth century a bellows with a valve which closed when the instrument was collapsed, thus forcing all the air out of the spout. When in the thirteenth century water wheels were used to run this type of bellows, a strong enough blast was produced to liquefy iron. Thus many of the impurities were removed from iron which previously had been hammered out of the spongy mass that had been obtained from less intense fires; what was more, liquid iron could be cast into various forms that earlier had been unattainable, like iron vessels, iron pipes, and even iron cannon.[6]

Inasmuch as cast iron is brittle and cannot be used for many purposes involving stress, as for example swords and cutting tools, a large amount of iron still had to be hammered or "wrought." To aid in the performance of this task, heavy beam hammers were by the twelfth century put into use. They were allowed to rest on a fulcrum, were raised by filling buckets attached to their lighter ends with water, and were allowed to fall with a striking force by dumping the buckets. Then, in the fourteenth century, trip hammers, activated by water wheels, as in the fulling machines, were applied to forging and made the task of hammering much more rapid. Moreover, a wire-drawing machine was developed in Nuremberg in 1350. Rolling mills were used in Germany in the fifteenth century. Rolling both reduced the amount of forging that had to be done and produced sheets of metal for making breastplates and wagon tires.

In spite of the almost revolutionary advances in metallurgy, textiles, and grain grinding, no technological innovations of the pre-modern period were of more importance in the general, if not in the economic, history of Europe than those made in printing and papermaking. Although there is

---

[6] Cast-iron cannon did not come into widespread use, however, till the sixteenth century. Early cannon, particularly the giant bombards (massive siege guns) were forged of iron bars and hoops, or cast of softer metals like bronze (fifteenth century). Often the largest guns were constructed right on the spot of a siege—an easier approach than transporting them about.

strong evidence that the idea of printing was borrowed from China, where printing from wooden blocks was practiced in the sixth century A.D. and from movable wooden characters in the eleventh century, specific printing techniques in the West differed enough from those in the East to suggest that they were not merely imported from abroad. What appears to have been a fairly autonomous development in Europe led to the use of wooden blocks in printing the elaborate capital letters which ornamented manuscript books in the late twelfth century and then in the late thirteenth century in printing entire pages. The first use of the latter technique was at Ravenna, Italy, which had been in close relations with Constantinople and to which may have come Eastern printing technology. In any case, printing from wooden blocks was a great improvement over handwriting and by the fifteenth century was in common use at Brussels, Ulm, Venice, and several other places.

The task of carving separate blocks for each page of a volume was, of course, enormous; thus it was logical that there should have been a search for a method whereby type once carved could be used over and over again. Finally, the quest for such a process resulted in the making of printing blocks for individual letters, the assembling of this type to reproduce whatever text was to be printed and after the printing had been completed the "knocking down" of the type for reuse. This use of "movable type" was attempted at a number of places—at Limoges in 1381, at Antwerp in 1417, at Haarlem in 1435, and at Avignon in 1444, but it was Gutenberg at Mainz who in the 1440s brought the technique to a point of successful operation, and it is to him that the credit for the invention is usually given.

Movable type was received with enthusiasm all over Europe in printing establishments which, not being hampered by guild restrictions, widely adopted it. By 1500 books were being produced in large quantities compared with earlier times and were being sold at low enough prices to be within the reach of vast numbers of people. Movable type "democratized" learning, just as iron had democratized metal tools in the Iron Age. It was one of the most important inventions of all times.

Perhaps movable type would not have had the effect that it did if it had not been accompanied by the development of a cheap material on which to print. Parchments made of hides, or "sheepskins," as they are still called by college students whose diplomas used to be printed on them, were expensive; papyrus, the ancient writing material of the Egyptians, was not available in Europe. The answer to the prayer of printers was paper.

The techniques of papermaking, even more than those of printing, were borrowed from the East. They were practiced in China as early as 100 A.D. and gradually made their way westward along trade routes dominated by Moslems, having appeared in Baghdad in 793, in Egypt in 900, in Sicily in

1109, in Spain in 1150, in southern France in 1189, in Italy in the thirteenth century, and in Germany in the fourteenth century.

The process of papermaking as introduced into Europe consisted of beating some fibrous material like linen rags, which had been softened by water, into a pulp, spreading the resulting mass in a thin layer on screens, which allowed the surplus water to drain off, and then pressing the substance on the screens into dry sheets.[7] The most laborious task involved in papermaking was the beating of the fibers to pulp, and it was to perform this work that Medieval Europe in the beginning of the fifteenth century made its greatest contribution to the industry. What was done was simply to rig up trip hammers—the third application of this device which we have cited—and to run them by water wheels. The hammers did the work of beating, much as in fulling and in forging iron. This development greatly reduced the cost of papermaking and also increased production to a point where there was a demand for a cheaper raw material. This was found later in cotton fibers and much later in wood pulp.

Finally, the printing trade needed more efficient presses. Although the screw press, similar to the "letter presses" seen in offices only a generation ago, was in use, it was slow-acting. Improvements were now made in it by changing the screw so that it would close the press with fewer turns (Figure 9).

Among other technological advances in the Middle Ages, the most important stemmed from clockmaking. Both the fine craftsmanship and the intricate gearing systems developed in this trade were of great value in the further development of mechanical contrivances of all kinds. Ever since the Bronze Age, time had been measured by hourglasses or water clocks, which worked on the principle of the amount of sand or water which flowed through a small aperture. Eventually, Moslems devised water clocks which would produce at stipulated intervals a mechanical puppet show, much as cuckoos appear at the end of every hour in our cuckoo clocks. Apparently, out of these mechanical accompaniments to the timekeeper itself came the inspiration for mechanical clocks.

By the thirteenth century European clockmakers were attempting to build mechanical timepieces and had come to grips with the principal difficulty in doing so—that of controlling and regulating the speed at which gears turned. Finally, they found a solution to their problem by the invention of an escapement that permitted a strategically placed gear to turn just so far and no farther per second and to control the escapement by a balance wheel. Just when these two inventions were first made is not

---

[7] Watermarks are obtained by designs placed on or in the screens. The fine lines of the screens can be seen in the paper upon which these words are printed by holding it up to the light.

clear, but they appeared in the famous Dover Castle Clock in England in 1344 and shortly thereafter were found in numerous places. At the end of the Middle Ages there was a real clock-building boom, every town believing that it was not up-to-date unless a clock adorned the steeple of the local church, the town hall, or the castle.

Still another industry in which notable advances were realized in the mMiddle Ages was glassmaking. Here the standard practice was to place a molten mass of silicon at the end of a hollow tube and to "blow" the glass until it was of the required thickness and to shape it by cutting and by bending it with forceps. At Murano near Venice and at Limoges in France, craftsmen achieved great skill in this technique and made their products famous throughout all Europe. In the tenth century they learned how to color glass, which made possible the stained glass windows that were to beautify high-vaulted Gothic cathedrals, like those of Chartres and of Paris. By the thirteenth century crystal glass was being made which was so clear that it was used for artificial jewels and so transparent that it was employed in the first eyeglasses of which we know. Then, in the fifteenth century, Murano craftsmen began to blow glass into cylinders which when cut and flattened made windowpanes up to twenty square inches. Thus, it was technically no longer necessary to set small pieces of glass in lead frames in order to let in light, although window glass did not become cheap enough for the common man until it began to be rolled in the sixteenth century. Finally, Venetians began to coat glass with lead to make a mirror and later substituted mercury for lead in order to get a better reflection.

In the closely allied pottery industry, the Middle Ages also made technical progress. Although pots were still turned on the potter's wheel in the time-honored way, the use of better clays and better glazes resulted in the manufacture of what were essentially new products. Thus, in Italy, the adoption of colors that had been employed in the glass trade led to the making of Majolica ware and to the production of the terracotta statues and friezes which were made famous by the Della Robbia family.

Still another flourishing trade of the second half of the Middle Ages was building. It was then that housing was constructed on a large scale in the growing towns and that most of the great architectural monuments which today attract admirers from all over the world were erected. With this great

Figure 9
Printing press of the seventeenth century. On this screw press only one sheet of paper could be printed at a time. The pressure was provided by the screw, turned by the worker. The bedplate with the type was rolled under the screw by turning the handle which the worker has in his left hand. A bedplate not in use is at *N.* At *EE* are probably cases of type. Ink was put on with leather-covered instruments at *M. From Vittorio Zonca, Il Nuovo Teatro, 1656.)

activity, it was only natural that stonecutters, masons, and carpenters should have advanced their arts. Quarrying was improved with better chisels and in the fourteenth century by the use of blasting powder. Masons made new uses of pulleys, derricks, and scaffolding. And workers in wood developed the mechanical saw for cutting logs into boards and timbers in the twelfth century,[8] the carpenter's plane in the fourteenth century, the brace and bit to replace the bow drill, water wheels to run grindstones, bolts and nuts to hold carriages together, and the wood-working lathe run by crank and treadle.[9]

Simultaneously great progress was also made in architecture and in the plastic arts for the adornment of great buildings. In both the Romanesque style and in the later Gothic, efforts to achieve height, size, and impressiveness created problems of stress hitherto unknown in the West. Gradually solutions to all of them were found, chiefly by the juxtaposition of arches and the use of flying buttresses. So expert did architects become that they were able to construct vaulted roofs out of masonry instead of wood, and one of them, Brunelleschi, was able to build the great dome of Santa Maria del Fiore at Florence without erecting a temporary support during the construction (1461). In sculpture, a development of techniques and craftsmanship led to the creation of some of the most famous masterpieces of all times, like the figures on the facade of the cathedral at Chartres, the doors of the Baptistry at Florence, and the works of Michelangelo. In painting, efforts to achieve movement, color, perspective, and realism led to the great masterpieces of the Renaissance in the Low Countries and in Italy.[10]

Scarcely an industry of any importance, hardly any aspect of life was without some change in the second half of the Middle Ages. In mining, pumps were improved in the urgent task of getting water out of the diggings—improvements which were to lead ultimately to the invention of the steam engine. In lighting there was the invention of the wax-and-tallow candle, which was much more efficient than the old oil lamps without chimneys. In distillation, methods were found in the twelfth century to get alcohol from wine, which was to provide the world with a new and powerful stimulant. In warfare, wheels were put under cannon to take care of the recoil and to give artillery more mobility; mortars were developed to lob balls over walls; and incendiary projectiles were made

---

[8] This was the so-called up-and-down saw. Previously logs had been tilted up in the air on a fulcrum, and a workman on the ground and another on top of the log laboriously pulled a long saw back and forth. The new invention was a saw worked up and down by a crank run by a water wheel. Circular saws were an eighteenth-century invention.

[9] Wood-working lathes had previously been turned by pulling down a flexible pole and using its recoil to rotate a spindle around which a cord, attached to the pole, had been wound.

[10] The first work devoted entirely to perspective was by the painter Piero della Francesca (1416?–1492).

more effective. And as by-products of dyeing and glassmaking, discoveries were made of the industrially important nitric, sulfuric, and hydrochloric acids.

Organization of urban industry

As medieval cities grew under the stimulus of commerce, political power came to reside in the hands of rich merchants. This was particularly true in the north where lords did not move into towns until the sixteenth century and so were not on the spot for the exercise of authority. It was also generally true in the Mediterranean littorals, for even if the lords lived in town, they usually engaged in trade and so had interests similar to those of the merchants.[11] Accordingly, the economic organization of town life and the economic policies of cities reflected the interests of rich wholesale traders.

The class character of regulations was particularly clear, as those affected the provisioning of towns with food and drink. Since the city fathers were exclusively consumers of foodstuffs, they wanted adequate and steady supplies at reasonable, if not at low prices. To achieve their ends they forced on both peasants and retail food merchants all kinds of restrictive rules, and these people had to submit to them because they depended on cities for markets. By the late twelfth century, among the rules imposed on them were prohibitions on middlemen, more exactly, on "regrating," that is, on buying goods for resale; on "forestalling," that is, buying goods before they reached the towns; and on "engrossing," that is, hoarding goods as a protection against rising prices or shortages in supply. Moreover, all food commodities had to be publicly exposed and for a certain period of the day sold only to burgesses. Butchers could not hide meat in their cellars; bakers could not store more grain than was normally needed for their own ovens. All traders in food were subject to rigid inspection, and defrauders were severely punished by having their goods confiscated, by fines, or by being banished from their trade or even from the city itself. Finally, maximum prices were sometimes established, and "quality inflation," that is, selling inferior goods at the maxima, was rigidly repressed.

While these regulations may be interpreted as an exercise of authority by town fathers, their more general significance must be underscored. They represent at once the great dependence of the medieval city on its

---

[11] In Tuscany and neighboring regions, these city-dwelling lords gave expression to their egos by building great towers, each trying to surpass the other. Such structures may still be seen in such places as Bologna, Perugia, and above all San Gimigniano.

agricultural hinterland and the continued uncertainty of life in a time when a severe winter or a too-wet fall meant starvation for many.

Scholasticism, the dominant philosophic system of the Middle Ages, had its practical side. Indeed it has been argued that modern economists searching for the origins of their discipline should look first to the sermons of now-sainted clerics of the Medieval period. The most consistent thread in scholastic economic thought is a horror of monopoly, especially regarding restraint of trade in foodstuffs. Perpetual exile was the recommended punishment for withholding foodstuffs in time of dearth. Scholastic economic thinkers fought restraint of trade in all markets, including labor markets, but the greatest passion was reserved for threats to the town's food supply. The urban citizen of the Middle Ages was not so comfortably isolated from agriculture as his modern counterpart. The great dependence of the town on daily shipments of food to the marketplace must have been a constant worry to townspeople only a generation or two removed from their own country origins.

The long-distance wholesale trade in foods was subject to less formal restriction by the towns because local livelihood was not at stake and because this trade was a source of considerable profit for the urban middle class. All that they required was that foreign suppliers sell through one of them, that is, through an official (licensed) broker or *Unterkäufer*, and that these same foreigners should not engage in retailing in competition with peasants. Local burgesses, who bought grain, fish, and wine at wholesale, were not subject to the same limitations. They might sell at retail and reap the profits derived therefrom.

Town policies regarding the food trade constituted a pattern which came to be applied to all retail trade and to local retail industry. As far as industrial goods were concerned, the rich merchants who dominated town life again wanted steady supplies of quality merchandise, fair prices, and peaceful industrial relations. Artisans, the chief producers of industrial goods for the local market, wanted reliable outlets for their products, just as the peasants did, and were willing to accept certain restrictions on their activities in order to get them. Thus, a kind of "deal" was made whereby town fathers granted a monopoly of business in the city to individual trades, sometimes even for the payment of fees, and in return demanded that artisans submit to the Church's principle of a just price (*justum pretium*) which meant, as we have seen, a fair or usual market price, and to a variety of regulations which would guarantee a high standard of product.

To these ends, regrating, forestalling, and engrossing were forbidden here, as they were in the food trade. Woolen cloth had to be "all wool and a yard wide." Night work was generally outlawed for fear that it would lead to inferior workmanship. Artisans had to work in shops facing the street, as they still do in many European trades, and to keep their goods continually in sight for public scrutiny. Craftsmen could not practice more than one trade in the belief that a "Jack-of-all-trades"is a master of none.

Nor did such rules constitute merely a paper program. They were strictly enforced. Artisans who broke the rules were severely punished·by fines and suspensions; in the case of repeated infractions, they might be subjected to the ignominy of having their shoddy goods exposed before their shops for all to see. Still worse, the artisan might be read out of his guild and hence prevented from practicing his trade. Although these rules did not entirely prevent cheats from such artifices as giving short measure, stealing customers' raw materials, or skimping work in general, they had considerable efficacy in maintaining honesty, quality, and fair prices.

The organizations among artisans which provided a means for maintaining craft traditions, for enforcing rules of production, and for regulating supply were the craft guilds. The origins of these institutions have been the subject of long dispute among scholars, some believing them to be found in the collegia of the Roman Empire and others in workshops of the lord. Still others, including the present authors, expect that they simply grew up to meet the needs of the times. At all events, by the end of the eleventh century artisans were forming fraternities (*fraternitates*) along lines determined by the goods produced for retail sale and were using merchant guilds or religious societies for their models. Before long these bodies were in evidence all over Europe and were being called craft guilds (*métier* or *jurande* in French, *arte* in Italian, and *Amt, Innung, or Zunft* in German). Thus there were guilds of tailors, bakers, cobblers, cabinet makers, blacksmiths, and boatmen. Each had a monopoly for the production and retail sale of its special products in the town—a monopoly sanctioned by public authority—and each was subject to the type of restrictions already mentioned. The fact of guild monopoly in the atmosphere of scholastic and civil abhorrence of restraint of trade is not as paradoxical as might be supposed. Within the guilds, competition among craftsmen was not discouraged; the main function of the guild "monopoly" was to prevent the encroachment of outsiders into the profession. For example, wine merchants were enjoined from trading in their used casks and barrels—an obvious threat to the coopers' guild. Woolworkers could not dabble in silk or cotton as these fibers were the provinces of other crafts.

Craft guilds gradually developed an elaborate organization of their own for the control of their monopolies. In order to regulate the amount of production and the quality of goods, they created an elaborate procedure for training labor and for limiting the labor supply. Thus to become a master craftsman and a full-fledged member of the guild who could produce goods in his own shop for direct sale to retail customers, it was necessary for a young man to serve as an apprentice to a guild master for a period, on the average, of seven years. During this time the master craftsman had at his disposal a worker, but in return he had to house, clothe, and feed his charge, and instruct him in the methods of the trade.

At the end of the apprenticeship, the trainee was supposed to be well skilled in his trade and to be ready to practice it as a wageworker, or as he was then called, a journeyman, a word derived from the French *journée*, meaning day. The journeymen worked for guild masters, but in some crafts and in some countries it was usual for them to travel around from place to place and from master to master to learn various regional "tricks of the trade." Journeymen masons often went on a *tour* of this kind to work on whatever large building was going up and to see the master-pieces of the building art, like the great cathedrals and public buildings. Even today, it is not unusual for French chefs to make a *tour de France* in order to learn how to prepare all the more famous regional dishes.

Eventually the journeyman might become a master craftsman. This step required qualifications other than skill in his craft and the production of a "masterpiece" which would give the guild wardens proof of his ability. The aspirant had to have enough capital to set up shop and to convince the guild that he would be able to pay his membership and other guild fees. He had to be married, for it was necessary to have someone keep house for him and his apprentices. And he had to be of good character and standing in the community, so that the guild could be reasonably sure that he would obey the regulations governing the trade. If he could meet all these requirements, he was taken into the craft and allowed to share in the monopoly of the market—to sell *good* goods at a fair price. If he could not, he remained a journeyman or turned to some other kind of work.

Furthermore, craft guilds built up detailed rules regarding production methods and selling procedures. Such measures were presumably designed to assure quality products, but inasmuch as guild members were jealous of one another and feared that some individual would get rich at the expense of others, these regulations aimed also to maintain economic equality among masters. Thus, all members of an organized craft were required to use the same techniques and were forbidden to introduce new methods unless approved by the guild. All masters had to work the same number of hours and have the same amount of equipment, because if one worked little and others much, or if some had few tools and others many, differences in wealth would soon appear. Finally, all were forbidden to advertise their wares, not even being permitted to sneeze to attract the attention of passers-by to their wares; all were prevented from selling to other than citizens of the town; and all were subject to price restrictions.

Naturally enough this standard pattern of urban industrial production for the retail market, with all its built-in rigidities, could not be and was not applied everywhere and in all trades with the same degree of thoroughness. In some cities rich merchants tried to suppress guilds, for fear that they would get so powerful that they would demand a voice in public affairs or even take over town governments. Such efforts were made, usually without success, at Rouen in 1189, at Brussels in 1240, and in practically all Flemish cities at some time during the fourteenth century. Moreover, the craft guild system never was applied to industrial workers in the countryside or to the growing class of unskilled workers in large-scale urban industries, such as the wool washers and beaters of Florence, the Ciompi.

In spite of all regulations which have been mentioned above, economic inequalities did grow up among guild masters, especially where opportunities for expansion were great. The rich enlarged their shops, took on more apprentices and journeymen than the poorer masters, and what was particularly significant, made it practically impossible for journeymen to become guild masters. More and more they endeavored to reserve their part of the monopoly to their sons, or to their sons-in-law, or to other close relatives by demanding impossible tests of aspirants or by requiring extraordinarily high membership fees. Thus, the rich guildsmen became in fact industrial employers, hiring workers for money wages and producing for profit.

Evidence of such changes begins to take form by the first part of the fourteenth century. In nearly all cities of any importance a distinction began to be made between the major and minor crafts, the major ones being where the transformation just described had taken or was taking place. In London there were the very wealthy livery companies which were far above the ordinary guilds in privileges and power. In Paris there were the Six Corps des Marchands. In Lucca there was the all-important Arte della Seta, and in Florence, the famous Arte di Calimala and the Arte della Lana. These last two organizations, like most of the others, kept the guild monopoly intact and used the word guild in their names, but neither was operated in the traditional guild manner. The few members of these bodies bought large quantities of raw material outside the town, thus breaking the rule against forestalling. They had the material worked up by artisans who were paid by the piece, contracted the job out to a master at a fixed-upon price, or took masters in as partners. They did the fulling and dyeing with machines that only a few could afford, thus violating restrictions on numbers of workers and equality of equipment, and they sold their finished products at wholesale to middlemen, thus breaking the rule of selling only directly to customers. The rich guildsmen even changed the organization of production, for instead of turning out everything in shops facing streets, they had some spinning, weaving, and knitting done in the homes of workers under what was called the domestic system and some done in fairly large establishments to which workers came, as in the modern factory system. In both cases, however, employers always kept title to the material being processed, whether it was raw wool or semifinished cloth, and more and more frequently they owned the means of production that the workers used.[12]

Under these conditions the status of workers was considerably altered. No longer could workmen look forward to membership in the guilds, unless they were fortunate enough to marry the "boss's daughter," or, better yet, a guildsman's widow. With the new dispensation, those who toiled were dependent upon wages for their existence. If there was no work because of the poor organization of supplies or because goods were not selling, their employers would drop them with little thought of the suffering which might be caused. If there was work, hours were long, being usually from dawn to dusk; wages were low, being just enough to provide a miserable standard of living; and working conditions were not good, even if one remained at home, because of poor light and little heat.

What proportion of the working class in the large cities had evolved to these conditions, it is difficult to say, but the numbers were not insignificant. At the beginning of the fourteenth century 10 percent of the entire population of Ghent is said to have been engaged in spinning or weaving, and half the craftsmen at Ypres to have been engaged in the manufacture of cloth. These proportions indicate clearly that masters must have been few and workers many. At all events, wageworkers were numerous enough so that they organized and agitated for the improvement of their lot. Journeymen began first to form loose groups, called *compagnonnages* or *Gesellenverbände*, to find work for their members and later to defend their interests in their relations with the masters. Urban wageworkers in the late thirteenth and fourteenth centuries initiated attacks upon the political monopoly of the commercial patriciate and made out of these efforts a real social movement. The revolt of the Ciompi at Florence (1378–1382), which was led by clothworkers, was of this character and so were the uprisings in many Rhenish, Flemish, English, and French cities.

As can readily be imagined, labor agitation of this nature was suppressed with vigor. Masters conspired to boycott workers who had disturbed the peace and cities formed leagues to prevent agitators from getting work within their walls. Finally, legislation of the budding political states shows efforts to contain labor. Both the English Statute of Laborers of 1350 and the French Royal Ordinance of 1351 aimed to prevent workers from conspiring to better their lot and set maximum wages which they could receive. These laws were promulgated in the period just after the Black Death when a severe labor shortage made havoc of the carefully controlled labor market of earlier years.

---

[12] In the domestic system, workers usually owned their spinning wheels and looms.

Just as there was no "typical" manor, in reality there was no typical guild; variations were as numerous as the number of cities and different guilds within them. Venetian guilds were formed originally as social and religious institutions (*scuole*) and only later became craft organizations. In Florence as elsewhere there were guilds of the rich and powerful (the Arte de Cambio was a bankers' guild) as well as of the humble. There were guilds of employers and guilds of employees. In their role as mutual aid and burial societies the guilds provided the earliest form of workmen's compensation and unemployment aid for their members. In some cities, guilds had a stultifying effect on technical progress as they fostered traditional practices and quashed innovation. But there were progressive guilds as well which encouraged technical change so long as quality was maintained and no threat to job security was involved. The guild system was, above all, an efficient system of industrial organization. If longevity is any measure of success, then the guilds were successful indeed, for, although they were subject to continuing change, like all institutions, they survived down to the Modern era.

Money, business, and the end of medieval growth

The development of money and credit

In the various phases of industrial expansion which we have been describing, the one common characteristic was an increase in the use of money as a medium of exchange. This was true in agriculture, in commerce, in industry, and in the employment of labor. Little wonder, then, that businessmen wanted money which was respected and which would be accepted over large areas. They wanted a money that was not being so continuously debased that debtors could always count on paying off their obligations in cheap money.

Under the circumstances, it is not surprising that monetary reform was the order of the day in the great commercial centers of the thirteenth century, nor that the lead was taken by the greatest of all such centers—Venice. The first move toward a hard-money policy was made in 1192 when a new coin, called the *grosso* or groat, was struck. The issuers of this piece of money took cognizance of the fall in the value of older coins and established the value of their coin at two grams of silver, which was approximately twelve times that of the existing penny. Thus came into being a shilling or sou which, as we have seen, had been only a book-keeping measure in Charlemagne's system. The groat proved to be just what creditor businessmen wanted and became so popular that all Lombard and Tuscan political jurisdictions struck similar coins of their own.

Beyond the Alps, efforts to create stable and standard moneys were inspired not only by rich merchants and bankers but also by monarchs who were endeavoring to establish their authority at the expense of rival lords. They saw in monetary reform a way to help commerce and, at the same time, by a kind of reversal of Gresham's law, a method by which they could drive the cheap money of the lords out of circulation.[1] Once this had been accomplished, lords would be deprived of an important source of income both from ordinary minting and from debasing the coinage, or, as we would say nowadays, from inflation. Thus, in England a stable penny was struck at the end of the twelfth century. In 1266 the French king, Louis IX, impressed by the great success of the Venetian groat, established the gros tournois (groat of Tours)— a coin that was joined a little later by the more valuable gros parisis (groat of Paris). These pieces, all twelve times the value of some penny, were favorably received by tradesmen and were adopted or imitated in Flanders, in the northern Netherlands, and in Germany, where they were known as Groschen.

Important as was the introduction of groats and shillings in their various forms, they did not entirely meet the needs of commerce, for any large sum in them was bulky and heavy and consequently hard to transport. Hence merchants requested the use of gold coins, which would be per value only a fraction of the weight of silver. Eventually their demands were heeded and gold began once more to be minted in Europe. The first of the new gold coins was struck by Frederick II, Holy Roman Emperor, whose brilliant Sicilian court was a center of art and learning. His gold augustales, struck in 1231, were because of their design and sharply etched lines real numismatic masterpieces of the Middle Ages.

The gold coins of Frederick II did not have, however, a wide circulation and were not adopted outside of Sicily. It remained for northern Italy with its relatively great volume of commerce to make gold popular (Figure 10). In 1252 Florence began to strike its gold florins, so-called because they had the floral emblem of the city, the lily, stamped on them. Shortly afterwards Genoa began to issue its gold ducats, from the Italian *duca*, meaning duke, and in 1284 Venice followed the example of its commerical competitor. Then Northern Europe fell into line, France issuing gold coins based on the gros tournois in the thirteenth century and Flanders and England following suit in the fourteenth. Inasmuch as these coins were equal in value to twenty silver groats or shillings, they were, in fact, pounds and thus gave reality to another of Charlemagne's bookkeeping fictions. Because they had considerable value and stability, they constituted a real blow to the minting activities of lesser territorial princes whose moneys could not

[1] This law, as stated by Sir Thomas Gresham in the sixteenth century, was that cheap money drives dear money out of circulation. In the short run, dear money is hoarded or goes into hiding if there is a chance of turning it later into stable money at a favorable rate of exchange, or into goods at advantageous prices. In the long run, however, cheap or unreliable moneys give way to sound, uniform coin because the risk of accepting light, debased coins is higher than for the good currency. But the long run is a long time. European circulation continued to be plagued by "black money" which was a constant source of inflation at the level of petty transactions. Major international trade could not tolerate this uncertain medium, and from earliest times gold coins of uniform fineness and weight were employed for large transactions.

Figure 10
Florins and ducats. It has been explained in the text that great commercial centers needed money in which traders could have confidence. Thus Florence created the florin (top) and Venice the ducat (bottom). The lily of Florence on the florin is of excellent design. The ducat shows Christ with a Doge against the sea, whence came Venice's wealth. *(From the Moneys of the World Collection of the Chase Manhattan Bank of New York. Used with permission.)*

compete with them. The future was clearly with moneys issued and guaranteed by centralized states.

Important to economic growth as were improvements in the coinage systems of Western Europe in the thirteenth century, the parallel development of credit instruments was of even greater significance for the long run. Such instruments provided ways for transferring debits and credits without the handling of money, the essential devices for borrowing funds on a large scale, and the means for businessmen to express their trust in one another, which is the basis of all transactions.

Of all the instruments of exchange the most significant was undoubtedly the bill of exchange.[2]   In its simplest form, it was both an acknowledgement by a buyer that he had received goods from a certain person for a stipulated sum and also a promise that he would pay the seller for them in a given amount at a specified place and subsequent time. Thus a bill of exchange written by a Fleming at Bruges for purchases made from a Venetian would read as follows:

> I, Hans Olbrechts, have accepted goods from you, Giovanni Cipolla, at Troyes, September 1, 1353, to the value of 1,000 gros tournois and I promise to pay you in Venice 1,100 *grossi* by June 1, 1354.
>
> (Signed) *Hans Olbrechts*

As can be readily seen, the Venetian merchant was hereby extending credit to the Flemish buyer—was actually financing the latter's commercial operations by allowing him time to sell his goods before paying for them.

---

[2] Its name comes from *bulla*, originally meaning seal and then by implication any document, and the fact that it almost always involved an exchange operation from one currency to another.

Payment of interest on the loan was concealed in the difference between the two sums mentioned or by the use of rates of exchange between two moneys which favored the lender.

This simple form of the bill of exchange was subsequently supplemented by the draft, in which three persons were involved instead of two. It was an order on the part of the buyer, Olbrechts, to use the case already cited, ordering someone owing him money, let us say in Venice, to pay by a given date the seller of the goods, Cipolla, what was due him. Therefore, this document would read:

> I, Hans Olbrechts, have accepted goods from you at Troyes, September 1, 1353, to the value of 1,000 gros tournois and I hereby direct Giuseppe Bellini to pay you, Giovanni Cipolla, 1,100 *grossi* in Venice by June 1, 1354.
>
> (Signed) *Hans Olbrechts*

Thus, not only was Cipolla extending credit to Olbrechts, but Olbrechts had already extended credit to Bellini. What was important here was that the network of credit relations in one document was being extended.

Finally, toward the end of the Middle Ages an addition was made to the draft which greatly added to its usefulness. If, in the case above, the third person, Bellini, agreed to make payment as specified by writing "accepted" on the face of the document, the draft became an *acceptance*. If Bellini was a responsible businessman of good standing, the acceptance might be used by Cipolla as security with which to raise funds. He might even take it to a banker and for a fee (later known as a discount) get his money at once. He had thus more opportunity to step out of his role as lender, if he were himself in need of funds.

Closely related to this document was the *lettre de foire,* or fair letter, which was developed at the fairs of Champagne. If a merchant, Du Pont, wanted to buy some silk goods from Lucchese, but was short of funds, he might ask Lucchese to trust him until the next fair. If Lucchese were willing, Du Pont wrote a *lettre de foire* in which he acknowledged purchase of the goods and agreed to pay Lucchese a given sum, including interest, at the next fair. If Lucchese were, on the other hand, reluctant to extend the desired credit, both he and Du Pont might go to a mutual acquaintance, perhaps a local money-changer, who would be asked to guarantee that Du Pont would make the payment. If he agreed, the *lettre de foire* was so written. However, it might be that Lucchese could not wait for his money, in which case the money-changer might lend the necessary funds to Du Pont and the *lettre de foire* would be written so that the sum which Du Pont paid back had a hidden interest charge in it. This was, in essence, a straight banking operation.

All of the credit instruments put together consituted means whereby those with initiative and courage would get credit for the conduct of their business. A lot of water had, indeed, passed over the dam since the time when most loans had been made by monasteries to lords for the purchase of consumers' goods. With the new instruments of credit, loans were of a business character; they were meant to be self-liquidating; that is, if the transaction as envisaged was carried out, the borrower would have the wherewithal to meet his obligation. Furthermore, most credit consisted of what today would be called commercial loans, for they were aimed to move goods and to be paid back in short periods of time. They were not usually made to finance capital equipment which could be amortized only over long periods. The new instruments provided ways for the easy transfer of funds and most importantly for hiding interest charges from clerical eyes. The prohibition against usury was still actively prosecuted. Still, a charge for the use of borrowed funds was essential both to encourage savings and to permit investment. The bill of exchange was the device used to dodge the prohibition against interest taking. Lastly, when credit instruments were transferred at discount or used to pay debts or to buy goods, money was created. For international commerce the effect of this new liquidity was as important as gold coin. In addition to instruments of credit, there developed other practices which we associate with banking services. At the end of each Champagne fair there was a period in which buyers and sellers came together to settle their accounts by clearing debits and credits among themselves without the use of money except to arrive at final balances. Thus, to take a simple case, if Olbrechts sold to Cipolla, and Cipolla sold goods of equal value to Dupont, then Dupont to Lucchese, and finally Lucchese to Olbrechts, the accounts of all four could be cleared in a face-to-face gathering of the principals by a mere canceling of claims. Such a practice greatly simplified the whole problem of payments.

Then, as has already been mentioned, money-changing became common: the many different kinds of coins necessitated exchange operations in nearly every transaction between merchants at any distance removed from one another; furthermore, so many of the coins in use were of such uncertain and changing value that persons with a detailed knowledge of them were needed to determine their worth. The first money-changers were merchants who engaged in exchanged as a side line to their commercial activities, but as their exchange business grew, it usually proved to be more profitable than buying and selling goods; hence they tended to specialize in the buying and selling of coins. Since some of them accumulated considerable wealth in the exercise of their trade, they had money to lend against such promises to pay as were contained in *lettres de foire,* drafts, and acceptances. When this happened, they had in effect become bankers.

Although some of them were Jews, whose religion did not proscribe interest taking from Gentiles, and some were natives of the places in which they operated, most of them were of Italian origin and were known in the North as Lombards.[3] Even to this day the numerous Lombard Streets which one encounters in cities throughout Western Europe indicate where these people plied their trade in the Middle Ages.

In the Lombard Streets, money-changers were not the only ones, however, who were performing some service connected with money. There were the goldsmiths, usually natives of the city in which they did business and generally members of a guild. They came to specialize in safe-keeping valuables for others in the safes or strongboxes which they had for protecting their own wares—a very important service in those days of uncertain law and order. Both goldsmithing and safekeeping were profitable, and eventually goldsmiths acquired funds that they could lend to others. In fact, they even lent money given them for safekeeping on the theory and experience that they needed to have on hand only enough to meet the expected, current demand of depositors. This practice led them, at least by the seventeenth century, to the issuing of "promises to pay," that is, "goldsmiths' notes," which, like modern banknotes, circulated from person to person. These "promises to pay," which could be paid by using the deposits of customers, came actually to exceed the amount of money on deposit. When this happened credit had been actually created by issuing paper—a very major discovery. But we are getting ahead of our story.

Still farther down our hypothetical Lombard Street, or at least around the corner from it in a little less respectable position, was to be found the pawnbroker.[4] To him came those who had some piece of personal property that they were willing to leave as security for a cash loan with the understanding that they could get their property out of "hock"—the place where it was kept—by paying back the loan plus interest.

Still farther on were the scriveners or notaries who drew up public and legal documents for those who could not write. In the practice of their trade they came to know a lot about everybody's business, and this knowledge gave them an opportunity to make deals for a quick profit to themselves. In time, they, too, had money to lend at a price to those who had a good proposition but not enough cash with which to execute it.

Somewhere along the street there were rich merchants who made another type of loan known as a "rent." This particular type of operation

---

[3] The role of Jews in medieval banking has usually been overstated. Although Jews were important here, recent scholarship has shown that, whereas their practice of taking interest was general, Christians took interest on such a scale that their competitors had little advantage in this regard.

[4] The three gold balls hung over the pawnshops today as a symbol of the kind of business transacted came into use in the Late Middle Ages. They represent *bezants* (gold roundels), the heraldic symbol for money.

developed from the fact that the rich for speculative purposes bought lands in expanding towns and built houses on them to rent to others. Sometimes these building speculators overreached themselves financially and had to borrow. Instead of borrowing on mortgage, they agreed to pay the person who lent to them specified sums at stipulated periods for as long as the lender lived. The amounts which the lenders received on these loans, which were very much like modern annuities, were known as "rents" and the recipients, *rentiers,* that is, people living off investments, which is the present-day meaning of the term.

Although there were cases of the untimely decease of *rentiers* because those paying the rents thought they had paid enough and took the appropriate action necessary to cancel their obligation, a similar kind of loan had a vogue in municipal and later in national finance. In order to raise funds, towns contracted to pay a lender at periodic intervals a "rent" on a loan for as long as the lender lived (a rent on one life) or for as long as he and a named heir lived (a rent on two lives). These rents became so extensive that cities sometimes assigned the administration of certain of their revenues to these *rentiers.* In 1164, for example, Genoa handed over some of its income for a period of eleven years to a society of lenders (*monte*) for sums that had been advanced. Then in the thirteenth century it consolidated its debt by selling rents, and finally it permitted these rents to be sold to third parties. It was to administer this kind of business and the city revenues pledged against rents that the first deposit bank in Europe, that is, a bank to receive deposits and to use them as a reserve against the loans it made, came into existence at Barcelona in 1401 and that the famous Bank of Saint George (Cassa di San Giorgio) was founded at Genoa in 1407.

Still other types of loans were created in connection with maritime construction and sea-borne commerce. In these trades the demand for capital was great, for both the building of vessels and the purchase of cargo and supplies entailed large outlays. Furthermore, in them there was either feast or famine, for although successful voyages paid off handsomely, the danger of total loss from shipwreck or pirates was ever present. What was wanted, therefore, was not only a way of borrowing capital, but also a method of dispersing risks. To a degree these needs were met by the bottomry contract, the respondentia loan, and the sea loan. The first of these was a loan for financing the construction of a ship and was secured by the vessel itself; the second was for financing trade and was secured by the cargo; and the third was for financing a voyage and was attractive because it permitted sharing in the profits. If all went well, these loans provided much-needed funds and paid lenders good returns. If disaster overcame a ship or its cargo, the loss was spread among both owners and lenders.

It was from these loans, especially the last, that underwriting developed.

An enterpriser would draw up a description of a voyage which he contemplated and would invite others to join him in putting up a part of the capital and in sharing in the profits. This they were to do by writing their names under his. If several "underwrote" the venture, both the risks and the earnings were shared, so that failure would not fall heavily on one person. Seldom was it that several voyages failed at once, as in the instance of Antonio's ventures in *The Merchant of Venice.* Sharing risks, which, as we shall see in more detail later, is the main principle in insurance, had so many advantages that it was extended in the seventeenth century to cover losses from fire and in the eighteenth, to cover hardships resulting from the early death of an insured person, that is, to life insurance.

In all these developments the borrower always gave the lender some consideration in one form or another for the use of capital. This premium on accumulated mobile wealth was crucial for the growth of the capitalist system and for economic growth under free enterprise. Although the Church fathers maintained a more or less fictitious opposition to the taking of interest in the later Middle Ages, all signs pointed to their losing the battle. Territorial princes gave permits for the establishment of "loan tables" in the commercial towns. The Papacy made use of bankers, upon the payment of fees or other charges, for the collection of Peter's pence, for the transfer of moneys to and from Rome, and for the general management of Church finances, and abbots, now not having funds to lend, borrowed from bankers when they wanted to purchase land or erect an extraordinarily expensive building. Moreover, no objections were made to some interest-taking methods, like that in "rents," on the ground that the lender ran a real risk of loss. Finally, it was clear from business practices that society, in general, condoned charging interest and that the Church would have to adjust its teaching to the world as it was.

Just what interest rates were in the later Middle Ages has been the subject of much discussion, and generalizations about them have varied widely because the great diversity of risks actually resulted in many different rates. For strictly business loans to persons with good credit ratings, the interest charge was around 5 percent per annum, but the risks might be so great or the borrower so little known or so unreliable that the rate would go up to 12 or 15 percent. Rates on loans to public authorities, like towns and monarchs, were usually high because their record of repayment was not good. Bankers might make loans to a king or a prince on condition that he would expel their competitors, usually Jewish bankers, from his territories, and then the rate would be low, but if they made a loan to a princess to ransom her captive spouse, or to a town to cover the expenses of war, or to a monastery to buy a piece of the "true cross," the rate might go to 50 or even to 100 percent. At all events, rates were high enough to make banking a very profitable business, and many great families, like the

Bardi, Peruzzi, and Medici became wealthy by it. Also, the risks were great and, as we shall see, two of the houses named above went under by overextending their loans.

Business organization

As business grew in volume, it was quite natural that the organization for the conduct of affairs became diversified. It was hardly to have been expected that the single owner-manager type of business enterprise, as found in the craft guilds, would be adequate for large undertakings. Thus, with the revival of business and the need for more working capital, partnerships, the favorite way for medieval businessmen to pool their resources, became more common. Frequently there were multiple partners, as in the case of the Bardi bank, where there were fifteen, and usually all participated actively in the enterprise. In the course of time, however, partnerships developed in which some of the partners were just investors (sleeping partners) and others were the active managers—an arrangement known as the commenda. Then, there were the merchant adventurers who pooled expenses on a trading voyage, but traded their own merchandise for their own account. Finally, in Genoa in the thirteenth century, there were cases where investors were allowed to buy *loca*, that is, shares, in the construction of a ship, very much as they were later to buy them in joint-stock companies, but that was a development of a later period.

The growing complexity of business operations made necessary, in turn, elaborate records and better bookkeeping methods. The first requirement here was for businessmen to know reading, writing, and arithmetic, and in point of fact burgesses created the first nonreligious schools in Western Europe expressly for teaching these subjects to their children. In the twelfth century city fathers began to shift the burden of these schools onto the taxpayers by making them municipal institutions and began also to have textbooks prepared in the various national languages to supplant the books in Latin which had hitherto been adapted from monastic schools. Indeed, record keeping was one of the important ways by which spoken vulgar tongues of Western Europe came to be put down in written form and became literary languages. It is not at all strange that the dialects of the great commercial centers should have achieved the status of national languages; that the early masterpieces of national literature, like Dante's *Divine Comedy*, should have been written in them; that the dialect of the London area should have become standard English; that the language of the Île-de-France and of the Champagne fairs should have become French; or that the dialect of Tuscany and especially of Florence should have become Italian.

Not only, however, did businessmen need to know how to read and write a popular language, but they also needed an efficient method for doing their figuring. Roman numerals, then in use, were exceptionally awkward to handle, as the reader can easily see for himself by trying to add MXL and CCVIII, or better, by attempting to multiply or divide them. Thus it was with enthusiasm that Western Europeans adopted Arabic numerals, which the Arabs borrowed from India. In the twelfth century, the use of these numerical symbols spread like wildfire throughout the business world, and the use of Roman numerals came eventually in our time to be limited to tombstones and academic buildings.

Finally, businessmen needed a better system of bookkeeping than had previously been in use—a system that would give them a clearer idea of their credit and debit positions both in general and in relation to specific persons. The answer to their need for such a method of accounting was double-entry bookkeeping, invented at the beginning of the fourteenth century and first described in detail by a Venetian, Lucas Pacioli, in his *Summa de arithmetica, geometrica, proportioni, et proportionalità* (1494). This method involved three sets of books: a daybook in which all transactions were written down in chronological order as they took place; a journal in which transactions were analyzed as credits and debits under such headings as cash on hand, accounts receivable, accounts payable, and goods in stock; and a ledger in which transactions were posted both as debits and credits by individuals. Under this system the two sides of the ledger always had to balance, inasmuch as every item was both a debit and a credit, and its totals had to agree with those of the journal. Men of affairs could thus ascertain whether or not their debits were larger than their credits, if their inventories were moving or frozen, if they were short of cash, or if they were extending too much credit. The books did not tell them, however, what their costs in certain classes of transactions and in specific goods were or what the running inventories were. Not until the twentieth century, when cost accounting was developed, were these kinds of information available. Only with cost accounting, however, were any notable advances made in the medieval system of bookkeeping.

Town economic policies and economic stagnation

In spite of all the improvements in the conduct of business which we have been describing, the economic scene displayed disturbing elements toward the close of the Middle Ages. One of these was the adoption by towns and by some territorial princes of restrictive economic measures. Another was an actual slowing down of economic growth in the fourteenth century and the beginning of general economic stagnation, although in certain areas economic growth continued in spite of the trend. A third was a drastic reduction in the population of Europe that created such a labor shortage on the land that some farmers, especially in Spain and England, were induced to take up sheepherding, which required fewer hands. And a fourth was, as we have seen, low agricultural prices until about 1450.

The restrictive policies of towns and monarchies began when guilds acquired political power and came to take a share in the determination of city affairs. These newcomers to the political scene were bent upon exercising to the full their monopolistic position at the expense both of merchants who brought goods to the city and of producers in the immediate vicinity of the town. In their little world it seemed to be to their advantage to keep out all competing goods and to raise prices to what the traffic would bear. Accordingly in towns where guilds had power, taxes on products from the outside were raised to prohibitive levels, and "foreign" workers were rigidly kept out.

Under the pretext of some exclusive right, perhaps extorted from a territorial prince for a bribe or by revolt, producers were prevented from opening up shops outside of the town boundaries, or from selling, except at fair time, any commodities that had not been produced within the walls. In 1314, Ghent, for example, forbade the sale within the city of any cloth that had been made within a radius of 3 miles of the town limits. In such widely dispersed places as Flanders and Florence, women spinners were required to sell the product of their labors to merchants in the towns. And in the former, legislation against rich manufacturers who produced for export became so hostile that in the middle of the fourteenth century the business of these people fell off, and many Flemish weavers migrated to Florence.

In a similar way, town particularism hampered large-scale commerce, for the guilds wanted all the business, wholesale as well as retail, for themselves. They harried wholesale merchants by adopting the "staple right" whereby traders passing through their towns were required to unpack their wares and offer them for sale to the burgesses, even though they might have wanted to sell them elsewhere and though there was no opportunity for selling them where they were stopped. In some places, too, boatmen's guilds claimed the exclusive right of towing all boats within their jurisdiction and even of transferring cargoes to their own barges. Fortunately, such policies were not everywhere pursued with the same vigor, especially in southern Germany, where capitalist industry was just beginning, in most of Italy, where the rich manufacturers wanted to trade outside and could compete with foreign products, and in England, where royal authority curbed the extreme protectionism of the towns.

Indeed, in places like England, where the territorial prince had considerable power, there began to appear policies which were designed not just for towns but for the entire realm. They were, in fact, embryonic state economic policies. The first indications of such measures were found in England, where in the early fourteenth century Edward II attempted to prevent the importation of foreign cloth, except for the use of the nobility. In 1331 Edward III tried to get Flemish weavers to come to England to build up the infant cloth industry and thus process at home the raw wool which had been going to Flanders. In 1381 the first of the English "navigation acts" was attempted by requiring goods in trade with England to be carried in English ships. Although this measure was unsuccessful, it was indicative of things to come. Then, in 1463, foreigners were forbidden to export raw wool from England and in 1464 Continental cloth was prevented from being imported.

Quite logically, such steps brought on retaliatory acts from the Low Countries. The Duke of Burgundy (1419–1467) prohibited the importation of English cloth in regular trade-war fashion. Furthermore, he used the infant-industry argument to create a fleet which would compete successfully with Hanseatic shippers. He subsidized the fishing industry, which was growing rapidly, in part, because of the invention of the herring cask in 1380, and he got a portion of the Hanse's trade in this great staple. He assisted Antwerp in its development as a port and thereby began the growth of a shipping center which was to take the place of Bruges and, in fact, to become the trading center of the Western world in the late fifteenth century.

These examples of territorial economic policies, which when adopted by national states in early modern times were to be lumped together under the term of mercantilism, might be expanded manyfold, but it is of no point to do so. What is important, however, is to realize that these restrictive measures coincided with a halt in the economic expansion of the West. Indeed, signs of economic stagnation were numerous in many places by the early fourteenth century, although all of Europe was not affected in the same degree. By then agricultural expansion to unclaimed lands either at home or on the periphery of Western Europe had virtually come to an end. Business at the Champagne fairs had fallen off and was not at once replaced by commerce at the important ports, like Bruges, and in 1343 a number of large Italian banking houses collapsed. Five years later the Black Death carried off no less than a third of Europe's population.

The limits of medieval growth

Scourge that it was, the plague of 1348 does not explain the failure of the European economy. In fact the economic downturn began at least a half-century before the plague. The fundamental problem was within the balance between population and food production. As we have seen, the source of demographic and economic expansion was a causal cycle of improved agricultural technology and increasing population. Technical improvements resulted in a larger, more reliable food supply. Improvements in real income, diet, and health encouraged population growth. With growing numbers of people came a heightened demand for agricultural and industrial commodities, as well as an increased labor supply to enlarge the areas of cultivation and to people new towns. Economies of scale and division of labor with attendant efficiencies accompanied the expansion, and increased market size induced wider commercial contacts on both regional and state levels.

Whether it is possible for such dynamism to continue indefinitely is a matter for speculation; in late Medieval Europe it did not. Finite limits to population growth were met in the form of pressure on food supplies. The open-field system, the horse collar and heavy plow, and the reclamation of new lands permitted a doubling of Europe's inhabitants, but beyond that point no new technologies were forthcoming from the rural sector. Rather, heightened food prices and greater uncertainties began to occur in the mid-thirteenth century, the apex of medieval prosperity. As one observer describes the situation, Europe at this moment was like a bather wading up to his neck in the sea. A declivity of inches meant that he would go under.

Europe began to go under in the years 1290–1320. A series of famines took a heavy toll. Cereal prices rose dramatically, and grain cultivation was temporarily expanded, not in new fields, but rather at the expense of animal husbandry and industrial crops. Simultaneously, a series of failures swept European banking. The taxing power of many rulers failed them and their default on loans spelled ruin for Tuscan banking giants like the Buonsigniori, Cerchi, and Frescobaldi in the 1290s. The turn of the century brought no respite. Population was on the downturn, and the cycle of medieval dynamism was reversing itself. The mining of gold and silver all but stopped. The textile industries of Flanders and Italy found themselves virtually bereft of buyers, the result of which was cutbacks and widespread unemployment.

One of the demands of the revolutionary woolworkers in Florence (1378) was that wool cloth manufacturers be required to sustain an annual production of 24,000 cloths per year to maintain employment, whereas a century before, 80,000 cloths per year was average. Years of crisis came with increasing frequency. One of the the worst was 1343, when Tuscan bankers again suffered default by bankrupt princes, and the greatest financial houses of Europe—the Peruzzi, the Bardi, and the Acciaiuoli—all crumbled.

In what light then shall we view the plague of 1348–1351? Westbound, rat-borne fleas carrying a combination platter of plague bacilli turned Italy into a peninsular graveyard in 1348. The disease spread northward and by 1351 killed off one-third of Europe's population, conservatively estimated.

Visitation of a plague to a locale caused instant death for many, followed by a short-lived euphoric chaos among the survivors, until grinding famine (owing to untended crops) finished the job. Town life stopped. Traditional law and religion lost all meaning. The economy ceased to function. In the countryside, so many animals died that even carrion-eaters would not touch them for their rottenness. Yet in England, for example, a horse formerly worth 40 shillings could be had for 6, a sheep for thruppence, and fowl for the finding. The suffering was at its worst in the towns —death traps by dint of overcrowding and unsanitary habitation.[5] Boccaccio's tale-tellers of the *Decameron* wisely ran for their lives to the hill-country as did every city-dweller who could afford to do so and who was not caught unawares.

The Black Death was neither the first nor the last great epidemic to befall Europe, though it was by far the worst. Its severity owed largely to the overextension of population to the very limits of agrarian support. Gradual adjustments to the demographic imbalance began earlier; population had been slowly shrinking as fertility fell. In the case of Pistoia, a town near Florence, the natural increase of the population had dropped to nearly zero as early as a century before the plague.[6] Even if slow reversal of demographic growth were the case for Europe as a whole, as a solution it clearly did not come soon enough. Although the Malthusian aspects of the great plague are still the subject of debate, it is safe to assume that, were Europe not treading water, demographically speaking, the epidemic might have been less catastrophic.

Medieval growth came to a tragic halt in the fourteenth century, but the later Middle Ages is one of the exciting moments in the economic history of man. From the ruins of Rome, and after a half-millennium of stagnation, Europe emerged as a dynamic economy. The technology of agriculture, commerce, industry, and business organization developed to such a high degree that medieval institutions and methods became the foundations of European economic activity until nineteenth-century modernization. Although economic history seems to delight overmuch in economic "revolutions," it is hard to deny that every sector of the European economy was indeed revolutionized in the later Middle Ages. There was an agricultural revolution (three-field agriculture), a commercial revolution (permanent

---

[5] Sample death rates for cities during the plague years were on the following order: Hamburg, 66%; Bremen, 70%; San Gimignano, 59%; Florence, 60%; Siena, 51%.

[6] David Herlihy, *Medieval and Renaissance Pistoia: The Social History of an Italian Town, 1200–1430* (New Haven, Conn.: Yale, 1967).

partnerships, bills of exchange, marine insurance, advanced accounting), and an industrial revolution (waterpower in forging, fulling, and paper-making).[7] We shall not see such a period of drastic change again until we make our way to England in the late 1700s when a new (but similar) series of revolutions begins.

The Renaissance paradox

In 1952 the historian Robert Lopez surprised his colleagues in art history by proposing that the cultural and artistic exuberance of the Italian Renaissance occurred during a great depression and was in fact unsupported by an economic "golden age" as had previously been assumed.[8] How inconvenient to abandon the idea that Renaissance architecture had been constructed on a foundation of good earnings and that the humanistic schools and sculpture academies were the product of increased leisure time, the gift of a beneficent and productive economy! Yet by the early Renaissance, the plain of southern Tuscany, a bountiful territory in the High Middle Ages, reverted to wasteland. Florence in the time of Michelangelo, Lopez indicated, had 30% fewer inhabitants than in the time of Dante. Throughout Italy the cloth industry was depressed and port traffic had contracted.

Where then did Renaissance culture flourish? In the palaces of the wealthy. Renaissance culture was high culture for the very few. Add together the names of the great humanists, artists, thinkers, and doers of the Renaissance and the list will be impressive but not long. Neither were the patrons numerous. From an economic standpoint, a Renaissance depression is no contradiction in terms; a few wealthy citizens sustained it despite the general hard times. A case in point was the Medici of Florence, the greatest of the patrons aside from the Church. But the history of their fortunes is a good indication that the Renaissance was no economic high point. The Medici bank, the foundation of the family's wealth, was the greatest in Europe in the fifteenth century, yet it was never so large as the Peruzzi and Bardi which failed in 1343. As the Medici became rulers, patrons, and poets, their control over the bank waned. Lorenzo the Magnificent, the greatest patron of Florentine culture of his century, "had no luck in commerce," according to Machiavelli. Other Florentine historians

---

[7] The term "revolution" is not used merely for dramatic effect; the word embodies the idea that economic progress is discontinuous, proceeding in spasmodic episodes. De-emphasis of "revolutionary" developments implies the opposite view, that secular growth is a steady accretion of improving techniques.

[8] Robert S. Lopez, "Hard Times and Investment in Culture," reprinted in *The Renaissance: Six Essays* (New York: Harper & Row, 1962). Lopez defines the years 1330–1530 as the Renaissance Period and so shall we. By the mid-fourteenth century Giotto and Petrarch had initiated new styles in art and literature and the *raison d'être* of medieval feudalism, heavy cavalry, had been cut down at Courtrai and Crécy.

more frankly indicate that understanding, not luck, was the lacking in-gredient. He lost contact with the bank, leaving its administration in the hands of an outsider to the family, a cardinal error for the head of a family firm. Under the control of Francesco Sassetti, the Medici bank began to crumble, and it seems likely that only by misappropriating government funds was Lorenzo able to stave off collapse until his death in 1492. Two years later the Medici were expelled from Florence.

No idea as potent as that of a Renaissance depression goes unchallenged for long. Naturally there are those who claim that the case is overstated. They point to the regional differences in the impact of the downslide, the paucity of accurate statistics, and the fact that the nadir of the depression came early in the Renaissance (mid-fourteenth century). Thereafter a slow but steady economic revival occurred. Whichever side is more accurate in emphasis, it is enough for us to be aware that it was the High Middle Ages, not the Renaissance period, that was the age of rebirth of the European economy.

The economic expansion
of Western culture
1500 to 1800

7

European discoveries and expansion— 1500 to 1700

Characteristics of Europe's economy in Early Modern Times

In order better to tell their stories, historians have established the end of the fifteenth century and the beginning of the sixteenth as the turning point between Medieval and Modern Times. Although Europeans who awoke on the morning of January 1, 1500, certainly noticed no great difference from December 31, 1499, and were totally unaware of arising in a new historical era, changes took place in the course of European history within the designated time span which were important enough to justify historians in their seemingly arbitrary periodization. These changes were (1) the development of humanism, (2) the growth of science as a method of attaining knowledge, (3) the Protestant Revolt, (4) forward steps in the rise of national states and of nationalism, (5) geographical discoveries overseas, (6) the beginning of the economic exploitation by Europe of the newly found lands, and (7) concomitantly the development of a large volume of distant commerce in staples which was crucial in Western culture's attaining a position of economic hegemony in the world. Each one of these changes had an effect on economic growth in Western culture, and hence each requires consideration here.

Humanism was an intellectual movement which had as its center of interest the ancient classics and largely through them a concern with things of this world, including humankind. It represented a definite trend away from theology and scholastic philosphy and toward physical, social, and political interests. It was manifested in painting by a shift from religious subjects to scenes of the flesh (and frequently in the flesh), in literature, by a spate of translations of Roman and Greek classics into modern languages and by stories of this world, like Boccaccio's *Decameron* and Erasmus'

Praise of Folly, and in architecture, by greater emphasis on lay buildings—palaces of lordly and worldly princes and public structures, like the Palazzo dei Medici in Florence, the Louvre in Paris, and the Rathaus in Bremen. With such changes came a more openly acknowledged interest in material well-being and a greater desire for wealth in order to procure those things which humanists held in high esteem. Although people might still be told that it was more difficult for a rich man to get into heaven than for a camel to pass through the eye of a needle, more and more appeared willing to take their chances on this score. Indeed, without wealth how could men create or enjoy those very things in the arts which the humanists were maintaining were the true marks of civilized people—were the real things worth living for?

The second of the big changes that mark the break from the Medieval to the Modern period was the development of science. For a long time men had been accepting, as true, statements by the Church Fathers or other great authorities, like Aristotle, and had been using these statements as premises in logical syllogisms to arrive at strange and even weird conclusions. Obviously results obtained were frequently in direct contradiction with what could be observed by the senses in nature and were of little use to the men who were concerned with material things—architects, engineers, or mathematicians. Clearly, men dealing with this world needed knowledge based on actual observations, upon regularities derived from controlled experiments, and wherever possible upon mathematical verification. They needed "science," which comes from the the Latin word *scire*, to know. They had to be able to identify events in sequence, to analyze interrelationships among these events, and to discover why and how they occurred in a given order. Once man had taken this attitude toward the real world, he was on his way toward mastery over his physical environment. This very mastery—the mastery of space by better means of transportation, victory over temporary shortages in food supplies, triumph over disease, and the turning to human use of vast quantities of animate and inanimate resources from quinine to coal—became in the mind of Western man another mark of civilization. Here again, economic growth, which was part and parcel of man's domination over his environment, came to be considered a necessity in the process of becoming more civilized.

The Protestant Revolt, for its part, contributed to the new turn in Western culture by breaking the authority or "university" of the Roman Catholic Church. For the study of economic history this was not without importance, since the Church's injunctions against taking interest and against the accumulation of wealth were further challenged and what remained of the Church's preachments regarding poverty as a virtue was attacked. In fact, some of the new religious sects, like the Calvinists, proclaimed the desirability of practicing thrift, or what in economic terms would be called saving for investment, in order to increase material well-being. Although Protestant behavior in matters economic was not essential to economic development, as is witnessed by the fact that economic progress was registered with apparently little distinction in both Protestant and Catholic countries, the Protestant ethic probably made it easier for the Protestant man of affairs than for the Catholic to bring his conscience into accord with his efforts to accumulate wealth. Furthermore, ethics rather than Catholic theology, that is, behavior of individuals in conformity with what was acknowledged to be the welfare of society rather than the dictates of the Church regarding the faithful observance of the sacraments, became a greater concern in Western culture than it had been earlier.

Still another aspect of the changes which were clearly being advanced in the century that marked the division between Medieval and Modern Times was the formation of dynastic states along more national lines. In brief, the national state is a political entity that embraces all the people of a nationality, that is, people who usually speak the same language or closely related dialects and/or are drawn together by common historical traditions or by similar literatures, music, and art. In this development away from governments by lay or clerical princes in those territories in which they could claim supreme authority and toward governments where people at least thought that they were bound together by common ties, the governed expressed some willingness to be joined together politically. This recognition of the doctrine of consent was eventually to contribute to the development of popular government, to a highly emotional loyalty on the part of the people to their nationality, and to policies for the strengthening of the nation-state. Although common economic interests, such as a desire for better police protection, standard business law, the abolition of local barriers to trade, and standardized weights, measures, and money, played some role in the formation of nationalities, national economic legislation tended to knit people together into some semblance of an economic unit, frequently at the expense of other national states.

Indeed, national states were to become divisive forces in Western culture and eventually to engage in wars which threatened to bring that culture to destruction. It is possible, but by no means certain, that a threat of attack from outside the culture or a common desire to perpetuate the culture may in our day bring national states into a working arrangement of some kind which will keep them from destroying themselves.

Fifthly, the end of the fifteenth and the sixteenth century can be considered a turning point in the history of Western culture, for it was then that Europeans made what were probably the greatest geographical discoveries of all times and began a movement known as the expansion of Europe overseas, which was to extend Western culture to large portions of the globe and which was to have a profound effect upon Europe itself. Within a generation Western Europeans brought within their ken more than half of the land mass of the world—Africa, India, the Far East, North America, and South America—and they developed practical routes for getting to the shores of each. They proved, what had long been believed, that the earth was round, and they were thereby able to explain empirically how by sailing westward one came to Eastern ports, the phenomenon of night and day, and the change of the seasons. Man had at a stroke found answers to problems pertinent to his control over the physical world and discovered an undreamed-of quantity of land to settle and of resources to exploit.

Sixthly, Europeans soon were taking advantage of their new opportunities. Not only did they bring in so many new products and such great quantities of well-known goods from the lands which they discovered that the imports had a veritably revolutionary effect, but they also picked up such quaint ideas about how man lived in a state of nature that these notions were to have a profound effect upon political thought and practice at home. Furthermore, they inaugurated a migratory movement, especially to the Western Hemisphere, which was to make prior migrations, such as those of the "People of the Sea" at the beginning of the first millennium B.C. and of the "barbarians" who came into the Roman Empire in the fourth and fifth centuries A.D., look like toy models. In fact, they began a process which was to carry Western culture to territories a hundred times greater than Western Europe—to an area that by the middle of the twentieth century was to have greater industrial and agricultural production and a much higher output per capita than the heartland of Western culture itself. So great was economic progress and material well-being to become in one part of this overseas area, i.e., the English-speaking section of North America, that this very region was to develop into one of the most important centers of Western culture.

Seventhly, Western culture so greatly increased its commerce in staples with distant lands that a veritable revolution was effected in the economic life of man. This trade led to a concentration of demand for goods in port areas and in certain specific industries, like textiles, builder's hardware, and firearms, which encouraged producers to turn out more goods and to take advantage of technological improvements in order to do so. Thus, as Adam Smith was so aptly to remark much later in his *Wealth of Nations,* the all-important division of labor (specialization of tasks) took on new dimensions in the neighborhood of commercial centers or where locational advantages for production of given products were particularly favorable. Furthermore, profits from trade permitted the accumulation of capital for investment in plant and enterprise and thus were an important supplement to industrial profits that were plowed back into plant as a source of *savings* for economic expansion. Commerce not only made such contributions to the rise of capitalism but also greatly furthered new types of business

organizations (the overseas trading companies led directly to the establishment of stock companies), played an important part in the creation of new
and more extensive credit facilites, and was a prime mover in the growth
of banks and banking.

In short, with the expanision of Europe overseas, Western Europeans
inaugurated a process whereby Western culture, especially in its economic
aspects, was to a greater or lesser extent to be borrowed by or foisted upon
every other culture of the entire globe until it might appear that the whole
world was destined to be Europeanized.

Indeed, the diffusion of Western culture's economy to other parts of the
world and shifts in the centers of leadership in Western culture resulting
from unequal rates of economic growth are basic aspects of our present
study.

Preparation for the great discoveries

The great discoveries of the late fifteenth and sixteenth centuries, which
were so profoundly to change the course of economic history, were in
actuality the culmination of a long process of acquiring geographical
knowledge and of developing shipping techniques for the mastery of the
seas. They provide an excellent example of how the accretion of knowledge and innovations in technology increase the range of opportunities for
alternative decisions.

As we have previously seen, late Medieval mariners had the compass
for giving them direction; the astrolabe, which helped them to establish
their positions in latitude, especially if they could go ashore to get an
accurate sighting; and astronomical tables, which were of some assistance
in guiding them across trackless wastes of water. They had fine maps, the
portulani, of those coasts which were much frequented by sailing men and
good techniques of cartography. And they had ships, especially the caravel
and the galleon,[1] steered by rudders and propelled in part by the inanimate
power of wind, which regularly made hazardous voyages, even to English
Channel ports.

With all this equipment, however, sailors would not have been so
anxious to probe the unknown seas if their curiosity had not been aroused
by snatches of geographical knowledge about far-off lands and by theories
regarding the shape of the earth. Many were clearly intrigued by the

---

[1] The caravel was a ship of about 50 tons, with three and later four masts, which carried lateen sails
and had a castle at the stern. The galleon, similar to the Portuguese *naus,* was considerably larger, broader
of beam, and more seaworthy than the caravel, and usually had castles fore and aft. See Carlo M. Cipolla,
Guns, Sails, and Empires (New York: Pantheon, 1966).

proposition that the earth was round, which was by no means a new idea in the fifteenth century nor one that was entertained only by the lunatic fringe. As far back as the sixth century B.C. Pythagoras had contended that the earth was round. Both Plato and Aristotle supported this contention in the fourth century B.C.; Eratosthenes of Alexandria had in the third century B.C. very ingeniously and with considerable precision calculated the circumference of the earth;[2] Claudius Ptolemy of Alexandria (second century A.D.) incorporated the idea in his summary of ancient geography which was passed on to the Christian world and was much in vogue in the fifteenth century. Indeed, Ptolemy made the thought of voyaging westward in order to get to the eastern lands in China especially tempting by understimating the earth's circumference and by overestimating the extent to which Asia protruded eastward toward Europe. Many fifteenth-century geographers, like Pierre d'Ailly in his *Imago Mundi* (1410), argued cogently that the world was round; many practical seamen, of whom Columbus was only one, read and were convinced by such scholars. Indeed, Columbus wrote in the margin of his copy of d'Ailly's book opposite the argument regarding the sphericity of the earth, "Yea, verily, the earth is round."

In the second place, late Medieval Europe had from time to time been set agog by tall tales of far-off places, of lands of great wealth, and of heathens waiting to be brought under the banners of Christ. Sometime after the Fourth Crusade, the legend of Prester John came into being and was subsequently revived at irregular intervals. Usually Prester John was represented as a Christian who had created a Christian kingdom in some barbarian land and was awaiting (this went on for three centuries) succor from the West. Somewhat later, vague reports trickled back to Rome from missionaries sent out to the Mongols of great lands awaiting the true word of God. Then there were the travels of Marco Polo of Venice—a man who spent the best years of his life, from 1271 to 1295, in China. As luck would have it, Marco was captured by the Genoese after his return and slapped into jail. There he had a cellmate by the name of Rusticiano of Pisa [Rusticello], who had done some work as a ghost writer and who apparently had that sixth sense that allows one to tell when a tale will find a market. In any case, after hearing Marco relate his adventures, he convinced his much-traveled friend that they should collaborate on a book that would tell of the East. The resulting work was a best seller. So successful was it, in fact, that imitators who had never traveled beyond their garden gates tried to outdo Marco in fanciful accounts of far-off places and

---

[2] Having learned that on the day of the summer solstice there was no angle of the sun at noon at Syene, near the Tropic of Cancer, Eratosthenes measured the angle of the sun at noon on the same day at Alexandria. This gave him the arc of a segment of the earth's circumference, the length of which was the known distance between Alexandria and Syene. His error resulted from the fact that the measurement of the distance from Alexandria to Syene was inexact.

thereby simply built up in the popular mind a belief in great riches awaiting the audacious somewhere in the unknown.

But if there were theories to be tested about the world, more or less wild
tales about people to be saved, and extravagant estimates of wealth to be
had for the taking, there was evidence close at hand of Eastern products
which brought good profits in trade. In fact, spices were being so widely
used to liven the taste of both food and drink in such quantities that there
seemed to be no question about profits if one could only get supplies.
Venice, however, was the only European power which seemed able to
secure deliveries, for it had made the necessary arrangements in the thirteenth century with the Arabs, who had dominated the Red Sea area, and
later with the Ottoman Turks, who captured Constantinople in 1453 and
Egypt in 1517. Although Venice had not taken undue advantage of its
monopoly, if one may judge from the fact that the prices of spices in
Europe did not go up after 1453, it was doing so well that many European
traders wanted to break into the field. Since the Eastern trade routes were
closed against intruders, the only possible way of horning in on Venetian
profits was to find an entirely new route to India or to the Spice Islands
of the South Seas.

For these various reasons, "for God, for gold, and for glory" (or curiosity), Europeans began to push out into the unknown Atlantic. As early
as the thirteenth century two Genoese brothers, Ugolino and Guido
Vivaldi, attempted (circa 1291), when Venice was sewing up the spice
route through the Red Sea, to find a route to India via Gibraltar. Then, in
1312, another Genoese, Lanzarote Mallocello, discovered one of the Canary Islands, which still bears his Christian name. Anonymous explorers
found the Madeira Islands (1330) and the Azores, or what appears to have
been the Azores, on contemporary maps (1351); and Catalan, Majorcan,
and Italian sailors probed along the African coast.

The first organized effort at exploration, however, was attempted by
Prince Henry the Navigator of Portugal (1394–1460). His imagination fired
by a campaign led by his father King John I in 1415 across the Strait of
Gibraltar and by the consequent seizure of Ceuta (1415), he decided that
African conquests offered great chances of profit and vast numbers to be
saved for Christ. Accordingly, he established at Sagres in the southwest of
Portugal a school of navigation to which he brought seamen, navigators,
and geographers. He founded colonies in the Madeiras and Azores, which
turned out to be profitable, and then pushed his men southward along the
coast of Africa. By 1434, the much-feared Cape Bojador had been rounded.
In the 1440s, Cape Verde was passed; and in 1457 the Cape Verde Islands
were discovered, and being uninhabited, settled. In the meantime, enough
gold was found, enough fanciful tales of a Christian kingdom, now located
in Abyssinia, were related, and enough natives were brought back as slaves

to whet the appetites of Portuguese and other European adventurers for further exploration.

For a time after the death of Prince Henry, the exploring activity of the Portuguese declined,[3] but it was eventually revived by Prince John, who became King John II. He guessed that the way to India lay around Africa and once of this mind relentlessly pushed his quest for the golden route. In 1487 one of his men got to India via the Red Sea and wrote from Cairo that the place to trade in India was Calicut on the Malabar Coast. In the same year, Bartholomeu Dias, under orders to round Africa, if possible, got far enough into the Indian Ocean to be sure of his great find—that Africa could be rounded. Then, in 1498, Vasco da Gama went all the way to Calicut and returned not only with the good news that India could be reached by an all-water route, but also with spices which are said to have brought a profit that paid the entire cost of his voyage sixty times over (Map 6).

While these discoveries were being made, another great find was in the making—that of the lands of the Western Hemisphere by Christopher Columbus. This man, who in his lifetime acknowledged himself a Genoese, made seamanship his profession and voyaged widely, certainly making the trip to England via Gibraltar and perhaps the trip to Iceland. These experiences undoubtedly nourished his *Wanderlust,* as did also his marriage to the daughter of a wealthy Portuguese who held grants of land in the Madeiras. At all events, although a man of little formal education, Columbus read widely of the *Travels of Marco Polo,* the stories of Prester John, the concept of the sphericity of the world, and the tale that in the Atlantic there was a great island, Antilia—a myth that may possibly have come from a Norse legend. Following Ptolemy, Columbus believed the earth to be much smaller than it is; following Marco Polo, he thought that Japan extended far into the Pacific; and following a Florentine scientist, Paolo dal Pozzo Toscanelli, who wrote a Lisbon priest that he believed one could get to Asia by sailing westward, Columbus believed that China could be reached by striking directly across the Atlantic.

In the course of time he developed an ambition to undertake such a voyage westward and sought support from King John II of Portugal. But John, who was heavily committed to the route around Africa, refused, and Columbus then turned to Spain for aid. For seven years he pleaded his suit in vain, but finally, after Spain had driven the Moors from their last stronghold in Granada and was free for other enterprises, his pleas were heard and assistance was granted. Somehow the necessary funds were

---

[3] In 1469 the Portuguese government did, however, give a trade monopoly in Africa to Fernao Gomes on condition that he would continue explorations there. He kept his bargain and got nearly to the Congo River, but his work lacked the drive of that of Prince Henry.

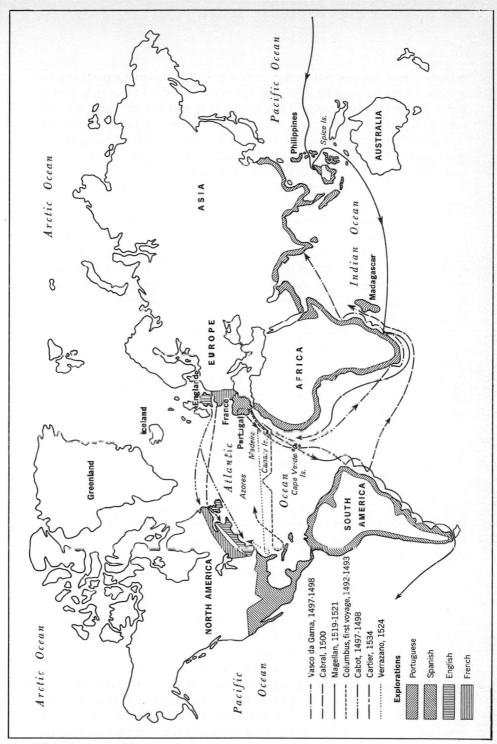

Pacific Ocean

Arctic Ocean

Arctic Ocean

ASIA

Philippines

Spice Is.

AUSTRALIA

Indian Ocean

Madagascar

EUROPE

AFRICA

England

Iceland

France

Portugal

Madeira

Azores

Canary Is.

Greenland

Atlantic Ocean

Cape Verde Is.

SOUTH AMERICA

NORTH AMERICA

Pacific Ocean

Pacific Ocean

Arctic Ocean

Vasco da Gama, 1497-1498
Cabral, 1500
Magellan, 1519-1521
Columbus, first voyage, 1492-1493
Cabot, 1497-1498
Cartier, 1534
Verrazano, 1524

Explorations

Portuguese
Spanish
English
French

Map 6
Voyages of Discovery—Late Fifteenth and Sixteenth Centuries

raised, largely by borrowing and certainly not by Isabella's pawning her jewels. A fleet manned by a crew of 120 was fitted out at the little port of Palos; in the late summer of 1492 the voyage was begun, and on October 12 the historic landfall was made at San Salvador in the Bahamas. Although Columbus thought that he had accomplished the amazing feat of reaching the Far East by sailing westward, he had, in fact, made a much more significant find—he had discovered a New World throughout which Western culture was to spread and to which economic primacy was to fall in the twentieth century.

Upon his homeward journey Columbus encountered bad weather off Portugal and sought refuge in the Tagus River near Lisbon. Apparently this circumstance gave the discoverer an opportunity, which he could not resist, to boast of his exploits to King John, who had so cavalierly refused his services a scant decade earlier. With real braggadocio Columbus told the Portuguese monarch of all his doings and of his discoveries, whereupon King John blithely laid claim to them on the ground of prior discovery. In consternation Columbus sent a messenger overland to Madrid to warn his sponsors of a trick, and they rushed a delegate to Pope Alexander VI at Rome, himself a Spaniard by birth, with a request to support their cause. Thus it was that the Pope issued the famous bull establishing the Papal Line of Demarcation around the world, granting to Portugal the unknown lands in the eastern half of the globe and to Spain those in the western half. Portugal, furious at this turn of events, threatened to go to war if the papal decision were allowed to stand. Fortunately, the principals had recourse to negotiations which led to the signing of the Treaty of Tordesillas (1494) and thereby to the establishment of a new demarcation line, which was more favorable to Portugal, 370 leagues west of the Cape Verde Islands, or at about the 46th meridian west longitude. This settled matters between the rival claimants, but latecomers to exploration, like Francis I of France, could well ask, and did, to see "Adam's will wherein he divided the world between Spain and Portugal."

Hard upon the voyages of Columbus and Da Gama, there were other explorations too numerous even to be listed here. Columbus made three more voyages before his death in 1506 and never gave up the idea that he had found a westward route to the Malay Peninsula. Pedro Alvares Cabral, sailing for Portugal, set off for India in 1500 but took such a westerly route in order to get full advantage of the trade winds of the South Atlantic that he struck the Brazilian coast, which he realized lay, according to the terms of the Treaty of Tordesillas, in the Portuguese sphere of influence. Amerigo Vespucci, a Florentine, took part in the Portuguese expedition of 1501–1502, which followed up Cabral's discovery of Brazil, and came to the conclusion that inasmuch as the new finds did not resemble any of the descriptions of the Far East known to him, what must be involved was the discovery of a *Mundus Novus*—a contention which resulted in this New Word being named after him.[4]

Then Ferdinand Magellan, a Portuguese who went over to the service of Spain because he failed to win promotion at home, sailed westward (1519) in order to claim the Moluccas for Spain and to avoid entirely Portugal's half of the earth. He got around South America by passing through the strait which bears his name, sailed up the west coast of the Americas for an unknown distance, and then struck out across the Pacific, which he, like most others of his day, thought to be narrow. Here trouble began, for provisions of both food and water were drastically inadequate for the months at sea. Nevertheless, the fleet reached the Philippines, which Magellan claimed for Spain and where the leader lost his life, and then dropped down to the Moluccas. Here, one of the three remaining ships, the *Vittoria,* was loaded with spices and took off for home through the Indian Ocean. Although badgered by further food shortages, the vessel reached Sanlúcar, Spain, in 1522, with eighteen survivors. In spite of the terrible losses, the voyage was considered a great success. Spain claimed the Philippines and the Moluccas, although it sold the latter to Portugal for the princely sum of 350,000 gold ducats (Treaty of Saragossa, 1529). The profit on the cargo of spices that got back is said to have exceeded the cost of the entire expedition. At last the world had definite proof that the earth was round.

The formation and exploitation of overseas empires

As soon as claims to the newly discovered parts of the world had been staked, the claimants made a mad rush to get what economic benefits they could from their finds. Not only was there a desire to recoup the heavy costs of exploration, but there was an almost unnatural lust in the haste with which the pioneers expected to get rich. Here was an interesting commentary both on the motives behind exploration and on the prevailing ideologies in the Western world.

The Portuguese, for their part, knew that they had a good thing in the spice trade to Europe via the Cape of Good Hope and vigorously set about making the best of it. First, they sought complete mastery of the Indian Ocean in order to prevent supplies of Eastern products from going to their competitors, the Venetians. This mastery they obtained when Francisco d'Almeida, in one of the most decisive battles of Modern Times—that of

---

[4] The letters which Vespucci wrote to friends on this subject became justly famous. They led a second-rate German geographer, Martin Waldseemüller, to propose that the new land mass be called America, for he thought that Vespucci was its discoverer. In 1541, the much more important geographer, Gerardus Mercator, prepared a map in which *America* was used for both continents in the Western Hemisphere, and this name stuck.

Diú in 1509—defeated a combined Arabic and Egyptian fleet, some whose ships, incidentally, had Venetian artillery and Venetian gunners aboard in order to protect the Republic's spice trade to the last.

Secondly, the Portuguese launched a plan, devised by Alfonso d'Albuquerque, their greatest colonial leader, to establish land bases for trade throughout the area of their operations. Thus they took Goa, which became the center of Portuguese power in the East, Malacca, the control point for spices, and Muscat and Ormuz, which dominated the Persian Gulf. Then their men pushed through to the Moluccas in 1512, thus being the first to discover the Pacific, coasted Formosa, and established contact with Java and Siam. In 1542 they visited Japan and in 1557 established a settlement at Macao, which was to be the oldest European possession in China (Map 7).

In this great eastern empire, the Portuguese had no thought of settling their own people, even in sparsely populated regions, or of developing an economy based upon the principles of productivity and economic growth. The Italian model of imperialism was so fixed in their minds and the opportunities of the East were so propitious that their one aim was to profit from trade—by buying cheaply and by selling dear. For the long term, this was a grave error, for it was not a difficult task for stronger powers to push the Portuguese out of their trading centers. For their part, natives were as willing to sell to representatives of one nationality as to those of another.

Then the Portuguese rulers made another serious mistake by declaring trade with the East a royal monopoly, contending that all the benefits should accrue to those who had financed the discoveries. As time was to show, Portuguese kings were unable to rise to the great enterpreneurial challenge. Not only were their losses great and their costs of administration heavy, but they could not prevent sailors and ship captains from trading on their own accounts or from ignominiously cheating them. Worst of all, they did not even try to distribute their Oriental products in Europe. They left this business to others, especially to the Dutch and Italians, who picked up cargoes at Lisbon and took them to various distribution points, notably to Antwerp. It was chiefly this trade that made the city on the Scheldt for a brief while the leading financial center of Western Europe. In the end Portuguese kings sold off their monopoly to the highest bidder, and when Portugal became a part of Spain (1580–1640), others, especially the Dutch, went directly to the East instead of to Lisbon for their spices, and Spain exploited the resources of its little neighbor for its own advantage. By then the height of Portuguese economic power had been passed.

The other part of Portugal's overseas empire, Brazil, like all the New World, presented a different problem from that of the East. Here, inasmuch as there was no existing trade to take over, recourse had to be had to other

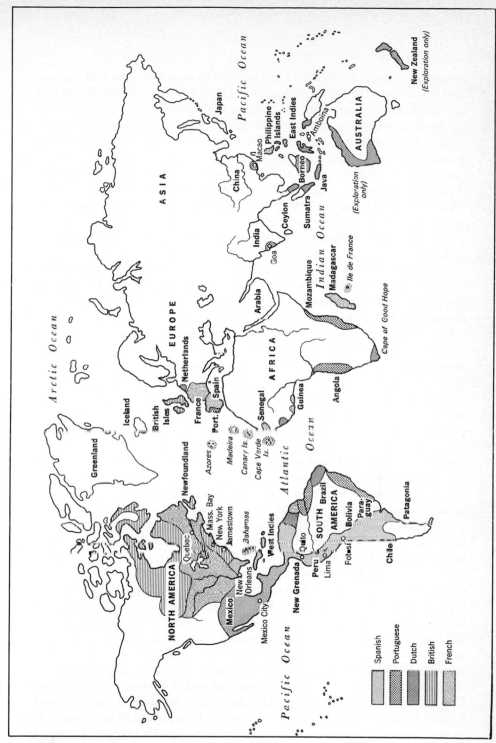

Map 7
European Overseas Empires at the End of the Seventeenth Century

means of realizing a profit on sums sunk in exploration. The first inclination was to hunt for the accumulations of gold and silver which rumor had
it existed in large quantities. Only when the possibilities of finding treasure petered out was serious attention given to settlement and production.

By 1532 Brazil had a small settlement and the land had begun to be
parceled out in holdings from the crown, each captaincy (*capitánia*) stretching 150 miles along the coast and indefinitely into the interior. Gradually
the captaincies were settled with Caucasians, Negroes, and Indians, who
cultivated sugar cane, cut brazilwood, and mined gold. Very shrewd economic forecasters of the time might well have guessed that this kind of
exploitation was in the long run to pay off better than one-sided trade in
luxuries.

The lands which the Spanish discovered in the New World were like
Portugal's Brazil in that they had no developed trade which could be
directed toward Europe and in that they were entirely unknown quantities.
Hence the first task to be accomplished was exploring the new lands,
which, given their size, was a formidable undertaking. The second task was
to conquer the Indians, if conquest is not too ambitious a word for what
was involved. These assignments fell to the lot of the adventurous *conquistadores.* Motivated by dreams of gold, hopes of glory, visions of God, and
in at least one case by a desire to bathe in a fountain of youth, these
intrepid pioneers had within a half-century spread out on the west coast
of the Americas from Chile to the Rouge River in Oregon, on the east coast
from Florida to the Argentine, and in the interior from Arizona and the
northern boundary of Mississippi, over all Central America, and to what
were to become the major centers of South America. Nor were the comings
and goings of these men fruitless. To a remarkable degree their searching
brought them the very kinds of rewards which they desired.

The first great success of the *conquistadores* was realized by Hernando
Cortés in Mexico. When this hardy man landed on the coast of Mexico and
heard stories of the great wealth of the Aztec Indians, he promptly burned
his ships so that his men would not take off and struck boldly overland
to reap his harvest. When he reached his destination, he found a people
with a fairly high degree of civilization and fabulous stores of gold and
silver, but a people who had never discovered iron, which impaired their
fighting effectiveness, and who offered up human sacrifices in such numbers to their gods that a revolt against the ruling minority was always
smoldering—a condition of which he hoped to take advantage. He discovered also that the Aztecs' chief city, located on the present site of Mexico
City, was built on an island in a lake and was connected to the mainland
by an aqueduct and causeway—a situation which proved to be vulnerable
to the Spaniards. Finally, Cortés encountered a friendly people who made
the great mistake of inviting the *conquistador* and his men into the town.

Once inside the city precincts, Cortés displayed a degree of perfidy that has become legendary. He took the emperor captive, expecting to start a revolt among the people against their leader, but on the contrary so aroused the populace that they turned on him and drove him to the mainland. There he calmly cut the city's water supply and the causeway over which its food came and waited for hunger to do its work. When the people were sufficiently weakened, he took the city (1521) and sacked it. His most important haul was the Aztecs' store of precious metals—an amount that did honor to the most fantastic dreams of his ilk.

The second great success story of the *conquistadores* was that of Francisco Pizarro. He had served under Balboa at the Isthmus of Panama and in the hard school of Balboa's murderer and successor, Pedrarias. Like many others, he heard the tall tales of high civilization and wealth of the Incas of Peru and like many before him was impatient to get at them. Finally, in 1532, he was able to realize his hopes. He penetrated the Incan empire with a small band of followers and immediately began a plot to get political power. He found a situation in which two brothers were disputing the succession to the throne, and by posing as arbiter between the two and then using the successful one as a puppet, he got the hold over the people which he wanted. When ultimately the natives turned against him, he defeated them without much trouble, for they, like the Aztecs, had not yet acquired iron and steel. It is said that Pizarro offered to let the emperor ransom himself by filling a room 22 by 17 foot and nine feet deep with gold ornaments. Once the treasure had been delivered, the Spaniard murdered the "ransomed" man in cold blood. When this take was melted down, it was found to be worth some five million American dollars of pre-1934 value.

Although these were the most famous exploits of the *conquistadores*, they were not the only ones of their kind. The civilized inhabitants of Guatemala and the Mayans of Yucatan were both subjected to the yoke of Spain; the Chibchas in the highlands of Columbia near Bogotá, famous for their fabled *El Dorado,* a man who according to legend was every year plated with gold and thrown in the lake, were conquered and robbed; and Venezuela and Chile were overrun. Then, when no more treasures remained to be seized and the conquering of more people seemed futile, the Spaniards turned to mining. They discovered a mountain of silver at Potosí, Peru, and went to work on it with vigor, as is attested by the fact that the roaring mining town of Potosí had 120,000 inhabitants in 1580 and was thus the largest city in the Americas. They also found fabulously rich mines at Zacatecas and Guanajuto in Mexico and lesser diggings in a hundred other places.

Although conquering, robbing, and mining were the chief economic activities of the Spaniards in the Americas during the sixteenth century, some interest was shown in agriculture. Spanish lords and gentlemen received large grants of territory and many of the grantees took off for the New World to make their fortunes off the land. They were largely responsible for the introduction into the Western Hemisphere of a host of domesticated plants and animals, in which America was extremely poor. The *conquistadores* introduced the horse, which gave them great mobility and thus one of their most distinct advantages over the Indians, while their successors brought in cattle, sheep, goats, chickens, and pigs. They also introduced into America sugar cane, wheat, barley, rice, rye, coffee, cotton, a number of garden vegetables, and fruits. They were the first to send back to Europe most of the things that America gave to the Old World— tobacco, chocolate, the "Irish" potato, Indian corn, quinine, the tomato, peanuts, and the turkey. They were largely responsible, because of their success in cultivation, for the initial increase in the use of sugar, rice, and coffee in the Old World. And they were chiefly accountable for the introduction of Negroes as slaves into the New World.[5] But the importance of permanent settlements in Spanish America in the sixteenth century should not be exaggerated, for in 1600 precious metals constituted 90 percent of the Old World's imports from the New and in 1700 the total Spanish population of the New World was only 150,000. Economic growth was largely a thing of the future.

While the Spanish and Portuguese were thus instituting the process by which their brand of Western culture was to become dominant in the Western Hemisphere from Mexico southward, and while the Portuguese in their exploitation of Eastern trade were beginning to make European economic life and European ways felt by Eastern cultures, the other great colonizing peoples—the English, the Dutch, and the French—who were eventually to do so much in spreading Western culture to non-European parts of the world, were also taking part in the expansionist movement. Their late start put them under a severe handicap, for by the time their first explorers set sail the routes to the East around Africa had been preempted by the Portuguese; the area of exploration for a way to Cathay via the South Atlantic had been monopolized by Spain; and the Treaty of Tordesillas had divided the whole undiscovered world between the two Iberian states. Although the opportunities for discovery, conquest, and glory thus seemed extraordinarily limited, the latecomers concentrated their efforts at first upon finding new routes to the Far East chiefly either via a northeast passage around Scandinavia and Russia or a northwest passage through or around the land mass of North America. Their efforts

---

[5] Indians could not legally be enslaved in Spanish America. They were, however, exploited in one way or another. By the *repartimiento* system Spaniards were given the right to all or part of an Indian's labor and by *encomienda*, the right to collect tribute, reminiscent of feudal dues, from Indians in given districts.

in the former direction bore little fruit, but those in the latter area took them to that part of the New World which was to become the wealthiest area of the entire planet. Furthermore, their failure to find new routes to the East led these powers to encroach upon Portugal's pathway around Africa, and to struggle among themselves for primacy in the colonial world.

In the French case the process of discovery was an excellent example of the accumulative effect of knowledge, each successive explorer building upon the foundations laid by his predecessor. Here, the chain of explorations began with Jacques Cartier, an experienced mariner from the Breton town of St. Malo, who in 1534 reached and claimed for France the Gaspé Basin. The next year he sailed up the St. Lawrence in the hope of getting through to China. When he saw water breaking in the river, he believed —or so it is said; the story is probably apocryphal—that he had succeeded and exclaimed *"La Chine!"*, thus giving a name to the rapids above Montreal which has stuck to them even to the present day (Lachine Rapids). Then Samuel de Champlain carried on where Cartier left off, founding a settlement at Quebec (1608) and exploring the Lake Champlain region and all the Great Lakes, which he claimed for France. Subsequently, a priest named Marquette and a trader, Joliet, went part way down the Mississippi and they were followed later by Robert Cavelier de La Salle, who reached the Gulf of Mexico and claimed all the land drained by the great Father of Waters and its tributaries for his King—*Le Roi Soleil*—Louis XIV. Thus the French carved out for themselves an empire which consisted of the heartland of America and Canada.

The English in their search for a route to China sent out an Italian, Giovanni Caboto, more commonly known as John Cabot, in 1496. He explored some of the coast of North America, thus giving England a claim to what was to become the Atlantic coastline of most of the United States. Then his son Sebastian, Martin Frobisher, Henry Hudson, and William Baffin one after another tried in vain to push around North America, discovering and claiming Newfoundland, Hudson Bay, and Baffin Bay, which were to give the English a hold from which they could contest the Canadian territory with the French. Finally, the Dutch, for their part, got a foothold at New York, thanks to the explorations of Henry Hudson (1609), who went up the Hudson River as far as what is now Albany.

These discoveries of the French, English, and Dutch were definitely disappointing, for they did not open up a golden gateway to the East or very promising lands as areas of settlement. The French could not at first cope with the cold and could get very little out of Canada except fish and furs. The English failed in their efforts to settle Newfoundland in 1582, and Sir Walter Raleigh was unsuccessful in his attempts to establish a colony at Roanoke Island, North Carolina. The Virginia Company's settlement on the James River, the Plymouth Colony, and the Massachusetts Bay Colony were at best only struggling outposts in the wilderness for some years after their founding. Indeed, advocates of permanent colonization and settlement, like the unsuppressible Richard Hakluyt at the end of the sixteenth century, seemed to be barking up the wrong tree. Even the Dutch colony at New Amsterdam was insignificant compared with what the Portuguese had in the East.

The French, English, and Dutch were not, however, content to admit defeat. From the first they had coveted Portuguese and Spanish colonial wealth and had speculated on how they might encroach upon it. Needless to say, cerebration on the problem led them to identical conclusions, for the range of possibilities was extremely limited. First, they agreed that they might do well to trade in Latin America, second, that there would be profit in plundering Spanish galleons on their homeward voyages, third, that they themselves could go to the Far East via known routes and get the spices which the Portuguese were selling to them at such a profit, and fourth, that they should take some of the less well-defended and apparently fertile lands in Central and South America and bring them rapidly into production of things, like sugar, that Europeans wanted. They tried all four of these solutions.

The story of what they did may be begun with the efforts of John Hawkins, an Englishman, to develop trade in slaves between the Guinea Coast and Spanish Caribbean colonies (both Spaniards and Portuguese had long used Negroes for slaves), and to bring back from the New World gold, silver, or merchandise in exchange for his human cargoes. Unfortunately the Spaniards did not like his plan, and when they caught him at Vera Cruz, they fired on his ships with such effectiveness that the poor man was just able to escape with his skin back to England. Inasmuch as peaceful trade seemed to be impossible, recourse was had to the next possibility— privateering. This profession fitted the personality and spirits of one of Hawkins' men, Francis Drake, perfectly, and he set out to harass the Spaniards in the West Indies. After a successful turn at this sport, he sailed around South America, up the coast of California, across the Pacific to the East Indies, through the Indian Ocean, around Africa, and thence back to England (1580). Plundering as he went, Drake sailed into port loaded with loot, much to the delight of Good Queen Bess, who promptly joined in his good fortune by helping herself to a share of the booty. Subsequently, other Elizabethan sea dogs took off on similar junkets, one of the most famous being that of Thomas Cavendish who held up Spanish galleons along the Spanish Main and also tried his luck in the Pacific.

Robbery on the high seas was, however, a precarious business at best and in this case contributed toward bringing on retaliations, of which the

Spanish Armada of 1588 was the most famous. Consequently, some among the latecomers wanted to try the third possibility of getting into the pioneers' colonial jackpot—going directly to the source of Portugal's spice supplies in the East. Thus would they get all the profit that was to be had from this trade.

That the Dutch should have been the first to have had recourse to this stratagem has a historical explanation. Netherlanders had obtained the lion's share of the trade of carrying spices from Lisbon to Antwerp and had made a very good thing out of the practice. The Netherlands, however, rose in revolt against Spain in 1566, and although the southern provinces were subdued, the northern provinces established their independence (1579). The upshot of this situation was that the Dutch cut shipping to Antwerp, while the Spanish, for their part, prohibited the Dutch from going to Lisbon to pick up Eastern products.[6] Thus excluded from a very profitable business, the Dutch had every incentive to go directly to the East for what they had previously obtained in Portugal.

Nor were the Netherlanders entirely unfamiliar with the routes which the Portuguese had laid out to India and the Spice Islands, for many of them had sailed on Portuguese vessels and one of them, Jan Huyghen van Linschoten, had published a well-known and fairly detailed account of his voyage. Therefore, it was with the expectation of success, if the Spaniards could be avoided, that a fleet set out under Cornelis van Houtman which reached Java in 1595 and thus proved that the Dutch could go to the source of spices as well as anyone else. This voyage was followed by a veritable flotilla of twenty-two ships that put out in 1598 to test whether the route around Africa or that around South America was the more feasible, thirteen ships heading for the Cape of Good Hope and nine for the Strait of Magellan. Since only one of the latter got back, the African route was decided to be the better of the two and was developed earnestly by merchantmen of the Dutch East India Company (founded 1602). One of this company's greatest colonial administrators, Jan Pieterszoon Coen, gained the upper hand in Batavia, Java, and the Moluccas; one of its great explorers, Abel Janszoon Tasman, discovered Tasmania and New Zealand and proved Australia to be an island. Their successors drove the Portuguese from Malacca (1641) and Ceylon (1638–1658). The Dutch established contact with Japan, which was the main relationship this country had with Western culture until the coming of Commodore Perry in 1854, and they founded a successful colony (1652) at the Cape of Good Hope, near the present city of Capetown, as the supply station for ships in the Indian trade.

---

[6] It will be recalled that Portugal became part of Spain in 1580.

Dutch inroads on Eastern commerce proved to be extremely profitable, and as a result the small nation of the Netherlands became the wealthiest state per capita in Western Europe during the seventeenth century. It did not, however, have everything its own way and was early confronted by competition from the English and the French. The former did, in fact, charter their East India Company two years before the Dutch did theirs and shortly thereafter sent merchantmen to the East for spices. At first the Dutch were not particularly hostile to the newcomers, for they appeared to be useful in subduing the Portuguese. But when the English attempted to establish themselves in the Spice Islands, the Dutch uttered a very emphatic "no" and were able to uphold their injunction with force. Thus the English turned their attention to trade with India and the Persian Gulf, getting a foothold at Surat in 1609, founding a station at Madras in 1639, securing Bombay in 1661, and establishing themselves at Calcutta in 1690. The French, for their part, planted small colonies on Madagascar and Reunion (1642), got footholds in Senegal and Guinea, where they could trade in slaves, and through their East India Company established posts at Surat and Pondichéry in India (1664), where they conducted a promising trade.

By the end of the seventeenth century trade in cotton, cotton textiles, and other Indian and Persian products was proving to be even more profitable than trade in spices, so the fact that the Dutch had excluded the English and the French from the Spice Islands was not of primary importance to the newcomers. Nevertheless, they waged war on the Dutch either together or singly from the middle of the seventeenth century to the end of the War of Spanish Succession in 1713. The small Netherlandish state could not stand this kind of attrition and it had to reconcile itself to limiting its activities. Its holdings in the East remained important, however, for they included Ceylon, Sumatra, the Celebes, the Moluccas, part of Borneo, New Guinea, the Malay Peninsula, and Java, where coffee growing became important. And in Africa it still had its colony at the Cape of Good Hope.

With the elimination of the Dutch from the real contest for power in the East, the struggle became one between the English and the French. Although these two peoples had been sparring at each other for some time, the struggle became particularly bitter after 1707, for then the collapse of the Mogul Empire in India left a vacuum into which both contenders rushed—and in their haste to extend their dominions they came headlong into conflict with one another. In the wars which ensued, waged under the leadership of two brilliant generals, Joseph François Dupleix and Robert Clive, the English emerged the victors at the conclusion of the Seven Years' War (Treaty of Paris, 1763). Henceforth the French were to remain in their few stations as traders rather than as colonizers. It was the English who would try to implant Western culture's economic practices and ideologies in India.

While these various tests of strength were going on in the Far East, still other attempts were being made by the colonial latecomers to profit from overseas expansion. For one thing, they all seized lands in the Caribbean area in the hope of producing goods which would supplement what was grown at home and in the expectation of trading with or of preying on Spaniards. Thus the Dutch took Curaçao and Dutch Guiana or Surinam; the English occupied St. Christopher or St. Kitts,[7] Bermuda, Barbados, Jamaica, the Bahamas, some of the Virgin group, and still others of less renown; and the French seized Martinique, Guadeloupe, the western half of Santo Domingo (now Haiti), and a number of lesser places. In most of these areas attempts were made to grow tobacco, but frequent oversupply of the market and consequent falls in price led eventually to less specialization—to the growing of rice, coffee, indigo, cotton, cocoa, and sugar. The last of these came to be the most important of all. It was to satisfy the sweet tooth of Europe that previously had had to rely largely upon honey, and it provided the ingredient of an entirely new alcoholic beverage—rum—that was to have wondrous effects on trade and on man.

Also, the French, Dutch, and English made more or less serious attempts to settle their lands in North America, but progress was very slow. In 1663 French Canada had only some three thousand French inhabitants and in 1763 but about eighty thousand, and New Orleans was in 1722 only a struggling village of five hundred. The Dutch colony of New Amsterdam, which was captured by the English in one of the many wars between these two peoples (1664) and rechristened New York, had only fourteen thousand inhabitants in 1760. And all the original thirteen English colonies along the Atlantic seaboard had a population of but 275,000 in 1700 and seemed destined to be hemmed in by the claims of the French in the north and west. The future, based upon production, was, however, theirs. And the French threat was removed at the time of the French and Indian War, or, as it was called in Europe, the Seven Years' War (1763), when France ceded Canada to England and Louisiana to Spain in compensation for that country's loss of Florida to England.[8]

By the middle of the eighteenth century, therefore, Western European culture had been carried to both North and South America and it looked as though it would eventually become dominant throughout the New World. It had come in contact with the cultures of the East and bade fair

---

[7] The French had part of the island until 1713, when they surrendered it to the English.

[8] Florida was returned to Spain in 1783.

to drag them into its economic orbit. What the economic impact of Europe on the rest of the world and of the rest of the world on Europe would be remains to be seen.

Economic consequences of European overseas expansion

A general statement

Of all the major movements which mark the transition of Europe from the Middle Ages to Modern Times, none was more pregnant with change than the expansion of Europe overseas. The impact of Europe on cultures beyond the seas and the influence of these cultures on Europe contributed much to giving the world the cultural configuration it has today. Yet in spite of its importance, expansion has been studied less and understood less than such other great developments of the sixteenth century as the Protestant Revolt, the rise of national states, and the development of capitalism and its institutions. The ramifications of the movement were so wide, its results often so subtle, and its action so intertwined with other forces that its complete significance has proved elusive. In the few pages at our disposal here, all that we can hope to do is to make clear the outstanding economic aspects of European expansion.

Undoubtedly the most important consequence of this movement was its marked impetus to economic growth. Overseas areas constituted a vast new market for all kinds of things from the motherlands, as is always the case in colonial undertakings, and the overseas areas gave the Old World supplies of goods that were to create entirely new industries. Secondly, the expansion of Europe led to the importation of so much gold and silver bullion into Europe that the prices of goods, based as they were on these metals, rose enormously. This price rise had a stimulating effect on business enterprise, but caused considerable social tension, particularly between lords of the land and those peasants who had long-term contracts with their overlords and whose obligations were fixed in money. Thirdly, the overseas movement tended to effect a shift in the center of commerce and subsequently of economic activity generally from the Mediterranean Sea area to the Atlantic seaboard—a shift that has been glorified with the rubric "Commercial Revolution." Fourthly, colonialism led to fundamental changes in business organization, for large-scale overseas enterprises required greater sums than could be provided by former institutions. In fact, European expansion is largely responsible for the coming into being of the stock company. Fifthly, from increased trade and an increased division of labor stemmed an ever greater use of money as a medium of exchange, and this increase led to important developments in banking practices. Lastly, the overseas movement contributed to changes in political, social, and, to some extent, economic ideologies which were to become integral parts of Western culture.

European price revolution, 1450-1650

The story of the economic impact of expansion on the Old World usually is begun with a consideration of bullion imports and the rise in prices, for these developments had effects which were pertinent to many economic, social, and political changes. Indeed, they had a bearing upon the increased use of money, on banking, on debtor-creditor relationships, on savings and investments, on economic growth, on the relations between serfs or wage workers and masters, and upon the costs of government and the raising of taxes.

Note should be taken, however, of the fact that prices began to go up well before bullion arrived in Europe from the New World. The reason for this was a general upswing in the secular trend which the European economy began to experience past the mid-fifteenth century. A recovering population put new pressure on agricultural resources, and an expansion of cultivation, buoyed by rising cereal prices, began. Under the pressure of demand for new food supplies, land reclamation projects multiplied, but the Continent's new hunger was not easily satisfied. The increasing use of horses in transportation made fodder scarce. More important, however, was the fact that the population of Europe increased by two-thirds between 1450 and 1650. Fueling the resurging economy early on was a spurt of new mining activity in Central Europe which increased the amount of money in circulation, a necessary concomitant of the inflationary times.

In France the price of wheat doubled from 1451–1500 to 1501–1550 and then nearly tripled in the following century as precious metal from the

Western Hemisphere arrived in quantity; the price of the same grain in England doubled from 1501–1550 to 1551–1600.[1]

From the second half of the sixteenth century on, the flow of bullion from the New World to the Old reached enormous volume, as can readily be ascertained from Table 2. If to the totals which were brought to Spain through official channels, 10 percent is added for what was smuggled in, if an undetermined sum is estimated for the production of the mines of Germany and Austria (like those of Joachimsthal and Salzburg), if allowances are made for the exportation of certain amounts of gold and silver to the East in payment for goods, and if the usual estimate of the Old World's store of bullion in 1500 is used, one will find that Europe's holdings of gold and silver more than tripled from 1500 to 1650. Furthermore,

Table 2 Spanish imports of fine gold and silver from America (in grams)

Period	Silver	Gold
1503–1510		4,965,180
1511–1520		9,153,220
1521–1530	148,739	4,889,050
1531–1540	86,193,876	14,466,360
1541 1550	177,573,164	24,957,130
1551–1560	303,121,174	42,620,080
1561–1570	942,858,792	11,530,940
1571–1580	1,118,591,954	9,429,140
1581–1590	2,103,027,689	12,101,650
1591–1600	2,707,626,528	19,451,420
1601–1610	2,213,631,245	11,764,090
1611–1620	2,192,255,993	8,855,940
1621–1630	2,145,339,043	3,889,760
1631–1640	1,396,759,594	1,240,400
1641–1650	1,056,430,988	1,549,390
1651–1660	443,256,546	469,430
Total	16,886,815,303	181,333,180

SOURCE: Earl J. Hamilton, *American Treasure and the Price Revolution in Spain* (Cambridge, Mass.: Harvard, 1934).

[1] It is important for today's student of prices to note that however "revolutionary" the Early Modern inflation was by the standards of the time, in modern-day terms, the rate of increase in prices was not large. A trebling of prices over a century involves an average annual rate of inflation of only 1.1%, a tenfold increase of only 2.4%. Today such a rate might be considered unacceptably low (but never too high) for a modern economy.

if a study of the area distribution of the newly acquired treasure is made, it will be seen that despite Spain's efforts to keep the gold and silver within its boundaries, precious metals went to all parts of Western Europe in payment for the difference between Spanish merchandise imports and its exports, that is, for the settlement of Spain's deficits in foreign trade.

As bullion came to be exchanged for goods, it lost value in terms of actual merchandise; that is, prices went up. This was because (1) supplies of gold and silver increased much more rapidly than the stock of goods, (2) the rate of circulation of money was accelerated with the boom in commercial transactions,[2] and (3) individuals, fearing shortages of goods or higher prices, used their free balances for immediate instead of future purchases.

From intensive studies of the price rise of the sixteenth century and the first half of the seventeenth,[3] it is clear that prices rose at different rates in different countries, that prices of some goods rose more rapidly than those of others, and that the prices of goods went up faster than that of services as expressed in money wages. As American bullion entered the market, its effects on prices were felt first in Spain and then in other countries almost in direct proportion to the extent of their participation in the new trade along the Atlantic seacoast. Prices, as expressed in gold and silver, first stopped rising in Spain as a reaction to the decline in the influx of bullion, to the fall in trade, and to the resulting deceleration in the rate of circulation of money, and then declined in other parts of the world (Table 3).

Furthermore, historical studies show that prices of staples, particularly arable farm products, rose earlier and more rapidly than other goods, such as timber, metals, and textiles.[4] Finally, wage series show that throughout most of Europe the rise of money wages was slow, lagging far behind price

---

[2] See p. 143.

[3] See especially the work of the International Scientific Committee for the Study of Prices. Among its publications are Earl J. Hamilton, *American Treasure and the Price Revolution in Spain: 1501–1650* (Cambridge, Mass.: Harvard, 1934); Henri Hauser (Ed.), *Recherches et documents sur l'histoire des prix en France de 1500 à 1800* (Paris: Les Presses Modernes, 1936); M. J. Elsas, *Umriss einer Geschichte der Preise und Löhne in Deutschland* (Leyden: Sijthoff, 1936); Sir William Beveridge, *Prices and Wages in England from the Twelfth to the Nineteenth Century* (London: Longmans, 1939); N.W. Posthumus, *Nederlandsche Prijsgeschiedenis* (Leyden: Brill, 1943); and see also Charles Verlinden (Ed.), *Dokumenten voor de Geschiedenis van Prijzen en Lonen in Vlaanderen en Brabant* (Bruges: "De Tempel," 1959).

In the last-named book, data (pp. 542 and 544) indicate that the rents on medium-size houses increased by a little over four times in Antwerp from 1500 to 1585. Wages of a mason's helper rose in the same city by nearly six times from 1500 to 1600. To be sure, Antwerp grew rapidly until Spaniards sacked it in 1576 and 1584–1585. For a more recent reinterpretation of Early Modern price history, see the works listed in the bibliography, p. 537.

[4] For a summary presentation of these conclusions, see Slicher Van Bath, *The Agrarian History of Western Europe,* pp. 98–131, 195–206.

increases. These facts reinforce the view that the inflation was caused by increased demand. Foodstuffs became dearer, compared with other products, as population levels rose; while increasing supplies of labor, the result of demographic growth, supressed the rise of wages. The net result was a falling, or at best static, real wage (Table 3).

Table 3. Composite index numbers of prices and real wages in Spain (base=1571–81)

Decade	Price index	Real wage index
1501–1510	33.26 (1501)	110.73
1511–1520	46.48 (1521)	122.19
1541–1550	56.02 (1541)	99.02
1571–1580	103.95 (1581)	100.49
1591–1600	143.55 (1601)	101.02
1611–1620	129.09 (1621)	124.89
1641–1650	116.53 (1641)	100.81

SOURCE: E. J. Hamilton, *American Treasure and the Price Revolution in Spain,* pp.279, 403.

The entire phenomenon of the price rise affected the lives of contemporaries so deeply that it was the object of much comment and some serious study. People of the times, in spite of their realization of what was taking place, were, however, at a loss to explain why it was occurring. Apparently it was not until 1568, when a French political philosopher, Jean Bodin, penned his *Reply to the Paradoxes of M. Malestroit,* that anything was published which approached a satisfactory explanation of the price rise. Bodin was the first in Modern Times to express the fundamental principles of the quantity theory of money; that is, if the quantity of money in circulation is increased without a comparable increase in the supply of goods, prices tend to react upward. It remained for later students to point out that an increase in the rate of circulation of money had the same effect on prices as an increase in the volume of money, and for still more recent scholars to stress that the course of prices is also conditioned by the rate with which people use their free balances for the present purchase of goods. Despite the theoretical sophistication of Bodin and his followers in later centuries, modern scholarship has turned away from the quantity theory of money and the role of bullion imports as an explanation of the price revolution. The inflation began in earnest as part of a pattern of general economic recovery around the beginning of the 1500s, long before any sizable additions to Europe's bullion stocks. This suggests in turn that the extraction of large quantities of precious metals in Central Europe, Mexico, and Peru was a result, not a cause, of the inflation, as the expanding European market came to require ever larger amounts of money in circulation.

As with all inflation, the price revolution benefited some elements of society although it hurt others. Contemporaries saw that the price rise favored debtors and penalized creditors. It was clear to all that debtors had to produce less than formerly to meet their money obligations, for they got more money per unit of what they produced. Thus a peasant whose various dues to his lord had been commuted to money payments found that his payments were much lighter at the end of the sixteenth century than had been those of his grandfather in 1500, because he had to grow only 3 bushels of wheat to realize the same amount of money that his forebear had gained with 10 bushels. Contrariwise, it was obvious that creditors were being paid off in money that bought only a fraction of the goods it had previously commanded. Thus a lord who received money dues established in the late fifteenth century could only buy a third or a fourth of the amount of goods with the same sum in 1650.

This situation led many lords to seek a revision of their arrangements with their peasants.[5] This was difficult to do if the peasant stood on his legal rights, but all too often the peasant lacked adequate legal advice or political power for a real defense. Thus lords were frequently able to change the terms of peasant payments and even in some cases to substitute a short-term lease of from five to fifteen years for the inheritable contract. In nearly all cases they were able to increase traditional dues that were not for specific amounts, as with heriot and relief, or to take undue advantage of practices, like that of *mainmorte* [mortmain]. As can readily be imagined, acts of this kind frequently led to troubles between lords and peasants which became so inextricably mixed with the religious sentiment of the sixteenth century that some of Protestantism had the appearance of a social movement.

In England, special circumstances created a particularly tense situation and a whole series of special social and economic problems. Here the price of wool went up with such amazing rapidity that the prospect of profits, together with a shortage of labor and low real wages, induced many large land owners to go into sheep raising. They were convinced that they could get far more purchasing power from their land in this way than they could by continuing to receive the much-depreciated (in real value) dues from peasants. However, to conduct the new type of agricultural undertaking successfully, it was necessary to have large pastures enclosed by fences and hedges, and to get the large pastures it was necessary to get rid of the

---

[5] It also helps to explain why so many lords were willing to strike boldly overseas in search of fame and fortune.

peasants and their rights to work small plots. This the land-hungry lords did by depriving their people of traditional privileges, like the right to turn out their livestock in the common fields, or by raising fees or leases to prohibitive levels.

By these and similar devices, it is estimated that in the sixteenth century about 5 percent of the English Midlands, where enclosures were the heaviest, was enclosed and that in a few counties the percentage ran as high as 10. It was so great that many of the people forced off the land were unable to find other employment and became public charges or beggars. Indeed, the increase in pauperism was so large in Elizabethan England that a system of poor relief provided by parishes came into being and begging was condemned as both a national calamity and a social nuisance. Moreover, enclosing went so far that government circles in London feared for the food supply of both the city and the entire nation and enacted legislation, like that limiting the size of flocks and prohibiting the conversion of arable land to pasture, to stop it.[6] Lastly, enclosures contributed to outbreaks and revolts, often in connection with religious and social movements, like Kett's Rebellion in 1549 and the agitation of the "Diggers" and "Levellers" in the seventeenth century.

In addition to the tensions thus caused in agriculture by the rise in prices, there were also troubles in industry between employers and employees. As a result, both apprentices and journeymen tried to get better terms from guild masters. Workers in the domestic system agitated for higher rates for their spinning and weaving, and laborers in large central shops demanded higher wages. In some places there were strikes and in others, riots. So severe, in fact, did labor troubles become that both France and England took legal steps to suppress them by forbidding strikes and by establishing maximum wage rates.[7] Obviously the decline in the real purchasing power of wages was understood, even if the policies adopted to deal with it left much to be desired.

That aspect of the rise of prices at a more rapid rate than wages, which, however, contemporaries did not understand, was what has come to be known as "profit inflation." Briefly, this was that with prices rising and wages lagging behind, profits tended to be larger; that is, they were "inflated," especially in those enterprises where wages constituted a high percentage of the total cost of production. Such a situation, at least in theory, increases the incentives of business entrepreneurs to augment their investments in capital equipment so that they can make more profit. In this way profit inflation is supposed to favor economic growth. Economic expansion depends, however, on so many factors of which the desire to

[6] The latter was repeated in 1593.
[7] See the Elizabethan Statute of Apprentices (1563) and the French decree of Villers-Cotterêts (1539).

increase profits is only one that profit inflation does not operate automatically in accordance with the theory. In Portugal and Spain, for example, conditions favorable to the making of larger profits seem to have had a limited influence on economic development, except in the case of investments in colonial enterprise and in sheep raising.[8] Its effect on industry was slight, partly because of a limitation of natural resources, a general unwillingness to save for investment, and an attitude, especially on the part of the nobility, that participation in industrial activity was degrading.

In the Netherlands, also, new investments were largely in colonial enterprises, like the East India Company, and in agriculture, where production was increased by new techniques that foreshadowed the "agricultural revolution" of the eighteenth century; but there was some investment in industry for the processing of colonial products, like chocolate, coffee, and spices, and for the production of ships and ship supplies. In France, the difference between prices and wages in the sixteenth and seventeenth century seems to have had but slight general effect upon commerce, industry, or agriculture. Nevertheless, the French took advantage of special situations to expand economic activity, as in the case of the slave trade, the refining of cane sugar, and the development of certain luxuries, like silk and glass.

Profit inflation undoubtedly had its greatest and clearest impact in England. In agriculture, production on large farms, even of wool that required little labor, was increased to take advantage of the opportunity to earn large profits. In commerce, new investments were made, as we have seen, in all kinds of enterprises from Drake's privateering to the establishment of overseas trading companies. And in industry, investments were placed in a whole list of trades, often at the instigation of Elizabeth's economic "brain truster," Lord Burghley. Many of these would undoubtedly not have been made, or they would not have been made in the same volume, if the likelihood of profits had not been good. Thus much new capital appeared in iron mining, in saltpeter and alum production, in brewing, in shipbuilding, and in coal mining, especially in the Newcastle area. In all these trades production increased remarkably and in all of them new techniques, which required capital outlay, were employed.

---

[8] The Mesta, a country-wide organization of sheep herders—a kind of national guild—had a strong position in this phase of agriculture and also in politics. With the extraordinary rise in wool prices, the Mesta increased output, having at its peak control of perhaps 3 million sheep. The organization arranged the migration of sheep from the coastal areas, where the animals were wintered, to the mountains, where they grazed in summer, the so-called "transhumance." It got rights to routes for these migrations and privileges to graze along them. It controlled pastures, and it secured favorable laws for the sale and export of wool. In time the success of the Mesta resulted in overgrazing and soil erosion and to conflicts with settled agriculturalists, whose interests were sacrificed. Hence the royal house, which had profited from the export of wool, had to refrain eventually from supporting Mesta policies.

The growth of commerce and the "Commercial Revolution"

With all the changes in agriculture and industry which occurred in the sixteenth century, clearly that branch of economic activity which experienced greatest growth was commerce. Just what the magnitude of that development was is impossible to state with precision, for reliable statistical information on trade is sadly lacking for this early period. From the movement of ships in the major ports, from a few cases where tax and customs returns are available, and from information regarding ship-building, we know that the expansion was very great. When one considers that Spain and Portugal received more gold and silver from overseas between 1500 and 1650 than was in existence in Europe at the former date and that much of this treasure went from the states of the Iberian Peninsula to other parts of Europe in payment for goods, one gets some conception of the extension of European commerce. To say that its total volume doubled within the first century of Modern Times would be a conservative statement.

Whatever the growth of European commerce may have been, it is clear that the greatest expansion was realized along the Atlantic littoral from Gibraltar to Hamburg and from Land's End in England to Newcastle-on-the-Tyne. Here were to be found the colonizing nations which were putting royal treasure and income from taxes into overseas explorations and colonial expansion. Here were the merchants who sought products for fitting out expeditions and for trading with natives the world over. Here were the places where colonial goods from the far corners of the world were marketed. And here, too, were the best ports of Europe, conveniently located for using the new routes around Africa and across the Atlantic.

Under the circumstances it is little wonder that places like Cadiz, Lisbon, Bordeaux, Rouen, Antwerp, Amsterdam, Bristol, and London grew by leaps and bounds. It is said that Lisbon's port on the Tagus River was, at its height in the 1540s, literally choked with ships and that Antwerp at its peak in the 1560s witnessed the passing up and down the Scheldt of 500 ships a day. Nor is it astonishing that in the thirty-year period prior to 1618, the number of English ships is said to have doubled and that in the middle of the seventeenth century the Dutch had a merchant marine estimated at four times the size of that of Italy, Spain, and Portugal combined.

So drastic was the shift in the center of international commerce from the Mediterranean to the Atlantic and especially to the North Sea ports that it has traditionally been called in the annals of European history the "Commercial Revolution of the Sixteenth Century." It was, indeed, one of the great locational changes of history, quite comparable to the transfer of the center of economic activity in Ancient Times from Greece to Rome, in the Medieval period from Rome to Byzantium, and in the twentieth century from Western Europe to the English-speaking part of North America. It meant that henceforth for some three hundred and fifty years important economic advances were to be recorded primarily within a 500-mile radius of Belgium. Here the most important economic innovations were to be realized, the greatest economic growth was to be attained, and the highest incomes per capita of the population were to be reached. It was this economic well-being that made possible Western Europe's political and cultural leadership in Western culture.

Important as the Commercial Revolution was, the impression should not be left that commerce elsewhere suddenly disappeared. Although the center of trade left the Mediterranean, commerce on the Middle Sea continued in considerable volume. All the leading commercial states of the seventeenth century—the Dutch, the English, and the French—had trading companies that exploited the possibilities of the Levant, and for a time they did reasonably well. Indeed, the early successes of the new North Atlantic competitors were made in the Mediterranean market. The Dutch, French, and English, by borrowing the industrial techniques of Southern Europe, were able to break the established trading monopolies of that region. These new competitors came into the market with woolens, glassware, printed books, soap, and metal goods—merchandise that was formerly sold exclusively by Venice and other Mediterranean producers. The Northerners began to take over commercial leadership by beating the Mediterranean traders in their own territory. Venetian observers in Constantinople wrote in dismay that English and Dutch woolens were driving Venice's woolens out of the marketplace. Worse yet, the newcomers sold shoddy goods at a fraction of the price of the fine, expensive Italian cloth, daring to mimic Venetian styles and colors. On occasion unscrupulous merchants would counterfeit the Venetian government seal of quality carried only by fine cloths from the city of St. Mark. Unwilling to cut costs and quality to match the new price competition, Venice lost her dominion over the Turkish trade. By the 1630s Venice's share in the Constantinople emporium was only one-fourth of the total trade, and England had become the new leader.

Venice did not collapse, however, like a punctured balloon. She survived the temporary Portuguese capture of the spice trade and the commercial and industrial reverses of the seventeenth century. She retained her importance as a regional center of banking and trade, and she retained enough vigor to play an important part in all the many coalitions to stave off the extension of Turkish power westward in the Mediterranean, especially that which defeated the Turks at the Battle of Lepanto in 1571 and that which gave Venice the Peloponnesus of Greece (Treaty of Carlowitz, 1699). The "decline" of Venice was a gradual and genteel one, befitting a lady of high station. And so, too, were the "declines" of Barcelona, Genoa, and Marseilles, if indeed, in the case of the last it is appropriate to speak of a decline.

The failure of Mediterranean trade to grow at the same rate as that of the coastal areas of the English Channel and the North Sea meant that those regions whose economy was based on commercial intercourse with the Mediterranean tended to stagnate. This was particularly true of south German cities, like Augsburg, Munich, and Nuremberg, and to some extent, of Swiss cities like Geneva. Even on the other side of Germany, in the Baltic Sea area, normal commercial activity seems to have been affected adversely. Here the Dutch began to supplant Mediterranean suppliers of spices and other Eastern products and to take the place of Hanseatic traders in bringing to the West both grain from Danzig and shipbuilding timber from Scandinavia. Then the herring, which for centuries had spawned in the Baltic, for some strange reason shifted their grounds to the North Sea during the sixteenth century. This was an important loss to the economy of the Baltic and a real gain for the Dutch, for herring was one of the few fish that was salted and pickled on a commercial scale for the large market created by Catholic rules against eating meat on Fridays and other days of abstinence.

Expansion and business organization

With the growth of commerce and of industry stimulated by the expansion of Europe overseas, business was confronted with problems of entirely new magnitudes. First and foremost, it was faced with raising amounts of capital which seldom if ever had been amassed for completely new undertakings. For example, as late as the beginning of the seventeenth century it took upwards of half a million dollars at 1955 prices to send a fleet of four ships totaling 1,400 tons to the Far East with a cargo. Then secondly, it was obvious that the newly proffered business opportunities, lucrative as they might be if they succeeded, entailed far more risk than the usual entrepreneurial venture. The English East India Company, for example, lost about one out of every four ships it sent out in the first years of its existence.

In the case of Portugal, the pioneer in the new trade, problems of financing and risk taking were partly met by declaring trade with the Indies a monopoly of the royal houses—a stand based on the fact that the rulers had financed the discoveries—for the monarch's revenues were supposedly adequate to provide capital and to sustain temporary losses. In the long run, however, this solution was not successful, for Portuguese kings showed themselves inept as businessmen and did not have large enough resources at their disposal. They made the great mistake of not organizing the distribution of spices within Western Europe for their own profit; they gave too great concessions in return for loans, as for example, an almost exclusive right for a time to the Italian house of Affaitadi to buy spices at Lisbon for sale in Antwerp. They lacked the resources to outfit large flotillas and/or to fight the French, the Dutch, and the English, and they were unable to safeguard their interests after union with Spain (1580).

The Spaniards endeavored to meet the exigencies of the new situation by erecting a mixed system of government and private enterprise. The state furnished the galleons to escort privately owned vessels which yearly made the trip as a fleet to the New World and back. This system seems to have worked well until Spain became so weakened by foreign wars that the government could not keep up its part of the arrangements. In the end, foreigners were able to break into the trade monopoly by smuggling and through the Asiento agreement and to operate successfully because of the lower prices which they could quote to the colonials.[9] From the early eighteenth century onward, Spain's trading position worsened rapidly, and in the early nineteenth century its colonies in Latin America, except for Cuba, became independent.

The English, Dutch, and French worked out still other arrangements to exploit the possibilities of overseas trade. Here the royal houses played but minor roles. The Tudors probably did not have the personal means to engage in trade on a large scale; the Stuarts in the seventeenth century were no better off, for the rise in prices increased the costs of government, higher taxes made the rulers unpopular, and this unpopularity involved them in a struggle for power. The Dutch, for their part, had no royal house, their form of government being republican. The French kings were so taken up in foreign conflicts or in questions of royal succession before Louis XIV, who reigned from 1643 to 1715, that none of them was in a position to turn his own fortune or that of the state toward commercial enterprise. Thus the main burden of organizing for the exploitation of overseas trade fell upon private entrepreneurs.

As we have already seen, late medieval experience furnished some hints as to what methods businessmen might employ to solve some of their problems. From the Mediterranean, enterprisers had the example of multiple partnerships, in which all the partners were active in management; of the commenda, in which some of the partners were merely investors and hence were known as sleeping partners; of loans secured by cargo or ship,

---

[9] The first inroad into the monopoly occurred when the Spanish sold the right to bring slaves to Spanish America to the Portuguese. This Asiento was surrendered briefly to the French in 1701, but the French lost it to the English at the Peace of Utrecht in 1713. In addition to the slave trade, the English had permission to send one ship a year, the *navio de permiso,* to the New World, and this offered a splendid opportunity for smuggling.

that is, the respondentia loan and bottomry contract, respectively; and of sea loans in which the lender advanced money to a shipper with the understanding that he would get a relatively large return if the voyage succeeded. Furthermore, sixteenth-century businessmen could profit from studying the case of those medieval traders who had banded together to get special commercial privileges from territorial princes and who shared common expenses of warehouses, hotels, and protection while traveling.

From medieval practice, therefore, as well as from common sense, it was clear that capital requirements for the new commercial enterprises could be provided in two ways: either by bringing capitalists together in the same enterprise as active operators or by bringing them together in undertakings in which they were strictly investors with no managerial responsibilities. When recourse was had to the former arrangement, the resulting form of business organization was the regulated company, as in the case of the English Merchant Adventurers, the Eastland Company, the Levant Company, and the later Muscovy Company. In each instance, merchants got monopoly rights to trade in certain areas; they pooled their resources to buy or hire ships, and they elected officials who laid down the main lines of every program. But merchants in these companies actually traded on their own, as in the Spanish case. With their own funds they bought goods which they wanted to take to foreign markets; they did their own selling; and they bought up foreign products for their home customers. They simply shared certain expenses to keep capital requirements of the individual to a minimum and to distribute risks of loss.

The regulated company had its drawbacks, for competition among members for business abroad was keen and the allocation of blame if a voyage failed led inevitably to animosities, recriminations, and dissolutions. Therefore, from the beginning of the seventeenth century, the alternative form of organization—combining the capital of investors rather than combining active tradesmen—became more common. Here the practice was for an entrepreneur or group of entrepreneurs who wanted to launch a specified business to issue shares of stock and to offer them to the investing public at a given price. Let us suppose that the English entrepreneur in a colonial trading venture estimated that the capital need of his project would be 100,000 pounds. To raise this sum a thousand shares at 100 pounds par value would be issued. The organizers would buy some of the shares, perhaps enough to keep control of the offices and policy-making bodies, each share having one vote, and sell the rest.

What investors had, then, was part ownership of a tangible business— of the actual property that the money might be spent for. If the business prospered and its property increased in value, they not only got a share in the earnings which might be distributed in the form of dividends, but they also profited by the fact that their stock would go up in price. If the business failed and were liquidated, they were liable for the debts of the company, but there were faint suggestions of limiting the liability of investors to what they had invested, an advantage that was to become regular practice in the nineteenth century.

This joint-stock arrangement was one of the most important inventions in business organization of all time. Its greatest advantage was that it could tap the savings of very large numbers who had liquid capital at their disposal and thus could bring together the sums that were needed for large enterprise. It furnished the public a way of putting its capital to work, even in small amounts, without involving the investors in complicated tasks; it limited investors' liability, and it permitted the stockholder to get cash when needed by the simple expedient of selling some or all of his holdings. Lastly, the joint form of business organization had the advantage of not coming to an end upon the death of any one of the owners, as did individually owned businesses. Those who inherited the shares of the deceased owners simply became the new owners, and the business went forward as though nothing had happened. This allowed very long-range planning and gave continuity to policies. In brief, the joint-stock company had so many advantageous features that the wonder is that it was not developed much earlier.

The first joint-stock ventures of which we know were attempted by the English for overseas trade in the middle of the sixteenth century, as in the case of the Guinea or African Company and Drake's voyage of 1577–1580.[10] Not until the establishment and success of the English East India Company, chartered December 31, 1600, did this form of business actually come into its own. This new concern was launched, interestingly enough, by men who had had experience with a regulated company—the Levant Company—and the first minutes of the Company were kept in the books of the Levant enterprise. For the first voyage of the East India Company the founders sold shares amounting to 68,000 pounds to some two hundred investors, then, when the ships got back to port, they divided both profits *and* capital among the stockholders. Obviously such temporary arrangements made planning difficult and the raising of sufficient funds both uncertain and expensive;[11] Thus, as the Company's ventures became more regular, a permanent capital was established and a permanent organization created (1657).

The East India Company was granted by its charter the privilege of being the only English concern which could trade in the East Indies. In

---

[10] Queen Elizabeth was one of the purchasers of shares in this venture, which explains why she was able to share in the profits, as we have seen above. She was so delighted when her investment paid off that she knighted Drake on the quarter-deck of his ship. The privateer became Sir Francis on the spot.
[11] Amounts needed for financing rose rapidly. For the third voyage, 1,629,040 pounds were raised.

addition it was charged with setting up its authority in places where it was to operate and in administering these areas. In brief, in return for a trade monopoly the Company was given the task of performing all the acts of government in those regions under its jurisdiction. That this arrangement was, at first, favorable to the Company there can be no doubt, for profits were high, the voyage of 1612 paying 220 percent on the investment. Nevertheless, there was another side to the ledger. The defense of the monopoly was expensive,[12] Administrative costs in the East were high, and waging war caused heavy losses. Nevertheless, the Company went forward, even emerging from the long war with the French (1756–1763) with its trading position strengthened. In fact, it was not until free-trade ideas became well established that the Company lost its trade monopoly (1833). Not until it appeared incapable of meeting modern colonial requirements in the Sepoy Rebellion of 1857 did it lose its function of colonial administrator.

Almost as old in the history of joint-stock companies as the English East India Company was the Dutch East India Company, chartered March 20, 1602. Like its English counterpart, this concern grew out of multiple partnerships organized much like the English regulated companies, and out of temporary joint-stock companies, created for individual voyagers to open routes to the source of spices in the East. Moreover, the charter of the Dutch Company was similar in many respects to that of the English. It provided that the Company should have a monopoly of trade in all the territory between the Cape of Good Hope and the Strait of Magellan. It bestowed upon the Company the right to exercise in this region all the privileges, prerogatives, and powers usually held by sovereign states—to seize and defend territories within its sphere of action, to make peace, to levy taxes, to administer justice, and to make local laws. Moreover, in addition to these delegated powers, the Company had the assurance of the support of the Netherlandish government in case of trouble, for the same persons who controlled the Company directed the affairs of state.[13]

Similar, however, as were the Dutch and English East India Companies in origin and charter, they differed fundamentally in structure and administration. Whereas the management of the English Company was controlled by stockholders, who elected a board of directors and officers, the Dutch concern was run by political appointees. So the general policies of the Company were laid down by a board of seventeen directors who were chosen from six local "chambers" on the basis of their importance. Thus

---

[12] In 1628 a rival group was granted the monopoly of trade in the East in return for a loan to the government of 2 million pounds. The original company was soon able to merge with these newcomers and to continue on its way.

[13] In return, certain of the Company's profits and a portion of the value of captured Spanish and Portuguese ships went to the government.

there were eight directors from the chamber of Amsterdam, four from Zeeland, and one or two each from Rotterdam, Delft, Hoorn, and Enkhuizen. The members of these local chambers, which conducted the local business of the Company, were selected by the Estates of the seven provinces. Even when fleets were fitted out, this political and decentralized character of the Company was maintained, each local chamber being charged with getting certain supplies and each assuming a proportion of the cost, again in proportion to its importance.

With this organization the Company achieved remarkable success. It took the spice trade away from the Portuguese and defended it successfully against both the English and the French. And when the spice business fell off, it found substitutes in coffee, tea, and cocoa. From 1605 to 1614 the Company paid dividends which fluctuated from 3 percent to 75 percent of the par value of its stock and during its entire existence, until its dissolution at the end of the eighteenth century, it averaged dividends, so it is said, of 18 percent.

With the excellent profit records made by both the English and Dutch East India Companies in their early years, it seems strange that the French did not rush immediately into competition with them. Not until 1664, however, did the French East India Company come into being, and then it was established largely through the initiative of Louis XIV's remarkable minister for economic affairs, Colbert. It was he who convinced a group of private entrepreneurs that France should go after the lucrative Indies trade, and it was his support that made the project feasible. He gave the organizers of the Company a charter with privileges and prerogatives similar to those of the Dutch and English Companies; he awarded them the assets of the French colony of Madagascar; and when the French investing public failed to take up but half of the 8.2 million livres of stock, it was he who got the King to give the concern the 4 million livres which were lacking.

Unlike the English and Dutch East India Companies, the French Company did not at first have a good record of earnings. During the first twenty years its losses were heavy, in part because of the Dutch War (1672–1678), but the Company was reorganized and kept doggedly on. It established trading posts, notably at Surat and Pondichéry, got into the importation of textiles, including cottons, traded with Siam and China, and in spite of many vicissitudes made progress. In the middle of the eighteenth century, it had reached a point of importance and power at which it could contest, under the leadership of its most brilliant colonial, Joseph François Dupleix, control of India with the English Company, which was at the time directed by one of its greatest leaders, Robert Clive. Although these efforts of the French Company failed and this institution subsequently declined until it vanished during the French Revolution, it might have been successful with greater support from the motherland.

In any case, the three great East India Companies thoroughly established the joint-stock form of business organization for colonial enterprise. It was employed in the Dutch West India Company (founded 1621), in the French West India Company (1664), and in such English enterprises as the Virginia Company, the Massachusetts Bay Company, and the Hudson's Bay Company. By the end of the seventeenth century, indeed, the joint-stock company had become so seasoned and its advantages so generally recognized that it was being used in domestic business undertakings like banking, mining, and even manufacturing, in fact, wherever the needs for capital were great.[14]

As joint-stock companies grew in number and in capital, the floating of issues of stock and the trading of existing shares became big business, so big, in fact, that a new occupation came into being—that of stockbroking. In the pursuit of their trade brokers assembled first at places where men of wealth congregated, such as at commodity exchanges, like the Royal Exchange in London (1571) and the Amsterdam Bourse (1611), or at coffee-houses, but eventually they founded exchanges exclusively for trading in shares, like the London Stock Exchange (1773). Here the business of stock trading gradually took form, including the practice of speculating on rises or falls in the price of stock. With the earnings of companies fluctuating widely and with many new concerns being established to undertake uncertain projects, like trying to find a Northwest Passage to China, "booms" and "busts" were frequent. The most remarkable of all such incidents was the South Sea Bubble, which burst in 1720. It was of such proportions and injured so many people that it put the joint-stock form of business organization under a cloud from which it did not entirely emerge until a century later.

Cultural consequences of European overseas expansion

So widespread were the effects of expansion of Europe overseas that hardly a single phase of European culture was left untouched by it. Nevertheless, it would be a mistake to consider all of the new trends in Europe's economic development as primarily the result of expansion. Thus, although colonial markets added greatly to trade, home markets far exceeded those of overseas areas, and hence the two should be treated together when consideration is given to the pressure which demand placed upon the means of production—to what is commonly called the Industrial Revolu-

---

[14] Among the first of the joint-stock companies for domestic enterprise in England were the Mineral and Battery Works Company and the Mines Royal Company for silver and copper mining.

tion. Similarly, the development of a money economy, of capitalism, and of capitalist institutions, accelerated as it was by colonial commerce and the importation of bullion from overseas, needs to be studied in the context of Europe's total experience and not simply as a phase of overseas expansion. Also, in spite of the fact that colonial trade contributed greatly to the rise of those cities which were to give Western civilization most of its styles of art, its social classes, its leading ideologies, and its patterns of government, it would be a mistake to discuss the rise of cities in terms of expansion alone.

Although such topics must be left for later pages, two subjects should be introduced here as consequences of the expansion of Europe. The first is the effect on European life of new products from overseas; the second is the impact of expansion on the European mind.

The introduction of cocoa from the New World in the sixteenth century, the importation of tea from the East in the seventeenth century, and greater supplies of coffee from the Near East, from Java, and later from the New World had an almost revolutionary effect upon the European's breakfast menu and upon his social habits. Henceforth, any one of these beverages was to oust wine in the early morning or to supplement the other usual breakfast drink, milk, especially in cities. Moreover, these new drinks led to the establishment of entirely new places for people to congregate for social intercourse—to the founding of coffeehouses (or cafés) and of tea rooms and chocolate shops. These became, to a greater extent than beer halls and wine taverns had ever been, social centers, writers' and artists' clubs, political forums, reading clubs, and even business offices. They were an entirely new institution for the dissemination of news and for the exchange of ideas.

Another product which was important to European life because of new supplies from overseas was sugar. This sweetening, much cheaper than honey, had much to do in making coffee, tea, and chocolate popular and had a revolutionary effect on cooking. It made possible and certainly more available to all economic classes a long list of pastries; it allowed the fabrication of a completely new line of sweet alcoholic drinks, the cordials and the liqueurs of the present day; and it permitted the expansion of the candy trade to unheard-of proportions.

America also gave the Old World tobacco and thereby provided Europeans who used it comfort, snob prestige, and nose and throat irritation. This weed was introduced into Spain in 1558, and somewhat later by Jean Nicot, whence the word nicotine, into France, and by Sir Walter Raleigh into England. In spite of considerable opposition to its use (Benjamin Franklin once said that if God had intended that man smoke he would have turned up his nose to provide an adequate draft), tobacco became ever more popular. The typical country squire of the seventeenth century is invariably pictured with a long-stemmed clay pipe in his hands. And the effete dandy of the same period is represented as preening himself with a pinch of snuff, belittling his social inferiors with a snap of his little snuff-box, and astounding the uninitiate with a prodigious number of sneezes.

Among new food products introduced into Europe from the Western Hemisphere, the potato was undoubtedly the most important. This lowly tuber, which came from the region between Columbia and Peru, has the supreme advantage of being one of the vegetables that one can eat day after day without fatiguing the taste buds. It provides more calories per acre than any other easily cultivated crop and some double that of any of the ordinary grains. Moreover, it can be grown on a variety of soils, can support different weather conditions, and is hardy in most climates. It was introduced into Spain in the sixteenth century, and Sir Walter Raleigh was instrumental in establishing its use in Ireland. In the latter half of the eighteenth century, as grain prices increased and the growing population was pressing upon the food supply, its use became more generalized upon the Continent. It is said that Louis XV wore the potato flower in his buttonhole to show that the plant was not poisonous and that Marie Antoinette had a potato corsage. Gradually the potato became a standard article of the European's diet, although in some places not until the nineteenth century, and some regions, like Ireland, became absolutely dependent upon it.[15]

Furthermore, the New World gave the Old three other staple foods: codfish, Indian corn or maize, and the tomato. Although the cod had been known in Europe before the sixteenth century, catches off the Newfoundland and New England coasts became so large and the dried and salted fish so well preserved that the fish could be marketed at remarkably low prices. Thus it became a regular part of the diet of the poor and to some extent took the place of herring on days of abstinence. For its part, maize became widely grown because of its large yield per acre as a grain for livestock, but entered human diets in only a few districts, like the Piedmont in Italy and Rumania. And tomatoes eventually became widely used to give flavor to numerous bland products, like pastas.

Among luxury food products, the Old World got the turkey from the New and the guinea hen from Africa, which added variety to the poultry menu and, as semiluxuries, came to be traditional meats on very festive occasions. Among medicines, Europe received several herbs, but quinine or Jesuits' bark for relieving fevers from Peru and opium for diminishing pain were of the greatest value. Among industrial raw products, it got a

---

[15] In Spain the potato was called *patata* from the word for sweet potato, *batata,* hence the English word for it. In Italy the potato was confused with the truffle (*tartufo*), whence the German *Kartoffel.* In the Netherlands, this tuber was called earth apple (*erdappel*) and thus reached France as the *pomme de terre.*

number of dyes, of which indigo was the most famous, and eventually large supplies of cotton, which was to revolutionize the textile trade.

The expansion of Europe overseas resulted, also, in the introduction of or greater supplies of many finished goods which the well-to-do acquired for comfort or for prestige. There were silks which went into elegant clothes, rugs, carpets, and hangings to cover bare floors and walls; fine porcelain (chinaware) to supplement that of Europe or to supplant the more common earthenware, and new perfumes to gratify the olfactory sense. There were cotton textiles from India and Persia, which gave rise to a style demand at the end of the seventeenth and beginning of the eighteenth century that seemed insatiable. And there were products from China, such as embroideries, fans, umbrellas, screens, porcelains, and the Sedan chair,[16] in such number that an entirely new style was created—the *chinoiserie* of the eighteenth century.

As these material things from realms beyond the seas were making their mark on Europe, knowledge, imagined or real, of these same regions was having an impact on European ideologies and attitudes. When Thomas More (1477–1535) penned his *Utopia* and Francis Bacon (1561–1626) wrote his *New Atlantis,* they not only placed their dream worlds overseas, but furnished them with what they imagined were some of the characteristics of life among American natives, including a much greater equality in wealth than existed in their Europe. Montaigne (1553–1592), Montesquieu (1689–1755), Voltaire (1694–1778), and Jean Jacques Rousseau (1712–1778) used the example of the "noble savage" to criticize many of Europe's man-made institutions and to plead for their obliteration; Thomas Hobbes (1588–1678), on the contrary, argued that life among savages was violent and that to emerge from a state of nature it was necessary to erect governments with power to maintain order. Expansion overseas also became a literary theme. The greatest of modern epics, the *Lusiads* by the Portuguese Luiz Vaz de Camoëns (1524–1580), sings of the voyage of Vasco da Gama.

In addition to imaginative and fanciful treatment of overseas lands, there were also factual accounts which tried to provide Europe with an accurate body of geographical knowledge. There was the Catholic missionary and staunch defender of the natives in Latin America, Bartolomé de Las Casas (1476–1566), whose *Brief Account of the Destruction of the West Indies* (1554) and *History of the Indies,* not published until the nineteenth century, are justly famous. There were the French explorers, Jacques Cartier (1491–1557), who wrote *A Brief Account of the Voyage Made to the Islands,* and Samuel de Champlain (1567–1635), who published several books of his explorations in the Great Lakes. There was Richard Hakluyt (1553–1616), who

---

[16] So-called because it was introduced at Sedan, France.

began the great collection known as *The Principal Navigations, Voyages, Traffiques, and Discoveries of the English Nation,* that was continued after his death by Samuel Purchas. And there was Gerardus Mercator (1512–1594), who constructed the most accurate and up-to-date maps of the sixteenth century and who invented the Mercator projection for showing the round world and its parts on flat surfaces.

In general, it is safe to say that contact with distant civilization made Europe more firmly impressed than ever with knowledge arrived at by observation and by verification—with efforts to explain, without recourse to the supernatural, why one event in a given series followed another. Furthermore, this contact made Europe more conscious of its own faults and desirous, as if to prove that it was superior to all the rest, of a society where people lived according to known and just laws, where it was possible to create and enjoy works of art of a universally recognized high order, and where there was economic security for all. In fact, relations with the rest of the world tended to make Europe formulate its concept of civilization.

Science, technology, and Early Modern industry

Science and technology in Western culture

Of all the remarkable aspects of Western culture, none is more distinctive than the Western knowledge of and control over physical things. Developments within the last 450 years have permitted the West nearly to triple its members' life expectancy at birth. They have made available for human use a variety of materials, whether located deep in the earth's crust or high in the heavens, that hitherto had been deemed of no importance. They have allowed the West to eliminate famines, to move mountains, to conquer distances, and to learn many of the innermost secrets of nature. All these things Western man has accomplished chiefly because of his science and his technology, crucial advances in which were made in the sixteenth and seventeenth centuries.

The essence of the new science was, as has already been mentioned, the acquiring of knowledge based upon accurate observation, upon the quantification of observations, and upon the verification of the data thus obtained by the use of mathematics and by repetition of the experiment or observation. This science was, furthermore, a system of knowledge in which related events were established as having taken place, in which events were arranged in a necessary sequence, that is, a sequence without which the events could not have taken place, and in which relationships between two events or among all events in the sequence, of both a qualitative and quantitative character, were accurately determined. Henceforth Western man was not satisfied with trial-and-error methods, with rules of thumb, or with supernatural explanations of what had happened, at least as regards material things. He wanted to have verifiable answers to what, why, when, where, and how an event had taken place and to be able to repeat or to observe again for his own satisfaction the event or events in question.

Science, like virtually all aspects of human endeavor, has an economic side in the sense that an individual's time is a scarce resource and that by devoting time and energy to scientific inquiry one must forego participation in other activities. Remuneration for scientific inquiry should in the aggregate and in the long run compensate for this expenditure of time and talent. However, in the Early Modern period, unlike today, scientific achievements were not quickly translated into profit-making advancements in the productive process. The rapid application of science to the demands of industry is a very modern development.

The years 1500–1700 were notable more for progress in "pure science" than for anything else. In the short space of two centuries new methods of seeking knowledge and a new attitude toward the physical world came into being. This "scientific revolution," as historians have come to call it, was among the greatest changes in the intellectual life of man. There was, to be sure, technological advance as well. But while science and technology progressed in parallel, their respective paths did not often cross. Science was largely aloof from immediate application, and technology advanced by the action of entrepreneurs and craftsmen who, without benefit of any grand design, saw profit in new power sources and equipment. The essence of the new technology was the development of ways of performing tasks by machines driven by energy from nonhuman sources and of ways of rendering materials, especially those of an inorganic nature, useful to humankind. Western man obtained from machines moved by mechanical power or chemical or physical reactions the services of a number of "slaves," which allowed him greatly to increase his output in terms of his own input of energy. Furthermore, the new technology enabled him to increase the supply of available materials by finding ways of rendering useful what was abundant in nature. Thus coal came into use as a source of energy to supplement wood. Iron and steel were developed as building materials to supplant wood and to strengthen masonry. Hydroelectric power was perfected to reduce the use of coal, and the fission of uranium bids fair to become a partial substitute for coal. Rayon and acrylic fibers are taking the place of silk and to some extent also of cotton and wool, and plastics have found a use in places where steel, wood, or rubber were once employed. It may have been that the new technology stressed quantity rather than luxury production, but it permitted a tripling of the population of Western Europe from the early eighteenth century onward and perhaps a quintupling of the goods available for human consumption per capita of the population.

The development of this technology and of the new science was long in coming. Both had roots in the Middle Ages, and deeper roots reaching back into the remote past of mankind. Medieval man had displayed an intense desire to know about all kinds of things, and although scholastic philosophers had endeavored to obtain knowledge by deduction from premises derived from such authorities as St. Augustine, the Bible, Plato, and Aristotle, their very curiosity, disputations, and doubts led to a search for other methods for finding the "truth." People of the Middle Ages had also displayed an interest in techniques and, as we have already seen, improved such contrivances as the water wheel, the windmill, and the horse collar, and developed new ways of transforming common and abundant materials into useful products, like sand into glass and iron ore by means of blast furnaces into cast iron.

From such beginnings, from the accumulation of much detail, and from an intensified interest in things of this world, there were realized in the sixteenth and seventeenth centuries new syntheses in both science and technology. In science the synthesis was brought about by a galaxy of intellectual giants. Among them was Francis Bacon (1561–1626), who made an appeal for direct observation and the use of inductive rather than deductive logic. There was Nicholas Copernicus (1473–1543), who advanced the theory that the earth revolved around the sun rather than the sun around the earth, which was a direct attack upon authority—a theory which was refined by Johann Kepler (1571–1630). There was Galileo Galilei (1564–1642), who carried on a number of experiments which allowed him to determine the rate of acceleration of falling bodies, to establish the isochronism of the pendulum, that is, that a pendulum makes its swings in regular intervals of time irrespective of the length of the arcs described, and to state that the trajectory of a cannon ball is a parabola. There was William Gilbert (1540–1603), who experimented with magnets and laid a foundation for electricity. There was William Harvey (1578–1657), who through painstaking research learned that the heart was a muscular pump and that blood circulated throughout the body. There was René Descartes (1596–1650), who believed that the physical world operated mechanically and who urged the use of mathematics to describe its movements. And there was Isaac Newton (1642–1727), who by his development of calculus, his statement of the laws of gravitation, and his enunciation of the laws of motion contributed much to the realization of Descartes' dream—establishing a conception of the world as a great machine.

To what extent the scientific revolution and the new synthesis in technology were related and acted upon each other, it is difficult to say. What is clear, however, is that both movements emphasized experimentation, exact observation, and mathematical expression of findings. Moreover, in both science and technology men manifested an intellectual courage without parallel. No problem seemed to be so difficult that it was automatically relegated to the category of the impossible and thus discarded. Men of the new science and of the new technology had confidence in their methods and were willing to tackle everything from explaining the entire cosmos to making water run "uphill." There is no doubt but that scientists made use of new techniques, like that of lens grinding, which made possible the telescope, for their observations and their experiments. And there is no question but that scientists gave expression to ideas, like that of using steam to force water up a spout, which were picked up by engineers. Not yet, however, were men of science concerned with solving technological problems, nor did mechanical technicians rely on men of science for overcoming their difficulties. Only much later did "pure science" and "applied science" begin to cooperate closely.

The technical developments of the Early Modern period serve to demonstrate the important fact that refinement of existing techniques can be an important source of productivity increases. Although some radically novel devices were invented at this time, most of the technical change was in the nature of improvement, not revolution. These advances in design and organization were no less original and no less productive for the fact that they were based on older techniques.

The technological spurt of the sixteenth and seventeenth centuries is to be further characterized by the fact that the widest and deepest industrial changes resulting from it seem to have been realized in England and Scotland, thus effecting a locational shift in the center of industrial activity to the north. Furthermore, the new technological methods of production stressed the output of staple goods for mass consumption. This was of great moment, for it launched much of our present concern with economic growth and it helped to establish the basic ideology in Western culture that all people should be free from want and should partake of economic well-being. Moreover, businessmen came to learn that production for mass consumption offered greater possibilities for making profits than luxury production for a select few, for the wants of the many are less quickly satisfied than those of a restricted elite. Thus there came about a concern for the purchasing power of the masses, for continuing investments in producers' goods to turn out products within the price range of large numbers of people, for effecting a division of labor and adopting of labor-saving devices, and for developing cheap materials to take the place of expensive ones. This emphasis upon quantity rather than upon luxuries was in keeping with Christian conceptions of welfare, with democratic ideas of well-being for all, and with capitalism's apparent need for expansion.

Coal and early industrialization

Without any question, one of the most crucial innovations of the sixteenth and seventeenth centuries was the use of coal as a major source of heat energy. Although coal had been known for centuries in China and had been the object of some commerce toward the end of the Middle Ages from Newcastle-upon-Tyne, from Nottingham, and from Liège in what was to become Belgium, coal was never used systematically and upon a relatively large scale in industry until the second half of the sixteenth century. Then, as is always the case with all major innovations, a number of factors came together in England in fortuitous proportions and timing to result in the widespread use of this combustible.[1]

Perhaps the most impelling of all the conditions conducive to the use of coal were (1) the need for a cheap fuel to take the place of wood and (2) the presence of coal near the surface where it could easily be mined and near water transportation that allowed its being moved at low cost. The need for heat energy in England was extraordinarily great. The relatively cold climate required the heating of living and working quarters for a large portion of the year. Here the people drank beer or distilled liquors, the manufacture of which required heat. Here it was necessary to have many windows to light up interiors enough to permit close work, and the manufacture of glass took a great amount of fuel. Here salt could not be obtained by the sun's evaporation of water from sea brine, so water had to be gotten rid of by artificial heat. Here there had recently been a considerable development of alum production, of gunpowder manufacture, and of smelting, all of which required charcoal, and of shipbuilding, which took a great amount of lumber.

Under such demand the price of charcoal soared and that of shipbuilding timbers increased elevenfold from 1500 to 1640. In most Continental countries, like France and Italy, for example, a local shortage of wood simply drove lumbermen or charcoal burners farther into the mountains for supplies that were often floated down streams to market. In England, the almost complete absence of uninhabited forests precluded such a solution to the problem of the shortage of wood; whereas the importation of lumber except for quality use, like Baltic and later American timber for shipbuilding, was not feasible because of transportation costs. Coal was an obvious answer to England's fuel problem. At no other place in Europe was this substitute source of heat so readily available as there.

Still another important factor in the use of coal in industry in England was a greater economic expansion than in any other place in Europe from the middle of the sixteenth century to the middle of the seventeenth. The absence of devastating warfare at home allowed resources to be turned into productive activity. Between 1540 and 1640, population rose from 3 mil-

---

[1] John U. Nef, *The Rise of the British Coal Industry,* 2 vols. (London: Routledge, 1932).

lion to 6 million, and this 100 percent increase put pressure upon the means of production to meet mass needs. And a number of new industries expanded very rapidly, like iron smelting by blast furnaces, the number of furnaces increasing from 3 to between 100 and 150 in this century.

On the other hand, most of the Continental countries were torn by dynastic and religious wars from 1540 to 1640. Spain failed, in part, to make essential investments in industry because of the diversion of resources to wars against the Turks, the French, and the rebellious inhabitants of the Low Countries. The Spanish Netherlands suffered from the Spaniards' crusade against it and from the subsequent cutting off of its commerce from the sea. The production of cloth at Hondschoote, for example, fell from 80,000 pieces a year for the period 1560–1569 to 8,000 pieces for the period 1646–1649; the population of Antwerp declined from 100,000 in 1577 to some 30,000 in 1650. Italy suffered a relative setback with the shift of the center of commerce from the Mediterranean to the Atlantic. France was torn by the Wars of Religion, and the Germanies were hard hit by the Thirty Years' War (1618–1648). The Northern Netherlands was the country with the best chance of rivaling England's development, but it turned its energies heavily in the direction of commerce and to industries without a mass-market appeal, like shipbuilding, and besides, it had no known resources of coal.

Still another reason for England's rapid industrial development from 1540 to 1640 was the relation between prices and wages. Henry VIII devalued the currency in 1536 and 1539, which caused a price rise, it should be noted, before the influx of metals from the New World began on a large scale. These devaluations had the effect of raising prices, but as was usual, wages did not go up at the same rate. Thus because commodity prices were up, real wages down, and costs of production in terms of prices low, the opportunity to make large profits encouraged entrepreneurs to undertake new business ventures. Apparently this situation gave a shot in the arm to English economic activity but was not protracted enough to drastically impair the purchasing power of the masses. Prices of goods consumed by the lower classes did not go up so fast as those consumed by the rich, probably because of technological improvements in the manufacture of staples that kept costs down. Moreover, from 1600 to 1640 wages increased as fast as prices of consumers' goods, those of miners even advancing at a more rapid rate than prices.[2]

[2] John U. Nef, *La naissance de la civilisation industrielle et le monde contemporain* (Paris: Colin, 1954), pp. 122ff. Also by the same author, "Prices and Industrial Capitalism in France and England," *The Economic History Review,* vol. 7, no. 2, pp. 180–181, 1937.

Furthermore, England's break with the Roman Catholic Church had some relevance to the country's economic expansion from 1540 to 1640. As we have previously seen, the Protestant Revolt did not cause a sudden change in attitude toward the accumulation of wealth or toward the approval of such capitalistic practices as the taking of interest; Catholic businessmen had for long been trying to get rich, and Protestant theorists did not adopt doctrines favorable to interest charges until after 1650. But the upset of the English Reformation did effect economic change. The seizure of Church lands and their sale or gift to laymen meant a greater economic development of these properties. Indeed, many of the new mining enterprises were on lands previously owned by the Church or religious orders, which had never shown any signs of exploiting them on a large scale, and many of the large entrepreneurial investments in coal mining were made precisely by the new owners of former Church lands. Finally, the Protestants, by stressing the desire to create a heaven on earth and thus of establishing a greater degree of economic well-being among the lower classes than had existed previously, gave a fillip to the production of consumers' goods for the masses.

Also, new investments in England seem to have been directed into industries designed for quantity production, whereas on the Continent such placements of capital were made especially in luxury trades. Thus, in France there was a development of silk industry, in the Netherlands of faience, and in the Germanies of silver mining, with production for the masses being carried on in traditional ways. In England, on the other hand, the greatest advances were made in such industries as glassmaking, brewing, salt refining, sugar refining, soapmaking, and the production of alum and gunpowder. Each of these industries adopted coal as its chief source of heat energy and thus gave an impetus to the use of a great resource that had been stored up over eons of time. The only major fuel-using industry that still relied on charcoal was iron metallurgy which, for technical reasons that were not resolved until the eighteenth century, could not employ coal.

New techniques in mining and metallurgy

The beginning of the use of coal on a fairly large scale in England at the middle of the sixteenth century had important consequences for future economic developments. Not only did coal provide man with an abundant source of heat energy, but it led to larger production units. It accustomed businessmen, because of the high cost of coal-using equipment, to make larger investments in industrial undertakings. It resulted in organizing larger bodies of labor and of effecting a division of labor, and it gave an impetus to the development of new techniques of production in the use of heat energy and in mining.

Another important source of technological change in the sixteenth century was the production of silver in Central Europe. During most of the Middle Ages, the greater part of this metal had been obtained from lead ores along the Rhine in the Germanies, in Bohemia, in Hungary, and in the eastern Alps. By the fifteenth century supplies from these sources had been greatly reduced because of the exhaustion of the mines but the demand for silver was increasing because of the need for making payments in precious metals for Eastern goods and because of the need for a greater volume of coins. Under the circumstances recourse was had to copper ores that contained silver, even though the recovery of silver was somewhat difficult. Silver had been separated from lead simply by heating the ore to the melting point of lead and then letting this metal flow off. Such a simple method of refining could not be used in the case of copper ore, so lead was mixed with it in order to absorb the silver, and the silver was subsequently separated from the lead. Thanks to this process carried on in the famous *Saigerhütte,* the production of silver and copper in Central Europe increased some five times from 1460 to 1540.

The mining of copper and silver ores and the mining of coal led to the driving of deep shafts, to the development of greater power-driven pumps to get water out of the diggings, to new hoisting techniques, to new power-driven machinery for crushing the ore, and to new smelting processes. Quite logically, therefore, some of the most remarkable feats in mining engineering in the sixteenth and early seventeenth centuries occurred in England and Central Europe and the leading work of the period on mining and metallurgy, *De Re Metallica* (1556), was by a German, Georg Bauer, who is better known by his Latinized name of Agricola.

Indeed, efforts to remove water from mines accounted for many important developments in machinery during the sixteenth century. Inasmuch as suction pumps, the best-known pumps at the time, could raise water only some 34 feet and mines ran down to 600 feet, the suction pump was employed only with the greatest difficulty. Agricola describes, however, a system in which suction pumps were arranged in series, one above the other, and all were worked by an intricate arrangement of levers driven by a water wheel (Figure 11). Such a mechanism was awkward, subject to frequent breakdowns, and not very efficient; thus the search went on for better methods of getting water out of the mines. Chains of pots, like those used in ancient times for irrigation, were tried, but they could not cope with large flows. Force pumps, in which a plunger forces water up a pipe, were introduced, but they broke frequently because of the high pressure on the sides of the pipe at the base of the column of water. Then balls of horsehair attached to a chain and drawn up through a pipe with its bottom end in a sump, that is, in water, were employed with some success. Also, Archimedes' screws, repeated several times, were used, but they, too, were not very satisfactory because of the heights involved, Finally, the problem of raising water, made still more imperative by the need of better water supplies for the rapidly growing towns and cities, led to the suggestion by

Figure 11
Pumping machinery. One of the most serious of early mining problems was to keep the diggings free of water. Pails on endless chains were used and later, as this picture shows, a series of vacuum pumps. They were activated by a series of levers raised and lowered by a "crank and shaft" arrangement. The shaft was turned by a water wheel. *(From Agricola, De Re Metallica, 1556.)*

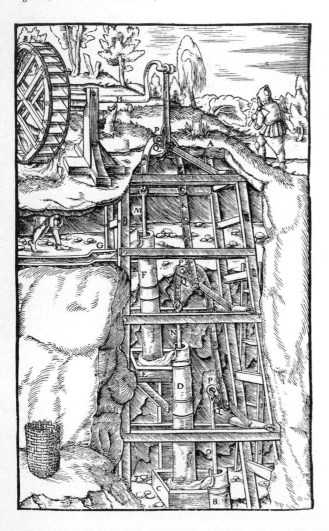

Baptista Porta in 1560 of filling a pipe with steam, of condensing the steam to create a vacuum in the pipe, and then of letting air pressure force water up the pipe to an outlet. It led, also, to a project by Solomon de Gaus in 1615 for a steam-driven fountain which was to operate much as a steam kettle with a long spout and a tight-fitting lid does when it throws water from the spout. Here were two principles which were to contribute very directly toward experiments that led to the invention of the steam engine in the eighteenth century.

Another important problem in mining is hoisting. For this work many ingenious devices were employed, such as the horse whim, whereby a chain to which was attached a bucket was wound around a drum that was revolved by the draft of horses. This machine involved heavy equipment and such novel gadgets as the friction brake to control the speed at which the bucket was lowered. Hoisting also led to an intricate device in which a water wheel 36 feet in diameter with two sets of buckets could be run forward or backward by a workman who controlled the flow of water to the wheel.

Once ore or minerals were on the surface of the ground, there were the problems of crushing, loading, and transporting. Carrying was greatly facilitated by the development of crude railways, which were usually just planks laid on the ground along which carts were run, and by the use of water-carrying whenever possible, even if this meant digging new canals, dredging rivers, building locks, or constructing docks. Many of the first "railways" ran from pit heads to nearby rivers, as from St. Etienne in France to the Loire, and many of the early coal mines in England were opened near the sea to get advantage of water transportation. Loading was done more and more by chutes and hoists; crushing or stamping ore was increasingly accomplished by water-driven trip hammers. Even Branca's proposal for an impulse steam turbine (1629) was portrayed as activating hammers for crushing.

Mining also involved engineering feats of shoring and of retaining-wall construction requiring great ingenuity and audacity. One of the most curious engineering accomplishments of the time was to be found at Culross, Scotland. Here Sir George Bruce, having acquired lands confiscated from the Church, discovered that he possessed rich veins of coal which ran under the sea. To exploit this treasure he built a pit head on the shore at a point that was underwater at high tide, but completely above the watermark at low tide. To protect the pit head at high tide he built a retaining wall; then he constructed a dock so that barges could be loaded directly from the mine at high tide; and finally he installed elaborate pumping machinery to keep the whole from being flooded.

The story is told that when James I was taken by Sir George to visit this mine the party went underground at low tide, when the encroachment of the sea was not easily foreseen. After having spent some time inspecting the shafts and galleries, the party emerged at high tide. When James I, who was not notable for physical courage, saw the sea all about, he began to cry treason. Sir George had to do some fast explaining to quiet his king.

While mining gave a stimulus to the use of machinery, to the adoption of mechanical power, and to remarkable achievements in engineering, innovations in the ferrous metal industry were being introduced on a scale which was to revolutionize methods of production and cheapen iron articles to a point where they would be within the reach of all. Here the crucial change was the widespread use of the blast furnace, which was greatly improved in the fifteenth century (Figure 12). No longer was it necessary to forge iron at great labor and with considerable waste of metal. It was now possible to separate the metal from most impurities by heating the ore to the melting point of iron and then letting it run off, much as in the case of silver smelting. This technique of smelting iron became firmly established in the period under discussion in the southeast of England, in the Midlands, in the Bishopric of Liège, and in Sweden. In these places, also, molten iron right from the furnaces was cast for a number of purposes, such as the making of anchors, nails, chimney placques, and kettles, or was run through rolling mills to make sheets for iron stoves and the like (Figure 13). These articles became exceedingly cheap by comparison with what they had been and were henceforth objects of mass consumption, but their price was to fall even more in the eighteenth century when technical difficulties that had prevented the use of coal in smelting were solved and this cheaper fuel to a large extent replaced charcoal. Then began that close affiliation between coal and iron that was to play such an important role in the subsequent development and location of industry.

Advances in mechanical techniques

Important as were the extended use of coal and the smelting of iron and silver in effecting changes in industry during the sixteenth and seventeenth centuries, other innovations were made which also tended to increase production for mass consumption. These consisted primarily in the development of power from falling water and the wind and from the application of this power to an ever-greater number of machines that could accomplish tasks which had previously been performed by man.

Evidence of the search for mechanical power and of mechanical contrivances is to be founded in the writing of all the great mechanical engineers of the day. Perhaps the most noteworthy confirmation of the trends of the age in mechanics is to be found in the *Notebooks* of Leonardo da Vinci (1452–1519)—painter, sculptor, anatomist, military planner, engineer, and genius extraordinaire. During his lifetime Leonardo filled over 5,000 pages with drawings of his conception of things, most of which he explained in

Figure 12
Sixteenth-century blast furnace. The blast furnace was a rather tall furnace in which a hot fire was provided by charcoal and a strong draft was induced by a high chimney and bellows. The furnace was charged from the top with charcoal and ore, piles of which lie in the right foreground. Mallets for breaking up the large pieces lie in the center foreground. In the left foreground is the ever-present anvil. Metal formed at the base of the furnace and was drawn off from the impurities which were either burned or came out as slag. *(From Agricola, De Re Metallica, 1556.)*

"mirror writing," that is, in writing that could be read only when reflected in a mirror, so that unscrupulous pryers into his affairs would be dis-

Figure 13
Sixteenth-century forge. There was considerable advance made in the technique of ironworking between the sixth century B.C. and the sixteenth century A.D. At the latter date a stronger draft was furnished by a taller chimney and by the use of large accordion bellows made of leather and worked by a water wheel. The smith is forming his bloom, however, much as at an earlier date. The tongs are the same and little change has taken place in the hammer and anvil. The smith in the foreground is probably shaping the product by hammering and is tempering the metal by dowsing it in water. *(From Agricola, De Re Metallica, 1556.)*

couraged. Even though the *Notebooks* were published only well after Leonardo's death, they were early read by many persons and had a considerable influence upon succeeding generations of technicians. Moreover, they provide a rich source for understanding the status of mechanical arts in the early sixteenth century.

Support, also, of the drive to make fuller use of water power and of machines is to be found in the work of Georg Agricola, to which reference has already been made in connection with mining; in Agostino Ramelli's *Le Diverse e Artificiose Macchine* (1588), in which many of Leonardo's suggestions are developed; and in Zonca's (1568–1602) *Nuovo Teatro di Macchine e Edifici* (1607), in which special attention is given to propelling such heavy machines as the fulling mill by power from water wheels.

In this period little improvement seems to have been made in the design of the water wheel, although Leonardo made suggestions which were preliminary to the invention of the water turbine in the nineteenth century. What was of particular significance were the ingenious uses to which the "overshot wheel" was put.[3] From Agricola and Zonca, one can get some idea of the many purposes for which water power was used for want of any other satisfactory source of great power, and one can also get some notion of the difficulties of using the water wheel to meet so many industrial needs (Figure 14). Moreover, it should be remembered that power from water depended upon an abundant and steady flow of falling water and hence was available only in certain places and even in them frequently only for limited seasons of the year. Water power was thus employed primarily in hilly or mountainous country and in industries in which the materials to be processed, like grain, could be transported with comparative ease to the source of power and the finished products then carried at relatively low cost to market.

The windmill had greater mobility than the water wheel, yet areas where strong and steady winds prevail are relatively few, and even in them calms occur often enough to make the windmill unreliable as a source of readily available power. Furthermore, the traditional windmill had certain technical weaknesses which limited its effectiveness in industry. The so-called post mill was actually set upon a post so that the mill could be turned in order that its arms could be made to face into the wind. Such an arrangement restricted the size of the mill and had other defects, such as making the mill hard to turn, getting out of level, and having a foundation that had to be repaired often. To overcome some of these difficulties

[3] The "overshot wheel" was one in which water fell on the wheel at the top. The weight of the water, as well as the force with which the water hit the wheel, turned the wheel. In the "undershot wheel," water hit the blades at the bottom of the wheel. Hence the force of the water was all-important.

Leonardo proposed attaching the arms of the mill to a turret atop the main mill that could be turned independently of the rest as need be. This

Figure 14
Grist mill driven by water. Advance in the milling of flour can be seen here by comparing this scene with that of the quern (Figure 8). Here is mechanical power at work. Energy is provided by falling water, admitted into a sluice at the gate *C.* The speed of the water turns a simple paddle wheel. The rotary power is conveyed by shafts and gears to the millstones. Grain is dumped in the hopper and falls down between the revolving stones, which have been cut with grooves on their contiguous surfaces. The flour is scooped out of the bin by the miller on the steps and is then bagged. *(From Vittorio Zonca, Il Nuovo Teatro, 1656.)*

proposal was worked out in detail by Ramelli and was actually put into practice by Dutch engineers in the late sixteenth century. It greatly improved the efficiency of the windmill, but wind as a source of power still left much to be desired.[4]

Although neither the windmill nor the water wheel was satisfactory enough as a source of mechanical power to discourage people from seeking an alternative source in steam, these two devices were used so widely that engineers came to devote much attention to problems of transmission of power. Da Vinci, for example, described shafts, pulleys, and belts. He probably invented the roller chain drive and improved the block chain drive and sprockets. He designed conical, spiral, and graduated gears; roller bearings to reduce friction; and universal joints. He made one roasting spit run with weights, as in contemporary clocks, and another which was activated by a propeller placed in a chimney to catch the rising hot air. He made steel springs to provide power and got regularity into some of the apparatus by employing the pendulum. A society which gave birth to all these devices was one that was using a considerable amount of power which was transmitted to machines.

In this period of "proto-industrialization" important inventions were also made on machines that turned out goods, although changes in this field were not so dramatic as those which were to be realized in the eighteenth and nineteenth centuries. In spinning, Da Vinci proposed the "flyer," which allowed spinning and quilling, that is, the twisting of fibers into thread and the reeling of the finished thread on a bobbin at the same time. This important step in making spinning fully automatic was put into operation about 1530 by Johann Jürgen, whose spinning wheel also had the treadle-and-crank arrangement so that the hands of the operator would be entirely freed of the task of propelling. Leonardo also designed power-driven silk reeling and twisting machines and a gig mill, improved by Zonca, for raising the nap on cloth.

Another important contribution to the machinery of the textile industry was the ribbon loom. It was so designed that the movements of the weaver in making one ribbon were automatically transmitted to the making of other ribbons. This apparatus appeared in Leyden in 1621 and by the end of the seventeenth century was in general use. As can easily be imagined, the ribbon loom was an intricate piece of machinery and a step in the attempts which were made to render weaving automatic. Then there was the all-important invention of a knitting machine or stocking frame by the Reverend William Lee (1589) that permitted making 1,000 or 1,500 stitches

---

[4] The fantail which would keep the arms of the mill always facing into the wind was invented in 1750.

per minute compared with 100 stitches by a fast hand knitter. Indeed, this invention threw such a fright into professional hand knitters that Lee became extremely unpopular in his native England and fled to France in hope of finding a more friendly environment for himself and his machine.

Considerable progress was also made in the sixteenth and seventeenth centuries in the clock industry, which produced, as we have previously seen, precise workmanship that was essential for the development of industrial machinery. Although public tower clocks had become common by the end of the Middle Ages, there was a demand for small, portable timepieces. These were made possible by the use of the coil spring, an invention attributed to Peter Henlein of Nuremberg in the last decade of the fifteenth century. The first clocks powered by springs did not, however, keep good time, for whereas the existing foliot balance and verge escapement had proved satisfactory when the mechanism of the clock was subjected to the constant force of weights, they were not adequate to control the variable force of an expanding spring.

Before a solution to this problem had been found, a new and urgent need for accurate timekeepers had come into being because of long-distance navigation of mariners in longitudinal directions. Navigators were for their own safety forced to establish their longitudinal positions with accuracy. Inasmuch as the determination of a point in longitude consists fundamentally in comparing the time where one is, established by "shooting the sun," with the time at some fixed point, let us say at Greenwich, it is essential to have an accurate timepiece in order to know exactly the time at Greenwich.[5]

After Galileo had discovered that a pendulum makes its swings in constant intervals of time irrespective of the length of the arc, he tried to employ the pendulum in a clock to be used at sea. Such a clock was partly built by Galileo's son (1642), and Huygens in the Netherlands built pendulum clocks for use on ships (1657, 1661). The great trouble with this principle was that the arc of the pendulum could not be controlled because of the motion of seagoing vessels. The use of a coil spring seemed to offer better prospects of getting an accurate navigational timepiece, and a return to it was eventually made. The uneven force of the spring was finally compensated for by the use of a balance wheel and hairspring, invented by the Englishman Hooke in 1658, the anchor escapement by Clement in 1680, and the deadbeat escapement by Graham in 1715; moreover, satisfactory methods for controlling the effects of temperature changes were developed by the Frenchman Le Roy in the middle of the eighteenth century.

---

[5] Astronomical observations by an observer at sea to determine the time at Greenwich had to be too precise to be depended upon. They were then not practical.

In both agriculture and industry any number of other devices were invented or proposed which were eventually to play a role in the mechanizing of production. In sixteenth-century Italy, Giovanni Cavallina invented a seed drill, the first important composite agricultural machine since the plow, which spread seed much more evenly than sowing by hand and which placed it under the soil where it could germinate quickly. In the cultivation of vineyards small plows, drawn by horses, were used to tear out weeds; in effect these were the immediate forerunners of the horse-drawn cultivator. And in the cultivation of the much-prized tulip in the Netherlands, much was learned of the use of fertilizers and of rotating crops which was to stimulate experiments that led to the agricultural revolution of the eighteenth century.

A list of some of the things not yet mentioned, which were included in Da Vinci's *Notebooks*, will give some idea of the ramifications of efforts in the sixteenth and seventeenth centuries to control physical environment. Thus we find both taps and dies for cutting threads on nuts and bolts, a machine for making files automatically, a flying machine, parachutes, wheel-lock pistols and muskets, breech-loading cannons, rifled firearms, a centrifugal pump, a hydraulic press, dredges, locks for canals, plans for draining the Pontine Marshes near Rome, and a canal from the Atlantic to the Mediterranean. To be sure, some of Leonardo's conceptions could not be realized until centuries later because of the need of preliminary work, improved craftsmanship, or a social demand for the product, but he opened vistas which stirred the imaginations of his successors.

Finally, the dissemination of information was greatly extended by the growth of printing—a means of communication which was especially important to the diffusion of technological information because of its ability to reproduce details with a minimum of error. Important printing establishments, like those of Plantijn in Antwerp, Kromberger in Spain, and Caxton in England, were founded throughout Western Europe and had a great financial success based, in part, on religious tracts connected with the Protestant Revolt and the Counter Reformation. In fact, this success allowed them to issue many works, notably the technical, which otherwise might have been too risky for publishers to undertake. For the most part, technological changes in printing came slowly after Gutenberg's great breakthrough, although new and famous type faces were developed, like italic by Aldus Manutius in Venice (1495–1515) and roman upper and lower case by Nicolas Jenson in France, and some improvements were made on the screw press to make operations faster. It was not, however, until the eighteenth century that presses were operated by compound levers and not until the nineteenth that typesetting machines were invented.

What the immediate impact of all these technological innovations was on actual production, it is difficult to say. What is clear is that machines increased the productive capacity of individual workmen and that although machine goods tended to be of inferior quality to the handmade, they were cheaper and appealed to the masses. Furthermore, machinery required larger investments and a more intricate organization of business than previously, and the existing types of prime movers with their centralization of power required the concentration of production in a given place. Some concentration of production was actually realized, but mostly in applications where the scale was large beforehand, such as international shipping, shipbuilding, foundry production, and, above all, mining. Capital required per mine in England rose from 100 pounds under Elizabeth to several thousand under the Stuarts, and a London brewery under Charles I had a capital of 10,000 pounds. The trend toward capitalist enterprise on a large scale, which was to attain such extraordinary proportions in the twentieth century, was clearly in evidence by the end of the seventeenth century.

The contraction of the seventeenth century

The Early Modern era was an age of economic concentration because of the increasing scale of enterprise and also because of breakthroughs in financing which permitted the amassing of much capital. In the back of our minds, however, we must remember that only a tiny percentage of Europe's population was participating in large-scale industry or commerce. The rural village and the small town were still the principal dwelling places, and agriculture was still the principal economic sector. In the seventeenth century the land was again becoming ungenerous. Following on the heels of the price revolution (which had tapered off in most areas by 1600) came a secular depression featuring diminished agriculture prices, reductions in cultivation and abandonment of land, sluggish demand, contractions in regional trade, curtailed population growth, and considerable social unrest. The depression was not so painfully severe nor so long-lasting as that of the fourteenth century, but it came a close second. By 1650 cereal prices had declined everywhere in Europe. The fall in industrial prices and wages was not nearly so bad, though there was a slump in rural and urban industrial production. The destructiveness of the Thirty Years' War (1618–1648) intensified the depression in Central Europe. At the nadir of the deflation, around 1660 to 1670, rye was selling in Central Europe for about one-half of its 1600 to 1649 price.[6] A *staro* of wheat in Modena, which sold

---

[6] Slichter Van Bath, *Agrarian History of Western Europe*, p. 209.

for as much as 400 *soldi* in the 1620s, went begging at 200 in the 1670s. In Strasbourg cereal prices dropped by 300 percent between 1640 and 1670. Predictably, land leases were shortened, tenant turnover became high, and agrarian improvement programs ground to a halt.

In a situation where the vast majority of the population makes its living from the land, an agricultural depression invariably means a contraction in aggregate demand for both agricultural and nonagricultural goods. The urban product of the seventeenth century contracted severely during the depression. In Venice, the output of woolen cloths dropped from a level of nearly 30,000 cloths per year in 1600 to less than 10,000 per year after 1670. In Beauvais, north of Paris, harsh and frequent famines made looms periodically creak to a stop.

The early 1600s was also a period of social turmoil: England, France, Catalonia, Switzerland, Portugal, the Netherlands, and Naples all witnessed upheavals between 1640 and 1660. Although the political circumstances in each case bear little resemblance one to the other, their concentration in time certainly suggests the probability of broad common causes.[7] We have seen outbreaks in the fourteenth-century city (the *Ciompi* revolt) and countryside (the *Jacqueries*), which came in times of economic hardship, but it would be too drastic a simplification to chalk up the crisis of the seventeenth century merely to falling agricultural prices. H. R. Trevor-Roper attributed the crisis to parasitic royal courts and to opposition to their extravagance in the more productive countryside. Marxian historians see the crisis as a series of related struggles to overthrow vestigial feudal institutions and privileges by emerging merchant capitalism and the more mobile elements of society. Others see the revolts (particularly those of France and Catalonia) as opposition to the newly centralizing modern state, which was extending its control under the efficient ministries of Mazarin and Olivarez.[8] The depression, alone, clearly will not suffice as an explanation of Europe's turmoil in the middle of the 1600s, but it was an important precondition. Whatever the form that discontent took, at its root was the inability of kings and peasants alike to sustain acceptable income levels.

[7] The civil wars in England and in France (the Frondes) were ostensibly internal power struggles. Naples, Catalonia, Portugal, and the Netherlands battled against deepening control by the Spanish Habsburgs. In Switzerland and Eastern Europe the crisis manifested itself in rural peasant wars.

[8] For full treatment of the seventeenth-century crisis see Trevor Aston (Ed.), *Crisis in Europe, 1560–1660* (Garden City, N.Y.: Doubleday, 1967); R. Forster and J. Greene (Eds.), *Preconditions of Revolt in Early Modern Europe* (Baltimore: Johns Hopkins, 1972); Roland Mousnier, *Peasant Uprisings in Seventeenth-Century France, Russia, and China* (N.Y.: Harper & Row, 1970); and A. D. Loublinskaya, *French Absolutism: The Crucial Phase, 1620–1629* (New York: Cambridge, 1968).

Establishing the capitalist system

Capitalism and its relation to economic growth

In the preceding chapters, devoted to economic developments in the later Middle Ages, to the expansion of Europe overseas, to the extension of commerce, and to the growth of machine industry, we have been discussing many of the changes which in their totality were to contribute to the creation of an economic system known by the generic term of capitalism. As can readily be seen from the name of this economic system, capital played a large role in the new ordering of material things. In all previous economic systems, capital (defined as resources which are not consumed but delegated to the productive process) was mostly in the form of improved land, timber, both private and public buildings, roads, and canals. Consequently this capital could produce only a limited amount of goods in any short period of time. Under modern capitalism, however, capital, which came from "savings" of a substantial part of annual production, consisted increasingly of machines, which could rapidly augment the output of goods, and of money and negotiable securities, which could be easily transferred from place to place. Furthermore, with a greater supply of money, which is a generally accepted medium of exchange, a store of wealth, and a measure of value, the entrepreneur could more readily acquire the means of production, buy raw materials, and hire labor for wages in an impersonal market in order to produce those goods and services which would bring him more capital or profits. Thus capital in the system which was coming into being had much greater mobility than the old and a much greater flexibility in its employment. The new capital had a greater marketability and liquidity; capital was employed more generally for producing goods and services than for current consumption; and it could more readily be gotten into the hands of those who had the entrepreneurial spirit for making profits because of the general acceptance of charging interest on loans and the rapid extension of the practice of lending.

Furthermore, under capitalism, the means of production came to be increasingly in the hands of the owners of capital instead of in the hands of workers; this allowed a planning of production on a larger scale than had been possible previously. This may have had adverse consequences for income distribution, but it was a more efficient arrangement, not only because of the increasing scale of production but also because entrepreneurs became specialists in the management of financial and industrial enterprise, an important aspect of the division of labor. Lastly, the development of the capitalist system meant that economic relations among people became more impersonal than they had been—that everything was regulated by a price system—and that one of the most important ideologies among people was the improvement of their material conditions. To recapitulate, capitalism came to be a system in which a relatively large amount of capital was mobile, transferable, and available at a price to anyone with good credit standing; in which capitalists hired labor for a wage in an impersonal market and sold what was produced for money; and in which the incentive to economic action was the desire for profits primarily for the improvement of one's standard of living or position in society.

The emphasis on individual well-being in this system and the desire for profits led at times to a disregard for the general welfare, but in fact under capitalism mankind was to achieve greater economic growth and general economic well-being than had ever been attained previously under any other system. Capitalism seemed to work best when there was an expansion of economic activity and this expansion, it was found, could be realized not only from reaching out to encompass more and more of the population of the world and by supplying an ever-greater variety of goods to society, but also eventually by increasing the purchasing power of the masses so that their demands would provide new opportunities for investment.

In the development of industry in England in the century from 1540 to 1640, there was a tendency toward mass production for mass consumption, as in the case of beer, and it was this very production that necessitated investments of capital in machines and factories and the hiring of labor for wages on a scale never before seen. In the expansion of Europe overseas, also, large investments were made in the hope of realizing profits in trading ventures, in colonizing activities, and in raids on native stores of bullion in the New World. In supplying society with a greater variety of goods, like window glass, gunpowder, and cast iron from home manufactures, or like cotton, spices, fish, and lumber from overseas, new opportunities were created for the use of capital in capitalist ways.

Such uses brought into being or strengthened in the sixteenth and seventeenth centuries certain economic institutions and practices that were essential for the proper functioning of the system. One of these institutions was money. Without money it would be extremely difficult, if not impossible, to effect savings, to have mobile capital, to invest as one would in time and space, to lend or to borrow for interest, to hire labor for wages, or to have impersonal economic relations regulated by a price system. With the vast quantities of gold and silver brought in from the New World and with new supplies of silver coins from the mines of Bohemia, Tyrol, and Hungary, Western Europe got large amounts of those very metals which were used in coin money. In addition, credit instruments, like bills of exchange and various "promises to pay the bearer on demand," came to perform more of the functions of money and thus to extend the use of a medium of exchange in economic relations.

Then with the development of capitalism a new fillip was given to banking. Bankers were primarily the ones to whom fell the task of amassing the savings of many persons in order to have quantities of capital large enough for financing vast undertakings. Banks were the chief lenders to those enterprisers who would attempt to produce more goods and services for profit. Banks did much of the transferring of debits and credits between individuals who had accounts with them (giro banking) and of transmitting funds over long distances. Also, from safekeeping services which bankers performed for the wealthy, banks developed two practices which were extremely important to the growth of the capitalist system. The first was that they would lend out at interest moneys deposited with them, for they soon came to realize that all depositors would not be likely to withdraw all of their deposits from the bank at the same time. The second was that they could issue "promises to pay the bearer on demand" which circulated like money. In the first instance, banks were able to put idle funds of depositors to work without the direct knowledge of the principals, and in the second case, they were able to *create* money, which was one of the major discoveries of Modern Times.

Finally, the capitalist system altered traditional forms of business organization. As the need for greater amounts of capital became real, the tendency was for individual entrepreneurs to band together in one way or another. This was done, as we have seen in an earlier chapter, by the formation of multiple partnerships, of companies of merchant adventurers who shared expenses but traded as private individuals, of *sociétés en commandite* in which some of the investors were sleeping partners with no responsibility for management, and of joint-stock companies in which many investors bought shares representing the value of the enterprise and received a pro rata portion of any earnings paid out.

With the development of mechanisms for effecting savings and making investments—two of the essential factors in economic growth—there was a greater use of money than hitherto and the creation of an extensive and delicate price system. These institutions made possible a greater exchange of goods and division of labor, which were two other important factors in economic growth.

The development of money and banking in Germany and the Low Countries

Although the various parts of the capitalist system—money, the price system, banking, the capitalist spirit, the making of investments for profit, and the impersonalization of economic relations—came about *pari passu*, banking was in a sense in the center of the new developments and epitomized the new ways of doing business. It was the most important means for bringing together savings from many persons and for making loans to enterprisers in the fields of both production and distribution. And banking was to become the principal agency for regulating the supply of money by the issue of banknotes and the extension of credit.

In the latter part of the Middle Ages, as we have already seen, banking became more important in economic life and various banking services, ranging all the way from pawnbroking to the making of large loans, became differentiated. In the first two centuries of Modern Times banking took new strides forward, assuming a particularly significant place in the economic life of those parts of Central and Western Europe where there were large-scale productive enterprises and extensive commercial undertakings. Augsburg in southern Germany, for example, became a banking center because some of the principal exploiters of silver mines were located there and because it was on the trade route between the Rhine and the Danube and between the Rhine and the overland trade routes with Italy. Antwerp became a second great center because it was the chief place for the distribution of spices in the west and north and for the export of textiles and metals from its hinterland to other places easily reached by ocean shipping. Amsterdam was a third center, being a successor to Antwerp in Eastern products after the Spaniards sacked the city (1585) and the Dutch had cut its shipping from the sea by controlling the lower reaches of the Scheldt. London was a fourth center because of the growth of industry for a mass market and the development of colonial and other ocean commerce. And there were other centers of banking at Genoa, Geneva, Barcelona, and Paris because of trade with distant places.

Of all of the bankers of Early Modern Times the Fuggers of Augsburg undoubtedly did the most business and were certainly the most picturesque. They were in their age what the Medici had been in theirs—and they illustrate well the way banking capital came into being and the kinds of business in which bankers engaged.

The first member of the Fugger banking clan of whom we have information was Hans, who came to Augsburg in 1380. He was a clothmaker and one of those individuals who in the era of guild production began to turn out products for more than the local market. He specialized at first in fustians, cloths made from linen and wool, but then turned to cottons made from raw materials brought from Venice. Apparently his wares enjoyed considerable favor, for upon his death he left a small fortune.

Hans's son, Jacob, continued in the cloth trade, and so did Jacob's sons, Ulrich, George, and Jacob, the latter becoming known as Jacob the Rich. They extended the family business to include woolens, silks, spices, and jewels. Their ventures prospered so that they were able to establish connections in Italy, the Netherlands, Silesia, Poland, and Hungary. By 1473 the Fuggers had members of the Habsburg family, the ruling house in Austria, as clients, and a little later they undertook to serve the Pope by transferring sums from Northern Europe to Rome. They adopted the best bookkeeping practices of their day and an excellent reporting system to keep abreast of events which affected business activity and to be informed of the credit standing of their customers.

Under the direction of Jacob the Rich (1459–1525) the Fugger fortunes flourished. This member of the clan engaged heavily in silver mining, and incidentally in copper and lead production, and made investments in that mining equipment and mining machinery to which reference has already been made. His primary activity, however, was in accepting deposits, in lending them out at interest, and in transferring moneys over long distances. The Fuggers, like the Medici before them, soon became involved in the finances of the Church. The passage of funds from parishes to bishoprics and from diocesan centers to Rome was the biggest financial operation of the time, and the bank which was favored with even part of the business could be confident of much profitable activity. These operations sometimes had their seamy side. The indulgence-seller Tetzel, a personification of abusive and dishonest Church practice, was accompanied everywhere by a Fugger agent who channeled the contents of the money chests to the local archbishop and on to Rome. Richard Ehrenberg, the great expert on the Fuggers, observed with justification, "Such was the business which led to the Reformation."[1]

Although many of Jacob Fugger's loans were for strictly business purposes, as the Italian bankers' before him, he was drawn into the practice of making political loans to emperors, kings, bishops, and towns. It is even

---

[1] Richard Ehrenberg, *Capital and Finance in the Age of Renaissance*, trans. H. M. Lucas (New York: Harcourt, Brace, n.d.), p. 73.

clear that Charles V used moneys borrowed from Jacob to influence electors of the Holy Roman Empire when he was chosen Emperor. For the time being, loans of this type did not backfire. Even though Jacob lived lavishly and engaged in such socially desirable enterprises as the building of the Fuggerei in Augsburg—a "garden city" for the poor—he left at his death what was undoubtedly the greatest personal fortune that had been amassed since Roman times.

Under his immediate successors, the wealth of the Fuggers continued to grow, but so, too, did their political loans. The financial needs of Charles V seemed to have no end, for he required funds with which to fight the French, the Turks, and the Protestants and with which to fit out armed escorts for ships trading to the New World. His successor, Philip II of Spain, had almost as serious financial problems, because of his wars with the Netherlands, and accordingly kept turning to the Fuggers for help. In 1560 the Habsburgs owed the Fuggers some 4 million gold gulden, or twice the fortune left by Jacob the Rich. In subsequent years the Fuggers had to take heavy losses on their political loans, and although they managed to play an important role in banking for a while longer, they dropped from sight as great bankers in the seventeenth century.

The Fuggers were not, by any means, the only large bankers of the sixteenth century. At Augsburg alone there were the Welsers, who financed overseas commerce, the Hochstetters, who got into the Lisbon-Antwerp spice trade, the Rems, the Manlichs, the Meutings, the Adlers, and the Haugs. In fact, all the main commercial centers had banking families of a similar kind.

Banking activity at Antwerp was particularly vigorous because of the large amount of distant trade in the city. This commerce had grown exceptionally fast after the middle of the fifteenth century, as foreign merchants moved from Bruges to Antwerp because of the special privileges granted them and because of the better port facilities required by the larger vessels which were coming into use. In fact, Antwerp's location was especially good, for the Scheldt was deep, and because it was a river, it provided a great expanse of wharf facilities. Moreover, the city was situated far enough from the sea to be safe from casual marauders but not too far to make access difficult, and it had access to a large hinterland via the Scheldt, its tributaries, and numerous canals.

In the early sixteenth century Antwerp came into its own, for it became the center in Western Europe for trade in spices and other luxuries from the East and in gold and silver from America. It also became the great entrepôt for Western and Northern European goods, like textiles, metal products, and ships' stores, which went to pay for Europe's imports. Finally, as a result of its commercial activity, Antwerp had a certain amount of industry, such as the making of glass, Majolica ware, sugar refining, printing in such famous establishments as that of Plantijn, and even painting, if that may be classified as an industry, with such great masters as Quentijn Matsys and the Breughels.

With all the business that was located at Antwerp it was only logical that there should have been banking. All of the major bankers, like the Fuggers, had important branches there, and there large local firms and many minor operators and merchants engaged in the business of borrowing and lending. Sometimes bankers and traders combined their resources to buy up large quantities of pepper in Lisbon, as was done by the Italian house of Affaitadi in 1552; sometimes they made large loans to the King of Portugal with the understanding that spices would subsequently be sent to them. They also financed smaller undertakings by lending on bills of exchange; they transferred credits between distant places; they "cashed" drafts; they lent to cities for public works; and they made loans to kings and queens in order to get favors or to take advantage of the high interest rates which were offered them.

For many years Antwerp was a thriving place, but eventually it fell victim to religious strife. When Philip II of Spain tried to keep his Netherlandish provinces from becoming Protestant, he unleashed a war that was long, bitter, and destructive. Antwerp was partially ruined, and what was worse, the Dutch were able to get control of the lower Scheldt and thus cut the city's access to the sea. As the latter condition persisted, Antwerp fell as rapidly as it had risen; it did not recover from second-rate status until the nineteenth century, when once again it became an important port.

With the fall of Antwerp, London and Amsterdam rose to prominence in the economic life of Europe. The former, with a good port well inland, had a thriving trade in wool and textiles and in those articles of mass production previously discussed. The latter rose to prosperity largely on the strength of the fact that it became Antwerp's direct successor as the European center of Eastern trade and had the added advantage of trading directly with the East instead of through Portugal or Spain. Like Antwerp, too, Amsterdam developed a certain number of industries of which the most important were shipbuilding, textiles, faience, and food processing, as in the case of herring.

Because of its great importance in trade, Amsterdam became a great money mart and a pioneer in banking practices. In 1609 it took a crucial step forward with the founding of the Bank of Amsterdam, an institution designed to put order into the confused monetary, banking, and payment conditions of the country. In these fields, indeed, there was almost anarchy, because the wars with Spain had led to the debasing of the many coins (there were, for example, fourteen different mints) and the influx of foreign merchants and bankers from Antwerp had introduced into the country a wide range of moneys and a new set of faces with varied credit standings. Under the existing circumstances, money-changers had a field day, but they gouged their customers to such a point that the business community rose up in wrath. At this point the city fathers decided that they would have to bring some order out of the chaos. Their method of doing so was the founding of the Bank. To the new institution they relegated by legislation a considerable amount of business, for they required that all bills of exchange over six hundred florins be payable only at the Bank, and they suppressed many of the private money-changers, thus forcing people with moneys to change to come to the official institution.

Strangely enough, the Bank of Amsterdam was not supposed to perform one of the major functions of banking—it was not supposed to make loans, although it did eventually lend to the city of Amsterdam itself, to the East India Company, and to the municipal pawnshop. Its main activity was the one for which it had been organized, that is, to bring order into the exchange of coins, to facilitate the transfer of funds, and to accept the deposits of customers. In pursuing these lines of business the Bank rapidly became one of the most important banking establishments in Europe. It controlled the minting of coins by providing the mints with gold and silver for making standard coins and by withdrawing debased money from circulation. It changed moneys at official rates and by honest weight, and it transferred, on the order of depositors, sums to the account of creditors by effecting changes on its own books—a giro banking operation. This latter service was so great a boon in the making of payments that the practice of withdrawing deposits from the bank fell into disuse. If a depositor wanted cash, he simply sold his "claim to money in the bank," or bank money, to another person, and there was always a market for this kind of money (it even sold at a premium) because of its convenience and the demands of those who did not have deposit accounts with the Bank.

The efficient services rendered by the Bank of Amsterdam contributed their share toward making Amsterdam the financial center of the world. Traders from all corners of the globe cleared their accounts here. Here was the greatest mart for gold and silver, in part, because after the middle of the seventeenth century both metals could be exported without serious difficulty. Here capital might be borrowed from private bankers at reasonable rates, if the loan were to be used in legitimate commercial activity. Here, too, were to be found businessmen from all over Northern Europe who had come to learn Dutch banking practices for the purpose of introducing them at home.

Money and banking in England and France

The next important development in the field of money and banking was taken by one of the direct offshoots of the Bank of Amsterdam—the Bank of Stockholm. This step was the issuing of bank notes. Whereas in Amsterdam depositors sold their receipts for what they had deposited in order to facilitate the making of payments, in Stockholm the Bank itself issued promises to pay (1661) which circulated for the making of payments. These promises to pay—these notes of the bank—were printed instead of handwritten; thus they were standardized, except for the serial number and date and the fact that they were issued in various denominations. They carried the following text:

> The bearer of this note of credit has a claim upon the Bank of Stockholm under number (such-and-such) for the sum of (denomination inserted here) copper money. This is hereby certified by us the undersigned, Commissioners of the Bank and Accountants, and also verified through the seal of the Bank hereto affixed. Given in the Bank of Stockholm, Year (such-and-such).
> (Amount in numerals)
>
> (Signatures) Seal.

Such pieces of paper were especially useful in Sweden, where coins were copper and extremely heavy, the largest, of 10 kroner, weighing 43 pounds and more common ones as much as 7 pounds. But they had a greater significance than being convenient—they permitted the Bank of Stockholm to issue more money than was on deposit, that is, to extend credit or to create money. This was an excellent thing so long as people had confidence in the notes—a confidence based on the Bank's ability to make its promise good—for it allowed an expansion or contraction in the supply of money according to the needs of the business community. In fact, the issue of bank notes was one of the major inventions of Modern Times.

Important as was the role of the Bank of Stockholm in the development of bank notes, undoubtedly the real success in the use of this instrument should be attributed to the English. In Britain, as elsewhere, merchants and public scriveners engaged in receiving moneys for safekeeping, in lending, and in transferring sums from place to place. Frequently these people might have so much coin on hand that they would take it to the Royal Mint in order to get the protection of the latter's vaults. This practice worked after a fashion until 1640, when Charles I suddenly refused to release the deposits of the merchants at the Mint until they had granted him a loan. This kind of a holdup antagonized the merchants, who henceforth entrusted their extra coin to goldsmiths, for these people also had strongboxes and vaults.

Goldsmiths had already been doing some lending and other banking business, as we have seen, and now with the new amounts left with them, they had an opportunity to expand their operations. They began to lend out at interest sums deposited with them on the assumption that all depositors would not want their money at the same time. This lending of other people's money proved so profitable that the goldsmiths began to encourage merchants to make deposits with them by paying interest on such sums, higher rates being paid for long-term than for short-term deposits. Unlike the Bank of Amsterdam, they allowed their depositors to withdraw their funds, but like the Dutch institution they permitted depositors to transfer sums from one to another by bookkeeping transactions, to write orders to pay a certain sum to a certain person, as in the modern check, and to sell their deposit slips, that is, to sell their claim to "bank money." From this last practice came the issuing of paper money in England.

The most important of the early forms of paper currency were the goldsmiths' notes. These notes were given to depositors in place of coin at the time of the withdrawal of funds, were issued in various denominations, and were essentially goldsmiths' promises to pay the bearer on demand a certain amount of coin. In the course of time these notes took the place of receipts for deposits, for they were more convenient, and assumed an important position as a medium of exchange. Soon the imaginative goldsmiths realized that they could issue notes up to a large percentage of deposits, as well as lend a large portion of the deposits, and that they could thus increase the amount of money upon which they could collect interest. In fact, from experience they learned that a coin or bullion reserve of 20 to 30 percent of their notes in circulation was sufficient to meet the calls of their depositors for cash.

For a time all went well with these operations, but eventually goldsmiths began to make political loans—loans to the Crown—and the kings' credit turned out to be poor. In 1672 the British monarch issued a "Stop of the Exchequer," which meant a stop to the payment of his obligations to goldsmiths. This action forced many goldsmiths to close their doors and destroyed public confidence in goldsmiths' banks and in goldsmiths' notes. Obviously a new solution to the banking situation had to be found.

For some time the possibility of creating a bank along the lines of the Bank of Amsterdam had been debated, and now the possibility seemed to have become a necessity. Only the Whigs appeared to fear the establishment of a strong public bank on the ground that it might lend money to the King and thus strengthen his position. Their hesitation was, however, removed with the change of the ruling monarch as a result of the "Glorious Revolution" of 1688–1689, which ended the reign of James II and brought the less autocratic William and Mary to the throne. Accordingly, the Whigs changed position, and the Bank of England was brought into being in 1694.

The fundamental plan for the Bank was worked out by a Scot, William Patterson. His proposition was that a group of private financiers would lend the government 1.2 million pounds at 8 percent in return for a charter, granted by Parliament, which would confer on them the right to accept deposits, buy and sell precious metals, borrow, lend, and transfer funds, discount bills of exchange, and *issue bank notes*. This plan was approved by Parliament, and the Bank finally began operations. At first the new institution encountered considerable opposition. The Tories disliked it because they regarded it as a Whig scheme and even tried to scuttle the Bank by offering the government a loan of 2 million pounds for approval of a bank with land as reserve. Their plan failed, but the Bank of England loaned the 2 million pounds promised by its rivals. Then the goldsmiths opposed the Bank for obvious reason that it would encroach on their operations. They tried to drive the Bank out of business by buying up the Bank's bank notes and demanding payment at once in bullion or coin. This "run" on the Bank might have worked, but the Bank refused payment to the raiders, and its action was sustained by the government.

Although private bankers continued to do business in England, the Bank of England was for a long time the only joint-stock bank in the land and the only one of its kind to enjoy the right of issuing bank notes. It engaged successfully, moreover, in all kinds of banking operations, although most of its business was in short-term loans to finance commerce, except for sizable loans to the East India Company and the South Sea Company. It weathered two serious financial storms in the early eighteenth century, once in 1720 when the South Sea bubble burst and once again in 1745 when the young Pretender marched on London and people suddenly decided that they wanted hard money instead of bank notes. After that the Bank, its prestige increased by the strength which it had shown in the crises, gained wide support. It attracted deposits from all sides, including smaller banks, and it lent money to banks when they were short of funds, thus giving stability to the money market, to financial institutions generally, and hence to business itself.

One of the many reasons which explain the greater economic development of England than of France in the eighteenth century was the fact that Great Britain had a superior banking system. Although the French were fully cognizant of the importance of a large, stable, "central" joint-stock bank, a great banking fiasco put joint-stock banking under a cloud for a long time. The fiasco in question is connected with the name of John Law. This personage was a Scot who had a firm belief that money greased the wheels of commerce. He came to France with a proposition that he be given a charter for a bank, patterned after the Bank of England, and his request was granted. He opened the doors of his establishment in 1716, began to accept deposits, transfer funds, make loans, accept bills of exchange, discount promissory notes, and most significantly of all, issue bank notes. Unlike the Bank of England, which pursued cautious policies, the Law Bank went overboard in issuing bank notes and in investing in wild speculations. Furthermore, from its very beginnings the Bank was on shaky ground, for only one-fourth of its capital was paid in and much of this was in the form of government securities of dubious value. Then bank notes were issued in such volume that the whole experience provided a classic example of overissue. In fact, notes in the amount of 148,560,000 livres were issued in the first two and a half years and 2,696 million livres worth of notes were outstanding in May 1720. In 1718 the Bank became a royal institution with the King as sole stockholder, and heavy investments were made in government securities. Finally, the Bank made large loans to a colonial trading company that Law founded—the Mississippi Company—and when this concern failed to make appreciable earnings, the prices of the Bank's stock and of the Mississippi stock stopped rising. Suddenly people lost confidence in Law's schemes and in the Bank's notes. Prices in the paper money went up, a run on the Bank began, and the joint-stock banking venture collapsed disastrously.

So horrendous was this entire experience that the French remained extraordinarily gun-shy of large banks, of paper money, and of stock companies throughout the eighteenth century and in some respects well into the nineteenth. Banking was carried on in France by private bankers who operated without the aid of a central institution that would take their deposits and make them loans when necessary in order to give flexibility to credit and stability to business. Not until 1776 was such a bank created by Turgot, the King's chief Minister, who was deeply interested in economic matters. Although the word "bank" was discreetly omitted from the title of the new institution, it being called Caisse d'Escompte, the Caisse operated much like the Bank of England. At long last France was on the way toward acquiring a sound banking structure, but again it ran athwart political considerations. The Caisse was forced to overinvest in government securities and collapsed during the French Revolution.

Money, instruments of credit, and the price system

Important as banking was, one should not lose sight of the fact that the very *raison d'être* of banks was to amass savings and to put them to work, and that these savings were in the form of money, which we have indicated several times to be a measure of value, a means of exchange, and a store of wealth. In many ways money should be regarded as the basic institution of the growing capitalist system, for without it the other characteristics of the new order would have been impossible. It was not that money was in and of itself new, but that it came to permeate all economic aspects of life and to more fully regulate relations among people. It was by means of a greater use of money that savings came to be effected more easily, that they were amassed more readily, and that they were invested more efficaciously. It was by a greater use of money that the owners of capital goods were able to bring together necessary materials, to hire labor for wages in an impersonal market without assuming responsibility for employees' welfare, and to sell finished products in an uncertain market in hopes of making profits, that is, of acquiring more capital. It was the extensive use of money that gave rise to an elaborate price system covering all scarce goods and services which were exchanged. And it was through money that changes in amounts of savings, investments, credit, and prices came to affect business activity, that is, to create business fluctuations or business cycles.

Considerable attention has already been given to money in the sixteenth century. We have seen that the European stock of those precious metals, gold and silver, used in coins increased three times from 1500 to 1650 and that this augmentation contributed to a greater use of money (Figure 15). The supply of "money" increased, however, much more than this because of the development of credit instruments which had economic effects similar to those of coins. Among the most important of these devices were the bills of exchange. They were, indeed, much like our modern checks and were widely used in distant trade, although in local transactions they were used sparingly, as is the check even today on the Continent. By being "discounted" by banks, bills of exchange served as a basis for loans, for the bank that paid the ultimate payee of the bill before its due date for a consideration was actually lending money at interest. And bills served as media of exchange, for once they had been accepted, we would now say endorsed, by a bank or merchant of good standing, they might circulate like coins.

Furthermore, the supply of money was increased by bank notes. Banks realized that they could issue "promises to pay" with deposits placed with them as reserves in a proportion of 1 to 5, that is, with a 20 percent reserve. Just how greatly the money supply was increased by this practice and by other credit instruments before the beginning of the eighteenth century,

Figure 15
Money of the seventeenth and eighteenth centuries. The first piece shown above is an early English check, or order, on Mr. Morris to pay a certain sum. The second piece is a John Law bank note. The third piece is one of the famous "pieces of eight," the Spanish milled dollar. It circulated widely in the American colonies. *(From the Moneys of the World Collection of the Chase Manhattan Bank of New York. Used with permission.)*

Money of the Seventeenth and Eighteenth Centuries. The first piece shown above is an early English check, or order on Mr. Morris to pay a certain sum. The second piece is a John Law bank note. The third piece is one of the famous "pieces of eight," the Spanish milled dollar. It circulated widely in the American colonies. *(From the Moneys of the World Collection of the Chase Manhattan Bank of New York. Used with permission.)*

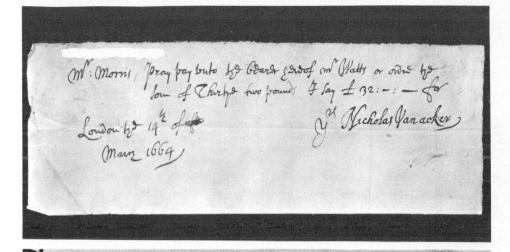

it is very difficult to say, but it is possible that by 1700 somewhere in the neighborhood of a third of all payments were made by these kinds of money and that the increase from 1500 was somewhat in the same proportion as that of bullion. In other words, the total supply of money from 1500 to 1700 may have increased as much as six times.

Public finance, insurance, bourses, bubbles

As more and more of the economic relations among human beings came to be expressed in terms of money, many older institutions became outmoded, and many new ones were brought into being to meet the exigencies of a money economy. In no phase of life was this more apparent than in public finance. No longer were payments in kind, in services, or in military support sufficient for kings and lesser lords to perform the functions of government. Wars could no longer be fought with armies composed of feudal knights and untrained peasants. They were fought by professional mercenaries who knew how to use the new firearms and the new tactics which were coming into being, and obviously the mercenaries had to be paid and provided with expensive matériel. Navies, too, became more costly with the development of specialized fighting ships with heavy artillery on board, and with larger numbers of ships in fleets. The Spanish Armada that sailed against England in 1588 was composed of 130 ships and 30,000 men; the Christian fleet that fought the Turks at the Battle of Lepanto in 1571 consisted of 250 galleys. Then costs of government went up as kings attempted to extend their sway over larger areas, to establish statewide administrative and legal systems, and to develop their economies by subsidies to entrepreneurs.

Under these circumstances changes in governmental revenue systems were the order of the day. Many of the old dues dating from feudal times were commuted to money payments, and rates were raised or new taxes levied on the consumption of products, like salt, wine, and beer, on outward signs of wealth, like doors and windows, on supposed incomes, on the heads of citizens (poll taxes), and on imported goods, especially luxuries, like silks and cotton prints, which cut into the business of local producers.

In spite of such changes, however, tax revenues failed to meet the costs of government, especially those arising from war, and governments resorted more and more to borrowing. Sometimes they combined tax reforms with loans, farming out certain taxes, notably those on consumers' goods, in order to get payments at once. Sometimes they granted privileges, like the right to establish a bank, in return for loans. Sometimes they had recourse to "forced loans," when other methods failed. And sometimes they tried to raise funds by making government loans attractive investments. This required keeping the government's credit good and interest rates high and/or by offering the public securities that had special advantages. One such type was the *rente* or the annuity, which was particularly popular in France. This kind of security had been used in late Medieval Times, as we have previously seen, to finance real estate and housing enterprises, but was now adopted on a larger scale. The *rente* consisted of a pledge on the part of the borrower to pay the lender in return for his moneys annual amounts for a given number of years, or for the life of the lender, or even in perpetuity, thus providing, if everything went well, a steady source of income to the lender. Then a variation on the theme of the annuity was developed which had a considerable vogue. This was the *tontine*, devised by Lorenzo Tonti, financial adviser to the French First Minister, Cardinal Mazarin, in the middle of the seventeenth century. According to his scheme, annuities would be bought by a "class" or age group of subscribers whose living members would receive a high rate of interest on the amount paid in by *all* members of the class until only a few members of the class remained alive, but the principal would be retired by the death of the subscribers. Thus those who lived longest stood a chance of getting large payments, while those who died early would get little, and their heirs would get nothing. People who entered into such an arrangement were, in effect, betting on their own longevity.

One of the early difficulties encountered with both annuities and tontines was that investors could buy an annuity on the life of a second person. Accordingly, shrewd financiers bought annuities on the lives of persons for whom the expectation of life was long. Thus they sought out young girls, on the theory that females live longer than males, in good health, who had had all the serious diseases of the time, like smallpox, diphtheria, measles, and mumps. Inasmuch as such a selection had not been envisaged by the founders of the tontines in their estimates of mortality rates, the costs of the scheme turned out to be much higher than had been anticipated. Yet the sale of *rentes* and annuities have remained important down to the present, and the abuses to which they were subjected have been gradually curbed. The element of chance in them attracted those with sporting penchants, and the investment features proved popular with those who wanted to make financial provision for their last years.

With the sale of these various types of government securities, public debts came into being. To be sure, princes had created debts from time immemorial, but in their cases it had been understood, at least in theory, that they would pay off their obligations. With the new public debts, there was no expectation that all securities would ever be completely retired. At most it was hoped that high-cost securities for short terms (the floating debts) might be replaced by low-cost obligations of long duration (consolidated debts). Just what the consequences of creating such debts were to be, contemporaries in the sixteenth and seventeenth centuries were not entirely sure. Some felt that the debts would impair the credit of governments and bring rack and ruin to the economies involved. Others thought that the debts would make little difference in economic activity or in government credit, if the states were able to meet their interest payments regularly. In actuality the effects of public debts depended very largely upon the purpose for which they were used. If they went into investments in productive enterprise, especially for goods of mass consumption, they contributed to economic growth. Unfortunately much of the sums obtained was used for conspicuous consumption, like that at the Court of Versailles, and thus stimulated luxury industries which had little impact upon raising national income per inhabitant. Other amounts went into war and war matériels that in and of themselves are destructive, although they may have been necessary for protection, and large sums were employed for the administrative business of government, which was notoriously inefficient.

Another institution which developed with the spread of an economy based upon the tenets of capitalism was insurance. As more and more goods and services became subject to monetary valuation and as the loss of property or of life caused greater hardships on individuals, it was quite logical that people should attempt to minimize the economic results of misfortune by sharing risks—by the device of paying premiums to a central fund from which they were to receive agreed-upon amounts in case of stipulated losses. Marine insurance, which had existed in the Late Middle Ages, became more highly developed and specialized, especially in England. There a group of marine underwriters assumed the habit of foregathering after the Glorious Revolution of 1688–1689 at a coffeehouse run by Edward Lloyd, and there they adopted the practice whereby several of them underwrote part of a risk on a ship, a practice which allowed them to handle very large policies. To assist them Lloyd began publishing *News* pertaining to shipping matters—a publication that became known as *Lloyd's List* in 1734 and in 1760 as Lloyd's *Register of Shipping*. Even to this day Lloyd's is a loose association of underwriters doing business together and insuring parts of a given risk.

Fire insurance, likewise, became organized in the first two centuries of Modern Times on the generally accepted principles of sharing risks. It appeared in Germany in the sixteenth century in the form of mutual-aid societies for rebuilding those properties of its members which were destroyed by fire. It developed in England after the Great Fire in London in 1666. One of the first companies there was the Fire Office, founded by a famous writer on economic subjects, Nicholas Barbon, which insured 5,650 buildings from 1686 to 1693. In England, too, there were fire mutual-aid societies, like the Hand-in-Hand Society and the Amicable Contributions for Insuring against Fire. In 1706 a company was founded that was absorbed by still another organization in 1709 to form the Sun Fire Office, a company that is in existence today.

Life insurance probably had its beginnings in marine insurance, when the life of a skipper was insured along with the cargo; in the sale of annuities, which provided experience with mortality rates; and to a lesser extent in bets placed by various individuals that a given prominent person would die before a certain date—a practice, incidentally, which had to be forbidden by law because of the number of murders to which it led. For satisfactory operation, life insurance required a knowledge of the laws of probability, which were worked out by Blaise Pascal in the seventeenth century, and of mortality rates, that is, rates at which people at different ages and in reasonably good health would die, information which was developed from empirical data in the seventeenth century. In the last years of that century life contracts began to be written, sometimes in conjunction with the sale of tontines. Then in the eighteenth century stable companies were formed to sell life insurance—companies that did a sizable business, especially in Scotland and England.

Still another institution of the growing capitalist system was the bourse or the exchange. Clearly, as more and more goods came to be sold for money, as government securities and the shares of stock companies became more numerous, and as insurance began to be more widely practiced, merchants and other men of affairs needed places to congregate for the transaction of business. To be sure, in certain trading centers of the Middle Ages, there had been essentially the equivalent of bourses, such as the Rialto at Venice and the Beurs at Bruges, but in the sixteenth century such marts became more common and more highly developed. Antwerp opened its famous New Bourse in 1531. Sir Thomas Gresham, having observed the Antwerp establishment, built an exchange in London (1571) as a private venture, an enterprise which was a direct forerunner of the Royal Exchange. The Amsterdam Bourse was opened in a new building in 1611, and bourses were established in other cities, like Lyons and Geneva. In part the bourses served as commodity exchanges, for merchants bought and sold there on the basis of samples and made contracts for future delivery. In part they were money markets where people could borrow and lend. In part they were security exchanges where businessmen could buy and sell stocks and bonds. And in part they were underwriting offices, for in them underwriters plied their trade.

As can easily be imagined, the presence of so many people with money, engaged in operations that almost always involved a certain financial risk, frequently led to wildcat speculative schemes and sometimes to downright frauds. At Antwerp a mania developed for betting on all kinds of events

—whether a given ship loaded with pepper would arrive safely in port, whether or not a given person would die before a stipulated time, whether or not the price of wool would go beyond a given point. or which one of two sparrows on a branch would first take flight. Some of these wagers had a direct connection with business, as in the case of a man who bet that a certain cargo of pepper would arrive in port, if he had an interest in the cargo or if he had a stock of pepper on hand the price of which would go down if the available supply of pepper were increased. Under such circumstances individuals would recoup some of their losses by placing their wagers in such a manner that by winning them they would cover some of the losses sustained if the ship did not arrive or if the supply of pepper were increased enough to bring the price of the spice down. On the other hand, many of these wagers were matters of sheer chance and could easily lead to crime.

One way to get rich on the exchanges was by taking advantage of fluctuations in prices. A person might buy a certain product in hope that the price of it would go up, sell "short," that is, sell what he did not then possess in hope that prices would go down before he had to deliver the product, or buy for future delivery in order to have goods at prices of which he was sure. One might also engage in arbitrage operations; that is, if the price of wool were much lower in London than in Antwerp, including costs of transportation and handling, one would buy in the London market and deliver in Antwerp.

If one wanted to get rich quickly, one might try to manipulate prices. This could be done by cornering the supply of a given product like wool, that is, by "cornering the market," and then by forcing users of the product to pay exorbitant prices because they had to have wool in their business. Prices might also be raised by spreading false rumors, or advantage might be taken of existing prices if one had advance information of events, like the loss of a ship of pepper or the declaration of war, which would affect business. Or prices might be manipulated by appealing to the gambling elements in society.

One of the earliest and most extraordinary speculative manias occurred in the Netherlands in the 1630s. Tulips had been introduced into Holland from the East and from Mediterranean Europe in the late sixteenth century and had met with much favor among the merchant classes. After the wars with Spain were practically over and people had more time to devote to the peaceful art of gardening, the prices of tulips began to go up. In 1633 a great rush to buy tulip bulbs began, for everyone thought that it would be possible to get rich from the cultivation of these tubers. For a time prices continued to rise, and as they did people began to go mad. They pawned their jewelry, mortgaged their homes, and sold productive enterprises in order to buy bulbs. Under this buying pressure prices of tulips soared, one much-prized type, a black tulip, going to several times its original value. In time a point was reached where there were few buyers at the prices demanded, sales fell drastically, and panic overcame the masses. The collapse came in 1637, bringing ruin to the greedy and a rich harvest for the canny few.

Then in the second decade of the eighteenth century there was a great wave of speculation, this time centered in France and England. In France the movement was connected with the name of John Law, who has already been discussed as the founder of a central bank which so overextended the issue of bank notes that the French lost confidence in his paper. In addition to the bank, Law attempted other ambitious projects. The first of these was the Company of the West, more commonly known as the Mississippi Company, which was founded in 1717, a year after the opening of the bank. The plan for this institution was actually devised by others than Law in order to mop up floating debt obligations of the state by selling stock in a company which eventually would profit from privileges granted it by the government. From the outset, the Company was given the exclusive right of trading with Louisiana, of developing mining interests there, and of importing a certain number of slaves. Then a year later it was granted a monopoly of the beaver trade in Canada. With these privileges in hand, the Company looked like a good investment and its stocks sold well from the very first. Its initial popularity went to the heads of its sponsors, however, and they began immediately to expand the scope of the enterprise. In 1718 they bought the tobacco monopoly in France. In 1719, when the name of the Company was changed to Company of the Indies, they took over other French trading companies—the French East India Company, the Guinea Company, the Company of Santo Domingo, the China Company, and the African Company; they even got the privilege of collecting those taxes which were farmed out, of minting coins, and of managing the public debt. Thus through the Company and the Bank, Law controlled the major part of France's trade with the East and with the Western Hemisphere, France's central banking, and France's public finance, and he had golden opportunities to make profit from the exploitation of a rich colony, of the beaver trade, and of the slave trade, to say nothing of tobacco and tax farming.

This extraordinary concentration was made possible by a simple but ingenious financial scheme. Capital of the Company was raised by selling shares for government securities or for notes of the Bank. In the case of government securities the Company received interest payments which it could use to finance its productive efforts and, by absorbing these obligations, strengthened the credit standing of the bonds which also formed part of the investment portfolio of the Bank. In the case of payment in bank notes, the position of the Bank was improved, because with the

Company holding large amounts of the notes the danger of a run on the Bank was reduced.

The success of the first sale of shares in the Company is to be accounted for in large part by the fact that government securities were selling at a large discount and holders of them felt that shares in the Company might be of more value in the long run. In the longer run, however, it was necessary for the Company to show earnings in order to keep the confidence of investors. This might have been possible if Law had pursued more cautious policies and if the stock of the Company had not become the object of a speculative mania. The French, particularly Parisians, and to some extent foreigners, too, got the notion that Law was a financial wizard and that his enterprises would succeed because of his Midas' touch. They began to bid up the prices of Company shares until a raging "bull market" in "Mississippi" stock developed. This was facilitated by the fact that the shares were transferable from person to person, that is, were made out to the "bearer" rather than to a specified person, and further by the fact that Paris already had an active money market. By December 1719, Company stock with a par value of 1,000 livres was selling at 10,000 livres, and Law was selling more and more shares—"watering his stock,"m as market operators were to call it in a later day.[2]

In January 1720, when the Company and the Bank merged, people actually rioted in the Rue Quincampoix in their efforts to buy stock. Once again individuals liquidated their possessions in order to get title to a part of Law's enterprises. Under such pressure, prices of shares kept climbing, but they finally reached "resistance points" beyond which buyers would not go. Some large speculators realized that the earnings of the Bank and the Company would have to be fabulous indeed in order to pay dividends on the stock equal to a reasonable rate of interest at the prices for which they were acquiring shares. Hence some of these investors began to sell blocks of their holdings, and these sales aroused the fears of others regarding the success of the Company's operations. Sales then came in volume, and prices of shares began to sag. Law tried to stop the avalanche of selling by forbidding speculation in the Rue Quincampoix and by throwing much of his personal fortune into the breach. But his efforts were of no avail. By July the "Mississippi Bubble" had burst ignominiously.

Although many gullible and greedy, but otherwise innocent, persons lost their fortunes in the collapse of this scheme, it did wipe out some of the government debt built up during the War of the Spanish Succession (1701–1713). More significantly, the Law debacle discredited joint-stock banking and the joint-stock form of business organization. The corporate

---

[2] The expression, "watering stock," came from a drover's trick of letting his cattle drink their fill immediately before a sale so that they would weigh more than if they were empty.

form went practically out of use both for banks and for other forms of economic activity, much to the detriment of French economic growth.

While these events were taking place in France, England was also having a paroxysm of speculation. The insanity in England began during the War of Spanish Succession. At that time France received from its ally, Spain, the right to the slave trade in Spanish America, the Asiento, which had previously been held by the Portuguese, and incidentally developed a certain amount of trade with Spain's colonies overseas. The English did not relish this turn of affairs and founded in 1710 a joint-stock company entitled The Governor and Company of Merchants of Great Britain Trading to the South Seas and Other Parts of America and for the Encouragement of Fishing. This was the full name of the South Sea Company.

This organization, like Law's in 1717, sold stock to raise capital and took government securities in payment for the shares. This operation permitted the funding of a portion of the government debt, that is, of taking short-term obligations off the market, and gave the Company a source of revenue that could be used for developing actual trade and for paying dividends. The Company might not have amounted to very much had it not received a most extraordinary windfall in 1713 as a result of the Treaty of Utrecht. In this settlement of the war, England instead of France got the Asiento privilege, which allowed it to sell 4,800 slaves a year in South America and to send a ship a year, the permission ship, to trade in the Spanish colonies of the New World. These concessions were bestowed upon the South Sea Company.

The Company's operations became exceptionally profitable, so profitable, in fact, that the price of South Sea stock went up. Thereupon the managers of the Company became emboldened and decided to take a leaf out of John Law's book. In 1719 they took over a government loan in a manner to make everyone who was a party to the transaction extremely happy. By their action the government effected a reduction in the rate of interest which it had been paying and received a bonus as well. In exchange for their bonds, bondholders got South Sea stock, which was going up in price, and the Company realized a sizable profit on the deal. This entire operation was so successful that the Company soon agreed to take over the entire public debt of England, save for the loans made the government by the Bank of England and the East India Company. The favorable issue of this gigantic undertaking hinged upon the rise in price of South Sea Company stock, so that holders of government bonds would exchange their bonds for stocks. The price of the stock did go up, but too fast and too high. Englishmen acted as though deranged in their efforts to acquire South Sea shares. They bid up the price of the stock from 129 pounds at the end of January 1720, to 1,050 pounds on June 24, 1720. This extraordinary rise carried the entire list of stocks into a raging bull market, East India shares, for example, going from 200 to 440 pounds in the first half of 1720. Worse, the wave of speculation brought into being a host of "bucket operators" who founded all manner of fly-by-night concerns in order to get into the stock-selling act. Some of these phonies were of the most brazen kind, like a company for improving the art, lately found out, of making soap, a company for making gold out of sea water, another for bringing fire from hell, and still another for "purposes which shall henceforth be disclosed."

The South Sea Company objected strenuously to this kind of competition and got a bill through Parliament—the Bubble Act (1720)—which forbade the founding of stock companies without an act of the legislature. Also at the urging of the Company, the government dissolved many of the harum-scarum concerns referred to above. In spite of such measures the prices of the shares of the remaining companies continued to soar, although their earnings did not warrant the increases. Even the crash in France did not bring investors to their senses. Finally, when the South Sea Company won a suit against four companies which were misusing their charters and thereby aired some of the worst abuses to which the corporate form was being subjected, speculators began to run for cover. In August the fall of prices began, South Sea stock going to 120 pounds in December and the shares of other concerns falling precipitously, some of them, indeed, vanishing with the companies themselves.

The crash was a resounding one. In the cleaning up afterwards, widespread corruption was uncovered in government and in politics generally, especially on the part of Whigs. Nevertheless, it was a Whig, Sir Robert Walpole, who did most of the hard work of putting things aright. He thereby won such a reputation that he was able to rule for twenty years as prime minister and to establish, incidentally, many of the practices of responsible ministerial government. He was able, moreover, to save for government bondholders about 60 percent of their investment, and he was successful in salvaging enough of the South Sea Company to keep the organization in business, eventually, however, with government securities as its only assets.

In England, as in France, the madness of 1720 threw a cloud over joint-stock organizations. The Bubble Act remained on the books until 1825, so that stock companies could be formed only with the consent of Parliament. In spite of this restriction, the English made greater use of the joint-stock form than did the French, and this fact proved to be an important asset in the industrial expansion of England in the late eighteenth and early nineteenth centuries—in what has come to be known as the English Industrial Revolution.

Mercantilism—the dominant economic theory of Early Modern Times

The theory of mercantilism

In every society, that is, in all groups of people living together who are so closely bound that there is a common desire to perpetuate the group, some at least rudimentary ideas exist concerning how economic affairs of the group shall be conducted. As the economy of a society becomes more complex and more highly developed, these elementary ideas become elaborated until they constitute a body of doctrines and are then glorified by the term "economic theory." Economic theory invariably reflects the environment from which it emanates and hence varies from place to place and in any one place at different times as the milieu itself changes. Moreover, theory inevitably conditions the economic practices and policies of a society, since, indeed, it is for this purpose that it is created. In almost all cases, too, economic theory is closely related to the question of economic growth, for its design is to explain how to attain specified economic goals, including improvement in material well-being, or to provide a rationalization for the lack of growth by deprecating material things and lauding existing conditions and even poverty.

As we have seen in passing, even the Medieval world with its economy of limited dimension had its dominant economic theory. The theory was part and parcel of Scholasticism, the major philosophic trend of the Middle Ages, which merged religious inquiry with Aristotelian logic. With religion at its base, the economic theory of the times was normative, not analytical. That is to say, it was less concerned with how economic behavior worked than with what "proper" economic behavior ought to be. Scholastic economics was a branch of the study of *distributive justice*, and it dealt with such issues as the impropriety of interest taking (and under what special circumstances interest was allowed), the just price, and the evils of monopoly. No one was particularly concerned with how the economic clockwork functioned as long as injustice did not cause starvation or contravene the tenets of Christianity. Scholasticism and its economic theory did not die with the Middle Ages. It remained an active minority branch of economic thought into the Early Modern period.

In the first two and a half centuries of Early Modern Times, mainstream economic theory was particularly influenced by five major developments: (1) great economic growth, (2) an enormous increase in the use of money, (3) the expansion of trade over long distances, (4) the acquisition of colonies overseas, and (5) the rise of national states. Accordingly, theory aimed to explain how growth was attained and what the roles of money, of commerce, of production, and of colonies were in effecting that growth. Especially characteristic of the theory, however, was that it sought as its primary goal not the direct welfare of all citizens, but the interests of those in specific lines of activity and more generally the economic strength of the state so that centralized control would be furthered and military power increased. Improvement of the economic status of the individual was a real, but a secondary, consideration in the theory of the times.

To all the economic theory from 1500 until well into the eighteenth century has been given the generic term *mercantilism*. This lumping is unfortunate, for as we shall see presently, both economic theory and practice varied widely from place to place and changed through time. Furthermore, mercantilism is a descriptively inaccurate term, because it implies that emphasis was put primarily on trade, whereas in reality stress was placed upon building the economy of the unitary state by the improvement of agriculture in primarily agrarian economies and by the development of industry and commerce. In brief, mercantilism in both theory and practice was economic state building and the use of the state to enhance the interests of policy makers, whether princes or private entrepreneurs.

The state intervened in all aspects of economic life, primarily by means of regulations to attain desired ends and to further the fortunes of those who had political power and influence. In and of itself this was nothing new, but the lengths to which one now went constituted a veritable innovation. The state engaged in an extensive amount of economic planning and also in a tremendous amount of control over private economic activity. Eventually, much of that state economic planning went awry, largely because it tried to keep alive uneconomic enterprises, because it curbed private initiative, because its red tape caused bitter hatred of the system, and because it engendered national rivalries which led to wars and the loss of the very purpose of the planning. In the eighteenth century mercantilism came under attack by new interest groups whose affairs were injured by mercantilist rules, by those who believed that greater economic growth would be attained if the state regulated the economy less and left it to the interplay of "natural law," and by those who thought that the economy of the state would be stronger if more attention were given to the welfare of the individual. The doctrines of *laisser faire* and of economic individualism were direct attacks upon mercantilism and mark the beginning of its end.

The mercantilism of Portugal and Spain

The use of political authority to regulate and direct economic activity had been resorted to on an important scale in Europe of the later Middle Ages. Towns adopted measures for encouraging and controlling production by the guilds within their walls and, in those places where business with distant places developed, for aiding larger-scale enterprises to get needed supplies, to have an adequate labor force, and to maintain lines of communication with foreign customers. Furthermore, towns and entire provinces adopted rules for provisioning their citizens with food in order to avoid shortages that might be caused by bad crops and by forbidding export to areas where prices of those goods which were needed at home were very high. Lastly, with the development in the fifteenth and sixteenth centuries of warfare in which fighting was done by mercenaries, silver and gold were hoarded in veritable war chests in order to have the wherewithal to hire soldiers in time of need.

Inasmuch as the conditions which gave rise to these various economic policies of the towns of the Middle Ages continued well into Modern Times, it is not surprising that the general tenor of the policies continued too. Guilds, for example, were not completely abolished in France until the French Revolution and hence exerted considerable influence on the government to maintain their monopolies, to restrain producers of different but competing goods, and to keep up the quality of products placed on the market. Manufacturers and traders sought governmental aid in furthering their endeavors, particularly in the newly discovered lands overseas. Famines remained a danger because of the poor means of internal transportation and hence led to a continuing of rules regarding provisions. And, as wars were fought on ever-larger scales and as war matériel became more expensive, governments had to have larger sums at their disposal for emergencies.

As national states achieved territorial unification by some lord extending his sway over other lords among whom he was *primus inter pares*, state economic theory and state economic practices began to take more definite form. This development was clearly evident in the case of Portugal. This small state, as we have seen, achieved territorial unification early and supported the efforts of several of its princes to explore the unknown areas of the South Atlantic. With the discovery of an all-water route to India, the Portuguese acquired almost overnight a most lucrative trade. Immediately the royal house claimed the exclusive right to this trade on the ground that it had financed the explorations and was the only agency in Portugal capable of exploiting the newly found riches. Accordingly, it instituted a number of regulations to keep out interlopers, and it conducted its commercial affairs with the idea of reaping a profit. This profit was to be measured by the amount of bullion that it amassed in its coffers, and bullion was to be obtained by having what came to be known as a favorable balance of trade, that is, by exporting goods to a greater value than was paid for what was imported.

By its practices during the heyday of its commerce with the East, Portugal established certain principles which were basic to mercantilist doctrine. The first of these was that colonies were to be exploited for the exclusive benefit of the mother country; the second was that all trade was to be regulated so that the metropolitan country would have an excess of exports over imports; the third was that national wealth was to be measured by the amount of bullion that a state had within its borders and therefore that precious metals should be accumulated at all costs.

These three principles, which were also found in the practices of Venice and Genoa in their trade with the Near East, became still more firmly entrenched in mercantilist theory by Spanish practice. Like Portugal, Spain was anxious to reap all the benefits of trade with its colonies which, as we have seen, proved to be rich in precious metals, the very stuff of national wealth, and so declared all commerce with the Spanish New World a national monopoly. In order to keep out foreigners trade was controlled by the Casa de Contratación, which ruled that all commerce between Spain and the Spanish colonies pass through specified ports in America, of which Porto Bello and Vera Cruz were the most important, and through a single port in Spain—Cadiz to 1503, Seville from 1503 to 1717, and then Cadiz once more. Licenses were required of all those who would go to the New World, and these were not granted to foreigners, nor for that matter to Spanish Jews, Moors, or converts. Ships going to and from the New World were made to sail in fleets to keep out interlopers and to ward off pirates. And the greatest pains were taken to prevent the gold and silver brought to Spain from leaking out to other states in payment for imports.

Spain was successful in acquiring large supplies of bullion, but the chief effect of them upon the economy of Spain was to make prices go up. Gold and silver had their usefulness, then as today, as stores of foreign exchange, that is, as internationally accepted currency. Spain's access to this form of wealth gave her potentially great purchasing power in foreign markets that might have been used to buy productive goods. Instead, much of this wealth was committed to troop payments for maintaining Habsburg rule in an overextended empire. Indeed, even when Spain became involved in disastrous foreign conflicts, all that she had was still not sufficient, and she could not buy what was needed for victory. By the Treaty of Münster (1648), the Dutch were given the privilege of trading with the West Indies, and by the Treaty of Utrecht (1713), as previously explained, the English were given a monopoly of the slave trade to the Spanish colonies and the right to send a ship a year to Porto Bello. Mercantilism as practiced by the Spaniards did not lead to great economic development nor toward material well-being. Few important Spanish economic theorists seemed to realize that production of goods and not hoards of gold were essential to national economic strength and to national defense.

The mercantilism of the Netherlands

With the economic decline of Spain, first the Netherlands and then England rose to positions of economic primacy in Western Europe, and France followed close behind them. The economic situations in which these states found themselves were profoundly different from those in which Spain and Portugal had been, and accordingly the economic policies which they followed and the economic theories that they spun diverged from those of their Iberian predecessors.

As we have already seen, the great economic growth of the Netherlands was based fundamentally on trade. Not only had the Low Countries developed a thriving commerce in exchanging local products and those of neighboring lands and seas for Baltic goods, but they had also reaped a rich harvest in bringing spices and other Eastern products from Lisbon to the west and north of Europe. Then, as has been stated above, when Spain tried to suppress Calvinism in its Netherlandish possessions in a long war that split the country into the southern (Belgian) provinces and the northern (Dutch) provinces, Dutch shippers, having been shut out of Lisbon, went directly to the East for the goods that had brought them such great profits in the past. There they carved out for themselves a colonial empire large enough to satisfy the hopes of the most imaginative burghers.

Because the Netherlands was a very small country with relatively little industrial activity and because its great prosperity had been achieved by trade, it was quite logical that cerebration concerning the basis of national wealth should have led to commerce and that state economic policies should have been concerned primarily with the exchange of goods. It was not a sheer accident that one of the greatest of Netherlandish legal minds should have argued for a *mare liberum* against the English contention of territorial waters and that the Dutch bent every effort to defend their commerce by force when it was attacked by jealous rivals in the seventeenth and eighteenth centuries. Thus Dutch mercantilism was characterized more than that of other people by its aim to facilitate trade. The Netherlands, unlike other contemporary states, levied almost no customs duties on imports, for it realized that multilateral international trade was in its interest, that tariffs hurt this trade, and that duties levied on imports tended to increase the price of goods in exchange and would thus be a disadvantage to the nation. This was a far cry from the usual high protectionism of mercantilism, yet it was practiced until the 1770s, by which time the peak of Dutch trading supremacy had passed.

Similarly, Dutch policy regarding the amassing of bullion differed fundamentally from that of Portugal or that of Spain. Although individual Dutch traders wanted to make money profits, Dutch statesmen and theorists recognized that the mere hoarding of bullion within the nation served no constructive economic purpose, except as a reserve behind credit instruments. They saw that the export of bullion was necessary to acquire goods that could be sold at a profit for still more bullion and hence permitted virtual free trade in precious metals. Thus bullionism was minimized in Dutch mercantilism in the interest of aiding commerce.

The Dutch, however, like the Portuguese and the Spanish, wanted to keep the benefits of Eastern trade exclusively for themselves. To this end, as we have seen, they established a trading company, the Dutch East India Company, to which was given a monopoly of this trade and the task of defending, administering, and exploiting the colonial empire. In other areas than the East, the Dutch also used the device of the trading company, as in the case of the Dutch West India Company and the Boards of Directors of Levant Commerce and Navigation, but in these places the Dutch were willing to forego attempts at monopoly and to compete with others as best they could. When the trading position of the Dutch began to decline relative to the English, it was not because of an inability to render services at low cost, but rather because of insufficient military force to withstand all the attacks that were directed against the Low Countries. From the middle of the seventeenth century onward the Dutch had to meet the onslaughts of the English, French, and Portuguese. They had to leave Brazil in 1661, New Netherland in 1667, and Ceylon and the Cape Colony during the Napoleonic Wars. In the Far East their trade fell off, for although they maintained their hold on the East Indian possessions, the narrow policies of the East India Company led to the disintegration of the organization and to its final dissolution in 1798. By the end of the seventeenth century, Dutch commerce had suffered an enormous decline relative to that of its leading rivals, although its gross volume held up fairly well. Dutch economic supremacy, built on trading goods produced by others, lasted little more than a century.

English mercantilism: a stress on production and trade

Portugal, Spain, and the Netherlands did not stress in their theory of economic state building the production of either agricultural or industrial goods. This was left to England and France, which ascended the scale of economic importance upon the decline of Dutch power. These two states had great productive potential, and because they lacked, at least at first, such trading opportunities as the Portuguese and Dutch enjoyed and found no Indians whom they could rob of hoards of bullion, as had the Spaniards, they set great store on production. To be sure, they recognized the desirability of a favorable balance of trade and the role that colonies might play in developing commerce, but their mercantilism was always tempered by emphasis on the critical importance of domestic industry.

Evidence of the significance given to production as the basis of national wealth was apparent in England in the sixteenth century. Then, William Cecil, later Lord Burghley, Secretary of State and Lord Treasurer in the reign of Elizabeth, resorted to all manner of expedients to foster industry. He encouraged the manufacture of munitions and ammunition so that England would literally be more powerful. He gave monopolies by letters patent, which were the origin of the patent system, to those who would undertake the mining of sulfur and saltpeter. He paid foreign workers in the metallurgical trades to come to England in order to teach their arts to local workers. He tried to preserve the forests along the sea coasts in order to guarantee a supply of timber for shipbuilding, and he encouraged the cultivation of flax and hemp and the making of canvas so that English carriers would have these much-needed products. And he even insisted that Protestant England eat fish on Friday so that the fishing industry, the training ground of sailors, would not be impaired. He made labor almost obligatory by the Statute of Artificers of 1563, and he endeavored to make business conditions so attractive to entrepreneurs that they would make capital investments.

In the seventeenth century, in spite of political disputes and revolution, the English continued to emphasize production in their plans for attaining national economic grandeur. With the Whigs, who generally were representative of business interests, becoming more powerful in politics, English economic rules became more and more positive in their direction of developing both output and trade. Guild regulations regarding the production of goods gradually waned; industrialists became freer to introduce new techniques of manufacture and to produce poorer goods in order to give more people products at lower prices. And a protective tariff was erected to preserve the English market for English producers.

Also in this century, however, the English placed great importance on the expansion of commerce, for the wealth that the Portuguese and the

Dutch had obtained through trade could not be ignored. This point is clearly made by economic writers of the time, like Roger Coke, whose *Discourse on Trade* (1670) had a great vogue, and Sir William Temple, whose brilliant pen and vantage point as English ambassador to the Netherlands were well used in the cause of lauding trade. So impressed did the English finally become with the importance of commerce in their economic state building that they fought the Dutch on several occasions in order to reduce competition from their rival; they founded overseas trading companies, like the English East India Company; and they enacted the famous Navigation Acts of 1651, 1660, 1663, and 1673.

These last-named laws indicate the lengths and the detail to which the English were willing to go to get more business for their nationals. The acts provided that no goods produced in Asia, Africa, or America (save for Indian goods) could be brought into England except in English ships or in the ships of an English colony, captained by an Englishman, and manned by an English crew. They stipulated further that goods produced in Europe had to be brought to England in English ships or in the vessels of the country in which goods were produced or in ships of the ports which were the usual outlet of these goods. They required that colonial produce from Portuguese and Spanish possessions had to be brought in from Portugal or Spain, which was a direct blow at the Dutch carrying business. They required that vessels in the English coasting trade be captained by Englishmen. They imposed heavier customs duties on goods brought to England in foreign vessels than in English ships. They "enumerated" certain articles, like sugar, tobacco, cotton, indigo, ginger, and dye-woods (the list was subsequently extended), which had to be sent from an English colony only to England or to another English colony. They stipulated that most foreign goods (wine was an exception) imported by English colonies had to be imported from English ports in English ships. And they placed special duties on some goods shipped from one English colony to another, like sugar from Barbados to New England for the making of rum. Here was a program worthy of the most exclusive system of the Portuguese or Spaniards for reserving markets, getting shipping, and making England the center of the entrepôt or warehousing trade of the world.

The end of commerce was not considered to be, however, as it had been in Portugal and Spain, the piling up of precious metals. In the many controversies over the English East India Company's practice of exporting silver in order to get goods which could be sold for more bullion than was exported, the argument seemed to favor the getting of more goods. As early as 1621, Thomas Mun, a director of the Company, published a pamphlet entitled *A Discourse of Trade from England into the East Indies,* which was followed shortly by his more famous *England's Treasure by Forraign Trade or the Ballance of Our Trade is the Rule of Our Treasure.* Here he argued so convincingly for the use of bullion to further trade instead of simply piling it up within the state that he won a large portion of his countrymen to his way of thinking. Sir William Petty, in his *Political Arithmetic* (1690), for example, contended that the real sources of wealth in any state were not gold and silver but land and labor. Nicholas Barbon, in his *Discourse on Trade* (1690) and his *Discourse Concerning Making the Money Lighter* (1696), tried to show how a useful stock of goods could serve a country better than a store of bullion. And Sir Josiah Child, Governor of the East India Company, maintained in *A Discourse on Trade* (1696) that the mere supply of gold and silver within a state was of no importance, but that it was essential to have low interest rates so that enterprisers would borrow capital for developing their activities. Even Charles Davenant, inspector general of imports and exports and an ardent Tory, insisted, in his *Discourses on the Publick Revenues and Trade of England* (1698), that the real value of money consists in its being a medium of exchange and therefore that it should be allowed to serve its appointed function. In the light of such arguments it is not strange that in 1663 England adopted what amounted to almost free trade in gold and silver.

In its commercial policy England endeavored in many ways to increase its productive capacity. It obtained in the Methuen Treaty with Portugal in 1702 an outlet for English woolens in return for Portuguese wines, and the English East India Company exported woolen goods at a loss in order to pacify woolen manufacturers who complained of the importation of calico prints. The Treaty of Utrecht, as we have seen, contained the important Asiento agreement, which gave England an increased market for its goods in Spanish America. Export bounties were paid on goods that England had in large supply and on which prices were low, a policy that found expression in the Corn Law of 1689, which provided for the payment of subsidies to those who sent grain abroad when prices were below specified levels. In 1721 the Calico Act forbade the importation of calicoes on the ground that these cheap and stylish fabrics from the Orient were ruining the woolen industry, yet unlike their French contemporaries, the English permitted production of these stuffs at home, the Manchester Act of 1735 being very explicit on the point.

Throughout the eighteenth century England continued to protect its industry with high customs duties, to reserve its colonial market for its own industrial goods, and to direct colonial trade to its shores so that it would have a good supply of raw materials for the entrepôt trade. Such measures contributed to England's economic growth and to the technological changes which constituted the Industrial Revolution. Under them England's foreign trade quadrupled in value from 1700 to 1789 and its industry, especially the cotton textile and metallurgical branches of it, grew by leaps and bounds.

In spite of this economic development there were Englishmen who writhed under governmental rules and regulations pertaining to trade and to some industries. Sir Josiah Child, to whom we have already referred, is alleged to have claimed that the economic laws of England were nonsensical, having been enacted by country gentlemen who were not even capable of administering their own estates. Bernard de Mandeville, a Netherlandish physician living in England, likened a national economy, in his *Fable of the Bees* (1714–1719), to a hive that prospered most when left entirely alone to operate on the *natural* principle of self-interest. And David Hume, the philosopher, attacked nearly all the sacred cows of mercantilist doctrine in essays published in 1752 and 1753. In his view, money was fundamentally a means of facilitating exchange and was to be regarded as national wealth only insofar as it could be used to grease the wheels of trade. In his opinion the term "favorable balance of trade" was a misnomer, for if it led to the accumulation of bullion within a country and prices went up, the high prices would discourage foreigners from buying in that country, exports would decline faster than imports, and bullion would flow to other areas, thus reestablishing a more equitable distribution of bullion and a closer real balance between exports and imports. That is, Hume considered that the amassing of bullion in extraordinary quantities in any one country was impossible because the price mechanism would cause precious metals to flow to those places where goods were cheap in terms of gold and silver. Hume also held that trade is of benefit to all those who are parties to a transaction, for through trade goods are moved about in such a way that each buyer ultimately gets what he desires. This being the case, he favored measures which would raise the general level of multilateral trade among nations, for doing so would be of benefit to England.

The greatest of all critics of the mercantile system was, however, Adam Smith, whose *Wealth of Nations* (1776) marked the true break between mercantilist and laisser-faire theory. Smith, like Hume, attacked all the dogmas of traditional mercantilism—bullionism, favorable balance of trade, tariffs, colonial regulations, and shipping monopolies. He believed that the wealth of a nation was to be measured by the fund of goods that it had and that this fund depended upon the goods and services which a state could produce or obtain in trade with what it had produced. He thought, also, that this fund could be increased if there were a greater division of labor among producers, that is, if each one produced those things which he could make most cheaply and from the sale of which he could obtain the wherewithal to buy the other things that he needed, instead of each trying to turn out goods to meet all his requirements. This principle of specialization in the production of those things in which one had comparative advantages (advantages comparable or superior to those of others who were making the same products) should be, according to Smith, applied on an international scale in order to get the best possible utilization of world resources and talents. If this doctrine were followed, not only England's economy, but that of the entire globe would be improved. To attain this goal, it would obviously be necessary for nations to allow their economies to function without governmental interference—for production and commerce to be free of all man-made impediments and encouragements that would disturb a market-determined division of labor. Eventually the English came to agree with the main tenets of Smith's doctrine, but this day did not arrive until the second quarter of the nineteenth century when England's productive advantages were so great that the economy had little to fear from foreign competition.

French mercantilism

The economic position of France during the two and a half centuries with which we are concerned here was more analogous to that of England than to that of Portugal, Spain, or the Netherlands. France had neither routes to the Far East that provided from the beginning a remunerative carrying trade nor overseas possessions with stores of precious metals in the hands of natives which could be seized. To be sure, the concept of bullionism played a role for a time in France, as it did in England, and so, too, did the idea of a favorable balance of trade. In fact, a royal ordinance of 1540, frequently reiterated thereafter, forbade the export of bullion as contributing to the "impoverishment of our subjects," and there was legislation to suppress the importation of luxuries, for "by their purchase great sums are drawn from our kingdom by foreigners." Yet, very early the French realized that economic well-being and national economic strength depended primarily on producing goods and services and that the concept of a favorable balance of trade was important not so much as a means of accumulating bullion as for indicating the competitive vigor of a nation's productive establishment. In the sixteenth century, accordingly, the French government offered subsidies, tax exemptions, grants of monopolies, loans, and letters patent to develop such industries as glass making, sugar refining, tapestry weaving, and woolen, silk, and linen textile manufacturing. Sully, Minister to Henry IV, stated in an oft-quoted passage that "feeding the flocks and working the land are the two sources of French nourishment—the real mines and treasures of Peru"; and Richelieu, Minister from 1624 to 1642, did his best to establish trading companies and to construct a merchant marine.

Moreover, early French theorists expressed opinions which were in line with the economic practices already mentioned. Jean Bodin (1520–1596), as we have seen earlier, criticized the amassing of precious metals as a national economic policy on the ground that by so doing the chief result was an increase in prices, while he stressed the importance of production in judging the economic strength of a nation. Barthélemy de Laffemas (1545–1611), Controller General of Commerce, recognized the usefulness of a supply of gold and silver for the conduct of state business and the desirability of having a favorable balance of trade, but he saw that the possession of funds and an excess of exports over imports depended on production. Of a similar mind was Antoine de Monchrétien (1576–1621), for he argued, "it is not the abundance of gold and silver, the quantity of pearls and diamonds, which makes states rich and opulent, but rather the things necessary for life. . . . " Therefore he urged state economic development of agriculture, industry, and commerce, the acquisition of colonies, and an international division of labor.

Important as were these early economic theories and state practices of the French, the climax of French mercantilism was reached during the ministry of Jean Baptiste Colbert (1619–1683). Colbert, the son of a cloth merchant of Rheims, became economic adviser to Louis XIV, France's great "sun king." For economic theory Colbert had little stomach, but in practical economic matters he had the greatest interest and enthusiasm. Like many of his French predecessors, he was a staunch believer in productivity. Regarding bullionism, he said that it was a "narrow and little principle, but that great things could be accomplished in its name." To obtain bullion it was necessary to build up the entire productive capacity of the state—and to this end Colbert actually devoted his entire career.

Colbert believed that foreigners would buy French products if the goods turned out were of high quality. To foster manufacturing he gave subsidies to industries, carried the policy of creating royal manufactories much further than it had been pushed previously, and did his best to introduce new industries. That there might be a sufficient labor supply he forbade the emigration of skilled French workers; he encouraged boys to marry before they were twenty and exempted families of ten or more from paying taxes, if none were priest or nun; and he conducted a severe campaign against begging, charity, and general indolence. In order to insure that French products be of high quality, he issued detailed specifications for goods and for the methods by which they were to be produced, an edict concerning the dyeing of cloth having, for example, 371 articles. He built roads, bridges, and canals in order to improve France's transportation system; he tried to make France a customs union, and although he failed, he paved the way for a reform that was realized during the French Revolution.

So far as foreign trade was concerned, Colbert believed that there was a given quantity of it and that if France were to increase her share, she would have to take something from others, and that the quickest way to get it would be to take it by force. "Commerce," he wrote in 1669, "is carried on by 20,000 vessels and that number cannot be increased. Each nation strives to have its fair share and to get ahead of the others. The Dutch now fight this war [of commerce] with 15,000 to 16,000 vessels . . . the English with 3,000 to 4,000 . . . and the French with 500 to 600. The last two countries can improve their commerce only by increasing the number of their vessels and can increase the number only . . . by paring away from 15,000 to 16,000 Dutch ships." He therefore approved of Louis XIV's first war on the Netherlands and gloated over the fact that in 1669 "this state is prosperous not only in itself, but also in the condition of want which it has created in neighboring states. Extreme poverty appears everywhere. Only Holland still resists." In 1664 he adopted for the area of the "Five Great Farms," which was most of the center of France, relatively low tariffs in the hope that "free trade" would give France more commerce, but he reverted to high protective tariffs upon the loud laments of producers who feared foreign competition (Map 8). He founded the French East India Company, which he hoped would wrest Indian trade from the Dutch and the English. He tried to secure colonies and to exploit those that France already had. In his efforts to colonize Canada he ordered soldiers there to marry and he sent out women in order that they might be able to. Prior to dispatching one of his colonizing cargoes he sent this characteristic message to his agents: "We prepare one hundred and fifty girls, mares, horses, and sheep [to send to you]."

Unfortunately for France, Colbert's efforts to develop the national economy were not crowned with unqualified success. He placed a great deal of emphasis upon the luxury trades and this was probably a mistake, for great economies have always given a relatively large place to goods of mass consumption.

England's emphasis on industrial production in mercantilism provided a head start for full-scale industrialization, particularly in mass-market products like cotton cloth. The French, who also strove for industrial self-sufficiency, concentrated on the manufacture of luxury products of high quality and value, though of limited marketability. By using tariffs to protect home industry and to isolate it from the vicissitudes of competition, the French created a "hothouse" manufacturing sector which proved to be a source of retardation in later centuries.

Colbert's economic planning suffered much from Louis XIV's wars of glory and of conquest. The treasury could not stand the burden of large military establishments and of aid to industry and to commerce, nor were the energies of the French people sufficient to carry on grandiose economic enterprises and war simultaneously. Although French commerce grew and the French merchant marine increased in size during Colbert's rule, the events of the seventeenth century indicated clearly that the future of France's economy was in production rather than the development of a great foreign commerce, like the Dutch, or the exploitation of colonies, like the Spanish.

In the eighteenth century France continued for long to practice "Colbertism," that is, its own brand of mercantilism. It maintained high protective tariffs, encouraged exports, and most characteristically of all, tried to bring the new industrial techniques which were being developed in England to France so that its comparative productive position would be maintained. Nevertheless, in France, as in England, several economic theorists raised their voices against so much government intervention in business affairs. In the first place, there were the so-called neomercantilists, among whom the most important were John Law, François Mélon, and François

Map 8
French Customs Barriers in the Seventeenth Century

Véron de Forbonnais. The distinctive feature of their doctrine was the belief that since money was the lifeblood of business activity, there should be a large enough supply of it, in coin or in paper, so that there would be a greater exchange of goods and hence a greater division of labor. Sound as this view may have been in an economy where commerce was still curbed by the limited use of a medium of exchange, it received a hard blow with the fiasco of the Law System.

A greater future lay in the doctrines of those who concentrated their energies in making direct attacks upon government economic rules and regulations. One of the earliest of such critics in France was Pierre de Pesant de Boisguilbert (1646–1714). He believed that there were natural laws of economics applicable in all times and climes and that they should be allowed to take their course without interference from political bodies. If this were done, French manufacturing would be relieved of restricting regulations, commerce would grow, and agriculture would be improved. A healthy equilibrium in international trade would also be created and simultaneously a more vital French national economy. Another in this group was Richard Cantillon, an Irishman in the banking business in Paris, who attacked the concept of the favorable balance of trade on much the same grounds as Hume and added the idea that there are cycles of national economic primacy which are created by economic laws and that to fly in the face of these laws is both foolhardy and useless. Also, Vincent Gournay (1712–1759), intendant of commerce and usually classed with the next group of which we shall speak, should be included here because of his activity in having the works of English writers critical of government intervention in economic affairs translated into French.

The hardest blows delivered at mercantilism, however, were those of the Physiocrats—literally those who believed in the rule of nature. The founder of this school was physician to Madame de Pompadour, François Quesnay (1694–1774). He had become profoundly impressed by Isaac Newton's attempts to explain the physical universe in terms of natural laws and by Harvey's theory of the circulation of the blood, whose marvels he had witnessed in his most famous patient. Like so many others of his age, Quesnay argued that if there were natural, eternal, and immutable laws which governed the physical universe, there must also be similar laws which operate in the social, economic, and political worlds and that social scientists, like physical scientists, ought to be able to discover these laws by the use of reason—by sitting down, by keeping cool, calm, and collected, and by *thinking*.

By the use of the method which he proposed for all, Dr. Quesnay set about the discovery of natural laws in economics. His finds were first published in articles in the famous *Encyclopédie*, but his system was more amply described in his *Tableau économique* (1758). Dr. Quesnay "discovered," or thought that he had, that agriculture is the fundamental source of wealth—the source of what he called the net product. Industry simply combines and transforms materials, and commerce moves them around; but cast a bushel of seed on the soil and it returns five bushels—an act of true creation! In keeping with this idea was a Physiocratic theory of economic classes which divided the population into three groups: the "productive class," meaning agriculturalists exclusively; the "proprietary class," comprising landlords who by dint of ownership rights are participants in the creativity of agriculture; and the "sterile class," composed of manufacturers, merchants, and everybody else.[1] According to the tenets of Physiocracy, goods and wealth circulated, on the analogy of blood in the body, among agricultural, industrial, and commercial segments of the economy, and this circulation was determined and regulated by natural laws. This being the case, and nature being assumed to be good, it followed that no man or man-made institution, like government, should interfere with nature's handiwork. Hence all governmental and guild restrictions on commerce, all rules pertaining to the production of goods, and all limitations on agriculture should be done away with. Man should adopt the policy of *laisser passer, laisser faire*—nature should be allowed to operate freely.

Although there were those who thought that it was perfectly "natural" for man to intervene in economic affairs to prevent himself, for example, from starving to death, or to get out of the way in case of a natural avalanche, Physiocratic ideas, especially those having to do with government regulations, had a considerable following. Popularity was given to this philosophy by such important figures as Dupont de Némours (1739–1817), Mercier de la Rivière (1720–1793), and Robert Jacques Turgot (1727–1781), Chief Minister of France from 1774 to 1776. During his term of office, Turgot abolished many of the old regulations pertaining to the commerce of grain and tried to get rid of the guilds, although he was removed from office before the latter reform was completely carried out. Thus in France as well as in England, traditional mercantilist theory came in for severe attacks, and even mercantilist practice was slightly mitigated. In France, however, the doctrine of free trade was to have less success in subsequent public policy, for France was not to have the strong competi-

---

[1] The foregoing suggests an observation about all economic theories: However abstract they may seem, they are always to some degree philosophic creatures of the society in which they are formulated. Just as Scholastic economic thought served a Church-oriented social order and mercantilist theory prescribed the economic tactics of emerging centralized nation-states, so was Physiocracy the appropriate economic theory of the land-oriented *ancien régime*. It is no intellectual accident that a conception of economy glorifying landed proprietorship and deeming sterile the enterprises of the city-bourgeoisie arose in the atmosphere of eighteenth-century Versailles.

tive position in production which the English acquired through the Industrial Revolution.

In most other European lands, French Colbertism was followed more or less closely, and in them it had much the same evolution that is had in France itself. It was introduced into Russia by Peter the Great (reigned 1689–1725) and was applied with energy by Catherine the Great (reigned 1762–1796). In the German states, it was preached by a group of writers, known as Cameralists, and was practiced by most states, especially by Prussia, where Frederick William the Great Elector and Frederick the Great endeavored to develop industry. Then, in the latter half of the eighteenth century, its basic principles came to be attacked by those who read English and French criticism and by local adepts of Physiocratism. The application of laisser-faire theories to domestic economic affairs and of free-trade principles to foreign trade was, however, retarded because of traditionalism and the rapid advances made by England in manufacturing.

Mercantilism and the colonial scene

Inasmuch as colonies played such an important role in European economic development during the period when mercantilist thought was dominant, it was only logical that economic state-building theories should have special relevance to the policies which were followed in overseas possessions. In the first place, mercantilism regarded the acquisition of colonies as highly desirable, for the Portuguese and Spanish cases, to say nothing of the Venetian and Genoese, provided clear evidence of the wealth that was to be gained from them. In the second place, mercantilists took the position, getting their ideas in part from the Venetians and Genoese, that their colonies existed exclusively for them and for their material benefit. This was the famous "colonial compact," or *pacte colonial*, as the French called it. From it were derived nearly all the details of mercantilist colonial theory —that trade between the homeland and its colonies should be reserved to the motherland, that this commerce should be carried in ships of the state or of the colonies concerned, that the colonies should buy whatever they could from the production of the homeland, that they should not produce for sale or for distant commerce what could be bought from the metropolitan state, and that they should produce and sell only what the mother country wanted.

Within the broad framework of the colonial compact the policies of the different colonial powers varied to meet different conditions both at home and abroad. In general, one set of principles was applied in cases where colonial production was developed to a point that provided articles for trade, and a second set dealt with actual settlement by Europeans and with economic development. The first category had to do mainly with the East, for a time with Spanish America, and in the seventeenth and eighteenth centuries with all America. The second concerned primarily the Americas, especially the West Indies and English North America.

In the case of the East, when the Portuguese found a new route to the source of supply of goods that had been coming to Europe for a long time as a virtual monopoly of the Venetians and Genoese, nothing was more natural than that they should establish a monopoly of trade over the new routes for themselves. Their problems were, first, to get sufficient supplies in the East by establishing bases and some control over the natives and, secondly, to prevent foreigners from learning of their secret routes and from breaking into the trade. The East was organized by Albuquerque, as we have seen, but keeping foreigners out was a more difficult and persistent matter, especially for a country with fewer than 2 million people.

The Portuguese trade monopoly in the East was a fragile affair, built on military enforcement of exclusivity, not on true advantages in cost savings (over alternative routes) or mobilization of resources. The Portuguese monopoly was, in fact, broken by the Dutch, who learned of the route to the East by sailing on Portuguese vessels. By means of the Dutch East India Company they established their sway over Sumatra, Java, the Moluccas, parts of New Guinea and Borneo, the lower part of the Malay Peninsula, which they eventually lost to the English in 1824, and Ceylon, which they also lost to the English in 1796. Moreover, the Dutch entered into trade with China via third-party ports, but from 1624–1642 to 1661 more directly via Formosa, and after 1729 at Canton; the Dutch East India Company had practically a monopolistic position in trade with Japan from 1638 to 1854, when trade was "opened" by Commodore Matthew C. Perry of the United States Navy; they founded a way station at the Cape of Good Hope, which they actually settled; and they had ports of call in the Persian Gulf, which allowed them to pick up coffee and to reach Persian and even Russian markets. For the administration of the Eastern trade they used the device of a joint-stock company with monopolistic privileges rather than a royal monopoly. Like their predecessors, however, the Dutch were concerned almost exclusively with trade rather than with settlement and economic development. Accordingly, they established trading stations and tried to get goods into them for trade. When they wanted a given product, they began by paying high prices for it, but when production of it was well established, they cut prices to the bone. This practice was followed both in the case of coffee, which the Dutch introduced into Java in 1700, and of sugar, which they had brought in somewhat earlier. In the case of some of the spices their policies were similar, but they sometimes went so far as to destroy plantations to prevent a contraband trade that threatened to develop as a result of the low prices which they were paying and the high prices which they charged in Europe. In essence, the Dutch were not seriously concerned with the economic development and welfare of their colonies, but rather with commerce in easily obtained goods that would give large returns.

The Dutch, again like the Portuguese, were faced with encroachments by states which had greater productive capacity at home and greater military and naval potential, namely, France and England. These powers were not successful in breaking the Dutch hold on the East Indies, but they did get established in India for what turned out to be the more profitable trade in Indian cotton goods and tea. Both these nations endeavored to create national monopolies of trade by using the system of private monopolistic companies, like the English East India Company (1600) and the French East India Company (1664). Like the Dutch, both were primarily interested in commerce rather than settlement and economic development. However, their attempts to get the lion's share of the trade brought them into a conflict that reduced French holdings in the East to a few minor ports (1763).

In the Western Hemisphere, mercantilist policies at first resembled those applied in the East, for the Spaniards' find of gold and silver stores provided articles of value for trade and the *conquistadores'* demands for supplies from home to allow them to rob the Indians more effectively created a market for Spanish goods. Thus Spain developed strict regulations so that it could reap all the benefits of trade. Not only did it require that all trade pass through control ports in Spain and America, as we have seen, but also that ships in the trade sail in fleets and that all foreigners should be kept out of colonial trade—a rule that broke down because of the need for slaves and the force of foreign powers. Although Spaniards introduced many European plants and animals into the New World, they did little to exploit the riches of their lands, except in the case of silver mining. They kept enterprising people like the Jews and Moors out of their colonies and granted land in large amounts to nobles and to missionaries, who had little stomach for the production of goods for commerce.

To be sure, eventually sugar and tobacco were grown in large quantities in Cuba, Haiti, and Santo Domingo, cattle were raised in the La Plata region, sheep in Peru, and indigo and cochineal for dyes in more tropical climes, but the economic life of all these regions was made miserable by Spanish rules pertaining to trade. For example, goods from what is now Argentina had for a long time to be transported over the Andes to Peru and thence northward and, along with all west coast products, across the Isthmus of Panama and then on to Spain. Worse perhaps, the Philippines were allowed to send only one ship a year to Mexico (Acapulco) for fear that too much silver would leak out in the China trade. This limitation on shipping not only restricted Spanish commerce in the Far East, but it hurt trade with Mexico. It meant that supplies in the Philippines ran dangerously low, that space on the ship was very dear, and that the transportation of goods was unnecessarily costly. Even in the West Indies and Central America the fleets sailed only twice a year, with the result that sugar and tobacco piled up, costs of warehousing were high, and shortages of European goods were periodic. Small wonder that colonial Spaniards traded with foreign smugglers to get rid of their produce and to secure the goods they needed at lower prices than they paid to their countrymen. New Englanders carried on a brisk trade with the Spanish West Indies; the Dutch broke through the Spanish colonial blockade so successfully that they had for a time what amounted to a monopoly of the Spanish cocoa trade. And when the English obtained the Asiento in 1713, they accomplished little more than getting legal recognition for what they had for a long time been doing illegally.

Only in the eighteenth century, when Spanish power was insufficient to maintain its colonial trade intact, did the Spaniards liberalize their regulations. By about 1740 individual vessels, called registered ships, were authorized to go to the colonies and to trade in any port. In 1764 a regular semimonthly mail service was established between Spain and the West Indies and La Plata. In 1765 trade was opened to all Spaniards; in 1775 they could trade in many ports in South America and after 1789 to all in Mexico. In 1778 the system of having all ships sent in fleets was abolished. These more liberal policies resulted in a considerable increase in the trade of Spanish America, but Spain was not to reap the full benefit from it, for in the early part of the nineteenth century, most of her American colonies were to fight for and to win their independence from a motherland that had given little serious consideration to their economic welfare.

The history of Portuguese policy in Brazil was not unlike the policies pursued by Spain in America. The Portuguese made grants to nobles of large estates, *capitánias,* which were fiefs of the Crown and which usually comprised 150 miles of coastline and an indefinite extension inland. The actual cultivation of the soil got under way slowly, but sugar was introduced in the sixteenth century and ultimately became a commercial crop for which the home demand was great—a crop which, incidentally, led to the bringing of the first Negro slaves to the New World. In the late seventeenth century the Portuguese began to push inland from the coast, for gold was found in the Minas Geraes districts in such quantities that in the eighteenth century Brazil accounted for nearly 80 percent of the world's production; diamonds were also discovered in such supply that Brazil was the main source of these stones until South African mines came into production in the late nineteenth century.

For a long time Portugal paid little attention to its American colony, although it endeavored, true to the principles of the "colonial compact," to reserve all of the trade with Brazil to itself. With the loss of their Eastern commerce and with the finding of gold and diamonds, however, the Portuguese began to take more interest in their possession, raising it in 1645 to the status of a principality with the eldest son of the King as Prince of Brazil, attempting to establish a monopoly of trade in gold, and making diamond mining a monopoly of the Crown. Because of their inferior military power, they were unable to keep out foreigners. The Dutch established themselves in Guiana, whence they traded with the colonists, and so threatened the entire possession that these interlopers had to be bought off with trading privileges in 1661. Finally, Portugal proved too small a power to hold Brazil. The colony declared its independence in 1822.

The Dutch in the New World pursued policies which were similar to those which they adopted in the East. Inasmuch as they were primarily a trading people, they acquired colonies largely for the purpose of carrying on commerce with the natives or of having bases whence they could conduct a smuggling business with the colonies of other powers. Netherlanders did not emigrate to any of their colonies in large numbers, and they showed relatively little enthusiasm for developing colonial agriculture. To be sure, sugar was grown in their West Indian islands, especially Curaçao, and grain was produced on the manors of the great patroons of Nieuw Amsterdam, but the main activity of the Dutch in the West Indies was trading with Spanish colonists, to whom they brought slaves, and in Nieuw Amsterdam, it was commerce with the Indians from whom they got furs in return for rum and supplies. They endeavored to give a monopoly of trade to the Dutch West India Company, which had some success from 1621 to 1648, but the nature of their commerce was more suitable for individual initiative than for the action of a large company. Unfortunately, Dutch citizens frequently pushed their enterprise rather far, with the result that the Netherlands was dragged into trouble with foreign powers—trouble that was augmented by rivalries within Europe. They had to leave Brazil, and they were forced out of Nieuw Amsterdam (1664) and out of a part of Guiana (1803) by the English. What remained to them was of little significance and the position of primacy which they had enjoyed in American trade gradually fell to the English and Americans.

As far as the French were concerned, they early realized how important colonies might be to their economy and, as we have seen, claimed Louisiana and Canada as a result of exploration and grabbed some of the less firmly held West Indian islands from Spain, notably Martinique, Guadeloupe, and Haiti. From the first, the French pursued colonial policies in the New World which conformed strictly to the basic principles of the colonial compact—that colonies existed exclusively for the benefit of the motherland and that trade should be reserved to French nationals. As in the East, so in the Western Hemisphere, the French attempted to control and develop their holdings by the creation of monopolistic companies. In the

West, however, these companies did not have great success: The monopoly of the French West India Company was withdrawn after five years, and the Company was liquidated between 1672 and 1674; the Canada Company and its successor, the Company of New France, had but brief existences, the latter passing from the scene in 1664. The necessity of developing production, the large capital investments required, and the lack of French emigration (there were only 7,000 white inhabitants of the French West Indies in 1642 and 3,000 in Canada in 1663) were greater handicaps than proprietary rule could cope with. From the third quarter of the seventeenth century onward, French holdings in the New World were governed as royal colonies, with the backing of the state at every turn.

In the course of time, the French were successful in getting production under way, particularly in the West Indies. Tobacco was grown there with success in the first half of the seventeenth century, and sugar, introduced in about 1640, became such an important commercial crop that the French islands became the veritable sugar bowl of France and of a large part of Europe as well. Then in Acadia, or Nova Scotia, as the English called it, a thriving fishing trade developed; in Canada, fur traders and to some extent lumbermen did a lively business. Even in Louisiana prospects were promising, with the establishment of a settlement in the Mississippi Delta in 1699 and the founding of New Orleans in 1713. In 1787, French trade with the New World was five times greater than its commerce with the East and comprised a little more than one-fifth of all French commerce.

Unfortunately for France, national rivalries for colonial trade were so acute that many of its overseas possessions were lost in the eighteenth century. The French had to surrender Acadia to the English in 1713 (they had obtained it in 1667). They ceded Louisiana to their ally, Spain, in compensation for the loss of Florida after the Seven Years' War (1763), and although Napoleon got it back in 1800, it was sold in 1803 to the United States. The French also gave up Canada to the English in 1763, retaining only two small islands off the coast, St. Pierre and Miquelon, and they lost Haiti during the Napoleonic period to native revolutionaries. They fell victim to the animosities engendered by the very policies of colonial mercantilism.

English colonial policy in the New World conformed, like that of other European nations, to the ideas contained in the colonial compact. As we have already seen, the Navigation Act of 1651 and subsequent measures reserved shipping between England and the colonies to English and colonial ships and required that many articles be exported exclusively to England and certain others be imported only from England. Furthermore, England paid bounties to stimulate production in the colonies of those goods which it lacked, like tar, pitch, hemp, masts, yards, and flax (1704), indigo (1749), potash (1751), and silk (1770).

In two important respects, however, English experience in the New World differed from that of its predecessors and profoundly influenced its colonial policy. First, Englishmen went to the colonies of North America as permanent settlers in fairly large numbers; the population of the thirteen colonies was 2 million in 1776. Secondly, these people in the New World, especially those of New England and the Middle Atlantic states, developed the production of many goods to which they were accustomed in the homeland rather than strictly "colonial" products. Not only did they consider themselves to be the equals of Englishmen at home and deserving of treatment equivalent to that of their fellow men in the old country, but they undertook the development of an economy that was to make them in certain respects commercial rivals of the English (Table 4). Therefore, when the English took steps to preserve the trading or manufacturing interests of some of their compatriots, the colonists felt sorely injured.

One of the fields in which the Americans had great success from early in their history was shipbuilding, for they had timbers for masts that were unequaled in the Old World and vast supplies of oak for frames and planking. In fact, on the eve of the American Revolution one-third of all ships flying the English flag had been built in America. Success in shipbuilding led directly to shipping, and American carriers, particularly those from New England, built up a lively shipping business, a flourishing

Table 4. Commerce of American continental colonies with England (annual averages, in thousands of pounds sterling, current value)

	Exports to England			Imports from England		
	1701–10	1731–40	1761–70	1701–10	1731–40	1761–70
New England	37	64	113	86	197	358
New York	10	16	62	28	92	349
Pennsylvania	12	14	35	9	52	295
Maryland-Virginia	205	394	468	128	207	491
Carolinas	14	177	330	22	94	262
Georgia			36		3	40

fishing fleet off the coasts of Massachusetts and Maine, and a thriving whaling industry throughout the Atlantic Ocean. In their carrying business, the Americans developed a trade in fish from New England and flour from the Middle Atlantic states to the West Indies, where these products were exchanged for sugar and molasses. The latter were brought back for refining and for the making of rum; then sugar and rum were carried to England, where they were sold so that manufactured goods could be paid for, or to Africa where they were swapped for Negroes for resale in the colonies. Moreover, American shippers carried tobacco and cotton from Virginia, South Carolina, and Georgia directly to England and brought back supplies for these colonies, but if they could not get a good return cargo, they simply sold their ships in England at a handsome profit and returned to begin all over again.

In all trade, except that to India, colonial vessels were treated as English ships, with all the same rights, privileges, and prerogatives, and they might even import wine as they would, for England had none for sale, and export flour freely, for England had at that time an abundant supply of the staff of life. But colonial shipping was hurt, especially that of New England, when the English West Indian planting interests decided Americans should not go to Spanish or French West Indian islands for sugar and molasses. Indeed, English sugar refining interests got into the Molasses Act of 1733 a heavy duty levied on *all* sugar and molasses going to the colonies on the ground that colonial sugar refining and rum making were hurting their business. In a similar way, many infant industries in the colonies were injured by legislation to protect the colonial market for English manufacturers. Thus the Woolens Act of 1699 forbade the transportation of wool, yarn, or woolen textiles from one colony to another. The Hat Act of 1731 forbade the export of hats (mainly beaver hats, which were then much in style) from one colony to another and a hatmaker from having more than two apprentices. The Iron Act of 1750 prevented the manufacture of iron and steel goods in America, although it permitted the free export of pig iron to England, and several laws prohibited colonies from aiding their own industries by means of subsidies.

For a time many of these rules were not rigidly enforced. Manufacturing developed in both New England and the Middle Atlantic colonies, while trade grew apace between England and the colonies (Table 5).

Table 5. English combined imports and exports
(Annual averages, in thousands of pounds sterling, current value)

	1701–1710	1731–1740	1761–1770
American continental	556	1,313	2,843
British West Indies	942	1,781	3,406
India	582	1,179	2,516
Ireland	579	1,045	2,850
Total Empire	2,802	5,751	12,651
Total Europe	7,673	10,555	11,740
Grand total	11,069	18,919	25,930

However, after the Seven Years' War, or the French and Indian War as it was called in America, the English took the position that the colonies should pay a part of the costs of the conflict that was waged for their protection and should not interfere with English economic development. Consequently, new taxes were levied and the older restrictions on colonial trade and manufacturing were enforced with some degree of rigidity. Thus the Stamp Act of 1765 required stamps on many documents in order to provide more revenue; the Sugar Act of 1764 reduced the rates contained in the Molasses Act, but these new rates were actually collected; and the Townshend Act of 1767 placed rates on several articles that were imported into the colonies. Such measures led to a great deal of bitterness, although it is clear that Americans profited by being members of the empire. In fact, one of the reasons why Scotland wanted to be united with England (1707) was to get the same privileges enjoyed by American shippers. Moreover, American commerce suffered after the Revolution because American ships no longer had the trading rights of English ships. Nevertheless, England lost what was to become the greatest economy of the world by a narrow policy that was derived directly from the colonial compact. Half a century later she repealed the Navigation Acts (1849) and gave her remaining colonies a greater degree of equality of treatment as far as economic development was concerned.

Two overriding issues govern historical discussions of mercantilism today. First, economic historians try to decide whether or not mercantilism was a "system"; that is, was there a consistent body of principles that mercantilist practitioners believed to be operative in the world, or, on the contrary, were the actions of mercantilists simply a series of *ad hoc* devices for bolstering state finances? Mercantilism varied so much, as we have seen, from country to country that if indeed there were a consistent underlying system, it is not easy to pick out. Second, the purpose of mercantilist policy is a matter of debate. Was it purely an economic adjunct to state-building, with the sole objective of increasing state power even at the expense of the general welfare? Or was mercantilism a policy of plenty which encouraged domestic productivity and a favorable balance of trade as sources of economic welfare?

"Mercantilism" is, it must be remembered, a historian's term. In the seventeenth century there was no International Mercantilist Association or "Journal of Mercantilist Theory." But this does not mean that mercantilism was unsystematic. In each of the national mercantilist experiences there were common tactical precepts. Emphasis varied from place to place. These precepts were:

1 International trade, *if properly conducted,* is a means to increasing the wealth of a state.

2 However, trade between nations in the long run is an antagonistic

relationship: somebody wins, somebody loses. To win is to achieve a net inflow of bullion; to lose is to pay out bullion.

3   Trade is a matter of national consequence, and so government participation is vital to direct the course of trade for national ends.

4   Colonial possessions are aids to winning wealth, either by direct exploitation of gold and silver mines (as in the Spanish example) or by providing a source of trade commodities (as in the cases of the Portuguese and Dutch) or by producing a market for trade (as in the English case).

On the relationship between wealth and power the economist Jacob Viner has formulated four tenets to which all mercantilist practitioners would likely have subscribed:

1   Wealth is essential for economic and political power.
2   Political power is essential to the acquisition or retention of wealth.
3   Wealth and power are each appropriate ends to national policy.
4   The separate aims of wealth and power are in the long run harmonious.[2]

To which we might add a fifth and final "law":

5   Wealth and power for a nation are essential for sustaining or improving the common weal.

The separate applications of mercantilist doctrine varied in emphasis, but all nations reasoned that power and wealth were united interests if for no other reason than that "money is the nerves of war." They saw that trade was the device for increasing wealth and that the welfare of individuals could not be improved in a poor and weak nation.

How does this doctrine differ from what came before and what followed after? To some degree the emphasis on bullion as the ultimate measure of wealth remains a special feature of the period although, as we have seen, the English de-emphasized it (and modern America is very concerned about it in the 1970s, as in the gold-drain problem). More important than bullionism is the mercantilist view of trade as a highly competitive game played on a national level with winners and losers. In Medieval Italy and Flanders trade was a matter between people or companies, not nations. Even in the late 1500s, when Venice knew very well that her livelihood depended on trade, her posture *vis-à-vis* competitors in the Mediterranean was essentially noncompetitive, and this cost her a hegemony in trade of 500 years standing.

---

[2] Jacob Viner, "Power versus Plenty as Objectives of Foreign Policy in the Seventeenth and Eighteenth Centuries," in *World Politics*, vol. 1, 1948, p. 10. Reprinted by permission of Princeton University Press.

What finally overthrew mercantilism as a doctrine was the intellectual defeat of the view of trade as antagonism. The idea that international trade meant mutual benefit, even for a net importing country, was the succeeding theory. This view became an integral part of Classical Economic Thought and the economic theory of Modern Times.

The modernization
of the Western
economy

The setting of the
Industrial Revolution

The Industrial Revolution: a revised view

In historical study, as in all branches of knowledge, views of certain periods or of certain developments sometimes become established in a wave of exaggerated statement and must subsequently be revised in the light of more sober judgment, more thorough analysis, and more abundant data. Thus it has been with the Industrial Revolution.

Time was when this great movement was considered to have been a very sudden transition in the production of industrial goods from handicraft to machine methods. This rapid change was conceived as having resulted from the invention of a few mechanical devices, especially textile machines and the steam engine—and that these inventions leaped full-blown from the heads of geniuses, all of whom were English. Above all, this earlier view gave the impression that industrialization happened in a historical instant, turning England into an island of mills and mill workers, and that the "Revolution" ended sometime in the nineteenth century.

In the course of time this conception of the Industrial Revolution, based as it was on a tendency to intensify the dramatic elements of a period of rapid change, came to be tempered by a more judicious appraisal of what took place, by a fuller knowledge of events, and by a more complete understanding of technological and social change. Now economic historians recognize that what we used to know as the Industrial Revolution is really only a part (though a very major part) of a long-term transformation in the life of man that has been more powerful and all-pervasive than any previous technological revolution. For want of a better term we call this transformation "modernization."

The changes that modernization wrought seem almost too numerous to catalog. If we limit ourselves to major economic changes and their closest correlates, we might enumerate the characteristics of European modernization as follows:

1   Industrialization—This represents the change from domestic or small-shop manufacturing to factory production for mass markets. Manufacturing now involves large amounts of capital equipment (relative to labor) and the mobilization of power sources of greater magnitude than was imagined possible before. Industrialization entails a skilled and disciplined labor force.

2   Urbanization—Associated with the concentration of industry in high-density units, like factories, is the shift of population from the relative dispersion of the agrarian village or small town to the metropolis. Large cities have existed, and do exist still, in the absence of modernization; but only when a preponderance of the population lives in cities and when cities exert a greater influence on society than rural areas does urbanization becomes a reality. This is a purely modern characteristic.

3   Revolution in agriculture—The support of a preponderantly urban population necessarily requires an agricultural sector with tremendous productivity, such that a minority of workers (less than 1 in 10 in modern America) can feed the cities. The crucial step in agrarian progress, the total elimination of fallow, was the major element in modernizing agriculture. The introduction of capital equipment, chemical fertilization, and new crops into European farming were important improvements, but they depended in turn on the preconditions of increased plot size and a fuller work year to be effective.

4   Incomes—Modernization implies higher per capita real incomes. The manifold increase in output of a modern economy, unless somehow demolished, given away, or kept by a very few, must ultimately redound to the population in the form of greater material wealth. Although in the short run investment in modernizing industry might involve sacrifices, the most basic characteristic of a modern country is the increased income level and improved standard of living of the population.

5   Demographic transition—We know from studying pre-Modern Europe that major changes in real income do not leave population growth unaffected. Since the beginnings of economic modernization the world's population has grown approximately fourfold (see Table 1, p.52). In industrial countries rising real income and improvements in the technology of health care, sanitation, and the control of disease depress mortality rates and encourage fertility. The result: a population explosion. Only as modern economies mature and city life becomes expensive (particularly for large families) does the impulse emerge for population growth to subside. We know as well that the growth of population has powerful conse-

quences for the economy. A growing labor supply can be an important source of growth. The mass market is the prime source of demand for modernizing agriculture, manufacturing, and service sectors.

6   Capitalism and the market economy—In European modernization the mobilization of economic resources (labor, capital, land, raw materials, entrepreneurial talent, and technical expertise) was accomplished by markets. There have always been market mechanisms of some sort, however rudimentary, but never before have they so thoroughly determined every aspect of man's life. Employment and wages now no longer depend on the occupation of one's father or on the traditions of artisan guilds, but rather on the supply and demand for labor, conditions which may change from year to year or even month to month with disconcerting abruptness. The communality of the pre-modern village ended as modernity spread. Ownership of the economy's physical resources concentrated into the hands of the urban middle class. The political revolutions of the late eighteenth and mid nineteenth centuries ended the privileges enjoyed by the aristocracy of the *ancien régime* and gave over to the middle class a position of political power commensurate with the new economic preeminence of the *bourgeoisie.*

7   Costs and sacrifices—low mortality rates and high levels of material wealth have their costs, like everything else. To attain them, modern society has paid dearly. The concentration and noisomeness of city life are the price of centralized production. The growth of suburban living in mature, modern countries is at best an expensive compromise. Spoiled land, fouled air, and poisoned waters have become by-products of industrial civilization because the market economy has placed a low premium on their preservation.

Despite a steady decline in the work week in the past century in advanced countries, modernization still entails a sacrifice of free time that rural societies enjoyed. The discipline of the factory (and the office) will not stand for periods of idleness. Social cohesiveness has been sacrificed for mobility, a requirement for the efficient allocation of labor. Often the results are alienation and destruction of social ties.

Obviously our brief catalog is not meant to be exhaustive; each point will receive fuller attention later on. Our list is offered at this point only as a prologue to indicate that the economic history of the industrial period is many times more complicated than the story of the spinning jenny and the steam engine alone.[1]

---

[1] A more thorough attempt at cataloging the correlates of economic modernization is to be found in Simon Kuznets, *Modern Economic Growth: Rate, Structure, and Spread* (New Haven, Conn.: Yale, 1966).

The desire for material betterment; savings and investments

However much economic historians may have altered their descriptions and analyses of the Industrial Revolution, they have all agreed that here was a movement entailing extraordinary economic growth. At no previous time of equal length in all human history had there been such a rapid increase in the production of goods per capita of the working force. Inasmuch as we are here confronted with the problem of economic growth, we are concerned with the same kinds of factors which we have seen contribute to economic development at other periods of time, namely, with the strengthening of ideologies for material improvement, with a growth in savings and investments, with an increase in effective market demand, with innovations in the productive arts, and with a dramatic increase in population which began before the revolution in production took place and continued long afterward.

Evidence of a greater desire for economic improvement was to be found on every hand. New men of wealth, dubbed "bourgeois" because, as we have seen in the growth of towns, those with recently acquired riches lived in the bourgs, were attaining higher prestige in society. Although Molière could poke fun at these late arrivals on the top rung of the economic ladder, the fact was that their positions of economic power gave them a considerable amount of authority in all walks of life. In the Netherlands, the chief patrons of the arts came from among the new men of wealth; from the late seventeenth century the chief subject matter of Dutch artists was scenes from bourgeois life, if not the bourgeois themselves. In England the Whig party, which drew its strength from the middle class, dominated the political life of the country from the ministry of Robert Walpole until near the end of the century.

In France, practically all the philosophers of the Age of Reason, like Voltaire, Jean Jacques Rousseau, and Diderot, came from the bourgeois class and in a subtle way preached the wisdom of material improvement. They argued that there were laws of society, just as there were of the physical universe, and they proceeded to tell mankind what they were. One of these laws was that man wanted to be happy, which is the traditional position of the hedonist. A second was that man had natural "rights," of which life, liberty, and property were the most fundamental. And a third was that in order to enjoy the good life, to be happy, man had to have wealth which he could accumulate and use, unfettered by tradition of man-made law. Here were the expression of an ideology, a means of attaining it, and an attack upon privilege.

A desire for material improvement came not only from such reasoning or from the observation that the bourgeois were assuming a more important position in public life, but also from the fact that almost the only way for a commoner to rise in a society dominated by a nobility that inherited its position was by acquiring wealth. It was only with money that titles of nobility could be acquired for themselves; and only with large dowries that they could marry off their daughters into the caste above.

That the ideology for material well-being was becoming more firmly established is evidenced by efforts to abolish laws and destroy traditions that prevented some persons from engaging in the more lucrative trades. Thus nobles gradually freed themselves from rules which forbade them from engaging in certain kinds of manufacturing and trade on danger of losing their titles. Artisans sought to break into monopolies of others, which led to a weakening of guilds. And entrepreneurs tried to sell to an ever-larger market in order to increase their earnings, which meant that they wanted the tariff unification of national states and the abolition of governmental grants of special privileges.

Then, too, the desire for material improvement was intensified by the development of special groups which formed because their members were thrown together in their efforts to better their lot. One of the most important of these groups was composed of those who left the countryside and went to live in cities, for they would not have made the change if they had not been highly motivated to acquire riches of this earth. Another group of the same kind was composed of those who broke their ties with their homelands and set out for wild and poorly known colonies overseas. Indeed, one of the reasons why the ideology for material betterment has been so strong in American life has been because the act of migration meant an autoselection of those who were urgently bent upon improving their economic status.

Finally, it seems that the desire for economic well-being grew *pari passu* with opportunities for economic growth, as had been the case so frequently in the past. Thus, as industrialization offered ever-greater opportunities for getting a larger supply of this world's goods per capita, everybody wanted more. Here was a two-way action in which the ideology for economic improvement contributed to economic development, and economic development fostered a desire for material betterment.

One of the branches of economic activity in which this reciprocal play of forces was most visible was savings and investment. In their desire to get on in the world, many people showed a willingness, if not even an anxiety, to put aside some of their earnings in order to invest in producers' goods that would make them still better off in the future. In some quarters, as among Calvinists in many lands and as among the colonists in America, leaders vigorously preached the virtue of thrift. One manifestation of this concern was the founding of mutual aid societies or, as they were called in England, "friendly societies," which were formed by individuals to help fellow members out in times of financial adversity. Estimates indicate that

England had some 7,000 such organizations in 1801 with 600,000 members. True savings banks also began to appear, the first one in England dating from 1804 and seventy coming into existence by 1817.

To those who were not accustomed to the amenities of life, a small improvement in their standard of living gave so much satisfaction that they were able to save income above a minimum of increased expenditures. In his quotations upon the diary of Samuel Walker of Rotherham, T.S. Ashton has given us an example of this phenomenon from an early stage of capital accumulation in industry:[2]

"1741. In or about October or November of the same year, Saml. and Aaron Walker built an Air Furnace in the old nailer's smithy, on the back-side of Saml. Walker's cottage at Grenoside, making some small additions thereto, and another little hutt or two, slating with sods etc., with a small Garth walled in: and after rebuilding the chimney or stacks once, and the furnace once or more, began to proceed a little, Saml. Walker teaching the school at Grenoside, and Aaron Walker making nails and moving and shearing, etc., part of his time.

"1743. Aaron Walker now began to be pretty much imploy'd, and had 4 shillings a week to live upon. . . .

"1745. This year Saml. Walker, finding business increase, was obliged to give up his school, and built himself a house at the end of the old cottage, then thought he was fixed for life; then we allowed ourselves ten shillings a week each for wages to maintain our families."

At this time the value of the concern was put at £400. But in the following year £100 was added by Jonathan Walker (a brother of Samuel and Aaron), £50 by John Crawshaw (who had previously been employed "as much as we could, at 12 pence per day"), and £50 by Samuel himself. Thus equipped, the partners set up at Masborough first a casting house and then, in 1748, a steel furnace. The story that Samuel Walker rose to fortune by stealing from Huntsman the secret of crucible steel has no foundation: it was not by such methods, but by unremitting labour, thrift and integrity that success was achieved. Year after year some addition, great or small, was made to the plant. In 1754 a warehouse was built, and a keel—characteristically called *The Industry*—was put on the river. Four years later the partners dug "a navigable cut" and "improved the road for Holmes to Masbro' and lanes towards Tinsley —Gloria Deo"; and in 1764 they added to their establishment "a large shop for frying pan makers." It was not, apparently, until 1757, when the stock had reached £7,500, that the Walkers allowed themselves a

[2] T. S. Ashton, *The Industrial Revolution 1760–1830* (London: Oxford, 1948), pp. 95–97.

dividend of £140; and throughout, the proportion of the profit that was distributed remained small. Thus it came about that by 1774 the capital had reached £62,500. Profits on the manufacture of guns during the American War, ploughed back as they were, had, by 1782, raised the figure to £128,000. In this year Samuel Walker died, but the policy laid down by him was continued by his heirs, and in 1812 the assets of Samuel Walker & Co. were estimated at £299,015, and those of a sister concern, Walker and Booth, at a further £55,556.

The case of the Walkers was not an isolated one. Many of the entrepreneurs of the Industrial Revolution came from families of the lower middle class, began as workmen, established their first enterprises from very modest amounts of capital, some of which may have been borrowed or provided by partners, and built their fortunes by plowing back their profits into manufacturing. Robert Owen, the great cotton manufacturer and the founder of a social reform movement based on community living and cooperatives, was the son of a saddler. He began his rise to fame and fortune as a workman and successful manager of a cotton mill. His initial capital came from a 100-pound loan from his brother, the plowing back of profits, and partnerships with established businessmen. James Watt, the inventor of the steam engine, was the son of a small merchant. He became a watch maker and what would be called today a laboratory technician at the University of Glasgow. He undertook the development of a steam engine with a small loan from a friend and continued by means of partnerships. And Richard Arkwright, the inventor of power-driven spinning and carding machines, was originally a barber, and got his capital from a loan from a friend and from a partnership with an established producer of hosiery.

In addition to the financing of economic growth with the capital of those who found saving easy because their increased earnings greatly exceeded what they were accustomed to spend on living and besides the plowing of business profits back into plant, economic development was also furthered by capital amassed by banks through deposits and earnings on loans. In England a network of country banks existed, managed by persons who intimately knew local entrepreneurs and were willing to provide credit to those whom they believed to be responsible businessmen and good risks. The main assistance which they gave was to discount bills, which allowed many a merchant to operate on bank capital and to pay manufacturers at once for goods delivered. Moreover, these banks issued bank notes of small denominations, which provided much of the necessary medium of exchange not furnished by the Bank of England, which still issued bank notes of large denominations. Then, there was capital acquired from land rents that went especially into certain types of undertakings, like coal mining in England, that were closely connected with land ownership. Capital amassed in commerce often went into productive equipment, as in certain branches of the putting-out system. There was capital, too, accumulated from small investors through the sale of shares. And there was capital gathered together through the collection of taxes, some of which got into the hands of investors in sizable amounts because it was paid out to the holders of large blocks of state bonds.[3]

The factors that induced the owners of these accumulations to invest their moneys in large amounts in industrial enterprises are extremely complicated. In the last analysis the chief reason was that high and relatively sure profits were to be expected from industrial undertakings. The new machines seemed to make possible a dramatic reduction in costs of production, and because of population growth, the market for industrial goods seemed to increase continuously. Moreover, a secular rise in prices from at least the middle of the eighteenth century to after the Napoleonic Wars gave a certain buoyancy to economic activity. Yet the rise in price and the failure of real wages to keep pace with this increase (a situation of "profit inflation") seems to have been of greater advantage to the farmer than to the industrialist and to have had more of an effect in agriculture than in industry.

Whatever the reasons for investments in industry may have been, however, it is clear that capital for investment was becoming more abundant and that it could be had cheaply if governments did not bid up interest rates by their own borrowing. In the case of England the legal rate was lowered, following market conditions, from 10 to 8 percent in 1625, to 6 percent in 1651, to 5 percent in 1714, and to 3 percent on "consols," or the consolidated debt of the kingdom, in 1757. In businesses with good credit ratings interest charges seem to have followed a somewhat parallel course, 5 percent having been common at the beginning of the eighteenth century and 3 percent in 1756. It is undoubtedly safe to conclude with T.S. Ashton: "The deep mines, solidly built factories, well constructed canals, and substantial houses of the industrial revolution were the products of relatively cheap capital."

Exactly what the increase in the formation of reproducible or man-made capital was during the Industrial Revolution and when that increase took place are difficult questions to answer because of the inadequacy of our statistical information. The best evidence available indicates that for England about 5 percent of national income was being invested by 1850. Inasmuch as the population of England and Wales rose by 50 percent

---

[3] This was true, at least in the case of England, where the public debt mounted to 861 million pounds in 1815, which has been established to have been 8 percent of the money income of the country. In the case of France, amounts of the tax leases to tax farmers almost doubled from 1726 to 1786.

between 1751 and 1801, the volume of trade increased threefold, and real national income probably went up by 200 percent, the rate of investment would have had to go up by 50 percent just to keep the capital stock at a level with population and would have had to double to account for an increase in national income. By 1800 the rate of investment seems to have been 6 percent of national income. The big spurt forward came with the building of railways.[4]

Market demand; labor supply

Although savings and investments are considered by many students of the Industrial Revolution to have been the most strategic factors in breaking down the rigidities of traditional methods of industrial production, the fact remains that people were motivated to save and to invest because they expected thereby to better their material conditions. Furthermore, it is clear that their expectations depended in large part upon an increase in the effective demand for certain goods—upon a market in which there was both a growing desire for goods and a growing ability to pay current prices for them.

The reasons for an expansion of demand were numerous. In the first place, population increased in all the countries of Western Europe. In France the number of inhabitants is said to have gone up from 20 million in 1700 to 26 million in 1789; in the Holy Roman Empire to have increased from 20 million in 1700 to 27 million in 1800; and in England and Wales to have gone up from 5 million in 1700, to 6 million in 1750, to nearly 9 million in 1801, when the first census was taken, and to 13 million in 1831. For all of Great Britain the population was 11 million in 1801 and 16 million in 1831.

The reasons for these increases in population are not clear and have recently been the object of considerable controversy and research. In part, they came from a reduction in the death rate, which for England went from 35.8 per thousand in the decade 1730–1740 to 21 per thousand for the decade 1811–1821. It seems likely that improved income levels and diet brought about by agricultural advances exerted the strongest influence by reducing mortality in the following ways:

1   Famines became less severe, and fewer persons starved in times of dearth.

---

[4] Phyllis Deane, *The First Industrial Revolution* (London: Cambridge, 1965), pp. 153–156; and Phyllis Deane, "Capital Formation in Britain before the Railway Age," *Economic Development and Cultural Change* (April 1961).

2   Year-round cropping provided a buffer against the impact of a single harvest failure or seasonal shortages.

3   Better diet meant lower infant and child mortality.

4   Improved real income meant that mortality-related goods, such as medicines, soap, plumbing, and sanitary facilities, became easier to afford.

5   Income gains in agriculture were, in some proportion, invested in social overhead capital (highways, canals, hospitals) which, too, affected the chance for survival of the sick and infirm.

It has been argued that the advances in medical techniques of the eighteenth century in England were the main cause of the first of the world's demographic transformations. But, in fact, the net results of new types of preventive therapy, advances in anatomic knowledge and surgical methods, and the advent of lying-in hospitals were, on the whole, slight. Hospitals served principally to isolate the contagious, and the effect of new treatments on morbidity was significant but of insufficient magnitude to engender the population boom.[5] It is also probable that at least part of England's episode of population increase was due to increases in fertility, though it is uncertain whether this effect was more powerful than the drop in the death rate as a cause of the demographic revolution. Higher real income and job opportunities on and off the land meant relative ease in setting up households and an increased ability to support larger families. This favorable condition prevailed in the English labor market until the last decade of the eighteenth century.

At all events, the increase in population meant that, given stable patterns of consumption, the need for goods went up in proportion to these increases. Thus in England demand doubled in the last half of the eighteenth century just because more people had come into existence. Perhaps demand was, in fact, more than doubled because the increase was so large that the increment could not be absorbed in existing housing and because new housing, particularly in cities, resulted in extensive building of public services, like roads. The larger number of young people meant an increase demand for clothing and food.

In Western Europe prices went up, reacting to the greater demand for goods and to an increased supply of precious metals resulting from new mining enterprises in Brazil. In fact, prices rose in France from an index of 100 in the period 1726–1741 to 164 in the years 1785–1789 and in England from 100 in the 1750s to 130 for the years 1790–1795. The rise in prices, particularly for agricultural products, put pressure on agriculturalists to

[5] T. McKeown and R. G. Brown, "Medical Evidence Related to English Population Changes in the Eighteenth Century, " reprinted in the valuable collection of essays, *Population in Industrialization,* Michael Drake (Ed.) (London: Methuen, 1969).

produce more and made competition for the ownership of land keener than ever. This explains in large part why a new enclosure movement got under way in England, why the peasants in France wanted clear title to the lands which they had had a traditional right to cultivate, and why tensions developed between peasants and manorial lords that were one aspect of the French Revolutionary period.

The growth of population had, as we have seen, a direct effect upon the textile trades because of the need for additional cloth, and upon building because of the need for more lodgings. Furthermore, the market demand for cotton textiles was increased by a style rage for cotton prints in the "Persian" or "Indian" manner, for interior decoration, for calicoes for ladies' wear, and for cotton sheets that began to replace linen on the beds of the gentry.

As Daniel Defoe wrote in 1708:[6]

We saw our persons of quality dressed in Indian Carpets, which, but a few years before, their chambermaids would have thought too ordinary for them; the chintzes were advanced from lying on their floors to their backs, from the foot cloth to the petticoat, and even the Queen herself at that time was pleased to appear in China and Japan, I mean China silks and calicoes. Nor was this all, but it crept into our houses, our closets and bedchambers; curtains, cushions, chairs, and at last, beds themselves were nothing but calicoes or Indian stuffs.

For its part, the demand for housing was augmented by the shift of population to cities, the creation of new cities around textile manufacturing plants and ports, and the movement of the wealthy from older sections of cities that were becoming blighted to new sections, as in the case of Paris. In England, completely new rural communities came into being to take care of peasants forced off their holdings by enclosures, and in France and the Low Countries new houses were constructed upon land that was being reclaimed from forest and sea to grow the food needed by the greater numbers of people.

The building of houses created a new market for builders' hardware, iron and steel tools, and construction equipment, thus giving a fillip to the iron and steel industries. This stimulus was fortified by a wave of canal and road building that meant a great demand for picks and shovels for stone drills and sledges, wheelbarrows, and equipment for canal locks. Finally, the struggle between England and France for colonial possessions and domination of the seas, the American Revolution, the French Revolution-

---

[6] Defoe, *Weekly Review,* January 1708.

ary Wars, and the Napoleonic conflicts meant an enormous increase in demand for munitions, ammunition, and naval fittings.

Another important consideration regarding the development of the market was that demand came to be concentrated on fewer producers. The urban dweller had a larger choice of persons to whom he might go to satisfy his wants and he tended to go to those who sold at lowest prices. Moreover, managers of big undertakings, like those in charge of the construction of a canal or the fitting out of a ship, and officers in quartermasters' corps preferred to deal with a few suppliers rather than with a multitude. This fact, and the great improvement in transportation owing to canal, road, and port construction, made possible a greater specialization of production by regions and by plants than had ever been possible before. During the Industrial Revolution in England the cotton textile industry became concentrated in Lancashire, iron production in the west Midlands, and salt refining along the coasts from Durham to Cheshire.

From overseas markets there came also an increased demand for goods, a greater specialization in products, and from the very nature of foreign trade an ever greater concentration of orders on a few merchants and from them, in turn, on a few producers. The tonnage moving through English ports increased, for example, over six times from 1700 to 1800 and the value of French trade, which on the eve of the French Revolution was about the same as the English, is said to have gone up from 215 million livres in 1716 to 1,153 million livres in 1787.[7] Thus the pressure of foreign demand on producers per capita in England was exceptionally great, for, as we have seen, the population of France was at this time nearly three times that of England and Wales. Some idea of the impact of foreign commerce on industrial production can be gleaned from Table 6, which indicates for the eighteenth and early nineteenth centuries a tendency for foreign trade to "lead" or grow faster than industrial production. In fact, for this period, the generalization is frequently made that commercial growth came before the development of new techniques of industrial production, although the reciprocal relations between commerce and industry were obviously very close.

The impact of increases in foreign commerce on industry was particularly great because of the great concentration of trade in certain goods. Thus in Great Britain in the years 1814–1817, the first for which pertinent records are available, 78 percent of all English home-produced exports were finished goods, and of these about 75 percent were textiles and 8

---

[7] Arnould, *De la balance du commerce* (Paris, 1791). An increase of some four times if adjustments are made for price changes. Also B. R. Mitchell and Phyllis Deane, *Abstract of British Historical Statistics* (London: Cambridge, 1962), pp. 278–281.

percent metal products, especially those made from iron. In the years 1814–1845, 70.4 percent of net imports, that is, imports including re-exports, were raw materials, and of this amount about half was destined

Table 6. Total British overseas trade and industrial production, 1700–1933 (1913 = 100)

Years	Total overseas trade	Industrial production	Index of relationship
1700–1709	0.5	1.3	38.5
1710–1719	0.6	1.4	42.9
1720–1729	0.8	1.6	50.0
1730–1739	0.9	1.7	52.9
1740–1749	0.9	1.7	52.9
1750–1759	1.0	2.0	50.0
1760–1769	1.3	2.0	65.0
1770–1779	1.4	2.4	58.3
1780–1789	1.5	3.1	48.4
1790–1799	2.4	4.3	55.8
1800–1809	3.4	5.9	57.6
1810–1819	4.3	7.2	59.7
1820–1829	5.3	10.0	53.0
1830–1839	7.5	14.7	51.0
1840–1849	11.2	20.2	55.4
1850–1859	19.0	28.3	67.1
1860–1869	27.3	36.1	75.6
1870–1879	41.4	48.1	86.1
1880–1889	55.3	58.1	92.2
1890–1899	67.1	68.1	98.5
1900–1909	80.8	80.3	100.6
1910–1913	94.8	91.8	103.3
1914–1918	74.3	88.4	84.0
1918–1926	85.1	81.9	103.9
1927–1929	103.1	100.8	102.3
1930–1933	86.2	94.1	91.6

SOURCE: Werner Schlote, *British Overseas Trade* (Oxford: Blackwell, 1952), p. 51.

for textile processing. In France, this kind of concentration of goods that were in mass demand and could be turned out in greater quantity by the aid of machines was less great, for the French specialized in the exportation of luxuries, art products, foods, and wines; yet even there the growth of textiles was marked and was to become more so as the nineteenth century advanced. From early in this process of industrialization, European states, which were to be in the vanguard of economic development, were to make goods for mass markets, were to import raw materials and foodstuffs, and were to process raw materials so that they could export finished products. It was in this manner that the industrial states of Western Europe came to be known as the workshop of the world.

The labor force

In any consideration of the great complex of factors which combined with a timing and in proportions that were propitious for effecting changes in industrial techniques, serious attention must be given to the labor force. It was necessary to have workers who were willing to be employed for money wages, who were capable of operating the new machines, and who were numerous enough to meet the demand of employers.

Until recently, historians of the Industrial Revolution were of the opinion that England was particularly forward in this regard. They pointed to the fact that the peasants, who had been forced off the land by enclosures, were now without land by which to maintain themselves and were so desperate for work that they would have taken a job from the devil himself.

This view has now been boldly challenged. Although English landlords did deprive peasants by enclosures of those holdings which they had long had the right to work and thereby took from large numbers of farmers their customary means of making a living, scholars now believe that most of those who were pushed off their holdings did not flock immediately to the industrial cities. Most of them settled in "new villages" and sought employment on enclosed farms, on reclaimed lands, on canal construction jobs, or on road-building projects.[8]

The view now held is that in the early history of the Industrial Revolution no great difficulty was experienced in finding an adequate supply of labor, irrespective of whether land reforms pushed peasants off the land or, as in France, attached peasants more firmly to their holdings. The increase in population meant that more persons were entering the labor force and were seeking jobs than could find profitable employment on the land. Even in the case of enclosures in England, it is probable that children of those who settled in the "new villages" could not always find work on the enclosed farms and eventually drifted off to the cities. Furthermore, a good many persons in the agrarian society of the last part of the eighteenth and early part of the nineteenth century were underemployed, and their departure from the land was not severely felt.

The structure of the English labor force was notable in one vital respect: Even before industrialization, a larger-than-normal percentage of the work force was engaged in nonagrarian pursuits. While it was usual in the seventeenth century for 9 out of 10 European workers to be engaged in

[8] J. D. Chambers, "Enclosure and Labor Supply in the Industrial Revolution," *The Economic History Review,* ser. 2, vol. 5, no. 3, pp. 319ff., 1953.

agriculture, in Britain at that time only 6 out of 10 were so employed. By 1801 the proportion of the work force employed in the agrarian sector had been reduced to one-third (and by 1951 to a mere 5 percent). This proclivity for specialization outside of agriculture was Britain's single greatest head start to modernization.

Just what real wages were in industry in the early Industrial Revolution has been the subject of considerable controversy. Although available data do not permit us to make categorical statements on the issue, some fragmentary evidence about living standards can be ventured. It would seem that during the earliest phase of economic expansion in the eighteenth century gains in per capita real income were made. Increases in national income as a result of increased productivity in agriculture were large, and patterns of consumption indicate broadly based improvement in living standards. Bread and vegetables, the staples of the lower-class diet, were plentiful, and prices remained stable until the last decades of the century in England. From about 1790 through the mid-nineteenth century English standards of living seem to have taken a turn for the worse. Although average real wages did not decline, according to such indications as we have, patterns of consumption reflected an inability of the urban masses to sustain living levels. Per capita meat and vegetable consumption declined, and the quality of urban housing deteriorated, and the problem of urban poverty was at its worst. It has been hypothesized that the benefits of high productivity in the industry had been nullified by the increase in population (7.5 million to 18 million between 1780 and 1850 in Britain). In England, as on the Continent, beginning in about the mid-nineteenth century, there was a consistent and undeniable upward movement of all indicators of living standards so that by the first decades of the twentieth century there could be no doubt that, except in backward regions, the entire population of Europe was living on a new plateau of economic prosperity.

In the early phase of modernization, real wages in industry, although somewhat higher than in agriculture, remained low enough and the supply of labor remained elastic enough so that early industrial entrepreneurs could estimate with some certainty what labor at what costs would be available to them. They could assume, further, that labor would work some fourteen hours a day for six days a week, which would mean a high utilization of plant, and would work with a regularity never before seen in the West. Moreover, in the early stage of industrialization no intermediary institutions, either governments or labor unions, stood between employers and their work force. Strikes or bargaining for higher wages was unknown. Until their repeal in 1825, the Combination Acts of 1799–1800 in England forbade trade unions. The Le Chapelier Law of 1791 in France outlawed trade unions until 1864. Similar legislation kept workers weak in most other countries.[9]

Undoubtedly the presence of an abundant labor force which earned more in agriculture than was being paid was a boon to industrial growth, for the extremely poor cannot buy goods which are placed on the market. If a growing demand from industrial labor had not existed, those who had surplus for investment would have been more reticent than they were to invest in productive enterprise. On the other hand, some shortage of labor in the face of growing demand seems to have encouraged the adoption of new ways of doing things—the introduction of more machines.[10] Indeed, in the United States where there has traditionally been a dearth of labor, the major characteristic of inventions has been devices to take the place of labor or to make labor more efficient, as is evidenced by the cotton gin, the assembly line, and "automation."

In every discussion of the supply of workers in the Industrial Revolution, one must take into consideration another aspect of the question, that labor was becoming much more mobile than it had been for centuries. With the breakdown of feudalism and the manorial system, workers in Western Europe were no longer legally bound to the soil, but were free to seek their fortunes where they pleased. With the adoption of the same machines in many places, techniques were standardized enough so that a worker could easily adapt himself to the requirements of employment in many places, and with improvements in transportation, especially by water, workers could travel at relatively low cost to seek jobs in distant places. Indeed, with the Industrial Revolution one of the greatest "movements of population" of all times took place, with people moving to cities chiefly within the same linguistic area, across the Atlantic to the New World, and in North America from the Eastern seaboard to the sites of mineral deposits, water power, and transportation centers further inland.

Although it is now thought that the enclosure movement gave England and Scotland no marked advantage over other lands in the matter of sheer numbers of workers available for employment, these two countries seem to have had a jump on all others in that their workers were freer than those anywhere except in the American Colonies from the confining restriction of guild regulations. In fact, in England most of the guilds in those industries in which mechanization was the most pronounced, that is, in the textile and metallurgical trades, had long since relaxed their rules, so that many workers could attain the full development of their potentialities and experiment with new methods of production.

[9] For a very judicious, up-to-date, and impartial discussion of real wages during the Industrial Revolution, see Phyllis Deane, *The First Industrial Revolution*, chaps. 9 and 15. Also see bibliography, p. 541.

[10] See the discussion of this point by H. J. Habbakuk, *American and British Technology in the Nineteenth Century: The Search for Labour-saving Inventions* (London: Cambridge, 1962).

Moreover, in England and in America payment on a piece basis, especially in the putting-out system, provided an incentive for workers to introduce improvements in their operations so that they could earn more. On the Continent, on the other hand, labor's range of opportunities was much more limited, for guilds continued in existence, for a long time successfully maintained opposition to new industries (cotton prints were not permitted in France until 1759), and curbed the development of the putting-out system.

Furthermore, England seems to have had some advantage in industrialization through having a relatively large body of moderately well-trained workers to run the new machines. Inasmuch as England and Scotland had thriving textile and metallurgical trades before the advent of machines and inasmuch as the first machines employed skills that were very close to those used in handicraft production, there were many workers who could move without delay into the operation of machines. In this connection, one should take note of the fact that in the spread of machine technology, those techniques which moved most rapidly and most easily to new areas were those which were close to handicraft techniques, in part because they could be used by workers with their handicraft skills. This was especially noticeable in the field of textiles, the new machines being the first of English inventions to be adopted by France, the first to make important headway in the United States, particularly in New England, and the first to be taken in by underdeveloped areas, such as Italy in the second round of industrial diffusion, especially after the middle of the nineteenth century, and in India, in the third round, especially after 1900.

But the greatest advantage which the United Kingdom possessed in the matter of labor was a goodly supply of workers at the most advanced technical levels. From the very outset of the Industrial Revolution a premium was placed upon men who could construct the new machines, repair them when they broke down, and make such complicated preparations for their use as setting warps in intricate patterns on mechanical looms.

Apparently the supply of labor with the highest skills was greatest where interest in investigation was most intense, where primary education was most widely developed, and where mechanical contrivances were widely enough developed to provide opportunities for advanced training. Although the study of "natural philosophy" was being greatly expanded in the British Isles, on the Continent, and in America during the eighteenth century, although new schools were being established to give instruction to the children of the merchant classes, and although some new industrial techniques were developed in France as well as in England, the British were undoubtedly leaders in all these respects. The universities of Glasgow and Edinburgh had no peer in matters of scientific inquiry and experimentation in the late eighteenth century and it was more than mere chance that James

Watt, a laboratory assistant at the former institution, should have become familiar with the expansive force of steam and the problems of its utilization as a prime mover in industry. The Scottish system of primary education was the best and most widely diffused of any in Western culture, and nonconformist academies adopted curricula that for the age were heavily weighted toward practical affairs. Thus it was not an accident that many of the early inventors and mechanics were Scotsmen—that, for example, seven of Watt's eight assistants in the business of setting up steam engines were Scots. Finally, as we shall see in more detail later, Britain was the pioneer in the employment on a large scale of new machines and productive methods, and thus provided greater opportunities than any other region for training in the highest skills.

From very early in the Industrial Revolution, people in foreign lands realized that the English possessed industrial techniques which gave them a cost advantage, and foreigners expressed a burning desire to acquire the new methods of production for themselves. Ideas traveled with great speed, with the result that general notions about the new machines were soon known to France, the Austrian Netherlands, the Rhineland, and America.[11] To get new machines actually constructed and set up for use in the lands of adoption was not, however, an easy task. Its successful accomplishment depended upon highly skilled workers, and they came to be actively sought after. The French offered large subsidies to anyone who could bring over English technicians, construct "English" machines, and put them to work. John Cockerill, the son of an English worker, built a great industry at Liège in Belgium for the construction of machines. Samuel Slater, who had been employed by Richard Arkwright, came to Rhode Island, where he went into partnership with local enterprisers to form the firm of Almy, Brown and Slater, and thus laid the foundation for a great textile machine industry. As late as the middle of the nineteenth century, the Amoskeag Mills at Manchester, New Hampshire, had a special recruiting policy in Scotland in order to get an adequate supply of highly trained technical men in their shops.[12] And the history of the introduction of machines in Germany and Italy is shot through with the names of foreigners who brought new techniques to these countries.

For their part, the English realized that they had knowledge and skills which were of such advantage that they should keep them to themselves. The extent of their concern is indicated by the following:[13]

---

[11] The French *Encyclopédie Méthodique,* published at the end of the eighteenth century, had several volumes devoted to a remarkable set of plates portraying a great variety of industrial and agricultural machines that had just come into being.

[12] Daniel Creamer, "Recruiting Contract Laborers for the Amoskeag Mills," *Journal of Economic History,* vol. 1, no. 1, pp. 42–57, May 1941.

[13] S. B. Clough and C. W. Cole, *Economic History of Europe* (Boston: Heath, 1947), p. 405.

... laws of 1774 and 1781 made it an offense to export tools or utensils used in manufacturing cotton and linen cloth, and to send abroad sketches, models, or specifications of textile machines. Similar regulations were applied to the secrets of the metallurgical trades in 1785 and 1786, and a general act of 1795 endeavored to prevent the leaking out of information about manufacturing techniques. Skilled workers were not allowed to go abroad after 1782; and if they did, they were to return within six months or lose their British citizenship and have their property confiscated. These British efforts to keep a national monopoly of their advanced techniques by a strict control were not completely abolished until 1843.

The availability of power and industrial raw materials

Important as were the supply of skilled labor, the demand for goods, and the investment of much capital in the process of developing mechanized industry on a large scale, the availability of industrial raw materials played a role in determining the specific places in which industry would be located. In general, it may be said that in so far as the transportation of materials used in manufacturing constituted a large element of final costs, industry tended to settle at places where the bulkiest and hardest to move materials were found, especially if they were much bulkier and much harder to transport than the finished products made from them.

At the beginning of the Industrial Revolution one of the most important locational factors was water power, for no other source could produce mechanical power so cheaply. Water had to be used where it was found, for not until it could be used to generate electricity could it be "transported" to other locations. Consequently, most of the early cotton textile centers among the industrial countries were found along rivers in hilly regions, as in Lancashire in England, along the Merrimack River in New England, in the Vosges Mountains in France, and later on the southern slopes of the Alps in Italy.

Other industries responded to other locational factors. The iron-smithing industry was located near ore outcroppings in forests; salt refining was centered near salt mines or salt marshes which had abundant fuel at their disposal; sawmills were in or near forests; and brickyards were near claybanks. Furthermore, inasmuch as water transportation was by far the cheapest form of carrying freight at the end of the eighteenth century, industries that involved the shipment of bulky and weighty products profited from being near good ports to take advantage of shipping by sea and from being located on an extensive inland waterway system in order to reach the largest possible source of supplies and extent of market. Those industries which required great skills, like watchmaking or machine-tool making, tended to be drawn to areas having specialized labor; those that depended upon style demand, like women's clothes, tended to settle near their markets both to be abreast of changes in demand and to have close contact with customers.

The exact force of the various factors determining location changed as new techniques made possible the generation of different kinds of power, the use of different raw materials, and the employment of new forms of transportation. Thus the invention of the steam engine gave a new mobility to the power plant and made the location of industry possible at any site where costs of transportation were low. The discovery of a method of smelting iron ore with coke took the smithing industry away from outcroppings of ore in forests and located it near coal mines, for the very good reason that some 5 tons of coal were used to smelt 1 ton of ore, and the finished product weighed much less than the ingredients which went into it. And the building of railways gave a flexibility to carrying that had never existed when main reliance was placed on water transportation.

England seemed to be particularly favored by Providence as regards those factors which were primary in determining the locations of industry in the second half of the eighteenth century. In the matter of raw materials it was especially blessed. It had, in the first place, large supplies of native-grown wool for the manufacture of a product that up until 1802 constituted Britain's most valuable export and for long thereafter remained one of the more important British items sold abroad. The large supply of native-grown wool, increased by the enclosing of land for pasture in the sixteenth century and the extension of sheep grazing in the Highlands of Scotland in the eighteenth, meant the existence of a kind of agriculture which could make profitable use of marginal land. It meant such a wide dispersion of raw material that household workers under the putting-out system could readily be supplied without high transport costs. And it contributed both to giving employment to "underemployed" women and children and to avoiding imports that would have given Britain a problem of settling foreign debts.

England also had large supplies of raw cotton at her disposal, for through military victories in India the British were able to get raw cotton from that source and subsequently to introduce cotton growing successfully in their American Colonies.[14] In the New World, commission merchants made the British desire for cotton widely known and after emphasis was taken from trying to grow long-staple fiber in the Sea Islands off the

---

[14] Southern plantation owners found that cotton could be grown on their lands more profitably than tobacco, with its widely fluctuating prices. Moreover, shippers already engaged in bringing "colonial produce" to England discovered that cotton could provide very lucrative cargoes.

coast and placed on growing short staple on the mainland, and after the invention of the cotton gin in 1793, supplies of American cotton for British jennies were great.[15] In 1821, of the 125 million pounds of raw cotton which Americans exported, 71 percent went to Great Britain, 11.5 percent to France, and 7.5 percent to other countries.

In the matter of sources of energy, England was also well endowed. Although other countries, especially Alpine countries, had superior potential supplies of water power, England had many small streams that could turn the wheels of that day and had a reliable enough rainfall to keep the streams almost as full as the Alpine torrents which were fed by mountain snows. As far as coal was concerned, however, England had a great advantage. The early development of mines around Newcastle, which were on the very shores of the sea, the consequently cheap transportation of coal to numerous ports of which London was the most important, and the use of coal in industry placed England far ahead of other countries in the utilization of a product which was to assume enormous proportions as a factor in location. France's output of coal was low in the eighteenth century, although its main field in the North was opened between 1720 and 1734; German production was almost insignificant, the first mine in the Ruhr Basin going into operation only in 1841. In 1840, Great Britain produced 31,024,000 tons of coal, compared with 3,929,000 tons for Belgium, 3,091,000 for Prussia, and 3,003,000 for France.

As far as iron ore was concerned, although Great Britain was only moderately well supplied, the country had been a leader in the late eighteenth century both in the per capita use of iron products and in the development of a new technology in the smelting and refining of iron. In England, there were many outcroppings of iron ore, but in the northern and central sections and in the great valley of Scotland coal was in close proximity to the ore—and this proximity provided a glorious opportunity for experimenting with coal, which was already being used for domestic heating and for such industrial purposes as brewing and as a fuel for smelting iron. Moreover, Swedish bar iron, which could be brought in from the Baltic at a cost equivalent to what it took to transport it 20 miles by land, was the main source for wrought-iron products and for steel and was worked up most cheaply on the East coast where coal was readily available. It was the eventual substitution of coke for charcoal which was to revolutionize the ferrous metal industry and to make iron products more plentiful and cheaper than ever before.

In relatively few other places were coal and iron found in quantity in

---

[15] As late as 1784, eight bags of American cotton were seized at Liverpool by customs officers on the ground that that much fiber could not have been grown in America.

such happy union. In the great Lorraine iron field, there was little known coal in the eighteenth century, and besides, at that time only limited amounts of alluvial ores were smelted because the abundant minette ores could not be worked satisfactorily with charcoal. In the Ruhr coal field, there was no iron. And in the American Colonies, where blast furnaces sprang up in such quantity that in 1775 they actually outnumbered those of England and Wales, vast supplies of timber made possible the working of deposits in New Jersey and the Adirondacks of New York. Only as the industry moved into Pennsylvania was coal used as a fuel, following examples out of Britain. Most smelting was carried on at forges wherever there were outcroppings of ore, water power to work the bellows, and forests to provide fuel, as in the Walloon parts of the Austrian Netherlands, in the Rhineland, in Lorraine, in Sweden, on the northern slopes of the Massif Central in France, and on the southern slopes of the Alps.

Transportation

A skilled and willing labor force and available power and raw materials were all quite necessary for early industrial development—necessary, but not sufficient by themselves. For unless inexpensive and efficient long-haul transportation services were available to distribute the fruits of industry, such fruits would never have been forthcoming. "Extension of the market" —a prerequisite for economic growth in any age—means being able to reach more consumers. The productivity of ocean shipping was a key factor in the extension of the Early Modern market and, as such, was a vital link in the chain of economic progress in those centuries.

The first great contribution to productivity in ocean shipping after the age of the galleys was made by the Dutch. Their innovation was a merchantman called a *fluitschip,* in English, a "flute" or "flyboat." Its appearance on the seas during the last years of the sixteenth century made older ship designs obsolete. Like many of the innovations of the Commercial Revolution the hallmark of the flute was low cost (see p. 148). Inordinately long for the ships of her day, she was light, buoyant, and almost entirely unadorned by the impressive but expensive superstructures of competing craft. Built with economy in mind, a Dutch flute might cost a third less than a ship of equivalent tonnage of English or French origin. Because of this, and because of the smaller crew a flute required, the freight rates of the Dutch in their commercial heyday were often 33 to 50 percent lower than those of other carriers.[16]

---

[16] Violet Barbour, "Dutch and English Merchant Shipping in the Seventeenth Century," in *Essays in Economic History,* E. M. Carus-Wilson (Ed.) vol. 1 (New York: St. Martin's, 1966), p. 249.

As we have seen, the heyday of Dutch commerce was not a long one; by about 1730 the mantle of supremacy in oceangoing trade had passed to England. The pace of improvement in the efficiency of ocean transport did not slacken. Naval war and piracy became somewhat more episodic, and the safety of sea lanes increased. Cargo carrying capacity rose as the requirements for crews, armaments, and other expenses diminished. It has been estimated that the productivity of ocean shipping increased at a rate of between 1/2 and 1 percent per year between 1600 and 1750.[17]

In the matter of ocean carrying, England was very well off. At the end of the eighteenth century it was estimated that out of a total of 4,026,000 net tons of shipping for all Western culture, Britain had 1,856,000 tons to 250,000 for France and 970,000 for America. Her great overseas trade meant that she had a vast organization both for selling her merchandise and for tapping the resources of the earth. Moreover, the navigation law, which required that certain materials should be brought to England in English ships, meant the development of an entrepôt trade which made England mistress of certain supplies. Liverpool, for example, came to be the center for trade in cotton, and this fact was of immense significance in keeping Lancashire mills supplied in times of shortages, as during the Napoleonic Wars.

Furthermore, the English recognized early the importance of improving their inland waterway system (Figure 16). Indeed, Adam Smith in an oft-quoted passage in his *Wealth of Nations* stated:[18]

As by means of water-carriage, a more extensive market is opened to every sort of industry than what land-carriage alone can afford it, so it is upon the sea coast, and along the banks of navigable rivers, that industry of every kind begins to subdivide and improve itself.

In the light of such opinion as this, it is not strange that the English began early to render their rivers more navigable and to build canals. Much of this pioneer work is associated with the name of James Brindley (1716–1772), an illiterate millwright. One of his first important accomplishments (1761) was building a canal for the Duke of Bridgewater from the Duke's coal mines to Manchester—a waterway that at one place was carried high in the air by an aqueduct. Subsequently Brindley joined Liverpool and the Mersey River with Manchester and built the Grand Trunk Canal, which joined the Midlands and North of England and had an outlet to the sea.

---

[17] Douglass C. North and Robert Paul Thomas, *The Rise of the Western World: A New Economic History* (New York: Cambridge, 1973), p. 137. See also Douglass C. North, "Sources of Productivity Change in Ocean Shipping," *The Journal of Political Economy,* vol. 76, pp. 953–970, September/October 1968.
[18] Bk. 1, chap.3.

Thus was launched a canal-building mania which provided Britain with one of the best inland waterway systems of the time and which, inciden-

Figure 16
Seventeenth-century gate lock. Economic growth required that there be a greater division of labor; and a greater division of labor demanded cheaper transportation. The use of the lock made possible cheaper inland transportation. This picture shows the boats apparently being raised. They have come into the lock from downstream through the gate C. As the gate B is opened, with C closed, water rushes into the lock from upstream. When the lock is full the boats will continue up the stream. Note that the boats are small and two of them are probably for short hauls. Note, too, that the gates are opened and closed by winches. Gate locks served also as dams, on gently flowing streams. *(From Vittorio Zonca, Il Nuovo Teatro, 1656.)*

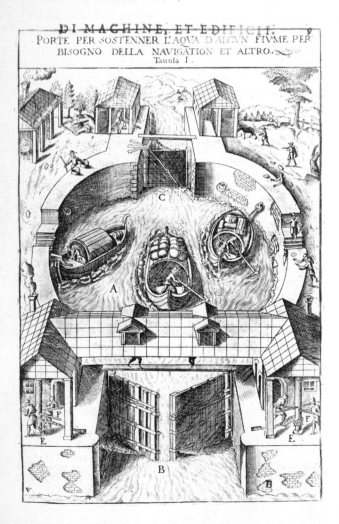

tally, gave a fillip to the joint-stock company, for canal entrepreneurs almost always employed the joint-stock form of business organization.

In the matter of roads, England also had some advantage, for a great wave of road building took place in the country in the eighteenth century. In an effort to lower costs of road construction below those involved in the laying of cobblestones or even slabs of stone, as in Roman roads, experiments were carried on in many places. The system which found most favor was probably hit upon first in Italy but was developed subsequently by two Scotsmen, Thomas Telford (1757–1834) and John McAdam (1756–1836), who in English historical literature have received credit for it. This new method consisted in creating a firm foundation by dumping fairly large stones in a roadbed and then covering these with smaller stones and covering the whole with gravel, slag, or even clay. Such a road could withstand heavy loads and much traffic. It was crowned in shape so that water would drain from it and was flanked by deep ditches that prevented water from washing away the road. This system of construction, which is the basis of road building even today, although asphalt and concrete have been substituted for gravel and clay for surfacing, was extensively used by turnpike companies which built toll roads as profit-making enterprises.

There was little progress in inland transportation elsewhere in eighteenth-century Europe, where reliance on navigable rivers and the network of Roman roads had gone largely unchanged for centuries. In France the interest in canal construction shown by Colbert had waned. There, as in the German states, internal tariffs, border crossings, and tolls were serious artificial barriers to the efficient transport of goods. Although there was some renewed interest in civil engineering during the Napoleonic period, improved transport facilities did not precede industrialization on the Continent. They came at a later date as part of the introduction of machines.

The Agricultural Revolution
and its aftermath

The nature of early growth in agriculture

The foremost characteristic of what we have come to call "modernization" is a rise in economic output, a rise entirely without precedent in history both in terms of the magnitude of change and in terms of the effect of change on every individual. But however dramatic the result, the beginning of the cataclysm happened in a way which is already familiar to us. Strategic innovations in agriculture caused increases in incomes on the land, and these became the basis for larger families and rapid population growth. The supply of labor thus increased, and the growth of demand for agricultural produce was sustained. As income gains outpaced population growth other sectors of the economy became sucked into the whirlpool of expansion; increasing demand for the products of industry and the services of the towns made the entire economy party to the boom. This is a pattern which we have seen before in the Late Middle Ages. In the Early Modern period it proved to be the agricultural basis for industrialization.

In the case of England (Table 7) we can see how the balance between population and agricultural output was maintained as both spiraled upward. Population, growing at about 6.4 percent per decade, doubled between 1700 and 1820. During this period the rate of natural increase bounded up from 5 per thousand per annum (1731–1770) to 12 per thousand per annum (1781–1820).[1] The jump was partly attributable to a diminishing mortality rate, the first incidence of "demographic transition"

---

[1] Simon Kuznets, *Modern Economic Growth, Rate, Structure, and Spread* (p. 42). The crude rate of natural increase is simply the difference between the birth rate (births per 1,000 population per annum) and the death rate (deaths per 1,000 population per annum).

in the modernizing world. The output of grains kept pace, roughly doubling over the same period. It is noteworthy that the growth of cereal production was smoother over the eighteenth century than was population growth, which proceeded slowly to about 1780 and then shot up dramatically. The effect of this end-of-century spurt was a powerful stimulus to the demand for foodstuffs, and advancing wheat prices mirrored the pressure on food supplies. Great Britain turned from a net exporter of grains to an importer of large quantities of corn in the 1770s, even as the productivity of her domestic agrarian sector continued to rise. After 1800 grain production increased at an astounding 15 percent per year. The English case represents, in microcosm, the basic relationship between population growth (as a source of labor supply and final demand) and the growth of output in early modernization.

Table 7. Population and agricultural output in England and Wales, 1700–1829

Decade	Population	Output of grains	Output per capita	Index of wheat prices
1700–09	5.8	14.8	2.55	105
1710–19	6.0	15.4	2.57	109
1720–29	6.0	15.8	2.60	99
1730–39	5.9	15.3	2.59	84
1740–49	5.9	15.4	2.61	84
1750–59	6.1	16.5	2.70	101
1760–69	6.6	17.0	2.58	117
1770–79	7.1	17.4	2.45	136
1780–89	7.5	18.6	2.48	142
1790–99	8.3	19.9	2.39	196
1800–09	9.0	21.1	2.34	
1810–19	10.3	24.4	2.37	
1820–29	12.1	27.9	2.31	

NOTES: Population (in millions of persons) and output of grains (in millions of quarters) are end-of-decade figures; index of wheat prices is a decade average.

SOURCE: Phyllis Deane and W. A. Cole, *British Economic Growth, 1688–1959* (New York: Cambridge, 1969), derived from tables 17 and 23.

The most significant consequence of the New Agriculture in the eighteenth and early nineteenth centuries was the increase in the output of foodstuffs in the West and the avoidance of famines by more reliable methods of production, better storage facilities, and better means of transportation. It was this better and more adequate food supply that, in part, made possible the great growth of the economy of the Western world and that was in part responsible for better nutrition and hence better health records than had ever before been achieved. The Agricultural Revolution, in short, has contributed much to the economic progress of the last two centuries. Historians, particularly those who have concentrated their attention upon the English scene, have been inclined to portray the coming of the New Agriculture as something sudden, which was carried out by a relatively few great agricultural reformers. They have regarded it both as a "Revolution" and as a necessary precursor of the Industrial Revolution.

The search for vividness and drama undoubtedly got the better of the judgment of scholars. More sober reflection and the consideration of agricultural change in a larger geographical sense and in a longer time sequence have led to a modification of the traditional accounts of European agricultural history from the seventeenth century to the nineteenth, just as they tempered the traditional views of the Industrial Revolution. Now scholars recognize that the Agricultural Revolution had long antecedents, that the New Agriculture was adopted slowly, and that it accompanied industrial change.[2]

Since the Middle Ages advances had been going on in European agriculture, particularly where farm produce was raised for market and where an interchange of ideas through commerce was possible. As we have already seen, the invention of the horse collar which rested on the shoulders of the animal greatly increased the value of the horse for draft purposes and for transportation. Indeed, the horse became the chief means of travel on land and the generally employed draft animal in large field cultivation. Sugar was introduced from the East by Arabs and was successfully grown in the Canary Islands. Rice, also from the East, appeared in the fifteenth century and was of considerable importance in the Po Valley by 1700. The lemon came to Sicily in the twelfth century, and the orange, somewhat later, was of importance by the fifteenth century. Buckwheat, which could be grown on poor soils, put in an appearance in the fourteenth century. Mulberry trees, on whose leaves silkworms feed, were introduced in the Late Middle Ages. Then with the discovery of America came maize or Indian corn, tobacco, the tomato, and most important of all, the potato. Improvements were also made in livestock, especially sheep and especially in Spain, with

---

[2] See, for example, J. D. Chambers and G. E. Mingay, *The Agricultural Revolution 1750–1880* (New York: Schocken, 1966); Eric Kerridge, *The Agricultural Revolution* (New York: A. M. Kelley, Publishers, 1967) which argues that the "Revolution" happened in the sixteenth and seventeenth centuries, *not* between 1750 and 1880; and the valuable collection edited by E. L. Jones, *Agriculture and Economic Growth in England 1650–1815* (London: Methuen, 1967).

the development of the Merino, which produced the best wool in Europe. But some improvements were also made with cattle, in some areas by importing better stock from neighboring regions.

Some crops were grown as commercial products rather than for consumption on the farm or the local market. Grain from the Baltic was perhaps the most famous, but wool was grown in England for the Flemish wool industry; flax was grown in Flanders; hops were produced for the brewing of beer from the Late Middle Ages, which made this drink easier to transport and to preserve; cole was raised in order to get the seeds for oil; the olive was cultivated on the Mediterranean littoral, also for oil; and the vine was grown, especially in the Bordeaux region of France, as a commercial product. Wherever agriculture was conducted for the sale of goods for profit in an unknown and uncertain market, and especially where such agriculture was of an intensive kind (high value of product per acre), farmers endeavored to improve their techniques in order to reduce costs and to raise output. Thus in the Po Valley big investments were made in drainage and irrigation works, and a light soil was enriched by the plowing under of humus. In the Bordeaux region horse-drawn implements similar to the cultivator were used to tear up the weeds between the vines. In the Netherlands and Flanders capitalistic farming predominated. There agriculture was at its most intensive, because of the concentration on horticulture from the early seventeenth century and because of the high density of population and the demand for foodstuffs (except for grains which were in part imported from the Baltic). Indeed, in the Netherlands the greatest synthesis of agricultural methods was made in Early Modern Times and it was from there that the English borrowed most of their practices which constituted the mechanical aspects of the traditional Agricultural Revolution.

Although Europe had a history of almost continuous technical progress in agriculture, two major obstacles obstructed the path of any monumental breakthrough in increasing yields. If the term "Agricultural Revolution" has any meaning at all it is in reference to the technological overthrow of these two barriers to progress.

The first of these barriers was small plot size, a condition almost universal in peasant agriculture in the Early Modern era. The disadvantage of this landholding pattern is obvious: Individual small farmers on small plots could never introduce sufficiently large amounts of capital equipment into farming practice to shift agricultural production upward to any major degree. In such circumstances, if more output were desired it could only be achieved by cultivating more land or trying to elicit modest increases in yield per acre by adding more seed or more labor. This condition is equivalent to manufacturing on a handicraft scale—there is no opportunity to introduce steam engines or other major capital goods into the productive process until the jump to large-scale factories is made.

In agriculture, as in industry, the jump first came in England. Small peasant holdings and common field remnants of feudal agriculture were absorbed and consolidated by large landholders and were literally "enclosed" with fences or hedges. Occasionally this was done by pact with the smaller landholders or tenants, but more often in the eighteenth century it required an act of Parliament on a petition for enclosure. The distributive aspects of this upset in traditional landholding patterns will be discussed elsewhere (p. 274). For the moment let us simply note that from 1700 to 1845, 14 million acres, that is, one-quarter of all the arable lands of England, were brought together. The cost of executing an enclosure for expanding landowners was not low. Indemnification to peasants, fencing, and purchasing the equipment for large-scale cultivation were all major capital expenditures. A reasonable mid-eighteenth-century figure for the cost per acre of enclosing was roughly 3 pounds. This means that the total cost of enclosing a small estate of 5 acres was about 15 pounds, almost equal to the yearly wage of an agricultural worker. Yet all indications are that these investments paid off handsomely. One observer calculates that the annual rate of return on investments in enclosure ran as high as 25 percent, this at a time when the interest rate on government debt instruments was well under 5 percent.[3] This payoff is just another way of expressing dramatic increases in the productivity of the soil per acre. The high returns enabled landowners to continue making capital improvements both on and off the land. The agrarian sector was a major source of eighteenth-century investment funds for construction of canals, roads, and irrigation projects. Enclosure and the increase in the scale of agricultural production was not, as we shall see, the sole reason for the burgeoning of food production. But for England it was as important as the development of the factory system in industry for creating the institutional preconditions for modernization.

The second great obstacle to expanded productivity of the soil was the idleness of arable land during fallow periods. We recall that the development of three-field agriculture in the Middle Ages reduced this idle time by 50 percent, but a given field was still left uncultivated every third season. There was no single instant in which fallow practices were revolutionized, but rather there was a steady reduction in fallow time throughout the Early Modern period. The greatest advances were made in the Low Countries, where land was precious and population density was high. Demand made increasingly intensive cultivation a profitable necessity

[3] Donald N. McCloskey, "The Enclosure of Open Fields: Preface to a Study of Its Impact on the Efficiency of English Agriculture in the Eighteenth Century," *Journal of Economic History*, vol. 32, no. 1, March 1972.

even though such forms of agriculture required more labor and capital per acre to be effective.

The number of crop rotations in the agricultural cycle increased and became more complex, often involving as many as six different crops on the same plot over a five-year cycle. Nitrogenous legumes, which served as vegetable or fodder crops as well as soil replenishers, became integral to fallow substitution. Heavy periodic manure-spreading replaced the unsystematic grazing of animals as a fertilization technique. In Flanders the costs of procuring and applying manure may have been more than half the total expense for raising a given crop. Other sources of fertilization, such as Peruvian guano and synthetic fertilizers, came in the nineteenth century and reduced the need to practice fallow almost entirely. Before this development, however, the English refined Netherlandish cropping practices to such a high degree that the Norfolk four-course system of rotation became diffused throughout Europe.

Rotations included industrial crops as well as food and fodder. In the Netherlands, flax, which exhausts the soil, might be followed by turnips, which had the advantage of breaking up clay soils; turnips might be followed by oats, which were used as a cover crop for clover or alfalfa; and when the clover, which was used for fodder, ran out after some five years, a return would be made to other crops. Sir Richard Weston, who was the first to describe Netherlandish agricultural practices for the English public in his *A Discourse on Husbandry Used in Brabant and Flanders* (1645), was much impressed by this system, which was not to be found in England.[4]

Yet the person who developed rotation into a system and so popularized its use that his work constituted an important part of the Agricultural Revolution was Charles, Viscount Townshend (1674–1738). As he addressed himself to the problems of his large estate, he became impressed with the wastefulness of the practice of letting a portion of the arable lie fallow every year and he dedicated himself to a search for a method whereby fertility of the soil could be maintained even if all the soil were made to produce a crop every year. He experimented with various plants which could be rotated with grains and discovered that by growing clover, which captures nitrogen from the air and returns it to the soil, and by cultivating turnips, which loosened the soil, an idea obtained from the Netherlands, he could get a good return on a piece of land every year. He became such a staunch advocate of using turnips in his rotation system that he was given the nickname "Turnip" Townshend, and he was so successful that many were inspired to follow where he led. The most famous of his disciples was perhaps Coke of Holkam (1752–1842), who

---

[4] Barnaby Googe's *Four Books on Husbandry* (1577) considered the growing of fodder crops as unusual. Turnips at that time were rare in England.

standardized a four-crop rotation on the lines suggested by Townshend, a practice which became known as the Norfolk system. Coke had so much success with it that the income of his estate was multiplied ten times within the span of forty years. This was a notable achievement even though it was abetted by a price rise and a favorable market. It did much to induce farmers to follow the new practice.

With the elimination of the fallow system, the demand for manure was greatly increased. This was particularly apparent in Flanders and the Netherlands, where leaving a portion of the land fallow was abandoned so early. There the feeding of fodder crops produced more manure than was available from pasturing. Farmers got "night soil" (human excrement) from the towns and villages, even at some distance, for transportation of heavy loads on canals was not much of a problem. They used considerable quantities of ashes from peat, which was a household fuel, and from wood. And they brought to their lands city garbage and from the early seventeenth century the refuse from the pressing of cole seeds. Their practices were picked up by the English, who added special twists as local conditions demanded. The most important of these was marling, that is, the addition of a lime soil to soils that showed signs of being acid (the appearance of moss). The growing of fodder crops and stall feeding, which resulted in a concentration of manure from cattle, was crucial in the success of rotation of crops.

The combined advantages of a larger scale and the elimination of fallow could be made to bear fruit only if other more "nuts-and-bolts" aspects of agrarian technology kept pace. We must remember that despite all our attention to revolutionary change in economic production, technology at its most basic level means solving very day-to-day problems by creating new tools or methods to widen bottlenecks or to remove stumbling blocks to greater efficiency. That conventional usage has come to associate "technology" with industrial machinery is a regrettable misconception. Technical innovation means any adjustment in a method of production whose effect is increased output from the same inputs of capital, labor, land, and raw materials as had been employed beforehand. In agriculture it can be anything from reorganizing the lay of the land (which will hopefully increase the yield per acre) to designing a plow which will dig up the earth faster (and thus give equivalent yields while reducing the necessary man-hours of plowing time).

Just how essential these technical improvements were to the improvement of agriculture can be imagined when one realizes that with oxen a farmer with a heavy plow could turn over only about a third of an acre a day (an acre is about the size of a football field). With horses he could plow about twice this amount, but the work was backbreaking, especially in stony ground where the plowman might be thrown head over heels when the plow pulled at a good clip by horses hit a stone. Harvesting with a sickle could advance at about a fifth of an acre a day, and with a scythe only a third of an acre. Threshing was winter work, but went ahead very slowly, a man with a flail being able to thresh four bushels a day, and the work seemed interminable. Winnowing was one of those dusty chores that made sufferers of hay fever beg for mercy.

In the eighteenth century a number of farm implements were invented to alleviate the load of farm work. One of the most important of these was the plow. In England the Norfolk plow was much lighter than the old and awkward swing plows. But the big advance was the development, also in England, of an entirely iron moldboard (1771), which was much more rugged than its wooden version, and then of an all-iron plow (also 1771). Improvements were also made in the harrow for the breaking up of the sod into fine soil and for sowing seed below the surface instead of just broadcasting it, which was an invitation to birds to help themselves. Concurrently, practical seed drills came into use, which allowed the sowing of certain crops in rows, and once they were in rows then it was possible to cultivate between them to keep out weeds and to create a dust mulch that would reduce the evaporation of water from the soil.

One of the pioneers in this work in England was Jethro Tull (1674–1740), who became famous for innovations in field husbandry. On his father's estate in Berkshire, he experimented with sowing seeds in rows, instead of flinging them broadcast, and with cultivating between the rows. In order to get seeds sown as he wanted them to be, Tull devised a seed drill, the direct ancestor of modern planters, and in order to cultivate more easily between rows he developed a "horse hoe" or horse-drawn cultivator, which he had seen at work in the vineyards of Languedoc in France. To give publicity to his innovations, he wrote two famous books which had a great vogue, *Horse-Hoeing Husbandry* (1731) and *The Horse-Hoeing Husbandry, or, An Essay on the Principles of Tillage and Vegetation* (1733).

Still another aspect of farming which came in for a change in the eighteenth century was that of raising livestock. Not only was there better fodder and more stall feeding, but serious efforts were made to improve the quality of animals. More milk, which was usually turned into butter and cheese,[5] was required as the population increased and more meat was needed for cities. Cattle fattening near markets came to be more widely practiced, for walking took off some 35 pounds per 100 miles and made

---

[5] Milk was mainly drunk by invalids. Peddling milk in London began in 1619. On the Continent up to World War II herds of goats could be encountered in Paris to provide milk on the spot. Raw milk was not very sanitary, and cows on the outskirts of towns were kept in miserable condition.

the meat tough and stringy. Oxen and cows became displaced as draft animals in livestock-raising districts so that the meat would be improved. And sheep were bred for better wool and more meat.

One of the pioneers in better breeding practices was Robert Bakewell (1725–1795), who began to manage his father's estate in Leicestershire in 1760. He experimented widely with new agricultural techniques and new crops, especially grasses, but he is best known for his efforts to improve breeds of sheep, horses, and cattle. Although the science of genetics had not yet developed, systematic knowledge was not needed to conclude that stock could be improved if animals having visibly desirable qualities were used for breeding purposes and if those with patently undesirable features were prevented from coming together in common pastures. Consequently Bakewell engaged in selective and controlled breeding in an empirical way and achieved considerable success. With sheep he endeavored to replace the rangy animal whose sole advantage was its ability to travel fast and far with a chunkier breed which would have more meat and wool—a breed that came to be known as the New Leicestershire. Similarly, he produced a better strain of beef cattle, the Dishley or New Leicestershire longhorn, and a bigger and stronger horse. At the Southfield livestock fair, which was near his home, the average weight of sheep increased from 28 to 80 pounds and that of cattle from 370 to 800 pounds between 1710 and 1795. Most of this increase is to be attributed to the success Bakewell had in breeding, although some of it may be accounted for by better feeds and stabling of animals.

Obviously all farmers did not adopt the new techniques with the same rapidity or the same avidity. The *métayer* or share-farmer was loath to make big investments on his land for fear that his lease would not be renewed at the same rent if he did; and many farmers did not have the capital to afford to experiment in new-fangled ideas. Yet the advances were popularized and gradually adopted, particularly at first on large farms where the family labor force had to be supplemented by outside help.

One of the most famous advocates of the New Agriculture in England was Arthur Young (1741–1820). He publicized the work of the innovators and carried on intensive propaganda in its behalf. His several books usually took the form of reports of agricultural procedures, which he observed as he traveled about. Those like *Farmer's Tour through the East of England, Tour in Ireland,* and *Travels in France* were highly informative, even though his observations were strongly flavored by his faith in the New Agriculture and by the physical comforts which he had enjoyed during the day on which he wrote. In 1784 he began publishing an agricultural review, the *Annals of Agriculture,* which became justly famous for the encouragement it gave to agricultural advances. In 1793 Young was appointed secretary of the Board of Agriculture, which was the first governmental department devoted exclusively to agriculture.

The interest which the New Agriculture generated was enormous, and for a time farming enjoyed a veritable style vogue. George III of England became known as "Farmer George" and contributed to Young's *Annals of Agriculture* under the pen name of Ralph Robinson. In France, not only did latter-day Physiocrats preach the virtues of the New Agriculture, but many leaders in society played at farming. Marie Antoinette had a miniature farming village in the Park at Versailles, Le Hameau; Catherine the Great of Russia, Lafayette, and George Washington exhibited an admiration for the homely virtues of farm life.

Other countries of Western European culture kept reasonably well informed of the success which the New Agriculture was bringing to England and fairly well abreast of English procedures. The French, for their part, knew about what was going on across the Channel, as is attested to by the inclusion in the famous plates of the *Encyclopédie* of detailed sketches of the new agricultural machines and by the success of the volumes written by Duhamel du Monceau between 1751 and 1760 on English agricultural methods. In Prussia, Albrecht Thaer not only published his *Introduction to the Knowledge of English Agriculture* (1798) and his *Principles of Rational Agriculture* (1809–1812) but also founded the first Prussian school of agriculture (1804). And in America, Jared Elliot, in his *Essays on Field Husbandry*, published from 1748 to 1762, made known to his compatriots the work that was going on in England; and Thomas Jefferson gave publicity to English agricultural techniques.

Furthermore, non-English lands made important contributions of their own to the Agricultural Revolution. A Frenchman, Parmentier, did much to popularize the potato upon the Continent by writing a famous book on the nutritional and gastronomic virtues of the lowly tuber. A German chemist showed, as early as 1747, that sugar could be obtained from beets, a discovery which was in the course of the nineteenth century to have a profound impact upon the sugar plantations of the West Indies. Americans, for their part, did important work in the selection of seed, especially of short-staple cotton, tobacco, and corn. And the French contributed much to the improvement of livestock by means of their breeding stations, especially of the Merino sheep on the estate of Louis XVI at Rambouillet, and to the development of veterinary medicine with two schools, established in 1761 and 1765.

However, as long as old landholding patterns persisted in continental countries, the spread of the Agricultural Revolution was thwarted there. Only as small-plot peasant monoculture gave way to large-scale multi-cropping agriculture did the bounty of the soil magnify.

Further application of science and mechanics to agriculture

The search for new agricultural methods thus carried forward in the eighteenth century was continued in the nineteenth at an ever-accelerated pace. The objectives of the searchers' quest continued to be to increase the fertility of the soil, to develop labor-saving machinery, to improve the quality of seeds and livestock, and to bring vast areas of virgin soil in overseas lands into cultivation.

As far as improving the fertility of the soil was concerned, enormous progress was made as a result of increased knowledge of the chemical composition of plants and therefore of those ingredients which were needed in the soil as food for plants. Pioneers in this work were Jean Baptiste Boussingault (1802–1887), Sir John B. Lawes (1814–1900) at the experimental station of Rothamsted, England, and Justus von Liebig (1803–1873). In the 1840s they discovered that plants consist primarily of phosphorus, potassium, nitrogen, and water. This knowledge made possible the abandonment of purely empirical practices of fertilizing and made possible after soil analysis the addition to the land of those very chemicals in which it might be deficient.

This scientific advance led directly to the use of so-called commercial fertilizers. One of the first sources of phosphates and nitrates was Peruvian guano (the droppings of birds), British imports of this material increasing from 1,700 tons in 1841 to 220,000 tons in 1847. Subsequently, phosphate rock was pulverized for farm use and sometimes was treated with sulfuric acid to make superphosphates. Also, linings of Thomas-Gilchrist furnaces, rich in phosphorous, were broken up for sale to farmers after Lorraine ore began to be smelted on a large scale (post–1878). Later nitrates also began to be obtained from mines in Chile; and potash, that from time immemorial had been secured chiefly from wood ashes, began to be mined in various places, especially at Stassfurt, Germany (1861), and later in Alsace. Moreover, the growing practice of stall feeding to take advantage of cultivated forage crops resulted in the saving and controlled use of manure, and hence the addition of much-needed humus to the soil.

In the realm of farm machinery great progress was made, especially in America, where labor was scarce, land abundant, and extensive agriculture was, with the opening of the Middle West, the order of the day. Here Cyrus H. McCormick and Obed Hussey developed successful reapers in the 1830s (Figure 17), using the principle of a cutter bar composed of double-edged knives moving in a reciprocating fashion through slotted fingers.[6] With the cutter bar, horse-drawn mowers for hay and reapers for

---

[6] It should be noted, however, that a Scot named Bell had previously anticipated the work of McCormick and Hussey but employed the principle found today in barbers' clippers.

grain began to replace the backbreaking scythe, especially where operations were large enough to warrant the investment and where labor was
in short supply. These machines, along with the twine binder (1878) and
the "combine" (combination reaper and thresher) of the 1880s, made possible "extensive agriculture," that is, farming large tracts with little labor,
as opposed to "intensive agriculture." It was, indeed, by extensive agriculture that the vast plains of the Americas and of Australia were put under
cultivation and that the lowest costs of production were attained in grain
growing.

Similarly, in the development of farm implements for tillage Americans
made important contributions to mechanization. John Deere, a Vermont
blacksmith who had gone "West" to Illinois, made plows with mold-

Figure 17
McCormick's reaper. Power for this machine was provided by horses that were attached
to the pole at the right of the illustration. The gears were driven by power from the
wheel which supported the machine on the ground. The gears gave a reciprocating
motion to the cutter bar. One may discern the pointed fingers of the bar. Sharp edges of
triangularly shaped steel attached to a thin bar slipped back and forth through slots in
the fingers. These "knives" cut the grain, which was gently pushed against the cutter bar
by large arms which revolved like a reel. The grain, after being cut, fell on the canvas
apron in the rear. *(From Lucy L. Wilson, Picture Study in Elementary Schools, New York: MacMillan,
1902. Courtesy of the publishers.)*

boards constructed of sheet iron which scoured, that is, freed themselves of dirt, better than those made of cast iron (1838), and then made the still better all-steel plow (1847). Somewhat later James Oliver built a combination cast-iron and steel plow (1870) that had great popularity in the Eastern United States, more than 175,000 having been in use by 1878. At this time, too, came sulky or riding plows, which eliminated the drudgery of holding the plow and walking interminable miles in a dusty furrow. Then after the War Between the States, when new lands were being rapidly brought into cultivation, disk and spring-tooth harrows were introduced, which had the advantage over the earlier spike-tooth type in that they did not break so easily or clog so readily and consequently did a superior job of pulverizing the soil. Finally, cultivators were improved by the use of steel and by the construction of sulky models (1856).

In addition to these horse-drawn implements, which were aimed at performing most of the work formerly done with scythe, spade, and hoe, threshing machines were improved to lessen the backbreaking use of the flail or to eliminate the rather repulsive practice of driving mules or horses hitched to rollers over the grain. Winnowing machines were perfected to remove the chaff from the grain and consequently to do away with the laborious job of throwing the grain and chaff into the air on a windy day in hope that the wind would take away the chaff and leave the grain behind. The first successful threshing and winnowing machine in America was invented by Hiram and John Pitts of Maine (1837). This contraption required a considerable amount of power, which was provided at the outset by horses pulling sweeps, but which subsequently was furnished by horses on treadmills, by water, and then by steam. It is estimated that by the use of this machine the productivity of man at this task was increased six times. Indeed, it has been said by authorities that by the use of all the devices here described, as well as of others like the seed broadcaster and the seed drill, the number of man-hours required per acre in wheat production in the United States was reduced from seventy-five prior to 1830 to thirteen in 1880 and that wheat production was increased some three to six times per man-hour.

Such dramatic achievements were made even more striking by improvements obtained through the use of better strains of seeds and better breeds of animals. Farmers came more and more to buy their seeds of seedmen; and seedmen, with more business on their hands, were able to search for varieties that would be hardy under extreme climatic conditions, to make selections of high-producing strains, and to experiment with cures for plant diseases. Agricultural botany flourished and its practitioners became ever more competent in their subject. After the Irish potato famine of 1845–1849, for example, they made an earnest effort to find a type of potato which would be resistant to blight. By 1880 they were able to list 175 varieties and through careful record keeping to select strains which in the midst of diseased plants had remained healthy. Moreover, new varieties of vegetables were introduced; these not only tempted palates but also increased vitamin intake.

As far as livestock was concerned, more breeds came to be generally known and the better ones to be favored by farmers. Breed associations came into being, for breeders found from experience that they could get better prices if their animals possessed standardized characteristics—characteristics which altogether too often were those of color and shape rather than of productive ability. Regions which imported stock, and this was especially true of the United States, exercised care in the selection of animals for the very good reason that the investment being made was large and costs of transportation appreciable. It was not an accident that many of the early breeds in America came from England, where selective breeding was most highly developed. From England came the Jersey, Ayrshire, and Guernsey among dairy cattle, the Devon, Durham, and Hereford among beef cattle, the Clydesdale among horses (the Percheron came from Normandy), and among sheep, an English variety of Merino, which was further developed in New England.

In all of this work both private and public organizations played important roles. The English created the famous experimental station at Rothamsted and the United States began its network of stations in 1857. Government departments of agriculture became common. The one in the United States dates from 1862, and the English Board of Agriculture was raised to the status of a ministry in the same year. Agricultural schools were founded in all the leading countries of Western culture. The Royal Agricultural College at Cirencester, England, was established in 1845. The French school at Grignon was set up during the July Monarchy, and the German institution at Hildesheim opened its doors in 1858. In the United States the first agricultural school was founded in Cleveland in 1855, but the greatest impetus to agricultural education came when, in 1862, Congress granted to each state from the public domain 30,000 acres for each senator and each representative in the House in order to promote "the liberal and practical education of the industrial classes." Furthermore, every nation had one or more agricultural societies for the dissemination of agricultural knowledge and for the defense of farmers' interests. Thus England had its Royal Agricultural Society, founded in 1840. France had its Société des Agriculteurs, Germany its Bund der Landwirte, and the United States its Patrons of Husbandry, more commonly known as the Grange (1867). Finally, each nation had agricultural periodicals, agricultural fairs, and agricultural books with which the farmer could keep abreast of the numerous advances continually being made in the agricultural arts.

Still another important change that took place in the agriculture of Western culture in the nineteenth century was the bringing into cultivation of vast tracts of virgin soil in the New World, South Africa, Australia, and New Zealand. As produce from these regions increased in volume and could be transported at low cost, it entered into direct competition with Western European output. Western Europe was thus forced to protect its agriculture with high tariffs, to shift productive effort to crops in which a great amount of labor per unit was needed, or to allow farming to deteriorate.

The magnitude of settlement of new land staggers the imagination. In the United States, from 1860 to 1900, about one-quarter of the entire country passed into private hands. This was a land mass equal to the combined area of Great Britain, France, Germany, and Italy. Much of this land lay west of the Mississippi River and included some of the most fertile soil in the world, particularly the black and prairie soils which lie between the longitude of Memphis, Tennessee, and that of Bismarck, North Dakota. In disposing of these rich acres, the government of the United States offered, under the Homestead Act of 1862, to give 160 acres free to the head of any family if the family would reside on and cultivate the holding for five years, or to sell the land to the head of the family after six months' residence for the prevailing minimum price, which was about a dollar and 25 cents an acre. In addition, the government made large land grants to railway companies to foster rail construction into the West in order to hasten settlement. And it made important grants of land to mining and timber companies to accelerate the exploitation of the nation's wealth.

In Upper Canada, later known as Ontario, the number of acres under cultivation quadrupled from 1842 to 1871 and with the building of the Canadian Pacific Railway by the government, settlement was made in the Prairie provinces. With the introduction there of hard red wheats and durum, which were hardy in cold climates, production grew by leaps and bounds, the three provinces of Manitoba, Saskatchewan, and Alberta eventually accounting for 90 percent of all the wheat grown in Canada.

In Australia, a territory the size of the United States, agricultural and grazing lands in use in 1882 amounted to 100 million acres, on which sheep and cattle did most of the work of getting fed by seeking wild grasses. In the Argentine, agricultural and grazing lands equal to about one-quarter of those of the United States were being exploited by the end of the nineteenth century.

Changes in European landholding

With the bringing into cultivation of large tracts of virgin soil overseas which produced for distant and unknown consumers, with the development of new agricultural techniques which required fairly important capital investments and large holdings, with an increase in the consumer's reliance upon the market for the acquisition of goods to satisfy his wants, and with a growing belief in the equality of man, with its corollary that the few had no *natural* right to exploit the many, two profound but diametrically opposite changes in the landholding systems of Western culture took place. On the one hand, large estates tended to be formed or consolidated where grains and livestock were produced for market and where the new agricultural techniques were most widely adopted. This was the case in the Germanies east of the Elbe River, in England, southern Italy, and southern Spain, to some extent in Denmark, and in the overseas lands mentioned above. On the other hand, small holdings predominated where peasants got title by political action and without paying indemnities to the land which they had had the right to work from time immemorial, as in France and those regions where French reforms were introduced during the French domination of the Revolutionary and Napoleonic periods, and in districts where dairy and poultry farming was or became general, as in Belgium, the Netherlands, Western Germany, Savoy, parts of Denmark, and the eastern part of the United States.[7] Whatever the size of the holdings, however, everywhere in Western culture the old seignorial system was on the way out and business transactions between farm workers and landowners came to be determined largely by money payments.

In England the chief characteristic of landholding change during the period of the Agricultural Revolution was, as has been said, the formation of large estates by enclosures. The rise of agricultural prices from the middle of the eighteenth century to after the fall of Napoleon and the development of a larger market for foodstuffs owing to the growth of population and the rise of cities made agricultural enterprise more enticing for those who aspired to greater gain. Furthermore, lords who were bent on supervising the growing of agricultural products found the old strip system to have many disadvantages: a field could not be drained or irrigated except with the consent of neighboring holders; land was wasted in roads; time was lost in going from field to field; disputes over boundaries were frequent; no winter crops could be grown because of the right of common pasture on the arable fields from August to February; and rules of cultivation were such that weeds from fallow land might sow their unwanted seeds on the fields of its neighbors.[8] Finally, English agricultural entrepreneurs recognized that to use the new machinery they had to have large fields to cultivate, because horse-drawn implements could not be

---

[7] In regions where the *métayer* or share-farming system continued to be practiced, as in Tuscany, ownership of the land was by large estates, but farming was by small units.

[8] See criticism of the open-field system by the Reverend John Lawrence, *A New System of Agriculture* (1726).

maneuvered in small strips and because only large-scale production could pay off the costs of expensive equipment.[9]

For these various reasons, lords enclosed fields. The legal aspect of this procedure was for a number of persons in a region, usually large landowners, to petition Parliament for permission to enclose land. A commission was then appointed to investigate the petition and to make recommendations to Parliament. Usually the large landowners favored enclosures and the small ones opposed them, but this was not always the case. At all events, enclosing forced uprooted peasants to readjust to the new order of things as best they could. Some of them were settled on consolidated farms on parts of the estate; others became farm workers on the enclosed lands of the lords; still others, especially the younger members of peasant families, went to commercial or industrial towns to seek employment.

In spite of the disruption which enclosures caused peasants, lords were able to execute their designs without recourse to physical force. In the seventeenth century, indeed, peasants frequently consented to giving up their rights in return for compensation, but especially from 1760 to 1845, enclosures were effected by private acts of Parliament, that is, by political force against which peasants had no redress. In 1845, moreover, the General Enclosures Act provided that subsequent decisions regarding the consolidation of land should be made by special commissioners, for the number of bills for enclosure were becoming too numerous for Parliament to handle.

For their part peasants were indemnified for surrendering their rights to the land which they worked. Freeholders, who had paid small quitrents to the lords to be free of other claims, were given the largest compensation. Copyholders, whose tenure was specified in a "copy" of the manorial roll and whose payments to the lord were not insignificant, got somewhat less; cotters, who held simply a cottage and perhaps a garden plot and who had rights on the common pasture, received still less; and tenants at will, who rented land from the lord at his pleasure, were sent off empty-handed.

The resulting concentration of landed wealth is apparent in Table 8. In 1873, it is said, half of the land of the country was held by 2,250 persons! Those lesser landholders and tenants who lost land rights became, for the most part, agricultural wage-workers. Because of the high demand for foodstuffs and consequently for rural labor, incomes in the countryside remained at a fairly high level despite the bitter injustice to those who lost rights to land, often rights of centuries' standing.

[9] On this subject consult Edward Lawrence, *The Duty of a Steward to his Lord* (1727) and the writings of "Turnip" Townshend.

Table 8. Division of land in England, 1873

Class of owner	Average area held by each owner, in acres	Area held, in acres	Percent of land held
Public bodies and wasteland		2,950,000	8.6
Cotters, less than 1 acre	0.21	150,000	0.4
Small proprietors, 1–100 acres	18.00	3,930,000	11.4
Lesser yeomen, 101–300 acres	169.00	4,140,000	12.0
Greater yeomen, 301–1,000 acres	498.00	4,780,000	13.9
Squires, 1,001–3,000 acres	1,708.00	4,310,000	12.5
Great landowners, commoners having over 3,001 acres	6,597.00	8,490,000	24.6
Peers	14,320.00	5,720,000	16.6
Total		34,470,000	100.0

England thus acquired the large fields which could be cultivated with less labor and more machinery, but it remained to be seen whether or not English agriculture could stand competition from the virgin soils overseas.

Across the Channel in France, changes in landholding were, as has been said, very different from those which we have just described. The evolution away from medieval agriculture had been slower there than it had been in England and the wealthier French nobles had been less concerned with the actual cultivation of the land than the English. They tended to rely for their incomes on money payments, services, and the delivery of goods by their peasants rather than on the raising of produce and hence were not in general desirous of enclosing. As prices rose in the eighteenth century (it is said that they went up some 63.7 percent from the period 1721–1741 to the years 1785–1789[10]), nobles tried to increase their revenues by more scrupulously than ever collecting what was due them, by attempting to revise the *terriers* or copyholds so that the obligations of the peasants would be augmented, and by increasing the share paid them by the *métayers* or sharecroppers. Such efforts created bitternesses which were accentuated by the fact that many of the *philosophes* championed the cause of the peasants and certain nobles granted concessions that made general reform seem to be possible. Voltaire, for example, inveighed against seignorial justice in which the lord sat in judgment of cases in which he was a party at interest and against *mainmorte personnelle,* by which peasant heirs could not inherit the rights to the holding unless living on the holding itself.

---

[10] C. E. Labrousse, *Esquisse du mouvement des prix et des revenues en France au XVIIIe siècle* (Paris: Dalloz, 1932).

In France, unlike England, pressure for the actual acquisition of land to cultivate came from peasants rather than from lords. Here peasant land hunger resulted from a high density of population on arable land, few opportunities for alternative employment, and an unequal distribution of land. In fact, it is estimated that whereas peasants constituted 90 percent of the population, they had the right to work for themselves only 30 percent of the land. In one way or another, to be sure, they worked most of the noble lands, which constituted about 27 percent of the total, clerical lands, which amounted to 15 percent, and the land held by bourgeois, which was 27 percent of the whole, but their wages or other remunerations were meager and they were generally discontented with their lot. In 1789, on the eve of the French Revolution, peasants wanted, as was made clear in their lists of grievances (the peasant *cahiers*), the abolition of the most arbitrary abuses under which they lived, the acquisition of more land, and clear title to the land which they had the right to work.

When Louis XVI called representatives of the three estates together in a national Estates General to find a solution to his pressing financial problems, members of the Third Estate, led by bourgeois, took the position that they were assembled to effect reforms and in the face of royal threats refused to disperse before reform was achieved. In the midst of the accompanying tension in which urban workers, particularly those of Paris, supported the Third Estate, a wave of mass hysteria, known as the Great Fear (*Grande Peur*) spread through the French countryside. In some strange manner rumors flew about that armed forces were coming to enforce harsh demands on the peasants, if not to slaughter them. To protect themselves against such dire, if false, threats, peasants began to attack noble châteaux and to burn manorial rolls (*terriers*) so that no records would exist to which new burdens could be added.

This agitation frightened noble delegates to what had been the Estates General but which had transformed itself into the National Constituent (Constitutional) Assembly in Paris. On the celebrated night of August 4, some of the nobles promised to surrender certain of their seignorial rights without receiving compensation and to give peasants clear title, free of all seignorial encumbrances, to their land upon payment of indemnities equal, as a rule, to the revenue which they would expect to get from a holding over a period of twenty years.

Although peasants at first rejoiced at these gestures, they were subsequently disgruntled because of the indemnity payments required and other reforms that were being realized by the urban leaders of the revolutionary movement. Only after further uprisings and when the urban revolution was threatened both by civil war and by attacks from abroad did peasants get clear title to their lands without the payment of any compensation, for their support of the Revolution was absolutely necessary. As a result, a considerable portion of the agricultural land of France was destined to be in small holdings on which many of the horse-drawn implements were not practicable and from which such small incomes were derived as to mitigate against owners' making capital investments in farming.

This was not, however, the only reform of the French Revolution which contributed to a system of relatively small holdings in France. Early in the Revolution, the state seized the lands of the Church on the grounds that they belonged to the people, and with them as a reserve, issued money (the *assignats*) in order to pay the pressing bills of the government. Church lands were to be sold in part for *assignats,* which would then be retired, and in part for regular currencies, which would be used to pay the growing expenses of the state. Although the scheme did not work as planned, *assignats* being issued in such large quantities that they could not be retired and that their value declined in one of the great inflationary episodes of Modern Times, land was actually sold. Some of it went to speculators and to wealthy persons who bought large parcels, because the terms of purchase generally required large and immediate payments, but probably more than half of it went eventually into the hands of peasants. Similarly, the lands of the nobles who fled France during the Revolution, the so-called *émigrés,* were seized by the state and sold; and steps were taken, the *Ventôse* decrees, which aimed to distribute among Revolutionary soldiers the property of the "suspects"—those suspected of being opposed to the Revolution—although not much land was disposed of under them. Of the land thus distributed, perhaps half was acquired by peasants and became divided into small holdings. Some was bought by "dummies" for nobles in order to keep their estates intact. Some was purchased by capitalistically inclined investors who wanted to farm for profit. And some wound up in the possession of speculators.

All subsequent efforts to the land reforms of the Revolution failed. The Napoleonic regime confirmed the Revolutionary disposition of Church lands by the Concordat of 1801 and it did nothing to return noble lands to their former owners. Even the "milliard des émigrés," an indemnity paid to nobles in the Restoration (1825), did not result in the reconstitution by noble families of large estates. Finally, the Code Napoléon is said to have worked toward a system of small holdings, for it specified that a father with one child should leave the child half his property; one with two children, two-thirds of his property; and one with three or more, three-fourths of his holdings. When reliable censuses of landholdings were taken in France, it was seen that France had, indeed, more small holdings than most countries, but there were still some farms of good size (Table 9).

French agriculture did not experience the sustained burst of technical change and expansion of output that occurred in England, despite France's great wealth in the Early Modern period. As we have now come to associ-

Table 9. Landholding in France

Size of holding, in hectares (1 hectare = 2.47 acres)	Number of holdings			
	1862	1882	1892	1908
Very small: less than 1		2,167,667	2,235,405	2,087,851
Small: 1–10	2,435,401	2,635,030	2,617,588	2,523,713
Medium: 10–40	636,309	727,222	711,118	745,862
Large: 40–100	154,167	142,088	105,391	118,497
Very large: over 100			33,280	29,541
Total		5,672,007	5,702,752	5,505,464

ate agricultural expansion with population growth we might expect that no demographic explosion took place in France in the nineteenth century, and such was the case. Although in the mid-1800s the rate of natural increase of the population of England and Wales was 11 per thousand per year, in corresponding years the French rate was 3 per thousand, and so it remained with slight variation well into the present century. The absence of the "critical spiral" of early economic growth (expanding agricultural incomes enabling early marriage and large families whose offspring feed the fires of aggregate demand) is the principal explanation for the relative stagnation of the French economy in the nineteenth century. In those years France worried about its static population. In an age of nationalism and international warfare, the problem took on added dimensions. Questions of "national virility" and the maintenance of army strength became serious issues. For these reasons, those branches of social science that deal with population movement and the sociology of the family are largely French creations.

Returning to agriculture, we can summarize the causes of stagnation in French farming in a phrase—small plot size. Even the *gros fermiers,* those farm managers who leased large tracts from absent landowners and mobilized labor and capital in a relatively modern way, could not muster the momentum to "engross." The power of ancient property rights and love of land was too strong to overcome, and the food market was too sluggish really to remunerate radical restructuring of the rural sector.[11]

In Germany, the landholding situation became more complicated during the nineteenth century than in either England or France because various

[11] In other words, the market was not extensive and dynamic enough to tempt innovators to overthrow established land-use patterns completely. Population pressure was not sufficient to enforce the additional risk-taking of agrarian revolution. To look at it another way, we might adopt Arnold Toynbee's conception of "challenge and response." He observed that small challenges often meet with no response at all. In England population growth was a major challenge to the food-producing sector of the economy, and the revolutionizing of agriculture was the enforced response. In France the livelihood of individuals was not threatened by rapid growth of population, and consequently no agricultural revolution was elicited.

states pursued different policies in the matter of peasant and land reform. In a general way, it may be said, however, that in Prussia east of the Elbe and in Mecklenburg, large farms were created by lords from their estates, that in Hannover, Schleswig-Holstein, Westphalia, and Upper Bavaria, large peasant holdings predominated, and that in the west and southwest, along the Rhine, the Main, and the Neckar Rivers, small holdings were the most usual (Table 10).

Table 10. Landholding in Germany

Area of tillage, 1907	Millions of hectares	Acreage of holdings, in percent			
		Up to 12.5	12.5–50	50–250	Over 250
East of the Elbe	13.9	8.5	22.7	28.5	40.3
West of the Elbe	17.9	22.0	40.0	30.0	8.0

The explanation for the differences in the various regions of Germany is to be found in the nature of the seignorial system in the three regions, the kind of agriculture best suited to the different soils and climates, and the character of reforms which were effected. In Prussia east of the Elbe, the lords traditionally had overseen production on their own lands. They grew grain successfully and found a ready market for it in Western Europe, whence they imported a variety of products such as salt, textiles, and wine. Thus they came to farm for profit rather than to hold land on which they could collect seignorial dues in kind or money.

Under this system of *Gutsherrschaft*, that is, the production of goods, the labor services of peasants were of extreme importance to lords and they made every effort to maintain serfdom intact. That they were successful in their endeavor is attested to by the fact that their peasants were usually not free to leave the lord's estate, had to render him many services, even the menial ones (*Gesindedienst*), such as work in the lord's kitchen and stables, and had to swear to him an oath of allegiance.

In spite of the extreme subservience of peasants to lords, a movement for reform got under way in the Germanies. Peasants agitated for freedom from seignorial restrictions and Prussian leaders came to believe, after Napoleon's defeat of their country, that they should get peasant support for a war of liberation by making concessions to them. Thus the edicts (1807–1809) of Baron vom Stein abolished serfdom, allowed peasants to leave the land, relieved them of *Gesindedienst*, and permitted them to buy land. At the same time, however, the lords saw to it that the process of reform gave them opportunities to create large holdings. Indeed, the Stein decrees stipulated that the lords had the right to consolidate holdings in large fields, if peasants were given land elsewhere on the estate, and to seize tenures which dated from the second half of the eighteenth century. Similarly, the reforms of Hardenberg, especially the edict of 1811, decreed that those peasants whose right to work a parcel of land was considered heritable could receive clear title to two-thirds of their holdings, but only on condition that the other third be surrendered to their lords. This rule, which in 1816 was declared applicable only to those who could perform *Spanndienst*, that is, could yoke a pair of oxen, other peasants being required usually to surrender up to one-half of their holdings in order to become full proprietors of the rest, played into the hands of the lords, inasmuch as it permitted them to increase the amount of land which they could farm for profit.[12]

In the rest of Germany the seignorial regime was more analogous to that of France, with the richer lords relying on payments from their peasants in kind or money for their incomes rather than on the production of crops for market. This was the system of *Grundherrschaft*. Thus when reform began in Western Germany, lords were less able to hold onto their lands since they stood in a weaker position both politically and economically than their neighbors across the Elbe. In those areas which the French deominated completely at the time of the Revolution, as on the left bank of the Rhine, reforms of the French type were applied wholesale and small peasant proprietorships were created. Here feudalism was abolished (1798) and peasants were given clear title to their holdings without having to pay any indemnity. The property of the Church and the lands of *émigrés*, in this case nobles who opposed the Revolutionary or Napoleonic regimes, were seized and sold.

In the area between the Rhine and the Elbe, as in the Kingdom of Westphalia where French influence was still great but less complete than in the Rhineland, land reform of the Napoleonic period was characterized by the abolition of seignorial dues with compensation.[13] This forced those without enough land on which to make a living to sell out and permitted the richer peasants to form medium-sized holdings.

In other European countries, landholding reforms followed one of the three patterns experienced in Germany. In Denmark, serfdom was abolished in 1788 and peasants were given title to the lands which they had

---

[12] The *Kossaten* and *Häuslern*, that is, the cotters, did not have their houses and garden plots granted to them until after 1850. Manors continued to be the administrative units in some legal respects until the reform of 1892.

[13] In Saxony, indemnity payments were made as late as 1907.

the right to work, but they had to pay compensation to the lords. Consequently there were small holdings along with large estates until after 1899, when lands of the state, of the church, and of some very large proprietors began to be partitioned. In Belgium and the Netherlands, seignorial dues were abolished during the French period of domination (1795–1814). Peasants got title to their holdings, and they were given opportunities to buy properties of the Church and of *émigrés*. In these countries many of the scattered strips were consolidated in unitary farms, especially where the existence of canals made access to dispersed pieces of land particularly difficult.

In Austria, Joseph II abolished serfdom by a decree of 1781, thereby giving peasants freedom to move about as they would, to own land, and to marry whom they pleased. After the Revolution of 1848, Austrian peasants were allowed to acquire land upon the payment of an indemnity. In Italy, although the King of Sardinia began peasant reforms in Savoy prior to the French Revolution, peasants were not freed from seignorial obligations until the French became masters of the land. Much of the arable land here remained in large estates, the latifondia. Small holdings predominated in such mountainous districts as Liguria, the Abruzzi, and Molise, but there were some medium-sized farms where agriculture was highly commercial, especially in the Po Plain with its silk culture, rice growing, and cheese making. In Sicily and Naples lords usually attended to the raising of crops in the *Gutsherrschaft* manner of the region east of the Elbe, but they were prone to use their profits in conspicuous consumption rather than in capital investments on their lands. In the Papal States and Tuscany, the *métayer* system, or as it is called in Italian, the *mezzadria*, predominated and consequently large estates were general and little was done to improve the land. Chief evidence of agricultural advance was to be found on the large estates of the Po Plain, where young nobles like Cavour and capitalist farmers made farming pay and were thus encouraged to keep their holdings intact. Both took advantage of the opportunity to acquire more land when the holdings of the Church and of religious orders were sequestered and sold after unification of the country (1860) (Table 11).

In Ireland, Spain, and Eastern European countries, large estates were general and reform was slow. In Ireland, except for Ulster, large holdings were owned mostly by absentee English landlords who had obtained their properties through conquest and who collected high rents from their tenants. Only in the face of strong opposition from members of secret societies, like the Molly Maguires, and of a 47 percent decline in the population in the seventy years after the potato famine of 1846, did the English government endeavor to establish better conditions for tenants by the "three F's" in the laws of 1870 and 1881—fair rent, fixity of tenure, and

Table 11. Landholding in Italy, 1945

Size of holding, in acres	Percentage of total acreage	Percentage of total units
Up to 5	83.3	17.4
5–25	13.6	24.2
25–125	2.6	23.3
125–250	0.3	9.1
250–1,250	0.1	17.3
Above 1250	0.07	8.7

freedom to sell leases. Not until 1903 did the British government create a fund to enable Irish peasants to buy land by making small annual payments.

In Spain, serfdom was abolished during the Napoleonic period and the Church and religious orders lost their lands in the late 1830s. Yet large estates predominated in certain parts of the country, notably Andalusia, and the breaking up of these holdings remained for long an important economic and political issue. Proposed land reforms of the Republic in 1932 had much to do with the unpopularity of the Republic among the conservatives and were arrested when this regime was overthrown in 1936.

In Rumania, serfs were freed in 1864 and were given an opportunity to acquire land in proportion to the number of oxen which they could harness. The compensation which they had to pay the lords, however, was so great that few could make payments and the land remained in large estates, 37½ percent of it being in holdings of 1,250 acres or more in 1905. In Hungary, serfs were freed in 1848, but they had to pay the lords such large indemnities that they did not acquire much land. Hungary was, therefore, a land of large estates and on them grain was grown so abundantly that in 1900 Hungary was the world's third largest exporter of wheat, ranking after the United States and Russia.

In the latter country, where serfdom had not reached its height until the end of the eighteenth century, peasant reform was not begun until about the middle of the nineteenth century. Then money payments, that is, quitrents, began to be substituted for seignorial dues. Serfs took violent action for reform, especially after Russia's defeat in the Crimean War, and landlords experienced such a shortage of labor that they were hiring some workers for wages and were beginning to think that the peasant system was uneconomical. In 1848, peasants were encouraged to buy land; between 1859 and 1866, 2 million serfs were freed on the estates of the Crown and an equal number on noble estates were emancipated by the edict of 1861. By the terms of this measure peasants not only were freed from seignorial dues but also, on the payment of an indemnity, were given title to the land which previously they had had the right to work. Inasmuch as many peasants did not have savings with which to pay the sums required of them, the state immediately provided funds in the form of state bonds to compensate the lords for their loss of seignorial dues and allowed the peasants up to forty-nine years to make reimbursement for these advances.

Unfortunately this peasant reform did not work so well as had been anticipated. Landlords, already heavily in debt (40 percent of their estates and 70 percent of male serfs had been mortgaged prior to 1861), were short of working capital for farming on a capitalist basis and sharply falling agricultural prices in the period 1873–1896 made their situation still worse. Under the circumstances in which they found themselves, they dumped the bonds which they had received at low prices. These sales did not suffice to meet their needs, so they began to sell land to the richer peasants, the kulaks. In fact, they disposed of some 59 percent of their lands before 1916.

Emancipated serfs, for their part, had great difficulty in making their payments to the state, especially because of the fall of agricultural prices which followed so soon on their having been freed. Moreover, because redemption payments seemed to be so burdensome, some peasants (15 percent up to 1880) did not even try to obtain land. In order to rectify this situation, the purchase of land was made compulsory in 1881 and payments were simultaneously reduced by 27 percent. Even so, many peasants were dissatisfied either because their payments were too heavy or because they had too little land. In addition, they suffered from periodic famines, like the one of 1891–1892. After Russia's defeat by Japan in 1905 and in the face of peasant agitation, some effort was made to meet these complaints. The state canceled all peasant emancipation payments. It built railways to aid the peasants in getting their produce to market, and encouraged the construction of storage facilities in order to provide more adequately for years of poor crops. Not until the Bolshevik Revolution of 1917, however, were attempts made on a large scale to satisfy peasants' hunger for land by the seizure of large estates.

Landholding in areas of Western culture outside Europe

In the great agricultural areas overseas which were settled by Europeans, the landholding problem was quite different from that in the Old World. In the new lands there was no firmly established seignorial system with its elaborate network of dues which were to be paid for the right to use the lands of the overlord, nor was there any shortage of land to meet the requirements of a discontented rural population. On the contrary, in most places there were vast unpopulated, or sparsely populated, territories where the major initial problems were (1) how to get people to settle on the land and (2) how the land should be divided among newcomers.

As a general rule, land in these territories in the period prior to the second quarter of the nineteenth century was originally granted to friends of the kings who had taken claim to it, to administrative officials, and to religious orders. These large grants were, as a rule, subsequently sold in order that the original grantee be able to realize something on his holdings. Sometimes these sales were in small lots to attract colonizers, sometimes in fairly large units to speculators who might subsequently sell them to actual farmers, and sometimes in large estates, if conditions of soil, climate, topography, and the market were such as to make large-scale operations feasible and profitable. As a rule, relatively large farms were created on these lands, and recourse was had to "extensive" rather than to "intensive" agriculture, that is, to the use of a large amount of land per worker and to practices that gave relatively low production per acre but high production per man-hour. Furthermore, extensive agriculture meant the use of cheap labor, as on the cotton plantations of the American South and the sugar plantations of Cuba, the adoption of a great amount of machinery, as on the wheat farms of the American Middle West and of Canada, or the raising of sheep and cattle on ranges where the animals did most of the work of feeding themselves, as on the ranges of America, Australia, and the Argentine.

In the United States the first grantees, like Lord Baltimore in Maryland, William Penn in Pennsylvania, John Mason in New Hampshire, and the Virginia Company, received large amounts of land. Subsequently these grantees disposed of parts of their tracts in order to have their lands settled. In the region from New England to Virginia the Colonies usually gave or sold land to yeoman farmers in amounts sufficient at the time to support a family, a fact which goes to explain the predominance even to the present day of the family-sized farm in this area. From Virginia southward, where cotton and tobacco culture thrived, buyers of land were capitalist farmers, and as a rule, they acquired large tracts.[14]

After the War of Independence, the United States sold public land in rather large units because the task of disposing of it in small parcels was very great. Indeed, many of the Founding Fathers, of whom George Washington was a good example, speculated in land by buying large tracts from the government and then selling it as opportunity permitted in small units. During the War Between the States, however, the government adopted what was essentially a new policy in disposing of public lands. In large part

---

[14] In the mountainous parts of these territories, plantations could not be operated and so the land was sold in family-sized lots.

to win the people of the Northwest to the Northern cause, the government passed the Homestead Act of 1862,[15] which provided, as we have already seen, that 160 acres would be given free to any head of a family who resided on or cultivated for five years his holding upon the payment of a small registration fee; or this same person might buy his land after a residence of six months at the prevailing minimum, about one dollar and 25 cents an acre. In some areas, 160 acres constituted too small a farm to sustain a family and so "homesteaders" sometimes sold their lands, which gave others an opportunity to form larger farms. Also it was possible for the farmer to get land under the Timber Culture Act (1873) by planting trees on part of it, under the Desert Land Act (1877) by irrigating it, or under the Timber and Stone Act (1878) by staking a claim for what was declared to be nonarable. Moreover, large amounts of public land went to interests which were later to sell great and even mammoth tracts to farmers. Thus the railroads got over 131 million acres from the federal government and another 51 million acres from states as subsidies. The states received some 203 million acres from the federal government to accelerate the making of public improvements and to support agricultural and technical schools under the College Land Grant Act of 1862. And some land was sold at public auction. Just what the landholding situation was, it is difficult to say, but according to the census of 1880 the average farm had 134 acres, whereas that of 1950 indicated an average of 200 acres. Two-thirds of the tracts reported in 1950 as farms were actually rural residences for town dwellers or rural laborers. Thus, producing farms had a much larger acreage than the national average. In 1880, most of the farms were worked by owners, only about one-quarter being operated by tenants.

In Australia, land was granted freely in large tracts until 1831; then it was sold at auction; and after 1847 some of it was leased with an option to purchase. In general the unit holding was very large because much of the land was only suitable for grazing. In fact, tracts were so large that the problem of squatters in remote parts became a major issue. In Canada, the family farm was characteristic of the Maritime provinces, Quebec, and Ontario, although farms ran somewhat larger in Quebec than in the other eastern regions because the French had once had a seignorial system with large holdings that was not entirely obliterated until 1854. In the Prairie provinces, however, where some 90 percent of all Canadian wheat came to be grown, land was sold in large units so that the average farm there is some 335.4 acres as compared with an average of less than 200 in the east. Then in Chile, 50 million of the 57 million acres of the country were

---

[15] The Preemption Act of 1841 had provided that heads of families who had settled on unsurveyed public lands of the frontier and who were squatters had the right to purchase their land at the minimum price when it was put on sale. This Act was repealed in 1891.

owned by about 2,500 persons at the end of the nineteenth century, and concentration in the Argentine was probably as great.

The impact of overseas competition on European agriculture

Although the four major phases of the agricultural history of Western culture from the end of the eighteenth century to the close of the nineteenth were (1) the introduction of horse-drawn machinery, (2) the use of science in the treatment of the soil, in the selection and care of plants, and in the breeding of livestock, (3) the freeing of serfs in Europe with the attendant formation of small holdings in France, Belgium, the Netherlands, and Western Germany and of large estates elsewhere, and (4) the bringing into cultivation of vast areas overseas, there was still another development of great importance—the impact of overseas competition on European agriculture. From the early 1870s grains and meat, especially mutton and beef, began to come into Western Europe in large quantities and at prices which European producers could not meet. Accordingly, Europeans had to adjust their operations to produce those things in which they could compete or they had to seek high protection by means of tariffs, embargoes, and other restrictions on imports. If recourse were had to the first solution, experience came to show that they could compete in those products which required a large amount of labor per unit, like fresh vegetables, fresh fruit, poultry, dairy products, and pork. If salvation were sought in protection, the price of such staples as wheat remained far above the free-market level and hence resulted in making the consumer pay a kind of subsidy to the farmer.

From at least 1817, Western European farmers had feared foreign competition, for at that time France had imported grain from the Ukraine at prices which were extremely low in order to meet shortages of famine proportions. Then toward the middle of the nineteenth century farmers became particularly apprehensive, for in 1846 England repealed its Corn Laws, that is, its protection on grains. France again imported wheat from Russia at low prices, and in the early 1860s most Western European countries reduced their tariffs on agricultural products as part of a general European movement to lower rates. The realization of these fears was postponed by the Crimean War (1853–1856), which closed the Baltic and Black Sea to Russian grain, by the American Civil War (1861–1865), which turned American energies to war, and by the brisk demand for home-grown food at relatively high prices because of the growth of population, buoyant price levels, and comparatively high purchasing power resulting from industrial expansion. In fact, the period from 1853 to 1873 was one of prosperity for European farmers.

Yet the threat of overseas competition was particularly great and it began to be felt after 1873. A reduction in ocean freight rates occasioned by the success of clipper ships, the appearance of iron tramp steamers, and a reduction in the cost of land carrying with the construction of railways into the belts of extensive agriculture, like the American Middle West, made transportation cheaper. Furthermore, the use of cheap labor in Eastern Europe, the mechanization of wheat growing in America, and the grazing of cattle on the vast ranges of wild grass permitted the importation of agricultural goods in Europe at derisory prices. The cost of transporting grain from Chicago to New York went from 33 cents to 14 cents a bushel between 1870 and 1881, that of transatlantic shipping fell from 20 cents a bushel in 1874 to 2 cents in 1904, the opening of the Suez Canal in 1869 reduced rates from Australia to London, and refrigerator ships and cars made possible the handling of meat in the 1880s. Then, to make matters worse for the European farmer, the general level of prices reacted downward beginning in 1873 and remained low until 1896—a period known as the "long depression in prices." In this period agricultural prices fell lower than industrial prices, which only added to the woes of the farmer. The great staples were particularly hard hit, the price of wheat for example dropping from a dollar and a half a bushel in 1871 to 86 cents in 1885, and for one day to 23 cents, whereas the price of meat declined by about 25 percent from 1873 to 1896. Meanwhile grain exports from North America increased from an annual average of 5.5 million bushels for the years 1851–1860 to 150 million bushels in 1880. The United States raised its exports of chilled meat from 1,095 hundredweight in 1874 to 1,275,948 hundredweight in 1889. Australia brought its exports of wool to Britain up from 38,018,000 pounds in 1850 to 505,197,000 pounds in 1910. Finally, China and Japan undercut European silk producers so drastically that the end of the growing of the silkworm in Europe seemed imminent.

The plight of European farmers was, moreover, made even more disastrous as a result of a series of misfortunes. In the first place, a number of bad years with too little or too much rain hurt grain production; rinderpest destroyed cattle in the 1860s; sheep rot took a heavy toll of sheep in the late 1870s; phyloxera, a minute, green insect, raised havoc with the vineyards of France; and an epidemic of disease destroyed silkworms. Under such circumstances it is not strange that in Great Britain 4 million acres out of a total of 23 million acres of arable went out of cultivation between 1876 and 1907, that the number of sheep in Germany declined from nearly 25 million in 1873 to 10,866,772 in 1897, that French wine production fell from 1879 to 1889 by two-thirds, and that French raw silk production fell by one-third.

Nor is it to be wondered at that farmers cried for tariff protection, that they organized politically to get it, and that their efforts were by the late

1870s producing results. The French Société des Agriculteurs managed to push through the famous Méline tariff of 1892. In Germany, tariff rates were raised in 1879, 1885, and 1888, and the Bund der Landwirte got exceptionally high protection in the agricultural tariff of 1902. Italy raised its rates in 1878, 1887, and 1891 and tangled with the French in the famous tariff war from 1888 to 1899. And even in free-trade Great Britain there was serious agitation led by Joseph Chamberlain and his "Fair Traders" for protection. Yet neither here, nor in the Netherlands, Denmark, or Finland, was a return to high tariffs attempted. These free-trade nations pursued the policy of changing their agricultural production to lines in which they could compete.

Undoubtedly the most drastic and dramatic adjustments to overseas competition were made in Denmark. There, at the beginning of the agricultural depression when wheat prices began to slump, farmers followed the old adage of "Down corn, up horn" and turned from the growing of grain to the raising of livestock, especially cattle. When, however, meat prices also went down, they did not send their herds to slaughterhouses but increased their output of dairy products. Beginning in 1875 they formed cooperative creameries to handle milk and to produce butter and cheese. The invention of the De Laval cream separator (1879) helped in the mechanization of creamery work and the practice of pasteurization, which followed Louis Pasteur's famous paper on lactic fermentation in 1858, and the making of butter by the addition of lactic acid and of cheese by the use of special cultures, allowed them to produce more efficiently and to standardize their products. Their buttermilk they used to fatten pigs, which they could raise at low cost, and they added poultry as a side line to take up the winter months when field work was light. For their products the Danes found a ready market—the English breakfast table which traditionally carried, along with porridge, bacon, eggs, cheese, and buttered toast. The value of Danish exports of these goods increased tenfold from the early 1880s to 1914.

To some extent the Netherlands followed the Danish example, and even in those countries which had tariff protection farmers made some alterations in production in the face of overseas competition. Gradually hogs took the place of sheep, the hog population of Germany rising from some 7 million in 1873 to over 22 million in 1907; the acreage given to the sugar beet in France nearly tripled from 1860 to 1914.[16] The acreage given to potatoes in Germany increased nearly 20 percent from 1880 to 1912; the

---

[16] The growing of sugar beets flourished after the middle of the century. Most countries gave subsidies to growers. The granting of bounties became so extensive that sugar-beet-growing nations signed the Brussels Convention in 1902, by which they agreed to stop paying export bounties and to punish by high tariffs those states which continued to give them.

production of fresh vegetables grew impressively with the coming of rapid transportation. The bovine population, largely in dairying, grew steadily in both France and Germany. Moreover, the holders of large estates acquired more machinery in an effort to reduce costs, as was being done in America, the number of mowing machines quadrupling in France from 1862 to 1892 and increasing some twenty times in Germany from 1895 to 1907, when the process of mechanization was most rapid. Finally, better field and animal husbandry brought an improvement in yields per acre and in production per head of livestock. Thus European agriculture was prevented from going into eclipse. Only in England was there for the moment little effort to save the farms and by World War I, England was producing less than 25 percent of its food needs.

The period of low prices, especially for agricultural products, was one of great agricultural expansion in overseas lands, as we have seen, but in spite of this growth and the inroads made on European agriculture, these areas experienced considerable discontent among farmers. The grumbling was particularly marked in the United States, where it took the form of agitation for better railway and shipping rates, demands for more liberal terms on which to get public land, and "campaigns for monkeying with the money," that is, for forcing prices up by inflationary policies. In Russia, the price decline made the emancipation payments more difficult, as we have seen, and led finally to the cancellation of peasant obligations. And in Canada it led to greater production on larger units. Finally, in 1896, a rise in agricultural prices saved the farmer from being crucified on a cross of depressed prices. During the experience of the Great Depression there had developed in agriculture a greater division of labor in the world, the satisfying of a greater proportion of Europe's needs by imports, and an improvement in agricultural techniques.

It is instructive to note that the depression of 1873 to 1896 differed from previous downswings insofar as agriculture was concerned. It was severe and of long duration, but the years of even the most severe trauma were not marked by famine and starvation as were pre-Modern depressions in Europe. Modern cultivation involves a small proportion of the labor force supplying food for the majority. By 1870 in most Western European countries the majority of the population had ceased to be engaged in agriculture (Table 12). Even during adverse climatic or market conditions, fertilization and mechanization maintained acceptable levels of food supply for both the countryside and its dependent cities.

The severest contrast between Modern and pre-Modern agrarian systems in Europe is that of England and Ireland earlier on, in the 1840s. The "hungry forties" was a bad decade for agriculture. In Modern England the forties brought privation and hardship, but no catastrophe. In Ireland one and a half million left the country and a half million died. *Phytophthora*

Table 12. Percentage of the labor force in agriculture, selected countries

Country	Percentage of labor force in agriculture	
	Mid–19th century	Mid–20th century
Great Britain	23 (1841)	5 (1951)
France	30 (1861)	20 (1951)
Belgium	24 (1880)	11 (1947)
Norway	49 (1875)	25 (1950)
Sweden	55 (1870)	19 (1950)
Italy	51 (1871)	35 (1951)
United States	68 (1840)	12 (1950)

SOURCE: Kuznets, *Modern Economic Growth,* p. 106.

infestans (the potato blight) was not the whole story. Between 1750 and 1840 the number of people in both England and Ireland doubled. But unlike "mother England," Ireland continued to rely on small-plot peasant monoculture. When the crop failure happened in 1845 the Irish were little better protected from disaster than their peasant counterparts in four-teenth-century Tuscany or seventeenth-century Beauvais. The difference between the English and Irish experience, was, simply put, modernization in agriculture.

Sizable areas of Western Europe remain pre-Modern even to the present day, but in no Western country has modernization been so retarded that famine poses a periodic threat to life. This is the ultimate benefit of agricultural modernity.

The mechanization
of industry

New techniques of the Industrial Revolution

The intricate interconnections among the various branches of human activity constitute one of the most baffling objects of study for social scientists. Investigators want to know what role economic phenomena play in
the creation of social institutions and in the formation of interest groups.
They want to know how social institutions and interest groups make their
weight felt in political life, how political action influences the minds of
men, how ideas and ideologies react on economic behavior, and so on in
endless variations. It is unreal to isolate one part of the exceedingly complex pattern of life in society and then to attribute all change to it. It is more
in accordance with what has actually happened through time to recognize
that "multiple factors" in various parts of the total scene account for great
movements in society.

Thus in the study of the Industrial Revolution the historian may separate mechanical inventions, chemical discoveries, and the development of
new techniques from their environment in such a way as to make them
seem to have sprung from nowhere, and thereby to make them appear to
have been the brainchildren of a few notable geniuses. Moreover, the
historian may make their adoption seem to have been in the vanguard of
change and thus suggest that all other phases of societal life, like ideologies, social groupings, and political parties, "lagged" behind techniques
and had to adjust to them.

As a matter of fact, however, most new ways of producing goods and
services have come about as the answer to well-defined and recognized
needs, as if to confirm the old adage that "necessity is the mother of
invention" and as if, indeed, new techniques "lagged" behind a social need

for them. Furthermore, the factors which contributed toward bringing forth new techniques were not only numerous but they came together during the Industrial Revolution for the first time in all history in just the right proportions and in just the right relationships to produce a cluster of new mechanical contrivances. Here is striking evidence of the importance of the doctrine of necessary concomitances, which is opposed to the traditional manner of thought that assumes a prior cause and subsequent effect, as in the simple syllogism.

The necessary and sufficient forces which were at work together in the environment which produced mechanized industry seem to have been (1) a desire for material betterment, (2) a considerable knowledge of mechanics, hydraulics, and metallurgy, (3) capital for investment, (4) a demand for more goods, (5) raw materials in sufficient and concentrated supply to be worked on a large scale, (6) methods of transportation to make possible the accumulation of supplies and to carry finished goods to market, and (7) workers who were willing to work for a daily wage and who were able to adapt themselves to new ways of doing things. In large measure these potentials for modernization in industry depended upon a dynamic condition in the economy: rising real incomes and rising expectations. High levels of demand for goods and the availability of funds for investment imply high income levels. More indirectly, rising incomes meant improving levels of health and education—key determinants of the quality of the labor force and of the fund of entrepreneurial talent. Finally, no stronger impetus to the desire for material betterment has ever been devised than income gains in the present which give a taste of better things to come. In light of these considerations, the contribution of a dynamic agrarian sector to the progress of industry must be reiterated. As we know from earlier discussions, the conditions for industrial advances were most adequately present in Great Britain, although to a lesser extent they existed in many places in the Western world, so that, in fact, mechanized industrial production was diffused fairly rapidly, once its advantages had become recognized.

England's advantage

Eighteenth-century England was the most fertile medium for industrialization for a variety of reasons. It has been justly observed, therefore, that modernization in England is the *worst* example for later modernizing countries to emulate, for, inevitably, backward countries face disadvantages that England did not suffer. On the other hand, the English had to start from scratch in many respects, whereas subsequent modernizers might borrow technology and save on the costs of developing new methods of production. Great Britain, the first industrializer, is clearly a special case. Her unique advantages may be briefly enumerated as follows:

1   The ongoing cycle of growing population and swelling agricultural output (p. 258) provided a source of expanding aggregate demand and investment funds.

2   England's heritage of specialization in pre-Modern trade and industry was an ideal "childhood" for an industrial nation. In the late seventeenth century as much as 40 percent of the labor force may have been engaged in nonagrarian pursuits; no country since has enjoyed such a favorable labor-force structure at the brink of industrilization.

3   Yet labor was not entirely abundant in early British manufacturing centers. Wages were rising in the eighteenth century, and this was a distinct advantage; it proved a great impetus to mechanize, substituting capital for labor in the manufacturing process. As we shall see, the massive gains in output of the English textile industry are largely traceable to the simple desire of entrepreneurs to reduce the number of hands engaged in making a bolt of cotton cloth.

4   Finally, the payoff for economic achievement at all levels of society was greater in England than elsewhere. At the lowest levels, exploitation was less severe in England than in pre-Revolutionary Europe, and the resulting more even distribution of income meant that one who worked to accumulate some wealth saw some likelihood in keeping most of it. True, labor was costly in such circumstances. British real wages were twice as high as wages in France in the eighteenth century. But the relatively higher purchasing power of the masses in England meant greater demand for those commodities that they could use and afford. Mass production of plain, uniform, utilitarian goods was the result.

Higher up the social scale, the British middle class was assured that as its members invested and accumulated wealth, social benefits would follow, making the risk and struggle for upward mobility worthwhile. Elsewhere in *ancien régime* Europe, *nouvelle richesse* brought revulsion and ostracism. The *bourgeois gentilhomme* was a comic figure in society, not only on the stage. How unsatisfactory it must have been to labor and to endure the threat of failure that attends entrepreneurship only to win derision! Wealth is never really its own reward. In England, the path to the elevated social status of the squirearchy and beyond was more open and the social rewards to economic endeavor for the middle class were more reasonable than on the Continent.

At the uppermost level of English society, those whose high station was due to birth rather than to ambition were at least not deterred from enterprise by the dictates of social convention. That a member of the upper classes might willingly soil his hands with agricultural experimentation, mechanical tinkering, or an active role in commerce without disgracing his station in life was virtually unique in England before the nineteenth century. Elsewhere in Europe the attitude of the aristocracy to gainful employment outside the army, Church, government, or landed estate had not changed measurably since the time of the fictional Lazarillo de Tormes (1500s), whose *hidalgo* master would sooner starve than work.

The combination of these social and economic factors made Britain the stage for the germination of industrial modernity.

Mechanization of the textile industry

In the early phase of the Industrial Revolution, the most far-reaching inventions were made in the textile, ferrous metal, and power-machine industries. The demand for the products of all these phases of production was great; all had the possibility of producing rich rewards for successful entrepreneurs, and all at the handicraft stage required extraordinary amounts of human energy and procedures which were extremely boring and repetitious. Moreover, technical changes in these industries had a profound effect upon subsequent industrial developments. Those in the textile trade did much to show the advantages to be derived from a division of labor, to establish production on a factory basis, and to turn out standardized goods for an unknown market. Improvements in the manufacture of ferrous metals and the consequent lowering of the price of iron made available a building material which was essential for the construction of machines that could withstand the wear and tear of rapid operation under heavy load. And the development of power plants, using inanimate materials that were in large supply, made possible the driving of machines which were concentrated in factories and the propelling of carriers that furnished safer, more adequate, and cheaper transportation.

Which branch of industry should be regarded as the pioneer in change is somewhat arbitrary, for innovations were visible at about the same time in various trades. However, inasmuch as some of the first of the more dramatic aspects of mechanization took place in the textile industry, especially in the making of cotton cloth, it has become traditional to begin the account of the Industrial Revolution with this industry.

That some of the first important changes in techniques in the eighteenth century should have taken place in this trade is not surprising. In the first place, textile techniques were already at such a point of development that only a few minor alterations had to be effected to render both spinning and weaving semiautomatic and to make the application of mechanical powers to these operations practicable. Inasmuch as many persons were familiar with existing textile techniques because of the widespread practice of spinning and weaving, the inventive talent of very large numbers was brought to bear on solving fundamental problems of cloth manufacture. Cloth was in great demand, for everyone used it and some, like the inhabitants of large cities and pioneers overseas, did not produce their own because of more pressing demands upon their time.[1] The textile trades were relatively free to use new techniques to reduce costs of production, for the putting-out part of the woolen business was not subject to guild regulations and the monopolistic guilds never existed in cotton because it was a new industry.

In the textile industry, the real bottlenecks of production were in spinning and weaving, for the fulling of woolens had been mechanized; cottons could be printed expeditiously with woodblocks on flat presses; and the hand operations of combing (straightening out such fibers as cotton) and carding (mixing short fibers in a fluffy mass so that they can be twisted) consumed little time. In spinning, the problems were that an operator had to "draw out" the fiber into a loose strand, then twist this strand by use of a revolving and falling weight, of a spinning stick or spindle twirled with the fingers, or, more commonly in Europe in the early eighteenth century, of a spinning wheel which was run by a foot pedal, and finally wind the finished thread onto a bobbin. This process was slow, tedious, expensive, and ill-paid. What was needed was a method of production which would mechanically perform some of all of these operations.[2]

In weaving, the main difficulty was "throwing" the shuttle through the strands of thread that constituted the warp and then of "beating" the thread left by the shuttle so that it would come compactly against the previous thread thrown (Figure 18). In the case of one weaver working alone, the width of a piece of cloth was determined by the distance to which he could reach to his right to throw the shuttle and then to his left to throw it back again; or in the case of two weavers working together, one at each side of the loom, by the distance that the shuttle would travel with one throw. In any case, the pace of these operations was slow, for the throws were fatiguing and between every throw the weaver had to pull the beater.

Because spinning and weaving were light enough to be practiced by anyone, even children, and because both tasks could be performed in odd moments of the day and in seasons when other work was slack, entire

---

[1] The West Indies and the American Colonies took 10 percent of English domestic exports in 1700 to 1701 and 57 percent in 1797 to 1798. Woolen goods accounted for about two-thirds of these exports at the beginning of the eighteenth century and for some 27 percent at its close. See Phyllis Deane and W. A. Cole, *British Economic Growth 1688–1959: Trends and Structure* (London: Cambridge, 1962), pp 30–34.

[2] The distaff or "rock" was simply a device for holding the loose fibers before spinning. It consisted usually of a multiforked stick.

Figure 18

Hand loom. This wooden hand loom of the early nineteenth century was used in Maine. The photograph shows the threads of the warp strung through the string heddles. By operating the pedals the heddles may be raised and lowered so that a shed is obtained between the alternate threads of the warp. Through this shed the shuttle passes with the thread which constitutes the woof. The beater, upon which the hand of the operator may be discerned, is pulled back toward the operator and pushes the thread of the woof back to make the material firm. *(Reproduced with permission of Textile World.)*

households, especially in country districts, became engaged in them. To take advantage of this available but widely dispersed labor force, certain textile merchants began to take raw materials to the workers, sometimes to provide the workers with spinning wheels and looms, to pay labor by the piece for processing their materials, and to market the finished products. This was the "merchant-employer" or "putting-out" system.

With the growth of "putting-out," the stimuli to improve techniques in spinning and weaving became ever more impelling, for here lay the chances for gaining larger profits or avoiding drudgery. Evidence of attempts to make existing methods of production more efficient can be seen in the improvements made during the sixteenth century in the so-called Saxton spinning wheel with its flyer, crank, and shaft power from a pedal, and variable speeds given to spool and spindle, and in the development of the Dutch loom in which the shuttle was driven to and fro by a crank device and which was used at least in Germany and England for weaving ribbons.

Not until the eighteenth century, however, were solutions found to be chief problems in spinning and weaving which would permit a marked increase in production per operative. When they began to be discovered, they appeared almost simultaneously in the two main divisions of cloth-making. The first major improvement in textile manufacture after 1700 was the "flying shuttle," an invention patented by the Englishman John Kay in 1733. Kay was intimately acquainted with the process of weaving and knew the blocks in the way of higher production, for he was not only a weaver but also a maker of "reeds" for looms—the comb-like device which holds the threads of the warp in place and which beats every thread of the woof. He is credited with having substituted steel wires for the usual wood, horn, or reeds used in "reeds" in order to eliminate breakage and warping (1730). But the greatest ingenuity which he displayed was in the invention of a mechanical device for throwing the shuttle back and forth. This flying shuttle consisted of a shuttle fitted with small wheels which ran in a wooden groove that was always exposed as the threads of the warp rose and fell. The shuttle was struck by hammers at either side of the loom, which were activated by the weaver who pulled a cord from his usual position on the weaver's seat in the middle of the loom. In this way one operator alone could drive the shuttle across a wide warp, and he could do so much more quickly than he had ever been able to do by throwing it by hand from side to side.

Kay's invention was to have profound consequences for the textile industry, but at the very outset it was unpopular with weavers who feared that it would put them out of work. In fact, the story is told that the weavers of Manchester were so hostile to Kay that he had to flee the city hidden in a woolsack and take refuge in France. Nevertheless, the flying shuttle was adopted so rapidly in England that the normal ratio of four spinners to one weaver was completely upset. Obviously, the supply of spinners had to be increased or new techniques of spinning had to be developed if full advantage were to be taken of the flying shuttle. The way out of the impasse was to be found in the invention of new spinning machinery.

Some promise of better spinning methods was held out in the early 1730s when John Wyatt, like Kay a professional mechanic and tinkerer, and Lewis Paul, the son of a French refugee who moved in high society, formed a partnership to develop a contraption made by Wyatt. This machine consisted of a series of rollers which were rotated in such a fashion that they gave to a loose strand of carded fibers a twist that made a thread, much as one could make such a thread by rolling fibers between the thumb and forefinger. Their machine, which was patented in 1738, was not a great success, for it broke down frequently and the thread made from it was weak because of insufficient twist. To remedy the latter deficiency the partners tried to combine the roller principle with that of the spindle, but they fell out before they had perfected their new machine. Nevertheless, they had hit upon ideas which were to be used in later spinning machines, but which had to be greatly elaborated before they were successfully applied in industry.

One of the chief contributors to this elaboration was James Hargreaves of Lancashire, weaver, carpenter, and millwright—and hence like Kay and Wyatt a tinkerer by profession. Not only was Hargreaves intimately acquainted with the technical problems of spinning and weaving, but he became interested in improving them. His first effort of this kind was made in 1762, when he was commissioned by a neighbor, the founder of the Peel textile fortunes, to construct a carding machine, probably after a design by Lewis Paul. His greatest contribution to the industry was, however, his "spinning jenny," named after his wife, which he patented in 1770 (Figure 19).

Tradition has it that the idea for his device came to Hargreaves when he observed that a spinning wheel which had tipped over kept on making thread while the wheel was moving and the loose strands were held in the fingers on the spinner. Accordingly he went ahead to build a machine which consisted of a rectangular frame resting on four legs, with a row of spindles placed vertically on the wheel instead of horizontally as had been the custom. Across the frame and facing the spindles were two wooden rails upon which a carriage that held loose bands (rovings) of cotton fiber on large spools could be moved backward and forward. A spinner was thus able with one hand to turn a crank that drove the spindles so that the yarn could be twisted and with the other to push the carriage which drew the thread when moved back and allowed it to be wound on a bobbin when it moved forward.

Figure 19
Hargreaves' spinning jenny. In the model shown above one may see the upright spindles which gave the rovings the twist. The carriage on top of the machine through which the threads went could be pulled backward and pushed forward, thus drawing out the thread to give it fineness. Mechanical power could be easily substituted for the man-operated crank. *(Reproduced with permission of Textile World.)*

Like the flying shuttle, the spinning jenny was a success. Yet it was soon evident that both devices could be made more automatic and that mechanical power could be used to drive the machines and thus relieve the physical burdens placed upon the operator. One of the most important steps toward the development of power-driven machines in the textile industry was the water frame, patented by Richard Arkwright in 1769. Arkwright, although a barber and wig maker by trade, was familiar with the process of making cloth and had a keen eye for opportunities for earning an extra penny. Possibly he knew of a plan for a power-driven spinning frame which had been developed by a certain Thomas Highs or Hayes, but at all events after a series of lawsuits he began in 1785 to produce water frames for spinners. His enterprises flourished to such a degree that he was able to brag that his fortune would be enough to pay off the national debt of Britain.

Hard on Arkwright's invention came a large cluster of other technical innovations in the making of cloth—a cluster which provides a classic example of how pressures for change bring forth inventive responses and how major developments in technology result from an accumulation of many details. In spinning, Samuel Crompton, the son of a yeoman farmer and a spinner and tinkerer by trade, produced the "mule," which was a cross between the roller and spindle methods of making thread—a machine that made such excellent thread that curious spinners bored holes in the inventor's shop in order to peep in on the secret device. About 1782 a machine was invented to make rovings at low cost, which was a significant step forward because both "mules" and "jennies" used rovings rather than the loosely carded fiber. Furthermore, Richard Roberts, a maker of machines, patented in 1825 the "self-actor," which provided for the automatic motion of the carriage in order to draw threads; John Thorpe of Rhode Island, the center of the textile machine industry in the New World, substituted (1828) for the flyer with hooks on it a flanged annular ring on a C-shaped traveler, which facilitated the winding of the thread on a bobbin and kept the thread under perfect tension.

In the application of mechanical power to weaving, the crucial invention was the "power loom," which was patented in 1785 by Edmund Cartwright. This young man, unlike his contemporary contributors of new techniques, was an Oxford-trained classicist and clergyman. He became interested in mechanics through stories which he heard from his parishioners and applied himself to the devising of an automatic power loom that could keep pace with the expected abundance of yarn from Arkwright's frames. Cartwright's fertile mind soon solved some of the major problems involved in producing the desired machine, and before the end of the century his original prototype was much improved so that it would not break threads while working at the same rate of speed as a hand loom. Still, the adoption of the power loom came about slowly, and in the years between the mechanization of the spinning phase and the wide diffusion of the power loom (after 1815) the hand-loom weaver was in command. During the Napoleonic period, when the cotton trade was upset by blockades of shipping, power looms were developed to a degree where two looms with only one child to oversee their operation could outperform a hand weaver by fifteen times. The weavers, who had been much in demand, were quickly cascaded to the depths of poverty and unemployment as the power loom took over permanently.

The weaving branch of textile manufacture got a loom which was capable of weaving figures and other designs in cloth—a loom that was the invention of the Frenchman Vaucanson and that was subsequently improved by Jacquard (1801). Finally, metal looms began to be made in 1803 and in the same year steam power was for the first time applied to the process of weaving.

In other phases of clothmaking, technical improvements were realized that contributed to the general movement of increasing output per unit of human input. Thus in carding, Richard Arkwright developed (1775) the "crank and comb," probably after the designs of others, which turned the carded fiber out in the form of a strand that could be made into rovings. The French chemist, Claude Louis Berthollet, developed a method of bleaching with chlorine which came to supplant the usual and more cumbersome practice of exposing cloth to the sun in order to make it white. Thomas Bell invented a cylindrical press (1783) for printing cloth, which embodied a principle that was eventually to be introduced into the printing of books (1790). And John Mercer developed a method of processing cotton that gave this fiber a silky feel—"mercerized cotton."

As these various inventions increased the production of cotton goods, the demand for raw cotton grew by leaps and bounds. Here, however, a real bottleneck existed, for picking seeds from the bolls was a slow and laborious task, one worker being able to clean only from 1 to 6 pounds of cotton per day. Some advance in overcoming this difficulty was made with the invention of the rolling mill, which would clean up to 25 pounds per day, but this device could only be used on long-staple cotton and long staple could be grown successfully only in a few parts of the region that supplied most of Europe's cotton—the Southern states of the United States.

A successful solution to the problem of picking seeds from cotton was finally found by the American Eli Whitney, a professional tinkerer and inventor, in 1793. His cotton gin, which consisted of circular saws with dull teeth that pulled cotton fiber through a comb so fine that the seeds remained behind, was capable, if manned by three men, of cleaning some 50 pounds of cotton a day. Inasmuch as this machine worked best on short-staple cotton and short-staple cotton could be grown in the upland Piedmont region of the American South, it was a great boon to that region's economy. It permitted the extension of cotton culture at the very time when a money crop was being sought to accompany tobacco. The gin was largely responsible for the increase of the cotton crop in the United States from 1.5 million pounds in 1790 to 85 million pounds in 1810,[3] and incidentally for the extension of the plantation system and of Negro slavery. It thus contributed much to the tension which developed between the Northern and Southern states, which led finally to the War Between the States.

These various inventions in the textile trades came, by the end of the eighteenth century in England and by the conclusion of the first half of the nineteenth century in Belgium, France, Germany, and the Northeastern states of the United States, to have a visible effect upon the character of industry. The machines were heavy enough to be housed in well-constructed and sometimes specially built establishments, which meant that they were actually concentrated in buildings that came to be known as factories. This concentration of production was accentuated by the fact that mechanized power, at first water and then steam, could not be provided economically unless it worked many machines at once. And the use of power and large supplies of raw materials coming from overseas meant that the location of plants had to be in hills where there was water power, at places where the raw material could be brought by water, and/ or where coal could be delivered at low cost. Power-driven machinery was most economical when machines were banked side by side and superintended by only a few workers. This need for concentration in industry destroyed the putting-out system, replacing disparate units of production with factories. Concentration of the machinery in large factories meant that investors who could mobilize large amounts of money for equipment came to own the means of production—one of the hallmarks of the capitalist system. The cotton textile industry began to relocate in advantageous sites, at such places as Lancashire and Derbyshire in England, on the banks of the Clyde in Scotland, around Rouen, Lille, and Mulhouse in France, at Ghent in Belgium, in the Rhineland near Krefeld in Germany, and along such rivers as the Merrimac in New England.

Of all the cotton textile centers of the world, Britain was by far the most important, primarily because of its leadership in the new techniques. In the first half of the nineteenth century, Great Britain consistently took more than half of all American exports of cotton, and usually more than half the

---

[3] Cottonseed oil began to be used for lighting (1818) and cottonseed cake as a feed for livestock (1821).

American crop was sent abroad. By the beginning of the nineteenth century British cotton textile exports were of greater value than its exports of any other product and in 1841 nearly twice as many workers were employed in the English cotton textile trade as in all the metal trades, ranging from the smelting of iron ore to the making of clocks.

The economic gains which fell to England as a result of the advances in the technology of making cotton cloth were the envy of other nations of Western culture and of manufacturers of other types of textiles. Some countries, notably France, sent industrial spies to England to learn the new techniques and gave subsidies to manufacturers who adopted the new machines or who employed English workers, skilled in the new ways of production, while certain political entities, like the Northern states of the United States, gave bounties to those who would improve local methods of spinning and weaving. Some entrepreneurs, like John Cockerill at Seraing in the Belgian Netherlands, and Samuel Slater in Rhode Island, made fortunes in producing machines patterned after those of England.

Producers of other kinds of textiles, for their part, showed evidence of a desire to lower costs by the use of power-driven machines and by developing new sources of raw materials. The jenny was used for spinning wool as early as 1773, although it was not widely adopted for this purpose until after 1785; the power loom was employed in the woolen trade in the first half of the nineteenth century; and wool was brought from Australia to the English market after 1818, one-half of all the wool that was woven in England coming from down under by 1850. Concomitantly, there was a shift in location of the British woolen industry from the southwest to Yorkshire, which gave the industry water power from the Yorkshire hills and cheap transportation through the ports of Liverpool and Hull and along the Liverpool-to-Leeds Canal and the River Humber. Similarly, in the United States the woolen textile trade tended to be located where there were port facilities and/or water power, as at Fall River and Lowell, Massachusetts, and in the Mohawk Valley of New York State. In France and Germany, mechanization of the woolen industry occurred mainly after 1850, and by that time the steam engine had been developed to a point where it could provide necessary power efficiently and where it was being used to make cheap inland transportation possible. Accordingly, in these countries the woolen trade remained to a large extent in traditional centers of production in order to take advantage of the supply of skilled workers, as at Rheims, Sedan, Elbeuf, Roubaix, and Carcassonne in France and at Aachen and Berlin in Germany.

In the manufacture of silk, mechanization also went on apace. Here the Jacquard loom, driven by mechanical power, came into general use and the ordinary loom for plain cloth began to be employed by 1844, especially at the great silk manufacturing center of Lyons in France. In the linen industry, the first successful spinning machine was patented in 1814 and the power loom began to be used extensively about 1840. In knitting, an improvement was made with the invention of the circular knitting machine by the Englishman Brunet and of the latch needle (1863), which made the application of power to knitting both possible and profitable. Then, in sewing, there was the invention in 1846 of the sewing machine by the American Elias Howe—a device which was to profoundly change the needle trades and to put the manufacture of clothing into factories.

Ferrous metallurgy and machine tools

Important as were the new techniques of the textile trades in awakening the imaginations of businessmen to the advantages of mechanizing industrial operations, in using power from inorganic sources to drive machines, and in concentrating production in factories, changes in the production of textiles were of no greater moment for the long-range effect upon industry than were those innovations which appeared in the refining of ferrous ores, in the making of steel, and in the transformation of these materials into useful objects. Because of improvements in these trades, Western culture, which had a complete monopoly of the new techniques, acquired a new "building material." Without this material, economic growth would have encountered an almost insurmountable obstacle.

In the refining of iron ore, the location of smelting has been determined by the relative costs of bringing ore and fuel together, for the raw ingredients in this process are bulky and cheap in respect to the finished product. In general, the tendency has been for smelting to be settled near supplies of fuel, for per ton of ore several tons of fuel have been needed. Consequently, prior to the nineteenth century, when charcoal was the fuel used in the iron trade, smelting was usually carried on in forests as close to ore outcroppings as possible. If woodlands were depleted of good charcoaling wood and if prices of charcoal rose to be inordinately high, the industry migrated to new sites, as in the case of England, where ironworking went from Sussex and Kent to Shropshire, the Midlands, and south Yorkshire between the sixteenth and eighteenth centuries. Such moves were expensive; and then in the late eighteenth century the industry was not certain of finding any area where charcoaling wood was plentiful. Obviously a substitute fuel for charcoal was needed to release the industry from its strait jacket.

Experiments to find a fuel to take the place of wood had become numerous in the seventeenth century, and invariably these experiments involved the use of coal. In its raw state, coal was not very satisfactory for working iron, because it did not provide a hot enough fire to permit the metal to run out of the blast furnaces into pigs; it had so much sulfur in it that it could not be used for casting because of resulting flaws; and it could not be used for making the almost pure malleable iron, known as wrought iron, for it rendered this product too brittle. What was required was some way to purify coal so that it would produce a hotter fire and would not contaminate the iron.

Credit for overcoming the deficiencies of coal must go to a Quaker ironmaster of Shropshire, Abraham Darby of Coalbrookdale. It was he who first reduced coal to coke by burning off its coal gas and many other impurities in an oven, much as wood was reduced to charcoal, and who used the resulting fuel in smelting. Partly because the coal which he employed, that is, Shropshire clod coal, made good coke and partly because his blast furnace was high and his blowing equipment extraordinarily powerful, his process proved successful (1709). Subsequently, coke fires were made hotter by the invention of piston air pumps (1761), which gave a stronger blast than bellows, and by the use of a blast of hot air—a change that was developed by J. B. Neilson in Glasgow in 1828.

Yet the use of coke in smelting was adopted with less speed than might have been imagined, although it was taken up more rapidly in England than in France or the United States. One of the chief reasons for the lag was that not all coal is good coking coal. Coke must be firm enough to hold up the weight of the ore and also porous so that air may reach all parts of the fire. Moreover, coke for smelting does not travel well, for handling tends to break it up into pieces which are too fine, and the costs of coking equipment were too high for small smelters. These facts help to explain why, as late as 1846, some three-fifths of the pig iron produced in France was smelted with charcoal, and in the United States not until 1855 did pig iron produced with coke surpass that smelted with charcoal, for wood was in relatively abundant supply.

Soon many other improvements were made in the production of iron goods. Coke was used to make cast iron, as in the case of pots, stoves, and even cannon, to heat pig iron before it was hammered to get malleable wrought iron, and to heat wrought iron prior to running it through grooved rollers (slitting mill) that turned it into rods. Furthermore, the making of wrought iron was accelerated by the discovery of puddling (1784), almost simultaneously by Peter Onions, an ironmaster, and Henry Cort, an Admiralty contractor. These men found that if pig iron was heated in a reverberatory furnace out of direct contact with fuel and if the molten mass were stirred or "puddled," many of the impurities would be burned off, thus rendering the usual amount of hammering unnecessary. Then, too, the production of wrought iron was facilitated by the invention by James Watt in the 1780s of the steam hammer, which could deliver 150 blows a minute of a weight amounting to 120 pounds, and by Henry Cort's development of a rolling mill that not only pressed out some of the carbon contained in the iron but had the advantage of producing iron sheets that could be used in boilers, as ship's plates, and for armor.

The use of coke on a large scale in processing pig iron accounts in part for the transfer of the ferrous metal-working industries to the proximity of coal. In the case of England the shift was clear, particularly in the making·of builders' hardware, like nails. In Belgium an important ferrous metals industry developed aroung Liège and in the province of Hainaut, where there was plenty of coal and where iron ore could be easily and cheaply brought by water. In France an iron industry was created under governmental encouragement and bounties near coal at Le Creusot—an industry, incidentally, based upon techniques brought to France from England by industrial spies and by English ironmasters like William Wilkinson. In the United States, there was a trend toward the concentration of the industry in the Pittsburgh area of Pennsylvania to take advantage of supplies of coal. And in the Germanies, by the 1840s the industry began to be located in the two main coal fields of the country, in the Ruhr Valley and in Upper Silesia. All of these areas employed the new techniques which had been so largely developed in England, but it took them a long time to overcome the advantage which the technological headstart had given the English. In 1865, for example, more than half of all the world's annual production of pig iron was accounted for by the United Kingdom.

In the making of steel, which was to be one of the most important branches of the ferrous metal industry, England also achieved an early position of primacy because of the development of superior techniques. There, toward the middle of the eighteenth century, Benjamin Huntsman, a clockmaker, mechanic, and general tinkerer, joined a multitude of experimenters who were trying to make a better grade of steel for watch springs. In his work he heated wrought iron in a crucible and added specific amounts of carbon in the form of pure glass in order to give his product the degree of hardness and ductility desired. This process was satisfactory for the immediate purpose for which it was designed, but steel produced by it was expensive because of the necessity of first making wrought iron and then of using a high-cost method for getting the requisite amount of carbon back into the iron.

The need for steel was, however, ever more pressing, for it was the only known metal which could stand the strains and stresses of the increased speeds at which machines were operated and of the heavier tasks that the new devices were called upon to perform. Cast iron was too brittle for railroad rails, drive shafts, and tires for wheels; wrought iron was too soft and pliable for a host of products ranging from nails to bridge beams. Yet the relatively high price of steel drastically limited its use—and this limitation threatened to hamper the growth of machine industry.

Under these circumstances ironmasters and trained chemists began an earnest search for a way to make cheaper wrought iron and hence cheaper steel. Thus it was that William Kelley, an American blacksmith from Kentucky, demonstrated in 1851 a method, which incidentally he did not develop to the point of practical application, whereby pig iron could be made into wrought iron without hammering, and to which carbon could be added to get steel. It was Sir Henry Bessemer, the son of a French refugee living in England, who developed this method into a practical system for making wrought iron and hence steel. He took out a patent for the crucial step in the procedure in 1856.

The Bessemer process consisted of driving a powerful blast of air *through* a molten mass of pig iron so that such an intense heat was produced that carbon and other impurities would burn off at the *"blow"* and a nearly pure iron would result. This was a big improvement over puddling in a reverberatory furnace, for in that system the fire was in a compartment of the furnace separated from the molten iron and carbon was burned out of the iron by the heated gases passing over it—a very slow process indeed.

The methods employed by Bessemer, in spite of all their promise, were not a great success at the outset. Ironmasters who made the heavy capital investments necessary to acquire the essential equipment frequently complained that the regulation of the blast was extremely difficult—that if they left it on too long it oxidized the iron so that it would not forge and if they did not leave it on long enough, too much carbon remained in the iron. Moreover, they claimed that no matter what they did the Bessemer process would not reduce their pig iron to wrought iron. In view of such complaints Bessemer went to work to try to find reasons for the difficulties encountered. So far as the length of the blast was concerned, he argued that from experience with the color of the flame from the blast one could determine approximately when to turn off the air and stop the action. So far as the failure of his method to reduce certain pigs was concerned, he had to admit that he had originally experimented with particularly good quality Swedish pig iron and that pigs made from ores with a phosphoric content could not be treated by his process. This was a severe handicap to many of the ironmasters of Staffordshire and the Midlands of England and of Lorraine in France, where ores contained large amounts of phosphorous.

The advantages to be derived from a cheaper method of making wrought iron, and thus steel, were so great and phosphoric ores were so abundant in many of the established metallurgical centers that experimenters were spurred on to surmount the shortcomings of the Bessemer process. They soon succeeded in perfecting a method of making steel directly after the "blow" had produced almost pure iron by simply adding to the still-molten mass an iron with a sufficient amount of carbon to produce the desired quality of steel. Then in 1866, Sir William Siemens, an Englishman of German birth, and two French brothers, Emile and Pierre Martin, developed an altogether new method for the industry—a method which became known as the Siemens-Martin process. This new procedure consisted of pouring molten metal into a shallow pan-like container—the "open hearth"—and then playing a mixture of gas and air upon it in order to burn off carbon and other impurities. Although this process was much slower than that devised by Bessemer, taking between seven and eight hours as compared with half an hour, it had several distinct advantages. It permitted the use of scrap iron. It could handle a greater range of ores, including those with a low phosphoric content; it yielded some 10 percent more of the metal input; and most important of all, it allowed testing for carbon content so that a more accurate control could be exercised in the production of steel of desired hardness and ductility.

Then, hardly had the Siemens-Martin process become a proved success than two English chemists, Sidney Thomas and P. C. Gilchrist, developed (1878) a method for satisfactorily smelting phosphoric ores. These men simply lined their furnace with magnesium limestone, which served to absorb the phosphorus or to turn it into slag which could be made to run off, thus permitting the refining to go on in the desired manner. Although in time the limestone lining of the furnace would become saturated with phosphorus and would have to be replaced, it could be broken up and sold as fertilizer.

Finally, other metallurgical chemists found that various qualities could be given to steel by allowing it with other metals—manganese to give it greater ductility, tungsten to make it hard, and chromium to prevent it from oxidizing. Obviously here was science serving as the handmaiden of industry.

All these technological changes had an enormous effect upon economic growth and upon the nature and location of the ferrous metals industry. They made possible a great reduction in the price of steel—it fell by 50 percent from 1856 to 1870—and thus made this metal available for a host of uses for which iron itself was not suitable. Furthermore, they came to the conclusion that coke was the absolutely essential fuel in refining iron; hence the industry was freed from forests and limited supplies of wood. The new techniques also determined that for a long time to come iron ore would be brought for refining to the proximity of coal deposits because of the larger requirements of coal per ton of ore. And finally, these men made possible the exploitation on a large scale of the hitherto little-used phosphoric ores of Lorraine and Luxembourg which are the greatest deposits of Western Europe and one of the most important of the world. The new techniques go far to explain why such great centers of the steel industry came to be located in the Ruhr Valley of Germany and in the Pittsburgh area of Pennsylvania and why the nexus of ore-coal relations came into being in the Lorraine-Ruhr area and in the Northern Minnesota–Pennsylvania–Ohio regions.

Dramatic as was the development of techniques in the refining of iron ore, it was scarcely more striking or more essential for the mechanization of industrial production than improvements in the methods for fashioning iron and steel into desired shapes. If industry had continued to rely upon the hammer and the anvil, upon files, clumsy molds, and man-driven drills and lathes, it would not have been able to make strong, long-lasting machines to perform industrial tasks accurately and efficiently.

Pressures for bettering the technology of metalworking began to make themselves felt almost as soon as iron and steel came into greater supply and industry indicated a need for sturdier machines. As early as 1774, John Wilkinson, a man of inventive mind and business genius—a kind of Arkwright of the metal industry—patented a drill for boring cannon which was of the utmost importance, for not only did it greatly improve this weapon and lead to more general use of firearms with rifled bores, but it permitted the making of accurate cylinders, so essential to the proper functioning of the steam engine. [4] Henry Cort, as we have already seen, patented the rolling mill in 1783, which made possible low-cost boiler plate and armor. Henry Maudslay invented (1797) his slide rest, which moved by an accurate screw device on an all metal lathe—a contribution to metalworking that greatly facilitated the accurate cutting of metal and that made possible such automatic devices as the screw-making machine. Thomas Gifford and S. Guppy developed nail-making machines in 1790 and 1796. The intrepid John Wilkinson launched an iron boat in 1787 and manufactured cast-iron pipe to carry water 40 miles to Paris. James Nasmyth developed milling and planing machines. Joseph Clement improved the lathe and the chuck for holding the cutting tool. And a certain Crawford, in 1837, "galvanized" iron, that is, he covered it with a coat of zinc to keep it from rusting—a process that was a forerunner of "tinning iron" (1879), which made possible the tin can.

These various inventions were the products of tinkerers and humble craftsmen who added detail to detail until they had something new—they were not for the most part the work of scientists who were hunting for "necessary sequences" to obtain definite ends or to test various hypotheses in their laboratories. In general, these inventions answered real social needs. They made possible a more extensive use of iron and steel, more efficient machines, standardization of types, and interchangeable parts— a development to which Eli Whitney in America made an especial contri-

---

[4] The drill was soon improved by a German, Breithaupt, who constructed a horizontal cylinder-boring machine in 1807 at Cassel. See Fritz Redlich, "The Leaders of the German Steam-engine Industry during the First Hundred Years," *The Journal of Economic History,* vol. 4 (1946), p.146.

bution. Finally, they did much to further the division of labor in the machine industry and the concentration of production in factories. John Wilkinson himself applied many of these inventions so successfully that he became in his day a veritable iron magnate. The Cockerill Company used many of them in its great machine shops at Liège, Belgium, and the German industrialist Borsig had such a large establishment for them that he employed 1,200 men by 1847.

The need for power—the steam engine

In few historical movements have the interrelationships of various developments been so striking as in the Industrial Revolution. As the story is told, it seems as though each new machine came into being when the need for it was great—that machine answered machine in a great contrapuntal symphony that gave rise to the most remarkable industrial advances of all time. Concomitant developments were indeed extraordinary, one set of conditions giving an impetus to the search for new techniques throughout a given trade or industry. Of all these concomitances, none is more striking than the invention of the steam engine—a device which was essential for driving the heavy machines which were coming into being and which had much greater locational mobility than the water wheel. It was, indeed, to free machines from the limitations imposed by the low "horsepower" of treadmills, by the fickleness of windmills, and by the arbitrary locations at waterfalls required by the water wheel.

The idea that motion could be obtained from steam had been known to the ancients, for evidence exists to show that Hero of Alexandria made a reaction sphere. Little attention was paid, however, to the properties of steam nor were any serious efforts made to make use of steam until the seventeenth century. It was then that Solomon de Caus (1576–1630), an industrious experimenter, discovered that if a tank filled with steam were closed and if the steam were then condensed a partial vacuum could be created. It was then that Giovanni Branca designed (1629) a turbine driven by steam. It was then, too, that experiments which were being pushed to improve pumps in order to remove water from mines led to the use of steam.

The first important step in the employment of steam for pumping appears on limited evidence to have been taken by Edward Somerset, later Marquis of Worcester, about 1663. At least in that year the Marquis and his heirs were given a monopoly of a "water commanding" engine for ninety-nine years—a contraption that seems to have been capable of raising water about 100 feet. We know of a certainty, however, that subsequently Thomas Savery, a British army officer, either made improvements upon the Marquis's device or came independently to design a very similar "atmospheric engine" (Figure 20). This machine consisted of a tank connected to a pipe that ran down into water and to another that ran upward. Following the principle laid down by Caus, a vacuum was created in the tank by condensing steam which had been introduced into it. Then when the valve of the pipe running down to water was opened, air pressure forced water up into the tank; and this water was, in turn, forced out of the tank and up the other pipe by steam pressure.

Although this machine had some utility for light work, it was not very practical for the most urgent pumping task of the times, the heavy job of

Figure 20
Savery's final steam engine. This was really an "atmospheric" engine. With valves *A* and *B* both closed, steam was admitted to the spherical chambers. This steam was condensed by running water over the sphere from the reservoir *C*. When a vacuum had thus been created, valve *A* was opened and atmospheric pressure drove water into the chamber. Valve *A* was then closed and valve *B* opened. Steam under pressure was then admitted to the chamber and water was blown up the vertical pipe. *(From A. Wolf, A History of Science, Technology and Philosophy in the Sixteenth and Seventeenth Century, London: George Allen & Unwin Ltd., 1935. Courtesy of the publishers.)*

pumping water out of mines. It had to be located within a relatively few feet of the level of the water to be pumped, it had to use higher pressures than existing equipment could stand; and its action was slow and inefficient. Consequently the search for better pumps went on, and very shortly considerable success was attained by a combination of principles already known. This new synthesis, the most crucial in the development of the steam engine, was effected by Thomas Newcomen, an ironmonger of Dartmouth, England, about 1708. The novelty of his work was that he used steam to work a piston within a cylinder in order to get an up-and-down motion. The piston was attached to a beam resting on a fulcrum, which was connected in turn with a regular atmospheric water pump. From Figure 21 it can be seen that, by lettting steam into the cylinder under the piston, the piston is driven upward. Then by condensing the steam to create a vacuum and by opening a valve at the top of the cylinder, air pressure will force the piston downward to its original position. In this way it was possible to pump water more cheaply than by any other method; hence the engine was a success for over fifty years. In time, improvements were made on the original design, valves being opened and closed automatically by a mechanism attached to the beam, and a safety valve, invented by Henry Beighton of Newcastle in 1717, was placed on steam boilers to reduce the danger of blowing them to bits by too high pressures.

Quite logically, the Newcomen engine attracted considerable attention among businessmen, mining engineers, and even professors of "natural philosophy," and experiments were conducted with it both for the purpose of explaining important principles and of improving it. It was not extraordinary that professors at the University of Glasgow, where instruction in natural phenomena was emphasized, should have used a model of the engine in the course of their lectures. Nor was it out of the ordinary that an instrument maker by the name of James Watt (1736–1819), who had a shop on the premises of the University, should have been called upon to repair and set up a Newcomen model for demonstration purposes.

While at his task, Watt made what in retrospect seems to have been a

Figure 21
Newcomen's steam engine. The nine "references," which form part of the design of this illustration, explain the operation of the engine. It should be added that within the cylinder 3 there was a piston. It was forced upward by the introduction of steam below it. This steam was condensed, creating a vacuum below the piston, so that when a valve at the top was opened to let in air, atmospheric pressure was enough to push the piston back into place. The beam activated a water pump. *(By courtesy of the Science Museum, Kensington.)*

The ENGINE for Raising Water (with a power made) by Fire

REFERENCES

—

1 The Fire Mouth under the Boyler with a Lid or Door.

2 The Boyler, Content 13 Hogſheads.

3 A Braſs Cylinder to Rarifie and Condenſe the Steam.

4 The Great Bars that Support the Houſe and Engine.

5 The Great Ballanc'd Beam that works the whole Engine.

6 A Lead Cyſtern fill'd by the Maſter Pipe.

7 Very ſtrong Chains fixed to Piſton and the Plugg and both Arches.

8 The Little Arch of the Great Ballanc'd Beam that moves the Sliding Beam.

9 The Sliding Beam mov'd by the little Arch of the Great Beam.

very elementary observation—that the chief defect of the Newcomen engine, that which made it particularly inefficient in the use of fuel, arose from the alternate injection and condensation of steam in the cylinder. Clearly, in order to prevent steam from condensing, at least in part, before the piston reached the top of its stroke, the cylinder had to be warm; conversely, on the return of the piston to its starting position at the bottom, the cylinder had to be cold in order to condense the steam. This meant an enormous waste of energy. Therefore, Watt began a search for a method by which this difficulty could be overcome. He hit upon it in 1765. His solution consisted of using a separate condenser which could be kept permanently cool, while the cylinder remained always hot. This single alteration increased the efficiency of the engine four times (Figure 22).

Important as this improvement was, however, the engine had to be further developed before it could have any significant impact upon the evolution of industry. This development proved to be exceedingly demanding in capital, technical skills, and entrepreneurial talent. John Roe-

Figure 22
Watt's steam engine. The affinity to the Newcomen engine (Figure 21) is clearly apparent, especially the action of the piston within the cylinder on the left and the communication of the up-and-down motion to the beam above. This model provided rotative motion by means of the "sun and planet" mechanism at the right of the center of the large wheel.

buck, Watt's first financial supporter, was so heavily drained of funds that he sold out his share of the patent, which had been taken out in 1769, to Matthew Boulton, a well-to-do businessman of Birmingham. In many ways, this was a fortunate occurrence, for Watt now had access not only to greater supplies of funds, but also in moving the scene of his investigations from Glasgow to Birmingham, he became established nearer to iron-works and machinists who were able to produce the parts which he needed and closer to the potential market for his product. In fact, his first engines were used primarily for pumping water to turn water wheels which ran bellows at ironworks and for pumping water out of iron mines. They were not, however, used immediately for pumping water out of coal mines, which can be explained by the fact that the engines at the beginning were leased rather than sold and that the royalty paid for their use was based upon the savings effected in fuel and that the cost of fuel was not great for coal mine operators.

Undoubtedly James Watt would have gone down in history as one of the great inventors of all time if he had made no other contribution to the atmospheric engine then that already described, but he saw great possibilities in the power of steam as a prime mover and he went on to realize them, encouraged as both he and Boulton were by Parliament's extension of their patent from 1775 to 1800. One of Watt's most pressing desires was to get rotary motion from his engine, but he was stymied for some time because patent rights kept him from using the "crank and shaft" system—a method employed for getting rotary motion on spinning wheels and today illustrated by the mechanism on the sides of steam locomotives. In 1781, however, he attained his desired goal with his "sun and planet" system—a device which consisted of putting geared teeth in the shaft that was driven up and down by the beam and by having these geared teeth engage a small geared wheel on the down stroke and running free on the up stroke. In 1782, he patented the double-acting rotative engine, in which steam and vacuum were used alternately at each end of the cylinder, and he adopted the principles of the expansive power of steam by stopping the flow of steam before the piston had completed its stroke, relying upon expansion to finish the job. In 1784 he introduced "parallel motion," whereby the piston rod was attached to the beam in such a manner as to let it move in a straight line; he added the throttle valve to regulate the flow of steam, and in 1788 he put a governor on the engine to give it greater regularity and smoothness of operation.

After a long, hard struggle filled with discouragement and reverses, the partnership of Boulton and Watt began about 1786 to prosper. By 1800 it had built and set up some five hundred engines both at home and abroad. These engines were still used chiefly for pumping water, even in the Paris waterworks, but they were also employed in iron mills, in textile factories, in breweries, and in a host of minor trades. In 1807 Robert Fulton propelled his *Clermont* on the Hudson River with a steam engine and as early as 1814 Robert Stephenson constructed a successful steam locomotive. The future of the steam engine was thus amply assured. Improved as it was by three important French inventions—the tubular boiler of Seguin in 1817, the pressure gauge of Bourdon in 1849, and the injector of Gifford in 1858 for getting water into a boiler that was under pressure—the steam engine was employed ever more widely. In 1850, Great Britain had 71,000 horsepower of steam in the cotton industry to 11,000 horsepower of water, and 54,000 horsepower of steam in other branches of the textile trades to 13,000 horsepower of water. In 1847, France had 5,000 steam engines with a total horsepower of 60,000, and in 1846, Prussia had some 22,000 horsepower of steam, 14,000 of which were in the mining and metallurgical industries. Clearly the age of steam had come.

Mechanization of other industries

Although the invention of the steam engine, the development of cheaper methods of making iron and steel, and the finding of ways for making cloth by machines were most crucial in bringing about the mechanization of industry on a large scale and the concentrating of it in factories, many other changes in techniques were realized which contributed to the Industrial Revolution. In all phases of production efforts were made to find ways for improving output while diminishing human input and for rendering useful the vast supplies of inorganic materials in the earth's crust without relying upon turning them into organic matter. More raw materials, more mechanical transformation of them, and more use of prime movers per employee were the aims in industrial change.

Although the steam engine was destined to be for long the most popular source of mechanical power, the water wheel continued to be important, especially where falling water was abundant, the flow steady, and coal scarce, as in Scandinavia, the Alps, New England, and the Piedmont region of the Appalachian Mountains. Moreover, water power continued to be used to the extent that it was because the old type of flutter wheel came to be supplanted by a much more efficient manner for harnessing the force of falling water—the water turbine, invented by the Frenchman Fourneyron in 1832. This turbine was particularly efficient in rendering useful large masses of water with slight fall or velocity, whereas the Pelton wheel was adapted for handling small flows at great speed. These two machines did much to keep alive the use of water power, even in those cases where factories had to be located at relatively inaccessible spots, until the development of electric power and high-voltage transmission made power from water more mobile.

Attempts to make the water wheel more effective were characteristic of the efforts of man to get machines to do work which had previously been performed by human hands. In lumbering and woodworking, for example, the circular saw, invented in Great Britain in 1777, was to revolutionize the use of wood. No longer was it necessary to employ handhewn timbers or to avoid using boards in construction because of the high cost and laborious task of sawing them with "up-and-down" saws worked by hand or water power. Henceforth they could be cut from logs with dispatch and accuracy. Furthermore, the band saw for sawing logs was invented in 1818, although it was little used until the end of the century. The rotary planer was patented in 1793; the Blanchard lathe, which turned pieces of wood against cutting disks in such a fashion that irregularly shaped objects, like ax handles and shoe lasts, could be produced, was invented in 1820.

In the paper industry, a dramatic step toward more rapid production was taken by the Frenchman Louis Robert, who invented (1799) a machine to make paper in a continuous strip. It actually took the wet ground rag pulp from the tank in which it lay, spread it on a fine wire screen, pressed out the water, dried the paper, and wound the final product on a roll. The sugar industry was improved by employing better evaporating equipment and the steam engine for running grinders; whereas the use of beets as a source of sugar during the Napoleonic period, when the Continent was blockaded from West Indian supplies, laid the laid the basis for an industry that was to make great progress after 1830.

Boulton, Watt's partner, developed a power-driven machine for stamping coins. Warfare was made more "mechanical" by the invention of the breech-loading and percussion lock guns (about 1807), the development of the revolver (1836), the rifling of cannon to give a projectile a twisting motion for greater accuracy, the invention of the machine gun by R. J. Gatling, an American, in 1862, and the development of the needle gun (1866) in which the charge was set off when the needle pierced the shell. Gunpowder was produced by a new mechanized process, devised by the French during the French Revolution, in which the various ingredients were pulverized and mixed by putting brass balls in a barrel and rolling the whole instead of by use of mortar and pestle.

Furthermore, the mechanization of communications was inaugurated with the independent discoveries of the electric telegraph by Samuel Morse in America and by Cooke and Wheatstone in England (1837). More rapid water transport was forecast by the invention of the screw propeller (1836). The turret lathe was patented in 1845. Compressed air began to be used in mining and the coal disk cutter came into being in 1852.

Remarkable as all these changes in the field of mechanics were, they were hardly more significant in the process of industrial development than the application of chemistry to industry. Progress in chemistry in the late eighteenth and early nineteenth century was little less than phenomenal. Although by the middle of the seventeenth century alchemists had become acquainted with most common metals, their alloys and salts, and although they knew about a few acids and the major alkalis, chemists had by the nineteenth century reached a point in their knowledge where they could explain chemical phenomena or attain desired results for industrial production. Henry Cavendish discovered the chemical composition of water (1784). A. Lavoisier found the nature of combustion. J. Dalton proposed the atomic theory (1803), indicating that all properties had fixed amounts of elements; Joseph Gay-Lussac described the elementary composition of organic matter (1811); and D. Mendeleev (born 1834) classified the elements.

With such work going on it is not be wondered at that practical-minded chemists began to make contributions to industry. Thus, Dr. John Roebuck of Birmingham (1718–1784) improved the making of sulfuric acid, which is basic to industrial chemistry. Claude Louis Berthollet developed prussic acid (hydrocyanic acid), used chlorine for bleaching, and discovered that potassium chlorate could be used in gunpowder in place of saltpeter. Nicholas Le Blanc discovered (1789) a way of making soda, the basic industrial alkali, from sea water. And Charles Tennant of England made a bleaching powder by combining chlorine and slaked lime (1797–1799).

Changes in structure and productivity

The effects of all these changes in mechanics and chemistry both upon economic development and upon society were enormous, yet they were only the beginning of a movement which has continued at an accelerated pace down to the present day. The new techniques made possible an increase in units of output per unit of human input beyond the wildest dreams of man. In Great Britain between 1780 and 1880, total product grew at a rate of 28 percent per decade and product per capita by 13½ percent. For Western countries which followed in Britain's path, rates of growth of total product were no less staggering: output doubled approximately every thirty years during the expansive years of Continental industrialization. Such growth of output made feasible a great increase in population, but even so, modern economies were able to sustain increasing rates of per capita output (and income). In all European countries which modernized between 1800 and the present, per-decade rates of growth of per capita product were well above 10 percent, although timing varied widely.[5]

[5] Kuznets, *Modern Economic Growth,* pp. 63–72.

Output per man-hour of labor quadrupled (at the very least) in Europe between the mid-nineteenth and mid-twentieth centuries (Table 62, p. 526).

The source of such aggressive growth was, of course, the new technology of the Industrial Revolution. The increasing *efficiency* of capital equipment, together with the ever-increasing *amount* of capital in the production process, created the material bounty that is the foremost characteristic of the Modern economy. Once basic precedents were set, the pace of change was super-fast. The application of steam engines to manufacturing in the mid-1800s quickly made pre-Modern power devices obsolete (Table 13). Likewise iron and steel attained absolute supremacy as the stuff of which capital goods were made, and in iron refining the complete shift to mineral fuels was accomplished. Mass-produced goods, such as cotton garments, were the ultimate products of the Revolution. The continuous reduction in the cost and selling price of such goods was the effect of industrialization that came closest to home.

In the earliest phase of modernization in eighteenth-century England the new technological innovations were designed to reduce labor costs. In the cotton industry the nature of the final product, the cloth itself, was largely unaffected by the application of the new machinery. The use of a

Table 13 Indicators of growth in European manufacturing capacity in the mid-nineteenth century

Country	Steam-power capacity	Coal consumption	Pig iron output	Raw cotton consumption
United Kingdom				
1850	1,290	37,500	2,249	266.8
1873	4,040	112,604	6,566	565.1
Belgium				
1850	70	3,481	145	10.0
1873	350	10,219	607	18.0
Germany				
1850	260	5,100	212	17.1
1873	2,480	36,392	2,241	117.8
France				
1850	370	7,225	406	59.3
1873	1,850 (1869)	24,702	1,382	93.7 (1869)

NOTES: Steam-power capacity is measured in 1,000 h.p. units. All other statistics are in thousands of metric tons. The 1873 statistics for Germany include the newly annexed territory of Alsace-Lorraine; French figures for that year do not.

SOURCE: David S. Landes, *The Unbound Prometheus: Technological Change and Industrial Development in Western Europe from 1750 to the Present* (New York: Cambridge, 1972), p. 194, table 4.

jenny or a water frame idled forty spinning wheels in forty rural cottages, but it did not significantly alter the nature of cotton thread. As each phase of the production process came to be mechanized, the challenge of back-logged supplies of semi-finished goods or backlogged orders for materials encouraged technological responses in other phases to break through existing production bottlenecks.

In the nineteenth century, with increased population growth and fewer large-scale wars, British supplies of labor became more responsive to the needs of a developing economy. The nature of European innovation thereafter did not, for the most part, emphasize the trait of substituting capital for labor but rather emphasized new and better products. Steel mills, machine tools, steam engines, and the like were not designed to reduce the number of operatives on the job, but they did effect qualitative and quantitative differences in the nature of output. Manufacturing became the leading sector of the economy, the predominant source of national product (Table 14). Predictably, national economic structures were transmuted to support the high-power sector. Manufacturing drew workmen, investment funds, and managerial talent, as productivity increases promised higher remuneration to productive factors. Western Europe became one vast manufactory as the greater part of human and material resources of society was devoted to mass production and as market demand fully kept pace with mushrooming supplies of industrial goods.

Table 14. Industry's share of national product
Product of industrial sector as a percentage of national product

Country	Early 19th century	Mid-19th century	Mid-20th century
Great Britain	23 (1801)	34 (1841)	56 (1955)
Germany		24 (1860–1869)	52 (DDR, 1959)
France	20 (1789–1815)	30 (1872–1882)	52 (1962)

SOURCE: Kuznets, *Modern Economic Growth,* pp. 88–93, table 3.1.

The revolution in commerce

Economic progress and the distribution of goods

On the preceding pages many instances have been encountered in which economic progress, defined as an increase in the supply of economic goods and services per capita of the population of a given area, was accompanied by a greater division of labor, but in no case was this characteristic of growth so marked as in the nineteenth century. Specialization of tasks among workers and also an extraordinary specialization of production among various areas of the world were greater than had ever before been witnessed in human history. An extraordinary growth of commerce allowed individuals and whole regions to become less economically self-sufficient than they had been; increased purchasing power permitted members of the economically lower classes to enjoy goods which had previously been beyond their reach; and interregional dependence brought new products into the market. In fact, the development of mechanized industry itself seems to have depended to a large extent on the growth of trade, for machine-made goods would not have been possible if large amounts of raw materials had not been amassed and the finished products disposed of through commercial channels.

In recent economic history an abundance of evidence exists to show that those economies which have experienced the greatest growth have had an exceptionally large proportion of their population engaged in exchanging goods rather than in the actual production of them. Thus, a comparison of the occupational distribution in the year 1931 of two countries like Britain and India, whose national incomes per capita were in the ratio of 6 to 1, indicates that the former had a much higher percentage in the service trades than did the latter (Table 15).

Table 15. Distribution of the working force in 1931 (in percent)

Occupation	Great Britain	India
Agriculture	6.1	70.50
Mining and manufacturing	38.0	17.15
Domestic service	8.1	2.70
Other	47.8	9.65

In like manner, in any given economy, as for example that of the United States, a greater concentration of the occupied population is to be found in trade, finance, and transport as economic progress is made (Table 16).

Table 16. Distribution of the working force in the United States (in percent)

Occupation	1850	1950
Agriculture	63.6	14.50
Forestry and fishing	0.4	
Mining	1.1	1.75
Manufacturing and mechanical industries	16.3	28.80
Construction		4.48
Transportation and communication	0.5	7.77
Trade	4.0	18.44
Professional services		.08
Finance and real estate		3.51
Educational, domestic, and personal services	12.2	9.23
Government not elsewhere classified		11.45

The increased division of labor, the accompanying dependence of the consumer on the market, and a growing tendency for various regions to specialize in the production of those goods in which they had a comparative advantage put pressure on agencies for the distribution of goods to improve their services: on transportation to better its methods of carrying, on communications to speed up the exchange of information, and on national states to change their commercial policies. The response to the new needs was remarkable. Retailing assumed a new place in the selling of goods and gave rise to new types of enterprises like the department store and the cooperative, while wholesaling became better organized and more important. In transportation great improvements were made in the older forms of carrying and new techniques came into being, like the steam locomotive, which provided at long last a cheap means of carrying heavy loads on land, and the steamboat, which made water carrying less expensive and more certain. Improved methods of communication resulted from the extension of postal services, from the invention of the telegraph, and from the establishment of extensive telegraph lines, including cables across the Atlantic. Finally, in this period so much credence was placed in the virtues of freer trade, if not of free trade, that many man-made hindrances to commerce were abolished.

The extension of the market

The extent to which a division of labor took place and to which people became dependent on the market is difficult to measure with any degree of accuracy, but several indicators point clearly the direction in which the economy was moving. First, the growth of population and a great increase in urbanization meant that more people were perforce dependent on the market for most of their economic wants. From 1800 to 1870 the population of the United States increased from 5.3 million to 38.5 million, and Europe's population just about doubled between 1800 and 1875. Moreover, the percentage of the population living in towns of 2,000 or more went up appreciably, being, for example, in England 51.3 percent of the population in 1851, in France, 28.9 percent in 1861, and in Germany, 35.8 percent in 1867.

Secondly, the amount of freight moving on canals and railways suggested a great increase in commerce and an extensive division of labor. For example, the number of tons of freight carried 1 kilometer on rivers and canals in France in 1847 was 1,760 million tons; in 1875, it was 1,964 million tons. Furthermore, in France the number of passengers carried 1 kilometer on railways in 1853 was 1,000 million and in 1875, it was 4,786 million, and the number of tons of freight hauled 1 kilometer rose from 1,000 million in 1854 to 8,136 million in 1875. In the United States, the railways carried 39,302 million ton-miles in 1881.

Thirdly, the great expansion of international trade indicated a growing specialization of production by regions. As can be seen in Table 17, this trade among nations increased nearly six times in the forty years from 1840 to 1880. Moreover, a very large part of this trade was accounted for by states in Western culture (Table 18), which meant that here was to be found the greatest regional division of labor.[1]

---

[1] One should add that the great number of political divisions in Western culture had a tendency to increase these percentages.

The Industrial Revolution and the rise in output of mass-produced manufactured goods presupposes a growth of consumption of great magnitude. The extension of the market was a necessary condition for the

Table 17. Total world commerce (in billions of dollars, contemporary values)

Year	Amount
1840	2.8
1860	7.2
1880	14.8
1900	20.1
1913	40.4

Table 18. Distribution of world trade (in percent)

Year	United Kingdom	United States	Germany	France
1840	32	8		10
1860	25	9		11
1880	23	10	9	11
1900	21	11	12	8

continuing growth of demand; its importance can hardly be overstated. Imagine, for the sake of example, a large department store in a present-day metropolis. How might it function in the absence of mass transit? The possibility of retailing on such a large scale clearly could not exist if the store's clientele were limited to only those persons who could comfortably walk to shopping. The scale of selling depends on the distance from the store to the boundary of points from which reasonable travel (in terms of cost or time) is possible. It is the same for interregional or international consumption. As the boundaries for "reasonable" transport expand with technical change, ever-greater numbers of persons fall within the circumference of access to markets and become potential consumers for merchandise of distant manufacture. Although international trade is nothing novel, its democratization was a fairly recent development. Formerly, as we have seen, transport costs were so high that only expensive luxury goods were worth shipping long distances, and the market for such goods was naturally small and selective. The revolution in commerce created such economies as to allow even the most inexpensive goods to travel long distances to broad market areas. The victory of transport techniques over the vagaries of weather and terrain meant that supplies of goods became continuous, and such practices as hoarding inventories or speculating on commodity supplies became less necessary to the market. The power of transportation technology to extend the market can be fully appreciated only when we consider that intermediate goods (raw materials, semifinished products, component parts) as well as finished goods are subject to the effects of increased availability in time and distance. The scale of both production and consumption depended absolutely on the new technology of transportation for continued growth.

Railways and waterways

Undoubtedly the most important new technique in the commercial revolution of the nineteenth century was the railway. It made possible the tapping of supplies in remote places. It carried bulk products cheaply to centers of population, and it had flexibility enough to reach the very maws of machines. Moreover, as we shall see later, the large amount of capital required for railway construction gave an enormous impetus to the joint-stock form of business organization and to such innovations as limited liability and preferred stock. Lastly, the vast volume of equipment which railways required spurred economic activity and also contributed much to business fluctuations because of the uneven rate of investment in railways.

The idea of applying the steam engine to transportation had found expression as early as 1769 in a cumbersome contraption fashioned by a Frenchman, Nicolas Cugnot, for use on roads. Subsequently, the Englishman Richard Trevithick constructed locomotives (1801, 1808), but his machines were designed for hauling around coal mines and had limited use. Finally, George Stephenson brought steam locomotion to the point of practicability, his *Rocket* attaining the exceptional speed of 31 miles per hour on a line from Manchester to Liverpool in 1830.

In spite of Stephenson's achievements, however, many engineering problems had to be solved before railroads could play an important role in commerce. At first, for example, the flanged wheels which were used to keep the cars on the track crept up on top of the rails on curves and some time elapsed before it was discovered that the wheels should fit loosely on the rails and that they could be attached to swivel trucks under the cars. Also, at first, the draft in the firebox was insufficient to keep up the steam pressure when the locomotive was not in motion—a difficulty which was overcome by forcing steam up the smokestack to create a draft. At the outset, too, brakes were uncertain affairs, being pushed against the wheels, and were not made safe and easily applied or released until George Westinghouse perfected the vacuum air brake in 1886. Furthermore, couplings were loose affairs which had so much play in them that when a train started the cars were yanked, particularly the last ones, so violently that passengers were toppled over backwards.

The comfort and reliability of rail service improved quickly. New steel rails were more resilient than brittle cast iron, especially when installed on wooden ties. Developments in bridge and tunnel engineering shortened distances and made travel safer (Chapter 18).

Rail building, more than any other nineteenth-century economic project, fostered the growth of heavy industry. The rail builders were industry's best customers, and we often find in the separate national histories of Western nations that railroad booms corresponded closely with periods of rapid industrialization. Belgian leadership in continental rail building was apparent as early as 1835, when the Brussels–Malines line was opened. In 1844 the Belgian rail network was completed at an estimated cost of 16,500 pounds per mile: an expensive enterprise which nevertheless paid off handsomely as German and French markets opened up to Belgian manufacturers thanks to the new rail linkages. As in the case of early American rail building, Belgium had to import the first equipment from Britain; but as the line progressed, domestic suppliers grew up to provide steel rails and car wheels, locomotives, and other equipment (Figure 23). Belgian leadership in early Continental industrialization dates from this rail building phase.

In Central Europe, Germany began work on rail lines thirty years before national unification. The first tiny lines inside German principalities were built with private capital, but after unification, it was the state, and particularly the military, which played the predominant role in rail systems' development and operations. More Spartan than the English railroads, the German lines were cheaper to build. Preliminary development of the technology had, after all, been accomplished elsewhere, and there were engineering precedents to rely upon. As early as mid-century the German states had developed the industrial resources to support railroad building internally.

In France the pattern was much the same, although private financing by stock issues, rather than by state funding, was the principal method of capital formation. In French industry, the diffusion of the three major innovations in steelmaking—the Bessemer process, the Martin process, and dephosphorization—was systematically linked to the demands placed upon the steelmakers by rail building. The railroads soaked up most of the steel produced by the new methods.[2] Linkages to engineering, bridge

---

[2] F. Caron, "French Railroad Investment, 1850–1914," in R. Cameron (Ed.), *Essays in French Economic History* (Homewood, Ill.: Irwin, 1970), p. 330. For other countries, see *Cambridge Economic History of Europe*, vol. 6, chap. 4.

building, and light and power technology also stemmed from the French rail boom.

In certain other European territories we find sequences of industrial stagnation with attendant slow development in the rail sector. Italy was such a case. Rail building was done at first with imported materials, and the impact on metallurgy and heavy manufacturing was slow to be felt. It is an overstatement to suggest that a boom in railroads was either necessary or of itself sufficient to induce growth in the capital-building sector of an economy, but it is certainly true that the demand for equipment created by railway development was a major impetus for the European capital goods industry.

By the third quarter of the nineteenth century, railways had become so successful that canal building fell off and the future of inland shipping began to look dim except for bulky products of low value, like grains and ores, and then chiefly on easily maintained rivers and lakes.[3] Henceforth canal construction was limited mostly to the building of connections between inland waterway systems and between oceans to shorten routes.

---

[3] Some strategically located canals, like the Erie, continued to prosper for a time. In 1860 this canal handled more tonnage than the New York Central, the Hudson River, and the Erie Railroads combined.

Figure 23
Typical passenger locomotive of 1871. This locomotive was built by Baldwin in America for the Camden and Atlantic Railroad. It had two large drive wheels for speed. *(Courtesy of the Association of American Railroads.)*

Thus a ship canal was constructed from Dortmund to Emden to facilitate getting products from the Ruhr to the sea; another canal was begun to connect the Rhine with the Danube via the Main. The Sault Ste. Marie Canal between Lake Superior and Lake Huron was improved (1896) to facilitate the shipping of iron ore from the Mesabi Range of Minnesota to the blast furnaces of Pittsburgh, Cleveland, and later Gary, Indiana. Of interocean connections the most famous were the Suez Canal, opened in 1869, which cut 4,000 miles off the haul from India to Western Europe,[4] the Kiel Canal, that was built across the Danish Peninsula to reduce the length of the route between the North and Baltic Seas, the Panama Canal, begun by a French company under the leadership of de Lesseps and completed by American interests in 1914, which shortened the water route from San Francisco to Liverpool by 5,666 miles, and the Corinth Canal across the Corinthian Isthmus in Greece (opened in 1893).

Shipping on navigable rivers continued to be important, particularly with the development of the steamboat, and was facilitated both by international conventions and by bold engineering undertakings. At the Congress of Vienna in 1815 a convention was signed to open international rivers to vessels of all countries. Agreements for the reduction of tolls not needed to maintain services were negotiated among the powers, and international commissions were created to regulate traffic on such important waterways as the Rhine (1831) and the Danube (1856). Many rivers were dredged and contained by levees or dikes in order to deepen their draught. The Scheldt River below Antwerp and the Lower Mississippi had such high levees that ships actually passed above the surrounding country. These levees allowed Antwerp to become one of the major ports of Western Europe and permitted New Orleans to receive in 1843 tonnage which was twice that handled in New York. Finally, shipping on the North, Baltic, and Mediterranean Seas and on the Great Lakes grew rapidly and coastwise shipping flourished.

Ocean shipping and international trade

Important as railway and inland waterway transportation was in tapping resources over large land masses, in bringing various complementary products together for processing, and in carrying manufactured goods from

---

[4] The British government had been instrumental in constructing a railway across the Isthmus of Suez in 1854. The canal was, however, built by an international company. The work was directed by a French engineer, Ferdinand de Lesseps. Disraeli bought for Great Britain almost half the shares of the Suez Canal Company with capital lent the treasury by Baron Rothschild. Partly to insure the life line to India, the British established a veiled protectorate over Egypt in 1882. The Suez Canal carried 20,275,120 net tons in 1912 and 33,446,014 in 1929, of which 65 percent was British.

industrial centers to widely dispersed consumers, ocean shipping was of extraordinary significance in the economic development of Western culture. It was a factor which fostered Europe's becoming the "workshop of the world," allowing that area to import raw materials and to export manufactured goods. Europe's economic primacy in the modernizing world stemmed from her capacity to acquire raw materials and reship finished manufactured products to distant sources of demand. The high prices for finished goods relative to raw materials (the "terms of trade") made Western nations rich and powerful. Intercontinental transport was the vehicle for the dominance of Europe. The relationship between European expansionism and technical prowess in navigation has roots in the sixteenth century, when outposts of Western rulership were extended the world over and intercontinental trade achieved a degree of regularity. With modernization, however, came the first intercontinental movement of materials of mass influence. Even diet was transformed by the new access to foreign foodstuffs.

The growth of ocean shipping was made technically possible both by improvements in sailing vessels and by the development of the steamship after the middle of the nineteenth century. The design of sailing vessels was improved, enabling them to carry greater burdens or, as in the case of clipper ships, of transporting passengers and perishable freight of high value at increased speeds. Furthermore, sail carrying costs were kept low, for vast resources of timber in the New World permitted the construction of vessels at low cost, and the use of iron (after 1832) and of steel (after 1879), which were in good supply in Great Britain, made possible the building of vessels of great durability cheaply.

Sailing vessels carried so well and at such low rates that they gave steamships stiff competition down to the late 1880s (Table 19), but there were also technical reasons why steam did not establish its supremacy over wind at an earlier date. The first steamships required so much fuel that they could not bunker sufficient coal to carry them on long journeys and have space left for a payload (the American-built *Savannah* crossed the Atlantic in 1819 in twenty-nine days but used steam for only eighty hours of the passage, and not until 1838 was a crossing effected exclusively with steam). Furthermore, paddle wheels were easily damaged by storms, and wooden construction limited keels to 300 feet. Thus, while steamships were used successfully first on rivers, lake, and inland seas for short hauls, they made little headway on the oceans.

Yet, the potentialities of steam propulsion were so great that inventors, engineers, and entrepreneurs strove to realize them. One of the greatest obstacles in their path to success was eliminated by the invention of the compound engine (1854), which led to the development of the triple and quadruple expansion engines—machines that reused steam two, three, or four times and saved so much fuel that they solved the problem of bunkering. Then, the screw propeller, invented in 1836 and first employed by the British Admiralty in 1843, permitted doing away with the vulnerable paddle wheel. Finally, iron and steel construction (the British East India

Table 19. Shipping tonnages, sail and steam (in thousands of net tons)

Nation	1850		1880		1890	
	Sail	Steam	Sail	Steam	Sail	Steam
Great Britain	3,396	168	3,851	2,936	2,936	5,042
United States	1,540	45	1,206	1146	749	197
France	674	13	641	277	444	499
Germany			965	215	709	723

Company began to acquire iron vessels in 1839) made possible such large vessels that there was ample room for steam equipment, fuel, and a cargo that would pay a good profit.[5]

As techniques of ocean carrying improved, shipping services on the high seas became greatly extended. Hitherto most carriers had been traders, like the East India Company, and transported cargoes for others whenever it was convenient for them to do so. In the first half of the nineteenth century, however, shippers came to limit their activities to carrying and at the same time became differentiated according to the services which they provided. Some of them would go anywhere at any time there was a cargo and thus came to be known as "tramp steamers." Others plied between stipulated ports but with no fixed schedules. And still others ran packets or liners, catered to passengers, and maintained regular schedules—services which were furnished primarily by great shipping companies, like the Cunard Company (1839), the French Compagnie des Messageries Maritimes (1851), and the American Collins Line, which reached its peak in the early 1850s. This division of labor in ocean carrying, together with technical improvements and an increased volume of business, permitted a considerable reduction in costs. In fact, charges of transporting grain from New York to Europe were cut in half from 1874 to 1884; charges from Odessa to the United Kingdom fell to one-sixth the former price just at the time when sail was giving way to steam.[6]

[5] Improvements in ship construction and in navigation were made continually. Ballast tanks were introduced to lessen rolling, ships were divided into watertight compartments, gyroscopic compasses which automatically controlled the rudder were adopted, and buoys and lights became more numerous and better regulated.

[6] See Douglass C. North, "Ocean Freight Rates and Economic Development, 1750–1913," *Journal of Economic History*, vol. 18, no. 4 (December 1958), pp. 537–555.

As ocean shipping grew, the various nations of Western culture came to attach new importance to the possession of strong merchant marines. They recognized in them not only a way to seek out new markets for their wares, to exploit new sources of supplies, and perchance to obtain colonies, but also a means whereby the nation could effect important earnings and enhance its striking force by giving more mobility to its fighting forces. Consequently most states encouraged both shipbuilding and shipping. To be sure, the old type of navigation act that restricted carrying between the motherland and distant parts, including colonies, to ships of the homeland and that kept foreign vessels out of a nation's coastwise trade were done away with, by Britain in 1849 and 1854 and by France in 1866 and 1869.[7] But new methods of assisting shippers were substituted for the old. Lucrative mail contracts were given to carriers who built ships to specifications that made them useful as fighting ships in time of war; outright subsidies were paid to shipping companies and to shipbuilders; and government loans on easy credit terms were granted to those who would venture in ocean carrying. Great Britain, for example, awarded important mail contracts to the Cunard Line and to some other shippers at the time when the transition from sail to steam was taking place and carriers were reluctant to risk their capital in what appeared to be a somewhat uncertain enterprise. Later, when Germany won the "Blue Ribbon" of the North Atlantic, that is, had the fastest ship in service from Europe to New York, Britain loaned Cunard 2.6 million pounds at 2¾ percent interest, which permitted the building of the *Lusitania* and the *Mauritania*, in order to regain the symbol of primacy. France, for its part, gave both mail contracts to shippers and direct subsidies to both shippers and shipbuilders (1881).[8] Germany, also, granted favorable mail contracts to its carriers, gave low railway rates on goods shipped abroad, subsidized its main lines, and after the Russian cholera epidemic of 1894 required emigrants from Russia and Austria to pass through quarantine stations maintained by the Hamburg-American Line and the North German Lloyd, which meant, in effect, that most of the emigrants sailed with these lines.

The assistance thus given by most of the Great Powers to their merchant marines had to some degree the desired effect, for the tonnage under their flags remained high. The United States, which gave its shippers little aid except for mail contracts, witnessed, on the other hand, a decline in the proportion of its foreign trade carried in its own bottoms from 66 percent in 1860 to 10 percent in 1914. Much of this fall was to be attributed to the

---

[7] The United States reserved coastwise shipping all through this period to vessels of American registry.

[8] The latter policy was not very successful, for at first the periods in which aid was given were deemed too short and later (1893) subsidies were based upon distance covered, which led to the construction of cheap sailing vessels that plied the waterways of the world more or less in ballast just to get the subvention. One company received more from the mileage subsidy than it did from freight. Hence, in 1902 subsidy arrangements were altered to favor steam construction and the actual carrying of goods.

lack of advantages in the building of steel vessels compared with those enjoyed when construction was of wood.

Shipping rivalries among nations were keen and competition among shipping companies was extraordinarily severe. So sharp did rivalry become, in fact, that individual companies made an effort to mitigate competitive practices of a cutthroat character by forming pools and combines. The first of these was among British carriers in the Calcutta trade (1875), but the most famous of all was the North Atlantic Shipping Conference (1908), which embraced the lines of various nations. By means of such associations, shippers endeavored to fix prices, to prevent rebates, and to compete for business by giving good service. National states condoned such practices, because the rates of members of the pool were but a little if any higher than those of nonmembers and because excessive shipping competition could lead to extraordinarily heavy drains on public treasuries.

At all events, ocean carrying, together with shipping on railways and inland waterways, accounted for a rate of growth in international trade which may even have exceeded that of the actual production of goods (Table 20). Furthermore, these exchanges among nations constituted an intricate network. Whereas earlier much of international commerce had

Table 20. Foreign trade per capita

Country	Period	
	1851–1853 (Swiss franc of 1853)	1929 (U.S. dollars of 1929)
Denmark		266.0
Netherlands	387	243.0
Switzerland	406	228.0
Great Britain	268	219.0
France	101	103.0
Germany	83*	100.0
United States		79.0
Russia	19	5.7

*Zollverein.

been bilateral (trade between two countries), exchanges of goods now became characteristically multilateral (trade among many countries). By means of what appeared, from a historical point of view, to be an exceptionally well-developed multilateralism, various economies got what they wanted and turned out what they could competitively best produce.

With the extension of multilateralism great economic inequalities developed between industrialized and nonindustrialized regions, as can be seen from Table 21. The explanation for the great differences in national income per capita of the gainfully employed among the various nations is to be found, in part, in the fact that the costs of turning out industrial goods were reduced more than those of producing agricultural goods and, in part, in the fact that large supplies of agricultural products from new regions came on the international market from the 1870s onward, which tended to keep agricultural prices low (Table 22).

Table 21. National income per person in work per year (in international units*)

Country	Period	Amounts
United States	1800	786
	1850	828
	1899–1908	1,319
Great Britain	1860–1869	707
	1894–1903	842
Germany	1805	114
	1854	406
	1894–1903	820
France	1800–1812	248
	1850–1859	426
	1900–1909	597
Japan	1007	100
	1897	101
India	1867–1868	132†

*One international unit is what 1 dollar would buy in the United States, on the average, in the period 1925–1934.

†Estimated.

SOURCE: Colin Clark, *Conditions of Economic Progress*, 2d ed. (London: Macmillan, 1951).

Patterns of consumption in countries of Western culture changed so greatly after the beginning of the nineteenth century and were so different from those found in countries of Eastern culture that the international comparisons given here accentuate the material inferiority of the economically backward areas. These comparisons do, however, indicate greater well-being in those more heavily industrialized areas which had an extensive division of labor than in the less industrialized.

With the development of multilateralism, exact balances among nations were never struck in the exchange of physical goods, because so many

Table 22. Index of wholesale prices, United States (1910–1914 = 100)

Year	All commodities	Farm products	Textiles
1865	185	148	266
1870	135	112	179
1875	118	99	141
1880	100	80	128
1885	85	72	105
1890	82	71	103
1895	71	62	79
1900	82	71	95
1905	88	79	96
1910	103	104	104

other items for which payments had to be made entered international accounts. Thus some nations performed shipping services, provided insurance, and did a banking business for others. Some received the expenditures of tourists; some, remittances from emigrants; some, earnings on investments; and some, cancellation of debts, which was actually a default. Thus the annual statement of foreign trade and payments of an economically advanced country, such as Great Britain early in the nineteenth century, indicated an excess of imports over exports, but large earnings from investments overseas, from insurance, shipping, banking, tourists, and emigrants were more than enough to cover such deficits. In fact, the British balance of trade and payments usually showed an excess of credits over debits (Table 23) and this excess made possible a growth of British investments overseas from early in the nineteenth century to World War I—an investment which was 1,302 million pounds in 1885 and 3,763 million pounds in 1913.[9] Similarly, French foreign investments increased from 15 billion francs in 1880 to 45 billion francs in 1914.

[9] See the series by A. H. Imlah, *Economic Elements in Pax Britannica* (Cambridge, Mass.: Harvard, 1958), pp. 70–75. His figures are reproduced along with other series in B. R. Mitchell and Phyllis Deane, *Abstract of British Historical Statistics*, pp. 279–335.

These relations among economically advanced states and the more retarded ones, together with an ardent nationalism in the former, account in large part for the revival of imperialism, particularly after 1873. As we shall see in greater detail later, Europeans came to believe that their economic interests would be furthered if they had political control over areas which could provide them with raw materials and markets for their goods and for their investment capital.

The balance sheet of a rapidly developing country like the United States indicated heavy borrowing abroad for investment, large immigrant remittances, which might be considered a cost of acquiring a labor force, payment on foreign borrowings, and an excess of exports over imports to get the wherewithal to make these payments to foreign creditors.[10] The international account of an economy having slow economic growth would show but little deficit for borrowed capital, heavy indebtedness for services, and some excess of exports over imports to pay for debts owed abroad (Table 23).

Table 23. Balance of trade and payments

Item	Great Britain (in millions of pounds) 1910	United States (in billions of dollars) 1896–1914
Merchandise	−159	+9.3
Investments	+187	−3.0
Services	+90	−7.2
Other	+35	+0.2
Unestimated		−0.3
Capital movement: Available for investment abroad	+153	+1.0

Although under certain circumstances an excess of imports over exports of physical goods might be economically justified, a belief that there was a special virtue in an excess of exports over imports persisted. This doctrine was particularly marked in those countries where the desire for material improvement was strong, where the realization that economic growth entailed industrialization was lively, and where the establishment of

---

[10] Foreign debt was also reduced by defaults or by declines in securities which were owned by foreigners. These items did not, however, appear in the balance sheets.

manufactures lagged behind that of other economies. It was preached by many statesmen and by a group of national economists, like Henry Charles Carey (1793–1879) in the United States,[11] Friedrich List in Germany (1789–1846), and Paul Louis Cauwès (1843–1917) in France. These theorists argued that to be economically strong and industrially powerful a nation must have a highly developed industry and well-rounded production; hence, national economic policy should assist economic growth with tariffs and subsidies.

The views of these men were opposed, however, by those who stressed the advantages to be derived from a division of labor and who consequently advocated free trade among nations and the nonintervention of the state in economic affairs at home. Most of these laisser-faire theorists were at first to be found in Great Britain, which had such technological advantages over other states that it had little to fear from foreign competition, especially in manufactures. There the doctrine of free trade enunciated by Adam Smith in his *Wealth of Nations* (1776) was elaborated by a brilliant group of the "classical school of economics"—by Thomas Malthus (1766–1812), David Ricardo (1772–1823), John Stuart Mill (1803–1873), and Alfred Marshall (1842–1924). Subsequently the free-trade faith was picked up and preached abroad by theorists like Jean Baptiste Say (1767–1832) and Frédéric Bastiat (1801–1850) in France. Even businessmen who were able to compete in the international market, like the Manchester manufacturers, the Bordeaux wine growers, and the cotton plantation owners of the American South, wanted low tariffs either to be able to buy cheaply what they needed or to get tariff concessions from other states so that they could sell more easily to them.

Already in the eighteenth century, as we have seen,[12] a current of *laisser faire* was flowing, which insofar as international trade was concerned was exemplified in the Eden Treaty (1786) between France and England—a trade agreement by which France lowered its rates on English textiles and Britain reduced its duties on French wines to the level of those on Portuguese wines.[13] Hardly was the ink dry on this document, however, than the French Revolution broke out (1789); this embroiled France in foreign wars that were not brought to an end until Napoleon's defeat at Waterloo in 1815. In these wars the French had extraordinary success upon the Continent, but they failed utterly in their efforts to bring the "island of

[11] Alexander Hamilton's *Report on Manufactures* (1791) had an impact on the thinking of these men.
[12] See chap. 11.
[13] Inasmuch as England's trade arrangements with Portugal, which were incorporated in the Methuen Treaty of 1702, gave Portugal favored treatment in wines, Britain lowered its rates on Portuguese wines after the signing of the Eden Treaty, so that the French did not get the equality of treatment which they had expected.

shopkeepers," as Napoleon called Britain, to its knees by military action and their chances of doing so seemed slight after their disastrous naval defeat at Trafalgar in 1805. Thus it was that France tried to bend England to its will by economic warfare—by constructing a closed economic system, known as the Continental System, against the English (Map 9).

The theory on which the Continental System rested was that England's economic well-being depended upon its export of manufactured goods and that if British exports to its principal market, the European continent, were cut off, industrialists would have to close their factories; workers would become discontented; the balance of trade would become adverse; the pound sterling would lose value; and the government would sue for peace. In the meanwhile, France would be able to gobble up the markets closed to Britain. The increased demand for goods would stimulate French manufacturing, and the growth of industry would augment France's economic, military, and political potential.

Almost immediately after France declared war on Great Britain (1793) the first stones of the foundation of the Continental System were laid. The Eden Treaty was annulled. A large number of English products were prohibited from entering the French market; in October 1793, *all* British goods were proscribed, and in September of the same year a blow was aimed at English shipping by requiring that all goods brought into France be carried in French bottoms or in the vessels of the country in which the cargo was produced. As Barere, the great tribune of the Revolution, stated, "Let us declare a solemn navigation act and the Isle of Shopkeepers will be ruined. Carthage will thereby be destroyed."

These rules were subsequently intensified and extended, especially in times of particularly hostile relations between France and Great Britain. Thus the tariff of 1796 was very harsh and new navigation laws were so rigorous that made-in-England buttons on the skipper's jacket were enough to cause the French to declare that a cargo was of British origin and a ship's putting in at a British port was enough to outlaw the vessel and to render it subject to seizure.

For a moment it looked as though such measures might accomplish their desired end and French hopes soared when the Bank of England suspended gold payments (1797). But England did not succumb to the attacks upon its commerce. When warfare was renewed after a brief interlude of peace (1802–1803), Napoleon applied the blockade with vigor and extended it to nearly the entire Continent (Berlin Decrees of 1806 and the Milan Decree of 1807). The English, for their part, declared by Orders of Council of 1807 a blockade of all ports from which Englishmen were excluded, outlawed all ships that tried to run the blockade, and required neutrals to go to a British port before proceeding to the Continent. This was one of the reasons for the War of 1812 between the United States and Britain. Fur-

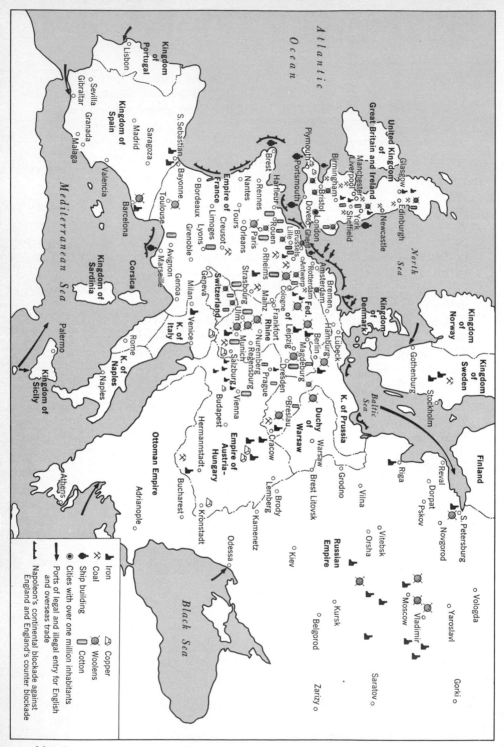

Map 9
European Economy at the Time of Napoleon

thermore, the British encouraged their shippers to break through the blockade and were so successful in getting them to do so that English goods were found on the Continent in such large amounts that French quarter-master corps bought English shoes in Hamburg for the French soldiers for their march on Moscow (1811–1812). Moreover, French industry was unable to take full advantage of the market reserved to it, especially in such things as cotton textiles made from the raw cotton which had to be brought from overseas. This failure so aroused the ire of the satellites that they abetted the English efforts to break the blockade. Eventually leaks in the Continental System became so great that Napoleon had to recognize them. At the end he turned the various restrictions on trade into a money-raising device by selling licenses for the importation of British goods.

Upon the defeat of Napoleon, the Continental System came officially to a close, but by the tariff of 1814 France prohibited a long list of goods. It raised rates in 1816 and instituted high protection with the corn laws of 1819, following the poor crops of 1816–1817, high prices for food, and the first large-scale importation of Russian grain. Even French shipping was favored with a flag tax (*droit de pavillon*), which was a charge levied on foreign vessels bringing goods of third nations to France, a *droit de tonnage*, which was a special tax per ton on foreign ships, and a *droit d'entrepôt*, which was an extra charge on goods that had been warehoused in other than their country of origin before they arrived in France—a tax aimed at England's middleman position in overseas trade. In England, agriculturalists demanded protection and got it with the Corn Law of 1815, which was revised slightly downward in 1828 with the Duke of Wellington's sliding scale. Industrialists worked behind a tariff barrier and had the advantage of laws designed to prevent the exportation of industrial secrets and the migration of skilled workers. In the United States, high protection was instituted in 1816, partly as a result of sentiments aroused during the War of 1812 against the commercial policies of France and Britain.

Yet, in spite of an apparently universal policy of protection, cogent arguments for free trade were being spun and certain interests, particularly commercial ones, took a firm position for lowering tariff barriers. In fact, commercial men in London signed a petition for free trade in 1820 and William Huskisson, who was President of the Board of Trade, that is, Britain's department of commerce, from 1823 to 1827 worked arduously for the abolition of the worst impediments to trade. He did much to abolish the Navigation Acts, opened trade with British colonies to foreign goods (1822–1825),[14] wiped out absolute prohibitions and prohibitive rates on

[14] The imperial preference system remained in force, however, until 1860; that is, Britain charged lower rates on equivalent goods coming from its colonies than on goods coming from foreign countries and its colonies collected lower rates on goods of British origin than on goods of foreign make.

imports, replacing them with duties that did not exceed 30 percent *ad valorem*, did away with prohibitions on the exportation of goods and with export bounties, and permitted the emigration of skilled workers (1824) and the exportation under license of industrial machines (1825).

The tariff reform movement was subsequently carried further by Robert Peel, who was Prime Minister from 1841 to 1846. As First Lord of the Treasury he instituted an income tax to furnish a substitute revenue for customs duties; then he cut the tariff (1842), allowed the exportation of machinery (1843), abolished the export duty on coal (1845), did away with the export duty on raw wool (1844), and, most important of all, repealed the Corn Laws (1846) when agricultural prices soared, especially in Ireland, following the potato famine of 1845.[15] Furthermore, he continued a policy begun by his predecessors of negotiating free-trade or freer-trade commercial treaties with foreign states. Britain supported Latin American nations in their efforts to get independence, and supported the American Monroe Doctrine (1823) to keep foreign powers from "intervening" in the affairs of the states of the Western Hemisphere. It negotiated a trade agreement[16] with the youthful state of Greece (1837) and another with centuries-old Turkey (1838). Britain got trade concessions from Persia (1836, 1857). It "opened up" China by the Opium War of 1840–1842, fought the Crimean War to keep the Danube and the Black Sea area open to its commerce, and won trade concessions from Japan in 1858.

Although free trade may have looked particularly good to Britain with its strong competitive position in industrial goods, most Continental countries continued protectionist policies during the first half of the nineteenth century. France maintained its rates at a high level during the July Monarchy—the so-called "Bourgeois Monarchy"—from 1830 to 1848. The United Netherlands adopted protection (1821–1822).[17] Prussia, although it enacted a relatively low tariff in 1818, began in 1833 to bring many of the German states together in a tariff union (*Zollverein*)[18] and thereafter raised its rates. Finally, the Kingdom of Sardinia, the most important of the Italian states, Russia, and Austria all had high customs duties.

---

[15] Agriculturalists, in general, opposed the repeal of the Corn Laws, for they feared competition from low-cost producers. They did not suffer from overseas competition until the 1870s because of the costs of transportation. The most ardent advocates of the repeal of the Corn Laws were to be found in the Anti-Corn Law League, directed by two free-trade enthusiasts, Richard Cobden and John Bright. The Chartists, who wanted an extension of the suffrage, also supported repeal.

[16] Most of Britain's trade agreements in this period were with the less economically advanced countries with whom England's trade was growing. Britain's exports to Continental countries did not go up much from 1815 to 1837.

[17] Belgium, which was united with the northern Netherlands from 1815 to 1830, introduced a sliding-scale corn law and a navigation act (1844).

[18] Inasmuch as Prussia had, as a result of the settlement at the Congress of Vienna, important territories which were separated from one another by intervening states, it was to Prussia's advantage to have a customs union so that goods going from one of its territories to another did not pay duties. The Rhineland province was the chief area separated from the rest.

By 1850, however, signs were abundant that ultraprotectionism was going to be modified. Not only was Britain moving toward free trade but many producers of raw materials and foodstuffs in several of the less economically developed countries, like the cotton interests of the American South, favored a reduction in tariff rates so that they could get manufactured goods more cheaply.[19] In fact, in the United States, tariff rates were lowered steadily from 1833 to the War Between the States. Some of the smaller nations began to reduce rates because much of their trade was perforce with other economies. The Netherlands virtually abolished customs duties from 1845 to 1877, Belgium greatly reduced its rates after 1851, and Sardinia did away with excessive forms of protection under the leadership of its great statesman, Count Cavour.

The crowning event, however, in this movement toward lower tariffs was the Anglo-French commercial treaty of 1860. For some time advocates of free trade in France and Britain had been preaching the advantages of lower rates. Finally, Michel Chevalier and Richard Cobden exerted their influence with Napoleon III and Gladstone, respectively, and persuaded the two men to have a commercial treaty negotiated. The resulting document not only provided for low rates but also stipulated that each signatory would extend to the other "most-favored-nation treatment," that is, would grant the other the lowest rates extended to any other nation. Subsequently, both France and England negotiated a whole series of trade agreements which contained the "most-favored-nation clause" with other powers and usually introduced some reduction of rates in them. Thus, through a network of most-favored-nation clause treaties, the lowest rates which Western culture had ever known became generalized.[20]

Reaction against these low rates set in, however, with the extraordinary depression in European agriculture after 1873. With low prices, with such misfortunes as phyloxera, sheep rot, and poor harvests, and with an influx of agricultural goods from overseas, European farmers began to clamor for protection. Then in those lands where manufacturing had made little headway, industrialists demanded protection for infant industries.[21] In Europe customs duties began to move upward with the Austrian tariff of 1878 and continued to mount until World War I. In 1910 the average rates on all imports, including those on the free list, were computed on an ad valorem basis to have been as follows: France, 8 percent; Germany, 8.4 percent; Italy, 9.6 percent; Spain, 13.4 percent; Russia, 38.9 percent; whereas the

[19] Canada moderated its rules by trade agreements (1857).
[20] In this same period many of the measures to protect national shipping were abolished. Thus the French did away with their surtaxes on foreign shipping in 1866.
[21] In the United States, the North, which had most of the country's industry, dominated the political scene and got protection.

rates on just dutiable goods entering the United States were 38 percent. Only the Netherlands, Finland, Turkey, and Great Britain continued to pursue free-trade policies.

As time went on states came to use special devices to keep out foreign goods when competition threatened. The French, for example, had two sets of rates, minimum and maximum, so that they could change their rates as they would and yet give minimum rates to those countries with whom they had most-favored-nation clause treaties and maximum rates to all others. Embargoes were resorted to in order to minimize foreign competition, sometimes under the guise of sanitary regulations, as when in 1885 Germany prohibited the entry of American pork, and sometimes to prevent one nation from "dumping" surplus products abroad at prices greatly below those charged at home. Sometimes, too, rates were made to apply to goods so specified that the products of one country had a preferred position. Germany, which had most-favored-nation clause treaties with France and Switzerland, thus gave Swiss imports an advantage by granting low rates to cows raised at altitudes of 1,000 meters or above. Moreover, to encourage exports, states gave subsidies, such as outright subventions at the time of exportation, subsidies on production, drawbacks, that is, payments to offset the duties levied on imported materials used in exports, and cheap transportation rates on national railways or shipping lines for carrying goods abroad. Finally, some nations which had colonies, especially France, Spain, and Portugal, adopted steep preferential rates,[22] although Great Britain and the Netherlands remained loyal to the principle of free trade in the administration of their empires.

One of the immediate consequences of protective commercial measures was the outbreak of tariff wars. Among the most acrimonious of these conflicts was that between France and Italy (1888–1899). Each nation believed that it had been particularly discriminated against in new commercial laws and consequently placed extra-heavy duties on the other's goods, used all imaginable obstructionist tactics, and even cracked down on loans from one nation to the other. Similarly, Russia and Germany were involved in a tariff struggle from 1879 to 1894, France and Switzerland were in one from 1893 to 1895, and Germany and Canada, from 1897 to 1910.

Tariffs also aided the creation of monopolies and selling agreements, because high protection allowed the formation of cartels which could establish prices without fear of having them undermined by foreigners. Moreover, tariffs usually meant higher prices on the domestic market and antiquated production methods.[23]

---

[22] Such preferential rates could not be applied to certain colonial areas because of international agreements. This was the case wih the Belgian Congo and Morocco.

[23] Within the larger economies, however, competition was often sufficient to prevent production from becoming moribund.

Tariffs were defended by asserting that they allowed certain industries to become established, that they mitigated shocks from sudden influxes of goods, and that they were a means of planning for increasing the economic and military potential of a nation. Furthermore, advocates of tariffs claimed that the free movement of goods required the free movement of people so that populations of those areas with no comparative advantages in production could move to areas where there was work.[24] Finally, protectionists pointed out that tariffs in this era were not so high that international trade was stopped and that a kind of world-wide division of labor was created in spite of them.

Developments in communications and marketing

With a greater division of labor both in domestic economies and in the entire world, and consequently with a greater dependence of the individual upon the market for goods to satisfy his needs, pressures were great to improve the means of communication and the methods of marketing. Business needed to know from day to day what prices were and to have the means of placing orders rapidly before conditions of trading varied. Sellers and buyers needed to have a market where staple goods could always be exchanged and where prices could be established through free negotiation. And both merchants and consumers needed places to which they could go to get the goods that they required.

Most important among improvements in communications from the end of the eighteenth century to the last quarter of the nineteenth were the extension of postal service, the invention and adoption of the electric telegraph, and the establishment of penny newspapers. Prior to 1800, letters were carried mostly by private enterprises, like the Turn and Taxis company in Austria and the early "express" companies in the United States. After 1800 national states began to create their own mail services and as they did so they introduced such reforms as standard rates for equal weights, low charges (the penny post was introduced into England in 1840), and adhesive stamps. Moreover, they greatly expanded postal services by opening post offices in every hamlet and they speeded carrying by entrusting the post to railways (England did so in 1838). How significant all these changes were can be imagined from the fact that the number of letters carried in France, for example, increased from 4 million in 1830 to 358 million in 1869.

[24] Their opponents maintained, on the other hand, that the free movement of goods served as a substitute for the free movement of people. Such an argument might have some validity in a place with goods to sell, like Britain, but made less sense in a poor region, like southern Italy.

Significant as such mass communications were for economic growth, speed of transmitting messages was often of extreme importance. Many a financial *coup* was made possible by advanced information about a crop failure, a military victory, or some other event that would have an impact on prices. Even before 1800 businessmen had used carrier pigeons to send information with dispatch, but such experiments were not very successful because the birds could not be trusted to fly to the right places. Then, they tried various types of semaphore systems to relay messages from place to place (the Chappe telegraph system, invented in 1793, was capable of transmitting messages from Strasbourg to Paris in six and one-half minutes), but such devices were of little use in fog and rain or darkness.

In the quest for a sure and rapid method of communication, experiments were made with electric signals as early as 1753, but not until the 1830s did the German Weber, the Englishman Wheatstone, and the American Morse make progress with this method. Finally, Morse succeeded in transmitting by electricity a message from Baltimore to Washington (1844) and thus got credit for inventing the telegraph. Almost immediately railways strung wires along their rights of way in order more efficiently and surely to control traffic, and those wires were soon used for sending private messages. In 1860 there were 126,140 kilometers of telegraph lines throughout the world on which 9 million messages were transmitted. In 1851 the first submarine cable was laid from Dover to Calais, and in 1866 the first transatlantic cable was put in operation. Then, at the end of the period at present under consideration, Alexander Graham Bell invented the telephone (1876) which was to facilitate communication still further, for it made the sender and receiver independent of "middlemen" and could be put at the beck and call of everyone.

Lastly, the diffusion of information important to business was speeded by the appearance of low-priced newspapers. Although daily journals of news had existed before 1800 (the first English daily dated from 1702), they were costly and were read primarily by the well-to-do in coffeehouses and other public places. The cylindrical press, introduced into newspaper printing in 1812 by the *London Times*, reduced costs, and the sale of advertising space provided a new source of revenue. By the middle of the nineteenth century the "penny" newspaper was well established and carried information useful to both the businessman and the consumer.

The craftsman who produced and sold goods in his own shop gradually disappeared, although in certain trades, like tailoring and shoemaking, the old form of organization died slowly. And the peddler who carried a small quantity of a large number of items of light goods from needles and pins to pots and pans began to be inadequate to the task of distribution. In their stead came the retail store, the first of which seem to have been for dry goods (mercers' shops), for colonial products (spices and teas), and for a large assortment of wares (the general store). These establishments were fairly common by 1800, but became ever more numerous as the century wore on. From a small dry goods store came the first department store, La Belle Jardinière of Paris (1830); another department store of Paris, Le Bon Marché (1852), adopted the practice of charging fixed and marked prices; and the house of Potin, a Parisian grocery establishment, developed a reputation for excellent quality and great variety at fair prices.

With the appearance of such retail establishments based on the profit motive, there also came into being consumers' cooperatives, founded on the principle that consumers would furnish the capital necessary for an enterprise and distribute among themselves whatever profit there might be from their purchases. The outstanding pioneer organization of this nature was founded in 1844 by a group of workers at Rochdale, near Manchester, England. This society, which furnished a pattern for cooperatives all over the world, was organized on the joint-stock company plan, with capital being furnished by the sale of stock to an unlimited number of members. The "co-op" sold goods at regular market prices, but at the end of the year made a distribution among its members in proportion to the amount of goods purchased. The success of the Rochdale experiment was so great that many cooperatives were established throughout Western culture both for distributing goods and for producing them.[25]

The development of retail selling by those who did not produce their wares created a problem of getting supplies, for manufacturers were numerous and the demand for goods was uneven. Thus there came to be a need for the services of middlemen between retailers and producers—for the wholesaler. Previously, what wholesaling there was had been done by merchants who brought goods to fairs, by traders, like the English East India Company, who sold their wares when they came into port,[26] and by specialists who had stalls in central halls, like the Blackwell Hall in London, the *Halles Centrales* in Paris, and the Washington Market in New York. Now wholesalers established warehouses in various areas where they kept stocks of goods, sent out "runners" or "drummers" to drum up trade among retailers, and so replenished the inventories of retailers.

---

[25] In 1929 consumers' cooperatives in Great Britain and Ireland had 6,168,984 members, or 10 percent of the population, and did a business of 216,967,000 pounds.

[26] Often these sales were "by candle," that is, bids were accepted so long as a candle continued to burn.

16

Finance capitalism: the revolution in investment and business organization

Capital investment and economic growth

The establishment of new means of transportation, of communication, and of distribution, the growth of machine industry organized in factories, and the development of a partially mechanized agriculture required an enormous investment of capital. Railways were notoriously expensive to get into operation because of the vast amount of land that had to be acquired, the need for extensive grading, the building of bridges and tunnels, the construction of terminals, and the purchase of rolling stock. In the English cotton-spinning industry, capital equipment per worker in handicraft production was about 5 pounds; whereas it was 118 pounds in factory production in 1892. Indeed, capital invested per gainfully occupied worker in Great Britain appears to have gone up some 50 percent from 1865, when many of the large initial outlays had already been made, to 1913.[1] The crucial facts here were that savings, which permitted human energies to be diverted from the actual production of goods for immediate consumption, were being effected and that these savings were being used to create capital goods, which would eventually make possible the turning out of still more goods. Just what the rate of saving or the rate of investment was in Western culture in the hundred years prior to 1875 is impossible to determine with accuracy. From what evidence we have, it would seem that capital formation in the United States was at the annual rate of about 20 percent of national income in the 1870s and in the United Kingdom at about 17 percent of national income in the 1860s.

---

[1] In the same space of time, national income per gainfully occupied worker increased some 70 percent. The capital invested per worker in Japan in 1913 was about one-seventh the amount invested per worker in France.

Economists are generally of the opinion that such savings and investments are extremely important to economic growth,[2] but because they have recently placed so much emphasis on the role of investment perhaps the introduction of a caveat here is in order. Investment cannot be considered to be the *single* cause of economic growth, nor in and of itself to have made economic development possible. As has been frequently stated in preceding pages, change in economic life takes place as a result of many factors operating concomitantly. One scholar has been so bold as to estimate that only about 10 percent of the economic growth in the United States during the eight decades prior to 1953 is to be attributed to the rise in the stock of tangible capital consisting of buildings, machines and other equipment, inventories, and foreign assets.[3] This estimate, if anywhere near actuality, indicates that the major proportion of economic growth depends upon changes in methods and in the organization of production, in short, upon technological change.

The distinction between capital deepening and technological change as sources of growth of output is not difficult to understand, but neither is it self-evident. Adding capital means an increase in economic input or factor utilization. Technological change, as we have previously defined it, means the ability to produce more output from a given level of input.

To explore the difference in microcosm we might choose the example of a single firm, such as Adam Smith's old, reliable pin factory. In that factory there are laborers and some machines which together produce pins. Supposing that an increase in pin production were deemed desirable, it could be accomplished by increasing the number of machines for cutting points, affixing pinheads, and so forth. If workers merely superintend machines, it might be that no new laborers need be hired, but still the cost of new machines would be heavy. How much more economical it would be if the same number of machines (or the same dollar value of capital) could be coaxed into producing more pins. This might be accomplished by rearranging them, by powering them more efficiently, or by changing the very nature of the machine. Although it is occasionally possible to improve efficiency merely by rearranging factor inputs in some more rational way (such as in an assembly line), more often technical change is embodied in a new generation of equipment. As long as the efficiency of the productive process is increased, technical change has taken place.

---

[2] Colin Clark, *Conditions of Economic Progress*, 2d ed. (London: Macmillan, 1951), pp. 506ff.

[3] Solomon Fabricant, *Economic Progress and Economic Change*, Thirty-fourth Annual Report of the National Bureau of Economic Research (New York, May 1954). From tangible capital are excluded consumers' equipment, military assets, land, and subsoil assets. See, also, Robert Solow, "Technical Change and the Aggregate Production Function," *Review of Economics and Statistics*, vol. 39, August 1957.

Business organization—the corporate form

One aspect of change that contributed greatly to national efficiency from the eighteenth century to the last quarter of the nineteenth was the growth in the size of economic enterprise. Industrial plants, railways, shipping companies, and department stores had to be large by comparison with earlier undertakings in order to exist at all. Inasmuch as optimum size was large, capital requirements were likewise very great. This being the case, the single owner-manager type of business no longer sufficed for large enterprises. It became necessary for many persons to be associated in order to get together adequate amounts of capital and to assemble necessary technical and managerial talents.

From the earliest days of the Industrial Revolution, partnerships were numerous. They came about, in some cases, because inventors then as now did not ordinarily have either the capital resources or the business acumen needed to exploit their finds. James Watt had to seek the assistance of Matthew Boulton to get his steam engine produced and marketed. Richard Arkwright, although probably more of an entrepreneur than an inventor, required capital aid from his wife and from Jedediah Strutt, whom he took on as a partner. And Edmund Cartwright had several partners in his efforts to launch his power loom.

In other cases, as we have previously seen, the resources of a single partner did not suffice for the task at hand and so multiple partnerships were formed. Some partners were chiefly investors and did not participate directly in the management of affairs. Such persons were known as "sleeping partners"; and their position received special status in the business form known as the *société en commandite*, for they were exempt from liability for debts of the concern. This type of company was recognized by the Code Napoléon (1802) and enjoyed particular favor on the Continent. Out of it grew the *société en commandite sur actions* (with shares), which, while retaining full liability of the partners who were active in management, gave an opportunity for relatively small investors to place their funds without incurring liability.

In England, however, the joint-stock company came to be developed more fully than the "sleeping partnership," and was, indeed, more adequate to meet the challenge of the times. The corporation was an excellent instrument for amassing large amounts of capital from numerous investors. It provided a way for investors to diversify their risks by placing their eggs in several baskets; and it had the advantage of "being perpetual," in the sense that it was independent of any one individual and could continue in operation despite changes in personnel at the top.

The joint-stock company had come into being, as we have seen, in the seventeenth century with the establishment of trading and colonizing ventures overseas, but then it went under a cloud following the mania of speculation in the second decade of the eighteenth century with the collapse of the Law system in France and the breaking of the South Sea Bubble (1720) in England. Indeed, joint-stock companies were not permitted in the two countries mentioned (by the Bubble Act of 1720 in England and by similar legislation in France) unless Parliament or the King granted the right by special act or charter. In France, the few such companies which actually came into being were suppressed by the revolutionaries from 1793 to 1795. Although the Code Napoléon allowed their creation, joint-stock companies had to be specially approved by the state and were so surrounded by a mass of red tape to prevent fraud that few entrepreneurs had recourse to them. In England, on the other hand, charters for the establishment of incorporated companies were given with increasing frequency as the eighteenth century progressed, especially for the building of turnpikes, canals, and bridges and in Scotland for the launching of insurance companies and even banks. Incorporated companies proved so successful and the need for more in order to take advantage of existing opportunities was so great that the Bubble Act was repealed in 1825 and incorporation by registration, if certain requirements were met, was permitted in 1844.

Hard upon this liberalization in England of the use of the joint-stock type of business organization, many speculative companies were founded which soon went under, but such adverse experience was not sufficient to discredit the corporate form. On the contrary, it was used ever more extensively. And it became ever more effective, especially by the addition of limited liability and of the preference share. Limited liability meant that investors would not be liable for the debts of a corporation in which they owned stock—a privilege based on the assumption that stockholders were running considerable risk in letting others use their capital. Limited liability was applied to the stock of most types of businesses in England in 1855 and 1856 but was not granted to the stocks of incorporated banks until 1858 and to those insurance companies until 1862.

The preference share, or preferred stock, as it is called in the United States, was stock which had a preferred position vis-à-vis common stock in that it received limited dividends before earnings were paid out on common stock and it had a prior claim on a company's assets in case of bankruptcy. It came into being from the fact that in launching certain types of businesses, such as factories and railways, more capital was frequently required than had been originally anticipated and sponsors of enterprises found that they could only get new investors to put money in their undertakings if they were able to offer additional securities that had a good chance of showing profits. So essential did the preference share seem to be for amassing capital to bring some enterprises to the productive stage that it was approved in a special case by the English Parliament in 1825 and given legal status in 1863.

The joint-stock company had so many advantages that it made headway in all parts of Western culture. As early as 1811 New York permitted the incorporation of companies engaged in certain types of manufacturing; both Connecticut (1817) and Massachusetts (1830) adopted the principle of limited liability; all states had some kind of law permitting incorporation by 1860. French legal restrictions were relaxed in 1867, and those of various German states were abolished after the founding of the Reich in 1870. So important did corporations become that to a marked degree economic progress was reflected in the number of joint-stock companies and in the amount of their capital. In 1844 England had 994 incorporated companies with capital of 345 million pounds; in 1840 France had 260. In 1867 Italy had 291 with paid-in capital of 1,192 million lire, and in 1870 Prussia had 276.

The increase in the use of the joint-stock form made necessary the establishment and expansion of stock exchanges—of marts where corporate securities could be readily bought and sold. There had to be places where new issues could be launched, where those with savings could place their funds, change their portfolios, or turn their holdings into cash. In London, stockbrokers who had been carrying on their activities at Jonathan's Coffee House moved first (1773) to the Stock Exchange Coffee House and in 1802 to the Stock Exchange. At the latter date the Exchange consisted of 500 brokers, but new members were accepted upon the payment of a small fee. Only later was membership restricted by charging aspirants large sums.

The French Bourse, which had been founded in 1724, was reorganized in 1816 with a membership of sixty persons and with a list of seven stocks. In the course of time, business expanded to a point where so many companies wanted a market for their securities and so many brokers (*agents de change*) wanted a place to operate that trading was permitted on the peristyle of the Bourse—an exchange that soon became known as the Coulisse. In 1889 trade in commodities was separated from trading in securities at the old Bourse, which became known as Le Parquet, and membership in this body was increased to seventy in 1898.

In New York brokers organized for business in 1792, but they did not found the New York Stock Exchange until 1817. Their business subsequently flourished so that in 1880 they bought and sold securities to the amount of 95,737 million dollars. In Berlin, Amsterdam, Vienna, and Rome similar developments took place, either with existing exchanges growing and becoming specialized in the handling of securities or new institutions being created. In 1887 stocks listed on European and American exchanges had a market value of some two and a half billion dollars.

Important as joint-stock companies and stock exchanges were in furthering economic growth, they made possible practices which came in for a considerable amount of criticism. Investors were usually absentee owners who exercised little real control over management despite their power to select members of boards of directors, to voice their views at annual stockholders' meetings, and, in extreme instances, to bring a minority stockholders' suit against the management. In general, stockholders showed such apathy toward their companies that management came to dominate affairs. In fact, a class of managers came into being whose members in the upper echelons frequently adopted a proprietary attitude toward the company which employed them. Sometimes these people, many of whom in this period were also investors in the companies for which they worked, used their power for their own benefit. They were in a position to give business to other concerns in which they may have had an interest, as was done in the case of the Union Pacific Railroad when its promoters let the actual construction contract at exorbitant prices to their own company, the Crédit Mobilier. Members of the management group could also speculate in the stock of their company, for they knew its value better than anyone else. They could unload their holdings if the stock were overvalued and threatened to go down, and they could "water" stock by issuing stock certificates to themselves at a nominal price.[5]

Still another criticism made of the corporate form was that it permitted the concentration of control of a large part of the economy in the hands of a few. This might be accomplished by a system of "interlocking directorates" in which some persons served as directors of several banks and business concerns. Thus a small clique could determine the line of credit that businesses would get, could refuse credit to competitors, and could acquire so much power that it could determine the policies of governments and even overthrow regimes which were hostile to it. Prior to World War I directors of the Dresdner Bank in Germany sat on the boards of about two hundred corporations; American financiers like George F. Baker, President of the First National Bank of New York, and John Pierpont Morgan, the great investment banker, held so many directorships that it is difficult to see how they could have done much else than go to directors' meetings. The *deux cent familles* which controlled the Bank of France dominated in turn a large part of big business in France.

Concentration of control might also be effected by use of the "trust"— a procedure made famous by the Standard Oil Company. In 1879, when the Company did about 90 percent of the petroleum business of the United States, holders of the majority stock of the various corporations composing Standard Oil placed their securities in the hands of trustees, receiving in

---

[5] *Poor's Manual*, a United States investment manual, estimated that in 1900, 1,250 million of the 3,100 million dollars' par value of stock in the hands of the public was watered.

return trust certificates. Thus the stockholders got a share of the earnings of the Company, had complete and permanent control of their concerns, and obtained greater freedom of action and greater privacy of operations than was possible in the ordinary corporation.

When this kind of trust arrangement was declared illegal (1890) in the United States and the term trust had become a synonym for large enterprise, other ways to extend control over businesses were found. In one of the new procedures, the organizers of a company limited the amount of voting stock issued and by owning a controlling interest in this small amount of stock dominated the affairs of the company. A second method involved securing proxies from a large enough number of stockholders to allow control of stockholders' meetings and election of their candidates to directorships. Still another device was that of the holding company, first sanctioned by law in the state of New Jersey in 1888, whereby a corporation was formed simply to own stock in several subsidiaries which actually produced goods or services. The United States Steel Company, founded in 1901, was essentially a holding company and was the first corporation to have a capitalization of a billion dollars. Finally, and least subtly, concentration of economic activity could be effected by the merger, which was simply the bringing together of two or more companies to form a new corporation. An indication of how mergers led to concentration is offered by such facts as the drop in the number of banks in England from 600 in 1824 to 250 in 1865, 55 in 1914, and 11 in 1937. In the United States in 1904, 300 of the largest corporations had two-fifths of all the capital in manufacturing establishments.

In instances where concentration of ownership or control was not possible, competition among businesses could be mitigated in other ways. One of these was by means of the "pool," which appeared first in Europe in the first half of the nineteenth century. This consisted usually of a loose agreement to maintain prices and to limit business to established quotas. A more formal arrangement was the cartel, one of the first of which was the Rhenish-Westphalian Coal Syndicate (1893) in the Ruhr. By the terms of the cartel device independent companies agreed to maintain established prices, to abide by quotas on the amounts of their sales, which were based upon productive capacity and size of investment, and to pay into the cartel treasury fines if the terms of the cartel were broken. Cartels had a particular vogue in Germany, where law did not ban monopolistic practices, in France after 1884, when the law forbidding agreements on prices was abrogated, and in international trade, where three of the most famous organizations were the dynamite cartel of 1886, the railmakers' cartel of 1904 and the North Atlantic Shipping Conference of 1908.

In England and the United States, not only the common law but also popular sentiment was hostile to monopolistic practices. Pools and cartels

were virtually outlawed, except in the case of the export trade and shipping and in railway carrying,[6] and a definite campaign was launched
against most monopolistic devices. In America a series of federal laws, like
the Sherman Anti-trust Act of 1890, declared any combination in interstate
commerce which was in "restraint of trade" to be illegal. What constituted
"restraint of trade" had to be decided by the courts. This turned out to be
a most difficult thing, especially when great combines were able to lower
prices and evidence could be presented to show that many of the most
efficient businesses were large ones.

To what extent antitrust legislation prevented wealth from becoming
concentrated in a few hands and monopolistic practices from being indulged in is difficult to ascertain. About all that can be said is that businessmen contrived to reduce competition, that identical prices for standard
products were often arrived at through trade association meetings without
any provable collusion having taken place,[7] and that the courts did not
find an inevitable correlation between size of enterprise and objectionable
practices.

The price system and money

Undoubtedly the assumption which lay behind much of the opposition to
monopoly was that competition was necessary to keep prices low; and
certainly the primary reason for the great concern with prices was that they
came to regulate many of the relations among men, to determine the
individual's ability to acquire goods and services, and to permit a division
of labor. So important did prices become, indeed, that much attention was
given to a study of how prices became established.

Since prices are expressed in money, it was obvious that both the supply
of goods and the supply of money were major factors in determining the
relationship between the two. It was also clear that, inasmuch as goods and
money were held by individuals, their willingness to part with the one in
order to have the other depended upon their respective desires for a long
list of goods and services, upon their purchasing power, and upon their
expectation of what prices would be in the future. It seemed reasonable,
too, that prices would be influenced by the number of sellers (monopoly,
duopoly or oligopoly) and by the number of buyers (monopsony, duop-
sony, oligopsony), by the velocity at which money circulated (a rate deter-

---

[6] In the United States the Webb Act of 1918 allowed exporters to make cartel agreements. Railway
pools were allowed by the Transportation Act of 1920.

[7] Among such bodies might be mentioned the Comité des Forges in France, that was something of
a cartel, and the National Association of Manufacturers in the United States, which was founded in 1895.

mined by the amount of payments made divided by currency in circulation plus demand deposits in banks), by costs of production, and by the possibility of increasing or decreasing the supply of both goods and money.

In the 100 years prior to 1875, prices were relatively stable, that is, indices of wholesale prices fluctuated within a range of 100 to 200, except in France during the French Revolution and in America during the War of Independence, the War of 1812, and the War between the States. In France, as has been mentioned in connection with the discussion of land holding, the revolutionaries issued *assignats,* treasury notes which were to be retired upon the sale of land in order to pay government debts. Once launched upon such a course, revolutionary leaders could not resist the temptation to continue issuing more paper; consequently assignats lost value steadily until in 1795 they were worth 5 percent of par, or stated in another way, prices in *assignats* had risen 2,000 percent. In 1797 the Directory repudiated the assignats as worthless and at the same time declared a "two-thirds bankruptcy," paying its creditors one-third of their claims in new bonds and two-thirds in *mandats territoriaux,* which were similar to the *assignats* and had no market value.

In the United States, the high prices of the Revolution were to be accounted for primarily by the issue of Continental currency in large amounts without sufficient backing. Some of the "Continentals" were retired in 1780 at the ratio of 40 to 1 and the rest in 1790 at 100 to 1. With the War of 1812, prices of imported goods rose to about double what they had been in 1800 and prices of domestic articles went up some 50 percent, partly because of interference with foreign trade and partly because of domestic expansion. With the Civil War the wholesale price index for ninety-two articles was at 71 in 1860 but 127 in 1865 (1913 = 100), owing to an increase in economic activity and to the issue of paper money which had no reserve—the so-called greenbacks.[8]

In spite of the relative stability of prices there were secular or long-term trends in price levels. Prices rose in the period 1721–1741 to 1819; then they reacted downward until about the middle of the nineteenth century. Thereafter they rose until 1873; they fell again until 1896; and they rose once more from 1896 to after World War I.

These long-term trends in prices, which contain within themselves changes of shorter duration that had to do with poor harvests or fluctuations in business activity, have usually been explained exclusively by a consideration of money. It is very probable, however, that because of population growth and war, the demand for goods increased faster than

---

[8] It should be added that Russia declared 1 metal ruble worth 3 rubles 60 kopecks of paper money in 1827. Austria declared an 80 percent reduction in the value of its paper in 1811 and a 60 percent reduction in 1816. In both instances, the value of the gold coins was brought down to the level of the paper money.

supply from early in the eighteenth century to 1819, that supplies increased outlays of capital occasioned by the building of railways and the diversion of energies from productive activity during a whole series of wars stretching from the Revolution to 1848, through the Crimean War, the War of Italian Liberation, the Seven Weeks War, the American Civil War, and the Franco-Prussian War, supplies of goods fell off in relation to demand from 1848 to 1873. With the development of production on a large scale overseas and the growth of ocean shipping by which quantities of overseas products entered the European market, supplies of goods more than exceeded the volume and velocity of circulation of money from 1873 to 1896. These statements are, however, deduced from the manner in which prices behaved and so they may be said to be almost tautological.

At all events, to arrive at a fuller understanding of prices it is necessary to consider in more detail another factor in the equation—that of the volume of money, the velocity of its circulation, and the value of the metal or metals into which currency was convertible. As can readily be imagined, the volume of money in circulation increased rapidly from the end of the eighteenth century to the last quarter of the nineteenth, for the growth of commercial transactions required greater amounts in order to effect payments. In the case of the Bank of France, for example, the note circulation went up from 69 million francs in 1816 (current values) to 251 million in 1847, and to 2,300 million in 1880. In addition, payments were also made in other negotiable instruments, which may be considered money, such as checks, bills of exchange, money orders, and letters of credit. In the English-speaking world, the check supplemented bank notes and coins. In England it came to be used to make half the total value of payments and in the United States in the post-World War II period it has been employed to make some 80 percent of the volume of payments.

Not only did the supply of money in Western culture increase at a rapid rate in the first three-quarters of the nineteenth century, but each unit of money assumed a bigger role in the making of payments, that is, the velocity of the circulation of money went up, especially money in the form of checks. The rate of turnover of bank deposits, calculated by dividing the volume of debits in a given space of time by the average amount of deposits outstanding in the period, appears to have risen in the United States from less than five before the Civil War to over twenty-five after World War I.

As money thus became more abundant and more efficient as a medium of exchange, it remained remarkably stable, as has been previously stated, as a measure of value; that is, prices fluctuated within narrow limits. This was accomplished, in part, by making money ultimately redeemable in gold and/or silver,[9] by varying the amount of bullion to be paid out as

---

[9] Payments in bullion were suspended in a few emergencies, but redemption of paper bank notes in metal was generally adhered to.

these metals commanded more or fewer goods, and by exercising some control over the supply of money, including both the volume and the velocity of circulation of money. Moreover, a consistent downward pressure on prices resulted from increasing industrial efficiency. That manufactured goods were becoming steadily less expensive was the most powerful deflationary pressure in the nineteenth-century economy.

Throughout most of the nineteenth century a major consideration of the makers of monetary policy concerned the selection of a monetary standard —the kind and amount of metal or metals in which currency should be redeemed. In 1774 the English adopted to all intents and purposes a gold standard, for gold coin became the sole legal monetary standard at the rate then defined by mint ordinances, but in 1816 the government formally decreed gold to be the only standard of value at the rate of 113 grains of fine gold to the pound, with silver coins issued only as tokens having very little silver in them.

Most countries, however, used at the time a bimetallic system. In 1791 the United States adopted a decimal system in place of the sexagesimal system of the pound and fixed the silver content of the dollar (a word derived from Thaler, which in turn came from the fact that much silver was mined in Joachimsthal in Bohemia in the sixteenth century) at 371.25 grains with a ratio of 15 grains of silver to 1 of gold. The French, for their part, decided in 1793 upon a decimal system of coinage, decreed in 1795 that the franc should contain 5 grams of silver 0.9 fine, and declared in 1803 that the ratio of silver to gold should be 15.58 to one. Other peoples of Western culture for the most part followed these examples.

Still other changes resulted in establishing monetary "unification" on a national basis and "national monetary sovereignty." Thus in the reforms of the hundred years prior to 1875 a single unit of national currency replaced a number of regional moneys. How important this was can be realized from the fact that during the Revolution France's two major livres were abolished in favor of the franc. In 1850 twelve different Swiss currencies were reduced to one. Following Italian unification in 1860 several different monetary systems were fused; and in 1875 nine different currencies in Germany were replaced by the bimetallic mark. Furthermore, the earlier custom of letting foreign currencies circulate more or less freely at home was abolished, so that henceforth the state considered itself sovereign in respect to money and the control thereof. So firmly did this concept come to be rooted and so important to the economy did the managing of money become that the surrender of monetary sovereignty constitutes a major obstacle to European unity plans of the post-World War II era and a major problem of international finance.

Whatever the final judgment of national economic policies, of which the monetary policy was only one, will be, the fact remains that those which had to do with metal standards operated with a fair degree of success and were not held to so rigidly that they could not be altered when conditions seemed to justify a change. Thus during the first half of the nineteenth century the bimetallic arrangements functioned well, for although gold increased somewhat in value no great difficulty was encountered except in the United States, where in 1834 the mint ratio was changed to 16 of silver to 1 of gold. After 1850, however, fluctuations in the respective prices of gold and silver were great enough to have a serious effect on the established ratios and consequently on the use of metals in money, for the hoary doctrine of Sir Thomas Gresham that cheap money drives dear money from circulation operated with inflexible rigor. Changes were then made in the ratios and the metal contents of currency units.

The supply of gold greatly increased following the discovery of gold in California and Australia in 1848 and 1849. The annual average world output of gold went up from 15,740,000 dollars for the period 1801–1850 to 121,210,000 dollars in the period 1851–1855. Under these circumstances gold lost value in terms of silver, with the result that gold began to flow to bimetallic countries, driving silver out of circulation; silver began to flow to silver-standard countries like some of the German states and India. Commodity prices rose by 25 percent from 1850 to 1866. At the latter date gold stopped losing value in terms of silver, although there was no reduction in production, which indicates the importance of other factors than the amount of precious metals in the price equation, and gold and silver returned to their former relationship of about 15½ to 1.

During the years when gold was cheap in relation to silver and the white metal was taking flight from countries with a bimetallic system, there was a danger that silver coins would entirely disappear from circulation. To prevent such an eventuality, most of the countries concerned simply reduced the fineness of silver pieces; the United States took such action in 1853 and most of the continental countries west of Germany followed suit. Inasmuch as they did not act together, however, exchange rates were upset and silver fled from one country to another depending on how high it was valued. To bring some order out of the resulting chaos, Belgium proposed the formation of a monetary union whose members would have similar coinage systems and identical metal content of coins. This proposal led to the founding of the Latin Monetary Union in 1865; this had as members France, Belgium, Italy, and Switzerland, and after 1868, Greece. Moreover, Spain, Romania, Finland, and several South American and Central American states collaborated with it. Efforts were made to get England and the Germanies to join the Union but England refused on the ground that she was not a bimetallic[10] country and Germany was not wanted by France after the Franco-Prussian War (1870).

While these attempts to put more order in the monetary systems of Western Europe were being made, events were working toward the adoption of a gold standard. In 1873 Nevada silver mines began to produce and shortly thereafter silver began to become cheaper in terms of gold, the ratio shifting from 22.10 to 1 in 1889 to 32.57 to 1 in 1893. Under these conditions it became the turn of gold to be driven out of circulation and for silver to be used widely in actual coins. In this instance, however, monetary experts were ready with a remedy for the new malaise—they simply advised going on a gold standard to maintain the stability of prices. Thus Germany and Holland adopted the gold standard in 1871 and 1873; the Scandinavian Monetary Union, which included Denmark, Sweden, and after 1875 Norway, followed suit upon its formation in 1873. The Latin Monetary Union suspended the minting of silver coins except as tokens in 1874, thus adopting the "limping standard," that is, taking gold as the real measure of value, with silver limping along behind.

Bimetallism was, indeed, in full retreat from 1873 onward, having almost no supporters at the International Monetary Conference at Cologne in 1881 or at Brussels in 1893. There were those, however, who attributed the downward march of prices to the use of gold as a measure of value and who advocated the "unlimited coinage of silver." Proponents of this idea were to be found, logically enough, among miners of silver and among representatives of debtor groups. They were particularly strong in the United States, where they had enough power to secure the passage of the Bland-Allison Act (1878), which required the Secretary of the Treasury to coin into dollars not less than 2 million nor more than 4 million dollars' worth of silver each month, and the Sherman Silver Purchase Act, which provided that the Secretary of the Treasury should buy 4.5 million ounces of silver bullion each month and issue in payment for it legal tender known as the "Treasury Notes of 1890."[11]

With the depression of 1893, the demand for gold in payment of silver coins or certificates was so great that the gold reserve of the Treasury of the United States was threatened. This fact, plus the continued fall in prices, gave the advocates of the free coinage of silver an opportunity to push their cause. It was then that William Jennings Bryan, the Democratic candidate in the presidential campaign of 1896, advocated the unlimited

---

[10] In 1857 a convention was held at Vienna among Central European countries to establish uniform currencies. The basic coin was to be the Thaler of 18.66 grams of silver. Inasmuch as gold coins were not given legal status, the members of the union were on a silver basis. Austria withdrew from the group in 1867.

[11] Under the Bland-Allison Act 378,166,000 dollars' worth of silver or silver certificates (notes payable in silver) were issued. Under the Sherman Act 156,000,000 dollars' worth of silver bullion was acquired.

coinage of silver at the ratio of 16 to 1. In an impassioned speech he promised that "mankind would not be crucified upon a cross of gold."

Such flights of oratory were not sufficient, however, to carry the day; and the Republicans won the election with promises of a "full dinner pail" and their platform of sound money. By 1900 they had adopted gold as the legal standard, but contrary to Bryan's gloomy expectations prices did not go down. New supplies of gold were coming into the market as a result of a more adequate exploitation of South African deposits, the use after 1890 of the cyanide process of getting gold from ore,[12] and the opening of gold fields in the Klondike (Canada), in Alaska, and in Siberia. These new supplies plus the greater use of negotiable instruments, like checks, resulted in a larger supply of money. This fact, together with the extension of a demand for goods, tended to push prices upward in a secular trend that was to extend through World War I.

Banking

The actual provision of money was a function of the banking system and of national states. More and more, banks not only performed their traditional tasks of furnishing means for safeguarding funds, of accumulating the saving of many, and of making loans to entrepreneurs, but also they came to control credit and thus to influence the rate of business activity.

The most influential institutions in the formation of credit policies were "central banks"—a term which did not, however, come into use until the twentieth century. These were semipublic bodies; that is, they were organized as stock companies but were chartered by states according to terms that allowed the state certain controls over them, such as naming the governors and vice-governors and borrowing from them. In the course of time central banks became less concerned with making profits than with providing money to meet the needs of the commercial world and to give stability to the entire monetary and credit structure of the economy. They became, in time, prepared to extend credit to other banks which might be threatened with insolvency, especially if their assets were good but not readily marketable. Gradually they got monopolies of the right to issue bank notes[13] and were in a position to *create* money in order to have the

---

[12] This process recovered some 90 percent of the gold in the ore as compared with 60 percent from the mercury method.

[13] The Bank of England's notes became legal tender in the financial crisis of 1797. In 1826 country banks were not to issue notes for 5 pounds or less. In the Bank Charter Act of 1844 the right of issue was concentrated in the Bank and the country banks gradually lost their rights of issue so that by World War I the Bank of England was the sole bank of issue. The Bank of France was the sole issuer of notes in Paris from 1806. During the Revolution of 1848 and the financial turmoil accompanying it, the Bank's notes became legal tender and the Bank became the sole issuer of bank notes. The Bank of Italy became the only bank of issue in that country in 1926.

wherewithal to lend. They have been likened to fire departments which try to prevent fires, send out fire engines to put out conflagrations once started, and make at their own volition an almost inexhaustible supply of extinguishing fluid.

In the first half of the nineteenth century an important controversy raged regarding the amounts of notes to be issued and the basis for determining those amounts. The two rivals were the "currency school" and the "banking school." Although members of both groups approved the idea of an automatic monetary system in which the value of the currency was related to precious metals, they differed in how to create and run this system. The adherents of the "currency school" wanted to treat bank note money the same as metallic money. Thus if gold flowed out of the country, the money supply (note issues) should be contracted just as it would be if only metal money existed. Thus banks would restrict credit and curb the exuberance of entrepreneurs and consequently prevent financial crises.

Supporters of the "banking school" contended that unfavorable exchange rates were the result of bad harvests or other temporary catastrophes and that the restriction of credit did not solve the problems facing the economy. In fact, they held that the contraction of credit in such circumstances only made matters worse and generated crises. They advocated a supply of money commensurate with the needs of the business economy.

In England, the principles of the "currency school" triumphed in the Bank Charter Act of 1844. According to its provisions the Bank of England could issue bank notes up to a total of 14 million pounds sterling (15 million after 1875) with first-class securities as backing, but for every bank note issued in excess of that sum the Bank had to increase its reserve of bullion by an equal amount of precious metal (a pound of gold for every pound of bank note). This meant a very limited and inelastic money supply and created certain hardships. In fact, in the emergencies of 1847, 1857, and 1866 the Bank was temporarily allowed to exceed the legal limits on notes issued against securities and in 1890 managed to borrow 2 million pounds in gold from the Bank of France to weather a storm.

The English banking system was able, however, to devise ways to overcome the rigidities imposed on it by law. By encouraging the use of checks, the Bank of England actually fostered another medium of exchange, as we have already seen, which greatly added to the volume of money in circulation. Furthermore, by extending or restricting credit to other banks, which were its chief clients, it could do much to regulate in turn the bank credit extended to business and thereby to control business activity and the need for money. Thus in times of great expansion, the Bank of England raised its discount rate (in the panic of 1866 it was pushed up to 10 percent) and in times of depression the Bank reduced it (from 1894 to 1896 the rate stood at 2 percent)[14] in hope of returning the economy to an even keel.

Furthermore, the credit situation in England could be influenced by the Bank's "open market" operations. If the Bank bought securities in the market, it provided the business community with more funds with which to do business; if it sold securities, it absorbed money and hence took away from the business community some of the media of exchange with which to operate.

In France, the central bank, the Bank of France, was founded in 1800 by Napoleon.[15] Its issue of bank notes was based upon the "banking principle" rather than on the "currency principle." This meant that instead of the issue of notes being limited to a low maximum and the deposit of bullion required as a reserve for notes issued over this ceiling, notes would be issued with commercial paper as the main reserve. Consequently as more commercial paper came to the Bank for discount (it did business with other banks and directly with businessmen), note issue could be increased, and when less came in, the note issue would be restricted. Such a system, although it required the maintenance of rather large reserves so that calls made on the Bank could always be met,[16] gave the French economy a large and flexible money supply. This was important inasmuch as checks, in spite of their convenience, never developed widely in France and businessmen discounted small bills. Yet, the Bank of France could regulate the supply of money by altering the discount rate. It could control credit by decisions to accept or to refuse commercial paper for discount,[17] because it dealt directly with businessmen as well as with banks and operated branches all over France.

In most of the other countries of Western culture, central banks came into being which pursued policies similar to those of the Bank of England or of the Bank of France, or adopted procedures which were a compromise between these two. The Reichsbank in Germany is an example of the third group. Although it followed the banking principle of the French, did business directly with individuals as well as with banks, had many branches, and had to maintain a one-third reserve of metal or treasury bonds

---

[14] This practice also had an effect upon foreign money markets. If the English rate were high, foreign gold went to London in search of profits; if it were low, English gold went into foreign investments in hope of getting better earnings.

Unfortunately the changes in the discount rate did not come early enough nor were they drastic enough to prevent business fluctuations. They were usually remedial rather than preventive.

[15] It was placed on a more solid and realistic basis in 1806.

[16] In 1847 they were half of the note issue.

[17] This was one of the reasons that the Bank of France did not have to change the discount rate so often nor so drastically as the Bank of England.

against its total issue of bank notes, it could exceed this limit if it paid a 5 percent annual tax on the excess.

In the United States, however, central banking had a hard time of it. To be sure, the First Bank of the United States acted as a central bank from 1791 to 1811, but its charter was not renewed, partly because of the conservative policies which it pursued and partly because state banks, supported by a basic "states' rights" sentiment, hoped that they would be the lucky recipients of lucrative government deposits. When Congress decided not to renew the charter of the First Bank, many banks were chartered by the states, their number increasing from 86 in 1811 to 246 in 1816. Unfortunately these banks overextended themselves and in 1814 all of them outside of New England were unable to pay out specie for their bank notes. Because of the crisis, the fact that the government was required to take state bank notes in payment of taxes and bonds, and the demand of the Treasury for a central bank, which would receive its funds on deposit and transfer them from place to place, Congress finally reached the decision to establish a new central institution. In 1816 it gave the Second Bank of the United States a charter for twenty years.

The course of the Second Bank was extremely stormy. At first it was grossly mismanaged, and subsequently, under the direction of Nicholas Biddle, it became a political football between those interests, especially in the West and South and in Eastern cities like New York, led by President Jackson, which favored states' rights, feared moneyed interests, or resented the leadership of Philadelphia, and Eastern interests, represented by Biddle, which desired stable money and "sound" banking policies. From this match of wits and power, President Jackson emerged the victor and consequently blocked a renewal of the Bank's charter (1832). Again banks chartered by states began to appear on every hand, especially in parts of the West which were so sparsely settled that it was alleged "wildcats were the only customers." The policies of many of these banks, now dubbed "wildcat banks," were, in fact, so wild that this term became synonymous with loose banking practices.

In the ensuing years banking suffered by the absence of a lending institution of last resort and by a laxity of state supervision. The government experimented with the so-called Independent Treasury System, whereby it placed its money in vaults in customs houses and mints, thus keeping capital idle and not providing for regional needs. Only with the coming of the War Between the States, when more conservative business interests were in power, when the need for federal governmental supervision of banking was more urgent than ever, and when the government wanted to sell more of its bonds, were important reforms effected.

When the South repudiated its debts to the North, the financial stringency was so severe that many Northern banks failed, especially in the

Mississippi Valley. Furthermore, the fact that there were 12,000 different types of bank notes in circulation, many of which had been issued by bankrupt or discredited banks, made even those who usually favored cheap money realize that reform was needed. Consequently Congress passed the National Bank Act of 1863, which provided that every bank that accepted federal regulation could deposit government bonds with the Treasury of the United States and issue bank notes with these bonds as security.[18] This privilege, heavy federal taxes on the bank notes of state banks after 1865, and a decision to deposit government funds with national banks curbed wildcat state banking.[19]

The National Bank Act remained in operation until 1913.[20] Although it was an improvement on what had existed before, it left much to be desired. The system of reserves tended to bring deposits of banks to New York, which forced the New York banks to maintain large liquid assets. As these assets were often lent at call on mthe New York Stock Exchange and as they fluctuated widely, they constituted an unnecessary element of instability. Furthermore, the concentration of reserves in New York meant that some parts of the country were poorly served when it came to financing great seasonal activities, like moving the wheat crop. Most important of all, however, the supply of bank notes under the National Bank Act arrangements did not expand and contract in unison with business needs, but with the amount of government bonds in the market and their market value.[21] Had it not been for the concomitant growth in the use of checks and the elasticity which this practice gave the volume of money, stringencies would have been much greater than they were.

Central banking became in time very crucial to the monetary and credit structures of every country where it existed. Yet ordinary banking business—the receiving of deposits from customers and the making of loans —was obviously fundamental to economic development and the functioning of the capitalist system. The institutions engaged in this kind of activity were differentiated both by the way they acquired funds and by the type of loans which they granted. Thus in "private banks" capital was provided mostly by rich owners or partners, whereas in joint-stock banks it was raised by the sale of stock. Savings banks were characterized by the

---

[18] At first bank notes could be issued in volume up to 90 percent of the market value of the bonds, and not beyond a limit of 300 million dollars. In 1875 this limit was removed, but country banks were required to maintain a 15 percent reserve against bank notes, whereas for banks in reserve cities, the reserve requirement was 25 percent.

[19] Furthermore, the National Bank Act provided a way for banks to use greenbacks, unsecured paper money in the amount of some 450 million dollars that had been issued to finance the war, for this currency could be used to buy government bonds. This fact tended to bring greenbacks up to par.

[20] When the Federal Reserve System was created.

[21] Banks did not retire their notes as a rule to meet seasonal demands, so there was little contraction. To hold low interest government bonds against the day when more money would be needed was not profitable.

fact that their deposits were in small amounts. Deposit banks were distinguished by the fact that they specialized in handling commercial deposits which could easily be "withdrawn" by the writing of checks; trust companies were set off because of their specialization in the administering of other people's property.

On the lending side, there were investment banks, which made long-term commitments to business enterprises and sometimes held large blocks of their stocks or bonds; there were also commercial banks making short-term, self-liquidating loans to businesses, mortgage banks lending on mortgages, and last, but by no means least, banks doing a mixed business.

At first most of the great banks were private banks, *les hautes banques,* as they were called in France, like the Rothschilds, the Barings, the Hopes of Amsterdam, the Bleichröders of Berlin, Mallet Frères in Paris, and Morgans of New York, but the trend was in favor of joint-stock institutions, for they provided a way of amassing great amounts of capital and a method of limiting an investor's liability. The Société Générale of Belgium, founded in 1822, was one of the first of such organizations. In England the monopoly of the Bank of England on joint-stock banking was broken by an act of 1826, which permitted joint-stock banks outside a sixty-five-mile radius from London; and these banks came to account for from one-fourth to one-fifth of all bank notes issued.[22]

The success of these early experiences with joint-stock banking led to many imitators, such as the Crédit Lyonnais (1863) and the Société Générale (1864) in France, the Diskontogesellschaft (1851) in Germany, and Lloyd's in England (1899).

As time went on, joint-stock banks displayed a tendency to merge. The number of banks in England fell from 600 in 1824 to 55 in 1914, and to 11 in 1937, when five-sixths of the country's banking was done by the "big five"—Midland, Westminster, Lloyd's, Barclay's, and the National Provincial. In Germany the famous "D" banks—the Darmstadt Bank (1870), the Diskontogesellschaft (1851), the Deutsche Bank (1870), and the Dresdner Bank (1872)—were reduced in 1932 to the Danatbank (a fusion of the Darmstadter and Dresdner) and the Deutsche, which had absorbed the Diskontogesellschaft.

With the trend toward joint-stock banking and toward mergers, there was also a drift toward mixed banking. With a few great banks, except in the United States where in most states bank branches were limited by law, it was inevitable that banks should amass funds in many ways and make many types of loans. Moreover, concentration on long-term investments

---

[22] An act of 1833 permitted joint-stock banks within the 65-mile radius, but these banks could not issue notes. In 1844 joint-stock banks might be founded without special act of Parliament. These banks got limited liability by acts of 1859, 1862, and 1879.

had brought both grief and scandal in its wake. In England, Overend, Guerney and Company went under in 1866 because it entered into promotion ventures which froze its assets. Baring Brothers, which had gone heavily into Argentinian bonds and found in 1890 that these securities could no longer be moved at a profit, was saved only by a committee of bankers, organized by the Bank of England, which gave Baring time to unload its holdings and an opportunity to reorganize as a joint-stock bank. In France, the Crédit Mobilier, a joint-stock institution organized by the Péreire Brothers in 1852, financed the building of railways, the establishment of the French Line, and the reconstruction of the Rue de Rivoli. It engaged in such questionable practices as paying dividends out of capital and foundered when money became tight in 1866 and there was no market for its assets. Finally, in America, Jay Cooke and Company failed (1873) because of being overextended in Northern Pacific Railway securities, which would not move.

On account of such experiences most of the great banks leaned toward commercial banking, yet their portfolios, that is, their list of investments, held substantial blocks of government bonds, large amounts of business securities, and some mortgages, in addition to very large holdings of discounted bills. Specialized banking persisted, however, with the continuance of such investment banks as the Banque de Paris et des Pays Bas (1872) in Paris, of mortgage banks, like the Crédit Foncier (1852) in France, and of savings banks. Such new "specialists" came into being as postal savings banks, whose main purpose was to encourage thrift, and the German innovation, the Schultze-Delitzsch Banks, which were cooperative credit societies to serve small businessmen, and the Raiffeisen-Hass group, which were made up of rural credit cooperatives to finance farming.

In the aggregate these various banks came to constitute a tremendous power in the economic world. In France, the Bank of France had such a powerful position and its stock was so closely held that it was said two hundred families could dictate to whom credit should be extended, even to the point of refusing loans to the government if it were in hands hostile to them.[23] In Germany, the Dresdner Bank claimed before World War I that its directors sat on the boards of more than two hundred corporations, thus participating in making policies for these businesses and determining the bank's line of credit to them. And in England, bank loans, especially for commercial activities, did much to determine the directions in which the economy expanded. So important did the part which banks played in the economies of the Western world become that some observers characterized the capitalism of the West from about 1870 to at least the Great Depression of the 1930s as finance capitalism.

[23] Francis Delaisi, *La Banque de France aux mains des 200 Familles* (Paris, 1936).

Public finance

With the development of the capitalist system, the state took on more and more tasks that required the outlay of funds. Not only were the expenses of defense much greater than they had been, but public authorities assumed the responsibility of providing for education, for public works like roads, railways, and harbor installations, for merchant marines, and, especially in those countries which were slow to industrialize, for economic growth in general. As a result profound changes had to be made in public finance. Existing tax structures had to be revised, for either they did not furnish sufficient funds or they did not have desired economic effects. The excess of expenditures over receipts was so large that every state had a large funded debt. Government spending became so great that it could stimulate business booms.

The extent of the demand on governments for funds is well illustrated by the French case, where expenditures of the national state increased from 900 million francs (current value) in the early 1830s to 5,067 million francs in 1913, or by that of England where expenditures rose some 370 percent from 1850 to 1913 and amounted to about 20 percent of national income. Some idea of the nature of expenditures may be gathered from Germany, where federal, state, and local branches of government allocated in the fiscal year 1913–1914 31.9 percent of outlays to the military, 19.3 to education, 8.6 to highways, 8.6 to debt service, 7.7 to welfare, 3.7 to police, and the remainder to a host of other services.

To raise funds to meet the new demands central governments relied primarily on customs receipts, excise and stamp taxes, and borrowing; local governments had recourse to property taxes and licenses on business. In Great Britain of the early nineteenth century two-thirds of the tax revenue of the royal treasury came from customs and excises, whereas local governments got some 95 percent of their revenue from taxes on property.

In many countries, expenditures exceeded receipts because existing tax rates could not be pushed up fast or far enough to meet growing needs, and spending jumped suddenly beyond all reason because of such events as war. Borrowing became the order of the day, accordingly, and public debts grew alarmingly. That of France, for example, more than doubled from 1848 to 1871. In that country exceptional expenditures became so important that a double-budget system was adopted (1881), one for ordinary receipts and expenditures and the other for extraordinary (non-recurring) receipts and expenditures—a practice that was followed by many other countries.

The desirability of balancing governmental budgets, at least for recurring expenditures, was so generally recognized that tax reforms were steadily sought. In general, demands for tax changes were conditioned by such social and political considerations as a desire to make all citizens contribute a share to the public purse without losing the votes of any one group, to distribute the tax burden according to ability to pay, and to make assessments on actual wealth and not on arbitrarily determined amounts or upon sums arrived at by bargaining. Furthermore, there was a general tendency to favor, at least in theory, direct taxes (property, income, or inheritance taxes), which would be paid by the person taxed, instead of indirect taxes (excises, customs duties, and licenses), which could be passed on by the taxpayer to others. In Great Britain, an income tax was instituted in 1799 under the stress of war, but it was subsequently abolished, only to be reestablished in 1841. It was made "'progressive," that is, heavier according to the size of the income, in 1909. This impost was so remunerative that it provided two-thirds of the national government's income by the post-World War I period. The United States adopted an income tax during the Civil War, but dropped it in 1872, when needs for revenue were less urgent, and reintroduced it only in 1913 following the adoption of an amendment to the Constitution that settled the question of the tax's legality. Prussia adopted an income tax (1851, 1891) and a progressive tax on property (1893); the German Reich instituted an income tax in 1913 and France, in 1917. An inheritance tax was experimented with in Britain during the French Revolutionary and Napoleonic Wars, was reintroduced in 1853, and extended in 1894 and 1909. A similar tax was levied in Germany in 1906, was used temporarily in the United States from 1862 to 1870 and from 1894 to 1902, and was made a fixture after World War I. France, for its part, was slow to effect tax reforms but came to rely heavily on indirect taxes and permitted taxes to be levied on the "apparent value" of things.

Business fluctuations

Despite increases in economic well-being resulting from the mechanization of industry, the development of production in new lands, the extension of commerce, and the division of labor, modern capitalism had its flaws. One of the most important weaknesses of the new system was that it seemed to generate within itself forces which led to business booms and to business depressions. Fluctuations in business activity were, in essence, nothing new, but prior to the nineteenth century they appeared to have been caused mainly by forces that were not strictly economic, like weather and war.

In the nineteenth century, however, things changed. Patterns of periodic, endogenous ups and downs in the Western economy became increasingly manifest. Respecting no national boundaries, the recurring cycles of prosperity and contraction obviously were not caused by governments or forces outside the economic system. Beginning in the early nineteenth century, economists began to explore the internal workings of capitalism to try to find the causes for fluctuations. A Swiss historian and economist, J. C. L. Simonde de Sismondi, originated the idea of "underconsumption," an insufficiency of aggregate demand, as we might say today, as a cause of depressions. Karl Marx, in his critique of capitalism, detailed an elaborate theory of endemic cycles of boom and bust, ever more severe as capital became concentrated in the hands of fewer and fewer persons, leading to eventual entropy and the destruction of the system. In later years, groups of empirical economists examined the record of business fluctuations and determined that, in fact, several different types of cycles, each caused by a different set of factors, were simultaneously operative upon the Western economy. These different classes of cycles may be summarized as long waves, long swings, and business cycles.

We know next to nothing about long waves; they are the most difficult fluctuations to perceive and measure and the most difficult to explain. Nikolai Kondratieff, after whom the phenomenon is sometimes named, found evidence of three long waves in European modernization: the first from roughly 1780 to the 1850s (peak at 1810–1817); the second wave, rising to a peak at 1870 to 1875 and followed by a decline to the last decade of the century; and the third, rising to the period of World War I and falling through the 1930s. Kondratieff found evidence of these cycles in such varied statistics as agricultural and industrial wages; production and consumption of coal, pig iron, and lead; and interest rates.[24] In spite of such scrutiny the long wave remains but a name for a set of observations, for the cause of such long-term fluctuations has not been successfully pinpointed. A possible source of long-run variation in the economic life of a capitalist economy is the bunching of innovative activity. Joseph A. Schumpeter, a Vienna-trained Harvard economist, observed that as epochal innovations or technological breakthroughs are made, the resulting high profits induce successive enterpreneurial activity, investment, and a general burgeoning of the economy. These spurts are of sustained duration and only as imitators cause profits to fall does the cycle swing downward. The timing of points of inflection in European long waves lends some credence to the idea that critical innovations underlie major upswings. Europe's first long wave corresponds at the outset to the spread of early developments in agriculture, the cotton industry, and steam-power technology. The rise of the second wave seems to parallel breakthroughs in steel and chemicals, and the turn-of-the-century wave is inaugurated by shifts in power technology to electricity and internal combustion.

[24] See Nikolai D. Kondratieff, "The Long Waves in Economic Life," *Review of Economics and Statistics*, vol. 17, no. 6, November 1935.

Within the long waves, smaller cycles of eighteen to twenty-five years' duration have been charted. These long swings, building cycles, or Kuznets cycles, as they are called, result from the interaction of population changes and economic behavior. With favorable economic opportunities, a generation of workers may find employment and household formation easy to accomplish. International migration and flows of investment funds are attracted to the "constructive"economy. Within the context of this prosperity, marriage and child rearing can proceed without economic hardship to new families, and household budgets can sustain greater numbers of children within the family. Eventually, with the saturation of the labor force and diminishing employment opportunities, this phase of the cycle must end; but replication of the upswing in the future becomes likely. It is programmed into the economy by the "lump" in the age distribution created by favorable fertility conditions. As this "echo generation" proceeds through various phases of the life cycle, the impact of its demand is strongly felt in residential and capital construction, in general levels of economic activity, and in the labor market. The eighteen- to twenty-five-year duration of the cycle is reflective of a generational lag "baby-boom children" coming of age and entering the labor market themselves. Long swings have been found to exist in immigration patterns, flows of investments across international boundaries, balance-of-payments statistics, and home and plant building.

The shorter the fluctuation, the easier it is to perceive. No one can easily sense where he stands in a long wave; charting long swings is accomplished with greater precision. Still, the man in the street has no feeling for the effect of such movements upon his life. Business cycles, the short four- to eight-year fluctuations, are another story. Everyone knows about them and feels their effect directly. Workers know that employment levels and the growth of wages depend upon them. Investors get stomach ulcers worrying about them. Words like "prosperity" and "depression" have become part of the parlance of modern life. According to the late Wesley C. Mitchell, one of the great analysts of the business cycle, the short fluctuations had four phases, each of which was characterized by forces that led to the next phase. These may be described as follows:

1 *Expansion.* Expansion comes on the heels of *revival.* It is characterized by an increase in production, a higher level of employment, higher wages, bigger profits, and greater consumption of goods. Prices rise and businessmen are optimistic about the future. More capital is invested in plants and equipment.

2 *Recession.* As expansion gathers momentum by the interaction of the forces listed above, it reaches a point where the economy is handling as much volume as it profitably can. Costs of production increase. Manage-

ment becomes less efficient; interest rates are up; and prices reach a level so high that some buyers put off purchases. Plant expansion is curtailed and the makers of producers' goods begin to suffer. As these manufacturers close their plants, purchasing power is reduced and workers are laid off. Similar conditions soon appear in other industries. Banks begin to worry about the loans which they have made and start to call them in.

3 *Contraction.* Pessimism now sets in among businessmen. Prices go down; production declines; profits are reduced; bank loans shrink; and unemployment becomes more general.

4 *Revival.* With the contraction of business, less money is needed to conduct affairs and interest rates go down. Management tries to cut waste and to reduce costs. Prices become so low that certain groups, especially those on fixed salaries, begin to buy. Retailers start to build up their inventories. Factories improve their organization and begin to renew their equipment. Bankruptcies become fewer. Prices are more stable and show a slight inclination to rise, and confidence begins to return. Before long the economy enters the phase of expansion and the experience begins to repeat itself.

Business fluctuations showed many variations in detail from this basic pattern. Some of them were short and "mild"; others were long and "deep." In every one some segments of the economy developed against the general downward trend. In general, it may be said that periods of prosperity were longer and periods of depression were shorter in times of secularly rising prices, as from at least 1801 to 1820, from 1850 to 1873, and from 1896 to the end of World War I, and that the reverse was true in times of secularly falling prices, as from 1820 to 1850 and from 1873 to 1896, this last period being known as the Great Depression in prices.

A detailed analysis of business cycles from the end of the eighteenth century to the last quarter of the nineteenth century is not possible here, but a word about them is essential for an understanding of economic growth and for an appreciation of some of the social and political history of the times. One of the last fluctuations of the old type of depression resulting primarily from poor crops, which in turn were caused by bad weather conditions, began in France in 1787. Exceptionally disastrous harvests in 1787 and 1788 raised prices suddenly; in July 1789, they reached the highest level of the entire century. Economic conditions improved in 1791 and 1792, but then political tampering with the economy became so extensive, foreign and domestic strife was so great, and crops were again so poor that business activity was retarded during the Terror (1793–1794). In England, the fall of exports was so large that gold was drained away until the Bank of England had to suspend specie payments (1797). Subsequently the Continental blockade worked so much havoc that there were crises in both France and England. So bad did things get in France that

Napoleon lost much of the support which he had previously enjoyed in the business community; in England, industrial production was so slack and industrial wages so low that there were serious riots (Luddite Riots of 1811–1812). In 1815 economic activity lagged because of the unsettled political situation and the brief renewal of war which ended with the battle of Waterloo in Belgium.

Following the restoration of peace, business conditions improved somewhat, but poor crops in Western Europe in 1817 made food prices high, those in England going up with those in France. Concomitantly, English manufacturers were having difficulty moving all of their output and Continental producers were having trouble meeting the competition of the English. In both places there were unemployment and wage cuts. Consequently the years 1818–1819 were depressed, with the latter being marked by the Peterloo Massacre at St. Peter's Fields at Manchester, when the Yeomanry Guard charged a workingmen's mass meeting. Even in the United States business suffered, largely because of a decline in European demand for cotton and other New World products. Subsequently, business activity increased, but English speculation in South American trade and American cotton and an accompanying expansion of industry led to a crisis in 1825–1826 and to a mild recession on the Continent and in America.

In 1830, business on the Continent was somewhat disturbed by revolutions, but the building of new plant in Europe and speculation in America, both in westward expansion and in commercial crops, made money tight. Thus when President Andrew Jackson issued his Specie Circular in 1836, requiring that all public lands be paid for in specie, the bubble of good times burst in the panic of 1837. Recovery soon followed, however, with the railway building boom of the 1840s, but this in turn came to an end in 1847–1848. Industrial prices had risen extraordinarily high because of the increased demand, and agricultural prices had gone up dramatically with the poor crops and the Irish potato famine of 1846.

When stable political conditions were reestablished following the revolutions of 1848, business began to expand once more. Railway building was resumed and there was a great expansion of the ferrous-metal industry. Prices went up, and so, too, did wages and the costs of production, until finally businessmen began to lose faith in the future and started to restrict their activity. In 1857 there were many bank failures, a fall in the price of stocks, a decline in commodity prices, unemployment, and in the United States, a series of failures among railroad companies.

Recovery from the Panic of 1857 was rapid because of the further expansion of railways, the introduction of Bessemer converters, the building of iron steam vessels, and a series of wars.[25] This movement came to

---

[25] These included the War of Italian Unification, the Austro-Prussian War, and the American Civil War.

an end in 1866, just after the conclusion of the war in America, when new supplies of cotton in the world market brought the price of cotton down so suddenly that an important English bank, Overend, Guerney, and Company, failed.

Again revival set in, with railway construction going forward, with the opening of the Suez Canal, with the introduction of the Siemens-Martin process of making steel, with a building boom in Germany, and with an expansion in ocean shipping. By 1873 prices reached a higher level than at any time in the previous half-century; wages and profits had risen fast, and capital had become dear. This time a recession was triggered by the failure of the American bank of Jay Cooke and Company (1873), which had overextended itself in railways and which enjoyed such a good reputation that a newsboy was arrested in New York for crying, "Read all about it. Failure of Jay Cooke." In the crisis several European banks had to close their doors; stock market securities collapsed, and prices, especially those of agricultural products, fell drastically.

This time recovery was slow, but some improvement had been made by 1882, when the failure of a French bank, the Union Générale, tightened the money market. Subsequently an improvement in business was registered, but a new setback occurred in 1889 and 1890 with the breaking of the Panama Canal Company scandal (1889) and the near-failure of Baring Brothers (1890).[26] Not until 1896, when prices began to go upward in a new secular trend, was business said to be good again. In 1903 to 1904 money was exceedingly tight and a "rich man's panic" occurred; 1907 to 1908 saw another stringency of funds, although the pace of business did not slacken much. There was expansion from 1913 to 1914, when the entire operation of the business cycle was disturbed by war.

In the face of this new phenomenon, governments did not stand idly by, waiting for what many held to be a "self-adjusting economy" to right itself. From early in the nineteenth century, states, usually through their central banks, endeavored to curb excessive speculation by raising the discount or rediscount rate in the hope that higher interest rates would curb business expansion. Conversely, when times were bad, the banks forced interest rates down and lent more liberally in order to encourage expansion. Such measures were not, however, particularly effective, for they were not always timed correctly and did not have enough leverage to influence business policy. Hence they were supplemented in given instances with efforts to extend or contract the amount of money in circulation by the issuing or purchase of government bonds, by public works projects, of which the Freycinet Plan in France (1879) was one of the first, by attempts to bolster up faltering institutions, as in the case of Baring

---

[26] The depression hit America in 1893.

Brothers, and by colonial expansion, which in the long run, it was hoped, would provide a necessary outlet for European goods, capital, and people. Yet, neither an understanding of nor a control over business fluctuations was realized, as the Western world was to learn to its sorrow in the 1930s.

New risks and insurance

Fluctuations in business activity were not, however, the only new risks which emanated from the economy. As men became more and more dependent on money to satisfy human needs rather than upon the produce of their own labors and of their own means of production, relations among individuals became more and more impersonal. Those paternalistic attitudes which had been adopted by the lord toward his serfs or by the guildmaster toward his journeymen and apprentices disappeared with the payment of wages, the ownership of capital goods by entrepreneurs, and the organization of production by large units. Workers, especially urban ones, and small businessmen and their dependents came to rely almost exclusively on current earnings for existence. Savings were too small to carry these people over more than short periods and they had few opportunities[27] for alternative employment. If the head of a family died, dependents could seldom expect anything from his former employer. If some member of a family became unemployable because of injury, disease, or old age—and dependents from these causes became more numerous as the average age of populations became greater and work became more dangerous—dependents fell as almost a dead economic weight on the family. In an agricultural society such persons might frequently be put to performing easy or unskilled tasks. They might be fed by putting a "little more water in the soup," and they might be housed in a loft or stable. In cities such expedients were, however, impossible. Even in bourgeois families, current earnings were necessary, for although there might be some savings to live on, they were usually not enough to last very long if the standard of living to which the family had become accustomed were to be maintained.

To meet the essentially new exigencies of economic existence, efforts were made to share the risks at first through private efforts and later through governmental intervention. At the outset, workers created mutual-aid societies whose members agreed to help those among them who were stricken with misfortune; the more well-to-do developed life insurance and annuity arrangements to ward off the effects of the worst hazards

[27] In the United States in 1944, nearly one-third of all families effected no savings; in 1957 only 13 percent of Old Age and Survivors' Insurance (governmental "Old Age" insurance) beneficiaries had assets of 5,000 dollars or over.

—death and old age. Then later on, labor began to clamor for state-sponsored insurance, which was initiated in Germany in 1883.[28]

The most fruitful principle for meeting the new risks was that of insurance. It was based on the following conditions: that several persons have an interest of some kind that is susceptible of pecuniary estimation, that these persons would incur a loss if that interest were destroyed or impaired by the occurrence of designated perils, that an insurer assume from the above-mentioned persons the risk of loss, that such assumption be part of a general arrangement to distribute actual losses among a large number of persons bearing similar risks, and that as a consideration of the insurer's assumption of risk, the insureds make a ratable contribution, known as a premium, to a general fund from which losses are paid.

Insurance, as has been seen, was used particularly in shipping in the Late Middle Ages. Subsequently, it was extended to cover the lives of masters of ships for single voyages. The closely allied arrangement of buying an annuity developed in the seventeenth century. Then, in the eighteenth century, life insurance companies began to be founded, especially in Scotland and England, the first important one being the Society for Equitable Assurances on Lives and Survivorships (1762). Thence, life insurance spread to other parts of Western culture, the first company in France being founded in 1819, the first in Germany in 1827, and the first in America to continue in operation to the present day in 1843. By 1885 the amount of life insurance per capita in the United States amounted to 41 dollars. In 1942 it was 989 dollars.

This insurance just mentioned was taken primarily by the well-to-do, and efforts of the working classes to get similar relief through mutual-aid societies were at best only moderately successful. Because of this situation, workers began a drive for state "social insurance." Their requests were at last heeded in Germany where Bismarck, who was anxious to take the wind out of the sails of the Socialists, was ready to ingratiate himself with the workers. In 1883 he instituted sickness insurance; in 1884 he introduced workmen's compensation laws; and in 1889 he founded an Old Age and Security Insurance scheme—the "security" here being against disability caused by certain diseases like tuberculosis.

These laws, although diverging somewhat from the principles of private insurance, minimized losses to individuals through the sharing of risks. Contributions to the funds from which benefits were paid were made not only by those who stood to benefit in case of loss, that is, by the insureds, but also by employers and the government. Furthermore, whereas workmen's compensation placed liability on employers for injuries to workers

[28] See the discussion of Bismarck's policies, below.

which occurred in the course of employment, employers covered their risk of loss by paying premiums to private insurers. Gradually society was developing a means of assuming responsibility for the unfortunate—a method that subsequently was to be greatly extended.

The anticapitalist reaction—theory

The genesis of Marxian anticapitalism has its theoretical origins in a rather academic issue: What is value and how is it created? In capitalism, as we understand it today, the market determines the value of a commodity, and the market price is determined by the combined behavior of sellers and buyers: supply and demand. We understand costs to be the key determinants of supply schedules, and costs represent payments to several factors of production. Labor receives its wage; investors in land or capital receive some rent or interest payment to remunerate them for abstaining from consumption; and entrepreneurs take profits in payment for their abilities to mobilize production and for the risks they endure. In actual practice the departures from this simple model are manifold. No market is truly "perfect," which means that in almost all cases buyers or sellers have some degree of arbitrary control over prices. Nonetheless our basic ideas of income distribution and economic justice still depend on this framework. In the middle of the nineteenth century Karl Marx challenged the legitimacy of the market as a device for income distribution.

Marx was born in Trier on the French-German border in 1816. He was raised in an environment of intellectual vigor, the son of a successful lawyer who had abandoned Judaism and a family rabbinic tradition for a diet of Kant and Voltaire. After an early career of scholarship, journalism, and radical activity which made him an exile from Germany and France, Marx eventually settled at the reading room of the British Museum in London to complete his task of analyzing capitalism. *Das Kapital*, the product of these labors, was both a treatise on economics and a history of economic development. At its foundation is the labor theory of value, which contends that the value of a commodity is determined by the labor that goes into its manufacture and nothing more. Marx recognized the existence of markets and market prices in capitalism and called such prices "exchange value." Exchange value, however, need not reflect the true value of commodities: uncultivated land, for example, may have a market price and therefore exchange value, but, according to Marx, this price form is imaginary; the land is without value, for no human labor has been incorporated into it. From this theory derives the Marxian view of economic justice. As only labor produces real value, only labor merits remuneration. Profits, rent, and interest would therefore be unjustifiable payments, representing exploitation of workers by the industrial middle class, those who are in control of the means of production. This divergent view of economic justice is the most fundamental difference between Marxism and capitalism, even to the present day.

The Marxian scenario for capitalist development projected ever-worsening conditions for workers. According to Marx's economic theory, the difference between the subsistence wage that a worker produces (and is paid) for his own bodily survival and the total labor that goes into his product is "surplus value," and this is appropriated by the capitalist, the very source of his profits. Capital (in the form of equipment) is a multiplier of surplus value, for it enables workers to produce more goods in a given time. As capitalists individually continue to invest in the hope of increased gain, the rate of profit is driven downward, and their recourse is to increase the exploitation of laborers. As wealth flows in ever-greater proportions into the hands of fewer and fewer capitalists, finite limits on the ability of society to consume the products of industry emerge, and periodic phases of overproduction become endemic in the economy. As unemployment grows and the incomes of proletarians diminish, a point of no return is reached and workers overthrow the rule of the middle class by violent revolution, leaving the means of production in the hands of the workers. What follows the deluge, in theory, is a communist society in which the market prices of goods are equal to their labor value and the rule of income distribution is, "From each according to his ability, to each according to his needs." Class antagonism, the motive force in history from the time of the ancients, as Marx saw it, would end, and man's more recent dependence on the market would also pass away.

Marx and his collaborator, Friedrich Engels, were not the first ones to envision such a model society as a replacement for the ills of the industrializing world. From the time of the French Revolution, socialist thinkers devised, and occasionally put into practice, alternative social and economic orders that would abolish privilege in favor of collectivism and centralized management. While the following of the early socialists was never large, some experimentation on a small scale did take place. Followers of the ideas of Robert Owen and Charles Fourier left what they thought to be the stultifying social order of England and France to experiment with communal life. Most of these communities dissolved soon after their founding. In the *Manifesto of the Communist Party* of 1848, the program of revolutionary Marxist communism, Marx and Engels reviled the "utopian socialists" for their limited programs and shortsightedness—"pocket editions of the New Jerusalem," Marx called the Fourierist *phalanstères* and the little Icarias (communities patterned after Étienne Cabet's 1838 *Voyage to Icaria*). Instead of imaginary utopias, Marx offered scientific socialism, a construct of general laws governing historical change and forecasting those changes in the future, together with a program for enforcing the transition to socialist society.

The anticapitalist reaction—practice

Before 1850 the cause of reform and redress of workers' grievances against the new industrial system was pursued only sporadically and without significant effect. Without organization among the ranks of the new factory workers (or for that matter within the residual work force of the countryside), the fate of this cause rested almost exclusively in the hands of others. The social conscience of Europe in the early period of modernization was represented by reform-minded conservatives, often members of the aristocracy, and a very few middle-class reformers. The old labor-force organizations, the guilds, the trade clubs, the journeymen's organizations (compagnonnages, in France), and the trade unions (federations of trade clubs) had either died a natural death with the end of handicraft manufacture or had been killed off in the orgy of suppression that spread through Europe after the French Revolution. In England the Combination Acts of 1799 and 1800 provided heavy punishments for protest activities; the French Le Chapelier Law of 1791 quashed the compagnonnages, and in Italy strikes were regarded as no different from political rebellion until mid-century.

In the face of repression, the only recourse for the disaffected was the anonymous protest of furtive mass violence. The machine-breaking rampages of the Luddites were such a response. Fueled by low wages and unemployment, the fury of the poor was vented by acts of sabotage and factory burning; it was not a mass movement, but the coordination and effectiveness of the Luddites suggested some degree of local organization. However, no success ever attended programless agitation, and violence was met with further repression: "gagging bills," suspensions of habeus corpus, spying, heavy sentences. Following the Peterloo Massacre in 1819 the infamous Six Acts were passed in England, signaling the apex of repression with a widespread abolition of civil rights and press freedom.

Soon after this period, radical-minded workers in England became involved in middle-class causes, such as Corn Law repeal and the parliamentary reform movement. The ostensible purpose of the Anti-Corn Law League was to reduce the price of food by allowing for grain importation (p. 340). Although this worthy goal enlisted many workers in the cause, it would not be overly cynical to mention that when dealing with the Manchesterian manufacturers, anti-Corn Law spokesmen were quick to point out that lower grain prices meant that wages could be driven down. Parliamentary reform became part of the radical working-class platform (such as it was) in England after new city growth distorted representation. Great industrial cities had almost no representation, while deserted villages might have two Members of Parliament chosen entirely at the will of the local landlord. Under middle-class leadership, reform bills were brought to Parliament and twice defeated. Popular riots followed. In 1832 reform was enacted, and the franchise was extended to all those who owned or rented a house at 10 pounds or more. This criterion effectively shut out the working classes from participation in the electoral process, while it admitted the *bourgeoisie*, a major disillusionment for lower-class radicalism. Popular participation stemmed from a false conception of the cause of distress among workers. People still thought that high grain prices and political corruption caused the distressful condition of urban and rural workers. Through no fault of their own, workers failed to realize that even if corruption or the high cost of bread were somehow eliminated, the unrestrained economic power of employers left them with little hope for improving their lot. Lower-class radicalism did not come to grips with modernization, property rights, and economic justice until later in the century.

The reorganization of workers began about mid-century. In England, the Amalgamated Society of Engineers, a prototype for modern labor unions, was formed in 1851. The Universal German Workingmen's Association was formed in Germany under the leadership of Ferdinand Lassalle, a charismatic radical whose Workers' Program was a vulgarization of the Communist Manifesto (or so it was deemed by Marx). The Workingmen's Association survived Lassalle's premature death (in a duel over an amorous adventure), and Lassallean unions were formed along with small Marxist unions and other local workers' groups. In France, the orientation of early unions was highly political. These groups developed slowly, suffering from the severely repressive reaction to the Paris Commune (the revolt of radical forces in the municipality following the defeat of France in the Franco-Prussian War). Toward the end of the century European unions burgeoned as the local craft organization gave way to wide representation of factory workers in industrial unions. By 1910 there were 3 million union members in England and over a million members of unions in France and Germany. In newer industrialized countries, such as Italy and Russia, unions also developed but on a smaller scale. Additional power was gained as unions formed national federations whose councils had the power to mobilize political resources and to call general strikes.

On the political front, socialist parties grew during the latter part of the century, and most were of Marxist orientation, although organizations varied from the tightly knit German socialists to the factionalized French and more anarchist Italian and Spanish movements. International meetings of European socialists were often riven by sectarianism, but the common threat of antiradical repression, which came in a wave over Europe following the Paris Commune, did much to keep the factions from destroying each other. By the end of the century most leftist political parties abandoned their revolutionary posture and worked for social reform within the system, although orthodox Marxists decried such revisionism. This new stance improved the prospects for reform; even the Catholic Church, the staunchest voice for conservatism in Europe, acknowledged the legitimacy of the union movement and advised greater attention to problems of welfare and economic justice.[29]

Governments also devoted attention to welfare and economic justice. In the Modern period these programs might be traced back to the English poor laws or, perhaps more properly, to the Factory Acts of 1833, the Mine Act of 1842, and the Ten Hours Act of 1847 which, championed by social-minded aristocrats and middle-class reformers, put limits on the severity of conditions in which women and children might be employed. Sporadic legislation enforcing minimum standards in health, housing, and education was passed by municipal governments, but only after 1880 did the idea of comprehensive national programs for social welfare develop. In Germany, Bismarck's odd co-optation of leftist reform resulted in a program of old age, sickness, and workmen's compensation insurance, the first of its kind. Other European states patterned their early welfare legislation on the German model. Austria passed a workmen's compensation plan in 1887, and Denmark, Italy, Norway, Spain, and Holland followed suit in the next decade. Social-minded governments legislated standards for child labor and working conditions and put an end to the fine system and the payment of wages in kind. These programs were important not only for the immediate effect of reform on life in the industrial city but also as the precedent for state intervention in the relationship between employer and employee. For the first time the national government became the guarantor of minimum acceptable conditions of housing, wages, work environment, and, ultimately, a minimum standard of living. As this goal was approached in the twentieth century, the "welfare state" was born in Europe.

---

[29] This appeared in the encyclical *Rerum Novarum* issued by Pope Leo XIII in 1891. The Church remained the antagonist of socialism, however. In 1949 Pope Pius excommunicated all communists and subsequently declared socialism also to be irreconcilable with the Catholic faith.

17

The new economy comes of age—
1875 to 1914

The continuation of earlier trends

By 1875 the main features of the new economy in Western culture had taken shape. Economic improvement per capita of the population had become a strong and generally accepted ideology. Greater amounts of goods per unit of human endeavor were steadily being turned out by the more extensive use of machines, by the use of mechanical power, and by a more intensive division of labor. Greater amounts of materials had become available for human use in the Western world not only by increasing the production of growing things but also by exploiting the resources of the earth's crust and by drawing on reserves from a very large portion of the globe on an unprecedented scale. Greater amounts of capital were becoming available for creating more producers' goods. And man was so increasing his knowledge of the physical world that a greater control of that world seemed certain. To an ever-increasing extent consumers relied on the market for the satisfaction of their numerous wants rather than on a diversified production of their own. They used money as a medium of exchange to get what they desired, and they came to realize that money was an important factor in regulating relations among human beings. Lastly, ownership of the means of production, especially in industry, came to be concentrated to a greater degree than formerly in the hands of investors, whereas workers came to rely for their livelihood more and more on current wages rather than on the sale of the output of their own production.

After 1875 and at least up until World War I all these new aspects of Western culture's economy continued to develop and to have wide repercussions in society. Economic growth came to be regarded, in fact, as an integral part of the new economic systems. Compared with that of periods prior to the Industrial Revolution, the rate of economic growth was remarkable. From 1875 to 1914 the national income of the United Kingdom at fixed prices more than doubled and the national income per capita increased by 60 percent. The national income of Germany about trebled in these nearly forty years, and the national income per capita of those working about doubled in both Germany and the United States. Technological change, which, as we have seen, was the primary source of economic growth, proceeded at an accelerated pace. So profound were the changes in the methods of manufacturing that some observers are willing to classify the later nineteenth century as an entirely separate phase of European modernization. This is an exaggerated view, for although the nature of the devices of production changed radically, the basic causal processes were no different from those of earlier years. Steel took over from iron and wood as the main material of manufacturing. The reciprocating steam engine, which was the prime mover of early machines for industry and transportation, began slowly to give way to electric and internal combustion engines. At last science became the handmaiden of industry, and the chemist's laboratory replaced the machinist's workshop as the primary site of new product development.

Moreover, in the period 1875 to 1914 certain new developments took place which set off this span of years as distinctive. One of the most important of these new departures had to do with the spread of the new economy to other parts of Western culture. At the beginning of the Industrial Revolution, as we have seen, change took place primarily in a triangle with apexes in England, Belgium, and northern France, but then it spread to New England and the Middle Atlantic states of the United States, to Germany, to Bohemia, to Austria, and to northern Italy. Only in selected industries, as in the textiles for which there was a steady local demand, and in mining and lumbering, for the exploitation of natural resources, was there extensive mechanization of industry beyond these areas. Thus, in Europe, Germany, France, the United Kingdom, Italy, Belgium, and Sweden accounted for 83 percent of all manufacturing production in 1870 and for 74 percent as late as 1913.[1] Similarly, in the United States, the New England, Middle Atlantic, and Eastern North Central states accounted for about 75 percent of all value added by manufacture in 1913.

This concentration of industry in Western Europe and in the northeastern United States resulted in great regional inequalities in well-being, for the very good reason that the real produce (value of goods produced) per man-hour in industry and trade was about twice what it was in agriculture.

---

[1] Derived from League of Nations, *Industrialization and World Trade* (League of Nations, 1946), p. 13. See also Francis Delaisi, *Les Deux Europes* (Paris: Payot, 1929).

Hence, people in the so-called economically backward areas strove to develop industry, if, indeed, they were motivated to improve their material status. Thus it was that Americans threw themselves with such abandon into industry, that Germany put so much of its energies into industrial development from 1870 to 1914, and that certain areas on the periphery of Western culture, like Russia, and a few completely outside it, like Japan, endeavored to mechanize their production. Inasmuch as such efforts were not without success, manufacturing grew at a faster pace than world trade[2] and the older industrialized nations of Europe had their percentages of world manufacturing reduced, which indicated that their potentials for growth were relatively not so great as those of certain of the less-industrialized areas of the world (Table 24).

Table 24. Percentage distribution of world manufacturing production

Period	United States	Germany	United Kingdom	France	Russia	Italy	Canada
1870	23.3	13.2	31.8	10.3	3.7	2.4	1.0
1913	35.8	15.7	14.0	6.4	5.5	2.7	2.3
1936–1938	32.2	10.7	9.2	4.5	18.5	2.7	2.0

Period	Belgium	Sweden	Finland	Japan	India	Other countries	World
1870	2.9	0.4			11.0		100.0
1913	2.1	1.0	0.3	1.2	1.1	11.9	100.0
1936–1938	1.3	1.3	0.5	3.5	1.4	12.2	100.0

SOURCE: *Industrialization and Foreign Trade* (League of Nations, 1945), p.13.

Accompanying these changes was a great accentuation on nationalism in Western culture. Various people, drawn together by cultural ties, came to believe that they had the mission to glorify, develop, and perpetuate the elements which bound them together, that they could do this successfully only if they constituted independent, sovereign states, and that to attain their finest hour they would have to achieve some semblance of material well-being.

As at least a partial consequence of nationalism, national states began to pursue economic policies which were admittedly selfish, and their na-

[2] In the period 1876–1880 to 1913 world manufacturing grew fourfold, whereas world trade in primary products did not quite triple. (*Industrialization and World Trade*, p. 14.)

tionals began to spin theories to justify such action. The ultimate aim of national economics seemed to be to make the state, if large, as economically self-sufficient as possible, or at least to develop the national economy to the limit of its potentialities. The main instrument for realizing these ends seemed to be protective tariffs, although some states were willing to grant subsidies to promising industries and some were ready to acquire colonies to supplement the potential of the homeland. In fact, the "new imperialism" of the 1875–1914 period was motivated by a curious mixture of nationalism and a desire for expansion. It became particularly violent during the "Great Depression" from 1873 to 1896.

Lastly, in the period from 1875 to 1914, the impact on society of the new economy became clearer and more pronounced. The occupational distribution of populations in the more highly industrialized countries, like Great Britain, indicated that a larger percentage of the population was engaged in industry and services (Table 25), which meant, given the structure of these two branches of the economy, that a large proportion of the population was being hired for wages. Concomitantly there was a considerable concentration of wealth, as indicated in Table 26, although whether or not this was greater than in days of a predominantly agricultural economy is debatable.[3] Lastly, inequality of income shares and unsatisfactory working conditions produced effective reactions to the trend of capitalist development by engendering permanent workers' organizations and political militance (Chapter 16).

The consequences of urbanization

In all countries where manufacturing and services became predominant and agriculture employed a smaller and smaller proportion of the labor force, a "rural urban shift" occurred (Table 27). This population movement happened in three ways: families moved from the country to nearby towns, or families moved long distances across national boundaries in an international migration stream from poor rural circumstances into distant and foreign cities, or natural increase (the excess of births over deaths) in the new industrial cities outpaced demographic growth in the countryside. The general reason for the shift to urban living was, in a nutshell, the centralization of the work force. With the advent of the factory system,

---

[3] In terms of the long-run history of European modernization this concentration of income distribution was a limited phase. The general trend was toward the leveling of inequalities. In the United Kingdom during the time period spanned by Table 26, the top 5 percent of persons on the income scale received a 43 to 48 percent share of national income. By 1957 the wealthiest 5 percent accounted for only a 14 percent share of national income after taxes. (Kuznets, *Modern Economic Growth*, p. 208.)

a widely dispersed labor force was no longer feasible, and the new urban agglomerations grew up naturally around industrial sites. The pace of city growth in nineteenth-century Europe matched the rapid growth of manu-

Table 25. Occupational distribution in Great Britain

Year	Sectors		
	Agriculture, forestry, fishing	Manufacturing and mining	Services: trade, transport, domestic and personal, government
Distribution of working population, %			
1871	15.1	43.1	41.8
1911	8.3	46.4	45.3
1931	6.0	45.3	48.7
1970*	4.0	46.0	49.0
Distribution of national income, %			
1868	23.0	41.6	35.4
1911	9.8	32.4	57.8
1930	3.8	36.8	59.4
1970†	3.1	44.4	52.5

* United Kingdom.

† United Kingdom, origin of gross domestic product at factor cost.

facturing, and this hasty process gave rise to the early industrial city. The new urban working class crammed into shoddily built tenements without adequate provision for sanitary facilities, water supplies, paved streets, and protection against crime and fire. Often one or two firms came to control the local economy and political life of the newer industrial towns—a circumstance which invited exploitation. Among the displaced masses of the new cities the stability of old ways was sundered; crime, divorce, suicide, and insanity rates went up. The severity of these dislocations seemed to be related to the pace of growth. In England, where the industrial transformation was most rapid, towns like Birmingham, Manchester, Leeds and Liverpool virtually exploded in size. London grew more slowly, but its poorer quarters suffered the same pangs of overcrowding, privation, crime, and disease as other centers. Elsewhere in Europe, where industriali-zation was a longer and more imitative process, the dislocations of the rural-urban shift were less severe. In France the growth of Paris overshad-

Table 26. Distribution of wealth in Great Britain, 1911–1913 (persons twenty-five years and over; contemporary value of pound)

Wealth, in pounds	Persons per group		Capital per group	
	Number, in hundred thousands	Percentage of whole	Amount, in millions	Percentage
Total	18,745	100.0	6,008	100.0
100 or less	16,218	88.37	400	10.3
100–1,000	638	8.7	624	10.0
1,000–5,000	379	2.1	963	15.7
5,000–10,000	77	0.4	598	9.7
10,000–25,000	54	0.3	875	14.0
25,000–100,000	25	0.1	1,170	18.7
Over 100,000	5	0.03	1,378	21.6

owed regional centers, creating a geographic imbalance that plagues the country to the present day. Such sites as Mulhouse, the Alsatian textile center, became typical industrial cities. In Saxony, the Ruhr Valley, and in Prussia, similar centers arose. Further south, Milan and Turin took on the aspect of the classic industrial city only around the turn of the twentieth century, in time with Italy's delayed modernization.

Life in the new urban centers was not all bad; if it had been, the growth of cities would not have persisted. As we have mentioned, the urban worker earned consistently more than his rural counterpart. Even the older artisan-type crafts, which did not rely on a concentrated work force, moved from towns and rural villages to major urban centers. The growth and centralization of populations in cities gave rise to broadened local markets and economies of scale which have since been the most powerful attraction of city life. That London has opera companies and symphony orchestras, myriad museums, many institutions of higher learning, and a restaurant for every recherché taste, while Dairytown has none of these, seems obvious and logical: Such diversity is a function of size. Large cities provide a wide variety of experience as well as a variety of employment opportunities, and this has been one of the principal reasons for continued city growth. The centralization of services is another significant characteristic of cities, one closely related to rising real income that attends modernization. As people earn more, their purchasing power increases, and, it can be argued, their time becomes more valuable in a financial sense. Under

Table 27. Urban populations in selected countries as a percentage of total populations in 1880

Country	Percent urban population
England and Wales	67.9
Belgium	43.0
France	34.8
Germany	29.1
United States	28.6
Denmark	28.0
Norway (1875)	18.3
Canada	15.9
Sweden	15.1
Russia (1897)	15.0
Switzerland	13.3

SOURCE: United Nations, *The Determinants and Consequences of Population Trends*. Population Studies, No. 17 (New York: United Nations, 1953), p. 109.

such circumstances, people prefer to "specialize," paying others to perform everyday tasks for them. Today one rarely sees physicians or executives washing their own cars or doing their own housework. This is an obvious example of such behavior. Modern city inhabitants in general were more specialized than other groups, and therefore urban life became more costly and more dependent upon the sale of services as the number of city dwellers grew.[4]

One very important change that urban life created in the family was that children became expensive to have and to raise. Living space for large families was not costly to provide in a country cottage, but it could be terribly expensive in a high-rent city dwelling. In the countryside children became contributors to the family income at an early age by helping with the farm chores; in cities this was less the case.[5] Finally, it was the nature

---

[4] Kuznets, *Modern Economic Growth*, pp. 273–275.

[5] In the earliest phases of industrialization child labor in the cities was commonplace. In fact, for certain tasks the nimble fingers of six- to eighteen-year-olds might be preferred to the slower hands of adults. Children under sixteen represented 10 to 15 percent of the early textile industry work force. Life for factory children was in many cases a continual horror of mechanical dangers, overwork, heat, occupa-

of modern urban society that upward mobility required advanced education. Secondary school and university diplomas carried little weight on the farm, but they were often obligatory for good employment in modern cities; and the costs to families of putting children through years of schooling were enormous, both in terms of tuition and in terms of incomes (of adolescents) foregone during this elongated maturation period. All of these factors made the determination of family size very much an economic decision. The purposeful limitation of family size in urbanized nations became commonplace.

The expensiveness of children in cities relative to the countryside explains to a large degree the demographic transition in its final phase. As we have said (p. 234), developments in medical technology, better sanitation, and the growth of real incomes in early modernization had the effect of drastically reducing the pre-Modern high death rate; and, as fertility remained at high levels, a population explosion was the result. But as modernized economies matured and the preponderant social influence became the city, fertility rates dropped as families began to limit the numbers of children in line with budgetary constraints. As this happened the rate of increase of populations slowed to a point where the total populations grew barely at all. Today the most modern countries are those whose population growth rates have approached zero, while those areas of the world which have benefited from mortality-reducing techniques but have not achieved full modernization continue to suffer explosive rates of demographic increase. Underlying Western culture's curtailment of population growth was, above all else, urbanization.

Further industrial change

In the expansion of industry during the years between 1875 and 1914 so many important innovations were made that designating the most strategic is exceedingly difficult. Yet there is little doubt that among the very important changes was the introduction of ways of making steel which permitted an enormous expansion in the output of this product (Table 28) as well as a dramatic reduction in price.[6] In 1870 the United States produced only

tional disease, and fear of fines and punishment. The English law of 1833 which stipulated a maximum twelve-hour work day for children under eighteen years old was considered a boon to child workers! Elsewhere in Europe circumstances were not different, often worse. But as countries achieved economic maturity, the widespread use of children as factory hands diminished to the point where child labor remained in force only in primitive handicraft occupations, as it was under the putting-out system before modernization. In the interim period of early modernization, urban children made an important contribution to family incomes among the poorer segments of society.

[6] The Bessemer (1856), Siemens-Martin (1867), and Thomas-Gilchrist (1878) methods contained the fundamental changes in manufacturing procedure. The rolling mill was also improved, especially by increasing its speed of operation.

100,000 long tons of steel compared with 1 million long tons of wrought iron; in 1890 this country turned out 10.2 million long tons of steel to 3 million long tons of wrought iron. Moreover, the price of steel rails in Britain went down from about 42 pounds a ton in the late 1850s to 6 pounds 10 shillings in 1881, and to 3 pounds 15 shillings in 1895. Steel was the building metal *par excellence*. It was employed ever more widely as different kinds of steel were produced to meet specific needs. Among the most important of the new types of steels was tool steel, which was hard enough to cut most other metals. The first steels of this kind were produced by Robert F. Musket (1811–1891), who got high carbon steel by adding spiegeleisen, a pig iron rich in manganese, to the iron in a Bessemer converter after the "blow." The most successful tool steel was, however, produced by an American, Frederick Winslow Taylor (1856–1915). Taylor, who was also the "father of scientific management," was able in about 1906 to produce a steel alloy containing chromium and tungsten, which allowed the tripling and even quadrupling of cutting speeds and the working of metals to much finer tolerances. As the price of steel diminished, it became an economical material for the construction of bridges, the skeletons of skyscrapers, and pipelines. Likewise copper production grew by leaps and bounds because of its excellence as a conductor of electricity. The manifold uses of aluminium, tin, and iron alloys (from combination with nickel, manganese, tungsten, and chromium) were developed around the turn of the century.

Among the categories of innovations which contributed to industrial growth should be placed achievements in mechanical engineering. Among them were the multispindle lathe in which several pieces could be worked

Table 28. Production of steel (millions of tons)

Country	1870	1913
United States	0.04	34.4
United Kingdom	0.24	8.5
France	0.09	5.1
Belgium		2.6
Luxemburg		1.4
Germany	0.14	20.5
Austria	0.02	2.9
Russia	0.01	4.6
Italy		1.0
Sweden	0.01	0.6

on by the same operator; and then there was the automatic lathe in which several tools were brought to bear on the work in succession. Also, friction in bearings was greatly reduced by ball and later roller bearings (about 1880), the starting effort being lowered from 830 pounds with shafting to 0.9 pounds with roller bearings. Better lubrication with petroleum products was also important in the reduction of friction, especially with the introduction of forced lubrication with grease cups, screw-down oil plungers, and oil pumps. Nearly all machine shop tools were improved, but none more than the universal miller (1861), which could cut uneven pieces, including spirals, and the universal grinder, which had cutting stones the shape and size of the piece desired. The clutch became a practical instrument for engaging a stationary piece of machinery with a moving one, which eliminated the dangerous practice of slipping belts on and off pulleys and allowed mechanical power plants to activate heavier loads. Spinning was improved by the yielding bolster (1878), which allowed an increase in revolutions of the spindle from 5,000 to 20,000 per minute. Looms were made more efficient by the development between 1881 and 1885 of a mechanism for the automatic changing of bobbins and for stopping the machine when a thread broke. Here was a forerunner of the "automation" of the post-World War II era (Map 10).

On every hand mechanical devices appeared to make human labor more productive and more accurate. The typewriter was made more practical in 1868 and the adding machine in 1888. The stem winding watch, that eliminated the elusive winding key, was patented in 1848. A sewing machine for shoes came onto the market after the 1850s and made possible a greater division of labor in the boot and shoe industry.

Printing was speeded by the invention of the monotype machine, which perforated paper by pressing of keys and which set type from the perforated paper, by the Mergenthaler linotype machine, about 1885, which made possible the mechanical setting of type in line-length slugs, and by the development in the 1880s of rotary presses with a capacity for printing nearly 100,000 copies of eight pages per hour.

The communications industry was improved by Alexander Graham Bell's invention of the telephone in 1876, by the printing telegraph (1856), by Michael Pupin's method of extending the range of telephony by placing induction coils at intervals along the line, and by Guglielmo Marconi's invention of the radio in 1896. And the munitions industry was revolutionized by a multitude of innovations—the rifling of cannon (1859), breech-loading cannon (following 1860), the machine gun (invented by R. J. Gatling in 1862), the needle gun, in which the charge was set off by a needle that perforated the shell (1866), the hammer-and-lock, breech-loaded rifle (1860s), and rifles with magazines (1880).

In a great many of the new industrial processes to which reference has been made, chemistry played such an important role that it is not amiss to speak of a chemical revolution. Indeed, throughout the period under

Map 10
The Industrial Revolution of the Nineteenth Century

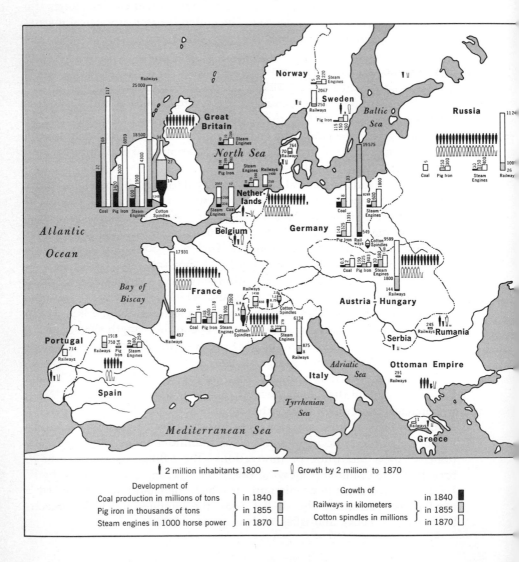

| | 2 million inhabitants 1800 | — | Growth by 2 million to 1870 |

Development of
Coal production in millions of tons } in 1840 ■
Pig iron in thousands of tons } in 1855 ▢
Steam engines in 1000 horse power } in 1870 ▢

Growth of
Railways in kilometers } in 1840 ■
Cotton spindles in millions } in 1855 ▢
} in 1870 ▢

discussion better cultivation of crops, converting natural products to useful goods, and finding substitutes for products in short supply depended largely upon a knowledge of chemistry. This knowledge was greatly increased after Dimitri I. Mendeleyev (1834–1907) in Russia and Lothar Meyer (1830–1895) in Germany formulated the periodic law based on atomic weights (1869).

Immense progress was made in producing soda, the most generally used of alkalies, and of sulfuric, the most widely employed acid. As we have already seen, the production of soda was first augmented by devising a method for getting it from common salt instead of the ashes of plants, but costs of manufacture were reduced after 1863 owing to the invention by Ernest Solvay, a Belgian, of a new way of processing salt and toward the close of the nineteenth century by the development of the electrolytic process.[7] So important did common salt become that its use was a barometer for the state of development of the chemical industry in any area.

Sulfuric acid, which is used in nearly every heavy chemical industry—in the preparation of fertilizers, in papermaking, in explosives manufacture, and in rubber—is made by combining sulfur dioxide with air and water. Until about the middle of the nineteenth century sulfur came mostly from Sicily, but some dent was made in this regional monopoly by the use of pyrites, of which Spain had a large supply, and was completely broken by the opening of sulfur wells in Louisiana in 1908 and in Texas at a somewhat later date.

Of the other basic chemicals, nitrates, potassium, and phosphates were the most important. All of them attained economic importance as fertilizers following Justus von Liebig's discovery of the chemical composition of plants (1840s). Moreover, nitrates, essential to the growing explosives industry, became of strategic importance to economic growth after the discovery of potassium nitrate, which was in short supply, and following Alfred Nobel's success in overcoming the dangerous aspects of using nitroglycerine to make dynamite (1863) and in combining nitroglycerine and gun-cotton to make smokeless powder (1887). For most of the period under survey, potassium was mined at Stassfurt, Germany, and in Alsace. Phosphate rock was obtained from North Africa, from Florida, and from smelting phosphoric iron ores, and nitrates were had from Chile and Peru, although on the eve of World War I, they began to be obtained from the air by the fixation process, invented by a German chemist, Fritz Haber (1868–1934).

The ramifications of the chemical revolution were almost infinite. They touched a host of common goods, like friction matches (1833), safety

---

[7] This process had the advantage of producing large quantities of chlorine, which was in demand for bleaching and papermaking.

matches (1855), photography (Louis Daguerre had the first practical success with his daguerreotypes in 1839), photoengraving (1860), and motion pictures (Thomas A. Edison, 1893).[8] They included the founding of an entirely new and great industry, rubber, which was made possible by Charles Goodyear's discovery of a way of vulcanizing rubber by the use of sulfur (patented 1844)[9] and by the amassing of great quantities of latex from the tropics, especially from the Belgian Congo and the East Indies. They embraced the decomposition of coal tar to get dyes (synthetic alizarin in 1869, indigo in 1880, Congo red in 1884, sulfur black in 1894), to produce synthetic medicines (from aspirin to camphor), and to make available perfumes, germicides, insecticides, artificial flavors, resins, and tanning materials. They even extended to the discovery of radium by Pierre and Marie Curie in 1910 and to the realization of the possibility of changing one element into another.

The economic advantages to be derived from chemistry were so obvious that the leading states of Western culture vied with one another to solve new riddles or to obtain as rapidly as possible solutions to problems discovered by others. In the first half of the nineteenth century leadership in chemistry was seized from France by England, but in the last quarter of the century Germany, thanks in part to the absence of a patent law, assumed a position of primacy which it maintained until well after World War I (Table 29). At all events, the wizardry of chemistry was throughout this period almost an exclusive monopoly of Western culture, and this gave the West a great economic and power advantage over the rest of the world.

New sources of power

Using chemical processes to wrest ever-greater quantities of economic goods from nature and employing ever more machines required the employment of constantly increasing amounts of energy. The overwhelming proportion of the energy required was produced by coal, although water power, petroleum, and natural gas became of some importance (Table 30). Consequently those areas that produced coal in large quantities or could acquire this "black gold" by water transportation at low cost had a distinct industrial advantage over all other regions (Tables 31 and 32). Coal had,

---

[8] Edison showed his first pictures in illuminated slot machines. Images were first projected on a screen by an Englishman, R. V. Hall (1895).

[9] In 1914 the rubber industry ranked twenty-seventh in the United States in terms of value added by manufacture. By 1856, the market offered a host of rubber articles: rubber boots, rubber carriage tires, and rubber sheets.

indeed, such a strategic importance in the location of industry that every great coal-mining area, like the western Pennsylvania–Ohio or the Indiana–Illinois regions of the United States, the Ruhr Basin in Germany, the

Table 29. Production of selected chemicals in 1913 (in thousands of metric tons)

Country	Salt	Sulfuric acid	Nitrates		Phosphates	Potassium
United States	4,364	4,743	647	(sulfate of ammonia)	3,883	56
Germany	2,077	1,704	1,700	(sulfate of ammonia)		1,788
Chile		20	2,016	(nitrate of lime)		
France	1,282	1,000	155		180	531
United Kingdom	2,284	924	301			

Walloon provinces in Belgium, the north of France, and later the Donets Basin in Russia, became great industrial centers.

Table 30. Relative importance of sources of heat energy in the world, 1913–1948 (in percent)

Area	Year	Coal and lignite	Oil	Natural gas	Firewood	Water power
World	1913	74.1	4.5	1.4	17.6	2.4
World	1948	54.8	24.6	7.3	7.2	6.1
United States	1889	87.0	4.5	6.5		2.0
United States	1948	46.1	30.0	11.5		12.4

SOURCE: E. W. Zimmermann, *World Resources and Industries* (New York: Harper & Row, 1951), p. 454.

Because coal was extensively used and expenditures for it constituted such an important percentage of final costs, efforts were made early to extract it more economically and to burn it more efficiently. Mining was improved by better pumping and ventilating machinery, by the use of mechanical elevators, by greater use of mechanical transportation both below and above ground, by pneumatic drills, by better and safer explosives, by the coal loader (1903), by conveyor belts (just prior to 1904), and by the safety lamp. The use of coal was, for its part, made efficient by

Table 31. Production of coal (in millions of metric tons)

Year	World	Belgium	France	Germany	United Kingdom	United States	Russia
1871	230	13.7	12.9	29.3	117.4	42.5	
1880	330	16.9	18.8	47.0	147.0	64.8	
1913	1,214.4	22.8	40.8	190.1	292.0	571.1	
1955	1,504.1	29.9	55.3	131.8*	225.1	447.5	276.1
1960	1,987.0	22.4	55.9	143.2†	196.7	391.5	374.9
1962	1,986.4	21.2	52.3	141.9†	200.6	395.5	386.4

*West Germany.
†These figures are for East and West Germany.
SOURCE: E. W. Zimmermann, *World Resources and Industries*, p. 471; and *United Nations Statistical Yearbook*, 1963, pp. 168ff.

extensive processing of coal before it was finally consumed, by improvements in smelting techniques, and by advances in coal-using equipment.
In power production, feeding the fire was made easier by mechanical

Table 32. World coal resources by continent, 1956
(in billions of metric tons)

Continent	Total
North America	4,149.4
Europe	2,440.9
Asia	1,167.6
Africa	230.9
Australia	173.5
Central and South America	3.2

SOURCE: E. W. Zimmermann, *World Resources and Industries*, p. 466.

stokers (early twentieth century). Combustion was bettered by new designs of furnaces to handle small or powdered coal, and more heat was captured by improvements in the arrangements of the tubes in boilers. Furthermore, the compound and triple-expansion steam engines, although known in principle in the first half of the nineteenth century, began to effect phenomenal savings in fuel and incidentally to make steam power feasible for long sea voyages (circa 1870). Lastly, still greater efficiency of steam was obtained by Sir Charles Parsons' development of the turbine (1884) in which steam acted first upon a large vane wheel and then passed through slots in the casing to work another vane wheel, and so on until its expansive power was largely spent.

Important as coal became in providing for the insatiable appetite of industrial economy, it received significant support from both water power and petroleum. Falling water assumed a new position in the power field with the development of improved devices to transform its energy into mechanical motion. Pelton wheels, used for high pressures and small heads, were perfected to a point where 85 percent of the energy of the falling water was captured; and water turbines, efficient for handling low pressures with large volumes of water, were improved and widely adopted. For its part, petroleum began to assume a position of importance with the invention of the internal combustion engine, perfected by N. A. Otto of Cologne in the late 1860s, by Gottlieb Daimler in 1883, and by Rudolph Diesel in 1892.[10] Although petroleum had begun to be important as a result of technological changes in lighting, it came into its own as a source of mechanical energy.[11] In fact, petroleum production jumped from almost nothing in 1850 to 5,730,000 barrels in 1870 and to 407,544,000 barrels in 1913, with most of the output coming from the United States and from Russian Caspian wells.

Although both the steam engine and the internal combustion engine gave considerable mobility to mechanical power and freed industry from locating at water power sites, there was an active demand for still greater mobility of power. Some means was needed to make it available to everyone, both young and old, for performing a myriad of tasks from lighting lamps and running sewing machines to drilling teeth and propelling railway trains. Fortunately electricity provided what was required.

In the eighteenth century numerous experiments had been made with electricity and in 1800 Alessandro Volta (1745–1827) had actually made an

---

[10] Diesel's engine used cheaper and heavier oil for fuel and got the material fired not by an electric spark, as in the gasoline engine, but by compression. All of the heavier distillates have a flash point that is determined by heat and compression.

The diesel engine came to be widely used as a stationary engine because of its efficiency, whereas the gasoline motor, because of its lightness, was adopted usually in vehicles where it had to transport itself.

[11] The lamp with wick and chimney (invented 1784) was a great success, but fuel for it, whether lard or whale oil, became so dear that a search was made for a cheaper substitute. This quest led to petroleum. Kerosene, made from the simple distillation of petroleum, turned out to be just what the lighting industry wanted, whereas oil obtained in the process of refining proved valuable for lubricating the points of friction in machines, thus replacing all kinds of oiling devices, that ranged from slabs of suet to cans of dripping lard.

electric battery. The practical value of electricity was not foreseen, however, until Michael Faraday changed an electric current to motion (1821) and showed that an electric current could be generated by revolving a copper coil in a magnetic field. It was not until 1867 that Werner Siemens made public his invention of a dynamo,[12] not until 1879 that electricity was used to drive the first locomotive in Berlin and that Thomas A. Edison made public his first carbon filament lamp,[13] not until 1882 that the current was turned on for the lighting system in New York, not until 1883 that Thomas A. Edison brought the generator to its essential modern form by the use of carbon brushes, and not until 1897–1898 that Niagara generating plants were put in operation. Even then problems of transmitting this form of energy were extraordinarily vexing. They were not overcome until the transformer was invented, high voltages of alternating current were employed, and much of the direct-current generating plant was scrapped.[14]

In spite of all handicaps the electrical industry grew rapidly after 1900, generating capacity in the United States attaining about 10 million kilowatt-hours in 1913. Great electrical equipment companies, like Siemens-Halske and the Allgemeine Electrizitäts Gesellschaft in Germany, the Thomson-Houston Company in France, the General Electric Company in the United States, and the British General Electric Company and Metropolitan-Vickers in Great Britain, came into being.[15] Constantly, new uses were found for electricity, as in electrolysis, electric furnaces, X rays, and fluoroscopes.[16] And electric motors began to revolutionize factory production by being built into machines, to make possible the decentralization of some specialized industries that did not have large transportation costs in relation to their price, like the shirt and blouse trades, and to provide clean urban rapid transit systems. Electricity was, indeed, the great boon of the age.

With all of these innovations in the field of power continual attention was given to how work could be organized for more efficient production. In general, in this period a high correlation was found between, on the one hand, optimum production and, on the other, maximum-sized establish-

---

[12] At approximately this time electric motors were announced independently by Sir Charles Wheatstone and S. A. Varley, a classic example of the way social needs bring forth inventive responses.

[13] Sir Humphrey Davy had invented the arc light in 1809, which was used after 1850 for lighting public places. The great disadvantage of the arc light was that it required frequent servicing because the carbon poles between which the current arced burned out.

[14] Not until the 1890s was transmission up to 200 miles practicable and not until this distance was spanned was it possible to build large-scale grids to take advantage of different-sized loads at different times of the day and at different seasons of the year. Successful high-power transmission was chiefly the work of Marcel Duprez (1882) and of Sebastian Ferranti (1889).

[15] In 1913 Germany made 34 percent of the world's electrical equipment and the United States, 19 percent.

[16] The X ray was the invention of W. C. Röntgen in 1896.

ments, amounts of horsepower per worker, and capital investment per worker. Economies of scale had proved themselves and had spelled the doom in most trades of the small handicraft operation, even in tailoring, which persisted where labor was low-cost. In Germany in 1882, 55.1 percent of the gainfully employed were in establishments of five workers or less, 18.6 in groups between six and fifty, and 26.3 in those engaging more than fifty, whereas in 1907 these respective percentages were 29.5, 25, and 45.4. In France, the amount of horsepower per establishment increased five times from 1852 to 1912. And in the United States the amount of capital per wage earner about doubled from 1879 to 1913.[17]

With the greater capital investment per worker, more care had to be taken to make labor efficient. Waste of time and effort had to be eliminated wherever possible. The productivity of workers in industry, which incidentally doubled in the United States from 1870 to the period 1909–1911, thus came to depend not only on the amount of power per worker or on the machines at his disposal, but also on the extent to which tasks were subdivided in making standardized products in which parts were interchangeable and on the organization of work in the productive process. The problem of labor efficiency had long been apparent in the cotton textile trade, but a new and more conscious effort in this direction was made after 1895. In that year the "father of scientific management," Frederick Winslow Taylor, published a famous paper on "A Piece Rate System," in which he advocated payments for accomplishing parts of jobs that would reward the particularly efficient and penalize inept or lazy workers. Moreover, he prepared time and motion studies which would show how jobs could be broken down into their essential elements in order to increase output and avoid accidents.

At the same time and connected with Taylor's program, experiments were conducted with the moving assembly line. In the manufacture of watches and sewing machines, the practice had been to bring parts together in one place and for one worker or a small team of workers to put them together to form the finished product. In 1913, Henry Ford decided to try a moving assembly with the product "growing" as workers, stationed along the endless chain or belt, performed some specialized task. His trials demonstrated that the time required to assemble an automobile chassis could thus be lowered from 12½ to 1½ hours; the extension of this idea made possible in large part a reduction in the retail price of the car from 950 to 290 dollars. This price permitted in turn the tapping of a mass market and an increase in the output of Ford cars to 250,000 per year on the eve of World War I.

[17] See Colin Clark, *Conditions of Economic Progress*, p. 486.

Trade, transportation, and empire

As has been repeatedly emphasized in preceding pages, increases in quantities of both agricultural and industrial goods would not have been possible if there had not been great specialization in production both by areas and by individuals. Furthermore, this specializion—this division of labor —would, in turn, not have been possible had there not been an enormous expansion of transportation and exchange facilities and a consequent growth of trade. Indeed, the extensive market is one of the most distinctive characteristics of the economy which Western culture developed in the nineteenth century.

In the growth of trade, railways and ocean shipping played particularly crucial roles. Railway building, which had done so much to stimulate economic activity in the second and third quarters of the nineteenth century, was continued until the earlier industrialized regions had dense networks, and overseas lands had lines which reached across vast unsettled or semisettled areas, across the United States and Canada, down the length of Africa from "Cairo to the Cape," from "Berlin to Baghdad," and to remote districts of South America and Australia. So universal was the recognition that railways were necessary for economic growth and also for military operations that states proved ready to provide the necessary capital for construction if private financiers would not or could not do so. Especially in areas such as Russia and South America where economic growth was retarded, railways had to be financed by public bodies; and even in some Western European states, notably in Germany, railways were nationalized in order to get faster construction or more efficient operation.

Some idea of how extensive railway carrying became can be gleaned from the facts that in the United States railway mileage increased from 94,665 miles in 1876 to 379,508 miles in 1913, that passenger miles went up from 12 billion in 1890 to 35 billion in 1913, and that ton-miles jumped from 76,207 million in 1890 to 301,730 million in 1913, that is, to 3,017 ton-miles per capita of the population. In Germany, the railway network grew from 17,360 miles in 1875 to 37,820 miles in 1910; and freight carried one mile reached 34,906 million tons or 503 tons per capita at the latter date.

Increase in shipping also developed rapidly, especially when iron and steel were used in the construction of hulls (after 1879), when triple and quadruple expansion steam engines began to be employed (1881 and 1894), and when the screw propeller began to replace side paddle wheels (after 1860). In the United Kingdom steam tonnage increased from 168,000 net tons in 1850 to 10,443,000 net tons in 1910, whereas sail tonnage declined from 3 million net tons in 1890 to 850,000 net tons in 1913. In 1914 the leading carrying nations of the world had over 20.5 million net tons of steam vessels, 96 percent of which belonged to Western culture.

Such developments help account for the fact that world trade increased about threefold from 1876–1880 to 1913; and the trade of heavily industrialized nations, especially small ones which thus had to rely heavily on exchanges with others, increased enormously. Thus the per capita foreign trade of the Netherlands went up from 80 dollars in 1851 to 1853 to 243 dollars in 1929, that of Great Britain from 54 to 219 dollars, and that of Russia from 4 to 5.7 dollars. In some cases, as in Britain, where in 1914, 25 percent of all manufactured goods was exported, foreign trade was essential for existence. And even in other nations, like the United States, where exports constituted some 10 percent of production, a sudden decline in foreign trade could upset the total economy.

With the spread of new ways of producing goods throughout Western Europe and to other parts of the world, there were shifts in the shares of trade accounted for by individual nations. These changes are indicated in Table 33. The United Kingdom, which had had such a large share of this trade because of its head start, began to lose ground proportionately to other more recently industrialized countries. The international division of labor became more highly developed, and a network of world trade and payments developed that allowed for the distribution of goods which some areas had in surplus to other areas where these goods were lacking and allowed for the settling of accounts among these areas.

Table 33. Percentage shares of world trade, 1840 to 1938

Year	United Kingdom	United States	Germany	France
1840	32.0	8.0		10.0
1913	17.0	15.0	12.0	7.0
1938	13.0	10.7	9.2	4.7
1948	12.6	10.8	2.6	5.5
1962	8.0	10.9	8.2	5.0

SOURCE: *Industrialization and Foreign Trade* (Princeton, N.J.: League of Nations, 1945); and *Statistical Yearbook* (United Nations, 1965).

In the conduct of trade, the countries of Western Europe which had become industrialized earlier developed an excess of imports over exports, but earnings on investments abroad, on shipping, banking, and insurance services, on emigrant remittances, and on the tourist trade were such that most of these nations had plus balances in their total trade and payment accounts. Hence they had moneys to invest abroad—and invest they did. These investments constituted an important element in the diffusion of Western civilization's economic system to the rest of the world.

During the last third of the nineteenth century, after a period of relative quiescence in European interest overseas, an orgy of extraterritorial expansionism swept the Western world. Within thirty years some 10 million square miles of territory fell under the formal or informal control of European nations. Moreover, Europeans informally staked out markets for their industrial products and for their investment funds in countries that were fully independent. In some cases, the aims of imperialism were not at all subtle: plundering raw materials and exploiting foreign labor began in the hope of quick, massive profits. The International Congo Association, founded in 1878 with King Leopold II of Belgium at the helm, was an enterprise created for such a purpose, though despite a high demand for rubber in the industrial world, the venture never succeeded. Occasionally the lust for empire was entirely bereft of reasonable economic motives, as in the case of Italian pretensions to empire in Ethiopia. The prestige motive and the urge to follow the leader, to which so many nations succumbed, seemed so lacking in good sense that the economist Joseph Schumpeter was moved to label imperialism as "objectless" and "atavistic." Often, however, the less blatant forms of imperialism had the highest degree of economic content. The British protectorate in Egypt, the German influence in Turkey, and the American acquisition of the Panama Canal Zone each protected large investments in vital transportation systems.

The pattern of European investments abroad was characterized, in general, by the financing of social overhead capital, extractive industries, and borrowings of governments. The British portfolio consisted mostly of holdings in temperate-zone areas of prior European settlement that were in the early stages of modern economic development (Table 34). Less than half of the sterling value of investment went into imperial territories. British investors preferred private equities and bonds to government securities, and transport and public works projects to manufacturing and other industrial enterprises. Often investment was directly linked with the sale of British products, as in the case of selling railroad equipment to British-financed railway development projects. Exports and investment flows thus fluctuated together in the manner of the classic business cycle. Similarly, the French made heavy financial commitments in Russia for rail construction, as did the Germans in Turkey. This investment posture benefited developing areas of the world outside Europe, although the joint problems of excess indebtedness and foreign control remained long after the investment projects were completed. For European investors benefits were realized in terms of higher rates of return than domestic investments paid, as well as the creation of new sources of industrial demand abroad.

Why then colonization? With the opportunities available to Europeans for investing, buying, and selling within less-developed nations, where did the profit lie in formal annexation? Speaking in terms of national incomes, colonies were for the most part bad business. The costs of military incursions and colonial management far outweighed the value of plunder or monopolistic advantages in the colonial marketplace. The answer to this question lies largely in the politics of special interest groups within the

Table 34. Geographical distribution of foreign investments in 1914 (currencies, 1914 values)

British	
	Millions of pounds
Within the Empire:	
Canada and Newfoundland	514.9
Australia and New Zealand	416.4
South Africa	370.2
India and Ceylon	378.8
Other colonies	99.7
Total	1,780.0
Outside the Empire:	
United States	754.6
Argentina	319.6
Brazil	148.0
Mexico	99.0
Other Latin-American investments	190.0
Russia	110.0
Spain	19.0
Italy	12.5
France	8.0
Germany	6.4
Rest of Europe	62.7
Egypt	44.9
Turkey	24.0
China	43.9
Japan	62.8
Rest of world	77.9
Grand total	3,763.3

French	
	Billions of francs
Russia	11.3
Turkey	3.3
Spain and Portugal	3.9
Austria-Hungary	2.2
Balkan states	2.5
Italy	1.3
Switzerland, Belgium, and Netherlands	1.5
Rest of Europe	1.5
French colonies	4.0
Egypt, Suez, and South Africa	3.3
United States, Canada, and Australia	2.0
Latin America	6.0
Asia	2.2
Total	45.0

German	
	Billions of marks
Austria-Hungary	3.0
Russia	1.8
Balkan countries	1.7
Turkey	1.8
France and Great Britain	1.3
Spain and Portugal	1.7
Rest of Europe	1.2
Africa (including German colonies)	2.0
Asia (including German colonies)	1.0
United States and Canada	3.7
Latin America	3.8
Other areas	0.5
Total	23.5

power structure of Western nations. During the depression (1873–1896) certain industrial groups began to push for "insured" markets where risks might be lower than in open, international competition. This was a strong argument for colonization, but only when the special groups could make the governments act in their private interests. In other cases groups within the government, the military, for example, or the foreign office, used the excuse of global strategy to move policy in support of their more limited aims of bureaucratic survival. In the United States, the powerful group of sugar manufacturers and the Department of the Navy each was behind imperialist ventures in the Far East and in Cuba. The sarcastic portrayal of British colonial administration as "outdoor relief for the upper classes" has a ring of truth to it. Noncolonial powers, without making expenditures for conquests, could buy colonial products at nearly the same prices as colonial powers, although they may have suffered a lack of prestige in the community of European nations which seemed at the time to measure national strength and virtue in square miles. In general, the "new imperialism" paid off only to limited sectors of the economy, and it is likely that the European man in the street would have been better off economically had his government eschewed the temptations of dominion over foreign lands. Exotic products and industrial raw materials for his welfare might as easily have been his through the normal market mechanism. Neither was he the beneficiary of investment abroad. In fact, it may be that even the wealthy who did invest abroad lost out in the long run.

Borrowers sometimes simply defaulted on their obligations and the lenders got nothing for their pains. In other cases, debtors paid in a currency which did not have the same purchasing power as that which they had borrowed, or they bought up their own securities when the prices of their obligations had fallen far below par. The largest of such defaults came after World War I, when, for example, the U.S.S.R. repudiated the debts of the Czarist regime, when inflation, especially the hyperinflation in Germany, permitted the settling of foreign debts at a great discount, and when many foreign securities seemed like such poor investments that their prices fell to unconscionable lows. Such reductions of foreign debt were significant enough to make it probable that the earnings on most foreign portfolios, in spite of their higher interest rates, were in the long run considerably less than on loans made at home.

For the most part, however, the governments of lending nations engaged in investments abroad as a means of winning friends, of increasing their nation's prestige, of getting access to sources of raw materials, or of winning markets, and gave little thought to the probability that they were strengthening potential enemies. Their policies regarding merchandise trade were, however, radically different from those pertaining to lending, if, indeed, they were not diametrically opposed to them. Most nations of Western culture believed that they should be economically strong, both for the defense and for economic well-being; economic strength required high productivity of industrial goods, and economic expansion required protection of the home market. Furthermore, in most states some segment of the economy, frequently agriculture, was suffering enough from foreign competition to create an interest group that demanded protection. With the long depression in prices from 1873 to 1896 prices of grains and raw materials fell more than prices for industrial products and trade in manufactured goods, as a percentage of trade in primary products, declined. (See Chart 2.) This meant that farmers, industrialists, and producers of primary products were all looking for remedies to the situation and for relief for their particular circumstances. Many of those involved became convinced that the power and authority of the state should be used to cushion the shock of sudden changes emanating from the operation of the free market economy. Thus a combination of economic nationalism, of vested interests, and of state paternalism led to an attack, as we have seen, on the low-tariff policies adopted in the United States in 1833 and in Europe in 1860.

Protectionism had the general effect of hindering the division of labor, although customs barriers were not insurmountable; hence for the entire economy of the world, it was undesirable. Furthermore, in some cases protection led to higher domestic prices for goods than those obtaining in the free world market, but in large economies, like the American, competition among domestic producers was at that time usually sufficient to prevent such results. Protectionism is also said to have contributed to the formation of monopolies at home and to dumping abroad, such effects having been particularly marked in Germany. On the other hand, tariffs helped to keep production of individual nations diversified, which may have been an asset in time of war, and they eased the shock of change, which was becoming more violent in the forty years before 1914.

Some exponents of free trade have argued that because tariffs curbed trade and because trade served as a substitute for the migration of people to areas of greater food supply, tariffs contributed to the great migration of Europeans between the years 1850 and 1930, when some 40 million persons moved overseas. Undoubtedly this argument is somewhat spurious, for Europe's trade grew faster than its population. Emigration on a large scale began in a period of low tariffs, and until 1895 the largest number of emigrants came from free-trade England. Whatever the truth regarding this issue, however, the fact remains that in this period what was undoubtedly the greatest migration of all time took place—a migration that meant a diffusion of Western culture to many parts of the earth, especially to the New World, to Australia, and to New Zealand.

The problems of depression and decline

Several complex and unsettled issues dominate the attention of economic historians who study the last quarter of the nineteenth century. A "Great Depression" is said to have happened during the years 1873–1896. Yet, while certain indices of prices and industrial production clearly show real declines, the evidence varies so greatly from country to country and from sector to sector that the picture of the period as a true episode of depression is very much in doubt. To make matters more complicated still, the latter 1800s were years of pronounced changes in the economic leadership of Europe. England was forced to relinquish her unique status as the world's workshop and give way to up-and-coming competitors such as Germany and the United States during these years. Why this was so is uncertain. Was there, in fact, a "Great Depression" in the European economy or just a series of intermittent business slumps and recoveries? Did Great Britain's economic decline happen because of the depression or had her rate of progress just become somewhat slower than that of Germany and other new competitors?

The period of years that goes by the name "Great Depression" or "long depression in prices" was marked by severe business-cycle fluctuations. After the panic of 1873 a six-year downswing hit all of Europe. In Germany, real wages declined, unemployment and the incidence of strikes ran high, and the use of iron and coal dropped by 50 percent from the level of former years. A similar spasm, though not so severe, occurred in Britain. In both countries, as well as in most others in Europe, a recovery followed between 1879 and 1882, only to be succeeded by a second business downturn (1882–1886), a second recovery, and a third cyclical slump from 1890 to 1894–1896. Did these cycles add up to a depression? With respect to prices, the answer is affirmative. Price indices for at most all countries show a continual deflationary trend throughout the period. Agricultural prices shrank most severely; rural wages stopped rising in the early 1870s; and the European countryside was the scene of much hardship. However, we must keep in mind that the *entire* nineteenth century was an era of falling prices—the longest and sharpest deflation that the Western economy had ever experienced.[18] This was not a cause of hardship, but of improved well-being. Falling prices from the time of the fall of Napoleon to the *belle epoque* resulted mainly from the unprecedented improvements in productivity that brought more goods to more people for less money than had ever been possible before. In fact, as we have just noted at length, even the so-called depression years of 1873-1896 corresponded to a spurt of innovative activity. Lower prices for foodstuffs were due in part to the importation of cheap North American grains, facilitated by the new marine steam engines. The age of steel and plastics gave Europe a range of new merchandise which was produced efficiently and sold for low prices. The "long depression in prices" may have signaled (or perhaps disguised) a time of rising productivity. Even in England, where the new technology was less evident than elsewhere, prices fell steadily throughout the period as na-

---

[18] This most important point is made by David Landes, *The Unbound Prometheus; Technological Change and Industrial Development in Western Europe from 1750 to the Present* (New York: Cambridge, 1972), pp.233–234.

tional income and wealth grew. Aside from price, every index of economic activity reflected clear, upward motion.[19] Even the consumption of food staples and the index of real wages rose. Unemployment, at times, however, was also high, especially in basic capital goods industries.

On balance the period 1873–1896 is best characterized as a deflation in prices unaccompanied by the usual hardships of a business depression, except in certain parts of the economy. Wages did not fall faster than prices, and so real incomes of industrial workers were not diminished. Unemployment cropped up with occasional severity, and incomes in agriculture were hurt more than other sectors. Generally, suffering was not very great or protracted for the European population, although the cyclical disturbances during these years and their effects—idle capacity, layoffs, failures of small firms, and crises of investor confidence—were somewhat more severe than run-of-the-mill business fluctuations.

Great Britain was a special case. Depression or no, sometime between 1873 and the First World War she lost ground and experienced a decline in her domestic rate of growth and in her share of world markets relative to other countries. As Germany pioneered the new technology, Great Britain seemed content to rely on old methods and old equipment. Many contemporary English observers who saw German products supplant British ones in the markets of Asia, Latin America, Western Europe, North America, and even within England herself, blamed England's entrepreneurs for the competitive fiasco. Businessmen seemed to behave as if Britannia still monopolized the world's trade. They were distinctly unaggressive in comparison with other merchandisers, often unwilling to accommodate their products or the style of their salesmanship to the new competition that confronted them. When German merchants went abroad, they armed themselves with a well-stocked sample case, sales catalogues in local languages, and fashionable but inexpensive merchandise. The English made no such concessions to foreign consumers' tastes. Their wares were of the highest quality but very expensive and generally devoid of color or fashion consciousness. Much frustration was caused by the fact that deceitful competitors would counterfeit famous English brands and hallmarks (like those of the respected Sheffield cutlery-makers) and pass off shoddy goods at bargain-basement prices as if they were English. In a manner of speaking, both the market and the reputation of British manufacturers were thus stolen at once.

At home, the technology of production did not change with the times. English entrepreneurs appeared content to continually reuse old but workable capital equipment, rather than to reinvest in newer and more efficient machinery. Industrial retardation seemed to stem from this peculiar British

---

[19] A. E. Musson, "The Great Depression in Britain, 1873–1896: A Reappraisal," *Journal of Economic History*, vol. 19, 1959.

resistance to new methods, such as standardization and scientific management. How different this behavior was from the vigorous entrepreneurship of the early Industrial Revolution in England! Some authors, in fact, saw British complacency and traditionalism to be a result of a generation of managerial elite who inherited businesses instead of building them. Social pretensions and genteel education made for an unfavorable outlook on business, with its sweaty problems and nerve-racking risks.

The case against the late nineteenth-century British entrepreneur has not been fully proved. The idea of keeping old equipment alive and working proved to have been more economical for individual firms than replacing it with new machinery, although the overall effect of this practice on national productivity was unfavorable. Other evidence suggests that what happened to England was largely beyond her control to change. The 1870s marked the technical transition away from the profitable employment of iron and steam, the foundations of British industrial technology. Vast mineral resources, newly discovered in Germany and the United States, drastically lowered production costs for these new rivals. Protectionism cut off England from expanding foreign markets. It is also noteworthy that there were inherent disadvantages in being the first to industrialize. Britain, in a sense, had to carry the cost of research and development; other nations borrowed technology, only later developing their own—far cheaper than starting from scratch. That Britain was at the apogee of industrial development twenty years before the first real signs of competition also helps to explain her ingrained behavior. For those who start from next to nothing, it is easy to be flexible and to enjoy high rates of growth. A late start was the most basic advantage of the Germans and Americans in the last years of the nineteenth century.

Britain's relative industrial retardation is a matter of fact. Little else about the subject is so certain. Arguments about the failure of John Bull, entrepreneur, are persuasive, and yet it is also easy to be convinced that there was more than a hint of inevitability about England's passing of the torch. She was Europe's unchallenged industrial mistress for a century and, in time, all such advantages must disappear, or so it would seem. There is a hint of irony, too, in that the very tactics of the new competitors which caused such anguish and rage in England—the imitation of style and technique, the falsification of trade markings, the aggressive and underhanded selling—were the very same devices that England had employed with much success in the earliest days of *her* rise to commercial prominence (p.148). As the debate about the causes of England's failure in the Victorian age continues to flare, it is important to keep in mind that her decline was relative, not absolute. Although her role as workshop of the world diminished, the well-being of her population continued to improve, in step with the rest of the Western world.

Crises in the economy
of Western culture—
1914 to 1974

18

International, economic, and social strains and stresses

The nature of the crisis in Western culture

Western culture's economic development in the hundred years prior to 1914 was little less than phenomenal, but in the ensuing thirty years the economy of this culture area was to undergo severe stresses and strains. In the first place it was to experience two "world wars," which from the point of view of the culture itself could be classified as "civil wars." These internecine conflicts destroyed inestimable amounts of wealth and greatly lessened the volume of goods and services which might otherwise have gone to support creativity in the arts, to establish a greater control over the physical universe, and to permit more orderly and just relations among men. Indeed, there were prophets of doom who thought that wars among nation-states of Europe would undo the West, much as wars among city-states of Greece had undone Grecian civilization. Even if one did not have such extreme views, one had to recognize that the two world wars were major factors in upsetting the West's economy and in creating economic problems of the first magnitude. Indeed, it is hardly an exaggeration to say that the two world wars of the first half of the twentieth century were the chief forces of economic change of the period. On these grounds the wars and their effects must be given a major place in any general economic history of these years. Although for purposes of theoretical analysis the economist may ignore political and social changes, the economic historian must treat of them when they impinge upon his story.

In the second place, the economy of Western culture was upset in the period under discussion by a major economic depression. As we have previously seen, the capitalist economic system, prodigious as it was in achieving economic growth, displayed a tendency to generate forces within itself which brought on business depressions. In 1920 to 1921 there was a minor "post-war "economic crisis, but from 1929 to 1936 there was a downswing of the business cycle that was of catastrophic proportions. Industrial production in Europe, excluding the U.S.S.R., declined by 30 percent from 1929 to 1932. In the United States, national income fell by some 50 percent from 1929 to 1933 and did not gain its pre-depression level until World War II. Unemployment was rife, suffering was great, and tensions among interest groups stretched to the breaking point. Indeed, the Great Depression of the 1930s aroused doubts as to the intrinsic viability of the capitalist system, made apparent the absolute necessity of taking measures to prevent a repetition of such a calamity, and led in some quarters, notably in Italy and Germany, to changes that boded ill for civilization, as the vast majority of the West understood it.

In the third place, the development of the West's economy had resulted in such changes in the relative economic and political position of interest groups in society that new theories had been spun to rationalize the place of each and deep-seated animosities had been created among them. Economic power had definitely passed from hereditary landowners and from Churchmen to those who owned or directed industrial, commercial, or financial enterprises, and political power within national states had shifted in the same dirction. Consequently, many wageworkers had come to feel that they were being exploited, or at least that they were not being given adequate consideration in the operation of the free-market economy. As a result, many of them adopted an attitude that was either hostile to or highly critical of their employers and to some extent of modern capitalism. They organized both trade unions and political parties in order to "slug it out" with employer groups. Furthermore, these "new groups" were in at least partial conflict with others which represented some ideology of an earlier time, whether it was a royal house, a social "caste," a sectional institution, like slavery in the United States, or an established church. The structure of the new society was, indeed, complex and full of stresses and strains. In addition, the extreme division of labor in the economy and in society, with all the benefits which it brought, had resulted in making everyone dependent on everyone else. If anyone failed to perform his appointed task, the entire economy could be dealt a severe blow, if not, indeed, brought to a standstill. With many persons being in strategic economic position, the chances of irresponsible elements taking action for personal advantage at the sacrifice of the whole society were greatly increased.

In the fourth place, the West seemed to be in crisis because of shifts in the location of power both within its own area and in the entire world. For a multitude of reasons the economic center of Western culture shifted from Western Europe to the English-speaking portions of North America, and this shift created a separate set of tensions. The Old World was loath to recognize, much less admit, its relative loss of status; the New was not altogether willing or prepared to assume the responsibilities which went with becoming the most powerful area on earth. The Old World was not quite willing to effect the changes which were indicated, if it were to avoid conflicts which all feared would deliver it its *coup de grace,* and not quite ready to cooperate closely with the New, now the center of power.

The fact that while Western culture was in crisis other cultures were increasing their power and their hostility to the West added to the West's predicament. In a very short time, the U.S.S.R. created both an economic and military potential which was adequate to make the West fear for its safety. Colonial areas sought independence from European overlords, for they had acquired the doctrine of nationalism from the West, learned some of the West's techniques of making war, and realized that the West was greatly weakened by war and social dissension. Finally, what boded particularly ill for the West was the fact that several other cultures, of which the Russian was the leader, seemed to be encroaching on the West or the West's "spheres of influence." Dangerous as such a threat was, it seemingly had the effect of forcing the West to pull itself together, to recognize its weaknesses, and to do something about them.

World War I

The first major evidence that the West was beginning to decline from its pinnacle of power was World War I. This conflict was estimated to have cost, including both losses and current wartime expenditures, 603,570 million dollars—this at a time when the national income of the United States was around 50 billion dollars. It occasioned the mobilization of 65 million men between 1914 and 1918; of these, 9 million were killed, 5 million reported missing, 7 million permanently disabled, and 15 million more or less seriously wounded.

That Western culture should have become involved in such a holocaust is one of the tragedies of Modern Times and one that requires solemn reflection. The war was so apocalyptic that one may ask with reason why such civilized humans as Westerners considered themselves to be should ever have become involved in it. Although this query has elicited millions of words of explanation and certainly millions of hours of investigation, a summary answer may be put simply. Tensions among national states had become acute, as suggested above, for the very concept of nationalism, implying as it did a sense of superiority and a special mission of the nationality, created rivalries among nations. These rivalries led to the adoption of hostile policies—policies which included matters economic.

Nations which had close commercial relations and mutually profited from economic exchanges lined up against each other, in part, because of a desire to gain some advantage or to prevent some advantage being taken of them.

Yet, tensions arising from economic forces certainly did not precipitate the conflict. The crucial decision was taken, or blundered into, because certain leaders with the power to unleash the dogs of war became convinced that there was no other way adequately to safeguard their nations' prestige or to bring their nation its much-wanted glory.[1]

In 1914 leaders on both sides were convinced that the war would be short and that a quick victory would therefore redound to their fame and fortune. They never dreamed that the war would cause so much destruction nor that it would threaten the very foundations of Western culture. Their pride and their certainty about the future course of events led them to ignore one of the fundamental tenets of civilization—the creation of orderly relations among human beings according to known and just rules of behavior.

At the outset, World War I was a war of movement with great mass armies marching and countermarching in an effort to wipe out the enemy, but by December of 1914 the forces on the Western Front, where the ultimate decision was to be reached, had dug in and a war of position ensued. Thenceforth the conflict was to a large extent one of economic potentials.[2] In this contest the Allies tried to deprive the Central Powers of overseas imports and overseas markets by means of a maritime blockade, while the Central Powers endeavored to achieve the same results by means of submarine warfare against Allied shipping, and ultimately against all shipping to Allied nations. Both sides created governmental control of their economies for the purppose of concentrating all energies upon the war. And both engaged in a considerable amount of economic cooperation in order to mobilize all the materials necessary for war and to use them in the most effective way possible.

The Allied blockade of the Central Powers was drawn very tightly.[3] Not only were German and Austrian shipping driven off the seas, but all

---

[1] Undoubtedly certain events arouse political leaders, as individuals, to fighting anger. Yet it should not be deduced from this that man is a fighting animal and has a biological need to fight, or that wars are consequently inevitable. Leaders, in taking hostile steps toward others, could rely on the powers of nationalism to provide them popular support, but they usually forgot that the same force was operative among their potential enemies. It should be added that popular support came also from a desire for excitement and from emotionalism rather than from sheer nationalistic pugnacity. See *The Nature of Conflict, Studies on the Sociological Aspects of International Tensions* (Paris: UNESCO, 1957).

[2] On the Eastern Front and in the Balkans the war continued to be a war of movement. The defeat of Russia by the Central Powers was a hard blow to the Allied cause, but it was not decisive. Similarly, the front in the Balkans was fairly fluid and sapped the strength of the Central Powers, but Allied victories there were also not decisive.

[3] France forbade the importation of enemy goods on September 27, 1914, and the exportation of all goods to the enemy on April 4, 1915. Stopping neutral trade with the Central Powers was difficult. The Declaration of Paris (1856) had laid down the rule of international law that neutral flags covered enemy goods, except contraband, that a blockade must be effective, and that neutral goods, except contraband,

possible land routes were blocked, contraband lists were extended until they included even food, and embargoes were placed on many commodities going to neutral countries adjacent to the Central Powers for fear that the goods would leak through to the enemy. The Allies invoked the doctrine of "continuous voyage," under which contraband goods billed for a neutral country were declared as destined to go to the enemy. In addition, firms suspected of trading with the enemy were blacklisted, and trade with neutral countries bordering on enemy lands was limited to shipments to trusted merchants.

Such measures were not without effect, especially after the tightening of the system in March 1915. German imports fell to about two-thirds of their 1913 level. Shortages of food were so great in Germany that in the winter of 1917 turnips became such a staple in the human diet that the year was dubbed the *Rübenjahr.* Rubber stocks became so depleted that at the end of the war many motor trucks were rolling on steel tires; fats needed in explosives were so short that housewives were requested to strain their dishwater to capture whatever grease it might contain; and petroleum products both for lubrication and for internal combustion engines were at the last almost nonexistent.

On the other hand, the Central Powers' war on Allied commerce was also effective. On February 4, 1915, Germany declared that the waters around the British Isles were a war zone, that enemy vessels would be sunk in this area without warning, and that neutral ships should keep clear of it. Subsequently many merchantmen were sunk, including the British *Lusitania,* on May 7, 1915, with several Americans on board. But to make the U-boat campaign more effective Germany announced, on January 31, 1917, that it would begin an unrestricted and ruthless war on shipping. By the autumn of 1917 the Allies had lost 11 million out of a total of 25 million gross tons which they had had in April 1915; Great Britain lost during the entire war 7,760,000 gross tons out of a total of 19 million. New ship construction was unable to keep pace with such losses and stocks of certain goods fell perilously low. Indeed, in March 1917, England had a wheat stock sufficient to meet consumption demands for only eight weeks.[4]

Shortages thus created in the economies of the belligerents, as well as the very nature of the war itself, led the participants to engage in governmental economic planning and in controlling economic activity. Prior to

were not liable to seizure. The Declaration of London (1909) specified that a blockade must not extend beyond the ports and coasts of an enemy country, that is, could not be conducted on the high seas. Great Britain, Germany, and Austria-Hungary were not signatories to this rule, but the latter two states agreed to it during the war because it was to their advantage to do so.

[4] Mention should also be made of the fact that the Central Powers blockaded Russia by controlling the Baltic Sea and by having their ally, Turkey, close the Strait. Russian imports declined to about two-fifths of their prewar value.

1914 little thought had been given to such war measures, except as regarded transportation, the mobilization of men, and the production of war materiel, for military men thought in terms of short wars. Hence national economic planning, which was to become so important in later years, developed piecemeal during the war.

This movement was begun by Walter Rathenau, a German industrialist, who early in the conflict became convinced that there would be severe shortages of strategic raw materials. He founded the *Kriegs-Rohstoff Abteilung* (War Raw Materials Department), which tried not only to increase the production of those goods in short supply, but also to develop substitutes for materials which could not be obtained abroad, to control the allocation of goods, and subsequently to determine the very uses to which these materials should be put. In other countries there were similar bodies, sometimes composed of trade associations, sometimes consisting of representatives of government, of employers, and of employees, as in the case of the British Control Boards, and sometimes limited to governmental officials.

Also, shortages of labor resulting from having so many men under arms forced states to create controls over manpower. One of the first things which governments did was to make military service more selective, that is, to take men for military duty who could be best spared from an economic point of view. They had learned during the early phases of the war that to draft men irrespective of their special skills might result in a reduction in the production of the sinews of war and that men at the front were of little value if their firepower were limited because of matériel shortages.[5] Women, retired men and youths of premilitary age were enticed to accept productive work.[6] France and Britain imported colonial workers. The German government had the power under the National Service Law of December 5, 1916, to order all men between the ages of seventeen and sixty to work at prescribed tasks. All belligerents drew workers from neighboring countries by offers of high wages.

Furthermore, problems of food supply, which were particularly serious, owing to the fact that all the major belligerents except Russia and the United States were food-importing countries, caused still further governmental intervention. Food control boards were created, food prices were regulated, and some foods were rationed either by limiting the amounts available to individuals or by forbidding the sale of a given product except on specified days.

In the case of the Allies, shortages of food were so great that they did

[5] Germany and France withdrew skilled machinists from the army in 1915, for example, and Great Britain, shipyard workers and stevedores in 1916.

[6] France had 29 percent more women in industry in July 1917 than in 1914.

much to effect Interallied economic cooperation. Early in the war England and France learned that in their anxiety to buy food abroad they were bidding up prices to their mutual disadvantage; later they realized that, with shipping in such short supply, they would have to pool their tonnages if they were to feed their people. Accordingly, combined Anglo-French boards were created for making joint purchases, an Interallied Wheat Executive was set up in November 1916, and the all-important Allied Maritime Transport Council for the allocation of tonnage to meet the most urgent needs was established (November 1917). Here was a form of international economic cooperation which was to be extended to almost all of Western culture in the economic reconstruction after World War II.

Also, problems of war finance pushed governments deeper into economic planning, into controls, and into Interallied cooperation. All belligerents levied new taxes, many of which were to have some effect other than the mere raising of revenue and thus constituted an interesting example of functional finance. Accordingly, excess profits taxes were designed to curb war profiteering; luxury taxes were aimed to prevent productive energies from being diverted from essentials; and consumers' taxes were used to curb the consumption of goods in short supply or to discourage the manufacture of goods that detracted from war production. Finally, all belligerents had recourse to new rates to get more revenue. France and Russia adopted the income tax. France introduced a tax on business transactions (turnover tax), and Great Britain levied customs duties. French doubled its tax revenues from 1914 to 1918, and Great Britain increased its threefold.

Heroic as such measures were, however, they were not sufficient to cope with the enormous demands of the maw of Mars. Consequently, all states had to resort to borrowing. If treasury securities were held by private individuals, borrowing had no great economic consequences. But if they were held by banks, especially central banks, they became the base, the reserve, for increasing the money supply or for the extension of credit. Thus they had an inflationary effect. As a matter of fact, prices rose considerably during the war in all belligerent countries. Thus in Germany, the amount of money in circulation increased some five times and prices about doubled. Among the Allies, however, the situation was somewhat relieved by considerable Interallied borrowing, the more financially able lending to the hardest pressed.[7] When hostilities had ended, about 15 percent of the Allied costs of the war had been met by Interallied loans. The United States had lent other Allies 7,077,100,000 dollars; Great Britain was a creditor for 7,014,500,000 dollars; and France had assisted others to

---

[7] These "loans" were in effect booking arrangements representing delayed payments for deliveries of goods. They were not funds that permitted a free choice of acquiring goods in the world's markets.

the extent of 2,237,600,000 dollars. Such pooling of resources explains, in part, why the exchange rates of Allied currencies remained at about their prewar ratios until after the conflict (the French franc in terms of the dollar declined from only 5.18 at par to 5.45 in December 1918).

At the end of the war the economic strength of the Allies was apparent on the fronts as well as in banking houses. The enormous resources of the United States and of the British Empire, and the ability of the Allies to draw upon the reserves of the entire world because of their domination of the seas, tipped the scale against the Central Powers. The Germans became aware of the predicament into which they were getting themselves and made an all-out effort to stave off disaster by throwing their weight after a long build-up against the Allies in March 1918. This desperate effort carried them to the Marne, but not beyond. Henceforth, they were literally crushed by a superior force—a force determined by a greater economic potential.

The economic consequences of the war

In an economic sense, however, the difference between victor and vanquished in the fall of 1918 was not very great. Losses in men and goods had been immense on both sides. For four years, the belligerents had devoted their energies to destruction, with the result that an important part of Europe's capital equipment had been destroyed or worn out.

Of perhaps even greater significance for the long run than the ruining of physical plant and the diversion of energies from construction to destruction was the fact that the war had resulted in innumerable economic dislocations. New tensions had grown up between employers and employees. Some resources had been so exhausted that shifts in the location of production were necessary; and industries had been started to meet the needs of war which were not viable in peacetime. Patterns of international trade and payments had been so drastically altered that the traditional flow of goods and methods of making payments had become impossible.

Immediately after the conflict—when social structures were weakened by the displacement of people, when rapid demobilization of armies with no provisions for the employing of ex-soldiers, was taking place, when patriotic fervor relaxed, and when there were great uncertainties about the future—leaders of the lower classes in several places attempted to seize control of political power. In Russia, they succeeded in overthrowing the Czarist regime (October 1917) and setting up a communist state. In Hungary, they created a very short-lived communist dictatorship under Bela Kun (1919). In Italy, workers occupied factories and a few large estates (1920). Existing regimes were done away with in Germany, Austria, Bulgaria, and Turkey. In France, Great Britain, and the United States, there were numerous strikes. In Central and Eastern Europe, there were demands for land reform which envisaged the breaking up of large estates. Such troubles contributed directly to the continuation of low production, which in Europe was some 23 to 30 percent less than it had been in 1913, and to the economic depression of 1920–1921.

To make matters worse, some wartime economic expansion required agonizing readjustment. Great munition plants had to be retooled as arms were beaten into plowshares. Allied shipyards, which had striven so valiantly to keep pace with sinkings, had to be cut back, and untold amounts of war matériel from gas masks to airplane motors had to be dumped. Moreover, the production of many basic commodities, like copper and wheat, had been so greatly increased that prices for them fell greatly and remained low throughout the 1920s.[8]

Difficult as were the readjustments to meet peacetime conditions and enormous as was the task of reconstruction, a return to the production levels of 1913 was effected with amazing rapidity. In France, which was one of the most ravaged nations, the index of industrial production attained its prewar figure in 1924 and the index of agricultural production reached its prewar position by 1925. In fact, by 1926 all leading European countries, including the U.S.S.R., had gotten back, as far as output was concerned, to what they had achieved in 1913. This was a remarkable tribute to the recuperative powers of modern technology.

A return to the *status quo ante* was not, however, effected with such dispatch in all branches of economic activity. Especial difficulty was encountered, as has already been said, in the field of international trade and payments, or more precisely in that delicate structure of multilateral movements of goods, payments, and investments whereby the accounts of nations were settled. For one thing, the "workshop of the world" nations had lost some of their markets during the war and had difficulty in regaining them. British exports in 1921 were half what they had been in 1913 (at 1913 prices), whereas United States manufacturing production was 22 percent and Japanese was 76 percent greater in 1920 than in 1913. For another thing, Western European nations had to replenish their stocks of imported industrial raw materials before they could get back into full production, and they had to bring in large quantities of foodstuffs to make up for the deficiencies caused by war. Furthermore, these same nations had reduced earnings from shipping services, from earnings on foreign investments, and from banking and insurance services. As late as 1928 the ten

---

[8] In the United States the acreage planted to wheat increased 25 percent from 1914 to 1919, for example. Much of this increase was in the Southwest on land that was to be partially ruined by erosion during the droughts of the 1920s.

most highly industrialized countries of Western Europe had a bare plus balance in current trade and payments.

The international trade and payments situation was finally made worse by still other disturbing factors. For a time the terms of trade, that is, the relationship of prices for imports compared with prices for exports, were unfavorable to Western Europe, so that Western Europe had to export more goods to pay for a given amount of imports than it had before the war. The creation of new states and hence of new tariff boundaries impeded the flow of goods in established patterns of production and distribution. The fear of political instability hindered the making of international loans. Curbs on immigration, like the American act of 1921,[9] created maladjustments in the supply of labor. And as though these difficulties were not enough, the entire international trade and payments picture was distorted by reparations and war debts.

Reparations and war debts

At the conclusion of the war, the European victors wanted Germany to pay all Allied war damages and all the Allied costs of the war. The United States, however, took the position that the payment of war damages would be all that Germany could manage if she were to be returned to full membership in the economy of Western Europe. Inasmuch as such a difference of opinion existed at the Peace Conference and there was then no possibility of drawing up a bill for war damages, the fixing of the amount of reparations was left to a special commission which was to submit its figure by May 1921. In the meantime, Germany was to pay the equivalent of 5 billion dollars in commodities, securities, and gold to cover the costs of the armies of occupation.[10] Furthermore, it was to surrender part of its merchant marine, to build 200,000 tons of shipping per year for five years for the Allies, to deliver a certain amount of livestock, railway equipment, and coal, and to give the Allies most-favored-nation treatment for five years. Incidentally, the blockade of Germany was to be maintained until the peace treaty was signed, a stipulation which was a very bitter pill for Germany.

The reparations bill which was submitted in 1921 called for the payment of 33 billion dollars, or four times what American experts at Paris had

---

[9] This law set quotas on the number of immigrants to be admitted to the United States in any one year. Each country was allowed a number based on 3 percent of its nationals living in the United States in 1910, although people of some countries were actually excluded. This law favored immigration from Northern Europe and limited it from Southern and Central Europe.

[10] Dollars are given at current value. Any of the sums mentioned which might be in excess of the costs of occupation were to be credited toward reparations.

thought to be feasible. This sum was to be paid over thirty years in fixed installments of gold marks plus 26 percent of the proceeds of German exports plus reparations in deliveries of physical goods—the so-called reparation in kind. Here was a burden so great that the German budget, then almost in balance, was faced with a large deficit. Germany began to issue paper money on a vast scale in order to meet governmental expenses; the German mark began to fall in international exchange, and Germany was soon the victim of runaway inflation.

Before the end of 1921 Germany informed the Reparations Commission that it could not meet its 1922 installments. Payments went into default, and the French and Belgians occupied the Ruhr (1923) to force collections. When this effort proved unsuccessful in the face of Germany's passive resistance, the Allies appointed a new reparations commission, chaired by an American banker, Charles G. Dawes, to try to bring some order out of the existing chaos. From the first the Dawes Commission was handicapped, because it was not empowered to alter the total bill. It did produce a plan, however, that reduced annual payments to sums considered to be within Germany's capacity to pay, extended the period over which reparations would be collected, and suggested sources of revenue for these payments.[11]

The Dawes Plan had no built-in magic; in essence it was simply a device for prolonging the agony. Soon Germany again had trouble in meeting its payments. In the new emergency another commission was appointed with another American, Owen D. Young, as chairman. The Young Plan of 1929 provided for both a reduction in annual payments and a lowering of the total bill, but it went into operation just as the economy was going into a tailspin. Under the stresses of the depression, a continuation of the reparations comedy was out of the question. In 1932 the parties involved signed the Lausanne Agreement that to all intents and purposes put an end to the reparations issue.[12]

Closely related to reparation as a major influence upon international trade, current payments, and capital movements were Interallied war debts. These obligations were contracted, as we have seen, during the war, but they were increased immediately after the Armistice by the sale of war stocks and the granting of further loans for immediate relief and reconstruction. Thus in 1922 the United States was a net creditor on war debts for some 10 billion dollars, Great Britain for 4.5 billion dollars, and France for 3.5 billion dollars. Britain and France wanted to distinguish between pre-Armistice and post-Armistice obligations on the ground that the for-

---

[11] It also proposed the withdrawal of France and Belgium from the Ruhr.

[12] Reparations from the other Central Powers were treated in the same way as those with Germany, but they were not a major problem, because they were not very large.

mer should be considered as part of a common war effort. The United States, however, insisted on collection, for it accepted the view expressed in President Coolidge's "They hired the money, didn't they?" Accordingly, Great Britain and France granted large concessions to their debtors and acknowledged loss of the aid given to Russia, but the United States tried to collect, making adjustments only upon interest charges and periods of payment. Because of this American policy, France and Britain insisted as long as they could on the payment of reparations and they finally agreed to abrogate their claims on Germany only on condition that they were no longer responsible for war debts.

In the payment of any obligation, a debtor nation must have things of value and must be able to transfer these things to its creditor. A government usually obtains whatever it uses for payments by taxing its people for by borrowing both at home and abroad. The transfers may be in the form of gold and silver, foreign moneys, securities, merchandise, and services. In any case, however, the creditors must be willing to receive what the debtor has to give.

Immediately after the war, Germany was able to amass a certain of precious metals, foreign securities, foreign moneys, and stocks of goods to sent to claimants on reparations account. At that time, too, when everything was in short supply, the Allies were willing to receive what was offered. Up to the Dawes Plan the Allies received on reparations account some 8.5 billion dollars, including a considerable amount in kind, although estimates of the total figure have varied widely. By 1924, however, Germany had little more in the way of gold and silver, foreign securities, or foreign moneys to transfer. The only way that it could get them was by exporting more goods and services than it imported or by borrowing abroad. The reparations claimants did not want the Germans to get any of their markets,[13] nor were they so willing as they had been to be paid directly in kind. In fact, they grumbled because German shipyards were building ships on reparations account while their own lay idle and British coal miners complained that German coal deliveries on reparations account to Italy were hurting their exports. Consequently, actual deliveries of goods, which had played an important role in the Dawes Plan schedule of payments, were cut drastically in the Young Plan. Then, what was of particular significance for the reparations problem was that Germany had a deficit in its foreign trade and payments from 1924 to 1930 of 8,250 million dollars. Yet it paid in this period some 2,620 million dollars.

Payment of war debts presented the same problems as did payment of reparations. Easily transferable values were in short supply, and each

---

[13] France rejected a proposal by Louis Loucheur whereby Germany would have reconstructed the devasted regions. Both French capital and labor wanted this business and work for themselves.

creditor was reluctant to receive goods which would compete with its own products. Yet, here, too, payments were made, the United States Treasury receiving from all debtors some 2,735 million dollars in spite of the fact that those payers had unfavorable balances in current trade and payments with the United States. From Table 35, below, one may easily see the extent of reparations and war debt accounts from 1924 to 1931.

Table 35. Total receipts and payments of principal countries on reparations and war debt accounts, July 1, 1924 to June 30, 1931 (in millions of dollars, current value)

	Receipts from		Payments to			Net position
Country	Germany	All principal debtors	United States	Great Britain	Total	Excess receipts (+), payments (−)
Great Britain	564.9	881.3	1,122.1		1,122.1	−240.8
France	1,426.0	1,426.0	220.8	197.1	417.9	+1,008.1
Italy	203.2	203.2	33.0	107.1	140.1	+ 63.1
Belgium	182.2	182.2	39.8	12.2	52.0	+130.2

How reparations and war debts were paid in view of the overall deficit in the trade and payment accounts of the payers is an interesting question. The answer is to be found in the fact that during the period under consideration the United States, and to a lesser extent, Great Britain, France, Switzerland, and the Netherlands made capital loans to Germany. Germany in turn paid her creditors by means of the funds thus put at its disposal. As the claimants on reparations accounts were paid, they reduced their war debts. The upshot of the story was that Germany paid in reparations from the beginning of the Dawes Plan about three-fifths of what it borrowed abroad and reinvested the other two-fifths for its own account outside its frontiers. The recipients of reparations passed on to the United States to reduce their war debts about half of what they received from Germany. Finally, American private investors wound up holding German securities of doubtful value. From 1914 to 1930 the United States shifted from being a net debtor for 3 billion dollars to that of being a net creditor for 11 billion dollars, in addition to being a creditor for unpaid war debts.

Inflationary movements in the post-World War I period

The postwar pattern of multilateral trade and payments was badly distorted by reparations and war debts—a distortion that would have been much worse, incidentally, if American loans had not been forthcoming. Furthermore, international trade and capital transfers were also upset by currency inflation. Uneven rates of inflation of various currencies resulted in great discrepancies between exchange rates and prices, consequently in heavy buying in areas where exchange and price advantages were to be found, and in sudden flights of "hot money" from a monetary area with a weak currency to another with a strong currency, that is, one that was not in danger of becoming depreciated.

The extraordinary inflationary movement of the 1920s had its origins in the war, when governmental expenditures so greatly exceeded receipts from taxation and borrowing from individuals. What governments did to keep their bills paid was to give "promises to pay" to banks of issue. The banks, in turn, increased the supply of money with these "promises to pay" as reserves. With more money in circulation without a corresponding increase of goods for sale or of savings, prices were bid up, as can be seen in the accompanying chart.

The most extreme inflation was that in Germany. The amount of money in circulation during the 1920s was five times what it had been in 1914. The public debt was up twenty times; prices had about doubled; and then reparations put a tremendous burden on the public treasury. The exchange rate for the dollar, which had been about 4 marks to the dollar in 1914, went to 14.8 marks to the dollar in May 1921, to 62.6 marks in November, and eventually to some 62 billion marks on October 30, 1923 (Figure 24). Prices soared, although they lagged behind exchange rates, until the mark became virtually worthless. In fact, the mortgage indebtedness within Germany of the preinflationary period became less in terms of paper marks than one glass of beer. Debts, including those represented by bonds and mortgages, were thus wiped out, but so, too, were insurance policies, savings accounts and all forms of wealth the value of which were determined by the value of the currency.[14] Order was only reestablished when a new bank of issue, the Rentenbank, was created—a bank that used as "reserves" large agricultural holdings and business properties pledged for the purpose by their owners. This was a temporary arrangement to provide the country with a usable medium of exchange and measure of value pending the accumulation of more traditional reserves for a new Reichsbank.[15]

[14] Some of these obligations, like life insurance policies, were subsequently "revalued," for insurance companies had properties, like real estate, that did not lose value during the hyperinflation.

[15] The new Rentenmark was declared equal to approximately 24 cents. The new money held this rate and German prices conformed to it.

France, for its part, emerged from the war with a monetary problem not unlike Germany's. Although it did not have reparations to pay, it did have war debts to settle and devastated areas to reconstruct. In the accomplishment of the latter task it spent money lavishly on the assumption that

Chart 1

Wholesale Prices, in National Currency, of Forty Basic Commodities in European Countries and the United States, 1910–1936.

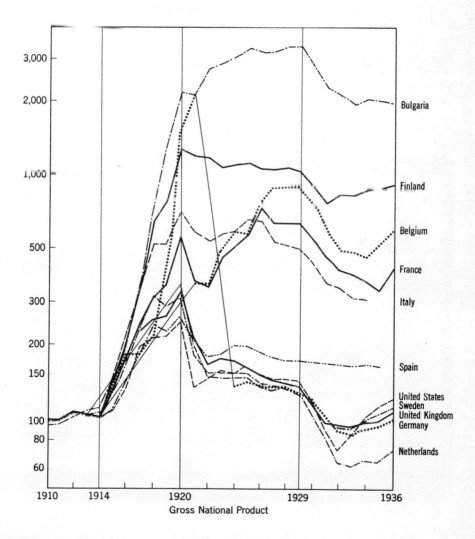

Gross National Product

reparations would cover all the bills. When this blithe expectation proved illusory, the supply of money was increased more rapidly to meet expenditures than was the supply of goods, and prices went up. As the French realized what was taking place, some of them sent capital abroad, changing their francs ("hot money") into apparently more stable dollars, Swiss francs, pounds sterling, or Dutch florins—a process which weakened the franc in foreign exchange. By 1926 the French franc, which had been worth about 20 cents in 1914, was bringing only 0.389 cents in New York. In the extremity Henri Poincaré, who was to become known as the "savior of the franc," made a herculean effort to bring the French budget into balance, slowed up the flight from the franc, forced some of the "hot money" back to France, and finally stabilized the franc at 0.392 cents.

Figure 24
German inflation money. This bank note is for 2 billion marks. Before such notes could be printed, the face value of existing notes was raised by stamping new values on them. Even so, an ordinary businessman had to carry bundles of money in large billfolds or brief cases in order to have enough to carry on even small transactions. *(From the Moneys of the World Collection of the Chase Manhattan Bank of New York. Used with permission.)*

One of the curious aspects of inflation was that prices did not rise at the same rate that a currency in the process of being inflated lost value in exchange for hard currencies. Thus, in the interval between the time a currency fell in terms of another money and the time national prices had risen to the level of international prices at the new rate of exchange, goods in the inflationary country were cheap for the citizens of countries with stable currencies. For this reason, American tourists flocked to France in the 1920s because they could travel there very cheaply, and many French goods had a strong competitive position for a time in the Swiss market. Consequently inflation gave a shot in the arm to exports—a spurt which could not be maintained—because of a price advantage in which the exporting country did not get full value for its goods. In the domestic economy that was experiencing inflation, investments usually slumped. Concentration of plant increased as those with stores of hard currencies abroad repatriated their moneys to buy up properties at low prices,[16] and many small businessmen and small savers lost heavily. It is probable that inflation so weakened the lower middle class economically and so discouraged it that its members were willing to listen to the proposals of extreme remedies offered to cure the ills of society—to the arguments of Socialism or Fascism. Indeed, the middle economic class was less effective than it had been in bridging the gap between the very wealthy and the wageworkers. Thus, inflation had important social and political consequences, as well as being a disturbing factor in trade and payments. In its mild form it may have contributed to economic growth by "forcing" a certain amount of capital into investment, but its extreme form it was certainly a deterrent to economic growth.

---

[16] The enormous holdings of Hugo Stinnes, which are said to have employed at their peak some 600,000 workers, were built up in this way.

Economic growth and economic depression

Economic expansion in the interbellum period

In spite of distortions in the system of multilateral trade and payments, in spite of inflations, and in spite of wartime destruction of life and property, the first half of the interbellum period was one of economic expansion in Western culture.

Yet the rate of economic growth in Europe (excluding the U.S.S.R.) was less than what it had been from 1880 to 1913 and decidedly less in the United States than what it had been (Table 36). Moreover, some production was to replace what had been destroyed or worn out during the war and hence could not be considered as much of an increment to the stock of human goods of 1913. Nevertheless output per employed worker went up; the number of hours worked per year went down; and Western man had more leisure to devote to other interests than the sheer making of a living.[1] Moreover, there were more people to partake of the leisure,[2] with the greatest growth being registered in Southern and Eastern Europe and in the United States. Finally, populations were getting older, with the result that a larger percentage of populations were within the productive ages of fifteen to sixty-five.[3]

In the interwar period the greatest strides in production per man-hour were made in industry and services rather than in agriculture. As can be

[1] The average annual rate of industrial growth as a percentage, 1913 to 1936–1938, of output per man in Western Europe was 1 percent and of output per working hour was 1.8 percent.
  In the United States the rate of growth in the same period was 1.3 percent per man and 4.4 percent per working hour.
[2] During World War I the population of Europe fell some 2 million.
[3] There were not yet enough unproductive aged to constitute a serious economic burden.

Table 36. Indicators of economic growth, 1880 to 1962

	Europe							
	1880	1913	1920	1929	1937	1950	1960	1962
Population (in millions)	247	340	338	365	387	391	427	434
Production of five grains								
(millions of metric tons)	85	117			115	106	124.8*	
Industrial production index								
(1938=100)	27	71	55	91	102	124		
(1953=100)							89	164.7 184.8

	United States							
	1880	1913	1920	1929	1937	1950	1960	1962
Population (in millions)	50	97	106	122	129	151	179	186.5
Production of five grains								
(millions of metric tons)	68	105			92	139	171.1	
Industrial production index								
(1938=100)	15	70	85	126	130	225		
(1953=100)							82	119 130

*1954–1956, all grains.

seen from Table 37, productivity per man-hour in agriculture was only about half what it was in industry, and in industry it was less than in the service trades.

Various explanations have been offered to account for these differences.

Table 37. Real product per man-hour (in dollars at 1926–1934 prices)

Year and country	Agriculture	Manufacturing	Services and small-scale manufacturing
United States:			
1909–11	0.181	0.402	0.782
1939–41	0.282	1.070	1.241
Great Britain:			
1904–10	0.145	0.176	0.411
1937	0.200	0.353	0.669

SOURCE: Clark, *Conditions of Economic Progress*, pp. 316–317.

It has been said that farmers have "hidden" incomes, as from family gardens and housing, and "psychic" income, like fresh air, a variety of jobs, and time out of the working day for partaking of "rural pleasures." Nevertheless, it seems that prices paid for industrial goods and services indicated that those in these branches of the economy were in a stronger position in society to get more per unit of human input than those in agriculture.

Under the price conditions which existed, it is not surprising that the occupational distribution of the population continued to show percentagewise a drift away from agriculture to industry and the services. In Europe (excluding the U.S.S.R.) there was an increase from 1913 to 1940 of 40 percent in the number of workers employed outside agriculture. In the United States, the trend away from agriculture and toward the services was very striking. The occupational distribution of the population in America, as illustrated in Table 38, when considered along with productivity per occupation (Table 37), provides further evidence of the extraordinary results which can be achieved by an extreme division of labor.

Increases in the division of labor were made possible primarily by an extension of the market economy, by an expansion in the use of money as a medium of exchange, by improvements in transportation made possible by the motor truck, the motor car, and high-tension electrical transmission lines, and by a greater specialization of skills as work became more technical. Sales of goods through stores increased at a faster rate than income and population. The number of ton-miles carried by American railroads went up from 301.7 billion in 1913 to 740.5 billion in 1944 under the pressure of war, that carried by motor truck increased from almost nothing in 1913 to 48.5 billion in 1940, that by inland waterways (including the Great Lakes) rose to 117.3 billion in 1940, and that by pipelines to 71.3 billion in 1940. The amount of electricity generated in the United States increased from 24.7 billion kilowatthours in 1912 to 146.5 billion kilowatthours in 1937, and to 279.5 billion kilowatthours in 1944, which meant that large amounts of power were available in many more localities

Table 38. Percentage distribution of gainful workers by occupational divisions in the United States*

Occupation	1850	1860	1870	1880	1890	1900	1910	1920	1930	1940†	1950†	1965†
Agriculture	63.6	58.9	53.0	49.4	42.6	37.5	31.0	27.0	21.4	16.8	14.5	6.1
Forestry and fisheries	0.4	0.4	0.5	0.6	0.8	0.7	0.6	0.6	0.5	0.3		
Mining	1.1	1.6	1.4	1.7	1.9	2.4	2.6	2.6	2.0	2.08	1.75	.08
Manufacturing and mechanical industries	16.3	18.2	20.5	22.1	23.7	24.8	28.5	30.3	28.9	22.4	28.8	25.2
Construction										6.58	4.48	4.1
Transportation and communication	0.5	0.7	4.2	4.8	6.0	6.7	7.1	7.3	7.9	7.78	7.77	5.6
Trade	4.0	4.0	6.8	7.9	8.8	10.6	9.7	10.1	12.5	13.4	18.44	17.5
Public service (not included elsewhere)	12.2	12.1	0.7	0.8	0.9	1.0	1.2	1.7	1.8			
Professional services	12.2	12.1	2.6	3.2	3.8	4.1	4.6	5.1	6.7			
Domestic and personal service	12.2	12.4	9.7	8.8	9.6	9.7	10.1	8.0	10.1			
Clerical occupations			0.6	0.9	2.0	2.5	4.6	7.3	8.2			
Finance and real estate										2.9	3.51	4.2
Educational service										3.15		
Other professional service										4.35	9.23	12.4
Domestic service										4.89		
Personal service										5.81		
Government not elsewhere classified										3.17	11.45	14.1
Not allocated										6.19		

*These are the gainfully employed over fourteen years of age. The data are related but not completely comparable because of changes in the collection of information.

The total labor force in 1965 was 56.5% of the total population. About 5% of the labor force was unemployed.

†Revised headings.

SOURCE: *Statistical Abstract of the United States, 1965.* Information for other countries may be obtained from *Demographic Yearbook,* United Nations (New York: United Nations, 1964), pp. 19ff

than before. Finally, the increasing specialization of tasks in the United States finds confirmation in the fall of the proportion of common laborers (other than farm laborers) in the total working population from 14.6 percent in 1920 to 10.7 percent in 1940, in the growth of technical education, and in the increased numbers going to school, especially to advanced educational institutions.[4]

New industrial technology

Accompanying the ever more extensive division of labor in the realization of greater productivity per man was the development of a technology based upon the tried and proved principle of using more machines to perform human tasks, the driving of these machines by mechanical power (Figure 25), the standardization of products, the "rationalization of production" along lines prescribed by scientific management, and the development of processes for rendering useful to man ever-increasing amounts of inorganic substances.

Among the new machines which now came into general use were rotary kilns in the cement industry, continuous rolling mills in steelmaking, and the electrical furnace for making various products where the elimination of impurities resulting from the combination of coke was especially desirable. Among new products that contributed to economic growth were airplanes, which greatly facilitated travel and the transportation of goods

Figure 25
Modern cotton spinning. The progress in the art of making thread has been enormous over the last two hundred years. This picture might be compared with those showing spinning in Ancient Greece (Figure 1) and on the Hargreaves jenny (Figure 19). The principles have not, however, changed much. The twist is provided by rollers (center of the picture) and by a revolving spindle. *(Courtesy of Burlington Industries.)*

---

[4] In the United States, the number of university students per thousand of the population went up from 4.21 in 1913 to 7.88 in 1930, and in France it rose from 1.040 in 1910 to 1.881 in 1932.

high in value and low in weight,[5] radios, which not only created an entirely new and vast industry but also opened a new era in mass communications, and business machines, which made the record keeping imposed by the extreme division of labor both more accurate and more efficient.

Production was further increased by a whole series of new processes, many of which were made possible by a greater use of chemical research. Thus in the refining of petroleum, it became possible to obtain a larger percentage of the commercially desirable gasoline by cracking, that is, by heating the raw material under pressure in the presence of a catalyst. Nitrogen in large quantities began to be obtained from the atmosphere by fixation, wood pulp was bleached by new and more economical methods, aluminum was refined by lower-cost procedures, and rayon-making processes were continually improved. The invention of plastics gave mankind an entirely new product that was to find employment in a great array of things from clothing fibers to automobile bodies. The development of mechanical (chemical) refrigeration allowed greater concentration and a greater division of labor in the production and distribution of fresh or frozen fruits, vegetables, and meats. And new methods of low-cost packaging produced profound changes in marketing, especially in foods, where the self-service supermarket forecast the store of the future.

Increases in production resulting from rationalization were to be found on every hand. Sometimes the steps taken were to eliminate unprofitable enterprises, as in the British coal-mining industry in which an official Coal Mines Reorganization Committee was created (1930) to shut down uneconomical mines. Sometimes rationalization operated to step up production by the use of the moving assembly line, by a better layout of work to reduce human movements, and by a more extensive use of power tools. In coal mining a greater employment of the conveyor belt, cutting machines, compressed air, and electric transportation about doubled the output per man-hour in the United States from 1914 to 1940. Sometimes rationalization took the form of introducing material-saving methods rather than laborsaving devices, as in the use of coal, where more and more coal was processed before being burned. In the Ruhr, by 1938 about 85 percent of all coal was coked. Furnaces were constructed so that they could be fed by mechanical stokers or by blowing coal dust into them; fuel economies were so extensive that the amount of coal needed to produce 1 kilowatthour of electricity in central stations in America fell from 7.05 pounds in 1899 to 1.25 pounds in 1946. At times rationalization meant

---

[5] Revenue miles flown in the United States' domestic traffic went up from 4,318,087 in 1926, to 110,101,039 in 1940, to 208,969,279 in 1945, and to 687,614,000 in 1955.

making such innovations as the placing of diesel engines in ships to save space and the inconvenience of soot. At other times it meant introducing friction-reducing devices, like roller bearings in existing machines. Sometimes it meant rearranging work so that there would be a continuous flow from start to finish.

Lastly, production was considerably increased by the standardization of products—a step that was necessary to realize the advantage of mass production. All too frequently custom had resulted in the continuation of various types of goods that served no useful purpose and satisfied no style demand. Thus in German coal mining 100 different models of picks had been in use before World War I and some of them had been produced by handicraft methods, whereas only three different types had any functional purpose and these three could be produced on a large scale and at a great reduction in cost. The standardization of automobiles by such far-seeing entrepreneurs as Henry Ford in America and André Citroën in France contributed much to making the automobile an article of mass consumption. A reduction in the number of types of coal cars in Germany from 175 to 3 effected an enormous saving. Standardization of sizes gave a fillip to the ready-made clothing industry. Standardized products generally made possible the chain department store, which greatly reduced the costs of distribution.

Changes in agricultural production between the wars

The great strides forward in industrial production were not matched in Western culture by advances in agriculture. In Europe, agricultural production at the end of the interwar period was only some 20 to 30 percent greater than in the 1909–1913 period, and in the United States, it was only some 30 to 38 percent greater. Increases in output per worker were larger in industry than in agriculture in Britain, the former having risen 200 percent from the eve of World War I to the eve of World War II and the latter only 20 percent. Even in the United States, where farmers did particularly well compared with other countries, production per worker in agriculture went up only some 40 percent from 1910 to 1935.

The chief reason for the relatively small growth in agricultural production per worker was lack of mechanization of operations. This lack may be explained by the very nature of farm tasks, many of which do not lend themselves readily or completely to mechanical performance. Furthermore, mechanization required capital investment which was beyond the means of small farms and which could not under existing conditions be amortized by farms on marginal lands. Finally, in the interbellum period the fact that agricultural prices fell much lower than industrial prices and that profits in agriculture were low tended to discourage risk capital from doing much to modernize farms.[6]

In spite of all these difficulties some mechanization did take place in agriculture. Electricity was widely installed on farms and used to perform many tasks in addition to lighting. More sanitary methods were employed in handling milk. On-the-farm refrigeration made possible the better handling of other perishable products. Field machines were more widely used, and the tractor effected a veritable agricultural revolution. The introduction of a field power plant required the use of whole series of subsidiary machines, like plows, harrows, seeders, cultivators, and harvesters. And they necessitated large enough farms to permit the full use of the equipment if a profit were to be made.[7] The extent of the tractor revolution may be seen in Table 39.

Table 39. Tractors in Europe and the United States

Area	Number of tractors in thousands			Hectares of land per tractor		
	1930	1939	1951	1930	1939	1951
Europe	130	270	963	1,277	615	171
United States	1,020*	1,597*	3,800	217*	138*	53

*Including Canada.

Furthermore, agricultural output was increased by a greater use of commercial fertilizers, by better strains of plants, and by better breeds of and better feed for livestock. World production of potash (K_2O content), excluding the U.S.S.R., increased from 2,320,000 metric tons in 1936 to 6.3 million in 1956, that of phosphate rock went up from 9,087,000 metric tons in 1936 to 24.9 million in 1956, and that of nitrogen fertilizers rose from 2.4 million metric tons in 1938 to 6.3 million in 1956. Seedsmen marketed carefully prepared and selected seeds, including hybrid seeds, which provided hardier, healthier, and more productive plants. A 10 percent increase in corn production in the United States from 1938–1940 to 1945 was

---

[6] In the United States the "parity ratio," that is, the ratio of what farmers received for their produce divided by what they paid for goods purchased (1910–1914 = 100), fell to 55 in 1932 and did not exceed 100 until well into World War II. In Germany, the index of wholesale prices for agricultural goods dropped from 100 in 1924 to 60 in 1932, while that for agricultural machinery never went below 86.

[7] Cooperatives might buy machinery for the use of their members. Individuals with equipment might do custom work for others, or governments might set up tractor stations for collective farms, but none of these systems proved particularly successful.

attributed to hybrid seed alone; yields of all crops showed some increase except in those places where there was a great increase in marginal land under cultivation. Lastly, animal geneticists discovered that certain animals could produce offspring with special characteristics, such as laying more and larger eggs, producing a large quantity of milk, or having bigger cuts of desired meat. And by an ingenious method of record keeping they were able to determine what animals should be bred. One hybrid breed of poultry produced 17 percent more eggs than its parents and one herd of cows increased its milk production by 20 percent in twenty years with no change in feed.

In spite of a certain success in increasing yields of crops and of animals, farmers were badgered by a multitude of problems in the interbellum period. In the first place, measures to augment production required capital outlays that farmers frequently met by borrowing. Then, with the fall in agricultural prices and with the changed relationship between the prices which they charged for what they sold and those which they paid for what they bought, their predicament became grave. In Germany, the interest burden borne by farmers increased 236 percent from 1924 to 1932, and in the relatively good year of 1928 debt payments and taxes are said to have taken 69 percent of farmers' income. In the United States, 27.8 of every thousand farms with mortgages had their mortgages foreclosed in 1924. Such conditions led in most places to governmental price-fixing arrangements, to subsidies to farmers, to tariff protection, and to governmental loans for farming. In the United States, the government guaranteed prices on designated goods, beginning in 1933, in order to maintain a given level of parity;[8] in Great Britain, a traditional fortress of free trade, high tariff rates were levied on basic agricultural imports.

In the second place, agriculture was upset by shifts in diets and changes in the patterns of international trade. From the period 1910–1913 to the period 1934–1938, when the population of Europe increased 13 percent, the consumption of wheat and rye per capita of the population fell by 9 percent. Because people ate more animal products, fruits, and vegetables, most of which could be produced advantageously in areas of intensive agriculture, grain-growing areas were put under a handicap. Their salvation lay in mechanization and large-scale operations. Then, to make matters worse, the greater decline of agricultural prices than of industrial prices placed nations that specialized in agricultural exports at a disadvantage. Thus the net exports of five major grains from the United States and Canada fell by two-thirds from 1925–1929 to 1934–1938 and those from Russia fell from 10.5 million metric tons in 1909–1913 to 1.2 million in 1935–1938. Denmark, an agricultural exporting nation, experienced a de-

[8] See p.436, n.6.

cline in its exports from an index of 149 in 1929 (1913=100) to 81 in 1933. Britain, an industrial exporting nation, saw its index of finished goods exports fall from 163 in 1929 (1913=100) to 124 in 1933.

Part of the difficulty of international trade in agricultural products could be accounted for by government agricultural policies, for many nations embarked on definite plans to increase their self-sufficiency in foodstuffs. They not only adopted high tariffs, but also regulated imports by quotas and currency controls, engaged in land reclamation projects,[9] and granted subventions of various types in order to stimulate the kind of production desired. Such programs usually resulted, however, in high-cost products, prices of wheat in Berlin and Paris being about twice what they were in Liverpool or the United States in 1935, and the programs did not lead to complete self-sufficiency, as can be seen in Table 40.

Table 40. Self-sufficiency in foodstuffs, 1937

Country	Percent of total consumption produced at home
Great Britain	25
Netherlands	67
Germany (1934 boundaries)	83
France	83
Italy	95
U.S.S.R.	101
United States	95

Furthermore, in order to take care of a certain number of the unemployed and to retard the rural exodus, most states favored small farms and the breaking up of large estates. Nevertheless, the drift of population from the countryside to the city continued and production on small farms remained high-cost except for crops which required a great amount of labor in relation to the value of the product. Thus poultry farming, dairying, truck farming, and small-fruit growing continued to be conducted successfully on small farms, but not grain growing, sheep raising, or beef-cattle

---

[9] In the Netherlands, for example, a dike was built across the mouth of the Zuider Zee. In Italy, drainage projects like that in the Pontine Marshes and irrigation systems like that in the Puglia Plain added appreciable amounts of arable. In the United Kingdom, the amount of arable was increased by 40 percent from 1934–1938 to 1948–1952, chiefly by taking land from pastures and forests. In the United States, a contrary movement was under way; that is, an effort was made to reduce arable so that crops which could not be exported would not be grown.

grazing. From an economic point of view, it seemed desirable that governmental agricultural policies should be flexible enough to aim for greater general economic output per capita and not simply to be temporary supports for high-cost producers. At least, this seemed desirable as long as world production of food was sufficient to meet people's needs, as long as this food could be distributed by multilateral trade, and as long as alternate ways for a more effective use of labor and capital existed.

The Great Depression of the 1930s: its nature

Despite growth in agricultural production, industrial expansion, and the remarkable economic recovery after World War I, undoubtedly the single most important event of the interbellum period was the deep economic depression of the 1930s. It disclosed with glaring lucidity a failure of Western man so to organize his economy that moments of "boom and bust" would be eliminated. It gave great impetus to state intervention in economic affairs, or put negatively, to a marked decrease in the free operation of economic forces. It gave a fillip to the creation of the "welfare state" —to a recognition that political entities should be responsible for the material well-being of their citizens—and to state participation in economic activity, to state ownership, operation, and control. It created, or drew so taut, social and economic tensions within states that to some segments of society regimes based on force seemed eminently desirable to preserve "order." And it augmented rivalries among states, as indicated by the coining of such catchphrases as the "have-not" versus the "have" nations, and it thus contributed directly to World War II.

Economic depressions, as phases of the business cycle, were obviously not new in Western culture, but the one of the 1930s was exceptional because of its impact on all parts of the West and because of its extreme severity. Although the downward movement of the curve of business activity was first manifested in the United States, declines soon set in in every economy of Western culture. Real national income fell in the United States from 100 in 1925–1929 to a low of 68 in 1931, which was comparable to the decline in national income in France during World War I. It declined in Germany to 80 in 1932; in France, it went down to 91 in 1936. Unemployment in the United States rose from 429,000 in 1929 to nearly 12 million in 1933 out of a total labor force of 48 million. For all of Western Europe, unemployment rose from 3.5 million in the period 1921–1925 to a seasonal peak of 15 million at the end of 1932. In the extreme case of Germany, at the latter date 43 percent of the labor force was without work. In the United States, bankruptcies increased by a third from 1929 to 1932. Wholesale prices fell from 95.3 in 1929 (1926=100) to 64.8 in 1932; the index of industrial production declined from 311 in 1929 to 192 in 1933, and the index of investments fell from a high of 178 in 1929 (1920=100) to 50 in 1933. World trade declined by more than 20 percent from 1920–1929 to 1931–1935.

Although the factors which contributed to the steep fall in business activity were exceedingly numerous and their interrelationships extremely complex, it is possible to indicate some of the main forces that led to the disaster. In the first place, production of some goods, like the grains, copper, and cotton in the United States and of war matériel in all belligerent countries, was greatly expanded during the first world conflagration, but the effective demand for these goods, at least where they were being produced, fell off drastically after 1918 and adjustments in the immediate postwar depression of 1921 to the new situation were not adequate.

In the second place, rapid expansion of plant took place in the "torrid twenties," as Western Europe bent its energies on reconstruction and the United States developed its industry to meet demands that could not for the time being be satisfied by Europe. In the third place, reparations, war debts, inflation, and subsequent stabilization, frequently at exchange rates that were unrealistic in terms of prices, upset both international and domestic trade and subsequently had an effect upon production. And in the fourth place, a stock market boom in the United States carried the index of 421 common stocks from 100 in 1926 to 225 in September 1929, while speculators borrowed money at 10 percent in order to buy stocks that at current earnings would have paid them only 2 percent at existing prices.

Although under these circumstances wages and wholesale prices of most commodities remained fairly steady and agricultural prices were decidedly weak, rates at which entrepreneurs borrowed money to expand business activity became higher; the general costs of doing business rose to a point at which entrepreneurs hesitated to go more deeply into debt to increase the output of goods which they feared would not be absorbed by the market. In fact, buyer resistance began to be apparent in several lines and some inventories became excessive after 1926. Then in September 1929, the "bubble" on the New York Stock Exchange burst. Between September 3 and November 13 share values on the Exchange fell by 30 billion dollars[10] and by June 1932 had reached an index of 34 (1926= 100). This decline turned the earlier optimism of businessmen regarding the future of business activity into rank pessimism, if not into panic. It induced lenders, especially banks, to restrict their loans and to demand repayment whenever possible, but some, like the *Creditanstalt* in Austria,[11] did not act

[10] They had gone up 51 billion dollars in the twenty months preceding September.
[11] This bank had been founded by the Rothschilds in 1855. It It was large and hitherto had been successful.

soon enough and failed, bringing down with them many of their creditors. Bank failures and restrictions on credit set up a chain reaction which forced many businessmen to close their doors and thus to turn their workers into unemployed.

What governments should do in the face of such a large-scale economic breakdown was not clear, although it soon was only too apparent that they had to do something. They could not rely on the free operation of the system to make the necessary readjustments in a short enough period of time to prevent social unrest and perhaps the overthrow of existing political and economic regimes. All states of Western culture soon adopted the position that political intervention in economic matters was essential— that they had a responsibility for the welfare of their citizens, which is a basic tenet of the "welfare state," and that they must, by whatever means they had at their disposal, get their economies to function properly once again.

Moreover, it soon became abundantly clear that the economic problems of the day would not be attacked on an international basis for the good of all, but that they would be dealt with by individual nations taking unilateral action. Thus economic difficulties tended to worsen international economic relations, and they aggravated political tensions among states. In fact, they contributed much to the situation from which World War II erupted.

Just how far states should go in establishing controls of their economies and what administrative machinery should be created to give economic direction were practical issues throughout the 1930s. There were those, especially the Communists and some Socialists, who believed that the system of private capitalism had outlived its usefulness and that in its place should be created a system in which the state would own and manage the means of production and distribution for the well-being of all. Then there were those, the Fascists, who held that the interests of the state were superior to the interests of the individual, that economic policies could best be formulated by representatives of interest groups under Fascist control —employers, employees, and state officials—organized for each major industry, and that, although the institution of private property should be preserved, the state should aid, control, or seize properties in order to increase its economic and military strength. Lastly, there were those who thought that the economic situation could be saved without any structural changes, but by temporary governmental assistance to private concerns, especially by loans, tax relief, and limiting supplies of goods going to market.

The proposals made by Communists were not adopted in any part of Western culture. Property owners were generally opposed to them and nonpropertied, salaried workers were not generally convinced of their efficacy. They ran counter to a well-established respect for private initiative, and they, as practiced by the only state which followed them, the Union of Soviet Socialist Republics, became entangled with concepts of dictatorship. In Russia not only had the state taken over the chief means of producing and distributing goods and services, but it had concentrated on the development of basic industries necessary for the production of more machines and the sinews of war rather than on the production of goods to satisfy human wants. Moreover, the Communist Party, which numbered only 2 million out of a total population of 170 million in 1936, and Joseph Stalin, who dominated the Party from 1925 until his death in 1953, determined policy, enforced it relentlessly, and permitted only members of the bureaucracy to enjoy a really high standard of living. Many Socialists were of the opinion that the millennium of which they dreamed should come by gradual reform and they were willing to make compromises with their plans for reaching their ultimate goal by accepting immediately and peacefully attained advantages. Indeed, during the depression of the thirties Western European Socialism shifted from the rigidities of Marxian logic and Marxian ultimates to a kind of reformism based on economic planning and the welfare state.

Changes proposed by Fascists were not so drastic as those advanced by Communists and had the support of persons already in high authority in certain countries of the West. The model to which these supporters of authoritarianism, statism, and corporatism looked was that of Italy, where the Fascists of Benito Mussolini had seized power in 1922 to prevent, so they claimed, the triumph of international Socialism and where they had created, under the stress of labor difficulties and retarded economic development, a corporate state.[12]

The state where dictatorship along Fascist lines was most completely established was Germany. There National Socialists under Adolf Hitler came to power in 1933. All labor unions were done away with as in Italy, and were replaced by the state-controlled Labor Front. Property owners were organized according to their calling into the Estate of Trade and Industry, the Estate of Transportation, or the Estate of Agriculture; artists, teachers, professional men, and journalists became members of the Chamber of Culture. In fact, however, the entire entire economy was run by the dictatorship, with Hermann Göring as the chief economic potentate after February 1938.

---

[12] Society was organized into "corporations," that is, bodies representing employers, employees, and the Fascist Party for the major categories of economic activity. By 1934 there were twenty-two such bodies. They were to handle labor disputes, plan the activity of their division of the economy, and provide representatives to the legislative body of the nation. Fundamental decisions were, however, made by political leaders.

In other states, where the traditions of representative government and the right of individuals to life, liberty, and property prevailed, such extreme attempts at political control of the economy were not made. Yet in these states there was considerable agitation for reforms either in the direction of state socialism or of authoritarianism and there were many new policies adopted which deviated widely from liberal political and economic theory and practice.

The Great Depression: the remedies

Whatever political expedient was used to meet the existing crisis, economic measures in various countries had a considerable degree of similarity. To meet credit stringencies occasioned by the collapse of stock prices and by the calling in of loans by banks, most states declared brief debt moratoria, had their central banks extend credit, created specialized lending agencies to assist the hardest-pressed branches of their economies, devalued their currencies in an effort to raise prices, to reduce the burden of debt, and to encourage exports,[13] and limited imports by raising customs duties or by adopting import quotas.

In the United States, for example, banks were temporarily closed in March 1933, when Franklin D. Roosevelt was inaugurated President, and they were only gradually reopened as they could show evidence of being able to meet their obligations.[14] Furthermore, more power was given to the Federal Reserve System in order to regulate the flow of credit and presumably thereby to exercise control over business activity. In France, the number of governmentally appointed representatives of the Board of Regents of the Bank of France was increased (1936) in order to insure the adoption of more socially desirable credit policies; in Belgium, the bank reform of 1935 aimed at greater liquidity for banks, better management, and a control of the money flow to influence the course of business activity.

Among the countries which devalued their currencies were those whose moneys were used widely by various countries for reserves, which meant that pressure was put on many currencies to come into line with the leaders. The United States reduced in 1933 to 1934 the value of the dollar

[13] Higher prices meant, for example, that if a farmer raising pigs got 12 instead of 6 cents a pound for his porkers, he could pay off whatever debt he had with half the number of pigs than at the lower price.

Devaluation was expected to give temporary encouragement to exports in that prices would not go up as fast as exchange rates. Some states, especially Germany, attempted to stimulate exports by giving special exchange rates for the purchase of German goods and by making bilateral barter agreements.

[14] Federal Deposit Insurance was instituted by the Glass-Steagall bill on June 16, 1933. It insured deposits up to 5,000 dollars.

in terms of gold by 41 percent. England left the gold standard in 1931 and subsequently devalued by 30 percent. France devalued in 1936 and again in 1938 and the Netherlands and several other nations in 1936.[15]

In the United States, immediate relief was given to the unemployed by creating the Civilian Conservation Corps (1933) for reforestation, flood prevention, and soil erosion control, by launching a public works program (Public Works Administration, 1933), by setting up a Works Progress Administration (1935) for the employment of intellectuals and artists as well as manual laborers, and by beginning work on such great projects as the Tennessee Valley Authority and large dams in the West.[16]

In Europe, unemployment insurance schemes helped alleviate the plight of workers, especially in Great Britain, where 63 percent of the gainfully employed were covered and where public moneys were used to continue payments beyond existing reserves. In most states, however, public works projects were resorted to as unemployment continued to be a serious threat to social and political order. In Italy, considerable numbers of men were used on draining swamps and building roads. In Germany, many men were absorbed by the remilitarization of the country. In the Netherlands, workers found jobs in conjunction with the reclamation of the Zuider Zee (Figure 26). And in France, they were employed in building the Maginot Line, a heavily fortified military line facing Germany from the Swiss border to the Ardennes, or in constructing such dams as the Genissiat on the Upper Rhône River.

Of greater long-range significance was the practice of states to buy securities of ailing business concerns or to lend them so much money that governments acquired a direct voice in business management. In the United States, the Reconstruction Finance Corporation with resources of 4 billion dollars was established (1932) by the government to make loans to business concerns. In Italy, the Institute for Reconstruction of Industry (IRI) was set up (1933) to give financial assistance to Italian industries— an action which was so enormous that by 1937 the state had an interest in 40 percent of all Italian corporations. In France, the government lent money to all its important shipping companies, to civil aviation concerns, to railways, and to banks. Great Britain made loans to complete the construction of the *Queen Mary*. Austria guaranteed to cover the obligations of the *Creditanstalt*, and Germany financed such projects as the hydrogenation of coal in order to have a national supply of gasoline.

---

[15] A World Economic Conference was held in London in June 1933, but it failed to bring order into the chaos of money. In 1937, the United Kingdom, the United States, and France made a Tripartite Agreement to keep steady the relationship of the dollar, pound, and franc.

[16] Also set up were the Federal Emergency Relief Administration (May 1933) to supplement direct relief provided by individual states and the Civil Works Administration in the winter of 1933-1934 to provide temporary employment on public works.

Figure 26
Land reclaimed from the Zuider Zee. The reclamation of land from the
Zuider Zee was pushed as a public works project during the depression
of the thirties. This picture shows farms established on the land. The
salt has been leached out and production has begun. Land is distributed
equally among the three religious divisions of the Netherlands—
Protestant, Catholic, and "humanistic." *(Courtesy of the Netherlands
Information Service.)*

In almost all countries, agriculture received very special treatment, because of the particularly disastrous financial plight of farmers, because of a desire to maintain a large farm population for sentimental, social, and political reasons, and in part because of a hope to attain greater national self-sufficiency in foodstuffs. In the United Kingdom, prices for the major grains were guaranteed beginning with the Wheat Act of 1932, and agricultural production was given protection of high tariffs and quotas, a policy which not only definitely broke Britain's low-tariff tradition but which also made possible a granting of preferential treatment to goods coming into the United Kingdom.[17]

Denmark endeavored to alter its agricultural production, reducing what it had exported and increasing what it had imported. Thus it brought down the number of pigs from 5 to 3 million by rationing the number which could be sold. It diminished the number of cattle by purchasing and slaughtering females with funds obtained by a tax on slaughter, and it increased the output of beet sugar until the country was self-sufficient. France gave subsidies to winegrowers for pulling up vines, discouraged the production of low-grade wines, limited the percentage of flour that might be obtained from wheat, and supported the prices of various agricultural products. Like the United Kingdom, the Netherlands gave up free trade by protecting its agriculture and, like Denmark, tried to shift production to meet domestic needs. And Germany expanded output, temporarily required farm laborers to remain in farming, and protected small holdings by the Inherited Freehold Act (1933)—a law which forbade owners from mortgaging their holdings, from selling portions of their farms, from breaking them up at inheritance, or from restricting production on pain of forfeiting their titles.

In the United States, where the market was glutted with staples and where prices had fallen to a ridiculously low level, President Roosevelt's New Deal aimed at bringing production more nearly into line with demand and at raising prices by placing a tax on processors, as was being done in England,[18] in order to get funds which could be used to compensate farmers who voluntarily reduced production. This restrictive policy raised a hue and cry as little pigs were done away with and big land companies got huge payments for not raising crops. But it was persisted in, for when the Supreme Court declared (1936) the enabling law to be unconstitutional on the ground that it infringed states' rights, Congress immediately passed the Soil Conservation and Domestic Allotments Act, which provided for payments from funds voted by Congress to farmers for diverting acreage from

---

[17] This system was inaugurated by the Ottawa Agreements in 1932. Hitherto members of the empire could give preferences to English-made goods, but the United Kingdom could offer no substantial tariff advantages in return.

[18] For example, 30 cents a bushel was charged on milled wheat.

overproduced crops to soil-conserving crops and for adopting soil-building practices (Figure 27).[19] Finally, the New Deal endeavored to lighten the financial burden on farms (about 40 percent of them were mortgaged) by creating the Farm Credit Administration, which made loans totaling 1.2 billion dollars from 1933 to 1936, and to reduce "agricultural slums" by resettling farmers who were living on submarginal soils to better lands.

In addition to all these efforts to deal with the depression, the states of Western culture took steps to bring some order into labor relations. In Italy[20] and Germany, strikes and lockouts were outlawed and labor contracts were virtually forced by the state upon governmentally sponsored organizations of employers and employees. In France, the doctrine of collective bargaining, that is, of contracts between business concerns and trade unions for entire industries, was accepted by the Matignon Accords (1936)[21] and compulsory arbitration was attempted. And in the United States, the National Recovery Act (1933) required labor codes (contracts) in all major plants, thus practically forcing the formation of labor unions. Then the Wagner Labor Relations Act (1935), passed when the NRA was found to be unconstitutional,[22] strengthened the bargaining position of labor.

All the various measures which were taken to cope with the depression involved a certain amount of economic planning and made apparent the necessity of "plans" if states were going to continue to intervene so extensively in their economies. Already economic planning had been given a considerable impetus in Soviet Russia, where exceptional economic progress was called for by successive five-year plans.[23] Moreover, planning had been widely publicized in both Fascist Italy and Nazi Germany, where it was inherent in the corporate state system. Even in many countries, like France, where the existing system remained intact, a step toward planning was taken by the creation of advisory economic councils. These bodies represented labor, capital, consumers, and the state and were created for the purposes of studying national economic issues and of making recommendations to the legislative and executive branches of government.[24]

[19] The new Agricultural Adjustment Act (1938) aimed particularly at supporting prices. Loans could be made to farmers for storing surpluses in years of high output. Marketing quotas were established if two-thirds of the producers of a crop in a district agreed. Parity payments were made to producers of some crops if the relationship between farm and industrial prices fell 75 percent below the average of prices in the period 1910-1914.

Furthermore, the Commodity Credit Corporation (1933) did some purchasing of commodities to regulate the market. It played its most important role, however, during and after World War II.

[20] In 1926.

[21] Matignon is the name of the palace of the Premier, where the agreement was signed.

[22] On the ground that Congress could not delegate legislative powers to the President.

[23] They were drafted by the "Gosplan," a planning bureau established in 1921, which was, in fact, a committee of the Council of Peoples' Commissars. It should be added that over-all planning was practically forced on the U.S.S.R. by its system of state socialism.

[24] Trade unionists in France had been particularly active in the campaign in favor of planning. The Confédération Générale de Travail proposed a planning body immediately after World War I.

The concept of economic planning was thus well established before 1939, although it was only after World War II that it became more than an expedient (Chapter 21).

Just as most of the measures used to deal with the depression involved planning, most relied upon considerable governmental expenditure as

Figure 27
Contour planting: The fields in the foreground have been contour plowed and contour planted. They contrast clearly with the solid field cultivation of the fields just beyond them. Soil conservation is aided by the planting of trees at crucial points where erosion might be great because of the runoff of water from the low spots in the contours. *(Courtesy of the United States Department of Agriculture's Photographic Service.)*

well. Policymakers came to realize that the very basis of the hardship was a vicious circle of insufficient *effective demand.* The key problem was that as unemployment grew, individuals cut back on consumption because those who were out of work could not afford to buy as much as before and those who still held their jobs saved all that they could in fear of being next off the payroll. As consumption fell, of course, production fell; plants became idle and more workers were laid off, further reducing the ranks of able consumers. Governments fought this cycle by injecting funds into the economy and putting people back on the job in public works projects and subsidized private enterprises. In 1936 a major contribution to economic theory helped increase the general understanding of these processes. John Maynard Keynes, a Cambridge economist, published in that year *The General Theory of Employment, Interest, and Money,* in which he demonstrated the importance of aggregate demand and its relation to employment. In lucid and engaging prose Keynes showed that governments possessed in their spending power the most powerful tool for combating cyclical downturns by being able to adjust the level of aggregate demand.[25] The power to tax, it was shown, could likewise be used to cool an overheated economy and to control too rapid growth and inflation. The present-day reliance on fiscal policy as a major economic stabilizer in capitalist economies stems directly from the experiences of the depression and the "new economics" of Keynes and his followers.

To the factors which thus contributed toward extending the state's role in economic life should be added two more—preparation for war and subsequently war itself. Up to the present time, war has been the single greatest economic activity of national states. Expenditures for national defense more than doubled in the United Kingdom, France, and the U.S.S.R. from 1937 to 1939, and probably the increases in Germany and Italy were even larger. In these states expenditures for defense appear to have averaged more than half of all expenditures immediately before World War II.

These large amounts of public funds were obtained partly by taxation, partly by borrowing, and partly by the issuing of paper money. Tax rates were pushed up, especially on income taxes. New taxes, like sales taxes and taxes on bachelors, were introduced, and a few capital levies, for example

---

[25] "If the Treasury were to fill old bottles with banknotes, bury them at suitable depths in disused coal mines which are then filled up the surface with town rubbish, and leave it to private enterprise on well-tried principles of *laissez-faire* to dig up the notes again..., there need be no more unemployment and, with the help of the repercussions, the real income of the community, and its capital wealth also, would probably become a good deal greater than it actually is. It would, indeed, be more sensible to build houses and the like; but if there are political and practical difficulties in the way of this, the above would be better than nothing." (*The General Theory,* 1964 ed., New York, Harcourt, Brace & World, p.129.)

Detractors of government deficit-spending policies contend that too many government projects "bury" money (or throw it away) without adequate social returns.

in Italy, were attempted. Taxes were raised to a point where in 1937 to 1938 they took 28 percent of national income in France and 23 percent in the United Kingdom.

Borrowing was also increased so that in many states the public debt exceeded national income, that of France being 71 percent in excess and that of the United Kingdom, 63 percent. And in nearly all countries state treasuries got advances in currency from banks of issue in return for promises to pay, or otherwise got moneys from the fiduciary system. An increase in the supply of money was thus effected without any increase in the production of goods—and this increase meant in the long run an increase in prices.

Thus in the period between the two World Wars the national state became an economic Leviathan, completely dwarfing the primarily political monster described by Thomas Hobbes in the seventeenth century. It tried to keep relatively orderly relations between capital and labor. It effected "savings" by taxing, borrowing, or extending credit to take the place of or to supplement private savings and investment when these were considered wanting. It endeavored to direct the distribution of goods in both domestic and foreign trade. And it moved in the direction of planning the entire economic life of its citizens. Such was the economy of Western culture when World War II broke upon it.

20

The economics of World War II

World War I and World War II compared

In many ways World War II was similar to World War I. Like its predecessor, it developed out of rivalries within the national state system —and these rivalries in both instances became crystallized into hostile blocs of Great Powers. Also like its forerunner, World War II was at the outset essentially a conflict among states in Western culture and thus from the point of view of the culture was a "civil" war. Furthermore, World War II, like World War I, developed into a war of attrition between two great economic potentials, which led to a new extension of state control over economic life. And like its precursor, World War II was enormously destructive. In fact, by one estimate, the total cost of the war, including destruction, amounted to 3,000 billion dollars. Expenditures for war materials alone came to 1,154 billion dollars. This was at least seven times the cost of World War I, and World War I had set a record in this respect. Casualties, both military and civilian, were said to have been 22,060,000 dead and 34.4 million wounded. Millions more suffered malnutrition. Over 30 million people in Europe were displaced by the conflict, and all ordinary economic relationships were gravely dislocated. World War II was a large edition of World War I. It was, indeed, a "total war."

In spite of similarities, however, there were certain differences between the two great World Wars of the first half of the twentieth century. In the first place, the Axis powers represented a set of ideologies which were more foreign to the basic tenets of Western culture than anything that Germany alone had stood for in World War I—the subordination of the individual to the state, a brazen duplicity in international relations without any regard for law or honesty,[1] and a disrespect for what the West called "human rights": life, liberty, and freedom of thought and of expression. In the second place, World War II germinated in the depression of the 1930s, when several states without great natural resources (Italy and Japan) or without overseas empires (Germany) considered themselves to be deprived of what should be theirs and adopted an avowed policy of territorial aggrandizement in the belief that thereby they would achieve economic growth.[2] Further, World War I and the dislocations that followed were partly responsible for the acceptance of wildly extremist and belligerent political ideologies that in turn led to the second conflagration. The political and economic instability that afflicted Germany, particularly in the years following the 1914 to 1918 war, and the unrealistic Versailles settlement had much to do with the appeal of National Socialism for large segments of the German population. Hitler's rearmament promised (and indeed achieved) renewed prosperity for the middle class of Germany, which had suffered both in the inflationary twenties and again in the depression. For industrial workers a virtual end to unemployment was realized. For those elements of society who felt the greatest frustrations from the scale and complexity of modern life, such as small farmers, shopkeepers, and artisans, Nazism proffered a return to old values of farm and village, an end to "cosmopolitan" influences, and a renewal of simple love of the fatherland.

The military issues

Although World War II began formally by Germany's attack on poland, September 1, 1939, forerunners of the conflict had been clearly in evidence since 1931. Late in that year Japan attacked in Manchuria China; subsequently it attempted a conquest of the entire nation. In 1936 Germany began the remilitarization of the Rhineland, contrary to the terms of the Versailles Treaty. Mussolini conquered Ethiopia. Germany and Italy sent forces to fight for General Franco in Spain, while the U.S.S.R. sent troops there to assist the Republicans. In 1938 Germany annexed Austria and, following the Munich Conference, took the Sudetenland from Czechoslovakia. In 1939 Germany annexed Bohemia and Moravia and set up Slo-

---

When Hitler informed his generals of his plans for attacking Poland, he said "No one will ask the whether or not he told the truth. In starting the war it is not right that matters, but victory."

[2] In his book *Mein Kampf*, Hitler had written: "We have finished with the pre-World War I policy of colonies and trade and are going over to a land policy of the future." He was also fearful of Russia. "The political testament of Germany must always be never to tolerate the establishment of two continental powers in Europe." He was much impressed by concepts of *Geopolitik*, as generated by a Swede named Kjellén and developed by a German, Karl Haushofer. He stated very frankly, "If the Urals with their incalculable wealth of raw materials, the rich forests of Siberia, and the unending wheatfields of the Ukraine lay within Germany, under National Socialist leadership this country would swim in plenty."

vakia as a protectorate, while Ruthenia was occupied by Hungarian troops. Germany seized Memel and a part of Lithuania. Italy annexed Albania, and Germany signed with Russia the famous Nonaggression Pact. By this agreement the signatories pledged to refrain from aggressive action toward each other for ten years; both carved out spheres of influence, the Russian being east of a line running from the west of Latvia and to the west of Bessarabia and the German being west of that line.

With Germany's invasion of Poland, events in Eastern Europe moved with lightning rapidity. Not only was the military operation a veritable Blitzkrieg (Warsaw capitulated on September 27), but Russia invaded Poland to "protect its frontiers," virtually established its dominion over Estonia, Latvia, and Lithuania, and launched a war against Finland that continued until March 1940. On the Western Front, however, action was initially almost nonexistent and so the war there, in contrast to that in the East, was dubbed a *Sitzkrieg* (Sit-down-war). The calm on the Western Front was, however, simply a lull before the storm. From April 9, 1940, to June 17, 1940, Germany overran Denmark, Norway, the Netherlands, Belgium, and France in quick succession. Italy, thinking that a final decision in the fighting had been reached, declared war on France and Britain. Hitler then turned his air force on Britain and simultaneously brought Romania, Hungary, and Bulgaria into line. Then Italy attacked Yugoslavia and Greece—an effort that was not brought to a successful conclusion until Germany lent a hand (April 1941).

In the meantime, Germany's air attack on Britain had not been equally successful. Although the raids did cause great damage, German air losses were enormous (2,375 planes up to the end of October 1940) and the Royal Air Force had managed to give the Germans a taste of their own medicine —and it was bitter stuff. Nor had Germany's submarine campaign been overwhelmingly effective, for although many ships were sunk (twenty-nine Allied ships went to the bottom in one week in March 1941), many ships were getting through. Moreover, President Franklin D. Roosevelt decided in the crisis to transfer a million tons of merchant shipping to Britain along with fifty overage destroyers.

From the Allied point of view, however, the most hopeful prospect for the future came from the fact that the Germans made the colossal blunder of invading Russia (June 22, 1941), and the Japanese, who were allied with Germany, had the folly to attack Pearl Harbor (December 7, 1941), thus bringing the United States into the war—a situation which Hitler had recognized in *Mein Kampf* as having been disastrous to Germany in World War I and to be avoided at all costs. Undoubtedly he thought that the war in the West was as good as over[3] and that Russia, an "uncooperative ally,"

---

[3] Hitler was so sure that he had Britain at his mercy that he ordered cutbacks in the production of war matériel. This action subsequently led to shortages in Germany.

should be dealt with before it became militarily any stronger. Germany's invasion of Russia, in spite of the fact that it led to the conquest in five months of an area three times that of the home country, sapped Germany's strength in manpower and matériel. Moreover, the United States provided the Allies with men and goods which were eventually to overwhelm the Axis Powers.[4]

The war of economic potentials

By December 1941, therefore, the Sitzkrieg-Blitzkrieg aspect of World War II was over, and the struggle became one between opposing economic potentials, as had World War I after November 1914. Some idea of the magnitudes of the opponents can be seen from Table 41. The Axis was aware of the preponderance in favor of the Allies; hence its strategy dictated an early, final decision. The Allies' plans, on the contrary, called for a holding operation pending a build-up of matériel and the training of fighting personnel—and then the delivery of a mighty blow.

The "war of economic potentials" had four distinct aspects. In the first place, it led to the "total mobilization" of the manpower and economic resources of each of the belligerents, to greater governmental controls of the various economies, and to more complete economic planning than had existed either in World War I or in the depression of the thirties. In the second place, it made urgent the reduction of the enemy's productive capacity by every possible means, especially by airplane and rocket bombings. The bombings in turn led to a policy of total destruction and this policy gave the last part of the war its most distinctive characteristic, that of a *Vernichtungskrieg.* Thirdly, it led the Axis to milk its conquered countries dry, and the Allies, because of their control of most of the seas, to draw upon the entire nonbelligerent world for supplies. And fourthly, it meant that because the Allies had to deliver goods and men overseas to fighting fronts the Axis powers could try to prevent such deliveries by submarine and air attacks on shipping—a repetition of the naval character of World War I.

The economic controls and plans which the belligerents established resembled those of World War I, but they were more rigorous and more inclusive. Rationing of consumers' goods, especially foodstuffs, was prac-

---

[4] Even before the attack on Pearl Harbor the United States was giving aid to the Allies. Although the Neutrality Act of 1935 required the placing of an embargo on arms to belligerents, it was gradually repealed. The United States sent munitions on a "cash and carry" basis to Britain and France (beginning November 4, 1939). Congress passed the Lend-Lease Act to send arms to the Allies in March 1941, and it permitted American ships to enter the war zones (November 1941).

ticed everywhere. In Europe, where food was usually imported, shortages were so great that the calorie intake of individuals was determined by one's

Table 41. Opposing economic potentials in World War II

Country	National income, millions of dollars at 1925–1934 prices	Percentage of world manufactures, 1936–1938	Population
United Nations*			
United States	66,203	32.2	131,669,000
United Kingdom	21,854	9.2	46,046,000
U.S.S.R.	17,230	18.5	170,467,000
China	?	?	450,000,000
Australia	2,543		6,630,000
Canada	5,084	2	11,507,000
New Zealand	691		1,574,000
India	?		382,000,000
Axis Powers and Axis-occupied countries			
Germany	17,580	10.7	79,375,000
Italy	5,320	2.7	42,919,000
Japan	8,171	3.5	73,114,000
Austria	1,013		†
Czechoslovakia	2,680		14,729,000
Poland	3,428		32,107,000
Hungary	1,205		14,683,000
Romania	1,471		13,493,000
France	12,480		41,183,000
Belgium	2,033		8,092,000
The Netherlands	2,624		7,936,000
Denmark	1,008		3,844,000
Norway	607		2,814,000
Yugoslavia	1,352		13,934,000

*The term "United Nations" was used during the war to indicate the Allies.
† Included in Germany.

nationality, one's age, and the extent of one's muscular output (Table 42). Such huge curbs were placed on fats, in great demand for explosives, that at one time British miners were entitled to one small cake of soap per month. Moreover, men of military age became liable for military service or other work. Every effort was made to use manpower effectively and to augment the labor force. In the United States, the number of civilian workers was increased, even though some 11 million men were under arms, by the employment of retired persons, women, and young people who normally would have been in school. Production was directed more and more toward war ends by governmental orders, by tax arrangements, by price fixing, by the directing of governmental investments, and by publicity. Finally, overall plans were laid down by governments for quantities and qualities of things needed for the prosecution of the war.

Table 42. Calories in normal consumer's rations per day

Country	1941	1942	1943	1944
Germany	1,990	1,750	1,980	1,930
Italy	1,010	950	990	1,065
Belgium	1,360	1,365	1,320	1,555
France	1,365	1,115	1,080	1,115
Poland	845	1,070	855	1,200

Under such controls and plans remarkable results were achieved. The United States increased its production of merchant ships from 342,000 deadweight tons in 1939 to 19,238,000 tons in 1943.[5] It stepped up aircraft output from 12,804 in 1940 to 49,761 in 1945. And in addition to all the war matériel it turned out, it was able to produce more civilian goods than it had prior to the conflict. Although the U.S.S.R. lost to the Germans territory accounting for 63 percent of its coal production, 57 percent of its steel, and 40 percent of its arable, it built up a new industrial area in the Urals and beyond the Volga. As a result its industrial output at the end of the war was down only 8 percent compared with that of 1939. Similarly, Japan's index of manufacturing production went from 100 in 1937 to 153 in 1944, and Germany increased its coal and lignite production by 30 percent from 1937–1938 to 1943–1944. In spite of such accomplishments, however, many mistakes in planning were inevitably made because of constant changes in estimates of the way the fighting was going, in types of equipment required, and in production facilities. The greatest blunder was undoubtedly perpetrated by Hitler, who ordered cutbacks in

---

[5] During the war the United States built a total tonnage equal to some two-thirds of the world's merchant tonnage of 1939.

schedules of production in September 1941, because he thought the war had been won. The resulting disorder was so extensive that a veritable crisis in German military supplies occurred in 1942.

In addition to establishing rigorous economic controls within their economies, the belligerents did their utmost to draw upon the resources of others and to pool supplies so that their stores would be used most effectively. In the case of the Axis powers, such policies meant a harsh exploitation of conquered areas and a veritable dictation by Germany and Japan of how materials should be distributed. After the defeat of France, for example, Germany seized railway rolling stock, rubber, stockpiles of gasoline, and nonferrous metals, required the payment of large indemnities which were used to purchase French goods out of current production and to acquire title to plants, established a favorable exchange rate for the mark so that Germans would be induced to purchase French goods, and set up a "clearing account" in Berlin, where sums owed France were allowed to accumulate. Furthermore, the Germans required the conquered areas to send them forced labor to such an extent that at the end of the war about one in every three workers in Germany was of this category. Lastly, Germany inaugurated its long-range plan for the Continent—a plan in which Germany was to be a great industrial center and its satellites were to supply her with foodstuffs and raw materials. In this way Germany aimed to keep her potential enemies in a perpetual state of economic subordination.[6]

In the case of the Allies, or of the United Nations, as they came to be called, Interallied cooperation became the watchword of the hour. Military action and material needs were determined in large part by the Anglo American Combined Chiefs of Staff in Washington (created February 1942) which collaborated with Russia and China by means of Allied Military Missions in Moscow and Chungking. Similarly, economic cooperation was effected by the Combined Shipping Adjustment Board (January 1942) in Washington, the Combined Raw Materials Board, the Combined Food Board, and the Combined Production and Resources Board. Then to avoid a postwar Allied war debt problem, a decision was reached to "lend-lease" materials among the Allies. Thus, the United States furnished its Allies up to July 1, 1945, with goods at a cost of 47,286 million dollars, with the United Kingdom and the U.S.S.R. receiving nearly equal amounts, and obtained in reverse lend-lease goods and services valued at 7,912 million dollars. Finally, the United Nations purchased heavily in the free markets of the world. The United States increased its imports at current prices by

---

[6] Japan's long-range plan for the East was not unlike Germany's. Japan exploited the "Co-Prosperity Sphere," that is, the areas which it had conquered, and intended to draw from the "outer zone" raw materials and foodstuffs and to process them in the "inner zone," Japan, Korea, Manchuria, and North China.

80 percent. The United Kingdom spent so much of its foreign investments that it became a debtor to a host of countries, including India, with which it had had for years a creditor position.

That the United Nations were able to draw on the resources of a large part of the earth and were able to maintain such a large volume of production accounts in a high degree for their final victory. Yet their superiority in matériel, especially as evidenced by firepower at the fronts, was for a long time in jeopardy. American mass-production methods required a long time to get under way and shipping losses were enormous. In fact, in 1942, 25 percent of the ships on the run to Murmansk to carry supplies to Russia were sunk and the loss of Allied and neutral shipping in 1942 was 8,338,000 gross tons.[7] Only when convoys were given adequate air protection from "baby flattops" after May 1943 did the submarine threat seem to be met. In desperation the Germans launched against Britain (June 1944) their famous rocket bombs, but these missiles were not accurate enough either to reduce drastically Britain's production or to destroy the vast depots of matériel ready for the trans-Channel invasion of the Continent (June 6, 1944).

Threatening as were German measures to curb Allied deliveries to war fronts and effective as was the Japanese war in drawing American supplies from Europe to the Allies' "second front," retaliatory measures of the United Nations were eventually overpowering. Not only did the Allies establish blockades of their opponents and blacklist firms which dealt with Axis powers, but they launched great air attacks against their enemies. They threw Germany and Italy out of North Africa and invaded the Italian peninsula. Later, they knocked Japan out of the war by dropping the first nuclear bombs.

The air forces of the Allies in the West flew nearly one and a half million bomber sorties to the Continent and dropped over two and a half million tons of bombs. At first both the British and American air forces tried daylight "pinpoint" bombing, but soon, because of heavy losses, gave up this tactic for saturation bombing. Consequently whole areas were laid waste. In August 1943, an attack on Hamburg destroyed one-third of all dwellings and killed between 60,000 and 100,000 civilians.[8]

Target priorities in this great air war changed with military exigencies, Early in 1943 special attention was given to submarine building yards and aircraft factories. In May 1944 oil plants became an objective of first consideration, and in September 1944 transportation was bombed heavily

---

[7] The total loss of Allied and neutral shipping up to June 13, 1945, was 21,141,000 gross tons, or about one-third of the world's prewar tonnage.

[8] Air raiders also took their toll of Axis shipping in the Baltic, North, and Mediterranean Seas, the Royal Air Force bagging 750,000 tons in the first half of 1942.

in order to prevent the massing of men and matériel to meet the invaders who had landed in Normandy in June. How effective this strategic bombing was has been the object of considerable controversy, but no one who visited the Continent, especially Germany, after the cessation of hostilities could help but be appalled by the extent of the destruction. In the case of oil plants, every major establishment was hit by July 1944, and the production of aviation gasoline fell from 175,000 tons in April 1944 to 5,000 tons in September. In the case of transportation, freight car loadings declined from 900,000 cars a week in August 1944 to 214,000 cars during the week of March 3, 1945, coal traffic was practically stopped by February 1945, and the movement of troops by rail became extremely slow and cumbersome.

In the Pacific, bombings of the Japanese homeland were begun in earnest with the conquest of Okinawa (April–June 1945), for thereby the United States got a base within easy striking distance of the central Japanese islands. Air attack reached its climax with the use of the first nuclear weapons. The atom bomb which hit Hiroshima was said to have killed 80,000 out of a population of 245,000, to have seriously injured another 80,000 and to have destroyed 60 percent of all buildings; the bomb dropped on Nagasaki killed 40,000, injured an equal number, and so demoralized the entire nation that the Japanese government decided at once to sue for peace.

In addition to the havoc wrought by strategic air and rocket attacks, there was the destruction by the more traditional weapons of land forces. All resistance points were heavily shelled and reduced to shambles, as at Cassino, Salerno, Anzio, and Pisa in Italy, at Cherbourg and Sedan in France, and at Saarbrücken and Aachen in Germany.

Thus the productive capacity of the Axis powers and their occupied areas was reduced at the very time when Germany's overextended lines were demanding ever-greater deliveries of goods and when workers on the home front were so driven that they needed more nourishment than they were getting to maintain their energies and more goods to keep up their morale. Through destroying the economies of their enemies and through increasing their own production of goods, as well as by victories in the field, did the United Nations win the war.

The economic consequences of the war

The destruction which has just been mentioned was one of the most obvious economic results of the second great war of the twentieth century. Desolation was the hallmark of the fighting, but in addition much capital equipment which remained standing had run down because of poor maintenance practices. Furthermore, Europe's stock of raw materials had become so exhausted and the long "pipelines" of supply had become so empty that some time and much capital were needed to fill them again. Finally, agricultural land that had not been laid waste had been over-cropped and deprived of its usual supplies of commercial fertilizers, and livestock populations had been depleted because of the pressure for food. Thus it is not surprising that both the industrial and agricultural production of the European nations had greatly decreased, whereas that of the overseas areas, which were sources of supply, as in the case of the United States and Canada, had grown at a rapid rate (Table 43). To be sure, some capital investment had been made in Europe during the war, but for the most part it was very spotty, Thus there was little expansion in materials-producing industries, like steel, in consumers' goods industries generally, in housing, or in transport, with the result that there were bottlenecks in these lines in the first years of reconstruction. What European economic expansion there was was limited largely to motive-power industries, especially in the smaller countries, and to the machine-tool industry, notably in Germany.[9]

Table 43. Indices of production

Country	Industry (1953 = 100)			Wheat production (1934–1938 = 100)
	1938	1946	1948	1947
West Germany	78		41	48
Italy	62		62	63
Austria	59		54	
Japan	88	24	38	
France	71	60	81	40
Belgium	71	63	87	
United Kingdom	71	72	83	
United States	36	67	78	191
U.S.S.R.	30	29	45	
Canada	41	69	79	129

In the United States, on the other hand, the expansion of basic industries, such as synthetic rubber, nitrogen, potash, magnesium, copper, salt,

---

[9] Motive power increased 23 percent in the Netherlands from 1939 to 1945 and by 35 percent in Denmark. Expansion of the machine-tool industry in Germany amounted to 75 percent from 1938 to 1943.

steel, and coal, not to mention agriculture, was very great. This was because the United States was the "economic arsenal" of the United Nations;
to fulfill its military task it had to expand plant and produce what it had
formerly imported. Thus at the end of the war the United States, and to
a lesser extent Canada and Australia, had productive capacity for the
things which the whole world was demanding.

Destruction, undermaintenance of plant, uneven economic investment,
and a great movement of expansion in the United States made Europe's
position at the conclusion of hostilities difficult enough to discourage the
most optimistic. Yet Europe's condition was made worse by heavy public
debts, by new waves of inflation, by an almost complete breakdown of the
system of multilateral trade and payments, by unfavorable terms of trade,
by territorial changes, by reparations demands, and, as we shall see in the
next chapter, by social and political disturbances.

Europe's public finance problems, which had been grave at the end of
the depression of the 1930s, became much more serious as a result of heavy
war expenditures. When a nation's very survival is at stake, public expenditures are increased with almost reckless abandon, for penny-pinching
policies have no place under the circumstances. Thus, the United Kingdom
augmented its expenditures from 1,147 million pounds in 1938 to 1939 to
6,190 million in 1944 to 1945; Germany increased its expenses nearly
eleven times, and other belligerents extended theirs in comparable proportions. Efforts were made to obtain a part of the sums spent from individuals
and corporations by either taxation or borrowing in order to reduce the
purchasing power of those who were buyers of consumers' goods, especially luxuries, and to curb the holdings of those who might make excessive profits. This policy was particularly pushed in the United Kingdom,
where the income tax was about doubled, with very heavy surtaxes on
large incomes, where tax revenues were increased three and a half times,
and where taxes covered about 25 percent of war expenditures.

As in World War, I, however, belligerents in World War II went to their
banks of issue for funds to meet their bills, giving these banks their
"IOU's"as security. With the new reserves thus furnished them, the banks
of issue increased the amount of money in circulation or the amount of
credit available to individuals in commercial bank deposits. In the period
from 1938 to 1945 these amounts ranged from four times for money in
circulation and three times for deposit money in the United Kingdom to
nearly twenty times for circulating money and seventeen times for deposit
money in Italy. Inasmuch as national income did not increase in similar
proportions, the "income velocity of money," that is, the rate of turnover
of money against final income, went up but little. Consequently the foundation was laid for a large increase in price—an increase which came for
the most part after the cessation of hostilities.

Equally calamitous was the international situation in trade and payments . Western Europe had liquidated so much of its external investments that whereas its earnings on these holdings in 1938 had equaled 32 percent of its exports, in 1950 to 1951 earnings on investments amounted to only 9 percent of what it sold to the rest of the world. Furthermore, Europe had accumulated new debts abroad, which required a 7 percent increase in the 1938 volume of exports in order to provide for repayment. Prices of what Europe sold the rest of the world had not risen so much as those of foodstuffs and raw materials which it imported (the disadvantage was about 15 percent in 1946) (Table 44). Earnings from shipping were down because of the loss of ships, and earnings from banking and insurance had also fallen, although to a lesser degree. In fact, Western Europe as a whole had to increase its exports by 80 percent over 1938 in order to pay for the same value of imports of that year.

Table 44. Indices of wholesale prices (1963 = 100)

Country	1938	1945	1950	1963	1969	1970	1971
United States	42	57	87	100	113	117	120
United Kingdom	30	50	78	100	121	126	133
France	4	13	70	100	116	124	127
West Germany	43		80	100	101	107	112
Italy	2	36	87	100	111	119	123
Switzerland	43	89	87	100	107	112	114
Belgium	23	76	88	100	113	118	117
The Netherlands	25	45*	82	100	117	124	125

SOURCE: *Statistical Yearbooks of the United Nations, 1956, 1965, 1973.*

*December 1946.

The difficulties of achieving this increase were particularly burdensome. To begin with, Europe had to fill the so-called "pipeline" of raw materials which it imported before it could start to export on a large scale; and importing required paying in foreign currencies, which Europe did not have. Moreover, Europe encountered more difficulty than formerly in selling its wares because the non-European world had endeavored to industrialize. Then, too, some of Europe's suppliers of foodstuffs, like the Argentine, had trouble in selling to Europe in prewar quantities because of Europe's efforts to produce its own food. Some areas, like Eastern Europe, were unable or unwilling to maintain exports to Western Europe of materials like petroleum. And some regions, like India, which were trying to industrialize, wanted heavy capital goods that could be obtained most readily from the United States.

For these various reasons Europe turned its own purchases more and more to the United States, although it had difficulty in selling its goods there because of American industrialization, mass production at low cost, and protective tariffs. To make matters worse, the United States had begun to produce materials that, before the war, it had bought in areas with which Europe had an excess of exports over imports and where Europe had thus been able to be paid in dollars. All of these changes resulted in a situation in which Europe bought more than formerly from the dollar area and the United States spent fewer dollars abroad in regions where Europe's trading position was strong. Thus Europe had a "dollar shortage," that is, a deficit in trade and payments with the dollar area. Because of this deficit Europe had to control its imports and could not permit the free convertibility or exchange of its moneys for other currencies. Consequently a serious handicap was put upon multilateral trade and payments both in the world and within Europe itself.

During the course of the war the Allies began to make plans to mitigate these difficulties in capital equipment, in trade, in payments, and in convertibility of moneys. In 1944 their representatives met at Bretton Woods, New Hampshire, to create two financial agencies which could provide credit for rebuilding what had been destroyed, for developing economically backward areas, and for stabilizing exchange rates. These agencies were the International Bank for Reconstruction and Development, with a capital of 9.1 billion dollars, and the International Monetary Fund, with a capital of 8 billion dollars. Furthermore, the American draft for the projected United Nations provided for an Economic and Social Council that was to sponsor an International Trade Organization, which would liberalize trade and thereby, perhaps, reduce international tensions.

Territorial changes, reparations, and war debts

At the conclusion of World War II the victors did not rush headlong into the making of formal peace treaties, as they had after World War I, for there was some feeling that a more reasonable and viable settlement would be possible after emotions had subsided during a "cooling-off period." Moreover, there had been enough differences between the U.S.S.R. and its Allies to induce the conquerors to postpone final decisions, that is, to keep the situation fluid, so that they might strengthen their respective positions or save face by procrastination if their views did not prevail. Yet, despite delay in negotiating a peace treaty with the major enemy, certain issues had to be resolved and what appeared to be temporary arrangements became in effect definitive settlements. Decisions regarding boundaries are a case in point, for they became in essence permanent and permitted a subsequent creation of spheres of influence. Inasmuch as trade between such spheres came to almost a standstill, territorial arrangements had an important bearing on the subsequent development of Europe and, indeed, of the whole world.

In the case of Germany, decisions were reached piecemeal well before victory was attained. They began with the Moscow Conference in October 1943, when the foreign ministers of the United States, the United Kingdom, and the U.S.S.R. decided that a European Consultative Commission should be created to determine policies regarding the military occupation of Germany.[10] It was this Commission which fixed the limits of the zones of occupation in Germany and thus drew the crucial line between the sphere dominated by Russia and that dominated by the major Allies. Essentially, this meant that Russia was going to be able to control the entire region eastward from the western line of its occupation zone; the Allied dream of a *cordon sanitaire,* consisting of Poland, Czechoslovakia, Hungary, and Romania on the European boundaries of Russia was shattered. Moreover, Russia's position in Eastern Europe was strengthened at the Yalta Conference (February 1945) and at the Potsdam Conference (July 1945). At the former it was agreed that the eastern boundary of Poland should be the "Curzon Line," which gave Russia a part of prewar Poland, and at the latter, that the western boundary of Poland was to be a line from the Baltic Sea west of Swinemünde and thence along the Oder and Neisse Rivers to Czechoslovakia and that the western boundary of Russia was to be a line running from the Gulf of Danzig north to Braunsberg to a meeting place at the frontiers of Lithuania, East Prussia, and Poland. Thus Russia not only increased its territory by 273,947 square miles and its population by nearly 25 million, but also attained a strategic position from which to bring pressure upon Poland, Czechoslovakia, Hungary, Romania, Bulgaria, and Yugoslavia, states which were to become Russian satellites.

At the Potsdam Conference, furthermore, the United States, the U.S.S.R., and the United Kingdom decided that peace settlements with Italy, Romania, Bulgaria, and Finland should be drafted by a Council of Ministers, made up of the foreign ministers of the U.S.S.R., the United Kingdom, the United States, China, and France.[11] Nevertheless, a confer-

---

[10] France was admitted to the Commission in November 1944. Incidentally, it should be noted that there was no question about the return of Alsace and Lorraine to France.

[11] Subsequently, the powers took the position that only those nations which had signed surrender terms with one of the defeated powers should participate in the drafting of the treaties. Thus the peace treaty with Italy was to be drafted by Britain, the Soviet Union, the United States, and France; those with Romania, Bulgaria, and Hungary, by Britain, the U.S.S.R., and the United States; and that with Finland, by Britain and the U.S.S.R.

ence was assembled at Paris on July 29, 1946, at which the Big Four (the United States, the U.S.S.R., the United Kingdom, and France) met with the Little Seventeen in order to make recommendations to the Council of Ministers regarding the final settlements.[12] In the discussions at this meeting the rivalry between the U.S.S.R. and the West became abundantly clear. Russia made every effort to win advantages for itself and its actual or potential satellites; the West consistently attempted to thwart such moves and to get favorable terms for its friends. In the treaties which were ultimately drafted and were signed at Paris on February 10, 1947, Yugoslavia was given Fiume and a considerable part of the Istrian Peninsula; Trieste was internationalized—a change that was to upset trade in this area and to disturb Italian-Yugoslav relations until Trieste, reduced in size, was returned to Italy (1954). Furthermore, Italy had to give up its colonies, which were to be granted ultimate independence, and to surrender the Dodecanese Islands to Greece. Hungary lost territory in southern Slovakia to Czecholovakia and had to cede northern Transylvania to Romania.[13] Bulgaria surrendered land which had been acquired with Nazi support from Yugoslavia. Romania had to give up Bessarabia and Bukovina to Russia. Finland had to cede the Province of Petsamo. The Saar was incorporated into the economy of France.[14] Then in a subsequent treaty with Japan, signed September 4, 1951,[15] Russia was given the southern part of Sakhalin Island and the Kurile Islands, which had been promised her at Yalta.[16]

Quite as important as the territorial changes effected by these treaties, so far as the subsequent economic development of Europe was concerned, were the clauses pertaining to reparations. The United States took the position that after the experience with reparations following World War I, it would be foolhardy to demand payments out of current production from the defeated states. It pointed out that, after the shortages of the immediate postwar period had been made up, special interests in each recipient country would be unwilling to receive goods and services and that there would be a general desire to have the vanquished powers resume their economic activity. Russia, on the other hand, insisted on reparations, for payments to a communist economy would not impinge on the interests of individuals and Russian losses had been so great that amends had to be made, even if of an avowedly punitive character.[17]

---

[12] The defeated states could submit their views concerning issues at stake and proposed terms.

[13] Hungary was reduced to its size of post-World War I. Approximately 3 million Magyars were in the regions taken from Hungary after World War II.

[14] The Saar was politically united with West Germany in 1956, but France was given a few economic concessions.

[15] The U.S.S.R., Poland, and Czechoslovakia did not appear at the signing.

[16] A treaty was signed with Austria on May 15, 1955.

[17] This position won support from those who wanted to curb Germany economically for an indefinite period. In America, Henry Morgenthau, Secretary of the Treasury, was the chief exponent of this position.

The reparations issue was raised at Yalta when the conflicting stands of the U.S.S.R. and the West became clearly evident. At that time Stalin demanded 20 billion dollars, half of which would go to Russia, to be paid over a twenty-year period. To this request Churchill and Roosevelt were flatly hostile, yet it was clear that some concessions had to be made and a compromise effected. This middle ground was reached at Potsdam. There the negotiating powers agreed upon the general principle that the war potential of Germany should be held in check by prohibiting the production of arms, ammunition, aircraft, and seagoing vessels and by limiting the output of steel, chemicals, and certain machines, but Germany should be left "enough resources to enable the German people to subsist without external assistance." From these propositions, the victors went on to establish a formula which the United States and Britain hoped would dispose of the reparations issue with dispatch and which Russia apparently believed was the best that it could get. It provided that the reparations claims of the U.S.S.R., out of which Polish claims would be covered, were to be met (1) by the dismantling and removal to the Soviet Union of certain German plants in the Russian Zone of occupation, (2) by removal of 15 percent of "such usable and complete industrial capital equipment . . . as is unnecessary for German peace economy . . . from the Western Zones of Germany, in exchange for an equivalent value of food, coal, potash, zinc, and so forth, as may be agreed upon," (3) by removal of 10 percent of industrial capital equipment from the Western Zones of occupation without payment, and (4) by an appropriate share of German foreign assets. Claims of the Western Powers were to be met by removals of plant from the Western Zones of occupation in Germany and from German foreign assets.[18] A reparations conference, held in Paris in 1945, established a schedule for the division of reparations, and an Inter-Allied Reparations Agency was created, with its seat in Brussels, actually to parcel out the booty. Finally, the Allied Control Council, composed of each commander-in-chief of the four occupying powers in Germany, was charged with overseeing the dismantling of plant.

Although these arrangements took care of the major phase of reparations, the Russians also insisted on payments from their lesser enemies. Thus in the treaty with Italy provision was made for reparations in the amount of 360 million dollars, of which 100 million was to go to the U.S.S.R., 125 million to Yugoslavia, 105 million to Greece, 25 million to Ethiopia, and 5 million to Albania. Furthermore, Hungary was made to pay 300 million to the U.S.S.R. and 100 million jointly to Yugoslavia and

---

[18] Russia was given complete control over German assets in Finland, Bulgaria, Hungary, Romania, and Eastern Austria.

Czechoslovakia; Bulgaria, 45 million to Greece and 25 million to Yugoslavia; and Romania and Finland were each asked to pay 300 million to the Soviet Union over eight years.[19] In comparison with the enormous bills presented after World War I, these sums seemed small. Yet, they were enough to keep animosities aroused, although they were not enough to be a major disturbing factor in the postwar period.

Similarly, too, sufficient foresight was exercised to avoid in the aftermath of World War II a repetition of the complicated and irritating issues of war debts. The American "lend-lease" formula meant in essence that no charge would be made for war goods sent to the Allies, principally the United Kingdom and the U.S.S.R.; and the other members of the coalition adopted similar stands. What debts were contracted, especially with the United States and Canada, by European nations were for relief and rehabilitation, but even after the conflict, as we shall see, the United States soon switched from lending to giving in order to help restore the economies of Western culture.

---

[19] The U.S.S.R. reduced in 1948 the sums demanded of Finland, Romania, and Hungary by 73 million dollars each. Russia got, however, as her price for making a treaty of peace with Austria, 10,000 tons of oil per year for ten years and 154 million dollars in goods, to be delivered within six years.

21

Economic recovery, expansion, and miracles

Chief characteristics of the postwar period

On the morrow of World War II the economic future of Western culture did not look bright. The destruction, dislocations of trade, and burdens of public debts already discussed weighed heavily on the people of Europe. In addition tensions among groups in society, especially between Communists and supporters of the existing economic system, threatened to tear society asunder. Fears that demobilizing vast armies and beating swords into plowshares would inaugurate a depression, as they had so many times before, made people hesitate to put their resources into productive enterprise. Discouragement and sheer physical weakness characterized many who had suffered mightily during the conflict.

Yet in spite of valid grounds for dire forebodings, the chief features of the history of Western culture in the postwar period were rapid economic recovery, then economic expansion, and finally an economic growth that was so amazing in some countries, particularly in Germany and in Italy, that it was regarded as miraculous. As can be seen in Table 45, all the countries of Western Europe had gotten back to or had surpassed their prewar levels of gross domestic product and then had gone on to raise their levels by from 34 to 78 percent in the ensuing five years. Furthermore, economic progress continued with no major setbacks, although a slowing-down in the rate of growth was experienced by some countries in the 1960s. American expansion was almost as dramatic as that in Europe, but percentagewise was not so astounding, for it started from a higher base. Lastly, economic growth was such that despite increases in populations it resulted in an augmentation of national income per capita and per man-hour worked, compared with prewar amounts, and in some equalizing of national incomes per capita among European countries.

Table 45. Indicators of economic expansion since World War II

Country	Index of gross domestic product at constant prices		
	1938	1949	1955
France	100	112	149
West Germany	100	100	178
Italy	100	101	150
Belgium	100	109	135
United Kingdom	100	113	134
United States	100	174	219

	Postwar GDP, billions of dollars			Postwar GDP adjusted for inflation		
	1953	1963	1970	1953	1963	1970
France	36.9	67.3	147.3	52.0	67.3	116.9
West Germany	30.4	78.4	186.7	32.7	78.4	177.8
Italy	16.8	39.1	92.7	18.1	39.1	77.9
Belgium	7.4	12.2	25.5	7.9	12.2	21.6
United Kingdom	41.3	73.2	119.8		73.2	
United States	333.2	528.2	986.4	360.2	528.2	941.5

* In billions of dollars, deflated by wholesale price index of respective country (base year = 1963).
SOURCE: Derived from *Statistical Yearbook of the United Nations* (New York: United Nations, 1956); and *Basic Statistics of the Community* (Brussels: E.E.C., 1971).

Remarkable as these changes were in view of what was thought to have been the catastrophic holocaust of World War II, Western Europe did not regain its relative economic or power position of prewar times either in Western culture or in the world as a whole. It had lost ground to the United States and Canada, on the one hand, and to the U.S.S.R., on the other. Although Europe, excluding the U.S.S.R., had nearly twice the population of the United States in 1950, it produced about equal amounts of coal and steel and lesser quantities of electricity, sulfuric acid, and grain. The national income of Western European states was less than that of the United States, and industrial output per capita was less than half the American average. For its part Russia with its satellites had become an economic and military colossus, and the U.S.S.R. had a greater rate of growth of gross national product than any of the "miracle" countries of the West. Lastly,

Chart 2

Percentage Distribution of World Commodity Trade by Regions (Selected Years). (From Frederic Dewhurst and Associates, Europe's Needs and Resources, New York: Twentieth Century Fund, 1961, p. 636.)

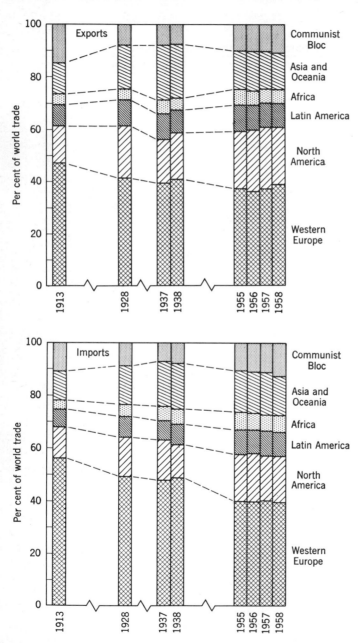

Europe's share of world export trade shrank from some 50 percent prior to World War I to about 35 percent for the years 1948–1950.[1]

The realization of the relative economic decline of Western Europe and the immensity of the task of reconstruction inclined most states to engage in some form of economic planning. In the Soviet Union, the centrally governed economy ("hard planning") became a nearly full substitute for the Western-style market economy. The government planning agency stipulated the production levels and prices for almost all goods and services according to forecasts and planning goals. In this fashion the direction of the economy was made fully subject to the will of the state. Activities deemed unimportant by political leaders were constricted, and most resources were allocated to heavy industry. The principal goal was to catch up with the West in the heavy-industry sector, and for a long while this required ignoring the demand for consumers' goods. Central planning solved two major problems for the Soviets: It avoided the uncertainties and fluctuations of the free-market economy by eliminating private investment decision making, and it provided the method for a workable economy without private ownership of capital, which was ideologically abhorrent. With these solutions came a host of new problems: to set prices and production quotas for thousands of goods in the absence of markets involved mind-boggling amounts of bureaucratic paperwork; without the incentive of profits, technical innovation was not readily forthcoming; no amount of planning could eliminate uncertainty in agriculture, which therefore remained a problem sector; finally, the deaf ear to the consumer meant that people had to endure long lines and empty shelves for even basic articles of human consumption.

In Western Europe planning did not replace the market mechanism, but the will to reduce uncertainty and assert national priorities caused governments to experiment with "soft planning," that is, the drawing up of general economic goals which were implemented only by moral suasion and the use of government facilities to bring industrialists, unions, and state representatives together outside the marketplace. In some countries, important segments of the economy were nationalized, as in the United Kingdom, France, Italy, and Norway, and the state could thus as entrepreneur determine what ends to achieve and how to attain them. In some nations nationalization was supplemented by an official planning commission—or such a commission might exist without nationalization—and this agency would then set up targets at which the economy was to shoot, try to sell its ideas to the business community, and get governmental economic

---

[1] Ingvar Svennilson, *Growth and Stagnation in the European Economy* (Geneva: United Nations, 1954), p. 169.

agencies to assist in its efforts to achieve its goals. Furthermore, economic planning was conducted by central banks, and these institutions became ever more important in adopting policies to implement economic plans. By controlling credit to those parts of the economy which should be expanded, they had a leverage of enormous power. Moreover, all governments tried to stimulate economic development by direct loans, tax policies, or "forced savings" for investment. Lastly, all states had in their planning a basic principle that the welfare of the individual is a fundamental responsibility of the state. Indeed, some, like France, even sanctified this doctrine by inserting it in their constitutions.[2]

Another characteristic of the postwar period was that communism became a great force in the world and worked to destroy the capitalist system, or to hinder its development. The calling of strikes of a primary political nature became in some countries a not uncommon thing. Russia and its satellites formed an economic bloc, which was formalized as the Council of Mutual Economic Assistance in 1949. The Western powers, for their part, formed a military alliance known as the North Atlantic Treaty Organization (1949) and several economic alliances, as we shall see in more detail on a later page. Thus a new situation was created in international political and economic affairs. Instead of four or five Great Powers existing in the world, which by shifting their allegiances could upset balances of power, two colossi, the U.S.S.R. and the United States, allied with states which could not alter basic alignments by changing sides, stood facing each other. These two blocs adopted such hostile stances toward each other that trade between them came nearly to a standstill. Each of the blocs endeavored to increase its economic potential by closer intrabloc economic ties.

Disruptive as such an alignment was to economic development, it was probably of less immediate relevance to economic recovery and growth than the breakdown of the worldwide system of multilateral trade and payments. For reasons suggested in the last chapter, Western Europe could not at once earn dollars with which to buy goods necessary to effect a rapid recovery (see Chart 4). Slow recovery would have made the threat of communism even more ominous than it otherwise might have been. To lessen this threat and thus the extension of Russian influence and power, the United States came to the assistance of Western European states. In 1947 it inaugurated the Marshall Plan, whereby it made huge gifts to its friends in Europe and subsequently in the rest of the world for their economic recovery and expansion.

Still other characteristics of the period since World War II emanate from

---

[2] "Economic Planning in Europe," *Economic Survey of Europe, 1962* (Geneva: United Nations, 1963), part 2, chaps. 4 and 5.

monetary problems. Immediately after the cessation of hostilities, moneys had to be revalued in line with public debts and central bank reserves, and consequently enormous price rises occurred. After this first flush of inflation, however, no new rush for devaluation of money to gain national advantage took place, but in nearly all countries a "creeping" price rise developed that was for most Western countries about 2 percent a year. Furthermore, in the monetary field the dollar and, to a lesser extent, the pound sterling were used extensively by central banks for their reserves; thus if either of these currencies showed weaknesses in the international monetary market, a danger arose that central banks would suddenly dump their dollars on the market in hope of buying more stable moneys or gold. This problem gave rise to a multitude of schemes for creating some kind of international currency to take the burden off single national currencies. As we shall see, the problem of international monetary flows has remained an unsolved problem, aggravating the difficulties of international trade.

The economic history of the last quarter century has also been marked by a new attitude of the Western powers toward the less economically developed parts of the globe. The old imperialism characterized by political domination came to an end, in some cases because of the hostility of the backward areas to the governing power; and in its place grew up a doctrine that economic relations with these areas could be maintained without political hegemony. Political colonialism gave way to what cynics called "dollar" imperialism. The morality of Western economic relations with the "Third World" was a tensely political issue. Although outright political domination of weaker nations had become passe, Western countries continued to exert much influence in the underdeveloped world. It is also true that the basic trade relationships had not altered greatly: the European economy bought agricultural products, extractive raw materials, and certain labor-intensive manufactured goods in exchange for capital equipment and other industrial commodities, benefiting from favorable terms of trade. However advantageous the European position seems, it is undeniable that many benefits have accrued to non-Western nations as well. Modern capital and technology of Western origin have helped to industrialize underdeveloped lands, as is abundantly clear from rates of industrial growth in non-Western regions, to say nothing of improvements in agriculture and the tertiary trades.[3]

Unquestionably the most important advantage for the rest of the world of intercourse with the West has been the rapid diffusion of mortality-reducing knowledge. The astonishing reduction of death rates in under-

---

[3] *Yearbook of National Accounts, Statistics, 1972* (New York: United Nations, 1973).

developed areas in the postwar period was directly due to the introduction of such techniques as DDT against malaria and other mosquito-borne diseases; vaccination and inoculation against cholera, smallpox, plague, and diphtheria; antibiotics; penicillin; and a host of other health measures. In Ceylon, by way of example, the death rate fell 34 percent in one year (1946–1947) and continued to fall thereafter, because of an anti-malaria campaign waged with the cooperation of the World Health Organization.[4] As Table 46 shows, these spectacular results have been widely duplicated. A significant difference in mortality between modernized and pre-Modern areas still persists due to differences in real income levels, but the trend is clearly in the direction of narrowing the gap.

Table 46. Crude death rates in selected countries, 1920–1969

Country	1920–24	1930–34	1946	1950	1960	1969
Non-European						
India	26.8	23.7	18.7	16.1		16.7
Japan	23.0	18.1	17.6	10.9	7.6	6.7
Egypt (U.A.R.)	25.7	27.1	25.0	19.1		16.5
Chile	31.0	24.5	17.2	15.7	12.5	10.6
European						
Belgium	13.7	13.5	13.4	12.4	12.9	12.7
France	17.3	16.0	13.5	12.7	11.4	11.3
West Germany	13.9	11.0	12.3	10.3	11.4	12.0
Italy	17.5	14.1	12.1	9.8	9.7	10.1
Sweden	12.4	11.7	10.5	10.0	10.0	10.5
United Kingdom	12.5	12.2	12.1	11.7	11.5	11.9

SOURCE: *United Nations Demographic Yearbooks, 1954, 1961, 1970* (New York: United Nations).

Economic planning and nationalization

From early in World War II all belligerents gave earnest thought to the economic phases of the aftermath. As we have seen, Germany had its plan to become the industrial heartland of an agrarian continent and Japan its dream of being the center of a "Co-Prosperity Sphere," but most countries

[4] Kingsley Davis, "The Amazing Decline of Mortality in Underdeveloped Countries," *American Economic Review*, vol. 76, May 1956, p. 312.

turned their thoughts of reconstruction and recovery not to projects for exploiting others, but rather to economic development with their own resources. Each of the various European governments-in-exile (most of which were set up in London) drew up plans for their recovery and their place in the brave new economic world. Some of these plans were hardly more than wishful thinking, as in the case of the Polish government's, for the chances of this government's being restored were not very good after the advances of the Russian armies through its territory. Some were very practical and quickly implemented, as in the case of Belgium's, for this government-in-exile had access to funds that allowed it to place orders for deliveries of goods immediately after entry to the country was possible.

One of the governments to go the farthest in wartime planning was the Free French under General Charles de Gaulle in Algiers. There the Committee of National Liberation had an economic committee which was required to draw up schedules of needs for lend-lease and other forms of Allied assistance for Algiers and later for France and thus by necessity got in the business of planning. Indeed, out of this group came the French Plan of Modernization and Equipment, which was developed under the leadership of Jean Monnet and came to be known as the Monnet Plan. In the United States planning was undertaken in order to avoid the usual postwar economic depression.

Although the schemes for recovery and development and methods for implementing them varied from country to country, considerable agreement existed on the main steps to be taken. Each nation realized that large savings out of current income had to be made to effect the necessary investments and that if the private sector of the economy could not furnish them, the state should. Each believed that basic segments of the economy should be developed first, rather than those that turned out consumers' goods, especially those that were not absolutely necessary for health. Thus in the Monnet Plan particular emphasis was put on the development of six basic branches of production—coal mining, the generation of electricity, ferrous metals, cement, agricultural machinery, and domestic transportation. Each recognized the importance of popular support for recovery programs if targets were to be hit. This support might involve hardships and sacrifices of well-being in the expectation that eventually Western Europe would regain its economic and cultural place in the sun and some semblance of its former political and military prestige.

Less agreement existed, however, on the means by which the needed savings and investments could best be made and by which people might be convinced of the wisdom of present sacrifices for future gains. The nationalization of private property had considerable support, especially in socialist circles, for ownership by capitalists of the means of production was believed to have led to the exploitation of the working classes, and governmental management was deemed no more inefficient than bureaucratic management by large corporations. To many it seemed that the power of the state to issue orders to all was needed to pull Europe out of its economic doldrums. Only from the state, it was thought, could the large sums needed for investment be obtained, and only by the state could these sums be properly allocated.

In some countries, the Resistance Movements had been particularly well supported by left-wing elements, and this had led to the making of promises for the nationalization of some sectors of the economy. Also, some industrialists had collaborated with the Germans to such an extent that the demands to seize their properties were very great indeed. These circumstances are well illustrated by the situation in France. There the Council of Resistance, with a strong Communist element, took a strong stand for nationalization, and there collaborators like Renault, who had large automobile interests, could easily be punished by expropriation. Inasmuch as the Provisional Government of General Charles de Gaulle needed leftist backing to bring certain industrial workers to his support, his government quickly and with little opposition nationalized the coal mines, electricity and gas, the Bank of France, the major commercial banks, insurance companies, the Renault company, and Air France.[5]

In the United Kingdom conditions were also propitious for nationalization, although they were different from what they were in France. There the Labor Party came to power in 1945 and in accordance with its principles proceeded to nationalize the Bank of England, the coal industry, gas, electricity, the telephone services, inland transportation, and the steel industry.[6] In Italy, the pattern of nationalizing was primarily for the governmental IRI (Institute for the Reconstruction of Industry) to hang on to the properties, or interest in properties, which it had acquired during Fascism, and then to expand its activities by investing in new plants. But in addition, ENI (a governmental company for developing petroleum and national gas) was allowed to continue; some wartime concerns were nationalized (for example, Alfa Romeo automobile company); the electrical industry was nationalized in 1962 as a gesture to Socialist parties when they were taken into a coalition government with the Christian Democrats. In Norway and Sweden nationalization was carried out by Socialist governments. Only in the Netherlands, Germany, Belgium, and the United States was there no wave of nationalization. In the last-named country, many of the emergency organizations set up during the depression of the 1930s were

---

[5] The railways had been nationalized under the Popular Front government, but compensation for them had not been completed. Some of the companies had continued in existence as investment trusts.

[6] British steel was denationalized in 1953, then was nationalized again under Harold Wilson in 1967.

liquidated, especially during the presidency of Dwight Eisenhower. In the United Kingdom, France, and Italy some 10 to 20 percent of industry became the property of the government and was operated for the benefit of the collectivity. Nationalization did not provide the great benefits expected by Socialists, nor did it prove to be the great bugaboo anticipated by its opponents. For the most part, nationalized establishments were run much as private concerns were—they were expected to return a profit.

Investments and labor

In all countries encouragement was given to investments in producers' goods, and as a matter of fact investments as a percentage of gross national product increased considerably over what they had been before the war (Chart 3). Encouragements took the form of giving borrowers extensive credit at low rates—a policy which was implemented by central banks—by providing investors with special tax advantages, such as freedom from taxes for a given period on new plant and exemptions from income taxes for certain investments, and by direct loans or other forms of assistance from governmental agencies. The role of the state in making loans increased greatly; 30 percent of investments in France from 1947 to 1951 came from governmental sources.[7] In general, investments tended to go into those branches of activity where opportunities for expansion were greatest and where social demand was the most pressing. Thus manufacturing and housing were particularly favored, but in certain circumstances some special activity, such as shipping in Norway, came in for exceptional treatment (Table 47). Although the correlation between investments and growth was very high, investments might be of such a character or put into such hopeless sectors of the economy that they had little effect on output. (Compare Table 47 with Tables 48 and 49.)

Besides endeavoring to encourage greater savings for investment, nearly all countries of the West engaged in massive campaigns to preach the doctrine of "productivity." The fundamental argument presented was extremely simple and easily understood by the masses of both employers and employees. It was that economic well-being is a highly desirable condition and that to achieve it more goods must be produced per unit of input. Here was a theory which was, on the one hand, to stimulate employers to get better equipment, to arrange their plants for more efficient production, and to try to establish better relations with their workers in their own interests.

---

[7] This rate of governmental investment was increased by the fact that Marshall Plan assistance was given out by governments.

On the other hand, it was to convince workers that increased output was ultimately in their own best interest as wage settlements and real income in general moved upward with increased productivity.

"Productivity" gave concrete expression to Western culture's basic tenet that one of the marks of civilization is a high level of material

Chart 3

Relationship between Gross National Product, Exports, and Investments at Constant Prices, 1947–1951 (1938 = 100). (From Economic Survey of Europe since the War, Geneva: United Nations, 1953, pp. 58ff.)

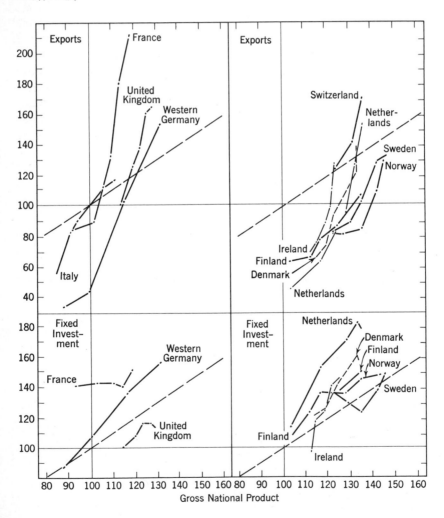

Table 47. Sectoral shares in employment and output in Western countries, 1949 to 1959 (A = percentage share of sector in employed labor force, average 1949, 1954, 1959; B = percentage share of sector in GDP, average 1949 to 1959)

Country	Agriculture		Mining		Manufacturing		Construction		Public utilities		Transport		Dwellings		Services		Total
	A	B	A	B	A	B	A	B	A	B	A	B	A	B	A	B	
West Germany	20.5	9.4	2.8	4.1	33.9	38.0	7.2	5.9	0.7	2.0	5.7	7.6		2.3	29.2	30.7	100
Austria	31.6	13.8	1.1	1.6	26.6	39.4	6.6	7.7	0.6	2.4	4.6	5.8		1.1	28.7	28.3	100
Greece	48.2	33.8	0.5	1.0	15.9	17.7	2.6	3.8	0.4	1.4	4.9	8.0		5.4	27.6	28.9	100
Italy	37.1	24.3	0.9	1.3	24.5	30.5	7.6	5.1	0.6	2.8	4.3	6.3		3.0	25.1	26.7	100
Turkey	81.0	46.1		1.3	9.5	9.7		5.4		0.5		7.4		3.7	9.5	25.9	100
Yugoslavia	67.0	29.0	1.0	2.2	10.4	33.5	4.5	5.7	0.2	1.1	2.1	6.8		1.4	14.7	20.2	100
Spain	45.7	26.5	1.6	2.0	18.2	22.2	5.1	4.7	0.5	2.1	4.0	6.6		3.2	25.0	31.4	100
Netherlands	12.3	12.1	1.4	2.3	29.5	30.3	8.2	6.5	0.9	2.3	6.8	9.1		2.7	41.0	34.8	100
France	26.5	11.5	1.5	1.7	27.8	35.1	6.4	6.6	0.4	1.1	5.1	5.6		2.6	32.4	33.9	100
Canada	18.5	9.5	1.7	4.0	25.3	25.2	6.7	6.2	1.1	2.7	7.4	9.4		4.2	39.3	35.8	100
Finland	34.9	23.1			23.5	35.2	10.7	9.1	0.7	2.3	6.3	7.0		3.8	23.9	24.5	100
Portugal	47.9	29.9	1.0	1.1	19.7	34.7	4.9		0.4	2.0	3.5	5.3		3.1	22.6	24.0	100
Norway	26.8	14.1	0.6	1.4	23.4	25.4	7.7	7.5	0.8	2.1	9.9	15.9		2.0	30.9	28.6	100
Sweden	17.8	7.8	0.5	1.9	32.1	35.9	8.4		1.0	2.3	8.1				32.1		100
United States	9.8	6.7	1.4	2.3	25.6	30.3	6.0	5.5	0.9	2.1	5.8	6.8		4.6	50.6	41.6	100
Denmark	24.2	19.4		0.3	29.6	27.1	7.0	7.0	0.6	1.7	7.0	9.5		4.7	31.6	30.3	100
Belgium	9.4	8.2	5.1	4.5	33.0	34.1	6.4	6.4	0.8	2.5	7.1	7.7		7.7	38.1	29.0	100
United Kingdom	4.9	5.0	3.6	3.5	37.9	35.6	6.3	5.9	1.6	2.1	7.4	8.0		3.9	38.2	36.0	100
Ireland	39.9	29.7	0.9	0.9	15.5	19.3	6.4	5.2	0.9	2.2	4.7	15.5		3.4	31.7	23.7	100

SOURCE: *Some Factors in Economic Growth in Europe during the 1950s* (New York: United Nations, 1964), chap. 3, p. 51.

Table 48. Sectoral shares of gross fixed asset formation in Western countries (percentage shares of each sector in gross fixed capital formation, average 1949 to 1958)

Country	Agriculture	Mining	Manufacturing	Construction	Public utilities	Transport	Dwellings	Services	Total
West Germany	8.8	4.3	23.8	2.0	7.0	14.8	22.7	16.6	100
Austria	13.8	2.1	23.5		11.8	13.4	19.8	15.6	100
Greece	10.5	1.9	14.8		9.9	14.2	34.6	14.1	100
Italy	13.0	2.2	23.9		7.1	19.9	21.9	12.0	100
Turkey	21.6	1.1	21.7		6.7	21.3	18.6	9.0	100
Yugoslavia	8.8	3.9	33.5	2.8	9.5	15.6	14.8	11.1	100
Spain	10.4		32.7				15.9		100
Netherlands	5.9	1.2	21.8	1.2	7.0	31.0	19.0	12.9	100
France	11.2	3.6	25.0	2.5	7.1	14.5	24.5	11.7	100
Canada	9.6	4.6	16.0	1.8	10.3	18.6	20.6	18.5	100
Finland	12.8	18.2		1.4	7.3	17.3	24.9	18.1	100
Portugal	12.5	2.1	21.2		11.1	16.9	20.2	16.1	100
Norway	8.8	0.8	16.9	1.3	8.5	36.2	16.5	11.1	100
Sweden	5.9	1.1	20.3	1.8	11.1	22.9	25.1	11.7	100
United States	6.6	4.1	20.2		7.6	14.3	28.6		100
Denmark	8.8		13.0		5.7	19.6	17.7		100
Belgium	4.1	3.5	25.7	2.0	4.3	16.8	26.5	17.1	100
United Kingdom	4.4	2.6	25.4	1.6	11.4	13.4	21.2	20.0	100
Ireland	13.8	1.1	16.6	2.0	10.8	16.9	20.1	18.7	100

SOURCE: *Some Factors in Economic Growth in Europe during the 1950s*, chap. 3, p. 51.

Table 49. Sectoral rates of growth of labor productivity in Western countries, 1949 to 1959

Country	Compound annual percentage rates of growth							
	Agriculture	Mining	Manufac- turing	Construction	Public utilities	Transport	Services	Total
West Germany	5.5	1.8	6.0	5.1	6.9	5.0	1.9	4.9
Austria	1.8	4.4	3.9	4.3	6.5	5.3	3.2	4.0
Italy	4.7	15.7	7.2	11.3	6.4	-0.6	1.3	4.9
Yugoslavia	4.0	2.6	2.9	1.9	5.5	2.3		4.4
Spain	4.3	2.9	2.7	6.6	10.5			4.5
Netherlands	3.8		4.9	2.1	6.6	5.0	1.9	3.3
France	4.9	5.1	5.1	1.0	9.1	6.2	2.7	4.3
Canada	5.9	9.0	2.7	1.6	4.9	1.8	-0.4	2.5
Finland	4.2		4.0	0.1	3.0	1.3	1.6	3.3
Portugal	1.5	-6.9	4.4		8.0	5.0	5.1	3.9
Norway	3.1	1.2	3.3	0.9	6.6	3.9	1.6	3.2
Sweden	1.7	-1.3	3.7		5.3			2.9
United States	3.7	4.4	3.4	1.8	7.8	3.5	0.4	2.1
Denmark	4.9		2.2	2.1	8.1	3.7		2.3
Belgium	4.6	0.5	3.7	0.2	4.1	4.3	1.3	2.6
United Kingdom	3.8	0.4	2.4	1.7	3.8	2.5	1.1	1.8
Ireland	2.5	11.7	2.5	1.6	4.1	0.1	2.7	2.5

SOURCE: *Some Factors in Economic Growth in Europe during the 1950s*, chap. 3, p. 57.

well-being because it not only permits freedom from want but also allows the enjoyment of the finer things of life. One measure of appreciation of these finer things, one likes to think, is the remarkable upsurge in attendance at institutions of higher learning since the war. In France the number of students enrolled in such schools went up from 75,000 in 1938 to over 282,000 in 1960 and 413,000 by 1965, and in the United States the number of students in colleges and universities rose from 1.1 million in 1930 to 5.6 million in 1965. Although much of the numerical increase was attributable to the increased size of the youthful population, the large magnitude of resources allocated to higher learning in the postwar period attests to the faith that the Western countries have placed in education as a source of both cultural and economic betterment.

Technology and demand

The boom in education generally made some kind of contribution to economic growth, although this contribution is difficult to measure in any precise way. The training of engineers was vastly expanded, and some correlation exists between their number and the rate of growth. (See Chart 4.) Furthermore, a larger percentage of the population was fulfilling state requirements for "compulsory" education, and this meant that the working force generally was more literate and thus able to learn more skills, and that more talents in the total population were being tapped. (See Table 50.) More moneys were being spent on research, and they give a strong presumption of being very important to economic growth.[8]

The greater amount of knowledge and skills that was being brought to economic processes made three important types of contributions to economic growth. The first was the development of new products. Among the most prominent of them were plastics, artificial fibers such as nylon and Dacron, detergents, jet engines, business machines, and computers. In and of themselves these goods did not bulk large enough in the total output to have made a great deal of difference; thus the effect of technology upon growth has to be sought in its other manifestations. The most discussed of these has been the introduction of laborsaving machines which have been made so automatic that the entire process has been named *automation*. This was the second type of contribution. Throughout history man has been looking for ways of getting greater output with less input, but in

---

[8] Obviously expenses of research may be reduced if one is able to borrow from the finders of new ways of doing things. See *Some Factors in Economic Growth in Europe during the 1950s* (New York: United Nations, 1964), chap. 5.

Table 50. Number of years of compulsory schooling, enrolment ratios, and students per teacher, by age groups, in 1948 and 1958

Country	Number of years in compulsory education	Enrollment ratios				Students per teacher		
		Age group 5-14		Age group 15-19	Age group 20-24	Age group 5-14		Age group 15-19
		1948	1958	1958	1958	1948	1958	1958
Austria	8		85	13	4		28	11
Belgium	8	92	95	32	6	26	20	16
Denmark	7	62	76	19	6	23	31	11
France	8	90	90	31	4	27	28	25
West Germany	8-9		80	18	5		34	23
Greece	6-8		75	17	3		41	20
Iceland	8		73	58	7		25	17
Ireland	8	88	93	20	4	36	32	14
Italy	8	63	79	16	4	27	22	12
Netherlands	8	84	86	33	5	34	33	20
Norway	7-8	73	77	36	10	26	25	17
Portugal	6	47	56	9	3	43	35	16
Spain	6	56	75	13	3	41	40	20
Sweden	7-8	73	83	32	11	21	22	21
Switzerland	7-9	75	79	23	3	30	27	22
Turkey	6	30	45	3	1	48	48	23
United Kingdom	10	92	99	18	4	30	26	13
Yugoslavia	8		66	17	4		32	20
U.S.S.R.	7-10		72	49	8		21	15
United States	9-12	93	90	66	12	33	28	17

SOURCE: *World Handbook of Educational Organization and Statistics*, 1st ed., 1951 (Paris: UNESCO, 1952); *Report of the Policy Conference on Economic Growth and Investment in Education*, Washington, D. C., October 16-20, 1961, part 2 (Paris: OEEC, 1962); and national sources.

recent times he has attained a level of technical sophistication that permits him to seek laborsaving devices as a regular part of economic life. His success in the postwar period has been phenomenal not only because of developing techniques but also because of war destruction which required the total replacement of plants. This latter fact reduced the ordinary reluctance of entrepreneurs in older industrial countries to modernize—a reluctance that is regarded as being of a structural nature. Even to list the changes which have been made would require a lexicon of no mean proportions.[9] They extend, in fact, from a continuous process for making steel,[10] to the making of Dacron thread by squirting the liquid resin through a hole (Figure 28), and to the computer, which can perform in a day mathematical operations which might take years or even decades. Then the third type of contribution has been that a great deal of attention has been devoted to the organization of production and to labor-management (personnel) relations. Scientific management of the Frederick Winslow Taylor type has not only been accepted but generally surpassed, for it is a known fact that organization can work wonders and that the lack

---

[9] See UNESCO *World Guide to Science and Information and Documentation Series* (Paris: UNESCO, 1961).

[10] In this process the molten metal is taken from the furnace and poured into a tall cooling tower where it is partially cooled by water until it takes the shape of a "bloom" (rectangular red-hot slab). It then goes to the rolling mill. Thus the task of forming blooms and reheating them for rolling is eliminated.

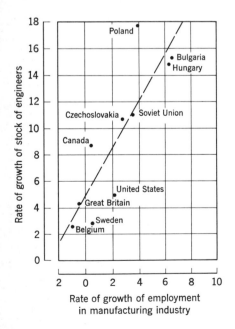

Chart 4
Comparative Growth of Demand for Highly Qualified Manpower and for Total Industrial Manpower in Selected Countries during the Fifties. (From Some Factors in Economic Growth in Europe during the 1950s, New York: United Nations, 1964, chap. 5, p. 16.)

of it, as in traditional building methods, is an enormous handicap. Similarly, it is obvious that the success of many a process depends upon the cooperation and even the enthusiasm of workers. Hence more consideration was given than formerly to working conditions and serious attempts were made to care for the welfare of workers by expanding pension plans and insurance coverage both at the governmental level and in negotiated contracts with private firms.

Economic recovery and expansion were also stimulated by a great increase in demand. Immediately after the cessation of hostilities, stocks of civilian goods were low or nonexistent; people were starved for a vast range of things which had been unobtainable during the conflict. Furthermore, the demand side of the economic equation was strong because of the extraordinary growth of population (Table 51). In spite of the war the population of Europe increased by 4.1 percent from 1940 to 1950, and in the United States the "baby boom" carried the population up from 1940 to 1949 by 13.1 percent to a total of 148,902,000 persons. From 1950 the population of Northern and Western Europe continued to grow at about 1 percent per annum and that of the United States by about 1.6 percent per annum, both largely from an increase in birth rates, although some

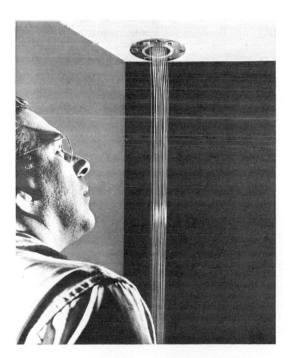

Figure 28
The production of man-made filaments for the textile industry. From tiny holes in a spinneret are extruded fine filaments which are twisted together to make a single end of continuous-filament yarn. The principle applies to nylon, "Orlon" acrylic fiber, "Dacron" polyester fiber, "Lycra" spandex fiber, and many other man-made yarns. When many filaments, as shown above, are twisted into a single thread, the yarn is known as continuous-multifilament. When the yarn is a single filament, such as the 15-denier nylon yarn in the majority of ladies' stockings, it is known as monofilament. *(Courtesy of Du Pont de Nemours and Company.)*

decline was registered in mortality rates. Because the saving and investment potential of these areas was great, this increase did not act as a drain
upon the economy but as a stimulus to it. It created a demand for clothing,
schooling, housing, and all consumers' goods and services. The population
increase that took place in Europe was itself due to economic recovery and
expansion. After the end of the depression and the devastation of the war,
rebuilding created a high demand for workers. With virtually no unemployment, entry into the labor force for young people became easy, and
these new workers could marry and start having children early in life. The
by-product of the economic surge to reconstruction was, therefore, many
new babies.

Demand was also generated by the desire of other parts of the world
for industrial goods and a number of tertiary services. The rest of the world
was bent on industrializing, which created a demand for the West's producers' goods, but it wanted to westernize in the sense of having many of
the consumers' goods of the West and the West's services, such as carrying,
insurance, and banking. Thus foreign trade, as we shall see in more detail,
played an important part in the West's recovery and expansion.

Especially did Europe rely, as it traditionally had, upon the importation
of foodstuffs and raw materials and the exportation of processed goods in

**Table 51. The growth of population in modern European countries
(mean population in millions)**

Country	1841–1845	1881–1885	1921	1940	1970	1980 (projected)
England & Wales	16.3	26.6	37.9	48.2*	55.7*	58.9*
Ireland	8.3	5.0	4.4			
Belgium	4.0	5.5	7.6	8.3	9.7	10.2
France	35.3	39.4	39.3	39.8	50.8	54.8
West Germany	29.5	41.0	61.3	69.8	60.7†	63.5†
Holland	3.0	4.2	6.9	8.9	13.0	14.5
Norway	1.3	1.9	2.7	3.0	3.9	4.2
Sweden	3.2	4.6	5.9	6.4	8.0	8.5
Denmark	1.3	2.0	3.3	3.8	4.9	5.3
Italy			37.7	43.8	54.5	58.4
Spain			21.4	25.8	33.3	
U.S.S.R.	76.8‡	121.5‡	190.0	242.8	277.8	

*United Kingdom.

†West Germany only.

‡European Russia only. 1921 statistic is actually for 1929.

SOURCES: W. D. Borrie, *The Growth and Control of World Population* (London: Weidenfeld & Nicolson, 1970),
p. 73; *Basic Statistics of the Community* (Brussels: Statistical Office of the European Communities, eleventh ed.,
1971), p. 14, table 1.

which it had embodied its skills. That it could continue to get raw materials from overseas was particularly fortunate, for many of its own resources were becoming exhausted or costly because of depletion, and with the exception of natural gas and some petroleum in Italy, France, the Netherlands, and in the North Sea off Britain, the resource base of the Continent remained much as it had been. Even coal could be imported from the United States, in spite of transportation costs, and sold at prices which were lower than the price of coal from the Ruhr. (See Map 11.)

At all events, once again many factors came together in a somewhat different but at the same time similar pattern and with a somewhat unexpected timing to give the West its rapid recovery and extraordinary expansion. The theory of necessary concomitants was once again shown to have validity.

In certain countries the record of growth was so extraordinary that it received the appellation of "miracle." In Germany the *Wirtschaftswunder* carried the gross domestic product from 112.3 billion marks in 1950 at 1954 prices to 289.2 billion marks in 1963 and manufacturing's share in these amounts from 39.6 billion to 130.9 billion. In Italy *il miracolo economico* took GNP from 11,697 billion lire in 1953 to 20,530 billion lire in 1963 at prices of 1958 and manufacturing's contribution from 3,186 billion to 7,721 billion in the same period. And in France *le miracle économique* witnessed the rise of GNP from 185.3 billion francs in 1950 at 1959 prices to 333.9 billion in 1963 and manufacturing's share from 51.1 billion in 1950 at prices of 1956 to 79.2 billion in 1959 and then at 1959 prices from 99.7 billion in 1959 to 126.6 billion in 1963.

Urban and regional planning

During the reconstruction period after the war, the growth of population and the continuing movement from the countryside to the cities and suburbs began to cause concern for the random way in which cities were growing. Urban planning was completely revitalized. The regulation of city growth became necessary in many European countries as postwar repatriation and immigration to industrial work centers threatened to cause instant slums. In England and the Netherlands, two countries with a long history of high population density and urbanization, town planning was most ambitious and most successful.[11]

---

[11] Maurice Crouzet, *The European Renaissance since 1945* (London: Harcourt, Brace, Jovanovich, 1970), p. 75.

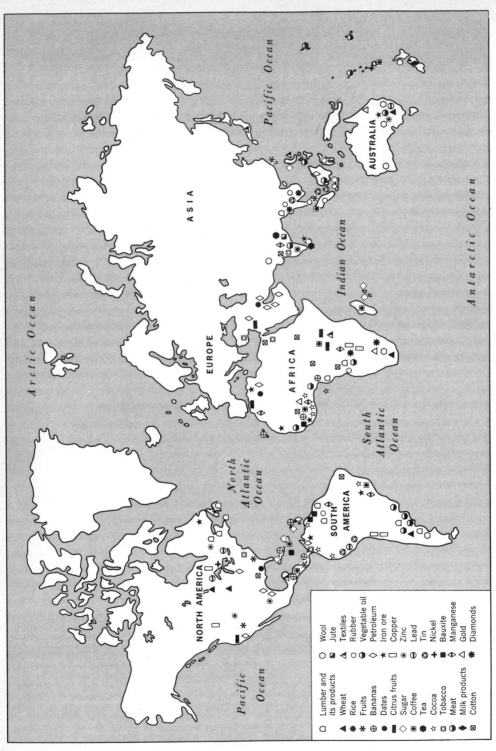

Map 11
Europe's Foreign Trade

In England, the Town and Country Planning Act of 1962 arranged priorities for the construction of new residential centers to avoid further overcrowding of London and other established municipalities. Likewise in the Netherlands new suburban centers were designed to absorb large numbers of people so that the old cities did not burst at the seams and sprawl randomly into the countryside. The durability and charm of older European residential buildings were such that there was no wisdom in demolishing large city tracts and erecting high-rise apartments in their place. This placed real limits on the absorptive powers of older cities.

The large numbers of semipermanent immigrant workers from Southern Europe that flooded postwar industrial production sites in north Italy, West Germany, France, and Belgium caused immediate housing problems. These unskilled workers from the Italian Mezzogiorno, Greece, Turkey, Spain, Portugal, Morocco, and Algeria—all areas of labor oversupply— came to the automobile works and factories in search of higher wages, often leaving families and rights of citizenship behind. Unprotected by the labor unions of host countries, which were naturally inhospitable to imported labor, and outside the pale of domestic welfare programs, these migrants were crowded into shantytowns (*bidonvilles*) where living conditions were wretched.[12] More recently, cooperation between European nations on this front, in keeping with the goal of free movement of labor, has caused much change for the better. Also, industrial and town planners have made provisions to accommodate the migrant work force.[13]

Planning on a still larger level to correct *regional* imbalances has been a feature of European economic programming since the end of the war and continues to rank high in the priorities of national governments and the European Economic Community (Chapter 22) to the present day. All but the smallest countries suffered some degree of regional inequality, but France and Italy were the most troubled. France, throughout its modern history, has been a country of two regions: Paris and everywhere else. In the 1960s the Paris region (2.2 percent of the country's land mass) held 15.8 percent of the total population and 27 percent of the urban population, including fully one-half of the nation's engineers and office workers, 70 percent of industrial research and development technicians, and 35 percent of the students.[14] There is no geographic reason for the super-concentration of Paris, just the historical fact that from the time of Louis XVI, French cultural life, business activity, and above all, administration increasingly

[12] Sergio Barzatni, *The Underdeveloped Areas within the Common Market* (Princeton, N. J.: Princeton, 1965), p. 138.
[13] On the role of the Common Market in improving the lot of migrant labor, see p. 516.
[14] Crouzet, *The European Renaissance*, pp. 80, 109.

centralized in the capital. The term *désert français,* used to describe provincial France, was hyperbole, but with an element of truth, so much greater was the desirability of settling in Paris. Meanwhile, economic backwardness afflicted peripheral regions such as Brittany in the west and Languedoc in the south (Table 52). Even fertile and hospitable regions failed to attract investment from both government and the private sector. Backward agriculture, underpopulation, and low capitalization in industry were the results.

Laws for regional equalization and development date back to the early 1950s. As economic planning progressed, financial encouragements for firms to settle outside of Paris were offered in the form of tax relief, investment loans, and outright subsidization.

In Italy the problem of regionalism was even more severe. While the *miracolo economico* catapulted Italy into the age of productivity, fully half the country, from Rome's region south to Sicily, languished in pre-Modern poverty. The southern work force was engaged in outmoded styles of farming, and agricultural underemployment was widespread. The south accounted for only a fourth of gross domestic product in 1969 (Table 53).

As in the case of France there were historical reasons for the severity of Italian regionalism. Under continuous foreign domination since the fall of Rome, the south was a virtual nonparticipant in the mainstream of Italian pre-Modern development. Unification brought little hope as the Piedmontese government seemed little different from earlier foreign over-lords. The Mezzogiorno was left behind by modernizing Italy, a trend that Fascism accentuated. Even during the years following World War II the dominant form of economic organization was latifundia agriculture (see Chapter 2!). The first serious commitment to regional equalization was the establishment of the *Cassa per il Mezzogiorno* (The Southern Development Fund) in 1950. Funds outside the ordinary ministerial budgets were provided for land reclamation and reforestation, road construction, irrigation and sewage facilities, tourism development, and land reform. Ancillary legislation forced major state industries to put at least 40 percent of their new investments in the south and encouraged private enterprise to follow suit. In 1960 the "Green Plan" for Italian agriculture aimed to improve techniques in cultivation and to adjust agrarian production to match domestic and foreign demand.[15] The increased level of economic integration of Europe in the 1960s benefited southern Italy by making a ready

---

[15] Shepard B. Clough, *The Economic History of Modern Italy* (New York: Columbia, 1964), p. 314. On underdevelopement in Southern Europe, see also Gustav Schacter, *The Italian South: Economic Development in Mediterranean Europe* (New York: Random House, 1965); and Barzanti, *The Underdeveloped Areas within the Common Market.*

market for wheat, tomatoes, olive oil, and citrus fruits more accessible, boosting farm prices. The overall Italian index of agricultural output rose faster in the 1960s than that of any other European country, and Italy's total exports to other Common Market countries rose from 1 billion dollars to nearly 6 billion between 1960 and 1970, the most rapid pace of export growth in the Community.[16] It is clear that the ongoing trend toward European integration has offered the greatest hope for correcting regional economic retardation on the Continent.

Table 52. Regional imbalances in France
(gross domestic product at market prices, 1962)

Planning region	GDP, $ billions	Percent GDP	GDP per capita, $
Paris	13.62	23.9	1,558
Upper Normandy	2.22	3.9	1,563
Lower Normandy	1.21	2.1	994
Picardy	1.85	3.3	1,230
Champagne	1.33	2.3	1,087
Burgundy	1.43	2.5	979
Central Region	1.88	3.3	995
Northern Region	4.81	8.5	1,298
Brittany	2.08	3.7	863
Loire Region	2.52	4.4	1,013
Poitou-Charentes	1.33	2.3	904
Lorraine	2.88	5.1	1,288
Alsace	1.62	2.8	1,207
Franche-Comté	1.10	1.9	1,159
Limousin	0.70	1.2	946
Aquitaine	2.68	4.7	1,130
Midi-Pyrénées	1.91	3.4	891
Auvergne	1.29	2.3	1,000
Rhône-Alps	5.15	9.0	1,242
Languedoc	1.61	2.8	987
Provence, Côte d'Azur, Corsica	3.70	6.5	1,158
Whole country	56.91	100.0	1,196

SOURCE: *Basic Statistics of the Community, 1971,* table 146.

---

[16] *Basic Statistics of the Community, 1971,* tables 19, 128.

**Table 53. Regional imbalances in Italy
(gross domestic product at factor cost, 1969)**

Region	GDP ($ billions)	Percent GDP	GDP per capita ($)
Piedmont	7.44	10.2	1,699
Val d'Aosta	0.18	0.2	1,651
Lombardy	15.41	21.1	1,849
Trentino–Alto Adige	1.08	1.5	1,286
Veneto	5.51	7.6	1,348
Friuli–Venezia Giulia	1.74	2.4	1,416
Liguria	3.33	4.6	1,778
Emilia–Romagna	6.13	8.4	1,599
Tuscany	5.08	7.0	1,470
Umbria	0.93	1.3	1,188
The Marches	1.58	2.2	1,158
Lazio	6.84	9.4	1,476
Abruzzi	1.18	1.6	982
Molise	0.26	0.4	781
Campagna	4.67	6.4	905
Apulia	3.51	4.8	967
Basilicata	0.51	0.7	815
Calabria	1.48	2.0	719
Sicily	4.56	6.2	935
Sardinia	1.47	2.0	983
Whole country	72.90	100.0	1,342

SOURCE: *Basic Statistics of the Community, 1971,* table 148.

22

Business fluctuations, international trade, and economic integration

The business cycle in recent times

The extraordinary recovery and subsequent economic growth were not accomplished in a straight-line progression, nor is it to be expected that economic growth will continue ever upward and onward without any falling back. Nor is it to be expected that growth will be so great that the planet will ultimately be so filled with goods and people that neither could move. In spite of some of the implications of economic theory, or statements on the subject by economists, growth has limiting factors, such as exhaustion of resources and the propensity of people to devote their energies to luxury goods or cultural activities rather than to producers' goods. Accordingly, no wonder should be expressed at the historical fact of uneven economic growth in the postbellum period and the appearance of business-cycle phenomena.

Immediately after the cessation of hostilities the much feared economic depression did not materialize. Recovery was, at first, fairly general in Western Europe with the notable exception of West Germany, where conditions were upset because of the Occupation and the lack of any definitive peace settlement. In this period inflation was a major problem, and steps taken to curb it had a depressing effect and led to a recognizable recession in the United States. This recession appears not to have been communicated to Europe,[1] but Europe did realign its moneys in 1949; and this alignment resulted in devaluations which had buoyant effects.

A setback in Europe's economic development was, however, experienced during the Korean crisis (1950–1953), because the terms of trade went against Europe; that is, the prices of foodstuffs and raw materials which Europe imported rose more than the prices of what Europe exported. (See Chart 5.) Also, during the Suez crisis of 1956–1957, ocean freight rates rose so much that Europe's trade was hurt. Then in 1958 and 1959 a recession hit most of Western Europe and America that had many earmarks of a mild business-cycle recession—a decline in investments, a rise in prices, a restriction of bank credit, and some unemployment. France devalued its currency in this crisis and reaped benefits from it. Most other countries sought recovery by expansionist credit policies.[2] Recovery was fairly general, but Italy experienced a recession when "an-opening-to-the-left" coalition government (left-wing Socialists were taken into a government headed by Christian Democrats) weakened the confidence of businessmen in the future and led to a flight of capital abroad. The sixties, and particularly the years 1966–1969, were years of unprecedented high growth rates in Western Europe, the United States, and Japan. Unfortunately they were accompanied by a growing inflation of monumental proportions, the most serious since the end of the war.[3] At the turn of the decade there was a reversal with a curious twist. Stringent austerity measures had been enforced by most governments in an attempt to hold down the rate of inflation. In 1970 these measures took hold on the world economy and a general recession resulted. However, the hoped-for result did not materialize, and inflation proceeded unchecked, a puzzling turn of events for economists and policymakers who termed the new condition "stagflation," a word every bit as distasteful as the circumstance it describes. As growth rates began to move upward again, *ad hoc* measures, such

---

[1] Angus Maddison in his "Growth and Fluctuation in the World Economy, 1870–1960," *Banca Nazionale Quarterly Review,* June 1962, p. 131, writes:
    European imports from the United States have been more dynamic and volatile than United States imports from Europe in spite of much milder European output fluctuations. Europe sends about 10 percent of its exports to North America, i.e., about 2 percent of European GNP. . . . Europe takes 28 percent of Northern American exports, representing about 1.1 percent of United States GNP and 4.1 percent of Canadian GNP. The popular notion that an American sneeze will give the world pneumonia is a fallacy. The United States tends to suffer more from European fluctuations than vice versa.
    See also Angus Maddison, *Economic Growth in the West* (New York: Twentieth Century Fund, 1964).

[2] It appears in retrospect that states tended to adopt meausres to restrict output when the chief problem was excessive growth of incomes. This was true in the United Kingdom in 1957 and was also practiced by the United States. Fear of wide fluctuations was very real and was reflected in these policy steps. Higher taxes on incomes would have been desirable, but politically they were difficult to levy.

[3] The United States dollar, French franc, and pound sterling suffered purchasing-power depreciation at rates of 4 to 6 percent per year. At these rates purchasing power declines 50 percent every fourteen years. See table 44, Chap. 20.

as multiphase wage and price controls imposed in 1971 in the United States and in 1973 in Italy, were used to break the ingrained inflationary psychology of the buying public.[4] The inflation was not only injurious to the Western economy by its effect on income distribution (reducing the purchasing power of fixed-money income groups like pensioners), but also, as we shall see shortly, because of the problems it caused in international trade and payments.

Labor

In the field of labor, six distinct developments have characterized the period since World War II. These are (1) a drive to create conditions of full

---

[4] "Inflationary psychology" is an important cause of the prolongation of inflation. A long episode of rising prices builds up a conviction among consumers that prices will always be higher in the future so that buying in the present appears imperative. This very palpable pressure on current demand pushes up prices, at once fulfilling consumer expectations and enhancing the inflationary trend. In small doses this syndrome is healthy, for it insures some degree of current demand for goods and services. But when the inflationary psychology reinforces an already overheated economy, the result can easily be a runaway inflation.

Chart 5

Terms of Trade[a] of the United States, the United Kingdom, and Nineteen Western European Countries. 1938 = 100 (From Economic Survey of Europe since the War, Geneva: United Nations, 1953, p. 12.)

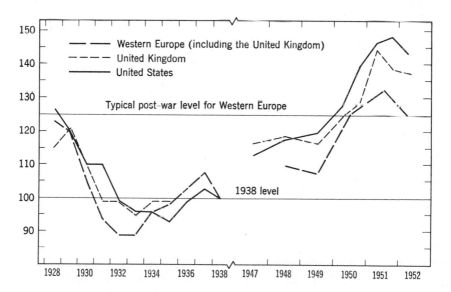

[a] The ratio of the import price to the export price index.

employment and a resulting decrease in unemployment; (2) an increase in wages and a concomitant rise in labor's standard of living; (3) the greater mobility of labor and the accompanying migration of workers from areas where work was scarce to those where there was a shortage, even over international boundaries; (4) a shift of workers from agriculture to the services and to some extent to industry; (5) an extraordinary amount of striking, even of a political chararacter, in spite of much attention to labor relations and to personnel management; and (6) the "hoarding" of skilled labor, that is, hiring workers even when they are not needed because of actual or expected shortages.

In the recovery from the war years, full employment was one of the important goals which planners set for their economies. As can be seen from Table 54, the unemployed as a percentage of the active population was dramatically reduced in most countries. This achievement was realized in spite of a considerable gowth in the work force because population increased and a greater number of women sought paid employment. Yet the proportion of the total population actually in work was somewhat reduced, for because of the baby boom after the war, a larger percentage of the population was for a time below working age and more people were going to school. Thus the age of the work force went up somewhat, which

Table 54. Trends in unemployment, 1949–1970
(unemployed as a percentage of active population)

Country	1949	1950	1955	1960	1965	1970
Austria	2.8	3.7	3.6	2.6	2.7	2.4
Belgium	4.9	4.8	3.2	3.0	2.4	2.9
Canada	2.9	3.6	4.4	7.0	3.9	5.9
Denmark	3.1	1.9	3.3	1.1	2.0	2.9
France	1.2	1.1	1.5	1.1		1.7
Italy	9.2	8.8	9.7	7.5	3.6	3.1
Netherlands	1.1	1.5	1.0	0.9	0.7	1.1
West Germany		7.3	3.9	0.9	0.6	0.7
United Kingdom	1.4	1.4	1.0	1.5	1.5	2.6
United States	5.8	5.2	4.2	5.4	4.5	4.9

SOURCES: *Some Factors in Economic Growth in Europe during the 1950s* (New York: United Nations, 1964), chap. 4, p. 7; *United Nations Statistical Yearbook, 1972* (New York: United Nations, 1973).

meant that more people with experience and skills were in work than previously. In the 1960s the trend began to reverse again. A desire to increase total family income, together with increased availability of day-care facilities for children provided by employers or governments, resulted in a renewed rise in labor-force participation by women. In 1970 about 38 percent of all women fourteen to sixty-five years old in Common Market countries were actively employed.

Labor was also better off than it had been before 1939. Although wages did not keep pace with rising prices in the immediate aftermath of the war, they ultimately climbed faster than prices to a point where they permitted a higher standard of living than formerly. This is reflected in Table 55, for a rising standard permits spending less on food and hence more on education, transportation, and entertainment.[5]

Furthermore, differential standards of living for workers by country diminished, in part because labor was more mobile than it had been in the interbellum period and had migrated from economically depressed areas to those which were booming, especially in industry and mining. In the fifties West Germany received some 2 million immigrants, many emigrating from East Germany for political as well as economic reasons; Switzerland received 340,000, mostly from Italy; and France took some 900,000, a large number of whom were from North Africa, particularly Algeria. Tiny Belgium has absorbed about 800,000 foreign workers and their families since the war, nearly a tenth of the total population in 1970. There were about 12 million transient workers in all of Europe in 1973.

With the movement of workers out of agriculture and into industry and the services, predominantly agricultural areas lost workers to urban areas. (See Map 12.) This was noticeable in the case of emigrants coming from Greece, Spain, and Italy and in the case of internal migrations within national boundaries. The classic example of such migrations is that of southern Italians moving to northern and central Italy. By 1961 some 1½ million persons had left the economically backward south and had gone north, where they did chiefly manual labor. Many who did get a skill may then have moved on to another area, like Western Germany, in search of higher wages. In general, then, labor shortages were mostly in the skilled trades, although for a time after the cessation of hostilities, shortages existed in mining and manual labor in the more advanced countries because nationals of these states were looking for better jobs.[6]

---

[5] International percentages are not strictly comparable, for in some countries education is generally provided by the state. Also, wages are not comparable internationally, because in some countries "family allowances," paid by the state from sums provided by employers and graduated according to the size of families, constitute a large part of the take-home pay but are not entered in statistical compilations as wages.

[6] See *International Migrations* (Geneva: International Labor Office, 1959), Studies and Reports, New Series, no. 54.

Table 55. Private consumption expenditures

Country and period		Food	Drink and tobacco	Clothing and footwear	Rent	Fuel and light	Consumers' durable goods	Other goods	Other services
					Percentage of total consumers' expenditures at current prices				
Austria	1951–1952	41.8	11.4	16.1	4.8	4.9		21.0	
	1961–1962	35.5	10.5	13.5	4.3	3.3		32.9	
Belgium	1953–1954	29.6	7.5	9.9	13.3	5.2	9.0	2.0	23.5
	1961–1962	27.1	7.2	9.7	11.9	5.2	10.8	1.8	26.3
Denmark	1951–1952	27.8	10.0	13.0	6.6	4.7	9.9	10.3	17.7
	1961–1962	23.9	10.1	9.0	8.1	2.4	17.2	10.0	19.3
Finland	1954	39.1	8.3	18.1	6.3	3.8	8.0	8.2	8.2
	1961–1962	36.3	8.7	14.2	7.4	3.0	10.1	8.5	11.8
France	1951–1952	37.6	10.2	14.5	3.4	3.8	7.2	4.1	19.2
	1960–1961	32.1	10.0	11.6	5.4	3.4	8.7	4.3	24.5
West Germany	1951–1952	42.7		15.1	6.4	3.5		32.3	
	1961–1962	37.4		12.4	8.1	4.1		38.0	
Italy	1951–1952	47.1	9.7	13.4	3.6	2.1	3.3	4.2	16.6
	1961–1962	41.9	10.0	9.5	7.5	2.7	4.3	3.8	20.3
Netherlands	1951–1952	34.2	6.7	18.2	6.3	5.3	7.8	3.1	18.4
	1961–1962	30.4	6.6	16.1	8.1	5.1	11.0	3.9	18.8
Norway	1951–1952	30.3	8.3	18.3	5.4	3.1	7.9	3.9	22.8
	1961–1962	29.2	7.9	14.9	8.4	3.6	10.7	3.7	21.6
Sweden	1951–1952	31.3	8.8	14.8	8.1	5.1	9.1	2.7	20.1
	1961–1962	27.9	9.4	12.8	9.7	4.5	11.4	2.7	21.6
United Kingdom	1951–1952	28.5	16.4	10.8	8.2	3.9	6.5	5.4	20.3
	1961–1962	26.7	14.5	9.6	9.5	4.7	8.7	5.0	21.3
United States	1951–1952	25.5	6.2	10.8	11.4	3.3	11.0	3.6	28.2
	1961–1962	21.1	5.3	9.2	13.3	3.6	10.5	3.6	33.4

SOURCE: *Statistical Yearbooks* (New York: United Nations, various years).

Map 12
The Demography of Europe

The post-World War II period has had an inordinately large number of strikes. In part, these have been owing to an increase in trade-union strength, which has made the strike a more effective weapon. In part, too, strikes have been resorted to because in a period of full employment workers have a better chance of success than in periods of hard times. At all events, in 1947 and in 1948 France suffered many strikes that resulted in 7 million man-days lost, which included strikes in coal fields that took out even maintenance men and resulted in flooding the mines. In 1952 the United States had strikes that cost 59.1 million man-days, and in 1955 the United Kingdom had a loss of 3,781,000 man-days.[7] Obviously such stoppages could wreck production, injure many innocent persons, and exert great pressure upon the state to intervene in the public interest. But labor, for the most part, remained immune to hostile legislation and to laws applied to employers which made them liable for collective acts in "restraint of trade," such as price fixing. Here was a power within the state of no mean proportion.[8]

Lastly, employment of skilled labor in industry and the services has tended to fluctuate less with the business cycle than was formerly the case. Because of labor shortages employers of skilled labor hoard workers. They hire them before their real need develops for fear of not being able to get them at the crucial moment, and they hesitate to lay them off when times are slack for fear of not being able to get them back. In addition, the costs of training skilled labor for specific tasks may be very great. As a result labor costs in the most advanced countries have tended to be like capital costs in that they continue in short-run bad times as well as in good, and thus they are considered by some economists as being "overhead costs."

Inflation, deflation, and monetary reform

Immediately after World War II all belligerents were confronted with the enormous problem of rising prices. During the conflict governments had gone heavily into debt in order to keep their current bills paid, and this debt in the form of government bonds was used as reserves by central

---

[7] Mention should also be made of the fact that collective labor contracts were becoming more common, that is, contracts for entire industries or for certain types of work. In these contracts "escalator clauses" became more common, that is, provisions for increases in wages as prices increased. Contracts had terminal dates, and thus periodically labor and management were given opportunities to bargain anew. Increasing wages had a tendency to encourage creeping inflation.

[8] An extraordinarily penetrating study of such powers within the state is Andrew Shonfield, *Modern Capitalism: The Changing Balance of Power of Public and Private Powers* (Fair Lawn, N.J.: Oxford, 1965).

banks to increase their issues of currency. Hence the supply of money ran way ahead of the supply of goods, and the result was an increase in what people would pay for what they wanted. Moreover, governments continued after the war to go into debt, for their tax systems could not be made quickly to yield more income and their expenditures were abnormally high as they endeavored to rebuild and to restore public services. Furthermore, governments did not want to restrict credit unduly, for to do so would discourage individuals from investing in plants for the restoration of production and for economic growth generally. And lastly, individuals were so convinced that prices would continue to go up that they turned their money currently into goods before it lost its purchasing power.

Policies adopted to meet the emergency varied considerably. Nearly all states tried for a time to enforce price controls, but only in rare instances, as in the United Kingdom, were such efforts really efficacious. Some states, such as Belgium in 1944 and Germany in 1949, effected "currency reforms," which consisted of making everyone exchange old money for new money. Such a reform frightened war profiteers or those who had evaded taxes from exchanging their old money, for if they did they practically gave themselves away and could be prosecuted. Furthermore, the reforms were carried out in such a manner that individuals were not paid what was due them all at once, and this withholding of money reduced the amounts which might be spent on goods.

Other states, especially France, Italy, and Germany, experienced dramatic price rises immediately after the conflict. As can be seen in Table 44, p. 462, the index of wholesale prices went up in France between 1938 and 1950 by 2,000 percent, in Italy by nearly 5,000 percent, and in Germany by so much that the statisticians gave up the task of trying to measure the amount. In France, the reluctance to attempt the heroic measures necessary to hold prices down were not taken, because it was easier politically not to do so. In Italy, the new state did not have the power or the expertise in governing to effect the needed reforms. And in Germany, the occupying powers had the real authority and did not act at once.

The United Kingdom and members of the sterling bloc, that is, states whose currencies were tied to the pound sterling by official exchange rates, had considerable success in holding down prices, but in so doing they kept the prices of their exports in terms of current exchange rates at levels which were disadvantageous to foreign buyers. In the United Kingdom, Belgium, and the Netherlands, the price rise was about 300 percent from 1938 to 1955. In the United States it was in the vicinity of 100 percent.

In all these countries, the changes in prices had the usual effect of diminishing the savings of lower-middle-class people who had invested in bonds, savings accounts, and life insurance. It allowed those who produced for the market to strengthen their economic positions.[9] It penalized those who received salaries which were not easily increased. And it hurt those who received wages, for prices rose faster than wages. From a social point of view inflation weakened the middle class and sowed discontent among workers.

From an economic viewpoint the uneven rates of inflation were very disconcerting to business and public finance. Although Gresham's law— that cheap money drives dear money out of circulation—has some validity, the conduct of economic affairs requires a medium of exchange that is stable enough to permit the orderly conduct of affairs, to make business decisions based on a predictable value of money (say, within 5 percent) for the coming production year. Accordingly, orderly moneys drive disorderly moneys out of business.

International trade and payments

Although recovery in production was realized with amazing rapidity after World War II,[10] dislocations in international trade and payments persisted with annoying tenacity. As we have seen, Western Europe's needs for imports were very great and its ability to export in the immediate postwar period was very limited.

The problem of foreign trade and payments had been anticipated during the war, and the United States stepped into the breach by helping to provide relief through UNRRA (United Nations Relief and Rehabilitation Administration) and by granting loans to its former allies. In fact, from the end of the war to August 15, 1947, the United States provided assistance totaling 8 billion dollars, distributed as follows: the United Kingdom, 4,400 million; France, 1,920 million; the Netherlands, 413 million; Italy, 325 million; and the remainder to other states, including Poland and Czechoslovakia. Furthermore, in the same period Canada opened a line of credit to the United Kingdom in the sum of 1,250 million dollars and the Bank for Reconstruction and Development and the Monetary Fund advanced 540 million.

Unfortunately these huge amounts were soon depleted and the credit of Western Europe nearly exhausted. Yet, it was generally believed that,

---

[9] This was the case if the prices of their goods held up in relation to costs of production and in relation to the prices of other goods. Prices of staple farm goods did not maintain their relatively high position, especially after 1951.

[10] It should always be borne in mind that much of postwar production had to go to replace what had been destroyed during the conflict and that, if there had been no war, there would probably have been economic growth beyond the productive levels of 1938. The rapid recovery achieved after both world wars should not give the impression that wars can be fought with economic impunity.

if foreign goods did not continue to flow to Europe, social and political disturbances would occur and that any profound upheaval might result in the establishment of Communist regimes throughout Western Europe. Such an eventuality was abhorrent to the traditionally dominant political groups in Europe and the United States, and they both sought a way out of the predicament.

At a crucial moment, George C. Marshall, American Secretary of State, stepped into the breach. In a now famous speech, delivered June 5, 1947, he stated,

> Europe's requirements for the next three or four years of foreign food and other essential products—principally from America—are so much greater than her present ability to pay that she must have additional help or face economic, social, and political deterioration of a very grave character . . .
>
> Before, however, the United States can proceed much further in its efforts to alleviate the situation and help start the European world on its way to recovery, there must be some agreement among the countries of Europe as to requirements of the situation and the part these countries themselves will take in order to give proper effect to whatever action might be taken by this government.

With great alacrity the British and French issued invitations to all European countries except Spain and the U.S.S.R. to a conference in Paris to draft a report which could be presented to Secretary Marshall.[11] On September 22, 1947, the conference submitted its findings to Washington, and American funds were immediately made available. The "Marshall Plan" became a reality.

The Plan provided for the creation of an Organization of European Economic Cooperation with headquarters in Paris, which had the duty of estimating requirements, of serving as a clearinghouse for national economic plans so that member nations would not work at cross-purposes, and of dividing American aid among the various members. Thus the OEEC practically forced its members to engage in some degree of economic planning and to integrate their plans. In order to estimate needs and have an objective measure for distributing aid, the OEEC decided that deficits in trade and payments, particularly dollar deficits, be used.

---

[11] In attendance were representatives of the United Kingdom, France, Austria, Belgium, Denmark, Greece, Iceland, Ireland, Italy, Luxembourg, the Netherlands, Norway, Portugal, Sweden, Switzerland—the fifteen states which ultimately agreed to join a movement of economic collaboration to which West Germany was added later. The U.S.S.R. forbade its satellites to attend for fear that they would be detached from her.

The OEEC became the Organization for Economic Cooperation and Development in 1961 with the admission of the United States and Canada.

Marshall Plan assistance was in the form of credits which participating governments could spend on imports. Individual businesses which purchased approved imports paid their governments for them in domestic currency and these sums went into the so-called counterpart funds. These counterpart funds were then used within the recipient countries for purposes approved by the receiving country and by members of American missions to these states.[12] Accordingly, not only did American aid help pay for imports, but proceeds from the sale of goods were funneled into projects for monetary stabilization and economic development.

The Marshall Plan was "programmed" to last five years, at the end of which time it was expected that Western Europe would be on its feet so far as trade and payments were concerned.[13] For various reasons, however, this goal was not attained. Some countries, instead of conscientiously trying to eliminate their trade and payments deficits, pursued easy credit policies toward importers on the theory that the greater their foreign deficits the larger would be their share of American aid. Furthermore, a business recession in the United States in 1949 led to a falling off of American purchases from Europe; the Korean War resulted in purchases which forced up the prices of many raw materials which Europe imported and hence made Europe's money deficit greater than it had been. The growing hostility between the U.S.S.R., on one side, and the United States and its friends,[14] on the other, caused the United States to be all the more anxious to preserve Western Europe from communism of the Russian kind.

On account of these conditions, American aid was continued (Table 56). In 1949, President Truman announced his "Point Four Program" for the development of economically backward areas both for their own material betterment and for providing more raw materials and larger markets for Western culture's economy.[15] In 1951, the United States passed its Mutual Security Act[16] for military assistance to friendly nations and for the purchase from them of military equipment for American forces abroad. Consequently American aid was more, although not exclusively, for defense rather than for economic reconstruction and it was extended to other than European nations, large sums going to the Middle and Far East.[17] In the greatest giveaway program of all time the United States made available

---

[12] These were the ECA missions (Economic Cooperation Administration).

[13] Amounts of American aid were to be progressively decreased in the last years of the Plan.

[14] The North Atlantic Treaty Organization (NATO) was formed in 1949 for collective defense. It included the United States, France, Denmark, Portugal, Iceland, Italy, the Netherlands, and Norway. Greece and Turkey were added in 1951. The Federal German Republic became a member in 1954. A joint military command was established at Supreme Headquarters of the Atlantic Powers in Europe (SHAPE).

[15] The United Nations undertook a similar program.

[16] This had been preceded by the Mutual Defense Assistance program of 1949.

[17] The Eisenhower Doctrine, enunciated in January 1957, was to give military and economic assistance to any nation or group of nations in the Middle East which requested help against overt aggression from any nation controlled by international communism.

Table 56. Distribution of U.S. foreign aid, 1945–1964 (in millions of dollars)

Net total for all regions and countries	97,283
Investment in international financial institutions	1,290
Under assistance programs	95,993
Military grants	33,841
Other grants, credits, and assistance	62,152
Amounts received by region	
Western Europe	23,919
Eastern Europe	1,636
Near East and South Asia	13,762
Africa	1,862
Far East and Pacific	13,880
American republics	4,931
Other Western Hemisphere	45
Other international organizations and unspecified areas	2,119
Amounts received by European countries and organizations	
Austria	1,088
Belgium-Luxembourg	664
Denmark	267
Finland	69
France	4,443
West Germany	3,056
Iceland	67
Ireland	132
Italy	2,883
Netherlands	830
Norway	243
Portugal	147
Spain	861
Sweden	87
United Kingdom	6,410
Yugoslavia	1,848
European Atomic Energy Community	31
European Coal and Steel Community	77
European Payments Union	238
Other and unspecified	478

SOURCE: *Statistical Abstract of the United States, 1965.*

to foreign peoples from 1945 to 1967 56 billion dollars, which was the equivalent of one-fifth of the country's national income in 1950. Of this amount, 37.4 billion dollars was for economic assistance and the remainder for military purposes. By 1963 aid had reached 96,671 million dollars.

There is no question but that this aid from America did much to restore multilateral trade and payments. The index of world trade (1953 = 100) went from 70 in 1948 to 113 in 1955; that of Western Europe rose from 45 to 127, and that of North America from 83 to 100. The recovery of Western Europe's export trade was particularly significant, for in the case of this area there was a high correlation between exports, investments, and economic growth. Yet Europe had lost ground percentagewise in world trade and still relied heavily upon imports of foodstuffs and raw materials for which it paid by exporting manufactured goods and services (Table 57).

**Table 57. Balance of trade of selected countries
(in billions of dollars)**

Country	1963	1970
United Kingdom	−1,642	−2,372
West Germany	+1,597	+4,735
France	− 643	−1,183
Italy	−2,534	−1,729
Netherlands	−1,005	−1,626
Belgium-Luxembourg	− 273	+ 242
Norway	− 748	−1,242
Denmark	− 250	−1,095
Sweden	− 186	− 233
Switzerland	− 825	−1,330
Austria	− 350	− 692
Spain	−1,212	−2,360
U.S.S.R.	+ 214	+1,061
U.S.A.	+5,908	+3,263

(Note: + denotes export surplus; − denotes import surplus.
SOURCE: *Basic Statistics of the Community*, table 62.

European prosperity was reliant on imported food and energy supplies, and economic growth in other areas of the world meant that competition for these supplies became more and more severe and that prices were constantly being bid up in the international marketplace. Between 1963 and 1970 total energy consumption in Europe increased by 42 percent, even as total energy production declined; consequently energy imports more than doubled in those years (Table 58). Regarding foodstuffs, Common Market countries in 1970 were largely self-sufficient in grains, vegetables, and dairy products, but these six continental countries were dependent on outside supplies of fish, citrus fruits, fats and oils, and protein supplements for fodder.

Table 58. Energy production and consumption in Western Europe in millions of metric tons of coal equivalents

Year	Total energy production	Total energy consumption	Net imports	Per capita consumption*
1963	576	977	419	2,906
1964	585	1,014	482	2,984
1965	574	1,045	527	3,049
1966	553	1,080	586	3,122
1967	537	1,094	625	3,141
1968	539	1,162	687	3,313
1969	542	1,245	854	3,522
1970	557	1,351	895	3,791
1971	585	1,384		3,878

*In kilograms of coal equivalents.
SOURCE: *United Nations Statistical Yearbook* (New York: United Nations, 1972).

Within Europe the problem of trade and payment balances took on an increasingly hectic and unstable character. "Gold Crisis" or "International Monetary Crisis" became frequent headlines, and of all the attempts at shoring up the system, none had fully succeeded. The Bretton Woods arrangement, which included the formation of the International Monetary Fund, determined that gold was to be restored as the primary international currency. Inasmuch as the dollar at that time was backed by nearly six-tenths of the non-Communist world's gold, it became a special currency whose worth could be trusted because of its hard backing and the strength of the American economy. A market in short-term dollar commitments outside the United States arose (the Eurodollar Market), making the dollar a "vehicle currency" for international business transactions and even central bank reserves and transfers. The international monetary situation assumed a degree of relative stability through the early 1960s. Germany had built up embarrassingly large favorable balance of payments; France had a bad debit position; then in 1962 and 1963 Italy had a big deficit in trade; and in 1965 and 1966 the United Kingdom had its turn. In these emergencies central banks and the IMF lent moneys to other central banks in order to keep their governments from yielding to the temptation of devaluing. But in the wings lay two ominous factors which threatened to throw the international payments mechanism into disarray. First, the growth of trade and the volume of international payments rose far more rapidly than the supply of gold, causing the price of gold to increase as the demand for reserves outran the supply. This put pressure on currencies which were pegged to gold at fixed prices, for to defend these prices, treasuries were forced to sell gold cheaply, thereby losing reserves in the process. Added pressure on gold supplies came from the private sector when, beginning about 1967, the electronics, aerospace, and jewelry industries, along with other private consumers, removed over one-third of the world's annual gold output from monetary uses. The second source of instability was the fall of the dollar from its position of absolute supremacy in the postwar monetary world. This came as a result of a chronically unfavorable balance of payments owing in turn to a rise in imports, worldwide military commitments, and unrelenting domestic inflation, which hurt United States competitiveness in international commodity markets.[18] As the United States paid out gold to cover payments deficits, the hard backing of the dollar softened and the possibility of devaluation made holding dollars less and less attractive.

Adjustment to the new monetary facts of life was difficult. Between 1967 and 1969, years in which both England and France were forced to devalue currencies and institute austerity measures to stem the tide of gold outflow, a new reserve asset came into being known as Special Drawing Rights (SDRs or "paper gold"). IMF member nations received annual quotas of SDRs and were able to use them to clear accounts along with, or in place of, gold. In 1970 it was determined that 9.5 billion dollars worth of SDRs would be created over three years, representing a 4 percent increase in the sum total of international reserves.[19] While this measure did

---

[18] It is noteworthy that the United States *balance of trade* remained strongly positive even as the *balance of payments* became unfavorable. The balance of trade as given in Table 57 represents net exports of goods and services minus net imports of goods and services. It is but one component of the balance of payments which also covers public and private unilateral payments (foreign remittances, foreign aid, government grants, and pensions paid abroad), military expenditures abroad, capital transfers (net investment abroad, purchases and sales of foreign securities, foreign claims on United States banks), and certain other international debits and credits. A negative (unfavorable) balance of payments results in the outflow of international reserve assets such as gold or "paper gold."

[19] R. E. Caves and R. W. Jones, *World Trade and Payments; An Introduction* (Boston: Little, Brown, 1973), p. 429.

not eliminate the pressure of increasing demand on the relatively constant supply of gold,[20] the prospect for improved international liquidity was much enhanced.

More problems remained to be solved, as the events of 1970–1972 clearly showed. The dollar was still widely held and traded in Europe, not only because of its role as a vehicle currency, but also because a high degree of participation by United States–based multinational corporations in Europe and around the world maintained the need for worldwide dollar payment facilities. Outstanding dollar holdings outside the United States rose to a condition of real oversupply in 1970, when an easing of domestic credit caused American banks to release Eurodollars onto foreign markets. Speculative pressure on the dollar ran high, and in August 1971 the United States suspended the convertibility of the dollar. To avoid depleting its gold stock the United States would no longer sell gold for dollars to foreign governments. Without convertibility, the dollar weakened in the money market. A formal devaluation later in the year, combined with earlier unofficial adjustments, left the dollar worth about 17 percent less than it had been a year before. At the same time the British pound and the Italian lira were devalued by about 10 percent, and the strong currencies, the German mark, the Swiss franc, and the Japanese yen, were revalued upward by 11, 18, and 24 percent respectively. Out of the chaos came a series of concrete proposals designed to reform world monetary order based on the framework of a strengthened IMF. The Smithsonian Accords of December 1971 quelled the wild fluctuations of major currencies that erupted when the convertibility of the dollar was suspended, and from these meetings came new rates of exchange that were created, for the first time, by genuine multinational negotiation. Also, a commission of twenty ministers was charged with formulating a major reform of the world monetary system. In 1973 at Nairobi, Kenya, a first draft of general proposals was issued recording the basic principles under negotiation. Despite outstanding differences of opinion,[21] it was generally agreed that reform was very much in order and that improved economic stability could be achieved without any drastic institutional change by promulgating a stable but flexible set of ground rules. The basic drift of these modifications would be to reduce the role of gold and national currencies as reserve assets and replace them with the SDRs, and to reduce the speed and arbitrary nature of exchange-rate revisions so as to do away with competitive devaluations and currency speculation.

---

[20] Before the official price of gold was about 35 dollars per ounce; in 1974 an ounce of gold sold for as much as 175 dollars in world markets.

[21] The most basic difference was between those countries—France foremost—which believed that reliance on gold and fixed rates of exchange insures stability, and others, including the United States, which emphasized flexibility through floating rates to adjust imbalances and favored decreased reliance on gold.

Insofar as Europe is concerned, we can see that two distinct phases in her monetary history have transpired since the war. The first was marked by the relative weakness of all European countries with respect to the United States, in terms of both trade position and currency. With the renewal of European productivity and trade competitiveness, this position was reversed and several European currencies achieved great strength, the Deutsche Mark being the foremost (Table 59). By the crises of the early

Table 59. The growth of official reserves (gold and convertible currencies) in the original six EEC countries (in millions of dollars)

Year	West Germany	France	Italy	Nether- lands	Belgium– Luxembourg	Common Market
1950	190	791	602	548	793	2,924
1951	455	616	774	554	1,054	3,453
1952	960	686	696	923	1,077	4,342
1953	1,736	829	778	1,163	1,088	5,584
1954	2,496	1,261	927	1,209	1,042	6,935
1955	2,935	1,912	1,167	1,223	1,147	8,384
1956	4,119	1,180	1,236	1,038	1,163	8,736
1957	5,114	645	1,355	1,009	1,142	9,295
1958	5,732	1,050	2,139	1,488	1,497	11,906
1959	4,522	1,720	2,988	1,339	1,222	11,791
1960	6,724	2,070	3,183	1,742	1,422	15,141
1961	6,527	2,939	3,557	1,715	1,657	16,395
1962	6,439	3,610	3,619	1,743	1,622	17,033
1963	7,098	4,457	3,181	1,899	1,802	18,437
1964	6,969	5,105	3,673	2,084	1,992	19,823
1965	6,353	5,459	3,867	2,058	1,996	19,733
1966	6,771	5,745	3,702	2,036	1,952	20,191
1967	6,850	6,108	3,819	2,268	2,202	21,247
1968	7,497	4,200	3,881	1,967	1,886	19,431
1969	5,679	3,833	3,855	2,090	2,232	17,689
1970	11,834	4,789	4,951	2,552	2,250	26,376

SOURCE: *Basic Statistics of the Community, 1971,* p. 185, table 143.

seventies Europeans came to own 45 percent of world gold reserves. These crises reduced the vestigial trading disadvantages imposed on America during earlier times while reducing the role of the dollar as a European super-currency. Hopefully, a third phase of stable but flexible monetary relationships has emerged from the years of crisis.

Tariff reform

The restoration of a system of mutilateral trade and payments was of prime importance after World War II. The main obstacles to such a restoration were the closing of the dollar gap, helping nations with large payments deficits, and national impediments to international trade, such as tariffs, import quotas, and exchange controls. Theorists frowned upon these obstacles to commerce, for they gave a high priority to the advantages to be obtained from an international division of labor. In line with their thinking several states proposed after World War II that an International Trade Organization be established as an agency of the United Nations, like the Bank for Reconstruction and Development and the International Monetary Fund, in order to work steadily for the removal of trade barriers. As a result of such proposals a General Agreement on Tariffs and Trade, popularly known as GATT, was negotiated at Geneva in 1947, and a charter for an International Trade Organization was drafted at Havana in 1948. These documents envisioned a liberalization of international trade by a general abolition of import quotas and exchange controls and an eventual reduction in tariff rates. The Havana charter was a watered-down version of a draft proposal submitted by the United States and did not find general acceptance. In fact, President Truman did not even present it to the Senate for ratification. Hence the ITO was never created, but its ends were sought by operating under GATT.

The reluctance of the members of the United Nations to effect trade reforms was very marked; most of them raised the traditional arguments for some kind of protection. European nations did not at first consider themselves strong enough to open their markets to competitors like the United States, whose productive plant had not been destroyed, or like Japan, where labor costs were low. Economically underdeveloped countries wanted and in many cases needed protection for their infant industries. Then, many feared that freedom to purchase goods in any market might result in such an outflow of national currency as to lead to inflation and to eventual devaluation.

In spite of such hesitations regarding the freeing of trade, some progress was made. Negotiating conferences were held (1949, 1951, 1960–1961), but the most famous of them began in 1964, following the United States' Trade Expansion Act of 1962, and became known as the Kennedy Round (of tariff reductions). From the outset the participating powers in the Kennedy Round agreed on an across-the-board cut of rates by 50 percent, but with the proviso that exceptions might be made because of national interest and that these would have to be justified and agreed upon—a very laborious and long-drawn-out task. Nevertheless real progress was made in freeing trade. Quotas were generally abolished; the almost free convertibility of currences was reestablished, or put another way, restrictions upon using national moneys with which to purchase goods abroad were removed; and tariffs were reduced on the average by about 35 percent (Table 60). The guiding principle of GATT negotiations was the "most-favored-nation clause," meaning that any trade concession granted in bilateral bargaining to one country became instantly applicable to all GATT members, at once eliminating inefficient discrimination between suppliers while checking the motive for retaliatory action by "unfavored" nations. GATT's great accomplishment was having prevented upward spirals of protectionism in the postwar period.

Table 60. Average tariff levels after the Kennedy Round (1972) in percentages

	European Economic Community[*]	United Kingdom	United States
Raw materials	1.0	2.0	3.6
Mineral fuels	2.0	0.2	3.7
Oils and fats	9.8	10.0	14.9
Chemicals	7.3	8.2	9.6
Semi-manufactures	8.0	9.4	8.8
Machinery and transport	8.5	9.7	5.9
Misc. manufactures	10.2	15.2	17.6
All products	8.4	10.2	9.0
All products before 1968	13.1	16.3	14.6

[*]Original six.
SOURCE: R. Broad and R. J. Jarrett, *Community Europe Today* (London: Oswald Wolff, 1972), p. 147.

Within Western Europe liberalization of trade was the order of the day as part of a program for economic integration. Tariff barriers on industrial goods moving between the customs union (the EEC) and the free-trade area (the EFTA) were fully dismantled in 1968, and protectionist pressures that arose in the early seventies were successfully thwarted. Much remained to be achieved: the Kennedy Round was a disappointment insofar as freeing international trade in agricultural goods and improving the position of developing nations, while Europe remained divided into two separate customs unions for largely nationalistic reasons. But the trend in tariff reform had been healthy; enlarging the benefits of freer trade contributed to real income gains for European consumers.

The economic integration of Europe

As Western Europe came to realize that its economic, political, and military position in the world had been greatly weakened, it began an earnest search for an explanation of the decline. It was obvious that the World Wars had been responsible in part for what had befallen the West and that to prevent a repetition of such catastrophes it was necessary greatly to improve relations among the nations of the Continent. Moreover, it was thought that an improvement of these relations could be effected by minimizing economic rivalries and tensions and that this happy state could be attained if Europe operated as an economic unit rather than as a number of independent pieces. Furthermore, there was general agreement that Western Europe should strengthen itself economically and that this was feasible given the area's resources, manpower, capital savings, and techniques. It was necessary, so it was thought, to increase production per capita. One important way of doing so was to create a larger market for European goods—a market that would allow producers to reduce the unit cost of their products by allowing them to increase volume. This doctrine of a larger market, although probably overstated, was preached with conviction by American leaders in the Economic Cooperation Administration, [22] was widely advocated by professional economists, [23] and became an obsession with certain European statesmen, like Robert Schuman of France. [24]

For these reasons efforts were made to realize customs unions of a few states, to negotiate arrangements to abolish the worst impediments to trade, and to create machinery to deal with obvious causes of tension. Thus, Belgium, Luxembourg, and the Netherlands formed a customs union known as Benelux and the Scandinavian states set up the Nordic Council

---

[22] See *Ninth Report of the E.C.A.* (Washington: Government Printing Office, 1950), p. 35.

[23] See, for example, François Perroux, *Europe sans rivages* (Paris: Presses Universitaires, 1954).

[24] For some time the smaller countries of Europe had favored freer trade within Europe because of their dependence on foreign markets. After World War II, the larger countries began to look with more favor on a European customs union, because their proportion of intra-European trade had declined more than that of small countries. The United Kingdom, however, hesitated to participate actively in plans for Western European tariff unification for fear that it would lose its preferential position with members of the British Commonwealth.

(1955) to propose reforms to member nations. The various states of Western Europe created the Council for Europe (1949), to which members of parliaments could come to discuss problems of common interest and to draft recommendations for legislation.[25] The North Atlantic Treaty Organization was established, following the signing of the Atlantic Pact (1949), to defend Western Europe against Russia. The Organization for European Economic Cooperation came into being, as we have seen, not only to divide American aid but also to exchange ideas regarding steps which had to be taken to foster economic growth throughout Europe.

Although attention was focused at first on the freeing of trade among Western European states, it was soon obvious that a unified market could not be established without envisioning "integration" of several kinds. Accordingly it was argued that in order to have freedom of movement of goods there would have to be freedom of movement of manpower and of capital and that there would also have to be a general equalizing of social security systems, of tax burdens, and of economic levels. Thus there developed a movement toward European economic integration—a movement that for the long run seemed to have much in its favor.

In the short run, however, there were several obstacles in the way of integration. For one thing, it ran smack into nationalism, which had been one of the greatest forces in Western culture in the preceding century and a half and which still had great potency. For another, the integration movement had to face up to the real difficulties involved in bringing together areas with such enormous economic differences as those of southern Italy and northern France. Dissimilarities in income per capita, in population growth, in systems of taxation, in social security systems, in unemployment, and in a thousand other things made for doubts that integration could ever be realized. The more highly developed regions feared that they would have to assume unreasonable burdens for people over whom they had no political authority, and the underdeveloped regions thought that they might be swamped with goods from regions with which they could not compete. In fact, a kind of circular reasoning developed by which integration was demanded to minimize economic inequalities and in which economic inequalities themselves made integration difficult.

Because of particular difficulties in establishing the freedom of movement of people and capital, the economic integration of Europe movement centered at first mostly on trade and payments. One of the greatest achievements of the early postwar days was the European Payments Un-

---

[25] An attempt was made to create a European Defense Community (1952), that is, a common European military establishment. It did not materialize because the French, the original sponsors of the project, failed to ratify the enabling act.

ion. From its inception the Organization for European Economic cooperation (OEEC) attempted to facilitate the multilateral settling of intra-European commercial accounts and after an unsuccessful start (1948) established the EPU in 1950. The Union provided for the fixing of "quotas" between each country and the Union. Up to the limit of its quota a country could pay its debits to the Union in its own currency, but beyond that amount it had to pay in gold and dollars. Again, beyond certain limits, a country had to receive payments for its credits in currencies of member states. Thus there were incentives for debtor countries to increase their exports or to decrease their imports and for creditor countries not to exceed given amounts.

In general, the EPU was a success. It had as members all the major countries of Western Europe, including the United Kingdom, and thus covered a large proportion of the trade of the world. Furthermore, it succeeded in progressively removing most of the quantitative trade restrictions in Europe so that, in 1956, 80 percent of European trade was free of them. Finally, it managed actually to settle accounts on a multilateral basis. Certainly, it contributed to an expansion of intra-European trade by some 90 percent between 1948 and 1951. On the other hand, the system resulted in certain rigidities, because when one country had a large and continuing credit, as was the case with Germany in the middle 1950s, or a large and continuing deficit, as was the case of France at the same time, the Union tried to establish a balance by permitting the reimposition of trade restrictions. Without the Union, however, the situation would undoubtedly have been much worse than it was.

Obviously the European Payments Union was not designed to accomplish more than a very limited task of settling international accounts and the ends of economic integration called for much more. It was thought by some that the most realistic approach to economic integration was to achieve it on a commodity basis. Thus there was created in 1951 the European Steel and Coal Community—an outgrowth of a plan proposed by Robert Schuman of France. This institution was to exercise sovereignty over the coal and steel industries of Belgium, France, West Germany, Italy, Luxembourg, and the Netherlands; that is, its decisions regarding coal and steel were to be binding on member states. Inasmuch as the Community was designed as a step toward political integration and inasmuch as it had to operate in its limited sphere much like a government, it was endowed with typical governmental institutions: a Council of Ministers to decide on major policies, an Assembly elected by member parliaments to serve in an advisory capacity, a Court of Justice to settle disputes and to rule on questions of treaty violations, and a high Authority to serve as executive. The Treaty of the ESCC provided for free trade in coal and steel among member states, for joint research, and for the abolition of cartels. Furthermore, a small percentage of sales of coal and steel was to be paid to the Community to cover its expenses and to provide funds for investments in the industries.

The European Coal and Steel Community was a success. It forced the most inefficient plants to close, notably the coal mines of the Borinage area in Belgium; it encouraged modernization of other plants, in part by making them loans; it helped to stabilize prices; and it tried to harmonize supply and demand. This experiment in placing authority over an industry in the hands of a supranational body was considered by some to be a poor test of integration. Such critics pointed out that coal and steel industries involved only some 3 percent of the labor forces of the participating countries; the need for freedom of movement of capital funds was mitigated somewhat by the use of Marshall Plan counterpart funds, and coal and steel industries had already cooperated on an international level to a considerable extent. Enthusiasts for economic integration looked at the ESCC, however, as a harbinger of better things and suggested that similar communities be established in a great variety of sectors from agricultural products (the Green Pool), inland transportation,[26] heavy chemicals, and nuclear energy.

The OEEC was particularly active in keeping discussions of integration alive, and these discussions finally led to concrete results. In 1957 the countries which had already formed the European Steel and Coal Community signed the now famous Treaties of Rome. One of the Treaties called for the creation of a European Atomic Energy Community, which immediately became known as Euratom, and the other provided for setting up the much more important European Economic Community. By the Treaty of Rome, Belgium, France, West Germany, Italy, Luxembourg, and the Netherlands agreed to the gradual establishment over a twelve-year period of the free flow of goods, capital, and labor among the participating powers. It provided further for the administration of the Community by a Council representing the governments of the treaty countries, for a Readaptation Fund which would bear 50 percent of the cost of retraining and relocating workers and of reconverting plants, for a European Investment Bank with a capital of 1 billion dollars, and for an Investment Fund of 600 million dollars for overseas territories of member states. By December 1957 this treaty had been ratified by all the powers concerned. The European Economic Community (EEC), more popularly known as the Common Market, and Euratom had come into existence.

This left a number of West European states out in the cold; thus they rather hastily improvised an agreement among themselves (the Treaty of

---

[26] The Inland Transport of the United Nations' Economic Commission for Europe made many suggestions for international collaboration in this industry.

Stockholm), which brought into being the European Free Trade Association (1959). This organization did not envisage the kind of integration contemplated by the founders of the EEC, but it did anticipate combined action to reduce tariffs.[27]

The history of Euratom is not complicated. This body created plants for the generation of nuclear energy, and it established research facilities.[28] The history of the other two organizations is, by contrast, very complicated. In brief, it may be said that they have both achieved important reductions of tariffs and that the EEC has established under certain conditions the free movement of workers. Movements are also afoot to reduce the differences in social security systems and in taxation. Major crises have, however, arisen. One was over the admission of the United Kingdom and other EFTA nations to the EEC. France vetoed this move twice when the bargaining became severe in 1963 and 1967. The other crisis was over subsidies to farmers for certain products, especially wheat. The farmers stood to take a loss with the establishment of common prices throughout the Community in preparation for having a common tariff on these agricultural products. This crisis became so tense that France withdrew its negotiators from the negotiations in process, and the entire organization seemed in danger. But the difficulties were satisfactorily resolved, and the EEC was able to proceed on its business.[29]

The accomplishments of these two bodies were great in reducing tariffs. As we have noted, the EEC was scheduled to become a customs union twelve years after the Treaty of Rome, and, in fact, the abolition of internal tariffs and the formation of a common external tariff was accomplished by July 1968, eighteen months ahead of time. Moreover, the Community reduced practically all internal barriers to trade and also facilitated the movement of both capital and workers across national boundaries.

The original six members of the Common Market agreed to a policy of tax harmonization. By 1972 all current members had adopted the *value added tax* (VAT) to replace a confusion of retail sales taxes, corporate profits taxes, and excises. The harmonization was deemed necessary because indirect taxes affect prices and thus can distort trade patterns. The VAT was a uniform, efficient, and comprehensive sales tax levied on the price at which all goods and services were sold, at all stages of production and

---

[27] The participating nations were the United Kingdom, Sweden, Norway, Denmark, Austria, Switzerland, and Portugal.
[28] The United Nations has published an important series under the title *Peaceful Uses of Atomic Energy* in sixteen volumes.
[29] The European Agricultural Guidance and Guarantee Fund was established to make payments to farmers. Its moneys come in part from individual member states and in part from import duties on agricultural products.

distribution.[30] Making business taxes uniform was a major step toward economic and possibly eventual political union.

Europe in its semi-united state was a formidable economic power in the contemporary world, conventional wisdom about the "decline of the West" notwithstanding. This can be judged in terms of the European role in world commerce. In 1970 the Inner Six sold 25.4 billion dollars worth of goods and services and the Outer Seven sold 17.6 billion dollars outside of Europe. So even omitting intra-European trade, Western Europe sold more throughout the world than the United States (42 billion dollars) or Japan and the U.S.S.R. combined (19.3 billion dollars and 11.6 billion dollars respectively).[31] This European economic power and influence has been in the process of enhancement, and it seems that Europeans are willing to abandon some of the trappings of nationalism to achieve this end. After two humiliating rejections at the hands of Gaullist France, Great Britain finally succeeded in joining the Common Market, together with Ireland and Denmark, in 1973. This was accomplished after much negotiation and with considerable swallowing of pride on both sides of the table. The accession took place with little fanfare, despite the historic significance of the occasion, on January 1, 1973, and the three new members became full partners with the original six in the Community. Even before this event an agreement had been signed which prearranged a slow reduction in trade barriers between the six EEC members and the rest of Europe.[32] In 1973 a 20-percent reduction of tariffs on industrial goods was effected, the first step toward total tariff-free trade in industrial commodities, which is scheduled for 1977. The immediate prospect therefore is a free-trade zone of 300 million people accounting for 40 percent of world trade—a potentially more formidable European economy than the world has seen since the nineteenth-century European economic hegemony.

---

[30] Theoretically the tax is levied on the value added to a commodity at each stage of transfer from raw material through wholesale exchanges to retail sale. Inasmuch as value added equals the price of output minus the cost of inputs at any production stage, the difference being wholly profits and wages, the VAT can be viewed as a tax on income distribution. See Alan Tail, *The Value Added Tax* (Maidenhead, England: McGraw-Hill (U.K.), 1972), p. 2.

[31] Broad and Jarrett, *Community Europe Today*, pp. 204–205.

[32] The remaining members of the European Free Trade Association stayed outside the Common Market for a variety of reasons. Austria was forbidden by treaty from entering a unifying arrangement with Germany; any move in that direction could have been vetoed by the Soviet Union. Finland falls within the Soviet sphere of influence and was pressured not to sign the free-trade agreement with the EEC. Sweden and Switzerland abstained from joining in order to conserve their stance of absolute neutrality, the Common Market being a Western bloc. The Community regarded the Portuguese government as undemocratic and therefore unacceptable for membership (as were Spain and Greece). Iceland did not seek to join; and finally, Norway was at the threshold of the Community, fully prepared to join, when a referendum in 1972 voted down membership by a small majority.

Map 13
Energy Sources

THE ECONOMIC INTEGRATION OF EUROPE **519**

Coal
Lignite
Petroleum and
natural gas
Pipelines
Under construction
Feeders
● Petroleum refineries
Ⓤ Uranium ore
⊛ Nuclear plants
✪ Nuclear plants
planned
△ Atomic research
centers
□ Geothermal
◉ Steam generating
plants
○ Water power plants
▬ Transmission lines

Gothenburg
Sweden

Denmark
Copenhagen

Great Britain

Heysham

Liverpool   Leeds

Ireland

Ipswich

London

Portsmouth

Wilhelmshaven   Hamburg
Groningen Emden
Netherlands   Hanover   Berlin
Amsterdam
Rotterdam   **Germany**
Antwerp
Dunkirk
Belgium   Brussels   Cologne

Rouen   Frankfort
on Main
Paris   Nuremberg
Orleans   Stuttgart
Strasbourg   Munich   Vienna
Rennes
France   Zurich   **Austria**
Nantes   Bern
Switzerland
Geneva
Lyons   Milan   Cremona   Trieste
Turin   Piacenza   Venice
Bordeaux   Ravenna
Montélimar   Genoa
Spezia   Florence
Pau   Leghorn   **Italy**
Toulouse   Nice
Marseille
Corsica
Spain   Rome
○ Madrid   Bari
Naples

Sardinia

Cartagena   Palermo Sicily
Gela

Challenges for Europe

However encouraging the growing closeness of the European Community may be, many major problems confront workers, businessmen, and policy-makers. Foremost among these are: competition with other world economic powers, including multinational corporations which operate on a world scale; the extreme vulnerability of the economic system; and the deleterious effects of industrial life, notably the degradation of the physical environment.

In 1967 a book was published in France, the title of which—*The American Challenge*—became a slogan for European men of affairs.[32] The author, J. J. Servan-Schreiber, argued that American business had "invaded" Europe, and because of organizational and entrepreneurial superiority, United States-based corporations threatened to become major owners of European industrial enterprise. The evidence he mustered was compelling. Between 1958 and 1968 American companies invested 10 billion dollars in Europe, representing over one-third of their total investments abroad.[33] American firms predominated in high-technology areas, controlling, for example, 80 percent of computer production and 95 percent of integrated circuit markets inside Europe.[34] There was much truth to the American challenge concept. Even the most casual observer could testify to the commercial and cultural impact of America on Europe in the quarter century following World War II. Ironically, however, a reversal in the trend began to take place soon after the publication of Servan-Schreiber's book. With the cheapening of the dollar relative to other currencies, American firms have become prime targets for European (and Japanese) investors.[35] No quick upset has taken place, to be sure; American holdings overseas (worldwide) outmatch foreign holdings inside the United States by a ratio of 6 to 1. However, there is recent indication that the American commercial presence in Western Europe has been a beneficial leaven for European entrepreneurship and that European corporations, when given the opportunity, engage in overseas investment in much the same fashion as their American counterparts.

International economic relationships in recent years have been complicated by the existence of corporations whose scale of operations is so vast that they transcend national boundaries. These multinational corpora-

---

[32] J. J. Servan-Schreiber, *The American Challenge* (New York: Atheneum, 1968), original published in France as *Le Défi Americain*.

[33] Ibid., p. 5.

[34] Ibid., p. 13.

[35] For example, Gimbel Brothers, a major United States retailing firm, was purchased by Brown & Williamson Tobacco Corp., a London-based company, in 1973; Switzerland's Nestle Alimentana purchased Stouffer Foods; and the Japanese conglomerate Mitsui & Co. acquired a half interest in the aluminum fabrications division of American Metal Climax.

tions pose serious legal and economic problems for all nations that host part of their operations. For disunited Europe the jurisdictional problems are especially acute. The magnitude of the multinational corporation can be seen from Table 61, which compares annual world sales of the biggest of these firms with gross national products of countries. The sales figure for the General Motors Corporation is larger than the GNP of all but twenty-two of the nations of the world! Note also that of the forty largest multinational corporations, over one-third are based in Europe. The Common Market, and for that matter the entire developed and underdeveloped world, has begun only recently to consider the effects of this development in business organization on factor markets, trade patterns, and global politics.

Table 61. National products and corporate sales compared, 1970

		GNP or gross annual sales ($ billions)			GNP or gross annual sales ($ billions)
1.	United States	974.1	25.	Pakistan	17.5
2.	U.S.S.R.	504.7	26.	South Africa	16.7
3.	Japan	197.2	27.	STANDARD OIL N.J.	16.6
4.	West Germany	186.4	28.	Denmark	15.6
5.	France	147.5	29.	FORD MOTOR	15.0
6.	Britain	121.0	30.	Austria	14.3
7.	Italy	93.2	31.	Yugoslavia	14.0
8.	China	82.5	32.	Indonesia	12.6
9.	Canada	80.4	33.	Bulgaria	11.8
10.	India	52.9	34.	Norway	11.4
11.	Poland	42.3	35.	Hungary	11.3
12.	East Germany	37.6	36.	ROYAL DUTCH SHELL	10.8
13.	Australia	36.1	37.	Philippines	10.2
14.	Brazil	34.6	38.	Finland	10.2
15.	Mexico	33.2	39.	Iran	10.2
16.	Sweden	32.6	40.	Venezuela	9.6
17.	Spain	32.3	41.	Greece	9.5
18.	Netherlands	31.3	42.	Turkey	9.0
19.	Czechoslovakia	28.8	43.	GENERAL ELECTRIC	8.7
20.	Romania	28.0	44.	South Korea	8.2
21.	Belgium	25.7	45.	IBM	7.5
22.	Argentina	25.4	46.	Chile	7.4
23.	GENERAL MOTORS	24.3	47.	MOBIL OIL	7.3
24.	Switzerland	20.5	48.	CHRYSLER	7.0

49.	UNILEVER	6.9	75.	BOEING	3.7
50.	Columbia	6.6	76.	DUPONT	3.6
51.	Egypt	6.6	77.	Hong Kong	3.6
52.	Thailand	6.5	78.	SHELL OIL	3.6
53.	ITT	6.4	79.	IMPERIAL CHEMICAL	3.5
54.	TEXACO	6.4	80.	BRITISH STEEL	3.5
55.	Portugal	6.2	81.	North Korea	3.5
56.	New Zealand	6.1	82.	GENERAL TELEPHONE	3.4
57.	Peru	5.9	83.	NIPPON STEEL	3.4
58.	WESTERN ELECTRIC	5.9	84.	Morocco	3.3
59.	Nigeria	5.8	85.	HITACHI	3.3
60.	Taiwan	5.5	86.	RCA	3.3
61.	GULF OIL	5.4	87.	GOODYEAR TIRE	3.2
62.	U.S. STEEL	4.8	88.	SIEMENS	3.2
63.	Cuba	4.8	89.	South Vietnam	3.2
64.	Israel	4.4	90.	Libya	3.2
65.	VOLKSWAGENWERK	4.3	91.	Saudi Arabia	3.1
66.	WESTINGHOUSE	4.3	92.	SWIFT	3.1
67.	STANDARD OIL CALIF.	4.2	93.	FARBWERKE HOECHST	3.0
68.	Algeria	4.2	94.	UNION CARBIDE	3.0
69.	PHILIPS ELECTRIC	4.2	95.	DAIMLER-BENZ	3.0
70.	Ireland	4.1	96.	PROCTER & GAMBLE	3.0
71.	BRITISH PETROLEUM	4.1	97.	AUGUST THYSSEN-HUTTE	2.9
72.	Malaysia	3.8	98.	BETHLEHEM STEEL	2.9
73.	LING-TEMCO-VOUGHT	3.8	99.	BASF	2.9
74.	STANDARD OIL IND.	3.7			

SOURCE: Lester R. Brown, *The Interdependence of Nations* (Foreign Policy Association, 1972).

Economic progress in the modern world is fragile and easily interfered with. Worldwide division of labor and interdependence for the supply of basic commodities have been among the most potent sources of high productivity in the international economy. But interdependence also means that an interruption in supply is quickly communicated to all branches of the world economy. A good example of this effect is the "Arab oil embargo," instigated in 1973. The oil embargo was set up by the Arab nations late in that year with the avowed purpose of shutting off supplies of petroleum to nations supporting Israel in the Middle Eastern power struggle. Cutbacks in crude-oil production quickly led to international shortages in transportation, energy supplies, and also manufactured goods, fertilizers for agriculture, and many vital services. It soon became apparent that, like all monopolies, the oil producers' power to withhold supplies enabled them to boost prices. By December of 1973 petroleum production had been cut back by more than 10 percent (by Arab producers) and the price had escalated a staggering 130 percent. Shortages were not limited to those countries singled out for "oil weapon" treatment. The effects of the supply shortage and price rise radiated, causing a slowdown in growth rates and an accelerated rate of inflation throughout the non-Communist world. While the economic edifice did not crumble, its fragility in the face of a relatively minor upset became all too apparent. The politics of the situation hurt Europe internally as well. As European nations (as well as Japan and the United States) abandoned any semblance of unity in the hopes of individually receiving special treatment at the hands of the oil producers' cartel, European integration suddenly seemed a long way off.

The third major challenge that confronts Europe, along with other developed countries, is the damage to land, air, and water resources that can result from irresponsible disposal of industrial waste products. Examples of industrial damage seem especially poignant in Europe, where often the "environment" includes not only natural resources, but also a man-made physical patrimony of great cultural achievement. Such a case is that of the Venetian lagoon at the mouth of the Adriatic Sea, where a modern industrial complex at Mestre-Marghera provides employment and energy in the form of refined petroleum products to north Italy while punishing the lagoon with a constant outpouring of noxious gases and waterborne waste. Statuary and architectural embellishments that withstood centuries of wind and weather in Venice have been obliterated in a decade. Workmen on the mainland wear gas masks daily as a matter of routine. The pattern has been repeated elsewhere. Beaches along the French Riviera and on the Bay of Naples have been declared unfit for bathing because of pollution levels in the water. Yet despite much irresponsibility and pessimism, progressive steps have been taken to inhibit further damage and reverse the effects of past mistakes. Cities like Bologna and Rome have banned automotive traffic from the most congested areas of their central business districts. The Scandinavian countries have pioneered in environmental-protection legislation and surveillance over industrial behavior. The surface has hardly been scratched as far as achieving victory over environmental degradation, for most of the work on the problem to date has been paperwork. It is nevertheless true that because of both legislation and public opinion, *social costs* have entered the calculus of business decision making, and communal resources, natural or man-made, should benefit from this change of mentality.

The end of economics is human welfare

In the study of economic history which we have been making together, the emphasis placed on economic development should not obscure the fact that the end of economic activity is to increase the material well-being of individuals. In fact, the measurement which we have used throughout this study to determine economic growth has been national income per capita of the population. In Western culture it is assumed to be desirable that this income be distributed with some degree of equity, that is, that the gap between the very rich and the very poor be narrowed. Therefore, as we come to the end of our study of the post-World War II period it is appropriate that we briefly consider personal income distribution and how that distribution has been made more equitable by social security systems and by taxation.

In spite of wars and depressions there was generally in Western culture an increase in real income per capita during the first four decades after World War I (Table 62). As can be seen from Map 14, the greatest successes were achieved where there was no great destruction from war.

After World War II, moreover, Western culture achieved some reduction in the inequality of income distribution. At least in the six countries for which information is available, the lower 60 percent of the income earners increased their earnings, and the highest 10 percent had their share reduced, the chief losses here coming from income from property.

Whether or not the changes in income distribution reflected structural change in the economy or were simply a function of full employment and prosperity is debatable. Nevertheless, it is clear that income taxes smoothed out income inequalities to a considerable extent.

Furthermore, social security systems were so greatly extended that they brought up the distributive shares of the lower income groups. In most Western European countries extensive health insurance, with generous medical benefits, was added to the usual sickness, invalidity, old age, maternity, death, and unemployment benefits. And in several places, notably in France and Italy, a system of family allowances was introduced whereby a worker's wage was increased according to the number of children he had. In France, social security benefits of all kinds were estimated to constitute nearly 30 percent of the French worker's total wage.

At all events, a degree of economic well-being was reached so that in the more advanced countries a considerable proportion of expenditures was for the finer things of life, and living standards were so raised that there was a marked extension of the expectation of life at birth.

The great socioeconomic problems for the future of the West are clearly whether prevailing standards of income per capita can be maintained or raised, whether a large part of personal expenditures will be for "civilizing activity," and whether the economic and military position of the West can be kept at levels adequate to cope with threats of force from without. These are issues which will test the leadership of the future.

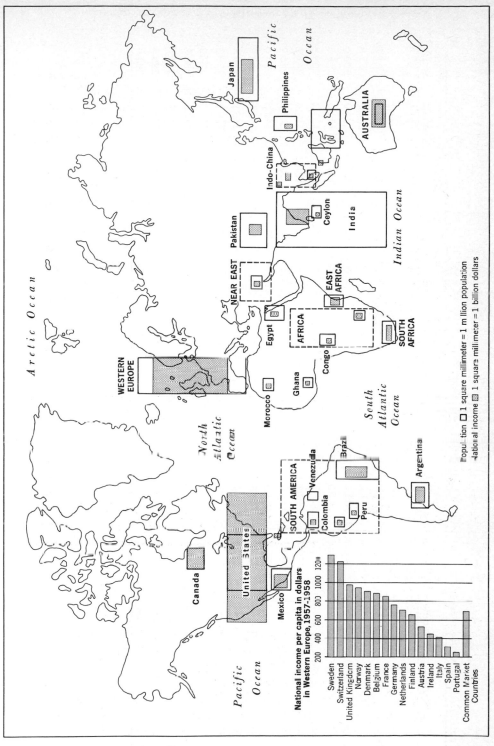

Map 14
National Income per Capita

Table 62. Output per man-hour in selected countries (1913 = 100)

	Belgium	Denmark	France	West Germany	Italy	Netherlands	Norway	Sweden	Switzerland	United Kingdom	Canada	United States
1870	42.1	33.8	46.3	42.3*	59.4		47.6*	32.2		52.3	41.5	37.3*
1880		41.9	53.9	52.9	63.4			39.5		56.9	51.6	
1890		55.3	68.8	67.8	65.3			49.5	70.1	82.5	59.3	61.2
1900		70.4	85.4	81.2	73.4	86.9	76.8	66.6		93.2	70.9	75.8
1913	100.0	100.0	100.0	100.0	100.0	100.0	100.0	100.0	100.0	100.0	100.0	100.0
1929	137.0	132.5	154.6	113.2	143.7	150.2	160.4	115.7	166.3	140.3	121.5	155.5
1938	144.2	137.1	178.5	137.1	191.1	145.4	194.8	151.1	183.1	167.9	121.2	208.8
1950	169.8	173.3	180.2	140.4	200.0	151.8	239.0	205.1	201.9	189.9	217.6	241.2
1951	174.7	174.9	189.8	153.8		156.3	247.6	204.8	210.1	192.6	227.3	246.2
1952	175.9	178.6	195.7	163.5		159.6	257.9	210.1	213.2	194.4	243.5	254.0
1953	182.4	186.4	202.2	169.8		169.1	263.6	219.8	223.0	199.6	250.4	262.7
1954	189.0	181.5	210.0	175.4		176.2	277.6	232.0	238.2	203.1	246.2	269.4
1955	191.6	182.3	221.0	188.1	243.9	185.7	284.8	241.4	250.9	205.8	259.5	276.3
1956	198.0	195.2	228.9	200.5		189.8	299.3	250.0	261.5	211.1	271.5	277.2
1957	202.3	204.5	239.4	213.1		193.8	307.4	258.3	268.2	214.9	272.5	286.5
1958	203.3	208.6	244.9	222.7		196.9	307.1	265.1	273.0	218.8	279.0	291.6
1959	211.0	217.8	251.4	234.2		205.7	330.1	281.1	284.1	223.4	276.6	296.5
1960	218.1	230.5	264.3	250.3	297.7	219.1	351.6	290.1	304.1	230.0	279.8	304.9

*1871.
SOURCE: Angus Maddison, *Economic Growth in the West* (New York: Twentieth Century Fund, 1964). p. 232.

Bibliography

The following bibliography is designed to assist both the student and teacher in pursuing the many subjects treated in this volume. It is, however, not conceived as an exhaustive guide to the entire literature of the economic history of Western civilization, but rather as an adjunct to the text. It is considered to be adequate for all levels of university students from undergraduates to graduates. Books that have particularly useful bibliographies are marked with an asterisk.

Bibliographical guides

There is no specialized bibliographical guide to all economic history. A most useful aid to locating bibliographies is Constance M. Winchell, *Guide to Reference Books,* 7th ed., Chicago: American Library Association, 1951 and supplements. *The Guide to Historical Literature,* New York: Macmillan, 1961, prepared by a committee of the American Historical Association, contains references of use to economic historians. The chapters of the *Cambridge Economic History of Europe,* London: Cambridge, 1941–1966, contain excellent selective bibliographies. The bibliographical appendix to volume 6 ("The Industrial Revolutions and After") is the most comprehensive, nearly 100 pages long.

Statistical compilations

Collections of quantitative data are available in yearbooks of all the major countries of Western civilization, such as the *Statistical Abstract of the United States,* the *Statistical Abstract for the United Kingdom,* the *Annuaire statistique* (France), *Annuario statistico* (Italy), and the *Statistisches Jahrbuch* (Germany). In some cases the statistical agencies which issue these volumes have published important historical compilations, like the *Annuaire statistique,* Paris: Imprimerie Nationale, 1947, and the *Historical Statistics of the United States, Colonial Times to 1957,* Washington, D.C.: Government Printing Office, 1960. See also Bertrand Gille, *Les sources statistiques de l'histoire de France des enquêtes du XVIIe siècle à 1870,* Geneva: Droz, 1964, and B. R. Mitchell and P. Deane, *Abstracts of British Historical Statistics,* London: Cambridge University Press, 1962. J. Marczewski, *Le produit physique de l'économie française,* and T. J. Markovitch, *L'Industrie Française de 1789 à 1864: Sources et méthode,* Paris: Cahiers de I.S.E.A., 1965.

The United Nations Organization has continued the policy of the League of Nations in publishing the very important *Statistical Yearbook* with international data. See also the *1964 Yearbook of National Accounts Statistics,* New York: United Nations, Department of Public Information, 1965. The various specialized agencies, like the International Labor Office, the Food and Agricultural Organization, the International Bank, and the United Nations Educational, Scientific and Cultural Organization, all issue separate statistical publications. The annual *Basic Statistics of the Community,* Brussels: Statistical Office of the European Communities, gives important comparative data for European countries.

Economic geographies

Economic geographies and studies of world resource patterns are published frequently as new information is amassed. An excellent study of resources is Erich W. Zimmermann, *World Resources and Industries,* New York: Harper

& Row, 1951. See also W. S. and E. S. Woytinsky, *World Population and Production,* * New York: Twentieth Century Fund, 1953. Other important studies of this character which also have some forecasts are J. Frederic Dewhurst, *America's Needs and Resources: A New Survey,* New York: Twentieth Century Fund, 1955, and J. Frederic Dewhurst et al., *Europe's Needs and Resources,* New York: Twentieth Century Fund, 1961. See also the works by Arnold B. Barach, *The USA and Its Economic Future,* New York: Macmillan, 1964, and *The New Europe and Its Economic Future,* New York: Macmillan, 1964.

The nature of history, economics, and economic history

The literature concerning the nature of history is abundant. For the philosophy of history one may consult with profit William H. Walsh, *Philosophy of History: An Introduction,* * New York: Harper & Row, 1960, and John Higham et al. *History,* Englewood Cliffs, N.J.: Prentice-Hall, 1965. For a history of history see Herbert Butterfield, *Man on His Past,* Boston: Beacon Press, 1960. For a statement on history in relation to other social sciences, see *The Social Sciences in Historical Study,* New York: Social Science Research Council, 1954; Fritz Stern, *The Varieties of History,* Cleveland: World Publishing, 1956; and Mirra Komarovsky, *Common Frontiers of the Social Sciences,* New York: Free Press, 1957. For an introduction to economics, consult a general elementary text like Paul A. Samuelson, *Economics: An Introductory Analysis,* 7th ed., New York: McGraw-Hill, 1967. For an appreciation of current trends in economics, see *A Survey of Contemporary Economics,* Philadelphia: American Economic Association, 1948–1952 (2 vols.); Simon Kuznets, *Modern Economic Growth Rate Structure and Spread,* New Haven, Conn.: Yale, 1966, *Six Lectures on Economic Growth,* New York: Free Press, 1959, and *Economic Growth and Structure,* New York: Norton, 1965.

For the history of economic theory, consult Charles Gide and Charles Rist, *A History of Economic Doctrines from the Time of the Physiocrats to the Present Day,* * 2d ed., Boston: Heath, 1948; Erich Roll, *A History of Economic Thought,* 3d ed., Englewood Cliffs, N.J.: Prentice-Hall, 1963; and Joseph Dorfman, *The Economic Mind in American Civilization,* * New York: Viking, 1946–1959 (5 vols.).

Regarding economic history, the student will find much food for thought in John Hicks, *A Theory of Economic History,* Oxford: Clarendon Press, 1969; Paul Hohenberg, *A Primer on the Economic History of Europe,* New York: Random House, 1968; Robert W. Fogel, "New Economic History: Its Findings and Methods," *Economic History Review,* vol. 19, 1966 (on new methods in the discipline); Douglass C. North and Robert Paul Thomas, *The Rise of the Western World; a New Economic History,* New York: Cambridge, 1973; Frederic C. Lane and Jelle C. Riemersma (Eds.), *Enterprise and Secular Change:*

Readings in Economic History, Homewood, Ill.: Irwin, 1953; Karl F. Helleiner (Ed.), *Readings in European Economic History,* Toronto: University of Toronto Press, 1946; Eleanora M. Carus-Wilson (Ed.), *Essays in Economic History,* London: E. Arnold, 1961–1963 (3 vols.); and S. B. Clough and C. Moodie, *European Economic History: Documents and Readings,* Princeton, N.J.: Van Nostrand, 1965.

Histories of technology and science

Inasmuch as works dealing with specific periods or individual machines will be cited later in chapter bibliographies, only general works are listed here. A good introduction to the theory of technological development is S. C. Gilfillan, *The Sociology of Invention,* Chicago: Follett, 1935. Also useful are William F. Ogburn, *Social Change,* New York: Viking, 1952; and John Jewkes, *The Sources of Invention,* New York: St. Martin's, 1958.

Among histories of technology, see the comprehensive work by Charles J. Singer (Ed.), *A History of Technology,* * Fair Lawn, N.J.: Oxford, 1954–1958 (5 vols.). Among other good studies are Maurice Daumas (Ed.), *Histoire générale des techniques,* Paris: Presses Universitaires, 1962–1965 (2 vols.); Abbot P. Usher, *A History of Mechanical Inventions,* Boston: Beacon Press, 1959; Samuel Lilley, *Men, Machines, and History,* * London: Cobbett Press, 1948; *McGraw-Hill Encyclopedia of Science and Technology,* New York: McGraw-Hill, 1960 (15 vols.); Richard S. Kirby, *Engineering in History,* New York: McGraw-Hill, 1956; Jacob Smookler, *Invention and Economic Growth,* Cambridge, Mass.: Harvard, 1966; Melvin Kranzberg and Carroll W. Pursell, Jr., *Technology in Western Civilization,* Madison, Wis.: University of Wisconsin Press, 1967; and Friedrich Klemm, *Technik, eine Geschichte ihrer Probleme,* Freiburg: Alber, 1954.

As an introduction to the history of science, one might well turn to Herbert Butterfield, *The Origins of Modern Science, 1300–1800,* New York: Collier Books, 1962; Alfred R. Hall, *The Scientific Revolution, 1500–1800,* 2d ed., London: Longmans, 1962; and René Taton (Ed.), *Histoire générale des sciences,* Paris: Presses Universitaires, 1957–1964 (3 vols.).

On the role of science and technology in industrialization, A. E. Musson and E. Robinson, *Science and Technology in the Industrial Revolution,* Manchester, Eng.: Manchester University Press, 1969; and A. E. Musson (Ed.), *Science, Technology, and Economic Growth in the Eighteenth Century,* London: Methuen, 1972.

History of population

Two general demographic histories are Marcel R. Reinhard, *Histoire générale de la population mondiale,* Paris: Montchrestien, 1961; and Roger Mols, *Introduc-*

tion à la démographie historique des villes d'Europe du XIVe au XVIIIe siècle, Gembloux: J. Duculot, 1954–1956 (3 vols.). For more analytic studies, consult W. D. Borrie, *The Growth and Control of World Population,* London: Weidenfeld & Nicolson, 1970; *The Determinants and Consequences of Population Trends,* Population Studies No. 17, New York: United Nations, 1953; Brinley Thomas, *Migration and Economic Growth,* London: Cambridge, 1954; Carlo Cipolla, *The Economic History of World Population,* 5th ed., Baltimore: Penguin, 1970; and E. A. Wrigley, *Population and History,* New York: McGraw-Hill, 1969. For important articles, see the following collections: D. V. Glass and D. E. C. Eversley (Eds.), *Population in History; Essays in Historical Demography,* Chicago: Aldine, 1965; D. V. Glass and Roger Revelle (Eds.), *Population and Social Change,* London: E. Arnold, 1972; and Michael Drake (Ed.), *Population in Industrialization,* London: Methuen, 1969. In this field the work of the modern French social historians must be included. The two prime examples are Pierre Goubert, *Beauvais et Beauvaisis de 1600 à 1730,* Paris: S.E.V.P.E.N., 1960; and Emmanuel Le Roy Ladurie, *Les paysans de Languedoc,* Paris: S.E.V.P.E.N., 1966.

History of money and banking

An excellent introduction to the history of money and banking is Carlo M. Cipolla, *Money, Prices, and Civilization in the Mediterranean World: Fifth to Seventeenth Century,* * Princeton, N.J.: Princeton, 1956. Interesting general views of money and its role in economic growth are Alfons Dopsch, *Naturalwirtschaft und Geldwirtschaft in der Weltgeschichte,* * Vienna: Seidel, 1930; and Marc Bloch, *Esquisse d'une histoire monétaire de l'Europe,* Paris: Colin, 1954.

Albert E. Feavearyear, *The Pound Sterling: A History of English Money,* 2d ed., Fair Lawn, N.J.: Oxford, 1963, is an exceedingly interesting account of a currency from its very beginnings to a recent date. See also, Paul Einzig, *The History of Foreign Exchange,* New York: St. Martin's, 1962; Sidney Homer, *A History of Interest Rates, 2000 B.C. to the Present,* New Brunswick, N.J.: Rutgers, 1963; Réné Sédillot, *Le franc, histoire d'une monnaie des origines à nos jours,* Paris: Recueil Sirey, 1953; and Carlo M. Cipolla, *L'avventure della lira,* Milan: Comunità, 1958.

General economic histories

Economic histories embracing the entire area of Western culture are extremely rare. Usually, economic histories are restricted to some geographical area or to a limited period of time. Of the more general works, see the multi-volume *Cambridge Economic History,* * London: Cambridge, 1941–1966, which was begun under the editorship of John H. Clapham and Eileen

Power and is being continued under the direction of M. M. Postan and H. J. Habbakuk. For the United States, the most modern and comprehensive work is Lance Davis, Richard Easterlin, and William Parker (Eds.), *American Economic Growth: An Economist's History of the United States,* New York: Harper & Row, 1972.

Economic history reviews

Many historical reviews carry articles pertaining to economic affairs, but the chief specialized journals are: *The Journal of Economic History* and *Explorations in Economic History* (United States), *The Economic History Review* (England), *Annales* and *Revue d'histoire économique sociale* (France), *Vierteljahrschrift für Sozial und Wirtschaftsgeschichte* (Germany), *The Journal of European Economic History* and *Economia e storia* (Italy), *Scandinavian Economic History Review* (Denmark), and *International Review of Social History* (Amsterdam). *Historical Abstracts* is a guide to economic articles in scholarly journals, and *The Journal of Economic Literature* provides synoptic reviews of economic publications.

National economic histories

Many of the works in economic history have been conceived as national histories for the very good reason that since the discipline of economic history has grown to importance, the national state has played a large role in forming economic policy and in determining the economic experience of individuals. Some of these national histories are listed here; others will be noted in the bibliographies of individual chapters.

The most extensive economic history of Britain is John H. Clapham, *An Economic History of Modern Britain,* * 2d ed., London: Cambridge, 1950–1952 (3 vols.). It covers the period since 1820. For a briefer version, see John H. Clapham, *A Concise Economic History of Britain From the Earliest Times to 1750,* London: Cambridge, 1949; and its companion, W. H. B. Court, *A Concise Economic History of Britain from 1750 to Recent Times,* London: Cambridge, 1954. Consult also Ephraim Lipson, *The Economic History of England,* London: A. & C. Black, 1937–1943 (3 vols.).

The leading economic history of France is that by Henri Sée, *Histoire économique de la France,* Paris: Colin, 1948–1951 (2 vols.).

For Germany, consult Friedrich Lütge, *Deutsche Sozial- und Wirtschaftsgeschichte,* Berlin: Springer, 1960; Gustav Stolper, *Deutsche Wirtschaft seit 1870,* Tübingen: J. Mohr, 1964; Gustav Stolper, *German Economy, 1870 to the Present,* New York: Harcourt, Brace & World, 1967; Walther Hoffmann, *Das Wachstum der deutschen Wirtschaft seit der Mitte des 19 Jahrhunderts,* Berlin: Springer,

1965; and Wilhelm Treue, *Wirtschaftsgeschichte der Neuzeit: In Zeitalter der industriellen Revolution 1700 bis 1960,* Stuttgart: Alfred Kröner, 1962.

For Belgium, see Henri Pirenne, *Histoire de Belgique,** Brussels: Lamertin, 1908–1932 (7 vols.); and Ben Serge Chlepner, *Cent ans d'histoire sociale en Belgique,* Brussels: Institut Solvay, 1956. See also J. A. van Houtte, *Economische en Sociale Geschiedenis van de Lage Landen,* Antwerp: Standaard, 1964.

For the Netherlands, the student will find useful I. J. Brugmans, *Sociaal-Economische Geschiedenis van Nederland,* The Hague: Nijhoff, 1961.

For Italy, see Shepard B. Clough, *The Economic History of Modern Italy,* New York: Columbia, 1964. Also Gino Luzzatto, *Storia economica d'Italia,* Rome: Leonardo, 1949. See also, Alfred Doren, *Storia economica dell'Italia nel medio evo,* Padua: Cedam, 1939.

For Scotland, Henry Hamilton, *The Industrial Revolution in Scotland,* London: Clarendon, 1932.

For Spain, Jaime Vicens-Vives, *Historia de España y America,* Barcelona: Editorial Vicens-Vives, 1961 (5 vols.), and Jaime Vicens-Vives (with Jorge Nadal Oller), *An Economic History of Spain,* Princeton, N.J.: Princeton, 1969.

For Sweden, see Eli F. Heckscher, *An Economic History of Sweden,* Cambridge, Mass.: Harvard, 1954; and Arthur Montgomery, *The Rise of Modern Industry in Sweden,* Stockholm: Almquist and Wiksell, 1939.

For Austria, see K. H. Werner et al, *Hundert Jahre öesterreichischer Wirtschaftsentwicklung, 1848–1948,* Vienna: Springer, 1949.

Among the many good economic histories of the United States, one may consult with profit Douglass C. North, *The Economic Growth of the United States, 1790–1860,* Englewood. Cliffs, N.J.: Prentice-Hall, 1961; L. Davis, R. Easterlin, and W. Parker (Eds.), *American Economic Growth* (cited above); and Shepard B. Clough and Theodor Marburg, *The Economic Basis of American Civilization,** New York: Crowell, 1967.

For a general economic history of Canada, see Hugh G. J. Aitken, *Canadian Economic History,** Toronto: Macmillan, 1956.

Chapter 1. Civilization, culture, and economic growth

For an introduction to these subjects, the student might consult Shepard B. Clough, *The Rise and Fall of Civilization,** New York: Columbia, 1957. In order to understand the anthropologist's views on civilization and culture and their relation to economics, see Alfred L. Kroeber, *Configurations of Culture Growth,* Berkeley, Calif.: University of California Press, 1944, and *An Anthropologist Looks at History,* Berkeley, Calif.: University of California Press, 1963; Clyde Kluckhohn, *Mirror for Man,* Greenwich, Conn.: Fawcett, 1961; and P. A. Sorokin, *Modern Historical and Social Philosophies,* New York: Dover, 1963. To learn how the sociologist sees the way that men living in society function, consult Robert M. MacIver, *Society: Its Structure and Changes,* New York: Holt, 1949. See also Robert K. Merton, *Social Theory and Social Structure,* rev. ed., New York: Free Press, 1965.

From the abundant literature on the subject of economic growth, one may consult with profit, for theory, Albert O. Hirschman, *The Strategy of Economic Development,* New Haven, Yale, 1958; Simon S. Kuznets, *National Income and Its Composition, 1919–1938,* New York: National Bureau of Economic Research, 1941 (2 vols.); Colin Clark, *The Conditions of Economic Progress,** 3d ed., New York: St. Martin's, 1957; Walt W. Rostow, *The Stages of Economic Growth,* London: Cambridge, 1960, and *The Economics of Take-off into Sustained Growth,* New York: St. Martin's, 1964; and Barry Supple (Ed.), *The Experience of Economic Growth: Case Studies in Economic History,* New York: Random House, 1963.

Chapter 2. Economic achievements in the Ancient world

Excellent surveys of the entire period are to be found in Gordon V. Childe, *Man Makes Himself,** 4th ed., London: Watts, 1965, and *What Happened in History,* rev. ed., Baltimore: Penguin, 1964. Among the standard works on the economic history of the Ancient period, one should note M. I. Rostovtsev, *A History of the Ancient World,* Fair Lawn, N.J.: Oxford, 1945 (2 vols.), and by the same author, *The Social and Economic History of the Hellenistic World,* Fair Lawn, N.J.: Oxford, 1941 (3 vols.), and *The Social and Economic History of the Roman Empire,** 2d ed. rev., Fair Lawn, N.J.: Oxford, 1963 (2 vols.). Also, Fritz Heichelheim, *An Ancient Economic History,* rev. ed., Leiden: Sijthoff, 1958–1964 (2 vols.); and Edouard Will, "La Grèce archaïque," in *Deuxième Conference Internationale d'Histoire Economique,* The Hague: Mouton, 1965, vol. 1, pp. 41–115.

Chapters 3, 4, 5, and 6. The Middle Ages

In addition to the more general works cited above, the more advanced student may want to push his studies into special phases of medieval life. One of the most stimulating scholars in this field has been Henri Pirenne, although some of his theories about development out of the "Dark Ages" have been questioned. Nevertheless, one will find useful Henri Pirenne, *Economic and Social History of Medieval Europe,* New York: Harcourt, Brace & World, 1956, *Medieval Cities: Their Origin and the Revival of Trade,* Garden City, N.Y.: Doubleday, 1956. See A. F. Havighurst (Ed.), *The Pirenne Thesis: Analysis, Criticism, and Revision,* Boston: Heath, 1958. Another stimulating scholar is Alfons Dopsch: *The Economic and Social Foundations of European Civilization,*

London: Routledge, 1953. On the early Medieval period, see Robert Latouche, *The Birth of Western Economy, Economic Aspects of the Dark Ages,* New York: Harper & Row, 1966, and Robert S. Lopez, *The Birth of Europe,* Philadelphia: Lippincott, 1967.

As an introduction to the agricultural economy on the Continent, one might begin by reading B. H. Slicher Van Bath, *The Agrarian History of Western Europe, A.D. 500-1850,* London: E. Arnold, 1963; Marc Bloch, *Les Caractères originaux de l'histoire rurale française,* Paris: Colin, 1956–1960 (2 vols.); Georges Lizerand, *Le Régime rural de l'ancienne France,* Paris: Presses Universitaires, 1942, and *Villages désertés et histoire économique, XI–XIIII siècle,* Paris: S.E.V.P.E.N., 1965; Georges Duby, *Rural Economy and Country Life in the Medieval West,* Columbia: University of South Carolina Press, 1968; Warren Ault, *Open-field Husbandry and the Village Community: A Study of Agrarian By-laws in Medieval England,* Philadelphia: American Philosophical Society, 1965.

On the subject of feudalism, one may turn with profit to F. L. Ganshof, *Feudalism,** 2d ed., New York: Harper & Row, 1961; James W. Thompson, *Economic and Social History of the Middle Ages, 300–1300,* New York: Ungar, 1959 (2 vols.); Marc Bloch, *Feudal Society,* Chicago: The University of Chicago Press, 1961.

The literature on industrial production is limited. See George G. Coulton, *The Medieval Village,* London: Cambridge, 1925; Emile Coornaert, *Les Corporations en France avant 1789,* 2d ed., Paris: Gallimard, 1941; Lynn White, *Medieval Technology and Social Change,* Oxford, England: Oxford University Press, 1962; and Bronislaw Geremek, *Le s..lariat dans l'artisanat parisien aux XIII* *–XV* *siècles: étude sur la main d oeuvre au moyen âge,* Paris: Mouton, 1968. On the other hand, literature on trade is extensive: Eileen Power and M. Postan (Eds.), *Studies in English Trade in the Fifteenth Century,* London, Routledge, 1933; Roberto S. Lopez and Irving W. Raymond, *Medieval Trade in the Mediterranean World,* New York: Columbia, 1955; and W. Heyd, *Histoire du commerce du Levant,* Amsterdam: A.M. Hakkert, 1959 (2 vols.).

Money and banking have also been extensively investigated. Philip Grierson, *Numismatics and History,* London: privately printed, 1951, and Carlo Cipolla, *Money, Prices, and Civilization** (referred to earlier under the History of Money and Banking) are good introductions to money. Regarding lending, see W. E. Lunt, *Papal Revenues in the Middle Ages,* New York: Columbia, 1934 (2 vols.); B. N. Nelson, *The Idea of Usury,* Princeton, N.J.: Princeton, 1949; Raymond de Roover, *The Rise and Decline of the Medici Bank, 1397-1494,* New York: Norton, 1966; A. P. Usher, *The Early History of Deposit Banking in Mediterranean Europe,* Cambridge, Mass.: Harvard, 1943; Gunnar Mickwitz, *Geld und Wirtschaft im römischen Reich des 4ten Jahrhunderts,* Helsinki: Centraltryckeri, 1932; J. G. van Dillen (Ed.), *History of the Principal Public Banks,* The Hague: Nijhoff, 1934; and Harry A. Miskimin, *Money, Prices, and Foreign Exchange in Fourteenth-Century France,* New Haven, Conn.: Yale, 1963.

Some idea of crafts may be had from Martin S. Briggs, *A Short History of the Building Crafts,* Fair Lawn, N.J.: Oxford, 1925; Henri Stein, *Les Architects des cathédrales gothiques,* Paris: H. Laurens, 1909; Eileen Power, *The Wool Trade in English Medieval History,* Fair Lawn, N.J.: Oxford, 1942; and Emile Levasseur, *Histoire des classes ouvrières et de l'industrie en France,* 2d ed., Paris: Arthur Rousseau, 1903-1904 (4 vols.). On slavery, see Charles Verlinden, *L'Esclavage dans l'Europe médiévale, Bruges: De Tempel, 1955.*

On population problems in the Middle Ages: Josiah Cox Russel, *British Medieval Population,* Albuquerque: The University of New Mexico Press, 1948, and *Medieval Regions and their Cities,* Bloomington: Indiana University Press, 1972; Charles Mullett, *The Bubonic Plague and England,* Lexington: University of Kentucky Press, 1956; and David Herlihy, *Medieval and Renaissance Pistoia: The Social History of an Italian Town, 1200–1430,* New Haven, Conn.: Yale, 1967.

The interesting debate on the end of Medieval growth and the "Renaissance depression" can be traced in: M. M. Postan, "Revisions in Economic History: The Fifteenth Century," *Economic History Review,* vol. 4, 1939: Robert Lopez, "Hard Times and Investment in Culture," reprinted in several places, among them the pertinent, Anthony Molho (Ed.), *The Social and Economic Foundations of the Italian Renaissance,* New York: Wiley, 1969; Robert Lopez and Harry Miskimin, "The Economic Depression of the Renaissance," *Economic History Review,* vol. 14, 1962, and, with Carlo Cipolla, *Economic History Review,* vol. 16, 1964.

Chapter 7. European discoveries and expansion, 1500–1700

Among the more general works, the best introduction to the discoveries is J. H. Parry, *The Age of Reconnaissance,* New York: New American Library, 1963. Also, see the publication of the Commission Internationale d'Histoire Maritime, *Les grandes voies maritimes dans le monde: XVe–XIXe siècles,* Paris: S.E.V.P.E.N., 1965; Lloyd A. Brown, *The Story of Maps,* Boston: Little, Brown, 1949; and Charles E. Nowell, *The Great Discoveries,* Ithaca, N.Y.: Cornell, 1960. Europe's advantages are stressed in Carlo M. Cipolla, *Guns, Sails and Empires,* New York: Pantheon, 1966.

Nearly all the explorers have been extensively treated in monographs. These are some of the more enlightening: Leonardo Olschki, *Marco Polo's Precursors,* Baltimore: Johns Hopkins, 1943; Henry H. Hart, *Venetian Adventurer: The Life and Times of Marco Polo,* Stanford, Calif.: Stanford, 1947; Edgar Prestage, *The Portuguese Pioneers,* New York: St. Martin's, 1933; C. R. Beazley, *Prince Henry the Navigator,* Putnam, 1923; Kingsley G. Jayne, *Vasco da Gama and His Successors, 1460–1580,* London: Methuen, 1910; Frederick J. Pohl, *Amerigo Vespucci: Pilot Major,* New York: Columbia, 1944; Charles M. Parr, *So Noble a Captain* [Magellan], New York: Crowell, 1953; Samuel E. Morison, *Admiral of the Ocean Sea: A Life of Christopher Columbus,* Boston: Little, Brown, 1942 (2 vols.); and John B. Brebner, *The Explorers of North America, 1492–1806,* Cleveland: World Publishing, 1964.

Hard upon the discoveries and explorations came trade and the first settlements. See Clarence H. Haring, *The Spanish Empire in America,* New York: Harcourt, Brace & World, 1963; Roger B. Merriman, *The Rise of the Spanish Empire in the Old World and in the New,* New York: Cooper Square, 1962 (4 vols.); Clarence H. Haring, *Trade and Navigation between Spain and the Indies in the Time of the Habsburgs,* Gloucester, Mass.: Peter Smith, 1964; Edward G. Bourne, *Spain in America, 1450–1580,* New York: Barnes & Noble, 1962; Lesley B. Simpson, *The Encomienda in New Spain,* rev. ed., Berkeley: University of California Press, 1966; James A. Williamson, *Maritime Enterprise, 1485–1558,*[*] Fair Lawn, N.J.: Oxford, 1913; John H. Parry, *The Spanish Seaborne Empire,* New York: Knopf, 1966, and *The Spanish Theory of Empire in the Sixteenth Century,* London: Cambridge, 1940; Charles R. Boxer, *The Dutch Seaborne Empire, 1600–1800,* New York: Knopf, 1965; Boise Penrose, *Travel and Discovery in the Renaissance, 1420–1620,* New York: Atheneum Publishers, 1962; and Ralph Davis, *The Rise of the English Shipping Industry in the Seventeenth and Eighteenth Centuries,* London: Macmillan, 1962.

Chapter 8. Economic consequences of European overseas expansion

One of the major consequences of the expansion of Europe to America was the acquisition by Europe of great amounts of precious metals, associated with a period of severe price increases. These increases have been investigated by an International Scientific Commitee for the Study of Prices. Among their publications are Earl J. Hamilton, *American Treasure and the Price Revolution in Spain, 1501–1650,* New York: Octagon Books, 1965; Henri Hauser (Ed.), *Recherches et documents sur l'histoire des prix en France de 1500 à 1800,* Paris: Les Presses Modernes, 1936; M. J. Elsas, *Umriss einer Geschichte der Preise und Löhne in Deutschland,* Leyden: Sijthoff, 1936–1949 (2 vols.); William Beveridge, *Prices and Wages in England from the Twelfth to the Nineteenth Century,* London: Longmans, 1939; and Nicolaas W. Posthumus, *Inquiry into the History of Prices in Holland,* Leyden: E. J. Brill, 1946–1964 (2 vols.). For a similar study, see Charles Verlinden (Ed.), *Dokumenten voor de Geschiedenis van Prijzen en Lonen in Vlaanderen en Brabant,* Bruges: De Tempel, 1959–1965 (2 vols.). For commentary on the causes and consequences of the inflation, see Peter H. Ramsey (Ed.), *The Price of Revolution in Sixteenth-Century England,* London: Methuen, 1971; and Aldo de Maddalena, *Moneta e mercato nel '500: la rivoluzione dei prezzi,* Florence: Sansoni, 1973.

Expansion also had an impact on business organization and the formation of joint-stock companies. See William R. Scott, *The Constitution and Finance of the English, Scottish and Irish Joint-Stock Companies to 1720*, London: Cambridge, 1910–1912 (3 vols.); and Charles H. Wilson, *Anglo-Dutch Commerce and Finance in the Eighteenth Century*, London: Cambridge, 1941.

Works of monumental importance (and monumental size) have been written on European commerce and its interaction with other facets of life around the time of the discoveries. Among the foremost are Fernand Braudel, *La Méditerranée et le monde méditerranéen a l'époque de Philippe II*, 2d ed., Paris: Colin, 1966 (2 vols.), and *Civilisation matérielle et capitalisme*, Paris: Colin, 1967; Pierre Chaunu, *Seville et l'Atlantique*, Paris: S.E.V.P.E.N., 1947–1958 (8 vols.); Ramon Carande, *Carlos V y sus banqueros*, Madrid: Sociedad de Estudios y Publicaciones, 1943–1967 (3 vols.); Herman van der Wee, *The Growth of the Antwerp Market and the European Economy*, The Hague: Nijhoff, 1963 (3 vols.). Also, Violet Barbour, *Capitalism in Amsterdam in the Seventeenth Century*, Ann Arbor: The University of Michigan Press, 1963; Brian Pullan (Ed.), *Crisis and Change in the Venetian Economy in the 16th and 17th Centuries*, London: Methuen, 1968; and Carlo Cipolla (Ed.), *The Economic Decline of Empires*, London: Methuen, 1970.

Chapter 9. Science, technology, and Early Modern industry

The development of the physical sciences was to have a great influence upon techniques and subsequent industrial processes. For the beginnings of science in the modern period one may use, in addition to histories of science mentioned earlier: G. N. Clark, *Science and Social Welfare in the Age of Newton*, Fair Lawn, N.J.: Oxford, 1937; and George Sarton, *Introduction to the History of Science*, Baltimore: Williams & Wilkins, 1927–1947 (3 vols.).

Some idea of the relationship between science and technology in this period may be had from Edward MacCurdy (Ed.), *Leonardo da Vinci: The Notebooks*, New York: George Braziller, 1958; and Georg Argicola, *De Re Metallica*, New York: Dover, 1950. See also, Arturo Castiglioni, *A History of Medicine*, 2d ed. rev., New York: Knopf, 1958; and Richard Shryock, *The Development of Modern Medicine*, New York: Knopf, 1947.

One of the pioneers in stressing an "early Industrial Revolution" in England is John U. Nef. See his *The Rise of the British Coal Industry,** London: Routledge, 1932 (2 vols.); *La Naissance de la civilisation industrielle et le monde contemporain*, Paris: Colin, 1954; and *Industry and Government in France and England, 1540–1640*, Ithaca, N.Y.: Great Seal Books, Cornell, 1957.

Chapter 10. Establishing the capitalist system

An old but good introduction to the subject of the beginnings of capitalism is Henri Sée, *Modern Capitalism*, New York: Adelphi, 1928. On the so-called capitalist spirit, see Max Weber, *The Protestant Ethic and the Spirit of Capitalism,* New York: Scribner, 1958; R. H. Tawney, *Religion and the Rise of Capitalism,* New York: New American Library, 1954; and Amintore Fanfani, *Le origini dello spirito capitalistico in Italia,* Milan: Vita e Pensiero, 1933.

Examples of business leaders in the period of early capitalism are to be found in Victor Klarwill, *The Fugger News Letters,* New York: Putnam, 1926; Richard Ehrenberg, *Capital and Finance in the Age of the Renaissance,* New York: Harcourt, Brace, 1928; and Yves Renouard, *Les Hommes d'affaires italiens du moyen âge,* Paris: Colin, 1949.

On economy and society in the Early Modern period, see Peter Laslett, *The World We Have Lost: England before the Industrial Age,* New York: Scribner, 1965; L. A. Clarkson, *The Pre-industrial Economy in England, 1500–1750,* New York: Schocken Books, 1971. Agrarian aspects are well covered by B. H. Slicher Van Bath, *Agrarian History of Western Europe, a.d. 500–1850* (cited above). Two collections of articles which adequately review the "general crisis" of the Early Modern period are Trevor Aston (Ed.), *Crisis in Europe, 1550–1660,* Garden City, N.Y.: Doubleday, 1967; and Robert Forster and Jack Greene (Eds.), *Preconditions of Revolution in Early Modern Europe,* Baltimore: Johns Hopkins, 1972.

Chapter 11. Mercantilism

The most penetrating study of mercantilism in recent times is Eli Heckscher, *Mercantilism,** rev. ed., New York: Macmillan, 1955 (2 vols.), although it has the defect of not giving consideration to Portuguese and Spanish policies. Another important study is Charles W. Cole, *Colbert and a Century of French Mercantilism,* Hamden, Conn.: The Shoe String Press, 1964 (2 vols.). It may be supplemented by his *French Mercantilist Doctrines before Colbert,* New York: Richard R. Smith, 1931, and his *French Mercantilism, 1683–1700,* New York: Octagon Books, 1965. A short statement of the problem will be found in chap. 1 of Shepard B. Clough, *France 1789–1939: A Study in National Economics,** New York: Octagon Books, 1964. Also, G. Schmoller, *The Mercantile System and Its Historical Significance,* New York: P. Smith, 1931; and Charles H. Wilson, *Mercantilism,* London: Routledge, 1958. For policies in Spain, see Earl J. Hamilton, *Money, Prices, and Wages in Valencia, Aragon, and Navarre, 1351–1500,* Cambridge, Mass.: Harvard, 1936; and by the same author, *War and Prices in Spain, 1651–1800,* Cambridge, Mass.: Harvard, 1947. An important historiographical review of the concept of mercantilism is D. C. Coleman (Ed.), *Revisions in Mercantilism,* London: Methuen, 1969.

For English policy, see Lawrence A. Harper, *The English Navigation Laws,** New York: Columbia, 1939; and on the relationship between policy and patterns of trade: Barry Supple, *Commercial Crisis and Change in England, 1600–1642*, London: Cambridge, 1964; and C. H. Wilson, *England's Apprenticeship, 1603–1763*, New York: St. Martin's, 1965.

Chapter 12. The Industrial Revolution

The best introduction to the Industrial Revolution is undoubtedly the small volume by T. S. Ashton, *The Industrial Revolution, 1760–1830,** 1st ed. rev., Fair Lawn, N.J.: Oxford, 1964, but see also his *An Economic History of England: The Eighteenth Century*, London: Methuen, 1961. An older but still useful and fuller study is that by Paul J. Mantoux, *The Industrial Revolution in the Eighteenth Century: An Outline of the Beginnings of the Modern Factory System in England*, New York: Harper & Row, 1965. One should read George N. Clark, *The Idea of the Industrial Revolution*, Glasgow: Jackson, 1953, as a corrective against exaggeration. See also, Phyllis Deane, *The First Industrial Revolution*, London: Cambridge, 1965; John U. Nef, *The Conquest of the Material World*, Chicago: The University of Chicago Press, 1964; and L. S. Pressnell (Ed.), *Studies in the Industrial Revolution*, London: Athlone Press, 1960.

David S. Landes, *The Unbound Prometheus: Technological Change and Industrial Development in Western Europe from 1750 to the Present*, London: Cambridge, 1969, merits attention as the most comprehensive comparative treatment of industrial modernization in Europe.

Studies of individual countries are enlightening on the factors which contributed to industrial change and to the whole problem of industrial diffusion both within a country and between countries. See John H. Clapham, *An Economic History of Modern Britain,** 2d ed., London: Cambridge, 1950–1952 (3 vols.); W. W. Rostow, *British Economy of the XIXth Century*, Fair Lawn, N.J.: Oxford, 1948; and Arthur D. Gayer, W. W. Rostow, and Anna J. Schwartz, *The Growth and Fluctuation of the British Economy, 1790–1850*, Fair Lawn, N.J.: Oxford, 1953 (2 vols.). See also, W. H. B. Court, *British Economic History, 1870–1914*, London: Cambridge, 1965; Phyllis Deane and W. A. Cole, *British Economic Growth, 1688–1959: Trends and Structure*, London: Cambridge, 1969; Walter Hoffmann, *British Industry, 1700–1950*, Oxford: Blackwell, 1955; and R. M. Hartwell (Ed.), *The Causes of the Industrial Revolution in England*, London: Methuen, 1967.

For France, see Arthur Louis Dunham, *The Industrial Revolution in France*, New York: Exposition Press, 1955; Charles Kindleberger, *Economic Growth in France and Britain, 1851–1950*, Cambridge, Mass.: Harvard, 1964; and Tom Kemp, *Economic Forces in French History*, London: Dobson, 1971.

For Belgium, see B. S. Chelpner, *Cent ans d'histoire sociale en Belgique*, Brussels: Institut de Sociologie Solvay, 1956; and F. Baudhuin, *Histoire économique de la Belgique, 1914–1939*, Brussels: Bruylant, 1944 (2 vols.).

For the Netherlands, see J. A. van Huotte, *Economische en Sociale Geschiedenis van de Lage Landen,* Antwerp: Standaard, 1964; and Izaak J. Brugmans, *Paardenkracht en mensenmacht; Sociaal-Economische Geschiedenis van Nederland, 1795–1940,* The Hague: Nijhoff, 1961.

The United States is dealt with in Victor S. Clark, *History of Manufactures in the United States,* New York: P. Smith, 1949 (3 vols.); Chester W. Wright, *Economic History of the United States,** 2d ed., New York: McGraw-Hill, 1949; and *Output, Employment, and Productivity in the United States after 1800,* New York: National Bureau of Economic Research, 1966.

For Germany, see Maurice Baumont, *La Grosse industrie allemande et le charbon,* Paris: Doin, 1928; Pierre Benaerts, *Les Origines de la grande industrie allemande,* Paris: Turot, 1933; William O. Henderson, *The State and the Industrial Revolution in Prussia, 1740–1870,* Liverpool: Liverpool University Press, 1958; Walther Hoffmann, *Das Wachstum de Deutschen Wirtschaft seit der Mitte des 19 Jahrhunderts,* Berlin: Springer, 1965; and Gustav Stolper, *Deutsche Wirtschaft seit 1870,* Tübingen: J. Mohr, 1964.

Switzerland is treated in William E. Rappard, *La Révolution industrielle et les origines de la protection légale du travail en Suisse,* Berne: Staempfli, 1914.

For Italy, see Rodolfo Morandi, *Storia della grande industria in Italia,* Bari: Laterza, 1931; and Gianni Toniolo (Ed.), *Lo sviluppo economico italiano, 1861–1940,* Rome-Bari: Laterza, 1973.

Finally, for Bohemia, see Herman Freudenberger, *The Waldstein Woolen Mill: Noble Entrepreneurship in Eighteenth-Century Bohemia,* Montpelier, Vt.: Capital City Press, 1963.

On the "standard of living controversy" mentioned in the text, see E. J. Hobsbawm, "The British Standard of Living, 1790–1850," *Economic History Review,* 2d. ser., 1957; R. M. Hartwell, "The Rising Standard of Living in England, 1800–1850," *Economic History Review,* 2d. ser., 1961; E. J. Hobsbawm and R. M. Hartwell, "The Standard of Living: A Discussion," *Economic History Review,* 2d. ser., 1963.

Chapter 13. The Agricultural Revolution

A good introduction to agricultural history may be found in N. S. B. Gras, *A History of Agriculture in Europe and America,* 2d ed., New York: Appleton-Century-Crofts, 1940; and Rowland E. P. Ernle, *English Farming, Past and Present,* 6th ed., London: Heinemann, 1961. See also B. H. Slicher Van Bath, *The Agrarian History of Western Europe, A.D. 500–1850,* London: E. Arnold, 1963; Charles K. Warner (Ed.), *Agrarian Conditions in Modern European History,* New York: Macmillan, 1966; and Folke Dovring, *Land and Labor in Europe, 1900–1950: A Comparative Survey of Recent Agrarian History,* The Hague: Nijhoff, 1956.

On the subject of landholding, see Georges Lefebvre, *La Révolution française*, 3d ed., Paris: Presses Universitaires, 1963; Jerome Blum, *Noble Landowners and Agriculture in Austria, 1818–1848*, Baltimore: Johns Hopkins, 1948; Friedrich K. Lütge, *Die mitteldeutsche Grundherrschaft und ihre Auflösung*, 2d ed., Stuttgart: G. Fischer, 1957; Charles S. Orwin, *The Open Fields*, 2d ed., Fair Lawn, N.J.: Oxford, 1954; J. D. Chambers, "Enclosure and Labour Supply in the Industrial Revolution," *Economic History Review*, ser. 2, vol. 5, no. 3; Robert Forster, "Obstacles to Agricultural Growth in Eighteenth-Century France," *American Historical Review*, vol. 75, no. 6 (October 1970); and Eric Kerridge, *Agrarian Problems in the Sixteenth Century and After*, London: George Allen & Unwin, 1969.

On the changing technology of farming: Eric Kerridge, *The Agricultural Revolution*, London: George Allen & Unwin, 1967; J. D. Chambers and G. F. Mingay, *The Agricultural Revolution*, New York: Schocken Books, 1966; E. L. Jones (Ed.); *Agriculture and Economic Growth in England, 1650–1815*, London: Methuen, 1967. See Ester Boserup, *The Conditions of Agricultural Growth*, Chicago: Aldine, 1966, for a theoretical approach to technical change in agriculture.

Chapter 14. The mechanization of industry

Specifically on the diffusion of industry, one should consult Shepard B. Clough, "The Diffusion of Industry in the Last Century and a Half," *Studi in onore di Armando Sapori*, Milan: Cisalpino, 1957; Charles Ballot, *L'Introduction du machinisme dans l'industrie française*, Paris: Rieder, 1923; William O. Henderson, *Britain and Industrial Europe, 1750–1870*, Liverpool University Press, 1954. For theory, Everett M. Rogers, *The Diffusion of Innovations*, New York: Free Press, 1965.

Among the specialized works on technology for this period, see Robert J. Forbes, *Man, the Maker: A History of Technology and Engineering*, New York: Abelard-Schuman, 1950; H. J. Habakkuk, *American and British Technology in the Nineteenth Century: Search for Labour-saving Inventions*, London: Cambridge, 1962; Sigfried Giedion, *Mechanization Takes Command: A Contribution to Anonymous History*, Fair Lawn, N.J.: Oxford, 1948; Jean Fourastié, *Machinisme et bien-être*, 3d ed., Paris: Editions de Minuit, 1962; and W. E. G. Salter, *Productivity and Technical Change*, London: Cambridge, 1960.

There are good studies of many of the industries in which rapid change was taking place. Among others, see Herbert Heaton, *The Yorkshire Woollen and Worsted Industries*, 2d ed., Fair Lawn, N.J.: Oxford, 1965; Erich Roll, *An Early Experiment in Industrial Organization: A History of the Firm of Boulton and Watt, 1775–1805*, New York: Longmans, 1930; F. X. van Houtte, *L'Evolution de l'industrie textile en Belgique et dans le monde de 1800 à 1939*, Louvain: Institut de

Recherches Economiques et Sociales, 1949; A. P. Wadsworth and Julia deL. Mann, *The Cotton Trade and Industrial Lancashire, 1600–1780,* Manchester, England: Manchester University Press, 1931; Neil J. Smelser, *Social Change in the Industrial Revolution: An Application of Theory to the British Cotton Industry,* Chicago: The University of Chicago Press, 1959; W. H. B. Court, *The Rise of the Midland Industries, 1600–1838,* Fair Lawn, N.J.: Oxford, 1938; Warren C. Scoville, *Capitalism and French Glass Making, 1640–1789,* Berkeley: University of California Press, 1950; William Woodruff, *The Rise of the British Rubber Industry during the Nineteenth Century,* Liverpool: Liverpool University Press, 1958; Theodore A. Wertime, *The Coming of the Age of Steel,* Chicago. The University of Chicago Press, 1962; and Howard G. Roepke, *Movements of the British Iron and Steel Industry, 1720–1951,* Urbana: The University of Illinois Press, 1956.

Chapter 15. The revolution in commerce

On roads and railroads, see H. Cavaillès, *La Route française, son histoire, sa fonction,* Paris: A. Colin, 1946; Ch. Dollfus and E. de Geoffroy, *Histoire de la locomotion terrestre,* Paris: L'Illustration, 1935–1936 (2 vols.); L. Génicot, *Histoire des routes belges depuis 1704,* Brussels: Office de Publicité, 1948; *100 Jahre deutsche Eisenbahn,* Berlin: Reichsverkehrsministerium, 1937; and Kimon A. Doukas, *The French Railroads and the State,* New York: Columbia, 1945. See also, Harold Bargor, *The Transportation Industries 1889–1946,* New York: National Bureau of Economic Research, 1951; Robert Fogel, *Railroads and American Economic Growth,* Baltimore: Johns Hopkins, 1964; and Albert Fishlow, *American Railroads and the Transformation of the Antebellum Economy,* Cambridge, Mass.: Harvard, 1965.

The literature on water carrying is abundant. For an introduction to the subject one might begin with Charles E. Fayle, *A Short History of the World's Shipping,* London: George Allen & Unwin, 1933; Adam W. Kirkaldy, *British Shipping: Its History, Organization and Importance,* London: Routledge, 1914; Gerald S. Graham, *Empire of the North Atlantic: The Maritime Struggle for North America,* 2d ed., Toronto: The University of Toronto Press, 1958; or David Budlong Tyler, *Steam Conquers the Atlantic,** New York: Appleton-Century-Crofts, 1939.

On French shipping, Charles de la Roncière, *Histoire de La marine française,* Paris: Plon, Nourrit, 1899–1932 (6 vols.); and Jacques Godechot, *Histoire de l'Atlantique,* Paris: Bordas, 1947.

For German shipping, W. Vogel and G. Schmölders, *Die Deutschen als Seefahrer,* Hamburg: Hoffman and Campe, 1949. See also, S. C. Gilfillan, *Inventing the Ship,* Chicago: Follett, 1935; the excellent book by Paul William Bamford, *Forests and French Sea Power, 1660–1789,** Toronto: The University of Toronto Press, 1956; Robert G. Albion, *Forests and Sea Power: The Timber Problem of the Royal Navy, 1652–1862,* Cambridge, Mass.: Harvard, 1926; John G. B. Hutchins, *The American Maritime Industries and Public Policy, 1789–1914,* Cambridge, Mass.: Harvard, 1941; and Louis C. Hunter, *Steamboats on the Western Rivers,** Cambridge, Mass.: Harvard, 1949.

For transportation in Spain, see David Ringrose, *Transportation and Economic Stagnation in Spain, 1750–1850,* Durham, N.C.: Duke, 1970.

The importance of national postal services in communications is described in L. Kalmus, *Weltgeschichte der Post, mit besonderer Berücksichtigung des deutschen Sprachgebietes,* Göttingen: Verlag für Militärund Fachliteratur, 1938.

Concerning commercial policy, see Aldo de Maddalena, *La politica commerciale estera degli Stati Uniti dal 1789 al 1812,* Milan: Cisalpino, 1953; Percy Ashley, *Modern Tariff History: Germany, United States, France,* 3d ed., New York: Dutton, 1926; Eli Heckscher, *The Continental System,* Fair Lawn, N.J.: Oxford, 1923; and William O. Henderson, *The Zollverein,** 2d ed., London: F. Cass, 1959. See also, Albert H. Imlah, *Economic Elements in the Pax Britannica: Studies in British Foreign Trade in the Nineteenth Century,* Cambridge, Mass.: Harvard, 1958.

Chapter 16. Finance capitalism: the revolution in investment and business organization

The role of finance capitalism is explained in George W. Edwards, *The Evolution of Finance Capitalism,* New York: Longmans, 1938; Andrew Shonfield, *Modern Capitalism: The Changing Balance of Public and Private Power,* Fair Lawn, N.J.: Oxford, 1965; and from a Marxist point of view, in Maurice H. Dobb, *Studies in the Development of Capitalism,** rev. ed., New York: International Publishers, 1964 [c1963]. Other studies include: Adolf A. Berle, *Power without Property: A New Development in American Political Economy,* London: Sidgwick & Jackson, 1960; Adolf A. Berle and P. Harbrecht, *Toward the Paraproprietal Society,* New York: Twentieth Century Fund, 1960; Bertrand Gille, *Recherches sur la formation de la grande entreprise capitaliste (1815–1848),* Paris: S.E.V.-P.E.N., 1959; and Peter Dickson, *The Financial Revolution in England,* London, 1967.

For the new types of banking, see Bertrand Gille, *Histoire de la Maison Rothschild. Des origines à 1848,* Geneva: Droz, 1965; Ralph W. Hidy, *The House of Baring,* Cambridge, Mass: Harvard, 1949; W. Gerloff and F. Neumark, *Handbuch der Finanzwissenschaft,* Tübingen: Mohr, 1952–1965 (4 vols.); and Rondo Cameron, *Banking in the Early Stages of Industrialization,* New York: Oxford University Press, 1967.

For studies of central banks, see John H. Clapham, *The Bank of England,* London: Cambridge, 1945 (2 vols.); Gabriel Ramon, *Histoire de la Banque de*

France, Paris: B. Grasset, 1929; B. S. Chelpner, *La Banque de Belgique,* Brussels: Lamertin, 1926–1930 (2 vols.); Esther R. Taus, *Central Banking Functions of the United States Treasury, 1789–1941,* New York: Columbia, 1943; Maurice Lévy-Leboyer, *Les Banques européennes et l'industrialisation internationale dans la première moitié du XIXe siècle,* Paris: Presses Universitaires, 1964; and Bray Hammond, *Banks and Politics in America, from the Revolution to the Civil War,* Princeton, N.J.: Princeton, 1957.

On stock exchanges and corporations: Francis W. Hirst, *The Stock Exchange: A Short History of Investments and Speculation,* rev. ed., London: Butterworth, 1932; George Heberton Evans, *British Corporation Finance, 1775–1850: A Study of Preference Shares,* Baltimore: Johns Hopkins, 1936. On the concentration of business, see Frances Cheney, *Cartels, Combines and Trusts,* Washington, D.C.: Library of Congress, 1944; Richard Lewinsohn, *Trusts et cartels dans l'économie mondiale,* Paris. Médicis, 1950; and, with different emphasis, Thomas C. Cochran and William Miller, *The Age of Enterprise: A Social History of Industrial America,* rev. ed., New York: Harper & Row, 1961.

On foreign investments, see Leland H. Jenks, *The Migration of British Capital to 1875,* New York: Nelson, 1963; A. R. Hall (Ed.), *The Export of Capital From Britain, 1870–1914,* London: Methuen, 1968. Harry D. White, *The French International Accounts, 1880–1913,* Cambridge, Mass.: Harvard, 1933; Rondo E. Cameron, *France and the Economic Development of Europe, 1800–1914,* Princeton, N.J.: Princeton, 1961; and Herbert Feis, *Europe, the World's Banker, 1870–1914,* New York: A. M. Kelley, 1964.

For a short course in business cycles, see the readings in J. J. Clark and M. Cohen (Eds.), *Business Fluctuations, Growth, and Economic Stabilization,* New York: Random House, 1963.

On the subject of insurance in this period: Charles Wright and C. E. Fayle, *A History of Lloyd's from the Founding of Lloyd's Coffee House to the Present Day,* New York: St. Martin's, 1928; J. Halpérin, *Les Assurances en Suisse et dans le monde,* Neuchâtel: Baconnière, 1946; and Shepard B. Clough, *A Century of Life Insurance,* * New York: Columbia, 1946.

As an introduction to the study of the history of modern public finance, one might read Sidney Ratner, *A Political and Social History of Federal Taxation, 1789–1913,* New York: Norton, 1942; Harold M. Groves, *Financing Government,* 6th ed., New York: Holt, 1964; Marcel Marion, *Histoire financière de la France depuis 1715,* Paris: Rousseau, 1914–1931 (6 vols.); and David H. Pinkney, *Napoleon III and the Rebuilding of Paris,* Princeton, N.J.: Princeton, 1958. Also, Eli Ginzberg et al., *The Pluralistic Economy,* New York: McGraw-Hill, 1965.

For social and economic analysis of the reactions to capitalism: E. P. Thompson, *The Making of the English Working Class,* New York: Pantheon, 1964; Karl Polanyi, *The Great Transformation: The Political and Economic Origins of our Time,* Boston: Beacon Press, 1944; E. J. Hobsbawm, *Industry and Empire:*

The Making of Modern English Society, New York: Pantheon, 1968; Edmund Wilson, To the Finland Station: A Study in the Writing and Acting of History, Garden City, N.Y.: Doubleday, 1940; and Peter N. Stearns, European Society in Upheaval: Social History Since 1800, London: Macmillan, 1967.

Chapter 17. The new economy comes of age

Inasmuch as this chapter deals primarily with the continuation of earlier trends, many of the works already cited are pertinent for the material covered.

On the "new imperialism" one will find useful Parker T. Moon, Imperialism and World Politics, New York: Macmillan, 1955. See also, Achille Viallate, Economic Imperialism and International Relations during the Last Fifty Years, New York: Macmillan, 1923; Percy E. Schramm, Deutschland und Ubersee, Brunswick: Westermann, 1950; and J. S. Bartstra, Geschiedenis van het Moderne Imperialisme, Haarlem: Bohn, 1958. See also, David Saul Landes, Bankers and Pashas: International Finance and Economic Imperialism in Egypt, Cambridge, Mass.: Harvard, 1958; A. G. L. Shaw (Ed.), Great Britain and the Colonies, London: Methuen, 1970 (as a preface to the problem); and Hans Ulrich Wehler, Bismarck und der Imperialismus, Cologne: Kiepenheuer & Witsch, 1969.

The literature on the workingman's problems becomes abundant for this period. See Edouard Dolléans, Histoire du mouvement ouvrier, Paris: A. Colin, 1936–1953 (3 vols.); Paul Louis, Histoire du mouvement syndical en France, Paris: Valois, 1947–1948 (2 vols.); Paul Cornut, Répartition de la fortune privée en France, Paris: A.Colin, 1963; J. Kuczynski, Labour Conditions in Western Europe, 1820–1935, New York: International Publishers, 1937; and, for conditions in Germany, see Alexander Gerschenkron, Bread and Democracy in Germany, New York: Fertig, 1966.

On various kinds of trade unionism see J. B. Duroselle, Les Débuts du Catholicisme social en France, Paris: Presses Universitaires, 1951; Jean Villain, L'Enseignement social de l'Eglise, Paris: Spes, 1953–1954 (3 vols.); Elie Halévy, Histoire du socialisme européen, Paris: Gallimard, 1948; George Lichtheim, Marxism: An Historical and Critical Study, New York: Frederick A. Praeger, 1962; Michael P. Fogarty, Christian Democracy in Western Europe, 1820–1953, * Notre Dame, Ind.: The University of Notre Dame Press, 1957; and George Woodcock, Anarchism: A History of Libertarian Ideas and Movements, New York: Meridian Books, 1962.

Other issues pertaining to the years 1875–1914 (including the "long depression in prices") are covered in: Peter Temin, "The Relative Decline of the British Steel Industry," in Henry Rosovsky (Ed.), Industrialization in Two Systems, New York: Wiley, 1966; Alexander Gerschenkron, "Economic Backwardness in Historical Perspective," in his collection of the same title,

New York: Praeger, 1965; and Donald McClosky (Ed.), *Essays on a Mature Economy: Britain after 1840*, Princeton, N.J.: Princeton, 1971. Also, J. D. Gould, *Economic Growth in History: Survey and Analysis*, London: Methuen, 1972; Hans Rosenberg, *Probleme der deutschen Sozialgeschichte*, Frankfurt: Suhrkamp, 1969; Helmut Böhme (Ed.), *Probleme der Reichsgründungszeit, 1848–1879*, Cologne: Kiepenheuer & Witsch, 1968; and Giorgio Fuà, *Lo sviluppo economico in Italia*, vol. 2, *Gli aspetti generali*, Milan: Franco Angeli, 1969.

Four varied interpretations of Great Britain's relative economic decline are: A. L. Levine, *Industrial Retardation in Britain*, London: Weidenfeld & Nicolson, 1967; R. J. S. Hoffman, *Great Britain and the German Trade Rivalry, 1875–1914*, New York: Russel & Russel, 1964; Donald N. McCloskey, *Economic Maturity and Entrepreneurial Decline: British Iron and Steel*, 1870–1913, Cambridge, Mass.: Harvard, 1974; and Derek H. Aldcroft (Ed.), *The Devlopment of British Industry and Foreign Competition, 1875–1914*, Toronto: The University of Toronto Press, 1968.

Chapter 18. International, economic, and social strains and stresses

By far the most comprehensive history of any war is James T. Shotwell (Ed.), *The Social and Economic History of the War* [World War I], New York: Carnegie Endowment for International Peace, published during the 1930s, in approximately 150 volumes. Among these, the following deserve special mention: Michael T. Florinsky, *The End of the Russian Empire* (1931); L. Grebler and W. Winkler, *The Cost of the World War to Germany and to Austria-Hungary* (1940); F. W. Hirst, *Consequences of the War to Great Britain* (1934); Pierre Renouvin, *The Forms of War Government in France* (1927); Arthur Salter, *Allied Shipping Control* (1921); Henri Pirenne, *La Belgique et la guerre mondiale* (1928); Luigi Einaudi, *La condotta economica e gli effetti sociali della guerra italiana* (1933).

On the reparations question, see Philip M. Burnett, *Reparations at the Paris Peace Conference from the Standpoint of the American Delegation*, 2d ed., New York: Octagon Books, 1965 (2 vols.); Bernard M. Baruch, *The Making of the Reparations and Economic Sections of the Treaty*, New York: Harper & Row, 1920; John Maynard Keynes, *The Economic Consequences of the Peace*, New York: Harcourt, Brace & World, 1920; and David Felix, *Walter Rathenau and the Weimar Republic: The Politics of Reparations*, Baltimore: Johns Hopkins, 1970.

On inflation following the war, the best works regarding German experience are Frank D. Graham, *Exchange, Prices, and Production in Hyperinflation: Germany, 1920–1923*, Princeton, N.J.: Princeton, 1930; and Constantino Bresciani-Turroni, *The Economics of Inflation: A Study of Currency Depreciation in Post-war Germany*, London: G. Allen, 1937. For France, see Martin Wolf, *The French Franc between the Wars, 1919–1939*,* New York: Columbia, 1951; Pierre Dieterlen and Charles Rist, *The Monetary Problem of France*, New York: King's

Crown Press, 1948; and *The Course and Control of Inflation*, Princeton, N.J.: League of Nations, 1946.

Chapter 19. Economic growth and economic depression

Claude W. Guillebaud, *The Economic Recovery of Germany, from 1933 to the Incorporation of Austria in March, 1938,* New York: St. Martin's, 1939; Louis R. Franck, *Les Etapes de l'économie fasciste italienne*, Paris: La Librairie Sociale et Economique, 1939; Gustav Stolper, *German Economy, 1870–1940: Issues and Trends*, New York: Harcourt, Brace & World, 1940; Frederick C. Benham, *Great Britain under Protection*, New York: Macmillan, 1941; and David E. Lilienthal, *T. V. A.: Democracy on the March*, New York: Harper & Row, 1953. See also, Simon S. Kuznets, *Economic Growth and Structure: Selected Essays,* New York: Norton, 1965; Angus Maddison, *Economic Growth in the West: Comparative Experience in Europe and North America*, New York: Twentieth Century Fund, 1964; Alfred Sauvy, *Histoire économique de la France entre deux guerres*, Paris: Flammarion, 1965.

On the great depression of the 1930s: Henry V. Hodson, *Slump and Recovery*, 1929–1937, Fair Lawn, N.J.: Oxford, 1938; John K. Galbraith, *The Great Crash*, 2d ed., Boston: Houghton Mifflin, 1961; and Moritz J. Bonn, *The Crumbling of Empire: The Disintegration of World Economy*, London: George Allen & Unwin, 1938.

Chapters 20, 21, and 22. The economics of World War II, postwar economic recovery and expansion, and business fluctuations, international trade, and economic integration

Most belligerents in World War II have prepared some kind of economic studies of their experiences. One of the best of this type is W. K. Hancock and M. M. Gowing, *British War Economy*, London: H. M. Stationery Office, 1949. See also, Louis Baudin, *Esquisse de l'économie française sous l'occupation allemande*, Paris: Médicis, 1945; and the publications of many Federal agencies of the United States, especially the Office of Price Administration. The impact of strategic bombing is interestingly portrayed in *The Effects of Strategic Bombing on the German War Economy*, Washington, D.C.: U.S. Air Force, 1945.

The effect of the war on American agriculture is competently treated in Walter W. Wilcox, *The Farmer in the Second World War*, Ames: Iowa State University Press, 1947. An excellent study of wartime migrations is Eugene M. Kulischer, *Europe on the Move: War and Population Changes, 1917–1947,* New York: Columbia, 1948; *International Migration, 1945–1957,* Geneva: International Labor Office, 1959; and Francis E. Merrill, *Social Problems on the Home*

Front: A Study of War-time Influences,* New York: Harper & Row, 1948. The story of relief is excellently described in George Woodbridge (Ed.), *UNRRA: The History of the United Nations Relief and Rehabilitation Administration*, New York: Columbia, 1950 (3 vols.). Also Karl Brandt, *Management of Agriculture and Food in the German-occupied and Other Areas of Fortress Europe*, Stanford, Calif: Stanford, 1953.

Certain important studies were made after the war to guide the constitutional assemblies or new governments in various states. Among these the Italian is extremely useful to the economic historian: *Rapporto delle commissione economica*, Rome: Instituto Poligrafico dello Stato, 1947 (4 vols.). Of a similar kind were the reports of the *Commissariat au Plan* [Monnet Plan], Paris: 16 rue Martignac, published annually since the war. For Germany, *Wirtschaft und Statistik*; for the United Kingdom, *Economic Survey*; and for Italy, *Review of the Economic Conditions in Italy*, published by the Banco di Roma, a ten-year summary which was issued in 1956.

Special studies exist for most countries. For Germany, see the excellent study by Henry C. Wallich, *Mainsprings of the German Revival*, New Haven, Conn.: Yale University Press, 1955; and André Piettre, *L'Economie allemande contemporaine: Allemagne Occidentale, 1945–1952*, Paris: Génin, 1952. For France, Edward M. Earle (Ed.), *Modern France: Problems of the Third and Fourth Republics*, Princeton, N.J.: Princeton, 1951; John and Anne-Marie Hackett, *Economic Planning in France*, Cambridge, Mass.: Harvard, 1963; Wallace C. Peterson, *The Welfare State in France*, Lincoln: University of Nebraska Press, 1960; and *La France Economique*, an annual survey of the economy of France published by the *Revue d'Economie Politique*. For Italy, see George H. Hildebrand, *Growth and Structure in the Economy of Modern Italy*, Cambridge, Mass.: Harvard, 1965. For the United Kingdom, see Arthur C. Pigou, *Aspects of British Economic History, 1918–1925*, New York: St. Martin's, 1947; Pauline Gregg, *A Social and Economic History of Britain, 1760–1965*, 5th ed. rev., London: Harrap, 1965; Reuben Kelf-Cohen, *Nationalisation in Britain*, New York: St. Martin's, 1959; and J. R. Dow, *The Management of the British Economy, 1945–1960*, London: Cambridge, 1964. For the United States, Shepard B. Clough and Theodor Marburg, *The Economic Basis of American Civilization*, New York: Crowell, 1967 (cited under National Economic Histories, above); John K. Galbraith, *American Capitalism: The Concept of Countervailing Power*, Boston: Houghton Mifflin, 1956; and Milton Friedman and Anna J. Schwartz, *A Monetary History of the United States, 1867–1960*, Princeton, N.J.: Princeton, 1963.

On the subject of inflation, see Arthur J. Brown, *The Great Inflation, 1939–1951*, Fair Lawn, N.J.: Oxford, 1955; Pierre Biacabé, *Analyses contemporaines de l'inflation*, Paris: Sirey, 1962; and Joseph M. Gillman, *Prosperity in Crisis*, New York: Marzoni and Munsell, 1965.

On the economics of peace, Redvers Opie et al., *The Search for Peace*

Settlements, Washington, D.C.: Brookings Institution, 1951; also René Albrecht-Carrié, *A Diplomatic History of Europe*, New York: Harper & Row, 1958.

For the broad view of Europe's economy since World War II, see Jossleyn Hennessy, Vera Lutz, and Giuseppe Scimone, *Economic "Miracles": Studies in the Resurgence of the French, German and Italian Economies since the Second World War*, London: A. Deutsch, 1964; Ingvar Svennilson, *Growth and Stagnation in the European Economy*, Geneva: United Nations, 1954; F. J. Dewhurst, *Europe's Needs and Resources*, previously cited. Since 1947, the United Nations Economic Commission for Europe has published annually an *Economic Survey of Europe*. Of these, see particularly, *Economic Survey of Europe since the War*, Geneva: United Nations, 1953; *Economic Planning in Europe*, Geneva: United Nations, 1963; and *Some Factors in Economic Growth in Europe during the 1950s*, New York: United Nations, 1964. Concerning the world economy, consult Gunnar Myrdal, *An International Economy: Problems and Prospects*, New York: Harper & Row, 1956; Angus Maddison, *Economic Growth in the West: Comparative Experience in Europe and North America*, New York: Twentieth Century Fund, 1962; Jan Tinbergen, *Shaping the World Economy: Suggestions for an International Economic Policy*, New York: Twentieth Century Fund, 1962; Alan T. Peacock and Gerald Hauser (Eds.), *Government Finance and Economic Development*, New York: McGraw-Hill, 1965; and Thor Hultgren, *Cost, Prices, and Profits: Their Cyclical Relations*, New York: Columbia, 1965.

Also see Alec Nove, *An Economic History of the U.S.S.R.*, Baltimore: Penguin, 1969; Jean-Jacques Carré, Paul Dubois, and Edmond Malinvaud, *La Croissance française: Un essai d'analyse économique causale de l'après-guerre*, Paris: Éditions du Seuil, 1972; Eric Roll, *The World After Keynes: An Examination of the Economic Order*, London: Pall Mall Press, 1968; Simon Kuznets, *Modern Economic Growth: Rate Structure and Spread* (cited above), and *Economic Growth of Nations: Total Output and Production Structure*, Cambridge, Mass.: Harvard, 1971.

To get a picture of recent developments in agriculture, consult Folke Dovring, *Land and Labor in Europe, 1900–1950: A Comparative Survey of Recent Agrarian History*, The Hague: Nijhoff, 1956; and on food, Merrill K. Bennett, *The World's Food*, New York: Harper & Row, 1954.

Studies on European economic integration include: William Diebold, *The Schuman Plan: A Study in Economic Cooperation, 1950–1959*, New York: Frederick A. Praeger, 1959; Gordon L. Weil (Ed.), *Handbook on the European Economic Community*, New York: Frederick A. Praeger, 1965; Finn B. Jensen and Ingo Walter, *The Common Market: Economic Integration in Europe*, Philadelphia: Lippincott, 1965; and Leon N. Lindberg, *The Political Dynamics of European Economic Integration*, Stanford, Calif.: Stanford, 1963; Steven J. Warnecke, *The European Community in the 1970's*, New York: Praeger, 1972; Dennis Swann, *The Economics of the Common Market*, Baltimore: Penguin, 1972; F. Roy Willis, *Italy Chooses Europe*, New York: Oxford University Press, 1971; and Roger Broad and R. J. Jarrett, *Community Europe Today*, London: Oswald Wolff, 1972.

On social welfare, see Leonard H. Goodman (Ed.), *Economic Progress and Social Welfare*, New York: Columbia, 1966. And on underdevelopment within Europe, see Gustav Schachter, *The Italian South: Economic Development in Mediterranean Europe*, New York: Random House, 1965; and Sergio Barzanti, *The Underdeveloped Areas within the Common Market*, Princeton, N. J.; Princeton, 1965.

All the international organizations having to do with economic affairs have important publications which assist the student in keeping abreast of economic developments. The United Nations is the richest source of such materials with its *Statistical Yearbook*, its annual surveys of various regions, its special publications on national accounts, demography, and health, and its occasional studies. But other organizations have excellent materials on special regions or on special subjects: the Organization for Economic Cooperation and Development, the European Economic Community, the International Monetary Fund, the International Bank for Reconstruction and Development and its affiliated International Development Association, the Food and Agricultural Organization, and the International Labor Office.

Index